CLIFFS N

HARDBOUND LITERARY LIBRARIES

AMERICAN LITERATURE LIBRARY

Volume 2

Civil War to 1900

11 Titles

ISBN 0-931013-14-3

Library distributors, hardbound editions:
Moonbeam Publications
18530 Mack Avenue
Grosse Pointe, MI 48236
(313) 884-5255

MOONBEAM PUBLICATIONS
Robert R. Tyler, President
Elizabeth Jones, Index Editor

Riverside Community College
Library
4800 Magnolia Avenue
Riverside, California 92506

REF PN 44 .C51 1990 v.2

American Literature library

FOREWORD

Moonbeam Publications has organized **CLIFFS NOTES**, the best-selling popular (trade) literary reference series, into a fully indexed hardbound series designed to offer a more permanent format for the series.

Hardbound volumes are available in a **BASIC LIBRARY**, a 24 volume series. The current softbound series (over 200 booklets) has been divided into five major literary libraries to help researchers, librarians, teachers, students and all readers use this series more effectively. The five major literary groupings are further subdivided into 17 literary periods or genres to enhance the use of this series as a more precise literary reference book.

Hardbound volumes are also available in an **AUTHORS LIBRARY**, a 13 volume series classified by author, covering 11 authors and over 70 Cliffs Notes titles. This series helps readers who prefer to study the works of a particular author, rather than an entire literary period.

CLIFFS NOTES HARDBOUND
LITERARY LIBRARIES
1990 by
Moonbeam Publications
18530 Mack Avenue
Grosse Pointe, MI 48236
(313) 884-5255

Basic Library - 24 Volume
ISBN 0-931013-24-0

Authors Library - 13 Volume
ISBN 0-931013-65-8

Bound In U.S.A.

Acknowledgement:
"**Cliffs Notes**" is a trademark of **Cliffs Notes Incorporated** who also hold the Copyright to all material contained in this volume, except the indexes created by Moonbeam Publications for this publication.

AMERICAN LITERATURE LIBRARY

Volume 2

Civil War to 1900

CONTENTS

THE AMERICAN

NOTES

including

- *Life and Background*
- *Introduction*
- *List of Characters*
- *General Plot Summary*
- *Summaries and Commentaries*
- *Critical Notes*
- *Character Analyses*
- *Questions*

by
James L. Roberts, Ph.D.
Department of English
University of Nebraska

INCORPORATED
LINCOLN, NEBRASKA 68501

Editor

Gary Carey, M.A.
University of Colorado

Consulting Editor

James L. Roberts, Ph.D.
Department of English
University of Nebraska

ISBN 0-8220-0164-0
© Copyright 1965
by
C. K. Hillegass
All Rights Reserved
Printed in U.S.A.

The Cliffs Notes logo, the names "Cliffs" and "Cliffs Notes," and the black and yellow diagonal-stripe cover design are all registered trademarks belonging to Cliffs Notes, Inc., and may not be used in whole or in part without written permission.

Cliffs Notes, Inc. Lincoln, Nebraska

CONTENTS

AUTHOR'S LIFE AND BACKGROUND

Henry James was a true cosmopolite. He was a citizen of the world, and moved freely in and out of drawing rooms in Europe, England and America. He was perhaps more at home in Europe than he was in America, but the roots of his life belong to the American continent. Thus, with few exceptions, most of his works deal with some type of confrontation between an American and a European.

Henry James was born in New York in 1843. His father, Henry James, Sr., had inherited a considerable sum of money, and spent his time in leisured pursuit of theology and philosophy. The father often wrote essays and treatises on aspects of religion and philosophy and developed a certain degree of mysticism. Among the guests in the James' household were some of the most famous minds of the mid-nineteenth century. Henry James was able to hear his father converse with people like Ralph Waldo Emerson, Bronson Alcott, George Ripley. The father was insistent that his children learn to approach life as widely as possible.

In the strictest sense of the word, Henry James had no formal education. As a youth, he had private tutors. Then in his twelfth year, his father took the entire family to Europe where they moved freely from Switzerland to France to Germany in pursuit of stimulating conversation and intellectual ideas. The world of Europe left an everlasting impression on the young Henry James. He was ultimately to return and make his home in Europe.

When the family returned from Europe, the elder James decided to settle in New England. He choose Cambridge because this was the center of American intellectual thought. Many of the writers of Cambridge, Boston, and nearby Concord where Emerson and Thoreau lived, were often visitors in the James household. It was here in Boston where James met the first great influence on his literary career. He established a close friendship with William Dean Howells, who as editor of one of America's leading magazines, was able to help James in his early efforts to write and publish.

In Boston, Henry James enrolled briefly in the Harvard law school, but soon resigned to devote himself to writing. His older brother, the most famous philosopher and psychologist America has yet produced, was also a student at Harvard, where he remained after graduation to become one of the most famous lecturers in America.

By the late 1860's, James had done some reviewing and had sold one work of fiction to *The Atlantic Monthly*. He also returned to Europe on his own to see the continent as an adult. He returned again to Cambridge and New York in the hope of continuing his literary career. But he gradually came to the realization that Europe was more suitable for his writings. Thus, in 1876, when he was in his thirty-third year, James made the momentous decision to take up residence in Europe. And with the exception of short trips to various parts of the world, he lived the rest of his life in and near London. Until 1915, he retained his American citizenship, but when World War I broke out, he became a naturalized citizen of England as a protest over America's failure to enter the war against Germany.

James' life and background were ideally suited for the development of his artistic temperament. Even though he was not terribly wealthy, he did have enough independent money of his own to allow him to live a leisured life. His father's house provided all the intellectual stimulation he needed. His father's visitors were the most prominent artists of the day, and James was able to follow the latest literary trends. In his travels, he moved in the best society of two continents and came into contact with a large variety of ideas.

With the above life, it is natural that James' novels are concerned with a society of people who are interested in subtle ideas and subtle refinements. There are no really poor people in his novels. He wrote about people who had enough money to allow them to develop and refine their higher natures. His novels develop with a deliberate slowness and conscientious refinement. Many critics and readers resent the deliberate withholding of information and the slow development found in the Jamesian novel, but James' life was lived with a high degree of leisure and refinement. And finally, James was the first American suited to develop the theme of the

American in Europe. By the time he made his decision to settle in Europe, he had made several trips there and had lived and attended school in several parts of Europe. Thus, the subject matter of most of James' works is about an American of some degree of innocence meeting or becoming involved with some European of experience.

But in spite of his decision to live in Europe, James remained essentially American in his sympathies. His greatest characters (or central characters) are almost always Americans. But at the same time, some of his most unpleasant characters are also Americans. But the important thing is that the characters who change, mature, and achieve an element of greatness are almost always Americans.

THE REALISM OF HENRY JAMES

Henry James has had a tremendous influence on the development of the novel. Part of this influence has been through the type of realism that he employs. At the same time, the most frequent criticism against James has been that he is not realistic enough. Many critics have objected that James does not write about life, that his novels are filled with people whom one would never meet in this world. One critic (H. L. Mencken) suggested that James needed a good whiff of the Chicago stock yards so as to get a little life into his novels. Others have suggested that James' world is too narrow and incomplete to warrant the title of a realistic depiction of life.

Actually, James' realism is of a special sort. By the early definitions of realism, James is not a realist. The early definitions stated that the novelist should accurately depict life, and the novel should "hold up a mirror" to life. In other words, the early realist was supposed to make an almost scientific recording of life.

But James was not concerned with all aspects of life. There is nothing of the ugly, the vulgar, the common or the pornographic in James. He was not concerned with poverty or with the middle class who had to struggle for a living. Instead, he was interested in depicting a class of people who could afford to devote themselves to the refinements of life.

Then what is James' special brand of realism? When we refer to James' realism, we mean James' truth to his own material. To best appreciate James' novels and his realism, we must enter into James' special world. It is the same as though we ascended a ladder and arrived at another world. Once we have arrived at this special world and once we accept this world, then we see that James is very realistic. That is, in terms of his world he never violates his character's essence. Thus, James' realism, in the truest sense, means being faithful to his character. In other words, characters from other novels often do things or commit acts that don't seem to blend in with their essential nature. But the acts of the Jamesian character is always understandable in terms of that character's true nature.

James explained his own realism in terms of its opposition to romanticism. For James the realistic represents those things which sooner or later in one way or another everyone will encounter. But the romantic stands for those things which, with all the efforts and all the wealth and facilities of the world, we can never know directly. Thus in James' novels, it is conceivable that man can experience the same things that his characters are experiencing, but in the romantic novel, man can never actually encounter the events narrated in the novel.

When James, therefore, creates a certain type of character early in the novel, this character will act in a consistent manner throughout the entire novel. This is being realistic. The character will never do anything that is not logical and acceptable to his realistic nature, or to our conception of what that character should do.

In later years, James in writing about *The American* thought that in one incident he had himself violated his realism. This concerns the Bellegardes. He later felt that the Bellegardes "would positively have jumped then...at my rich and easy American, and not have 'minded' in the least any drawback—especially as, after all, given the pleasant palette from which I have painted him, there were few drawbacks to mind." This then was the type of realism that James was concerned with—a faithful rendition of character in any given situation. And as with the Bellegardes, never to allow the characters to perform an action which would be inconsistent with the true nature of the character.

STRUCTURE

Almost all of James' novels are structured in the same way. There must be a center – something toward which all the lines point and which "supremely matters." This is essentially James' own explanation of his structure. The thing that "supremely matters," is the central idea of the novel or that around which the novel functions. In *The American,* the thing that "supremely matters" is the love affair between Christopher Newman and Claire de Cintré. Therefore, almost all of the scenes and action of the novel are designed to hinder or to bring to completion this romance.

James' creative process is also important to an understanding of the structure of his works. He begins his novels with a situation and a character. Many writers, like Nathaniel Hawthorne, would begin with an idea or theme in mind and then would create a situation and characters which would illuminate the basic idea. James' technique is just the opposite. He created a certain situation, and then he would place his character in this situation. Theoretically, then, James would sit back and simply observe what would happen when this character was confronted with this particular situation. Often, James said, he had no particular ending in mind when he began a novel. Instead, he would let the character and situation determine the ending. This allowed him more freedom, and allowed him the opportunity of "getting to know" his character by observing him in a series of scenes.

Thus, the central situation in *The American* is the arrival of a rich American in Europe in search of a wife. After his meeting with Claire de Cintré, the thing that "supremely matters" is his success in obtaining Claire for his wife. Thus we have the character, the situation, and the thing that "supremely matters."

We said above that all lines must point toward the thing which supremely matters. But these lines do not go in a straight line. This is not the way James structures his novels. Everything in the novel is aimed at the central situation, but he moves toward the center by exploring all the related matters. In other words, the structure could be best described by a series of circles circling the center. Each circle is an event which illuminates the center, but probes only a part of the center. Each circle then is often a discussion by several different people. For example, one character observes something and then goes to another person to discuss his observation. Then two other characters might discuss the same event. By the end of the various discussions, James has probed all of the psychological implications inherent in this particular situation. This would represent one circle. The discussions do not lead us directly to the center, but rather they fully illuminate one aspect of the circle. Then, we go to another event or situation which will be fully discussed before proceding to the next. Thus at the end of the novel, James has probed and examined every moral, ethical, and psychological aspect of the central situation, and the reader has seen the views of many people on the same subject.

Thus the structure of James' novels is circular in approach to the central subject, but every circle in some way illuminates the thing that supremely matters. Every incident functions to tell us more about the character or the situation. There is nothing that is superfluous or extraneous.

CAST OF CHARACTERS

Christopher Newman

A rich, thirty-five year old American who goes to Europe in search of culture and in hopes of finding a suitable wife.

Madame de Bellegarde

A proud and haughty member of the aristocracy. She is the person most opposed to Christopher Newman's marriage to Claire de Cintré.

Urbain de Bellegarde

Her oldest son who is in charge of the family. Along with his mother, he is proud and haughty and terribly aware of the honor of the Bellegarde name.

Marquise de Bellegarde

Urbain's wife who is more interested in enjoying life than she is in performing ritualistic and ceremonial duties.

Claire de Cintré

The daughter whom Newman wishes to marry. She was previously married by an arranged marriage and was supposedly terribly unhappy with her very old husband.

Valentin de Bellegarde

The youngest son who becomes a good friend to Newman and helps Newman in his suit for Claire de Cintré's hand.

Tom Tristram

An American whom Newman knew during the war. He is now married and lives in Paris. He spends all his time in an American club.

Mrs. Tristram

A sensitive and intelligent woman who, it is intimated, made a mistake in marrying Tom Tristram. She becomes a good friend and *confidante* to Newman and introduces him to Claire de Cintré.

Mrs. Bread

A servant or housekeeper in the Bellegarde household. She takes a liking to Newman and assists him later in his attempt to win Claire de Cintré.

Mademoiselle Noémie Nioche

A young flirt who uses her limited ability to paint in order to meet people to have liaisons with. She sells Newman a painting at much more than its worth.

Monsieur Nioche

The father of Mlle. Noémie Nioche who depicts himself to Newman as a gentleman caught in a series of misfortunes. He tutors Newman in French, and helps his daughter secure patrons.

Lord Deepmere

An English aristocrat who is distantly related to the Bellegardes. The Bellegardes would like Claire de Cintré to marry him.

The Reverend Mr. Babcock

Newman's traveling companion for part of a journey through Europe. He found Newman lacking in the proper "moral reaction" to the culture of Europe.

Stanislas Kapp

The person whom Valentin quarrels with and who fatally wounds Valentin in a duel.

Monsieur Grosjoyaux and Monsieur Ledoux

Acquaintances of Valentin who accompany him to the dueling ground.

The Grand Duchess

The theoretical leader of European society who likes Newman but whose allegiance must remain with the European aristocracy.

GENERAL PLOT SUMMARY

Upon his arrival in Europe, Christopher Newman begins to visit the various art galleries. In Paris, he meets, in the Louvre, a young girl who is making a copy of a great master. He prefers the copy to the original and offers to buy it. The young girl, Mademoiselle Noémie Nioche sells it to him at a much higher price than it is worth.

While at the Louvre, he meets an old acquaintance, Tom Tristram, whom he knew during the Civil War. He tells Tristram how much money he has made since the war and about his decision suddenly to drop out of the business and travel in Europe. When he suggests that he is on the lookout for a wife, Tristram tells him that Mrs. Tristram could help him. After several meetings, Mrs. Tristram suggests that he should court Madame Claire de Cintre, a very proud and inaccessible young lady who comes from one of Europe's oldest aristocracies. Later, Newman accidently drops in and Madame de Cintré is just leaving. She extends him an invitation to visit her, but when Newman arrives two days later, he is told that she is not at home.

The next day, Monsieur Nioche brings Newman the completed copy of the painting and is engaged to help Newman with French. The mademoiselle is to do some more copies for him. In a few days, Newman leaves on a tour of Europe during which he meets with a young unitarian minister from America. They compare their reactions to Europe and the young minister thinks that Newman is too liberal in his approach to life and art.

Upon his return to Paris, he calls on Madame de Cintré and finds her home. He also meets her brother Valentin and her sister-in-law, Marquise de Bellegarde. He apparently makes something of an impression on them. About a week later, Valentin pays Newman a visit. They discuss many aspects of European life, but whenever possible Newman brings the discussion around to Madame de Cintré. After a few more visits, the two men become good friends, and it is then that Newman tells Valentin that he wishes to marry Claire de Cintré. Valentin is shocked and thinks that Newman will not possibly be able to succeed, but promises to help him. Thus, after more visits, and as soon as possible, Newman proposes to Claire de Cintré. She is somewhat surprised and asks him to say no more about the subject for at least six months. Newman is encouraged because she didn't openly refuse him.

After the proposal, Newman meets the mother and the older brother, who are the head of the family. They are very cold and haughty, and look upon Newman as some type of curiosity. But at a later meeting, they tell him that he has permission to continue seeing Claire de Cintré.

One night at the opera, Newman introduces Valentin to Noémie Nioche. He tells Newman that the girl is not very honorable and that the girl's father knows this and consents to it. Newman is shocked and disagrees. Nevertheless, Valentin is intrigued by

Noémie's flirtatious charms. He plans to see her some more.

Sometime later, at a dinner party, Newman is introduced to Lord Deepmere, a distant relative from England. Lord Deepmere seems interested in Claire de Cintré. After the six months have elapsed, Newman proposes once again to Claire de Cintré, and to everyone's surprise, she accepts him. He wants to give a party, but the Bellegardes say it is their duty. At the ball, Newman is introduced to all of the aristocracy of France. The grand duchess, the titular head of European society, is delighted with Newman, but Newman is so happy that he does not notice that Lord Deepmere spends all of his time talking to Claire de Cintré.

Shortly afterwards, Newman is at the opera when he notices the presence of Valentin and Noémie and another gentleman. After a talk with them, Newman leaves. He later discovers that Valentin is going to fight a duel with the strange man over Noémie. Newman cannot understand this.

The next time he calls on Claire de Cintré, he finds her about to leave for the country home. She explains that she had written him a letter, but now tells him in person that she cannot marry him. Newman feels that the older Bellegardes have gone back on their promise. He wants to follow Claire de Cintré, but he gets word that Valentin has been fatally wounded in the duel and he must go to him. He finds Valentin still alive and tells him what happened between him and Claire de Cintré. Valentin is ashamed for his family and tells Newman to go see the housekeeper, Mrs. Bread, who possesses some type of knowledge which, if used properly, would force the Bellegardes to keep their word.

Newman goes to Claire de Cintré and tries to persuade her to marry him in spite of her family, but she tells him that she is resolved never to marry, and is determined to become a Carmelite nun. Newman goes to the Bellegardes and suggests that he has information which could damage them if they do not live up to their side of the bargain. They refuse Newman. He then goes to see Mrs. Bread, the housekeeper who has always liked Newman and who is strongly attached to Claire de Cintré. She tells him of a letter that the old Marquis de Bellegarde wrote on his death bed, telling how the son and wife had withheld his medicine from him which caused his death. He charges them with murder. Mrs. Bread then accepts Newman's offer to come and be his housekeeper. She leaves the Bellegardes despite arguments and threats against her.

Newman goes to the convent where Claire de Cintré is an apprentice. While there, he sees the Bellegardes, and confronts them with the letter. They are visibly upset, and the next day, Urbain comes to Newman and asks him to relinquish the document. Newman asks for Claire de Cintré's hand in marriage, but he is once again refused. Newman then decides that he must take his revenge.

He plans first to reveal his information to the grand duchess, but in visiting her, he recognizes their great differences, and says nothing. Soon afterwards, he leaves Paris and goes back to America, still desiring revenge. Later, he returns to Paris and suggests to Mrs. Tristram that he has something that could make the Bellegardes' life unpleasant. He then throws the slip of paper in the fire and watches it burn.

CHAPTER I

Summary

On a day in May, 1868, Christopher Newman was observing a young lady in the Louvre Museum making a copy of a famous painting. He was the type of American who often admired the copy as much as the original. He appeared to be perfectly relaxed and was, at thirty-five, at the peak of his physical health.

He only knew a few words of French and asked the young lady the price of her painting. He asked her to write the amount down, and when she wrote 2000 francs, he knew that she was asking much more than the picture was worth, but he told her to finish it and he would buy it. She wondered if he was kidding her, but Newman assured her, as best he could, that he was serious. At this time, the young lady's father, who could speak some English, appeared. The father was the "image of shabby gentility." He had had severe losses in business and had lost his courage. The father, Monsieur Nioche, arranges to bring the picture to Newman as soon as it is finished and dried. As they are about to leave, his daughter, Mademoiselle Noémie, suggests to her father that he offer to teach Newman the French language. Newman had never thought of himself as being capable of learning French, but he is pleased with the idea and it is arranged that M. Nioche will come to him, take morning coffee, and converse in French.

Commentary

As is typical in a James novel, it begins with the emphasis on the character placed in a certain situation and then allowing the situation to develop according to the nature of the character. As an individual, one of Newman's greatest attributes will be his natural and unpretentious honesty and forthrightness. His naturalness will later be contrasted with the European emphasis on formality and ceremony. Newman is seen here stretched out and reclining at ease as he watches the people making their copies. His ability to relax and to lounge, characterizes him as an American.

Newman's innocence and lack of experience are also suggested in this first chapter. As James characterizes him, Newman had "often admired the copy much more than the original." Thus, one of the things he must learn is to distinguish the worth of the original from that of the copy. In terms of the entire novel, he will later learn that Mademoiselle Noémie and her father are copies that he has overestimated, but this will be part of Newman's learning experience. Another of his qualities here emphasized is that he knew he was being overcharged for the copy, but did not seem to mind. He has a large soul which takes into account little discrepancies in people and is not bothered by them.

The quality most strongly emphasized is Newman's strangeness to these surroundings. Even though he is physically strong, the trip through the museum has almost exhausted him. This suggests that Newman is doing something that he is not accustomed to doing. In other words, as his name implies, he is the "new-man" discovering the old world. He is in a situation that is new and strange to him and we must watch to see how he reacts in these new situations.

He is reversing the voyage made by his name sake, Christopher Columbus.

Newman is later to learn that Mademoiselle Noémie is a flirt. The reader should be aware of this by the way James describes her glances at Newman. James will often devote a great deal of energy to describing his minor characters. M. Nioche is seen as a cringing man who has lost his courage. He is overly polite and obsequious, but for the first part of the novel, Newman is somewhat deceived about his character. Thus, part of Newman's education will involve his arriving at a recognition of M. Nioche's exact qualities.

CHAPTER II

Summary

Having bought his first picture, Newman felt a sense of difference and accomplishment. He then began to look around for another picture to buy, even though he knew he had paid too much for the first one. Then he noticed a man who looked familiar, and went over to him. It was Tom Tristram, a man Newman had known some years ago during the war. In their discussions, we hear that Newman has been in Europe seventeen days, and that Tristram has been living here for six years, but this is the first time that Tristram has been inside the Louvre. Newman can't understand this, because Tristram has just said that he knows Paris very well. But Tristram doesn't consider this the real Paris.

Tristram leads Newman out to a nearby cafe for coffee and a smoke. Newman envies Tristram for having a wife and home, but Tristram maintains that Paris is a place to be without a wife. Newman, however, suggests that he has lived alone long enough and would like to get married. He tells Tristram that he has made enough money now that he wants to see Europe and learn something about the world. He has come abroad to amuse himself, but he wonders if he knows how. Tristram volunteers to take him to an American club where they can play poker, but Newman revolts at this idea. He wants to hear fine music and see lovely sights and visit museums, churches, etc. Tristram doesn't really understand such "refined tastes," and Newman explains how two months ago, he was in competition with a man who had once done him a dirty trick. Newman was then in the position of making this man lose a large sum of money, but on his way to the stock market to close a deal, he became disgusted with the entire affair. He knew that if he didn't carry it through, he would lose sixty thousand dollars, but on the spur of the moment, he told his carriage driver to turn around, thus losing the sixty thousand. It was then that he decided to get out of business and learn to live, and this is why he came to Europe.

A man who could do something like that is outside of Tristram's comprehension, and he tells Newman that he must come and meet Mrs. Tristram who can understand him somewhat better.

Commentary

One of James' techniques as a writer is the use of contrast. The character of Tristram is used as a contrast to Newman. By seeing another American who devotes himself to playing poker in American clubs and who has never come to one of the great art galleries, we form already a better picture of Christopher Newman. James sums him up in one short stroke of the pen: "He looked like a person who would willingly shake hands with any one." In other words, Tristram is a person who has no taste, no wit, and not a great deal of intelligence. In his discussions of Europe, we see that Newman has learned more and profited more in seventeen days than Tristram has in six years.

We learn much more about Newman in this chapter. We see that he is a person who has the "desire, as he would have phrased it, to see the thing through." This is a typical Jamesian phrase used to suggest that Newman is the type of person who likes to investigate and delve into all aspects of life. Thus, James' novel also delves into every aspect of his subject before he finishes. Newman is also a person who, in the face of many difficulties did "see the thing through."

Furthermore, we find that Newman has made enough money so that he never has to work again. James always has characters who have enough money that they can devote themselves to refining their native talents, but notice that James refrains from saying exactly how much Newman has. This is left up to the imagination of the reader.

Another technique that James uses frequently is that of foreshadowing. In terms of the entire novel, Newman will later relinquish his great chance to get revenge on the Bellegarde family and will destroy a letter that could destroy the Bellegardes. This final action of the novel is foreshadowed by Newman's action with his business rival who had once played "a very mean trick" on him. Newman could have achieved a magnificent revenge on this man, but the idea of revenge filled him with mortal disgust. Thus, this scene prepares us for Newman's actions at the end of the novel. In other words, the reader should not be surprised at Newman's final action when we remember that part of his nature is revolted by the idea of revenge.

Furthermore, Newman says in this chapter that he wants "The best. I know the best can't be had for mere money, but I rather think money will do a good deal." The best later turns out to be Claire de Cintré, but it is also true that money is not enough to obtain her. As Newman keeps searching for the best, we must eventually realize that only within Newman himself is there the best for which he searches.

CHAPTER III

Summary

On the next day, Tristram took Newman home to meet Mrs. Tristram. Newman was fond of the company of women and welcomed the opportunity. Mrs. Tristram had a "marked tendency to irony." She had a very plain face, and had decided years ago to attempt to develop a great deal of charm to compensate for her lack of beauty. She had once been in love with a clever man who slighted her, and she "married a fool" out of some type of revenge, but she possessed "a spark of the sacred fire."

After a few talks with Mrs. Tristram, Newman and she became "fast friends." In their closer associations, he rapidly noticed that the Tristrams were not compatible. He also realized that the fault lay with Tom Tristram who seemed to live an idle and useless life.

As their acquaintance deepened, Mrs. Tristram often felt the need "to do something with" Newman. She pried information from him with the hope of discovering some way she could help him, but he seemed terribly self-contained. Finally, she told him one day that she would "like to put him in a difficult place."

After Mrs. Tristram tells Newman that he flatters her patriotism, she refuses to explain what she means, but advises him to always act naturally. If he is ever in a difficult situation, he is to do what comes naturally for him. Newman protests that there are so "many forms and ceremonies over here," but this is what Mrs. Tristram means—for Newman to cut through the rituals and come to the basic truth.

For the first time during their friendship, Mrs. Tristram brings up the subject of marriage. Newman tells her that he is anxious to marry, but wants to marry well, and he will be hard to please. His wife "must be a magnificent woman." Mrs. Tristram tells him that a perfect wife for him is already found and that she will bring them together. Mrs. Tristram asks him if he has a prejudice against European women, and Newman explains that he would marry anyone if the person pleased him.

In describing the person, who is named Claire de Cintré, Mrs. Tristram explains that Claire is not a great beauty, but "simply the loveliest woman in the world." She is not a "beauty, but she is beautiful" and she is half English and half French. Mrs. Tristram will not give an exact description, but maintains that "she is perfect." She warns Newman that Madame de Cintré has already been married once and doesn't want to be married again. It is Newman's job to make her change her mind.

At this point, Tristram breaks in and says that Madame de Cintré is a woman who is quite proud and haughty and not very good-looking. Her looks are the kind that one must "be *intellectual* to understand."

Some days later, Newman is calling on the Tristrams, and he accidently discovers Madame de Cintré as she is about to leave. With Mrs. Tristram's help, he is able to extract an invitation from this grand lady. After she leaves, Newman admits that she has a handsome face, but thinks she is more shy than proud. A few days later, he goes to the home, but is told by someone that "Madame de Cintré is not at home." As Newman leaves, he discovers that the man, who had seemed haughty to him, was actually Madame de Cintré's oldest brother.

Commentary

This chapter is devoted to introducing Mrs. Tristram who will play such an important role in the novel. She will become Newman's *confidante* (see section on the *Confidante* at the end of the book), and she will be the person who will introduce Newman to Claire de Cintré.

Essentially, Mrs. Tristram's function is to bring out certain characteristics of Newman and to illuminate the main character in some ways. She talks to him and by her probing questions we learn more about Newman as a character. She is also a complete contrast to her husband. It does not take Newman or the reader long to decide that Mrs. Tristram is far superior to her husband. For all of her faults, James still writes about her that she had "a spark of the sacred fire." This means that she belongs to the better type of people in the world.

In this chapter, James continues to use foreshadowing and irony. She says to Newman that she would like to put him in a difficult situation. Actually, by introducing Newman to Claire de Cintré, she involves him in a very difficult situation. Furthermore, she says that in six months she will see Newman in a fine fury, and Newman's pains and tumult that he endures at the hands of the Bellegardes are enough to put him in a fury.

James is also concerned with American innocence as opposed to European experience. This is first seen developing in this chapter. Mrs. Tristram advises Newman to always act naturally in all situations. This is Newman's (and the American's) great attribute –

the ability to act naturally, but in Europe Newman is confronted with "so many forms and ceremonies." Thus the difference between the American's naturalness and the European's experience will be seen on one level to be the difference between naturalness and formality, or between spontaneity as opposed to form and ceremony.

We also first hear of the fabulous Claire de Cintré in this chapter. There are two opposing views of her from the very beginning. First of all, Newman, in describing the woman he wants for a wife, says that she "must be a beautiful woman perched on the pile, like a statue on a monument." This is ironic because this description fits a woman who is not natural, who is more a work of art than a natural woman. Even Mrs. Tristram refers to her as "of a different clay." Tom Tristram says she is a "great white doll of a woman." Thus, James is already beginning to suggest that Claire de Cintré represents qualities that suggest art, form, and perfection rather than simplicity and naturalness.

We are also warned that Claire de Cintré's family are "terrible people" who are "mounted upon stilts a mile high, and with pedigrees long in proportion." We hear also that she has been married once and doesn't want to be married again. Thus, James is creating a situation where Newman will have to function in a manner and in a way that he has never before encountered. Thus, part of the suspense of the novel comes from our desire to see how this exceptional American will handle this completely new situation.

When Tom Tristram and Mrs. Tristram disagree about the value of Claire de Cintré , we, the readers, are already prepared to accept Mrs. Tristram's judgment of the situation, but we should not dismiss all that Tom Tristram says. When he comments that one must be intellectual to understand Claire de Cintré's beauty, he has accidently hit upon an important truth. Of course, Tom Tristram is not intellectual and therefore cannot understand Claire's beauty. Therefore, when Newman does respond, it suggests further qualities about the hero.

Mrs. Tristram tells Newman that he is "horribly western" and at the same time tells him that he "flatters" her patriotism. This implies a great deal about Newman. He is horribly western, because he is the natural man who is not affected by the manners, forms, and ceremonies of European society, but at the same time, Mrs. Tristram sees in Newman all of the good qualities that are represented by the American man and thus Newman flatters her streak of latent patriotism. That is, Newman combines all of the best qualities for which various Americans are known.

At the very end of the chapter, the reader is not aware of the fact, but Newman has met the Count Valentin and the Count Urbain de Bellegarde. The Count Valentin reacted in a friendly way and told Newman that he would see if his sister is "visible," but the Count Urbain said rather coldly that Madame de Cintré was not at home. Thus, our first exposure to these two brothers suggests the difference between their respective personalities.

CHAPTER IV

Summary

Some time later, Monsieur Nioche brings Christopher Newman the painting which is now completed and framed. Newman seems quite satisfied with the finished product. M. Nioche begins to complain of the difficulties of having an attractive daughter. Newman suggests that she get married, but M. Nioche explains that he doesn't have enough money for the proper dowry. Newman offers to buy six or eight more paintings from her and then she will have enough for a dowry. They then begin with the first French lesson.

On one occasion, M. Nioche expresses his fear for his daughter because his own wife had often deceived him. Newman decides that Madamoiselle Noémie should marry immediately and plans to meet her the next day at the Louvre in order to tell her what pictures he wants. M. Nioche is very embarrassed, but asks Newman to "respect the innocence of Mademoiselle Nioche." Newman finds this amusing, but assures the father he has nothing to worry about.

The next day he meets Mademoiselle Nioche and they walk through the Louvre with Newman pointing out the pictures he would like copies of. She tries to persuade him not to order certain pictures, and after he has completed his order, she calls him stupid and ignorant because he doesn't realize that her ability is not good enough to reproduce all the masterpieces he has ordered. She then confesses that she has no talent at all, but Newman says he is satisfied, and he suspects Mademoiselle of some ulterior motives in making the confession to him.

Newman finally asks her what she can do. She tells him that she has no talent for anything. He wonders why she continues then to deceive her father, but Mademoiselle Noémie affirms that her father knows that she has no real talent, however Newman is equally sure that her father believes in her. When she maintains that she can do nothing, Newman reminds her of his offer to buy a number of paintings, but Mademoiselle Noémie informs him that for a dowry of twelve thousand francs, she could do no better than marry a butcher or a grocer. He advises her not to be too fastidious and leaves her. As he goes, he realizes that Monsieur Nioche was correct when he feared that his daughter was a "frank coquette."

Commentary

During the course of the novel, Newman must learn. His encounters with the Nioches provide him an opportunity to learn something about the "shabby-genteel" life of the Parisian. During this chapter, he comes to one realization – that Mademoiselle Noémie is a "frank coquette." The reader should note that Newman thinks the father is honest and is deeply concerned over his daughter's morals. Later, he argues with Valentin about Monsieur Nioche's honesty and ignorance of his daughter's true nature. But we must remember that Newman is still the innocent American and has not yet acquired the experience necessary to evaluate the more subtle aspects of European natures.

Newman's desire to see Mademoiselle Noémie married parallels his own fate. At the end of the novel, he will meet her again in Europe and both will still be unmarried.

CHAPTER V

Summary

When Newman told Mrs. Tristram of his failure to see Madame de Cintré, she advised him to carry out his plan to "see Europe." He then began a long tour of Europe seeing the churches, monuments, pictures and other treasures of the continent. In Holland, he met a young American named Babcock who was a Unitarian minister. They became traveling companions.

After traveling together for some time, Mr. Babcock realized that Newman was a very noble person, but perhaps, he thought, Newman was too hasty to make judgments. Mr. Babcock thought Newman was not discriminating enough: "He liked everything, he accepted everything, he found amusement in everything." He considered Newman lacking in "moral reaction" and determined to break with Newman. He then explains to Newman how different they are: "You think I take things too hard, and I think you take things too easily. We can never agree." He tells Newman that "you are too passionate, too extravagant." Thus he leaves to "re-see" some of the things he has already seen and is confused about because Newman influenced his judgment. Some time later, Mr. Babcock writes Newman a letter, but the letter only confused Newman and rather than answer it, he chose an expensive little statuette in ivory and sent it to Mr. Babcock.

After more traveling, Newman realizes that he has been gone from Paris for four months. He still remembers vividly the gleam he saw in Madame de Cintré's eyes and wonders if he would not find more satisfaction in her eyes than in continued travel. He then receives a letter from Mrs. Tristram, and he replies that he will soon be returning to Paris. He tells her of Mr. Babcock, who found him too liberal, and then of an Englishman he traveled with who found him too virtuous and too "stern a moralist."

Commentary

James continues to give us more information about Newman. With every chapter we learn more about him. Here James uses the technique of contrast. In an earlier chapter, Newman was contrasted with Tom Tristram and by comparison was seen to be a far superior American, but the contrast left the possible interpretation that Newman was a prude when compared to Tristram. Now Newman introduces a real prude in the person of Mr. Babcock. Thus, by comparison, we see that Newman is very liberal. But again to keep the reader from thinking Newman too liberal, we hear about his English traveling companion who found Newman too moral and too stern. Thus when all things are considered, it seems that Newman is almost the perfect individual, being not too liberal and not too narrow-minded.

The inclusion of these characters who shed extra light on Newman is one of James' favorite tricks. He refers to these types of people as *reflectors* because by including them in the novel, they reflect something basic about the central character.

Newman's traveling has broadened him and increased his awareness of life. He now realizes things about himself and about other people that previously he would have thought impossible. For example, he sees through much of Babcock's fears, but doesn't judge him harshly. And he is not offended with either Babcock or the English companion for their criticisms of him.

More important is his realization about himself. He knew that he had never done a mean or ugly thing in his life, but he suddenly realized "that if he had never done anything very ugly, he had never, on the other hand, done anything particularly beautiful." Furthermore, he realizes that perhaps he can find more beauty in loving a beautiful woman than he can in seeing many sights. Thus his decision to return to Paris and Madame de Cintré.

CHAPTER VI

Summary

On his return to Paris, he trusted Tom Tristram to find some suitable rooms for him, even though Mrs. Tristram warned that the place would be hideous if Tom picked it out. But when Newman saw the place which was "gilded from floor to ceiling" and draped in various shades of satin, he thought the place magnificent.

Some time later, Mrs. Tristram tells Newman that she had met Madame de Cintré coming out of a church where she had gone for confession. She explains that the lady suffers rather harshly "from her wicked old mother and her Grand Turk of a brother." But according to Mrs. Tristram, Madame de Cintré's suffering illuminates her "saintliness and makes her perfect."

Newman wonders if Madame de Cintré is not free to do as she pleases. Mrs. Tristram explains that legally she is free but there is a moral obligation to the family. She fears that Claire de Cintré is being forced into another marriage because the Bellegardes are proud but very poor. Newman is tremendously affected by this news and wants to step in immediately and do something.

A few days later, Newman goes to see Madame de Cintré again, and this time meets her younger brother. Newman had previously thought the house strange, but this time he had a sense of wandering into a "strange corner of the world." During the conversation, her brother offers to allow Newman to "examine the house" promising him that it has many concealed and hidden things in it. Later, he meets Madame de Cintré's sister-in-law, who turns in surprise to Valentin and wonders why Madame de Cintré sees strangers now. She explains to Newman that she is the most modern of the family, and that Madame de Cintre is the proud one of the family. Newman turns to her and asks her directly if she is proud. She asks if he finds her so. Newman explains that she would have to tell him, because he would not know otherwise. He lets her know that he wants to see her again and she tells him to come often and even requests Valentin to invite him also, but Valentin first asks him if he is a brave man. Newman assures him that he is and then Valentin tells him in that case to come and visit again. Newman reminds him that he will be coming only to see Madame de Cintré.

Commentary

James is using a lot of foreshadowing in this particular chapter. First, there is the comment about Newman's new apartment that it was "gilded from floor to ceiling a foot thick." This will later become symbolic of the type of glitter or gild that Newman must learn to discern. Secondly, we learn more about Madame de Cintré and about her situation. She is described in terms of a bird or dove which "folds her wings." This will later be expanded to suggest that Madame de Cintré is similar to the wounded dove as she chooses to renounce this world. Thirdly, there is a suggestion that the house in which the Bellegardes live "looks as if wicked things had been done in it, and might be done again." This is an innocent statement in this context, but we later find out that the Bellegarde house hides many secret sins and of course their forcing Madame de Cintré not to marry is the wicked thing that will occur in this house. Carrying through with the analogy, James has Valentin later suggest that perhaps Newman would like to examine the house because there are many strange things hidden there.

When Newman enters the Bellegarde house "he had an unusual, unexpected sense of having wandered into a strange corner of the world." This is an extension of James' method of creating new and unusual situations for his characters, placing them in these new situations and then observing them. We see that Newman is awkward for a moment, but is soon master of the situation simply by being himself and pretending nothing. It is his quality of complete and direct honesty that serves him best in such situations.

CHAPTER VII

Summary

About a week after his visit to Madame de Cintré, Valentin came to visit Newman. At first, Newman had the impression that Valentin came to laugh at him, but he is very tolerant anyway. Valentin, however, explains that his sister requested him to come, and a request from his sister is a command for him. Newman notices how much he admires his sister and notices also that he resembles Madame de Cintré.

Valentin asks Newman's permission to ask a few questions. He wonders why Newman came to Paris. Newman tells him for pleasure, but that he is not having much fun; Valentin offers to aid him, but explains that he himself is a failure in the world. Valentin thinks it ironic that he offers his services to a man who has been a great success in life. Newman cannot understand why Valentin doesn't strike out on his own and do something, but Valentin finds this observation delightfully simple, and explains that things are different in Europe than in America. He explains also that there is nothing he can do and that he will probably go someday into a monastery.

During the next three weeks, Newman saw Valentin often and they soon established a firm friendship, and during this time, he often paid visits to Madame de Cintré but seldom found her alone. He continued to admire her and was convinced soon that she was the woman for whom he had been searching.

Once when Valentin visited Newman, he suggested a trip to see an Italian lady who was apparently beginning on a downward path. Valentin was interested in observing her. Newman suggested that perhaps someone should offer this lady some good advice, and suggested that maybe Madame de Cintré could talk to her. Valentin is almost horrified and tells Newman that his sister could never see this type of woman. Newman doesn't understand, and tempts Valentin to his apartment for a long talk.

Commmentary

This chapter is devoted essentially to establishing the friendship between Valentin and Newman. This friendship will be the means by which Newman will gain favor in Madame de Cintré's eyes and later the means by which he will discover the terrible secret about the Bellegarde family.

With Valentin, we find out that he considers himself a failure, but even as such, the "honor of name was safer in his hands than in those of some of its other members." This is later seen to be true when we find out how badly the Bellegardes treat Newman until even Valentin is ashamed of his family.

With this chapter, James is rapidly beginning to suggest some basic differences between the American and the European. "In America, Newman reflected, lads of twenty-five and thirty have old heads and young hearts, or at least young morals; here they have young heads and very aged hearts, morals the most grizzled and wrinkled." In this observation, Newman is suggesting a basic difference between the two. The American is essentially innocent but intelligent and willing to learn. But the European is already experienced and knows what to do in every situation, and is seemingly unwilling to attempt anything new; the difference is therefore presented in other ways. Newman sees nothing to prevent Valentin from striking out on his own. He doesn't understand how the name of Bellegarde can prevent a man from going out and earning an honest living. Furthermore, he doesn't know why Madame de Cintré is not free to go see a certain lady if she wants to. Thus, Newman has not yet learned about the restrictions imposed upon a member of the European aristocracy.

CHAPTER VIII

Summary

When Newman took Valentin to his apartment, he asked him directly to tell him something about Madame de Cintré. Valentin tells him that he cannot be objective because he admires his sister too much. He explains that she is the perfect combination of all the finest qualities of the world. She is kind, charitable, gentle, generous, and intelligent. She is both grave and gay.

Valentin then explains about Madame de Cintré's first husband. He was an odious old man of sixty years who had been guilty of misusing property that belonged to relatives. When he died, there were many court battles to gain possession of the property. Madame de Cintré found it so obnoxious that she promised her mother to do anything her mother asked her for ten years (except marry again) if she could drop the suit.

Newman asks about the marriage and is told how it was an arranged marriage. Madame de Cintré saw her husband only a short time before the wedding and turned ghostly white. She fainted at the wedding.

Newman reminds Valentin of his offer to render any service to him. Valentin tells him he is quite anxious to do so, therefore, Newman tells Valentin to make his sister think well of him. He then reveals that he wants to marry Madame de Cintré. Valentin is so surprised that he can say nothing. Finally Newman asks him to say so immediately if he must refuse. Again, Valentin wants to hear the request because he can hardly believe it. Newman explains that he wants only for Valentin to say a good word about him and he will do everything else; he promises to do everything in the proper form. Valentin finally says he doesn't know whether is he "pleased or horrified." Newman wonders why he should be horrified, and Valentin explains that Newman is not noble. Newman rejects that idea, maintaining that he is indeed noble. "I say I am noble. I don't exactly know what you mean by it, but it's a fine word and a fine idea; I put in a claim to it." Valentin asks for proof, for some title, but Newman says it is up to them to prove that he is not noble. For Valentin this is easy: Newman is not noble because he has "manufactured wash-tubs." Finally, Valentin tells him that what he means is that Newman is "not good enough."

Newman tells Valentin all that he expects of a wife, and all that he is willing to do for the right type of woman. For him, Madame de Cintré is his dream realized. All he wants from Valentin is a good word from him—for Valentin to tell his sister that Newman is a "good fellow" and "would make her a very good husband." Finally, Valentin is convinced that Newman is serious, and he decides to help Newman all he possibly can, but he warns him that it will not be easy—there are many forms and ceremonies to be observed. Furthermore, he warns Newman that the Bellegardes are an old and strange family: "Old trees have crooked branches, old houses have queer cracks, old races have odd secrets."

Commentary

This chapter elaborates on the character and nature of Madame de Cintré by having her brother praise her so highly, and as Mrs. Tristram had hinted early, Madame de Cintré is bound by some strange way to her family. Here we find out it is because of a promise that she made to the family. In her desire to drop out of the law litigations, when she found out about how corrupt her husband had been, we see in her actions and desires the same type of nobility recounted in Newman's earlier episode concerning the person who had played a dirty trick on him. Both Newman and Madame de Cintré would rather lose the money than be involved in situations tinged with vulgarity and immorality. Thus, she has made a promise to obey her family for ten years except that she will refuse to marry again. This information gives us the reason that Claire de Cintré cannot later defy her family when they refuse to accept Newman.

One of the essential differences between the American and the European is brought out in Newman and Valentin's discussion of the term "nobility." Newman, as the noble American, feels that he is as noble as any European, but for him this is an innate quality that men develop and live by. For him, others would have to prove that he is not noble, but for Valentin, nobility is something that is inherited. A man can be a perfect scoundrel as was Count de Cintré, but if he possesses a title, then he is automatically *noble*. It is earlier emphasized that the Bellegardes are among the most noble—the family nobility dates back to the eleventh century, and during this time there is "not a case on record of a misalliance among the women" of the family. A marriage between Newman and Madame de Cintré would therefore be considered a misalliance.

Throughout the entire chapter, Valentin is made appealing to the reader in spite of his brief spell of superiority and emphasis on nobility. This is a result of James' emphasis on Valentin's sincerity. He is one European who does not stand on ceremony and who does not employ forms and rituals in everything he does. Like Newman he acts with honesty and spontaneity. Even in his surprise and "horrified" reactions to the proposal, he remains a sympathetic character.

When Valentin accepts Newman as a suitor, his motivations are the best. He accepts Newman because he thinks Newman is indeed a fine person, and he is impressed that Newman thinks so highly of Madame de Cintré. This acceptance is based therefore on human values, whereas when the Bellegardes accept Newman as a suitor it is based solely upon the fact that he is immensely rich, a purely materialistic acceptance.

Several times during the chapter, Newman suggests that Valentin does not like his older brother, but Valentin says only positive things about the Count Urbain de Bellegarde. However, we know that he does in actuality despise his brother simply by the way that he alludes to him. Thus the forces are beginning to align themselves: Newman, Valentin, and Madame de Cintré as opposed to Madame de Bellegarde and the Count Urbain de Bellegarde.

At the end of the chapter, Valentin reminds Newman that "old trees and old races have strange secrets and crooked branches." This is again a bit of symbolic foreshadowing, for it is later discovered that the noble family has committed some rather terrible crimes.

CHAPTER IX

Summary

The next day, Newman goes to see Madame de Cintré. He must wait a long time before she comes in, but when she arrives, Newman is pleased to have her alone. He asks her if Valentin has spoken to her, and she says that Valentin has spoken quite well of him. Newman explains his position and tells her of his admiration for her and of his desire to make her his wife. She answers him that she has decided not to marry again. Newman requests her to see him more and not to reject him now—to think it over and wait before she refuses him. Madame de Cintré admits that she has not asked him to leave the house and never return. Newman emphasizes that Madame de Cintré is the type of person who needs to be perfectly free and, in marrying him, she would be perfectly free.

Madame de Cintré paused for a while and then admitted that Newman's comments had pleased her, but she asks him to say nothing more about the subject for six months. Newman is only too glad to promise.

A few hours later, he meets Valentin and tells him about the offer, and that Madame de Cintré did not accept the proposal, however, the fact that she is to continue to see him is, according to Valentin, a great "personal success" for Newman. He decides that he must present Newman to Urbain de Bellegarde immediately.

Commentary

In terms of a story of romance, many readers will view the proposal as rather quiet and unromantic, but with the nature of the characters, it could be no other way. We must remember that James is more interested in character, motivation, and states of mind than in exciting physical adventure.

As Newman is waiting for Madame de Cintré, he "wondered where, in so exquisite a compound, nature and art showed their dividing line. Where did the special intention separate from the habit of good manners? Where did urbanity end and sincerity begin?" These questions are, of course, central to the entire novel. Newman possesses natural goodness, sincerity, and good intentions, but he has not yet developed urbanity and art, that is, art in the form of observing the rituals and ceremonies so necessary in a formalized European society. Thus, we must begin to wonder how much of a combination of these qualities does Madame de Cintré possess. According to Valentin's description of her, she is the perfect combination of these opposing qualities.

CHAPTER X

Summary

Newman goes to Mrs. Tristram and relates his experiences with Madame de Cintré. Mrs. Tristram thinks it "is a great triumph." She is also surprised that Newman has gone so fast, and that he was not immediately thrown out.

Later, Valentin comes to conduct Newman to the house so as to meet the other members of the family. He warns Newman that his mother is not easily pleased. When presented to Madame de Bellegarde, Newman and she talk politely, both agreeing that each is ambitious and somewhat proud. She is very conservative in her manner and in her speech. She tells Newman that he must meet her oldest son who will not amuse him as much as does Valentin, but who is really much better. In a few minutes Newman meets the Count (Marquis) Urbain de Bellegarde who inquires about Newman's business activities. In a few minutes, Madame de Cintré enters and wants to attend a ball with her brother and his wife. This is, according to her mother, an inconsistent and strange action on Madame de Cintré's part.

When they have all left, Newman tells Madame de Bellegarde that he wishes to marry her daughter, but Madame de Bellegarde says she will not favor it. Newman tells her how rich he is and asks her if she will suffer it. She responds: "I would rather favor you, on the whole, than suffer you. It will be easier."

Commentary

This chapter continues to emphasize the difference between the American and the European. The reader should note the various ways by which Madame de Bellegarde is condescending to Newman. She makes various references to Americans as though they were some strange breed, and she speaks with a degree of coldness and distance. Urbain de Bellegarde is, as his name suggests, the epitome of everything that represents extreme urbanity. He was "distinguished to the tips of his polished nails and there was not a movement of his fine, perpendicular person that was not noble and majestic." But Newman and the reader immediately react against this person because he represents all form and ceremony without the touch of sincerity and honesty found in Madame de Cintré and Valentin. He represents the "incarnation of the art of taking one's self seriously."

We should be aware of how carefully James always has his characters say just the right thing, or else they say things which later become ironically true. For example, Valentin in urging his sister to attend the ball says that such "a beautiful woman... has no right to bury herself alive." Yet, at the end of the novel, the beautiful Madame de Cintré has done exactly that—buried herself alive.

CHAPTER XI

Summary

One day M. Nioche came to renew his visits with Newman. He expressed his great concern over Mademoiselle Noémie's actions, and Newman promises to look in on her at the Louvre the next day.

While wandering through the Louvre in search of Mademoiselle Noémie, Newman met Valentin who was there to conduct some dull English cousins through the most interesting parts of the museum, but they are late and at Newman's insistence, he joins him in the search for Mademoiselle Noémie.

When they find her, Newman wonders why she hasn't persevered and completed part of his order. She reminds him that she has no talent, and turns to Valentin to vouch for her that she cannot paint. Valentin advises her to give it up and try something else. After more polite conversation, M. Nioche comes to fetch his daughter. After they leave, Valentin admits that the Mademoiselle is very interesting and very attractive. Newman tells him that she is "a sad little adventuress" but Valentin thinks she is a great one. He realizes that "she has not as much heart as will go on the point of a needle," but this is an immense virtue.

Newman says he is not much concerned with the young lady, but he is worried about the father, but Valentin points out that the father is not worth the consideration. Newman maintains that M. Nioche is poor, but very high-toned and Newman is afraid that he will do harm to his daughter or to himself rather than suffer shame or disgrace. Again, Valentin gives a summary of the old man and tells Newman that he will survive and will probably end up living off his daughter's "ill-gotten" gains. Newman reminds Valentin that he is a cynic and that the only two virtuous men in Paris are himself and M. Nioche. If M. Nioche "turns out a humbug," then Newman will wash his hands of the entire affair. At this time, Valentin's English cousin shows up and he must leave with her.

Commentary

While many people think the episodes involving M. Nioche and his daughter are extraneous to the main action, these events are very central to Newman's development. First, he must learn about all aspects of European society before he can become the perfect American. From this couple, he learns gradually about duplicity. This is a part of his education. Until now, he has not possessed the ability or the exceptional sensitivity to detect all types of motivations. Valentin points out that M. Nioche is not so high-toned as Newman thinks the old man to be, but Newman now maintains strongly that he is right. This is again James' method of contrasting the European's experience as against the American's innocence. It will later be seen that Newman is wrong and has been deceived all the time. This is a part of Newman's education. These are things about which he must learn if he is to associate with people like the Bellegardes.

Furthermore, there is an implied contrast between Mademoiselle Noémie and Madame de Cintré, and from this point on, there will be the double love affair. One will be between Newman and Madame de Cintré on a rather high-toned plane, and the other will be between Valentin and Mademoiselle Noémie on a rather low level. Thus, in this chapter we have the introductions which begin this contrasting of love affairs, and the establishment of the rationale which will allow Valentin to be later killed in a duel.

CHAPTER XII

Summary

Three days after meeting the Bellegarde family, he received an invitation to dinner from the Marquis Urbain de Bellegarde. When he arrived, he was told that no one else had been invited. Newman asked Madame de Cintré if she enjoyed her ball, and she is taken aback when Newman answers for her that she had annoyed her mother and brother by going. Madame de Cintré admits he is right and warns him that she has "very little courage;" she is not, she says, a heroine.

Dinner was announced. It was simple but elegant and in perfect taste. During the dinner, Newman was uncomfortable and felt that the Marquis Urbain de Bellegarde was constantly in opposition to him. Newman, "for the first time in his life, was not himself." He suffered it through because he kept in sight the reward that he wanted so badly, Madame de Cintré.

After dinner, the gentlemen withdrew to the smoking room where Valentin burst out that he couldn't keep quiet any longer – Newman has been officially accepted by the family as a suitor for the hand of Clair de Cintré. He tells of the family council and other things which to the Marquis seem indiscreet. The Marquis explains that it was not an easy choice, but offers Newman his assurances that he will not interfere. "I will recommend my sister to accept you." But he suggests that Newman should receive the last word from the mother.

In the drawing room, young Madame de Bellegarde approaches Newman and tells him how she stood up for him in the family council. She suggests to him that she expects to take her revenge against the family through him. Newman is very cautious and the young Madame de Bellegarde reminds him that she could be a great help to him in many ways.

Madame de Bellegarde asks for Newman's arm and they retire to another room where she explains that they will not interfere, but the rest will remain with Newman. She feels compelled to tell Newman that they are stretching a point and doing him a great favor. Furthermore, she says that she shall not enjoy having her daughter married to him. Newman says he doesn't mind them not liking him as long as they don't back out of their promise. Madame de Bellegarde said that the word "back out...suggests a movement of which no Bellegarde has ever been guilty." She ends the interview by saying that she will always be polite to Newman but she will never like him.

In the drawing room, Newman tells Madame de Cintré that he he has been given permission to come often. She wonders if he didn't think it strange there was so much formality over his coming. Newman admits he doesn't understand it. Valentin arrives and congratulates him. He inquires about M. Nioche, and Newman had seen the old man that very day. M. Nioche had been particularly cheerful. This amuses Valentin because he tells Newman that Mademoiselle Noémie "is launched." She has left her father, and her father is still cheerful. Valentin now decides that he will see her.

Commentary

In this chapter Madame de Cintré tells Newman that she has very little courage and is not a heroine. Actually, when it comes later to a point of defying her family, it will be seen that she does not possess enough strength to do this and prefers to enter a nunnery.

At the dinner, Newman was not himself "for the first time in his life." Again, James' technique is to place his central character in a situation and watch his reactions. In this particular situation, Newman found that "the marquis was profoundly disagreeable to him" and that the marquis was a man "towards whom he was irresistibly in opposition." This is what causes Newman to feel uncomfortable. The marquis is a man of forms, phrases, and postures. He never speaks openly and spontaneously. These are rituals and ceremonies that Newman does not understand. Newman is an open, honest and sincere man. He cannot conceal his inner feelings. Thus to be around the marquis, he is uncomfortable because the two are diametrically opposite, and here is the contrast between the American and the European placed in its most direct statement.

The reader should be completely aware of the terms of the contract that the Bellegardes make with Newman. Everything in their promises suggest that they will never interfere with Newman and his suit for Madame de Cintré's hand. Later the Bellegardes use a small technicality to escape from the promise, but as Newman will later say, they will be acting dishonestly. Here, the Marquis even says he will recommend his sister to accept Newman. Later, however, they use the idea that they would not interfere with the proposal and when they do interfere, they remind him that they held their promise as long as they said they would, that is, until Madame de Cintré accepted him.

Newman, in his caution, fails to understand exactly what the young Madame de Bellegarde means when she offers him her friendship and says that through him she "expects to take" her revenge. Actually, later, she is able to render a great favor to Newman by arranging a meeting between him and the Bellegardes.

The chapter ends with the ironic comment about the Nioches. Here Valentin points out that Newman has been wrong, but Newman is so tense from his encounters with the Bellegardes that he doesn't care about the fate or downfall of M. Nioche. The point is, that in the midst of so much to be learned about Europe, Newman was certainly wrong in his evaluation of the Nioches, and as he accepts Madame de Bellegarde's word, he will later be wrong in believing her.

CHAPTER XIII

Summary

During the next six weeks, he went often to see Madame de Cintré. Their acquaintance deepened and Newman could see signs of her attachment to him.

Once with Mrs. Tristram, he commented on Madame de Bellegarde. He wondered if after all she had not sometime "murdered someone – all from a sense of duty, of course." But as wicked as the old lady seems to Newman, the marquis seems even worse.

One afternoon when he was calling on Madame de Cintré, he met an old English woman whom he later found out was Mrs. Bread. She pleads her old age and requests to be quite frank with him. She wants him to marry Madame de Cintré very quickly and go away to America. She implies that she knows things and that her information is worth something. Newman takes an immediate liking to her.

When Madame de Cintré enters, they discuss Mrs. Bread only a minute and then Madame de Cintré asks Newman about Valentin. She does not like the way Newman speaks of Valentin: she thinks it is with the kind of kindness that one shows to a child. Newman, however, protests that he likes Valentin too much to evaluate his feelings for the young man. Madame de Cintré closes the subject by telling of her foreboding that something is going to happen to her brother.

At their next meeting, Madame de Cintré asks Newman why he does not like her mother and brother. He explains that what is more important is that they do not like him, but he is not concerned as long as Madame de Cintré does.

While they are talking, the marquis enters, looking very exhilarated. He has with him a distant cousin from England, Lord Deepmere, who is a rather funny looking little fellow with a bald head, no front teeth and several pimples on his chin. It is apparent that the Marquis de Bellegarde is delighted with this cousin who has an immense amount of property.

Commentary

There is much use of irony and foreshadowing in this chapter. Newman's evaluation of Madame de Bellegarde is merely tossed off, but we later find out that she virtually did murder her husband; Mrs. Bread's suggestion that she has information worth something means only that she knows about this murder. As her name suggests, Mrs. Bread will actually be seen to be the salt (or bread) of the earth. She is a very plain but honest woman who wants to do the right thing.

Madame de Cintré's fear that something dreadful is going to happen to Valentin will also soon come true.

This chapter presents our first view of Lord Deepmere. Ironically the name suggests a deep sea or a deep person, but in actuality, Lord Deepmere borders on being somewhat of a simpleton. The reader should note the physical description. Physically, Lord Deepmere must look dreadful with his bald head, missing teeth, and pimples, but he possesses one great attribute that Newman does not have—he has a title making him a member of the nobility. Immediately, the Marquis de Bellegarde begins to regard him as a suitable husband for Madame de Cintré, and is delighted with his cousin even though we know Lord Deepmere has nothing to recommend himself except his title and his immense property.

CHAPTER XIV

Summary

Newman has kept his promise and said nothing for six months to Madame de Cintré, but now the time of waiting is over. He now speaks and tells Madame de Cintré that she is everything that he desires and more. She tells him that she liked him six months ago and even more today, but she reminds him that she is cold and "a coward." She continues by adding that she does not care for a brilliant, worldly life, but concludes that she thinks she could be happy with Newman because he is so different from anyone she has ever known.

Newman returns the next day and is met by Mrs. Bread. She tells him that nothing has been said, but she knows that he has been accepted. She reminds him to marry quickly and take Madame de Cintré away. She is still afraid.

When Newman meets Madame de Cintré, she tells him that she has not told her mother. Madame de Bellegarde is annoyed that she hasn't been told and asks that the marquis be sent for immediately. The marquis arrives and stiffly and formally congratulates Newman. Newman mentions that he is so happy he would like to shout the news from the rooftops, but Madame de Bellegarde is horrified at even the idea. Newman tells how he has already sent telegrams to America, and she assures him that her friends will not receive the news by telegram.

Valentin congratulates them, and wishes them happiness, but says that he adores someone he can't marry.

As Newman is about to leave, he says privately to Madame de Cintré that her family is not pleased. She is sorry about it but promises it will not become an issue between them.

When Newman next sees Mrs. Tristram, he tells about the telegrams he had received from America and how he had deliberately shown them to the Bellegardes "wanting for once to make the heads of the house of Bellegarde *feel* him." He tells of a party he plans to give in his "great gilded rooms." Mrs. Tristram finds this idea odious and delicious.

When he told Madame de Bellegarde of his plans, she turned pale and immediately told Newman that the Bellegardes must give a party first. As he was leaving, Valentin went with Newman and explained that his mother conceived the idea of the party on the spur of the moment so as to escape his party, but Newman is not bothered by this news.

Commentary

The reader should notice that James' method of handling the proposal scene differs from that of the average novelist. The scene is not filled with romantic sayings and happiness. Instead, there is a sense of almost fear. Madame de Cintré even mentions again that she is a coward. This repetition (she had said essentially the same thing in Chapter XII) begins to prepare the reader for Madame de Cintré's acquiescence to her mother's demands in Chapter XVIII. It is often by little remarks that James prepares the reader for some later action.

The proposal scene is followed immediately by an encounter with Mrs. Bread who adds an ominous note to the situation. Thus, to the careful reader, there are plenty of hints that things are not going as smoothly as Newman thinks they are.

Now that Newman is accepted by Madame de Cintré, he seems to explode. Or perhaps, more accurately, he seems to be less cautious than earlier. He is not disturbed that his telegrams to America are in bad form according to the Bellegardes, and he even delights in showing them the many responses he received. In his good nature, he is not even offended that his party was rejected in favor of one to be given by the Bellegardes. But we see that Newman is intent upon making "the heads of the house of Bellegarde *feel* him." This desire should be remembered in the light of what Newman could have done with revenge in a later chapter.

CHAPTER XV

Summary

Valentin gives Newman some more information about Mademoiselle Noémie. Newman found it disgusting to find he was wrong about M. Nioche, but he determined to seek him out one more time and find out for himself. He went to M. Nioche's address and was told that the old man was at a nearby cafe. Newman finds him drinking coffee with Mademoiselle Noémie.

Mademoiselle Noémie tells Newman that she has discovered that Valentin de Bellegarde has been making inquiries about her and tries to get Newman to take him a message, but Newman refuses to carry any messages. She reproaches Newman for their earlier relationship saying that he was not "gallant."

When Mademoiselle Noémie leaves, M. Nioche feels uncomfortable and tries to say that he meant his earlier protests at the time he made them, but now he just takes what she gives him. But, he maintains, he still hates it and can't forgive her for what she is doing.

The next time he sees Valentin, he admits that Valentin had judged the old man correctly, but still Newman is disappointed. Valentin, however, is very unhappy. He has formed a ridiculous infatuation for Mademoiselle Noémie even though he knows that she is not worth his attention. But she is, he says, charming and bewitching.

Commentary

Newman and Mademoiselle Noémie are both learning fast, but their objectives are quite different. Newman now learns that he was deceived in his opinions of both Mademoiselle Noémie and more important in his view of the old man. Thus Newman is learning something about deception.

Early in the novel, Mrs. Tristram had said that in six months she would see Newman in a fine fury of anger. Mademoiselle Noémie tells him that "It is something, at any rate, to have made you angry." Thus the one thing that can make Newman angry has now been discovered, that is, deception and especially deception in human relationships. Consequently, if he can be angry at being deceived in the relatively unimportant things like his relations with M. Nioche, then his anger must be tremendous when he is deceived by the Bellegardes.

The contrast between the noble love Newman feels for Madame de Cintré and the rather tawdry affair Valentin is having with Mademoiselle Noémie shows the difference between Newman's aims in life and those of Valentin. Even Valentin admits that his affair is a "striking contrast to your noble and virtuous attachment – a vile contrast."

CHAPTER XVI

Summary

The next days were the happiest in Newman's life. He saw Madame de Cintré every day. He also ran into the young Madame de Bellegarde and often had the impression that she wanted to say something to him—particularly something about how unpleasant her husband is. But Newman is determined not to do anything which would allow the Bellegardes to say he caused unpleasantness in their house.

Once Madame de Cintré warned Newman that she didn't come up to his ideal, but he refuses to believe it. She is everything he has ever looked for.

On the night of the grand ball, Newman is radiantly happy. He is ready to be friendly to everyone and to love everyone, even the Bellegardes. Madame de Bellegarde introduces him to a group of her friends, but all of them look somewhat alike to Newman. Thus, later when the Marquis Urbain de Bellegarde prepares to introduce him, he has already forgotten who these people were. When he is introduced to the Duchess ("The greatest lady in France."), he laughs uproariously at some of her remarks. She compliments him on obtaining the magnificent Claire de Cintré, and comments that the Bellegardes are very exacting people. She is not sure that at this moment she possesses their esteem.

Later when he meets Mrs. Tristram, he wonders if he is holding his head too high. Mrs. Tristram tells him little, but she has been observing M. de Bellegarde, and she feels that he doesn't like the entire proceedings. Newman excuses himself and goes to find Madame de Bellegarde. He finds her talking to Lord Deepmere who is embarrassed when Newman suddenly appears. Madame de Bellegarde tells Newman that she has been giving Lord Deepmere some excellent advice. Newman tells Lord Deepmere to accept her advice. Madame de Bellegarde tells Lord Deepmere to go and find Madame de Cintré and ask her to dance.

Newman tells Madame de Bellegarde that the ball is something he will always *remember*. She responds that she will never *forget* it.

She walks with Newman through the rooms, and then retires. Newman notices Madame de Cintré in the conservatory talking with someone and decides to approach her. Her companion is Lord Deepmere. When Newman approaches, Lord Deepmere becomes very red in the face. Madame de Cintré hints that they were discussing something that was to Lord Deepmere's credit but not necessarily to everyone's. After he leaves, Madame de Cintré emphasizes that Lord Deepmere is "a very honest little fellow." Newman asks Madame de Cintré if she is satisfied with him, and she answers that she is very happy.

Commentary

The chapter opens with a discussion between Madame de Cintré and Newman about Lord Deepmere. Without saying anything against him, it is apparent that Madame de Cintré finds him rather peculiar. Then Newman finds Lord Deepmere in conversation with Madame de Bellegarde and Lord Deepmere is embarrassed by the appearance of Newman. Then at the end of the chapter, Newman finds Lord Deepmere in private and agitated conversation with Madame de Cintré. Thus, his role in this chapter is central to the following actions in later chapters.

As Madame de Cintré says, blood is thicker than water. Earlier we had seen that the Marquis de Bellegarde was delighted to find Lord Deepmere. Then we must assume that he has plans for Lord Deepmere to marry Madame de Cintré. Then Madame de Bellegarde was apparently giving him the same advice. The conversation between the three is filled with double entendre or double meaning. Finally, we find Lord Deepmere in conversation with Madame de Cintré. Apparently from her remarks and from his embarrassment, he has revealed the advice that Madame de Bellegarde has given him. He is honest enough to reveal the possible treachery being perpetrated against Newman, and Madame de Cintré is wise enough to appreciate it and promises Newman that she will someday tell him, but she is also troubled. The reader should be aware of the subtle ways in which James allows the reader to know the above facts. It is not said directly, we must read into James' offhand statements what is not stated directly. For example, Lord Deepmere feels like going and getting tipsy. This is apparently not from a rejection by Madame de Cintré. There is nothing between them that would allow for such a reaction. Thus, he is probably disgusted with the duplicity of the Bellegardes. Likewise, Madame de Cintré would not say that the conversation was to "Lord Deepmere's credit, but it is not to everyone's" if Lord Deepmere had not conducted himself in an honorable fashion. She means it was good and honorable for Lord Deepmere to tell her of Madame de Bellegarde's advice but it is not to Madame de Bellegarde's credit to give such advice.

Newman, in his happiness, fails to catch many of the delicate and subtle occurrences at the ball. Thus, Mrs. Tristram has to employ her rather discriminating eye for detail and point out some things to Newman. But generally, Newman misses the nuances. For example, the young Madame de Bellegarde wants to say something to him, but Newman intentionally doesn't give her the chance. It is implied that she would inform him of the duplicity being perpetrated by the Bellegardes, but Newman fails to learn of this, simply because he refuses to participate in any sort of duplicity with the young Madame de Bellegarde.

James employes his technique of contrast again, by having the Tristrams meet the Bellegardes and by having Tom Tristram give his view of the old lady. He found her dreadful and wanted to say to her that he manufactured broomsticks for old witches. But Tristram's view of both Madame de Cintré and Madame de Bellegarde adds a touch of the real to our view of these people. Perhaps in Tristram's recounting of how nice Madame de Cintré was, we have a more real view of the lady than in Newman's accolades.

The reader should be aware also of the discrepancy between what Newman thinks of the French and what the French nobility think of themselves. Each thinks he is a distinctive noble, but Newman thinks they all look alike and has to warn M. Urbain de Bellegarde not to introduce him to the same people again. Newman's quality is best brought out by his natural reactions to the Grand Duchess. He thoroughly enjoys the duchess' sense of humor, but by reacting so honestly, he offends the Marquis de Bellegarde, who considers it perhaps a bit disrespectful. But the duchess is receptive to Newman and invites him to visit her. Finally, the reader should remember that this ball is the reason why the Bellegardes cannot allow the marriage. It is more than they can take when they see Newman among their most intimate friends.

CHAPTER XVII

Summary

One evening, Newman was attending the opera with a group of his American friends when he perceived Urbain de Bellegarde and his wife in another box. He plans to speak to them when he happens to notice Mademoiselle Noémie in a box somewhat further on. As he is making his way toward the Bellegarde box, he finds Valentin bemoaning his fate. Valentin tells him that he has realized what a fool he is for running after Mademoiselle Noémie but still admits that she is amusing and exciting. Newman changes the subject and talks to Valentin about going to America and occupying a position in a bank. He decides to go back and hear some more music while he thinks over the proposition.

Newman speaks to the Bellegardes on his way back, and Urbain makes a few remarks about the opera and leaves Newman with young Madame de Bellegarde. She wants him to promise to take her to an artist's ball because her husband would never condescend to go to such a place. She tells him how bored she is with her life.

When Newman resumed his place, he noticed that Valentin had joined Mademoiselle Noémie and her companion. At the next intermission, Valentin told Newman that he would be willing to try a position in America. As they are about to separate, Valentin is heading back to Mademoiselle Noémie's box. Newman tries to dissuade him, but Valentin explains that he has a special reason. Her companion has been insulting, and he must give the gentleman a chance to be openly insulting. It is, for Valentin, a point of honor.

At the end of the next act, he goes to Mademoiselle Noémie's box, and she is excited because Valentin and her companion are going to fight a duel over her. She is pleased because "that will give me a push." Newman is disgusted and leaves. He goes to Valentin who tells him that it is all arranged. Newman wants Valentin to drop it, but honor demands that Valentin continue with the arrangements. Newman requests permission to take charge, but as a future brother-in-law, Newman is not allowed to do so. Valentin leaves to find a second to accompany him to the dueling ground. Later he comes back to Newman and tries to explain how the thing is measured "by one's sense of honor." Newman objects because Mademoiselle Noémie is not worth testing one's sense of honor over. But Valentin cannot be changed in his opinion that his actions were the only possible ones.

The next day, Newman visits Madame de Cintré, and discovers that she has been crying. Valentin had been to see her and she has a foreboding that something dreadful is about to happen even though Valentin did not tell her about the duel. Newman does not feel that he has a right to tell her either.

Valentin dines with Newman the night before the duel. Again Newman tries to dissuade Valentin explaining that he is "too good to go and get" his "throat cut for a prostitute." But Valentin tries to explain the necessity of duelling and the necessity of his particular concept of honor. When they part, Newman asks only that Valentin return without damage.

Commentary

This chapter probably presents most directly the difference between the American and European's view of life, honor, forms, and ceremonies. Finally it is made clear that the European is more interested in how he will appear to the world than he is in any intrinsic values. The European sense of honor is built upon established forms and ceremonies while the American's sense of honor is built upon the proper perspective of any situation. Thus, Newman sees Mademoiselle as a prostitute undeserving of a duel by someone as important and valuable as Valentin. In other words, Valentin fights the duel only because he must preserve appearances and then he plans to go off to America. Thus appearances are more important to him than reality.

Furthermore, in Valentin's consideration of accepting a position in America, he is infinitely more concerned with how it would appear to others and how it would appear in his biography than he is in the usefulness and utilitarian value of actually doing something worthwhile. Throughout the entire chapter, while he is considering what to do with his life and while he is considering the proper forms to be observed in the forthcoming duel, he is never perplexed and never shows any signs of a failure to observe the correct forms and rituals. He even enjoys the music with perfect equanimity, and spends the evening before the duel discussing the proper ingredients for fish sauce.

Newman's reactions toward Mademoiselle Noémie have changed drastically during the course of the novel. At first, he wanted to help her, now he is disgusted by her desire to have two men duel over her simply because it will bring her publicity and "give her a push."

CHAPTER XVIII

Summary

The next morning, Newman went to call upon Madame de Cintré a bit earlier than usual. He was met by Mrs. Bread who told him that her lady was preparing for a journey and had left a letter for Newman, but she impulsively leads him up to Madame de Cintré's apartment. Here he finds Madame de Cintré already dressed for her journey. Madame and Urbain de Bellegarde are also present. Newman immediately felt as though he "was in the presence of something evil." He noticed that Madame de Cintré was in great distress. She announced simply that she couldn't marry Newman, and referred him to her mother and brother. They inform him that such a marriage is impossible and improper. He appeals to Madame de Cintré, but she says that she is "ashamed." She asks him to let her go in peace (or "death"), but at least to let her bury herself alone.

Newman then faces Madame and Urbaine de Bellegarde and reminds them of their promise not to interfere. But they maintain that they did not interfere; they simply commanded. This difference

Newman refuses to accept, especially after he has heard Madame de Cintré say that she is afraid of her mother. She then asks Newman to pity her and let her go alone. He promises to come to her later.

After she is gone, he accuses the Bellegardes of using some force on Madame de Cintré. But Madame de Bellegarde maintains that her only force lies in the obedience that her children show her.

They explain that they tried to carry the thing through, but after the ball, where they introduced Newman to their friends, they could not take it any longer. They can't accept Newman's antecedents, especially that he was engaged in commercial enterprizes. Newman appeals to them that he will leave the country or do anything they desire, but the Bellegardes are firm. They cannot allow Madame de Cintré to marry him.

After he leaves, he walks at random for a long time and finally finds himself near Mrs. Tristram's. He goes for a visit and she immediately knows that they have backed out. She admits that they are really aristocratic and points out that the Bellegardes want Madame de Cintré to marry Lord Deepmere. Mrs. Tristram also wonders what Valentin thinks about the entire situation. Then Newman remembers Valentin's plight and goes to his rooms where he finds a letter asking him to come immediately. He sits down and writes a note telling Madame de Cintré that he must go to Valentin who is "ill, perhaps dying," but he will come to her soon.

Commentary

Perhaps one of the greatest understatements of this chapter is made by Madame de Bellegarde when she asks Newman: "not to be violent. I have never in my life been present at a violent scene of any kind..." Yet, under all the calmness and quietness of this scene, there is a sense of impending evil and violence. It may be that Madame de Bellegarde only "commanded" her daughter to give up Newman, but for the sensitive reader, there is a sense of quiet violence present in these simple comments.

The reader should note that when Newman first enters, he feels that he is "in the presence of something evil." Furthermore, as he observes Madame de Cintré, he knows that she is terribly distressed. Perhaps her strongest statement concerning her family comes when she says "I am ashamed." This is the same thing that Valentin is to say in the next chapter concerning his family. But in this simple statement is an evaluation of her family that she has never before made. In her promise that she wants to bury herself, we are prepared for her future anouncement that she will enter the Carmelite nunnery.

As Mrs. Tristram points out later, it is not solely that the Bellegardes resent Newman's antecedents and commercial endeavors, but they also think that if they prevent this marriage then they can persuade Madame de Cintré to marry Lord Deepmere.

The reader should be aware of the Bellegarde concept of honor. They use a subtle distinction to justify themselves. They say that they had promised not to interfere until Madame de Cintré had accepted Newman. After that they felt they could not interfere, but could command. Like Newman's failure to accept Valentin's definition of honor, he refuses to accept this view of honor. Here Valentin agrees with Newman and apparently so does Madame de Cintré.

In the refusal of the Bellegardes to live up to their promise, the reader should see that the concept of honor, as adhered to by Newman, is far greater than the aristocratic concept adhered to by the Bellegardes.

CHAPTER XIX

Summary

Newman immediately catches a train to Switzerland where Valentin lies wounded. When he arrives, he is told that Valentin has already had the last rites of the church, and the doctor in attendance has definitely condemned Valentin. Newman hears how, in the first shot, Valentin intentionally shot to the side and only grazed M. Stanislas' arm, but M. Stanislas demanded another shot. The second time, Valentin fired aside, but M. Stanislas hit Valentin in the chest.

Newman must wait for some time before Valentin awakes. When he does, he says that he knew Newman would be there. He wonders if Newman is disgusted with him, but Newman tells him he is too sad to think of scolding him. Valentin asks about Claire de Cintré, but Newman tells him simply that she is in the country home in Fleurières; he wants to know why, but Newman doesn't tell him. Valentin knows that something is wrong, and insists upon knowing what. Newman tells him to get well and then he will tell him. When Newman tells Valentin that his wound is a mean way to end a man's life, Valentin asks him not to insist because somewhere deep down, Valentin agrees with Newman. The doctor comes in and asks Newman to leave.

Later that day, Newman is informed that Valentin is asking for him. Valentin tells Newman that he knows something is wrong about the marriage and asks him not to deceive a dying man. Then Valentin volunteers the information: "They have stopped" the marriage. Newman admits that Madame de Bellegarde and Urbain have "broken faith." Newman tells Valentin that Madame de Cintré is very unhappy; "They have made her suffer." Valentin asks for more information and finally tells Newman that he is ashamed for his family: "Here on my death-bed, I apologize for my family."

Valentin rests a while, and then calls Newman back to him. He tells Newman that there is a way to force the Bellegardes to "come round." There is a great secret, "an immense secret. You can use it against them—frighten them, force them." He tells Newman that his mother and brother once did something to his father, but he has been too ashamed to admit what it was. But Mrs. Bread knows and Newman is to go to Mrs. Bread and tell her that Valentin requests her to give Newman the information.

Commentary

The reader should notice varying degrees of honor and forms emphasized in this chapter. First, Valentin, while complying to the false concepts of honor involved in a duel, did do the gentlemanly thing and only grazed his opponent's arm and on his second shot fired way off to the side. He adhered to the right forms and honor to the last minute. Note also, that his companions are more interested or more concerned over the fact that Valentin had adhered to the strict code of honor than they are over the fact that Valentin is dying. Newman doesn't care for these fancy concepts of honor but only for the fact that his dear friend is dying.

It is Newman's concept of honor which prevents him from telling the dying Valentin about the Bellegarde's deceit. But Valentin is too perceptive, and he forces Newman to tell. Thus, James presents the scene in such a way so that Newman does not have to burden the dying man with his problems until he insists upon knowing.

As soon as Valentin hears about his family's deceit, he apologizes for the family; he is ashamed for them. His statements in the context take on immense importance. Valentin is lying on his deathbed dying by some concept of honor that he has always adhered to. To find out that his family has betrayed the same Bellegarde honor which is causing him his death is more than he can tolerate. Thus, this is one reason why he turns against his family. The other reason is the affection he feels for Newman and the deep love he feels for his sister whom he knows is suffering now at the hands of his family. Consequently, he reveals an immense secret concerning his family —a secret that he has been ashamed of, but he refers Newman to Mrs. Bread. As Valentin is dying, we are reminded of the earlier statement in Chapter VII that the "honor of the name was safer in his [Valentin's] hands than in those of some of its other members."

CHAPTER XX

Summary

Valentin died peacefully and Newman left so as not to see Urbain de Bellegarde. He received a letter from Madame de Cintré, and decided to drive down to the country home to attend Valentin's funeral and later see Madame de Cintré.

When he calls upon her, she seems greatly changed. She immediately admits that Newman has been greatly wronged, and she feels very cruel and guilty. Newman tells her that she is not obliged to drop him simply because her mother told her too, but she reminds him that she has always said she was not a heroine. Newman tells her that she is being false to herself and saying bad things about herself in order to cover up for her mother's and brother's wickedness. He reasons with her that the only reason she is giving him up is that her family has tortured her.

Madame de Cintré assures Newman that she is not giving him up for any worldly advantage. Newman knows this and even understands now about Madame de Bellegarde's duplicity in urging Lord Deepmere to court Madame de Cintré. Finally, Madame de Cintré admits that she is not indifferent to Newman, but what she is doing is "like a religion. There is a curse upon the house." She wanted to escape, but her family forced her to remember it. As she is about to go, Newman asks her where she is going. She tells him that she is going into a Carmelite nunnery for life. Newman begs and pleads with her not to take such a drastic step. He beseeches her never to lock all her charm behind an iron gate. She only reminds him that she can't live in the world and not be his wife. She feels this should help him understand her feelings for him. Newman takes her gently in his arms, and kisses her, but she soon forces herself free and hurries through the door.

Commentary

When Newman first sees Madame de Cintré in this chapter, she is described as having a "monastic rigidity." This suggests already her decision to enter the nunnery. The reader should be aware of the tremendous amount of tension in this chapter; both characters are filled with tension, but still control their feelings. This is that Jamesian violence under control.

At first Madame de Cintré tries to make herself seem weak and cowardly, so as to avoid making her family appear in a bad light. But gradually, Newman is able to break through all of her excuses for her behavior, and she finally has to admit that her feelings are based on fear of her family and, furthermore, it is fear that is like a religion. For this reason, there seems to be nothing that she can do but go into a nunnery. She cannot remain in a world filled with such evil, she can't defy the evil, and furthermore, by entering the nunnery, she is attempting to show Newman just how much she does love him even though she can't defy her family.

The fact that she allows Newman to embrace her at the end of the interview—the first physical demonstration of love in the novel—serves as a further proof of her deep devotion to him. It is, therefore, this mutual deep devotion which makes the love a tragic one.

CHAPTER XXI

Summary

Newman walks for a long time after the interview with Madame de Cintré. He cannot yet bring himself to give her up. He still thinks that if mother and son would drop their victim, she would still come back to him. He decides to have one more interview with Madame and Urbain de Bellegarde.

As he enters the chateau, he is met by Mrs. Bread who sympathizes with him. She tells him that Madame de Cintré left that morning for the nunnery and that she had only told her mother the night before. The Bellegardes are taking it rather hard. She asks for some last news of Valentin, and Newman asks her to meet him that night and he will tell her Valentin's last words.

When Newman meets the Bellegardes, he asks them to repeal their order because becoming a Carmelite nun is worse than marrying a commercial person. They refuse. Newman wonders if anything will force them. He tells them of Valentin's last words and his apology for the family. They refuse to believe it, and Newman warns them that he knows something about a crime. They refuse to talk to Newman any longer and send word by letter that they are leaving to confirm Madame de Cintré's desire to become a nun. That night he goes to meet Mrs. Bread at the appointed place.

Commentary

Newman is consumed with the idea of revenge in this chapter. Here he is not seen as the noble person he so often appears to be.

He reviews his case and decides that if he is objected to because of his commercial nature, then they have failed to take into considerations how far a commercial person can go in achieving revenge. But perhaps more important, Newman wants revenge for Claire de Cintré. He is convinced that the Bellegardes have used some kind of force on her. The reader should note that James never allows the reader to know what kind of specific force they used, but has left it to the reader's imagination. This is the same technique he often uses. We have never known exactly how rich Newman is, only that he is extremely rich. In other novels, James will have a person ill, but will never name the exact nature of the illness. This technique allows the reader's imagination to roam and makes the unsaid more important than the specific detail.

At this point in his desire for revenge, Newman still thinks that he can achieve his goal—the hand of Madame de Cintré. What he fails to note is that Madame de Cintré would probably not return to him now even if her mother were to release her.

The Bellegardes are, however, the true aristocrats. They are indeed shaken and frightened by Newman's utterings, but they still refuse to give in to him. Newman must go further before he can have his perfect revenge. But he has made them *feel* him.

CHAPTER XXII

Summary

At his meeting with Mrs. Bread, she tells Newman that the Bellegardes made Madame de Cintré feel wicked. She explains that Madame de Cintré knew nothing wicked about her mother, but that was because she was afraid to know, but Mrs. Bread wants to hear about Valentin. Newman recounts to her what Valentin had told him, and Mrs. Bread is shocked, but she is also touched that Valentin thought so highly of her and died with her name on his breath. Newman tells her that Valentin wanted whatever information she possessed so that he could force the Bellegardes to come round to him. He explains: "I have been cruelly injured. They have hurt me, and I want to hurt them. I don't deny that." He wants to bring them down. Mrs. Bread is worried about what Madame de Cintré would say, but Newman thinks she entered the nunnery so that he would have a free field to work in. Newman promises Mrs. Bread that she can come and work for him.

Mrs. Bread then tells Newman that she has harbored a grudge against Madame de Bellegarde for many a year. Once Madame de Bellegarde made some false accusations against Mrs. Bread and she has remembered these dishonors through the years. Now she tells how the elder M. de Bellegarde lay sick, and was supposed to take some medicine. Madame de Bellegarde wanted him dead because she wanted to marry Claire to the old Count de Cintré, but M. de Bellegarde opposed it. Thus, when the elder M. de Bellegarde needed some medicine, she poured the medicine out rather than give it to him. She left him later for dead, but he recovered enough to write a note telling what his wife had done. He gave the note to Mrs. Bread, and she has kept it through all these years. She can't read French, therefore, she doesn't know the exact contents of the note. She later goes to fetch the note, and when she returns, Newman reads it excitedly. It accuses Madame de Bellegarde of murder so that she can marry Claire to M. de Cintré, and the note is signed by the elder M. de Bellegarde.

Commentary

The reader should note that Mrs. Bread is not willing to divulge all of her information until Newman uses Valentin's request and Madame de Cintré's sorrow and suffering as an excuse. He also knows that Mrs. Bread admires him, and he explains why he wants the information. Finally, but not the least important, he offers her a place with him for the rest of her life.

Thus her story of the wicked deeds of Madame de Bellegarde and the note she has preserved through all the years provide the perfect mode of revenge for Newman. Now it is clear to the reader that behind all the forms and ceremonies, behind the sense of honor, aristocracy, and rituals, there lies a basic evil. But even now, Newman does not consider what Madame de Bellegarde did to her old degenerated husband as evil as what she is presently doing to Claire de Cintré. In the murder of her husband, she was, after all, murdering a dissipated old man, but with Madame de Cintré, she is destroying a potentially great personality – a lovely woman who has not attained her peak of perfection.

CHAPTER XXIII

Summary

Newman returned to Paris in order to plan and nurse his revenge. He walked to Madame de Bellegarde's and inquired if the lady had returned. He was disgusted to think that she would not receive him and he might have to resort to writing a letter. He returned home feeling rather tired. He began to think that nursing a vengeance was rather tiring.

While he was resting, Mrs. Bread was shown in. She tells Newman that she is all packed, and is anxious to get everything over with. She tells Newman that Madame and Urbain de Bellegarde have tried to see Madame de Cintré and could not. She describes the life of the Carmelite nun as something terrible. They wear coarse old clothes, sleep on the ground, and have no heat. It is the strictest of all the orders of the nuns. She tells him the name of the house which Madame de Cintré entered, and he plans to go some Sunday to hear the nuns even though one cannot see them. Newman sends Mrs. Bread off to select a room for herself, but she comes back saying that all of them are too nice for her.

The next day, she reports the difficulties she had in leaving the Bellegardes. She had sent her trunk down and had ordered a cab before she told Madame de Bellegarde. When Mrs. Bread told her that she was going to Mr. Newman, Madame de Bellegarde turned red and ordered Mrs. Bread to leave immediately, but she sent word down to the porter not to let Mrs. Bread out the gate. Mrs. Bread bullied the porter into opening the gate, however. Newman is excited because he now realizes that the old Madame de Bellegarde is frightened.

Later, he goes to see Mrs. Tristram who tells him that he is not himself. He asks her to do him a great favor. She is to go to some Abbé and get him permission to attend a service in the nunnery where Madame de Cintré is. Two days later he received the permission.

Commentary

Notice the fluctuation in this chapter between a strong desire for revenge and pure melancholy. During the first part of the chapter, we have a hint that Newman will not be able to harbor his revenge for a long time. Already it is too exhausting.

When Mrs. Bread arrives and begins to tell about the nunnery, Newman's desire for revenge fades and is replaced by a strong sense of sadness and melancholy. But on her second arrival when she narrates how she left the Bellegarde house, Newman suddenly realizes, from her report, that Madame de Bellegarde is disturbed and frightened. He moves back now to his desire for revenge.

This shift is represented in the last scene by Mrs. Tristram's remarks that Newman is strange and incoherent.

Early in the novel, Newman had thought the gilded rooms were magnificent. Now he says to Mrs. Bread that it is just so much tinsel and it will "all peel off of itself." Thus, Newman has been disillusioned about gilded rooms and the tinsel concept of honor found among the Bellegardes. He has, indeed, learned a great deal since his arrival in Europe.

CHAPTER XXIV

Summary

Newman goes to the nunnery on Sunday morning and is shocked by the bleak, barren stone. When he hears the nuns enter, they are singing or chanting, but it sounded more like a wail and a dirge. "It was hideous, it was horrible." Newman could stand it no longer; he rose and left. At the entrance, he came face to face with Madame and Urbain de Bellegarde who were just entering. Outside, he sees the young Madame de Bellegarde who motions to him to come to her. She wants him to know that she had nothing to do with the deceit and thinks Newman was treated dreadfully. Newman suddenly asks the young Marquise if she would delay her return so as to give him a chance to confront her husband and mother-in-law. She does even better. She tells that they are to meet her in a certain place in the park, and invites Newman to accompany her there.

After a time the Bellegardes are seen coming down the path. Newman stops them. They try to avoid the meeting, but Newman tells them they will regret it if they don't listen. Then he accuses Madame de Bellegarde of killing her husband. He tells her that he has a letter written by her late husband after she had left him for dead. Madame de Bellegarde asks to see the letter. Newman gives the Marquis a copy which he reads and turns pale. He assures them that the original is in a safe place. They wonder what he plans to do with the information. Newman tells them that he plans to show it to a few influential people. He says: "I mean to show the world that, however bad I may be, you are not quite the people to say it." Madame de Bellegarde pretends that it was not worth Newman's effort to stop them, and they leave. Newman feels that Madame de Bellegarde is indeed a "plucky woman."

The next morning, Urbain de Bellegarde calls at Newman's apartment and tells him that he and his mother think the document real. He asks that Newman destroy the note because it would only pain the friends of his late father to find out that he was apparently insane when he wrote such an outrageous note. Newman wonders what they will offer him. The Marquis says that they are giving him a chance that any gentleman should appreciate: "A chance to abstain from inflicting a terrible blot upon the memory of a man who certainly had his faults, but who, personally had done you no wrong." Newman reminds the Marquis that they don't consider him a gentleman. He then asks them to give him back Madame de Cintré, but the Marquis replies "Never!" He informs Newman that to reveal the contents of the note will be disagreeable but nothing more. After that, he leaves, and Newman thinks that he can begin to be satisfied now.

Commentary

The chapter opens with Newman's succumbing to a mood of grief and melancholy brought about by the appearance of the nunnery and the remembrance of the love he holds for Madame de Cintré.

When Newman first sees the Bellegardes, he notes that "they had not their grand behavior immediately in hand." This remark characterizes the entire chapter. For once, Newman has the upper hand in the matter. The Bellegardes are first of all terribly upset by Madame de Cintré's actions. To see Newman reminds them of their part in her terrible decision. Consequently, when Newman confronts them in the park with their terrible deeds, they are already troubled by their guilt in forcing Madame de Cintré into the nunnery. At the end of the interview, Newman is somewhat troubled that he did not get the best of the Bellegardes, until he realized that the old lady was only using a "very superior style of brazen assurance" to cover up for her guilt.

Newman is still learning. He discovers that the Marquis' defense is much more complicated than he had envisioned. Most important in this chapter is the Marquis' refusal to give back Claire de Cintré. The decisions which made them originally object to the marriage are still the same and will never change. This is especially true since the Marquis and Madame de Bellegarde are most concerned with the appearance of things. But for them the awkward and disagreeable charges that Newman can make are less objectionable than the marriage would be. This is the old aristocratic honor in its strongest form.

The reader should also note that the Marquis had previously preferred Lord Deepmere to Newman solely on the basis of the title that Lord Deepmere possessed. Yet as Newman refused to enter into an alliance with Madame de Bellegarde because of honor, we find here that Lord Deepmere has promised to return and carry on a minor affair with the young Marquise.

CHAPTER XXV

Summary

Newman calls upon the Grand Duchess and for a long time they talk about all sorts of impersonal things. He never has a chance to talk about the Bellegardes. Then an Italian prince is announced. She tells Newman not to leave because the prince might be a bore, but the prince turns out to have a lively and spirited conversation with the Duchess, and Newman is able to reflect that he has nothing in common with these people and since he cannot sympathize with them, it would be foolish to expect them to sympathize with him. He bids the Duchess goodby. Out in the streets, he realizes that to discuss the Bellegardes with anyone would be extremely disagreeable.

Later he dines with the Tristrams, and Mrs. Tristram discusses Madame de Cintré with him. She wonders if Newman could have been really happy, but Newman wanted the chance to try. Mrs. Tristram tells him that he needs to travel to forget it all. He agrees and packs up.

His first stop was London. Here after some days he meets, unexpectedly, with Mademoiselle Noémie whom he had avoided. Then he happened to sit down on the bench next to M. Nioche. It was fifteen minutes before Newman was aware it was the old man. M. Nioche said he didn't speak because he was ashamed. Mademoiselle Noémie returned on the arm of Lord Deepmere who had met her through Valentin. Lord Deepmere was somewhat embarrassed to be seen in her company especially since she was the indirect cause of Valentin's death. Newman was thoroughly disgusted and left immediately.

Commentary

For the first time since his betrayal, we are beginning to see the real Christopher Newman. Here also is the beginning of his renunciation. At the duchess', he begins to realize that revenge for the sake of revenge is not very rewarding. Furthermore, he realizes that the aristocracy has formed a bond from which he is definitely excluded. Before he is able to reveal his true intent, the prince arrives. The prince's visit gives Newman a chance to think things over, and also allows him to see the strong unity between the aristocracy. He sees the aristocracy as cold and superficial. It is an artificial world built of polite conversation which carries very little intellectual stimulation. He realizes that even if the Duchess would turn against the Bellegardes, this would not help his sense of despair. And finally, he is beginning to realize that unless he could regain Madame de Cintré, no revenge has any meaning for him.

In London he meets Mademoiselle Noémie and Lord Deepmere. Here then is the man the Marquis de Bellegarde preferred to Newman, and this man is associating with the prostitute who caused Valentin's death. This is James' closing comment on the nature and honor of the European aristocracy. Newman himself is innately disgusted with the woman and with anyone who would condescend to associate with her. Thus Newman has learned a great deal since the time when he first encountered her in the Louvre.

CHAPTER XXVI

Summary

Newman is still nursing a desire for revenge, but he does not want to be trapped in an act of revenge. He cannot escape the fact that he is the "good fellow wronged." But more and more he begins to see that the Bellegardes are suffering because they are in suspense as to what he will do with his secret paper. Perhaps the more he waited, the more the Bellegardes would suffer.

Newman travels to America, then across the continent to San Francisco. He told his friends nothing except that the lady had changed her mind. When further details were requested, Newman always suggested that the subject be dropped.

One day he received a letter from Mrs. Tristram. She told him that Madame de Cintré had taken her last vows as a Carmelite nun. That evening he started for Paris. When he returned to his Paris apartment, he told Mrs. Bread that he intended to remain forever.

He goes immediately to see Mrs. Tristram who tells him that Claire de Cintré is now transferred to another Carmelite nunnery on the Rue d'Enfer. She tells him that he did not travel long enough because he still looks dangerous if not wicked. Newman rejects the idea that he is wicked.

That night, he walked by the nunnery, where Claire de Cintré was "imprisoned." The nunnery only told him that "the woman within was lost beyond recall." As he remembered the depth of his love and the extremes of Claire de Cintré's punishment to prove her love, suddenly "the bottom had fallen out of his revenge." Then he was "ashamed of having wanted to hurt" the Bellegardes. "They had hurt him, but such things were really not his game."

He went to his apartments and asked Mrs. Bread to pack his bags. He tells her that he has decided never to return to Paris. He pays one more visit to the Tristrams. Soon Tom Tristram excuses himself to go to his club. Then Newman takes out the letter that the old Marquis de Bellegarde had written and throws it into the fire. He tells Mrs. Tristram that the piece of paper was his revenge because it contained a secret which would damn the Bellegardes if it were known. He explains that it is a very bad secret. Mrs. Tristram wonders if the Bellegardes were humbled. Newman explains that they pretended not to be but he knows that they were frightened and that is all the revenge he needs. Mrs. Tristram tells him that the Bellegardes probably counted on his being such a gentleman and their talent was not in bluffing but in their knowledge of Newman's "remarkable good nature." Newman turned to see if the letter was completely burned, but it was.

Commentary

With the passing of time, Newman has still done nothing about his revenge. He still feels, when he thinks of it, that he "was a good fellow wronged." And with this realization, he also came to another realization – that part of his revenge was leaving the Bellegardes in suspense as to when he would reveal the contents of the document.

Returning to America, Newman was unable to renew old acquaintances. He has learned so much in Europe and his experiences there have been so intense and so deep, that he feels unable to communicate these feelings to his old friends; thus, he says nothing to them. This need to communicate his feelings ultimately leads him back to Mrs. Tristram, the only person to whom he can speak openly about his wrong.

After talking to Mrs. Tristram and seeing the place where Claire de Cintré is imprisoned, he decides to leave Paris forever. When he goes to bid goodby to Mrs. Tristram, he learns that the Bellegardes have stayed in their country home ever since their betrayal of Newman. He realizes that they are now *feeling* him.

Newman's greatness and superiority is seen in these scenes. He now comes to realize that mere revenge is meaningless to him. If he could use his information to force the Bellegardes to give Claire de Cintré back to him, he would do so, but he knows now that he can never have her. Therefore, to make the Bellegardes suffer will not alleviate his own sufferings. In giving up his idea of revenge, he is renouncing a part of the world in the same way that Claire de Cintré renounced the entire world. But in both renunciations, the characters take on qualities which make them more important and more significant individuals.

The reader should remember that James has already foreshadowed this last act of Newman's. Earlier, when he had a chance to revenge himself on the man who had played a "dirty trick" on him, Newman had found the entire procedure distasteful. But the "dirty trick" played on him by the Bellegardes hurts much more. The point is that Newman is a consistent character with certain definite values. He only had to have time to realize that regardless of the degree of hurt or regardless of the magnitude of the "dirty trick" his own basic reaction will ultimately be the same.

James often ends his novels on a slightly ironic or ambiguous note. Thus at the end of *The American,* when Mrs. Tristram tells Newman that the Bellegardes were counting on his being gentleman enough to burn the letter, Newman looks to see if it is completely consumed. He resents perhaps that once again the Bellegardes got the upper hand. But still Newman would not have used the letter. He must remain constant to his values.

MEANING THROUGH SOCIAL CONTRASTS: THE AMERICAN VERSUS THE EUROPEAN

Henry James was the first novelist to write on the theme of the American versus the European with any degree of greatness. Almost all of his major novels may be approached as a study of the social theme of the American in Europe in which James contrasts the active life of the American with the mannered life of the European aristocracy. Embodied in this contrast is the moral theme in which the moral innocence of the American is contrasted with the knowledge and experience (and evil) of the European.

In its most general terms, ie., in terms which will apply to almost any Jamesian novel, the contrasts are seen as follows:

THE AMERICAN		THE EUROPEAN
innocence	vs.	knowledge or experience
utility	vs.	form and ceremony
spontaneity	vs.	ritual
sincerity	vs.	urbanity
action	vs.	inaction
nature	vs.	art
natural	vs.	artificial
honesty	vs.	evil

The above list could be extended to include other virtues or qualities but this list, or even half this list will suffice to demonstrate James' theme or idea in the use of this American – European contrast.

The reader should also remember that James uses these ideas with a great deal of flexibility. It does not always mean that every European will have exactly these qualities or that every American will. In fact, some of the more admirable characters are indeed Europeans who possess many of these qualities and in turn reject others. Because a European might possess urbanity and knowledge and experience does not necessarily mean that he is artificial and evil. And quite the contrary, many Americans come with natural spontaneity and are not necessarily honest and admirable. For example, Tom Tristram possesses most of the qualities assigned to the American character but he is not a particularly admirable character. Likewise, Valentin de Bellegarde possesses urbanity and adheres to forms, ceremonies and rituals, but he is nevertheless a rather admirable character.

In *The American,* the character who represents the American in the best sense of the word is, of course, Christopher Newman. The representative of the European in the worse sense of the word is the Bellegarde family.

When Newman arrives in Europe, he possesses an innocence simply because he has had to spend his earlier life making his fortune. He does not yet possess knowledge and experience in the world, especially in the European emphasis on the correct form and ceremony. But equally important, he is too innocent to see through the machinations of Mademoiselle Nioche and her father.

One of the great differences that is emphasized is the difference between the American's utility and the European's insistence upon form and ceremony. Early in the novel, Mrs. Tristram tells Newman that he is to do what he thinks right when confronted with any situation. But people like Urbain de Bellegarde know ahead of time what type of form and ceremony they will employ in any given situation. The American then acts spontaneously while the European has formalized certain rituals so that they will never have to confront an unknown situation. Thus, there is a sense of sincerity in the American's actions while the European is more characterized by a sense of extreme urbanity. Urbain de Bellegarde's first name is used to suggest his urbanity, and throughout the novel, we never see Urbain perform a spontaneous act – he is the epitome of the perfect and correct form. As Newman reacts spontaneously to the music of Mozart, Urbain de Bellegarde's reaction was formulated years ago. It will not change. Consequently, there is something false in his reaction while Newman's reaction strikes one as honest and sincere.

Furthermore, the American is a man of action. He has worked or he doesn't mind working. He is not afraid of labor. The European aristocracy have been bred to view work as vulgar. They are people of inaction. Valentin's great complaint is that there is nothing he is allowed to do. Because of the family, he cannot go into business or practice any trade. He must remain inactive while the American can enter into any type of pursuit.

The American's sense of spontaneity, sincerity and action leads him into natural actions. He seems to represent nature itself. On the other hand, the European's emphasis on form, ceremony, ritual and urbanity seems to suggest the artificial. It represents art as an opposing entity to nature.

Finally, these qualities lead to the ultimate quality of honesty vs. evil. When all of the American's qualities are replaced by all of the European's qualities, then we find that form and ritual are more important than honesty. Thus, the Bellegardes can actually murder out of a sense of adherence to form. James is not emphasizing that one should have all of one and not any of the other. The ideal person is the one who can retain all of the American's innocence and honesty, and yet gain the European's experience and knowledge. Valentin de Bellegarde is then great because he has the knowledge and experience, he has the form and ceremony and ritual, but he is not artificial because he reacts to things with sincerity and naturalness. Newman is becoming great because he has retained all of his American qualities but has learned a great deal about form and ritual and urbanity and has also gained a tremendous amount of knowledge and experience without losing his native virtues. Claire de Cintré's potential greatness is that she, like Valentin, possesses the commendable European qualities and shows a good inclination toward gaining or appreciating the American virtues.

SPECIAL JAMESIAN PROBLEMS AND INTERESTS

Central Intelligence and Point-of-View

One of James' contributions to the art of fiction is in his use of point-of-view. By point-of-view is meant the angle from which the story is told. For example, previous to James' novels, much of the fiction of the day was being written from the author's viewpoint, that is, the author was telling the story and he was directing the reader's response to the story. Much of the fiction of the nineteenth century had the author as the storyteller, and the author would create scenes in which certain characters would be involved, but each scene would not necessarily have the same characters in them.

James' fiction differs in his treatment of point-of-view. He was interested in establishing a central person about whom the story revolved. Usually, the reader would have to see all the action of the story through this character's eyes. This central character was called at times the "central intelligence" and at times the "sentient center." Thus in James' fiction, we have the central character of the novel, and it is as though the central character were telling the story because we see or hear about all events through him. We the readers react to certain events as this central character would react to them.

Every scene in the novel, therefore, will be a scene which reveals something about the main character, and usually he is present in every scene. As the *central intelligence,* his sensibility is the dominant aspect of the novel. In *The American* Newman is, of course, the central character. Every scene is limited to showing him involved in some type of situation, and every scene confines itself to the interests of this central character.

Confidante

James wrote fiction in an era before the modern technique of the "stream-of-consciousness" was established. In the modern technique, the author feels free to go inside the mind of the character. But in James' time, this was not yet an established technique. Thus, since James as a novelist wanted to remain outside the novel, that is, wanted to present his characters with as much objectivity and realism as possible, he created the use of a *confidante*.

The *confidante* is a person of great sensibility to whom the main character reveals his innermost thoughts (as long as they are within the bounds of propriety) and to whom he discusses his problems. The *confidante* is essentially a listener and in some cases an advisor. This technique of having a *confidante* to whom the main character can talk serves a double function. First of all, it allows the reader to see what the main character is thinking, and secondly, it gives us a more rounded view of the action. For example, after something has happened to the main character, he can often go to the *confidante* and in their discussion of the event, we the readers see and understand the various subtle implications of this situation more clearly.

The *confidante* is also a person who is usually somewhat removed from the central action. For example, Mrs. Tristram in *The American* is not directly involved in the central action of the novel, except that she does instigate the action by introducing the main character to the woman he later seeks to marry. But in some novels, the *confidante* can play a more important function in the main action.

Essentially, the *confidante* observes the action from a distance and comments on this action. She is a person of exceptional sensitivity and perception, who allows the main character to respond more deeply and subtly to certain situations.

Foreshadowing

James is a very careful artist who uses rather often and freely the technique of foreshadowing a later action. This means that he has given hints in the early parts of the novel about some important thing that is going to happen later in the novel. Thus, this adds a touch of realism to the novel because so many things have foreshadowed the main action that the reader should not be surprised to discover the action at the end.

The best way in which to see James' use of foreshadowing is to examine one or two central events which have been already foreshadowed. The most important thing in Newman's life, or his most important and unusual action, involves his burning of the letter which would condemn the Bellegardes as murderers. The average individual would have undoubtedly used this letter and received the revenge so desirable. But James has very carefully let the reader know that Newman is not the type of person who seeks revenge simply for the sake of revenge. The central scene which foreshadows Newman's later action, occurs early in the novel, immediately after he first meets Tom Tristram. He tells about a time that he was on the way to the stock market where he was going to get even with a man who had once played a very dirty trick on him. He tells how suddenly the entire idea of revenge became repulsive to him. And even though it meant that he would lose some sixty thousand dollars, he decided not to carry through with it.

For Newman the idea of revenge simply for the sake of revenge was obscene. He would have freely used the letter against the Bellegardes if he thought that by using it he could obtain Madame de Cintré as a wife. But since the letter would not help him gain his principal aim, he could take no pleasure in the revenge by itself. It would have been empty and meaningless. Aside, therefore, from this scene early in the novel, every aspect of Newman's character also attests to the fact that he would not be the type who drives for revenge. He has one thing that supremely matters in his life, and he functions solely to attain that end. When it is no longer attainable, he sees and feels no need for gratuitous revenge.

Madame de Cintré's action has also been foreshadowed. First she is frequently described as living the life of a nun. The Bellegarde house is frequently described as some sinister looking monastery. Even Valentin speaks of the high probability that someone in his or Madame de Cintré's situation would be best off in a monastery or nunnery. Furthermore, Madame de Cintré is described in terms of a person too good for this world. She has a quality of "other-worldliness" about her.

In general, when one reflects or rereads the novel carefully, he will find many samples of foreshadowing. Mrs. Tristram's statement early in the novel to Newman that she would like to see him in a difficult situation is later fulfilled. Madame de Cintré often said that she would never marry again. Thus, every action that is central to the novel has been prepared for by many hints and many types of foreshadowing.

The Renunciation Theme

Perhaps the most dominant idea that runs throughout all of James' fiction is the idea of renunciation. This is usually seen in a character who wants one thing badly and for some more noble reason, gives up the thing most desired for some other thing or for some other reason.

The use of this theme of renunciation implies that James' characters possess a certain quality or nobility in their character. This theme in *The American* is seen through Newman's refusal to take revenge against the person on the stock market who had once played a dirty trick on him. It is also seen more nobly in his refusal to use the letter which would have hurt the Bellegardes. This type of renunciation allows Newman to be viewed with a certain bit of nobility.

The main use of this theme is seen in Madame de Cintré's renunciation of life and entrance into the Carmelite nunnery. There is a type of living death involved in her renunciation. Of course, it could be maintained that she was the type of character who is too good for the world and that the only place for her would be in such a nunnery. But her actions are certainly indicative of James' use of renunication.

As most critics explain the action or as Madame de Cintré suggests to Newman, she would prefer not to live in the world if she could not become his wife. Since the latter course is blocked for her, there is only one thing that she can do and that is to enter the nunnery. Of course in choosing the most difficult and arduous order of nuns, her renunciation takes on a particular type of horror. Hers is viewed as a living death. The songs, the place, and the clothing are just the opposite of all the things which have been described in connection with Claire de Cintré.

Symbolism

James does not use symbolism in the way that modern authors do. His use of symbolism is perhaps more delicate and in one sense more obvious. There are no hidden symbols and no need to search for symbolic interpretations. He uses symbolism in the way that he uses foreshadowing. In fact, in a James novel, the two are closely related.

Symbolism is often seen in James' description of something. The apartment that Newman rented was at first described as being magnificent to him. But later as he learned more about the European way of life, he began to see that the "gilded walls" of the apartment were wearing thin, and finally that the gilding was peeling off. This simply symbolizes Newman's more increased awareness of certain aspects of European culture.

Symbolism is also used in describing a person. Madame de Cintré is often described in terms of a statue or a piece of ivory, and in terms of the dove who has folded its wings. These descriptions later become symbolic as Madame de Cintré does fold her wings and enters the nunnery where she lives a life that could be considered in terms of a piece of statuary.

Contrast

Aside from the use of *Social Contrasts* (see above section on this subject), James also used contrast in many other ways. Perhaps the most obvious is in his use of Mademoiselle Noémie and her father. In these people we have a tremendous contrast to the aristocratic European. Contrast is also used to point up or illuminate qualities of the characters. James gives us brief pictures of other types of Americans and by contrasting these other Americans with Newman, we get a better view of the noble qualities possessed by Newman.

CHARACTER ANALYSIS

Christopher Newman

Our first clue in analyzing Christopher Newman lies in his name. As Columbus discovered the new world (America), now Newman makes the reverse trip. He is the new-man discovering the old world. One approach to the novel is therefore through the concept of observing the actions of a new-man placed in an old, unfamiliar, and settled European world.

Throughout the novel, Newman is constantly developing and changing. He is, in other words, continually learning and experiencing, and thus the reader continually learns more about Newman, but there are certain qualities which Newman possesses throughout the novel.

Our first view of Newman shows him as a tall, relaxed, good-humored, and likeable American. The principal image connected with Newman is that of his stretching out his long legs and making himself comfortable. Throughout the novel, Newman is placed only in one situation where he is not himself or where he does not feel comfortable and that was the private dinner party given for him by the Bellegardes.

The first chapters also emphasize Newman's innocence or inexperience. In the museum, he preferred the copy to the original. During the course of the novel, we observe Newman losing his inexperience but retaining his innocence and "good nature."

Newman is also a man of extreme good taste. It is, to be sure, an undeveloped taste, but he does like and respond to the correct things. When Urbain de Bellegarde goes to hear a Mozart opera, he knows ahead of time what his reactions are going to be. Tom Tristram would not even bother to go to the opera. But Newman goes with no preconceived ideas and responds to the work with spontaneity and sincerity.

Through James' use of contrast, we also see that Newman is the almost ideal American. By contrast with Tristram, Newman is seen to be very moral, sensitive, and perceptive. There is such a contrast that the reader might immediately assume that Newman was somewhat of a prude. To avoid this impression, James sends Newman on a tour with a Unitarian minister who found Newman too advanced, too liberal, too rash, and too loose. Thus, by the series of contrasts, Newman is seen as an almost ideal person.

Newman's most valuable asset is his strong integrity. Even though he was not able at first to see through European duplicity because of his inexperience, when he gains the necessary amount of understanding, he is thoroughly disgusted with anything that is tinged with immorality. He is the self-made man who has made a large fortune without ever compromising himself. He is the thoroughly morally sound individual.

Newman is also a great human being. He laughs readily and enjoys all aspects of life. He is the sincere and spontaneous person who does not understand why everyone would not respond pleasantly to life. He enjoys giving happiness to others in many small ways, and he is always frank, honest and open in his relationships without being unpleasant.

In general, Newman, though inexperienced and innocent, possesses a strong intelligence and strong integrity. He is sincere and honest. He detests immorality and duplicity. He has sensitivity and perception, and he is a great man both physically and morally. He is James' ideal American.

Claire de Cintré

We hear about Claire de Cintré long before we get to know her. We hear that she is beautiful but not a beauty. Mrs. Tristram thinks that she is perfect in all ways.

James presents her as a representative of the aristocratic world in its best form. She is virtually a work of art. Many images of her are in terms of a cold statue of white marble. She possesses all the art and beauty but apparently needs Newman to give her life.

Valentin sees his sister as the perfect combination of many opposing qualities. She is half "grande dame and half an angel." She is also a mixture of pride and humility. Valentin says she "looks like a statue which has failed as stone...and come to life as flesh and blood."

All through the novel, people refer to her as being proud, but if she possesses this quality, she does not show it to Newman. Instead he views her as rather shy. But she does have pride. She knows the value of the Bellegarde name and will not think of marrying Newman until she is confident that he is worthy of that honor.

But she is humble also. She will not fight against her family and instead chooses to fold her wings and retire to the nunnery.

She is a combination of the European qualities of form, ceremony, ritual and urbanity. But she also responds warmly and in a friendly way to people. She makes everyone feel that she is interested in them.

She feels that her love for Newman is so great that she can only show it by renouncing this life. Even though she refers to herself as a coward, it takes a very brave woman to enter into the strict nunnery of the Carmelites. But for Claire, this was her only satisfactory way of showing Newman the extent of her love.

It may be said that Claire de Cintré was too good and too great for this world. Her beauty, intelligence, charm, and generosity are too much for this realistic world and can only be solved by entering the nunnery.

Valentin de Bellegarde

Even though Valentin is a European, he does possess many of the qualities and attributes associated with the American. As seen in his duel, he is truly European. His sense of honor, his sense of form and ceremony demand that he perform the duel. Even though Newman tries logically to reason with him, it is impossible to make Valentin retract. At the duel, he follows through as the perfect aristocrat would—he shoots off the mark intentionally. Valentin's European qualities are also seen in his dilemma created by his being a younger brother of a famous family. The honor of the family requires him to do nothing with his life. He feels that he cannot go into business and feels that there is nothing for him finally to do but go to a monastery. He is bound by the laws of the aristocracy and family.

He does possess other qualities, however. He responds to life and to people with frankness and spontaneity. He is quite natural in all of his relations with people. When necessary he is able to drop the forms and rituals and act as a natural man. These are the qualities which attract him to Newman and vice versa.

Early in the novel, it was reported that if the test ever presented itself, the Bellegarde honor would be safer in Valentin's hands than in anyone else's. During the course of the novel, this proves to be true. He is thoroughly ashamed of the way the Bellegarde family has acted, so ashamed that he apologized and offers Newman the chance to revenge himself. Thus, it is seen that Valentin is the European aristocrat who possesses a high sense of honor and integrity.

The Bellegardes

Madame and Urbain de Bellegarde represent the old order of the aristocracy. They are cold. They are content with their own limited circle of friends and desire no new experience and no intrusion upon their own way of life. They present, however, a formidable front to the world. We never see them acting in a friendly and spontaneous way. All of their actions are formal, reserved and distant. They represent the absolute form and ceremony. Their emphasis on form and appearance will lead them to commit any act, even murder, in order to preserve these old rituals. Thus, they murdered M. de Bellegarde partly because he was going to go against the old traditions of marrying his oldest daughter to a rich old count.

The Bellegardes are also very proud and very strong. They perform their acts with a certain knowledge that they are right and others are wrong. They are polished and refined to the point of being artificial, and finally as the name implies they are the "beautiful guardes" of old order of doing things.

Mrs. Tristram

Mrs. Tristram is a woman of great sensitivity and perception who has been somewhat embittered by some bitter strokes in life. She functions mainly in the novel as a *confidante* to Newman (See section on *Confidante*).

Once in her youth, she had been engaged to a clever man who had spurned her. She married Tom Tristram on the rebound. Even though she is American, she seems somewhat more of the European. She is able to come straight to a point without offending Newman or anyone, and she is able to take an idea and see more sides of it than is Newman who is perhaps too closely bound up in the idea. With these qualities, she fits well into her role of listening to and advising Christopher Newman.

QUESTIONS FOR EXAMINATIONS

1. What earlier scene in the novel helps explain Newman's refusal to use his letter for revenge against the Bellegardes?

2. What does Newman learn from Mademoiselle Nóemie and M. Nioche?

3. In what ways is the aristocratic Valentin similar to Newman? In what ways different?

4. If the Bellegardes had conceded to Newman's demands, would Madame de Cintré have married him?

5. What is Mrs. Tristram's relation to Newman?

6. Is Mrs. Bread essential to the novel? For example, could Newman have come by the letter in some other way?

7. Why is Madame de Cintré determined not to marry again until she accepts Newman?

8. How do Tom Tristram and the Reverend Mr. Babcock function in the novel?

9. Who is the strongest aristocrat, Madame de Bellegarde or her son Urbain?

10. Is Lord Deepmere essentially with or without integrity? Explain.

11. Why must Claire de Cintré obey her mother? Why is she afraid of her mother?

12. Did Newman have an obligation to Valentin to carry out the revenge?

NOTES

THE AWAKENING

NOTES

including

- *Life of the Author*
- *List of Characters*
- *Critical Commentaries*
- *Questions for Review*
- *Selected Bibliography*

by
Kay Carey, M.A.
University of Colorado

INCORPORATED
LINCOLN, NEBRASKA 68501

Editor

Gary Carey, M.A.
University of Colorado

Consulting Editor

James L. Roberts, Ph.D.
Department of English
University of Nebraska

ISBN 0-8220-0218-3
© Copyright 1980
by
C. K. Hillegass
All Rights Reserved
Printed in U.S.A.

1990 Printing

The Cliffs Notes logo, the names "Cliffs" and "Cliffs Notes," and the black and yellow diagonal-stripe cover design are all registered trademarks belonging to Cliffs Notes, Inc., and may not be used in whole or in part without written permission.

Cliffs Notes, Inc. Lincoln, Nebraska

CONTENTS

THE AWAKENING NOTES

LIFE OF THE AUTHOR

Kate Chopin was born in 1851 in St. Louis. The city was just beginning to gain a sense of commercial prominence in America, and Chopin's Irish father was ambitious to make a success for himself and his young family in this newly burgeoning American city on the Mississippi River. On Chopin's mother's side, the French influence matched Kate's father's Irish ambition and spirit; in fact, it was the unique combination of these two heritages which molded and fashioned Chopin's unique character.

Chopin's father was killed when she was four, and although his absence was a terrible, empty shock to the family, she was aware that her father had died in an attempt to unite an America that was daily becoming a greater nation. His death occurred as the result of an unfortunate accident causing the deaths of several of the city's most influential civic leaders. A key link in the Pacific Railroad was being completed when a catastrophic collapse of a bridge brought the celebration ceremony to a sudden halt.

After her father's death, Chopin was reared by a family of strong women—her mother, her grandmother, and her great-grandmother. They were all iron-willed and capable women, and they all had a strain of the romantic and the raconteur in them; Chopin was often entertained nightly by their many and varied tales of people and adventures.

Chopin met Oscar, her future husband, when she was seventeen. She had just graduated from the St. Louis Academy of the Sacred Heart, and Oscar was eight years older than she; he had left New Orleans to become a clerk in a St. Louis bank. He was immediately fascinated by Chopin's striking beauty and individualism when they met, and the two were soon married.

Not much is known about Oscar, but it is clear that he was not at all Like Léonce Pontellier, the stuffy husband of the heroine of *The Awakening*. Oscar's childhood had not been a happy one (his father was a possessive and jealous man, especially contemptuous of women), and as a result, Chopin was given an immense amount of personal freedom. This was fortunate, for her personality contained a deep desire for liberty that needed fulfillment. She was alive, alert, and excited by the vast opportunities and experiences which life had to offer in her rapidly changing and growing country, and Oscar was always very supportive of his wife's many interests and allowed her even the luxury of solitude—an unheard of luxury in those days, but a necessity to Chopin. Even on her honeymoon, she recorded in her diary the many delights she found in simple walks alone; she enjoyed glimpsing into other people's homes, meeting strangers, and imagining all sorts of histories and intrigues about the people she met. Yet, even with the generous allowance of money and freedom which Oscar gave to her, Chopin constantly rankled at being a woman in what was undeniably a man's world.

The young couple returned from their European honeymoon and lived in New Orleans for their first nine years. Its influence on Chopin's life and her writings is indelible. She absorbed every flavor and every nuance of this exotic American city. And while she was accumulating memories, she was also accumulating a family at the same time. Before Chopin was thirty years old, she was the mother of six children, and she was regarded by all who knew her as a good, thorough, and conscientious mother. Oscar, meanwhile, was having increasing troubles with his job as a cotton commissioner and, in 1880, his business failed so miserably that he was forced to move his wife and family to the small village of Cloutierville in the western, Cajun area of Louisiana. There, he ran a general store and managed a few small plantations, and it was by helping her husband that Chopin grew to love and absorb even more of Louisiana's richly mixed heritage of French, Negro, Spanish, and English ways of living. In this new Cajun country, Chopin adapted rapidly to a society that was strikingly different from the exclusive Creole and aristocratic social worlds of New Orleans. And it was about these people, these Cajuns, or Acadians, that Chopin eventually wrote most of her stories and sketches. It was fertile, untapped literary ore, and Chopin was immediately recognized as a master of interpreting its local color and character. In fact, her early reputation as a "regional writer" is partly responsible for her being ignored as one of America's finest fictional writers. Primarily, however, her lack of lasting, national recognition is due to the reception of her second novel, *The Awakening*, published in 1899. Her earlier novel, *At Fault*, had gotten rather good reviews, though by no means did it receive the acclaim that her short stories had received. But it was *The Awakening* which brought her to the attention of all the major critics and to the general American reading public. Mrs. Kate Chopin had written a scandalous book. Its heroine was a woman who found her husband dull, her married life dreary and confining, and motherhood a bondage she refused to accept. Chopin was blunt about her subject matter, and her critics were equally candid. They were outraged that Chopin had written about a woman who not only had sexual urges and desires, but felt that it was her right to have those drives satisfied. Such novels with similar subjects had been published in Europe, of course, but that was different. A French author could raise literary eyebrows and be tolerated, but because Chopin was American and, moreover, because she was a woman, the critics pounced on both her and her heroine, Edna Pontellier, as being evil and debauched. One critic declared that the novel was "strong drink" and that it should be labeled "poison." Chopin knew that her novel was daring, but she dared to publish it, never dreaming of the extent of furor it would cause. Her friends wrote her many letters of encouragement after its publication, knowing that she would be hurt by the critics' harsh words, but Chopin was more concerned about the book's future than she was about the controversy that it was causing at the moment. When libraries began banning the novel, however, Chopin's spirits sank, and she wrote a note of apology in a local paper. Its tone is courageous and positive and, at the same time, it is wry and satiric. "Having a group of people at my disposal," she wrote, "I thought it might be entertaining (to myself) to throw them together and see what would happen. I never dreamed of Mrs. Pontellier making such a mess of things and working out her own damnation as she did. If I had had the slightest intimation of such a thing I would have excluded her from the company. But when I found out what she was up to, the play was half over and it was then too late." The mocking tone of this overly polite apology is delightful, but it hides Chopin's true disappointment, and when the reviewers continued to attack both her and her novel, she wrote little more; yet she was never ashamed of the novel or of having written it. She simply felt that she had no further future as a writer. A widow by now, Chopin devoted the rest of her short life to her family.

The Awakening, a first-rate minor masterpiece, has only recently been rediscovered, and it and Chopin's other writings are at last receiving the long-neglected critical acclaim that they deserve. She has been compared to Lawrence, Gide, and Flaubert, yet all her writings and all her characters are distinctively American, remarkably contemporary, and have achieved prominence and recognition far beyond their initial status as romantic, local-color creations.

LIST OF CHARACTERS

Edna Pontellier

A handsome young woman of twenty-eight, she discovers during a summer vacation that she has led a pleasant, pampered married life, but that it has been a rigidly confined existence, and that her husband has always considered her to be his "property." She rebels and tries to find fulfillment for her psychological and social drives, as well as for her sexual drives. She is frustrated because no life-style in the 1890s offers her an alternative to the restrictions of motherhood and marriage; as a result, she commits suicide.

Léonce Pontellier

Edna's forty-year-old husband; he has a prosperous brokerage business in New Orleans, adheres strictly to the region's social conventions, and expects his wife to do likewise. All of the Pontelliers' friends consider Léonce to be "a perfect husband."

Robert Lebrun

A charming young man who spends his summers at his mother's resort on Grand Isle making the female guests feel "waited on." He begins an innocent intimacy with Edna Pontellier and flees to Mexico when he discovers that their friendship has turned to love.

Adèle Ratignolle

Edna's confidante at Grand Isle; she is Chopin's example of the perfect Creole "mother-woman." She is a well-organized, busy, home-loving mother of several children, and she thoroughly enjoys her role as a good wife and as a devoted and self-sacrificing mother.

Alcée Arobin

A young New Orleans "man of fashion." He is a good-looking, Casanova-type who is well-known for his amorous affairs with vulnerable women. He hopes to make Edna one more of his conquests.

Mademoiselle Reisz

In contrast to Adèle Ratignolle, she offers Edna an alternative to the role of being yet another "mother-woman." The old, unmarried musician has devoted her life to music and is considered to be somewhat eccentric because of her outspoken and candid views. She is genuinely fond of Edna and concerned about her young friend's confused, frustrated dilemma.

Madame Lebrun

After her husband deserts her, she successfully manages to run their summer resort on Grand Isle and support herself and her two sons, Robert and Victor. She is always fresh-looking and pretty, a "bustling" woman—yelling commands to the servants, sewing rapidly at her noisy sewing machine, and clad always in white, her starched skirts crinkling as she comes and goes.

Victor Lebrun

Robert's darkly handsome, spoiled brother; he is also Madame Lebrun's favorite son. At Edna's dinner party, one of her guests garbs Victor in a wreath of roses, and to Edna's wine-heightened senses, he seems to suddenly become the "image of Desire." The vision upsets Edna so greatly that she shatters a wine glass, and her party comes to an early, unexpected conclusion.

Raoul and Etienne Pontellier

Edna and Léonce's children. Edna is criti9ized unfairly by her husband for neglecting them. Léonce's mother is always anxious for an opportunity to take the children to Iberville so that she can tell them tales of Creole lore and save them from becoming "children of the pavement."

Edna's Father

The old Kentucky colonel did not approve of his daughter's marrying a Catholic and a Creole, and although he and Edna have a good time at the races when he comes to New Orleans for a visit, he is still severely critical of Edna's independence. When he leaves, he instructs Léonce to be more firm with Edna and to treat her with "authority and coercion." His other two daughters, Janet and Margaret, are models of submissive southern womanhood.

Mariequita

A young, pretty Spanish "spitfire" who flirts with both Robert and Victor Lebrun. Robert once gave Victor a sound thrashing for being too familiar with her and for giving the impression that he had "some sort of claim" on her. The young girl usually goes barefoot and is not ashamed of her broad, coarse feet nor the sand between her toes.

Doctor Mandelet

A semi-retired physician in New Orleans whom Léonce consults about his wife's lack of interest in housekeeping and her notions about the "eternal rights of women." Doctor Mandelet, who has a "reputation for wisdom rather than skill," advises Léonce to be patient and not to worry. To him, Edna is going through a "mood" that will soon pass.

Montel

A friend of the Lebrun family and unofficial beau of Madame Lebrun; he hires Robert for a position in his firm in Vera Cruz, Mexico.

Madame Antoine

Robert brings Edna to her house to rest after Edna has to leave Mass because of the oppressive heat and Edna's emotional exhaustion; she lives with her son, Tonie.

Mrs. James Highcamp

A devotee of the races and friend of Alcée Arobin.

CRITICAL COMMENTARIES

Chapter 1

The novel opens on a Sunday in summer, in the late nineteenth century. A New Orleans businessman and his wife are vacationing on Grand Isle, a popular Creole resort, fifty miles south of New Orleans; Mr. Léonce Pontellier is irritated by the mid-morning chatter of birds, his landlady's shrill commands to her staff, and a particularly noisy piano duet played by two children; he is anxious to return to his brokerage business in the city. His wife is swimming.

This Sunday tableau is typical of many American and British novels of that era. In such novels, the setting was described, and after the main characters were introduced, the action began. Chopin's structure for *The Awakening* fits this scheme, but she embellishes her narrative skeleton with a multitude of details that her enthusiastic, early critics labeled as "local color." To the critics and readers not familiar with the region, New Orleans and its Creole trappings were mysterious and exotic. Chopin, for example, begins her novel with a stylistic flourish: "A green and yellow parrot, which hung in a cage outside the door, kept repeating over and over: '*Allez vous-en! Allez vous-en! Sapristi!*' " Put in a historical context, this was a rather bold stylistic stroke for a female novelist, especially one who wanted to be taken seriously and whose theme in this novel is the discontent and revolt of a woman who refuses to pay the price that matrimony and motherhood demand.

The caged parrot, however, is not merely "local color," nor is the caged mocking bird on the other side of the doorway mere decoration. Both are symbols of the novel's heroine, Edna Pontellier, who will "awaken" in the novel and discover that she is caged in a marriage that does not allow her to grow or to become a mature, self-critical woman with a mind of her own and a sexual body of her own. Interestingly, Edna Pontellier's husband is only mildly irritated by the noise of the caged parrot; later in the novel, he will be confused and furious when he finds himself threatened by a wife who tells him that she refuses, as it were, to parrot the "right" phrases and refuses to perform what is expected of the wife of a well-to-do businessman. For the present, the caged birds which hang on either side of the resort doorway seem only a part of Chopin's local color, and we should realize now that she will thread them and many other motifs throughout her novel to give it dimension and texture.

The other local color accents in this first chapter—in addition to the French- and Spanish-speaking parrot and the summer resort being south of New Orleans—are the Creole landlady dressed in starched, crinkled white (a contrast to the silent lady dressed in black, walking among the cabins and saying her rosary), the nearby island of Cheniere Caminada, where Sunday mass is given, and the Pontellier's quadroon nurse, who follows the Pontelliers' two children around. Similar details frequently appear in Chopin's fiction; critics noted them and praised them. Yet it was not until *The Awakening* was published that they began to seriously consider the inner lives of the characters who lived in the midst of all this local color. Because Chopin was southern, and also a woman, critics read her short stories and pronounced them to be "finished," "charming," "delicious," and one even noted that she had "the dialect 'down fine.' " But *The Awakening* changed all that because the heroine is a woman who painfully comes to realize that many of the satisfactions of life are denied to her—precisely because she is a woman. Edna's awakening to the fact that she has no real identity and her subsequent revolt against this stifling southern status quo alarmed most of the readers and certainly all of the critics. The novel was said to be scandalous, and it was neglected and largely forgotten. Today, however, it has been recognized as a minor masterpiece, one of those small classics that is good literature and a joy to read and reread.

In Chapter 1, Chopin introduces us, first of all, to Edna's husband, and we hear about Edna from him before we see her for ourselves and are able to form our own impression. The man that Edna married is rather slender, has straight brown hair (parted neatly), a precisely trimmed beard, a slight stoop, and is forty years old. He is uncomfortable during this lazy summer weekend and is anxious to return to his business dealings in New Orleans. His first utterance is an "exclamation of disgust."

When we first see Edna through Mr. Pontellier's eyes, she is at a distance, and it is not precisely Edna whom we see. Far down on the beach we see only a white sunshade, or parasol, approaching. Under it are Edna and young Robert Lebrun, the landlady's son, whom Edna finds unusually fascinating. The mood of the lazy Sunday permeates this chapter as Chopin describes Edna's parasol approaching at a snail's pace, the gulf itself "melting hazily" into the horizon, and Edna and Robert seating themselves with "some appearance of fatigue," as they lean against the cottage posts. Mr. Pontellier says that it is "folly" to have gone swimming in such heat. His stuffy reaction reveals his characteristic indignation at his wife's childish and unladylike immaturity. He, of course, took a swim at the "proper" hour, at daybreak, and that is precisely why the morning has seemed long and never-ending to him. He feels out of place in this relaxed and peaceful pattern of his wife's Sunday morning, in the same way that he felt distracted by the early, noisy bustle around the Lebrun cottage.

"You are burnt beyond recognition," Léonce says to Edna. In other words, Edna has broken the social code which measures a woman's respectability by the cut of her dress, the length of her gloves, and in this case, by the color of her complexion. Edna is almost as dark as the racially mixed servants at the Lebrun's summer resort. Chopin then tells us precisely what Mr. Pontellier thinks of his wife: Léonce Pontellier regards Edna as "a valuable piece of personal property that has suffered some damage." Here is the key to Edna's predicament. Later in the novel, she will discover that she cannot be anyone's "personal property"; she cannot be the personal property of her husband or even of her children. She will refuse to be restricted by society, by her husband's code of confinement, or by the demands of her children.

Yet at this moment, when we first view Edna, she does not seem to feel particularly restricted by convention or by her husband's callous remark. She is enjoying the summer heat, the swimming, and she enjoys being the relaxed companion of young

Robert Lebrun. When Edna is swimming, she is free of all bonds on her. She even takes off her wedding rings before she goes swimming—and she does this in an age when most married women superstitiously never removed their wedding rings. Here, she blithely takes them off, and she delights like a child when she asks for her rings back, slips them on, and watches them sparkle on her tanned fingers. Note here that when she wishes to have her rings, Edna and her husband do not exchange a word. They have lived together long enough to anticipate one another's requests and to respond to one another's gestures. Mr. Pontellier understands what Edna wants when she raises her hands; later, she understands what he means when he shrugs an answer to one of her questions.

In her husband's opinion, Edna is a good wife, if a bit irresponsible. He is so confident of her faithfulness that he is neither irritated nor jealous at the pleasure she finds in the company of Robert Lebrun. But instead of swimming and joking with the boyish Lebrun, Mr. Pontellier would much prefer to be playing billiards with other men.

The first scene closes with Edna asking her husband if he is coming to dinner. He doesn't give her an answer; he shrugs his shoulders, and Edna accepts his non-verbal communication and "understands." Again, her prescribed role does not seemingly bother her too much here. Léonce allows her the freedom to go swimming, provides a nurse to look after their children, and gives her the freedom to enjoy Robert's company. Her husband's indifference doesn't bother her unduly. The prosaic reality of her marriage has become a habit, as has her passive response to it. As we might expect in any well-constructed novel entitled *The Awakening*, the heroine will first be viewed "asleep," as it were, before her "awakening" occurs. This is exactly what Chopin has done in this first chapter. She has shown us Edna Pontellier, and she has richly described Edna's two worlds—her exterior world (as a wife and mother) and her interior world (as a woman asleep—emotionally, intellectually, spiritually, and sexually), and the walls of both these worlds will topple before the novel is finished.

Chapters 2-4

By choosing, first of all, to describe Edna's eyes (the "mirrors of the soul" in nineteenth century literature), Chopin tells us precisely what Edna looks like and *how* she looks: Edna is a handsome woman, rather than a beautiful one. Her eyebrows are thick and horizontal, and the eyes themselves are the same yellow-brown color of her hair; they fasten onto an object and hold it. Edna's gaze is candid and frank, yet contemplative, and Chopin's description here is direct and clear-cut, very much like Edna herself.

After Edna's husband leaves for his club, Chopin focuses on Edna and Robert Lebrun, the young man whom Edna finds engaging. From Chopin's details, we realize that although Robert is the landlady's son, he himself isn't particularly well-to-do. He rolls his own cigarettes, for instance, because he can't afford cigars; the cigar which he has in his pocket is a gift from Edna's husband, a treat he has reserved for himself after dinner. Robert's youth is accented by his clean-shaven face, in contrast to Mr. Pontellier's bearded features, which fashionably connote money and status. Robert has a boyish air, and as we learn later, he is not terribly ambitious. We also learn later that Robert has a modest job in New Orleans as a clerk; there, his fluency in English, French, and Spanish is highly valued. Robert seems to drift through life; he is drifting this summer, as he has done for many summers, hoping something will happen to make this summer interesting, and Edna's presence, it would seem, has just accomplished that.

Robert's most prominent feature is his facial *expression*: his is one of open contentment, where "there rested no shadow of care." Edna's eyes contemplate, Chopin tells us, "lost in an inward gaze"; Robert's eyes reflect "the light and languor of the summer day." Chopin inserts an abundance of description here in order to slowly create a mood. Earlier, her tempo was busily paced to catch our initial interest. We looked at, listened to, and noted Mr. Pontellier's impatience and his disgust at the noisy birds, the soprano cawings of his landlady, and the piano duet by the Farival twins. Now Chopin shifts this scene to an andante mood as she leisurely delineates her two central characters—two people who value leisure, as they share the summer warmth of the Gulf and one another's presence. Edna plays with a palm-leaf fan, and she and Robert talk lightly about inconsequential things—the breeze, the pleasure they had while swimming, and the Pontellier children—all of the things that disgruntled Mr. Pontellier. The scene Chopin describes is a scene designed for lovers—which Edna and Robert are not, yet.

Throughout this novel, Chopin is never far from her narrative, and the early critics who charged her with "letting her stories tell themselves" or, on the other hand, of writing "analytical studies" failed to discern her particular style. One of the delights of reading Chopin's fiction is being suddenly aware, now and then, that we are hearing Chopin herself as she presents her characters and their problems. As an example, listen to her as she tells us about Robert: Robert "talked a good deal about himself. He was very young, and did not know any better. Mrs. Pontellier talked a little about herself for the same reason." The effect is dazzling. Chopin is being humorously intimate with us, while employing economy, conciseness, and a certain wise, wry humor. We have the feeling that she has a good understanding of her characters and knows and cares about the minor foibles of these young people. The effect is similar to Henry James' portraits, especially as she continues her description and tells us that Robert spoke of his intention of "going to Mexico in the summer, where fortune awaited him." Then Chopin offers us this neatly packed perception: Robert "was always intending to go to Mexico, but some way never got there." Succinct statements like this are electric with importance; we can predictably expect Robert either to continue his long-delayed daydream of seeking his fortune in Mexico, or else he may dramatically decide to stop his drifting and actually leave for Mexico. Already she has created suspense for us.

Edna and Robert's parting near dinnertime is casual; Chopin sustains the languid mood of the afternoon as Edna rises and goes into her room, and Robert joins Edna's children for a few last moments of play. There is a peaceful naiveté in the simple pleasure that Robert and Edna find in one another. Neither of them, of course, is aware that they have begun an innocent intimacy.

The charm of Chopin's introduction to the Lebruns' summer resort on Grand Isle and to the typical upper-middle-class Pontelliers abruptly ends when Léonce Pontellier returns late from his club and loudly reproaches his wife for her "habitual neglect of the children." His loud anger is unjustified; his railing at Edna is not motivated by his concern for the boys or by young Raoul's questionable fever. In this scene, Léonce acts "like a child," a patronizing accusation he frequently levels at Edna. He arrives home late, in high spirits, and expects Edna, "the sole object of his existence," as he likes to brag about her, to be awake and to adoringly listen to every word of his brusque joking about what happened at the club. He is angry that Edna is asleep, and he chooses to punish her with unwarranted charges that she is an irresponsible and negligent mother.

It is a temptation to make an easy villain of Léonce Pontellier. But he is no villain; in today's jargon, he is merely another example of a male chauvinist, a role not at all uncommon in his era. Léonce dramatically leaves the room of his allegedly sick child and orders his wife to tend to the child; meanwhile, he puffs on a cigar. His noisy concern for the child is enough responsibility for him in his role as a father and a husband. His responsibilities are practical; his duties include the brokerage business and making a living for the family. He has no time to either worry about his children's health or tend to their illnesses. Léonce believes both duties to be "a mother's place."

In this scene, it is significant that Chopin does not insert an editorial voice into the narrative. She presents the conflict between the Pontelliers quickly and cleanly. Instead of didactically denouncing Léonce's unjust actions, Chopin focuses more on Edna; she explores Edna's feelings after Léonce has finished his cigar and has fallen asleep. Edna is bewildered—and not merely about her husband's unjust outburst. She does not understand why she is suddenly crying; the fact that she is crying disturbs her more than her husband's angry insults. She feels lost but she is not absolutely lost; in particular, she is aware that she is allowing herself to succumb to a strange, deep mood. This is the first time that such heavy emotion has overwhelmed her and that she has let herself be *aware* that she is dissatisfied with her marriage and with Léonce. Her confusion dissolves her. She is slowly awakening in this sense. Until now, Léonce's upbraidings have never mattered particularly; Léonce has always been abundantly kind and devoted, as a generous recompense for her service to him as a wife and as a mother to his children. But tonight something new and different has suddenly happened, and Edna cannot fathom her strange sense of oppression nor does she even try to. It comes from "some unfamiliar part of her consciousness"; its anguish is vague, "strange and unfamiliar," and it consumes her. Of central importance is the fact that she *allows* herself to be engulfed in emotion.

Next morning, Mr. Pontellier leaves punctually in his carriage to catch the steamer to New Orleans; he will not return to Grand Isle until the following Saturday. Chopin, therefore, neatly concludes this chapter with a tableau of his leaving. Léonce's excitement builds as he anticipates a lively business week ahead of him, and he gives Edna half of his night's winnings as he leaves.

The effect of Léonce's leaving is liberating to Edna. Yet this feeling vanishes in a few days; Edna receives a box of candies from him, and the values of her mother and her grandmother and long generations of women before her cause her to graciously acknowledge that Léonce *is* a good man. Léonce gives Edna things; he is overly generous with presents to her. Edna is envied; people say that Mr. Pontellier is the best husband in the world. Not surprisingly, Edna decides that perhaps, after all, Léonce is a fine husband. Chopin's final comment here is that Edna "was forced to admit that she knew of none better"—that is, Edna knew of no better husband than Léonce. Perhaps this is true; perhaps Edna does not know of a better husband, but earlier in this scene we witnessed Edna beginning to feel the possibility that there *might* be something more to marriage than what she and Léonce share, something deeper in the relationship between a man and a woman than that which exists between her and Léonce. A sense of dissatisfaction, undefined and indistinct as of yet, has taken root unconsciously with her.

Perhaps some of this has to do with the setting. Compared to the rest of the women on Grand Isle, Edna is different. On the surface, Edna is a "good" mother and a "good" wife, but not in the way that Léonce, for example, is a "perfect" husband. Edna is not what Léonce expects her to be—that is, she is not like the "mother-women" here at Grand Isle. This term that Chopin uses to describe the Creole women is superlative, and its concept is central to the novel's theme. In the following chapters, we see Edna mingling with the other women and, as she does so, we gauge her against them. Grand Isle, it is clear, is a summer nesting place for mother-women while their husbands are working in New Orleans. One can see them fluttering about the resort, their protective wings protecting their brood of children. But not Edna. Her boys fight their own battles, overseen by their quadroon nurse who, when need be, buttons trousers for the boys and makes sure that their hair is parted on the proper side—all the little things that the mother-women do for their children.

As a perfect example of this mother-woman, there is none better than Edna's good friend, Adèle Ratignolle. Whereas Edna is handsome, Adèle is strikingly beautiful. Edna's yellow-brown hair is in contrast to Adèle's spun-gold hair that neither "comb nor confining pin" can restrain. Mothering, like her golden good looks, comes as easily and as regularly to Adèle as her successive birthings of babies. Nor does mothering seem to drain her energy. Adèle radiates gifted capability, whether she is tending her children or mending one of their bibs. Chopin captures the essence of Adèle as the mother-woman marvels over a pattern for a baby's winter drawers. Edna, in contrast, could not be less interested. She has never felt an impromptu, bubbling joy over the intricacies of a baby's winter drawers. She is capable of joy, but not about next season's baby clothes, and it bothers her that she feels that she should at least feign an interest in such things simply because she is a mother.

Although Edna has never taken the time to analyze her thoughts, she is aware that it is impolite to act disinterested in a friend's enthusiasms. But Adèle's passion for motherhood is only one of many things which Edna cannot explain or feel comfortable with. Equally puzzling is the Creole temperament. Edna Pontellier is the only non-Creole at Grand Isle, and she is not used to the community bond that exists among them—in particular, their "entire absence of prudery" and their "freedom of expression." These people have grand emotions—real and feigned—and share their feelings with the community; Edna does not. Her joys and her disappointments in life have been brief and certainly never tumultuous; usually she is evenly felicitious and somewhat guarded. Adèle can talk easily about a woman's "condition"; Edna is not even at ease when using this euphemism to describe a woman's pregnancy. Edna is bored with Adèle's patterns and she is shy about sexual matters. In contrast to the mother-women, Edna is a lady-child. But this summer, Edna is changing—a bit. She is astonished at the Creoles' frankness and their freedom of expression; the risqué books and stories which make the rounds of the guests amaze her sense of privacy. But she slowly begins to realize that their world is not a threat to her own and that their world is made up of wonders "which never cease." To a certain degree, all of this fascinates her.

But what Edna does not realize—yet—is that these women, while being free to discuss sexual matters, have given up their own unique identities. Their freedom to talk about sexual matters is natural to them because of its being relevant to marriage and children. They *seem* free, yet all of them have willingly conformed to the prescribed role pattern for the Creole wife and mother. Their frankness is not unusual to them; it is something they grew up with. And this frankness is not synonymous with freedom. Their frankness about sex and sexuality is merely a part of their evolving into mother-women; moreover, they have all conformed willingly. Edna feels alien because she could never conform so willingly to their role. She has conformed, certainly, for she has a prudish side, but she was reared to be a "lady." But Edna is also somewhat of an innocent, childlike rebel. She is most unladylike because she swims at whatever hour of the day she wants to, doesn't worry about how brown her skin becomes, and she is more than willing to let a quadroon nurse look after her children. In fact, it is her very individuality which is most striking about her, compared with the other women of Grand Isle.

Chapters 5-6

Because Edna is not one of the Creoles, she often watches them with a sense of fascinated detachment; for example, she thoroughly enjoys young Robert Lebrun's company, but her friendship with Robert is not as open nor as close as is Adèle's friendship with him. Adèle and Robert share a playful, spirited camaraderie. They joke, in Edna's presence, about Robert's "role" at Grand Isle; for the last two summers, Robert was Mademoiselle Duvigne's "knight" of sorts—that is, he pretended to be ready to serve her every whim, and he pretended to be inconsolable if her temper darkened. After Mademoiselle Duvigne died, Robert posed as the very figure of despair at the feet of Adèle, grateful for any crumbs of sympathy she might toss to him in his depression. It was a game of fantasy and romance for Robert and Adèle, fraught with gestures of grand emotions and grand passions—sensations which are alien to Edna. She sits on the edge of their mirth as they delight in teasing one another about broken hearts and tragic sufferings.

This scene helps us to better understand the "exotic" Creoles. Chopin wanted to show us the light and easy familiarity that existed between married Creole women and single men. The mere idea of jealousy makes Adèle and Robert laugh; the community shares its joys and its sorrows with all its members. And sexual jealousy for the Creoles, Chopin tells us, is virtually unknown. Jealousy, she says, is that "gangrene passion . . . which has become dwarfed by disuse." Chopin's comment here reminds us of Léonce Pontellier's attitude toward Robert; he feels absolutely no jealousy toward the young man. Likewise, Adèle's husband is not jealous of Robert and, therefore, this particular scene between Adèle and Robert should be compared to the scenes between Robert and Edna. The relationship between the young Creole man and Edna, the outsider, is "different." Robert does not feel free to exaggerate and boldly joke with her about "passions" which burn within him until "the very sea sizzled when he took his daily plunge." Throughout this novel, we must be continually aware that Edna is not a Creole; she has never experienced passion—real or imagined—nor has she ever discussed it, nor joked lightheartedly with anyone about it, especially the "hopeless passion" which Robert describes himself as being a tragic victim of.

This light bantering about "hopeless passion" is important to note here, for it is not wholly comic nor merely a part of Chopin's "local color"; it is an element which will play a pivotal role later in the novel when Edna becomes a victim of a passion that is, as it turns out, hopeless. Yet, at this moment, passion is a subject of romantic comedy, and while Adèle can laugh gaily at Robert's inventive richness, Edna cannot; she has never tossed through sleepless nights because of "consuming flames." She soon will, however, and thus, Chopin is preparing us for the change that is about to occur within Edna by showing us how foreign these feelings are to her at the present so that we can compare them with her later emotions, after she has begun to "awaken."

Edna has always kept her distance from strong emotions. So far in this novel, she has been largely an observer. She is not sure how much of Robert's bravado she can believe. More important, however, she is sure that she is absolutely incapable of such intense feelings as her friends joke about, and she is even a little annoyed when Robert touches her casually when she is sketching a portrait of Adèle.

Chopin's tableau of this trio begins to close as Edna breaks off sketching for the day and fills the open hands of her children with bon-bons. Chopin tells us that "the sun was low in the west, and the breeze soft and languorous." Edna notices that Adèle, the ideal mother-woman, is a bit flushed; she wonders if Adèle's lively imagination is responsible. Edna is extremely curious about this mother-woman. As she did earlier, she watches this mother-woman as she greets her children, showering them with endearments. The mother-woman leaves, and Edna is left feeling free from the pressing duties of all of the Creole mother-women. For this reason, she is coaxed by Robert into taking an evening swim.

Chopin accompanies the scene with words that are very much like ones she used earlier: "The sun was low," she tells us, "and the breeze was soft and warm."

Chopin speaks of the sea and the sea's waves and the waves of wonder that Edna feels as she tries to fathom the mysterious Creole nature and as she tries to understand her feelings toward the sea. Edna is slowly awakening to the fact that the sea is beginning to speak to her, making her aware of its caressing quality and the embrace of its solitude. This will signal the dawn of one of several of Edna's "awakenings." Chopin describes the feeling on this particular night as "a certain light . . . beginning to dawn dimly with [Edna]—the light which, showing the way, forbids it." Edna is a stranger to the bewildering symptoms of troubled dreams, anguish, and uncontrolled sobbing, just as she is a stranger to the sensuous, delicious delight of feeling the sea fold around her body.

But Chopin does not leave us with merely metaphors. She wants her readers to clearly understand what her novel will deal with—the ecstasy and pain of sensuality and of romantic and sexual passion, subjects which were revolutionary in her time, especially for women writers. Chopin states clearly that Edna was "beginning to realize her position in the universe as a human being, and to recognize her relation as an individual to the world *within* and *about* her" (emphasis mine). She also makes it clear that Edna is not undergoing a mere, or brief, sudden, shadowy insight into life, or even vaguely sensing a simple lesson in maturity. Chopin will be challenging Edna with complex ideas and with "a ponderous weight of wisdom." At twenty-eight, Edna will receive "perhaps more wisdom than the Holy Ghost is usually pleased to vouchsafe to any woman." This is a strong comment; obviously men of the late nineteenth century granted little wisdom to women. But here Chopin accuses even God Himself of neglecting to grant women unusual wisdom. Edna, however, is to be an exception and, as Chopin's readers, we are curious and interested to see how Edna will receive and cope with this "ponderous weight of wisdom."

The voice of the sea ends the chapter. Chopin calls it "seductive; never ceasing, whispering, clamoring, murmuring; inviting the soul to wander for a spell in abysses of solitude; to lose itself in mazes of inward contemplation." This passage could have come directly from Walt Whitman's "Out of the Cradle Endlessly Rocking," a poem published some forty years before *The Awakening*. In his poem, Whitman speaks of the rocking rhythms of the sea, its powerful call, and its ability to "soothe, soothe, soothe!" Chopin, like Whitman, is aware that the sea invites the soul to wander, as it pulses with its sensual, caressing wetness. For Whitman, the sea was a symbol of rebirth. It will offer Edna a retreat, for awhile, away from life, an opportunity to rock her body and soul into a peace that will prelude her awakening so that she will emerge freshened, strengthened, and reborn.

When Robert asks her to accompany him for a swim, she declines, then reconsiders. Convention rather forbids it—swimming at evening time—yet Edna rather wants to swim, and so she accepts Robert's offer. After all, why not? Swimming, to Edna, is frankly sensuous, and its sensuality is enhanced by the handsome young man beside her. A healthy *man* would not hesitate to respond to the sea, and Edna is beginning to question why she, simply because she is a woman, should deny herself this gratification or why she should let society deny it to her. Edna, as we noted, is beginning "to recognize her relation as an individual to the world within and about her." She is aware that she is a separate, unique individual; she is *not* a mother-woman and, at twenty-eight, she is beginning to view herself in an entirely new perspective this summer as she lives among the Creole mother-women on Grand Isle.

Initially, Edna simply enjoyed swimming in the sea, but now something new is beginning to happen; her moments are no ordinary moments. Edna is allowing herself to become part of an unconscious fusion with the sea, feeling the echoes and the restless pull of the sea's waves within her body. In Edna's body, remember, there was a sea itself, one in which each of her children was rocked; the waves and the pull of this Gulf sea invite Edna back to it, just as it has invited generations of beings who left it long ago. The sea has always held a certain mystery and mystique; men have always been fascinated by it, but perhaps no man can fully feel the magic of it as a woman can. Edna cannot explain nor fathom the lure she feels. She only knows that she enjoys allowing herself to respond to it.

This is a moment of epiphany for Edna. She realizes innocently, without intellectually analyzing her feelings, that this seemingly quite ordinary moment—her deciding to swim in the sea and to freely enjoy her new emotional feelings about the sea—is more than a simple "swim." She is aware of the intense cleansing and renewing sense of this moment. Chopin applauds Edna's frankly sexual and spiritual response to the sea. She does not caution her readers against its seductive hold; on the contrary, she urges her readers to listen to the cadence of her prose as she attempts to evoke the feeling of this moment as Edna steps into the sea, succumbing to its strength as it speaks to her soul and to her body, "enfolding [her] in its soft, close embrace." Edna will soon be awakened to a new and fragile sexuality within herself. At the same time this happens, she will begin to sense within the sea the vast solitude that is within her and within humanity. Her awakening, then, will be double-edged: it will delight her and it will open new depths for her, and finally it will become her consolation.

Chapters 7-10

After Chopin shows us Edna's mystical and sensuous immersion in the late evening sea, we witness Edna's relaxing her body and slowly releasing herself to new emotions and feelings. Then Chopin pulls back her narrative perspective and gives us some straightforward background exposition about the change that is to occur within Edna Pontellier. She tells us, for instance, that up to now Edna has always been a very private person, never given to confidences; even as a child, Edna had "her own small life all within herself." This small, private inner world, we realize, has continued to be characteristic of Edna throughout her adult life. She has whole dimensions of herself that she has not shared even with Léonce—nor with anyone else—until now. Now a vague, undefined possibility of a change occurring in her life has presented itself to Edna. This summer, she senses, will change the course of her life, and she is correct; neither she nor Léonce will ever be the same again.

At Grand Isle, she has allowed herself to be friendly with Robert—but only to a certain degree; it is therefore natural that she turns first to Adèle Ratignolle, another woman, when she feels the need to talk about herself. Adèle's unusual beauty so fascinates Edna that she believes that Adèle might perhaps be sympathetic to Edna's new, ambivalent feelings about discovering a new sense of beauty in living and, at the same time, a sense of confusion within herself.

As the two women walk along the beach, Chopin again contrasts them; their bodies seem parallels of their personalities. Adèle is "the more feminine and matronly"; Edna has "no suggestion of the trim, stereotyped fashion-plate . . . ." Chopin adds that "a casual . . . observer . . . might not cast a second glance [at Edna]." Chopin is cautioning her readers not to label Edna as a stereotype who will be "awakened" in this novel and suddenly "bloom." Her "awakening" is far more important than a cliched, romantic, physical change. Edna is *not* the usual nineteenth-century heroine; Chopin stresses this point continually. She is, in Chopin's words, "different from the crowd."

In yet another of Chopin's tableaus, the two women are sitting by the sea, and its force and boundless freedom strengthens Edna's resolve to talk about herself. Symbolically, she removes her collar and "opens her dress at the throat" before she begins to speak. The lady in black is in the background, Chopin's ever-present symbol of death and danger, as are the two lovers, the antithetical symbols of a secure life and love.

Adele instinctively senses that Edna needs to confess, and so she listens quietly as her friend reveals that sometimes as a young girl she could not resist reacting unexplainably to nature. One time, she remembers, she suddenly threw her arms outward, "swimming when she walked, beating the tall grass," and feeling as though she could walk on forever. She remembers that this was done on impulse. Usually she was not so spontaneous; she did not grow up that way. She grew up "driven by habit" and only now, this summer, have those feelings of childhood, those days when she wandered "idly, aimlessly, unthinking and unguided" returned to entice her. Adèle is clearly aware of how important this confession is to Edna and how different these new feelings are to her in contrast to her many years of living "by habit." Adèle is also aware that Edna does *not* withdraw her hand when Adèle covers it protectively;

ordinarily, Edna avoids any sudden physical contact, as she did when Robert accidentally touched her while she was sketching. Adèle even strokes her friend's hand reassuringly, freely allowing her mother-woman instinct to comfort this woman who feels troubled here among the Creoles; she realizes that Edna feels unable to share in the Creole community of familiarities and is terribly confused by what is happening within her.

Chopin then removes us from this scene again; to help us understand Edna more fully (Edna will allow herself to tell Adèle only so much about her past), Chopin speaks directly to us. She tells us that Edna was not altogether comfortable with her young romantic feelings when she developed a schoolgirl crush on "a dignified and sad-eyed cavalry officer"; later, when her family moved from Kentucky to Mississippi, she developed a romantic crush on a young man, but the infatuation was brief and he was already engaged; as a grown woman, she fell in love with the face and figure and photograph of "a great tragedian." Her first romantic kisses were given to the cold glass that contained his photograph. It is no oversimplification: Edna has never known real love or real passion.

Chopin tells us frankly that Edna's marriage to Léonce Pontellier was "purely an accident." Léonce fell in love with Edna, he pressed for an answer, and Edna was flattered by his "absolute devotion." She imagined that there was "a sympathy of thought and taste between them." But despite the fact that there was no romance between herself and Léonce, Edna could *not* be convinced to reject this Creole Catholic man. She married Léonce despite the violent oppositions of both her father and her sister Margaret. Edna had been proposed to by a man who worshipped her, and if she married him, she felt that she would have a "certain dignity in the world of reality"; thus she consciously chose to close the door on a young woman's "realm of romance and dreams," and that door has remained closed until this summer when, by accident, she discovered it open, exposing old memories and old feelings, but more important, revealing fresh new concepts about herself and her emotional and physical needs.

Until now, Edna has been "fond" of Léonce; similarly, "in an uneven, impulsive way," she has been "fond" of her children. But nowhere does Chopin mention that Edna has a deep love for either Léonce or for the children. In fact, the months which her children spent with Léonce's mother granted Edna "a sort of relief." But, as was noted earlier, Edna cannot tell all of this to Adèle; she has lived too long encased in years of inner privacy. Of necessity, Chopin must tell this to us.

Talking so candidly with Adèle is almost traumatic for Edna, and Adèle understands this. She understands that Edna's sudden decision to confide in her has "muddled her like wine, or like a first breath of freedom." Edna is suddenly weak when Robert appears with "a troop of children," and she must gather up the loose ends of her thoughts, her reveries, and rearrange her composure. Adèle is keenly sensitive to the pain and confusion that has been laced throughout Edna's confessions, and it is for this reason that she feigns having such aching legs that Robert must assist her while they walk back to the cottage. She senses that Edna is beginning to fall in love for the first time, and she knows that she must warn Robert. Adèle and Robert have an old comradeship, and being old friends, they can seemingly discuss anything, and the mother-woman within Adèle is as protective of Edna's tender new emotional awakenings as if Edna were one of Adèle's own children.

Adèle's request that Robert "let Mrs. Pontellier alone" is not received well. Robert realizes that his old friend is deadly serious, and he is momentarily disarmed; he is caught off-guard by Adèle's somber directness and, moreover, his pride is wounded when Adèle warns him that Edna "might make the unfortunate blunder of taking you seriously." Adèle's words sting because Robert has playfully toyed with married women for many summers, but until now he has not thought much about it; now Adèle has given Robert new insight into the emptiness of the "role" he has played and replayed in a long-running, trivial summer game. Before he leaves Adèle, Robert says with seriousness, softened by a smile, that she should not have warned him about Edna; rather, she should have warned him about himself, against *his* taking himself seriously. He leaves her then, and in the background are Chopin's familiar woman in black, looking even more ominously jaded, and the two lovers, seeming to be even more in love than ever. They are symbols, obviously, and are inserted here to prelude what is about to follow.

Robert's confusion, distraction, and irritation are apparent as soon as he enters his mother's house and hears the clacking noise of her sewing machine. Imaginatively, we can also hear the monotonous, mechanical clacking and parallel it with the monotonous, mechanical summer pattern that has been pivotal to Robert's summer years on Grand Isle. Yet it was a pattern which Robert enjoyed until Adèle made him realize how insignificant it was.

Robert inquires about the whereabouts of Mrs. Pontellier, and he reminds his mother that he promised to lend Edna the Goncourt. It is Robert now, not just Edna, who seems to be floundering. Ironically, Robert's life of simple spontaniety has been "driven by habit," just as Edna's life of bland sterility has been "driven by habit." And neither Robert nor Edna can fully understand nor grasp the changes that each of them instinctively feels is necessary for them. But Robert, however, seems far more alarmed and frantic than Edna, and when he remembers Adèle's capsule analysis of himself, it seems almost more than he can bear. It is easy to understand his thinking of Edna immediately; if no one takes him seriously, Adèle has said that Mrs. Pontellier might do so. The realization that he has been valued as no more than amusing summer entertainment is frightening to him. Like Edna, who is just beginning to discover how barren her life has been, Robert has suddenly viewed the deep void of his own life.

By accident that evening, he learns that an admirer of his mother is in Vera Cruz, Mexico, and has inquired about Robert's joining him in a business venture. By chance, Robert suddenly realizes that two people, for the first time in years, are considering taking him seriously—Mrs. Pontellier and Montel. Mrs. Pontellier finds him romantic and Montel considers him mature enough to be a business partner. The temptation to suddenly prove himself and establish a sense of his own manhood is overwhelming. He chides his mother for not telling him sooner of Montel's offer, and he searches for the Goncourt to take to Mrs. Pontellier.

After Adèle warns Robert about the danger of Edna's susceptibility to his charms, Chopin allows a few weeks to pass. It is now Sunday and an impromptu party of sorts is underway; there is music, dancing, an unusual number of people, and even the children are allowed to stay up later than usual. The Farival twins who once irritated Léonce Pontellier with their piano playing are at the piano again, and even the parrot is once again shrieking outside the Lebrun doorway. Recitations are being given, as well as a performance by a young, amateur ballet dancer.

Edna joins the ballroom dancing for awhile, but soon prefers sitting outside on the gallery in the Gulf moonlight, watching the "mystic shimmer" on the "distant, restless water." Her revery is short-lived. Robert is determined to tempt her and please her, and he does so in a way that makes her the focus of the evening. Robert promises to have old Mademoiselle Reisz play the piano especially for Edna; he knows that he can charm the quarrelsome, eccentric old woman into performing, and he does. Entering the hall with Robert, Mademoiselle Reisz requests of Edna what music the lady would like to hear. Robert carries off his role of summer cavalier well, providing Edna with a gift of music and assuring himself that Adèle was right: Edna does take him seriously, and she is romantically fascinated by him; she is not like the Creole women with whom he played empty games during the past summers. Edna, of course, is ignorant of Robert's motives, and she is embarrassed and overwhelmed by what he does and begs that Mademoiselle Reisz choose suitable music. The old woman is intuitive about Robert's motives and about Edna's feelings toward Robert.

What Edna hears unnerves her. Chopin tells us that Edna has responded to piano music before, conjuring up vague moods of solitude, moods of longing and despair as embodiments of her own confused emotions, but Edna is totally unprepared for the raw passion that Mademoiselle Reisz sets ablaze within her, sending tremors down her spine, invading her soul and, sea-like, "swaying it, lashing it." Edna seems, we feel, almost ready to faint, feeling the music beating against her. She trembles and chokes, and tears blind her. Significantly, old Mademoiselle Reisz is aware of how successfully she has accomplished magic with her Slavic, romantic music.

Yet while Edna is the most visibly shaken, the entire company is moved by the music, and suddenly it is as though Robert "arranges" yet another bit of evening entertainment in yet another attempt to be taken seriously. Chopin tells us that Robert proposed that they all go for a swim "at that mystic hour under that mystic moon" and that "there was not a dissenting voice."

Robert is definitely assuming a new, commanding role in the novel, and while he does not "lead the way" to the beach, Chopin tells us that he "directed the way." Yet even he is not sure of the rules of his new role, for he finds himself "whether with malicious or mischievous intent" parting the two lovers that Chopin has included in various scenes and dividing them, as he walks between them.

Edna can hear Robert's voice from afar, but she is confused as to why he does not join her. She does not understand his new attitude. Once they were comfortable companions, and suddenly he has become unpredictable, absenting himself for a day, then redoubling what almost seems to be a kind of devotion to her the next day. It seems as though he is deliberately choosing to tease Edna, for Chopin tells us that Edna has begun to miss him, "just as one misses the sun on a cloudy day . . . ." Clearly, Edna is falling in love with Robert, and he obviously is aware that she is doing so—becoming, in fact, seriously enamored of him. This is no longer the usual summer game of charade for him. Robert's attentions are being taken seriously by a monied, married woman, and he is enjoying his "seduction" of her; after all, he is a past master at such games.

It is now that we learn that Edna—all during the summer—despite all of her attempts, has never learned to actually swim. Despite her affection for the sea, she has never mastered it and while it lures her daily, it fills her with a "certain ungovernable dread." Tonight, however, all alone, she finds herself actually swimming for the first time in her life. The realization is overwhelming. Scarcely has she had time to adjust to Robert's generous attentions toward her than she was swept up by the power of Mademoiselle Reisz's romantic music, and now she discovers that she no longer has to "play" or "bathe" in the sea. Her emotions have been drained, yet she is giddy; she has gained a small bit of mastery—of herself and of the sea. It is almost as magical for her as Chopin has described the night as being.

Aware that she can actually swim gives Edna a new sense of freedom. She no longer needs a nearby hand. Her intoxication with her discovery makes her dramatically assertive; she wants to swim "where no woman had swum before," and she tries, swimming out alone, seaward, letting herself meet and melt with the pulsings she feels deep in the moonlit sea. Yet while she does not go any real distance, she goes far enough that she becomes frightened when she realizes that she might not be able to swim back. This is Edna's first encounter with the fear of death—yet another "awakening." But there is no one with whom she can share this terrible new discovery. Léonce is certainly not impressed that she can swim or that she is frightened. Not surprisingly, Edna chooses to leave him and return home alone. She is strongly affected by the rich magic of the music, by suddenly discovering the power of her swimming, and by the powerful fear that drowning is a possibility if one swims too far, alone.

Her senses are still swimming when Robert overtakes her; she is able to tell him, impulsively, exactly how she feels—of her exhaustion, of her joy, of her confusion, and of this night's being like a dream. She confesses that she feels possibly bewitched or enchanted.

Robert's response is dramatically on cue. He assumes the pose of a raconteur of Creole lore and interrupts her to explain that she has been singled out by a spirit that has "haunted these shores for ages." He fills Edna with romantic fancy, teasing her that perhaps the "spirit" that has found her may never release her. But he overplays his role; he gilds his fancy with too much embellishment, and Edna is finally hurt by his flippancy. Not being a Creole, she cannot respond with sufficient light wit and dash.

In the silence, Edna takes Robert's arm, then allows him to help her into a hammock. Both are aware that they are alone; she asks for her shawl, but she does not put it around her. Twice, Robert asks if he should stay until Mr. Pontellier returns and twice she says that he must decide. He smokes, they do not speak, yet she watches him, and in the silence, there are, Chopin tells us, "moments of silence . . . pregnant with the first felt throbbings of desire."

Robert leaves when the other bathers begin to approach, and when Edna says nothing, he believes that she is probably asleep. He could not be, ironically, more mistaken. Edna is fully awake, more awake than she has ever been in her life, aware of his body passing in and out of the strips of moonlight and, metaphorically, of his passing in and out of her body's desire for him.

Fittingly, Edna lies suspended in a hammock; she has learned to swim alone in the sea which she loves and which she now fears; she can almost joyously control this fierce natural power, yet she cannot wholly dominate it, for it fills her with a certain dread. Similarly, she has learned that her body has unloosened itself and she has let her emotions flow outward, unbounded; she has responded sexually to Robert's physical presence, yet, like the mysterious awe she has for the sea's power, she feels threatened by this new discovery of her sexuality because she cannot control what she does not understand. This night has engulfed her in multitudes of new emotions and discoveries. It is no accident that Chopin closes the chapter with Edna Pontellier suspended in a hammock, literally and symbolically suspended between a new reality and a night of magical awakenings.

Chapters 11-14

It is a combination of exhilaration, a surge of new courage, a trace of fear, but most of all it is a sense of new peace that fills Edna Pontellier as she lies alone in her hammock. She does not even speak to Léonce when he returns home. In fact, she does not even answer him initially when he questions her, and note here how Chopin's style parallels Edna's inward transformation; in her narrative, Chopin tells us that Edna's eyes "gleamed," suggesting clear, direct sight and, further, Chopin says that Edna's eyes, despite the late hour, had "no sleepy shadows, as they looked into his." This descriptive phrase is doubly significant. It underscores Edna's newly awakened state, and it stresses Edna's looking directly at her husband, facing him as an equal and even as an opponent. Her voice rings with new authority as she tells him *no*—she is not asleep. Edna is absolutely awake and newly aware of her aroused physical feelings and emotions. Her "Don't wait for me" is symbolic of her new sense of life's enormous potential. Edna is no longer Léonce Pontellier's childlike lady-wife; she is no longer in need of a man's presence before she can begin readying herself for bed. She has awakened to a new confidence and to a new assertiveness within herself. Chopin emphasizes the seriousness of the metamorphosis that we are witnessing by telling us that ordinarily Edna would have obeyed her husband "through habit," would have "yielded . . . unthinkingly . . . [like] a daily treadmill of . . . life." Understandably, Léonce is puzzled by his wife's "whimsical" defiance, especially when she repeats once again that *no*, she is not going to bed; she is "going to stay out here."

At this point, one must turn backward toward a time long past and consider not only the courage it took for Edna to defy her husband, but also the courage it took for Chopin herself to envision such a scene as this and create the character of a "dutiful, submissive" wife suddenly asserting a heretofore latent, unrealized willpower. For Léonce Pontellier, it must seem as though his wife is possessed and, to a degree, even Edna herself must feel a bit "possessed" as she realizes that "she could not at that moment have done other than denied and resisted" the force that she feels within her. The effect of Léonce's threat not to "permit" her to stay outside on the veranda is impotent, as is his derisive judgment that Edna's actions are more than "folly."

Léonce cannot comprehend the new voice he hears within his wife, a voice which has begun to articulate a new and independent identity. Heretofore, it has always been Léonce who has made all decisions, even minor ones. Now Edna has discovered the courage to hold her own nebulous future within her own two hands and, without rationally considering the consequences, she tells Léonce not to "speak to me like that again."

The silence is heavy. Léonce's preparations for bed are overly self-consciousness and nervous; he slips on "an extra garment," drinks two glasses of wine, and smokes several cigars. And all this time we are not even sure that Edna is conscious of her husband's puttering preparations for bed; she is experiencing a mildly chaotic ecstasy—"a delicious, grotesque, impossible dream." Truly, it must seem "grotesque"—Chopin's adjective is not too extravagant—for Edna Pontellier has come to the realization that it is *unnatural* for her to be dominated any longer by her husband. Chopin speaks of the "realities pressing into her soul" and of the "exuberance" exulting within her. Her words are suggestive of an intellectual, an emotional, and even a sexual climax within Edna; she has cut herself loose from the moorings of a life of attendance on monied, middle-class mores. Instead of stagnating in Léonce Pontellier's shallow marital confines, she has swum out and felt the cleansing power of new, fresh perceptions. She has never before sensed her own strength nor imagined that she could escape from an oppression which had always seemed a necessary dimension of a woman's lot.

After a few hours of feverish sleep, Edna's physical actions are not entirely strong. Chopin says that the cool morning air "steadied somewhat her faculties," but Chopin does not let her readers worry that Edna's "folly" (so termed by Léonce) was only momentary. Edna is as triumphantly awake in these morning hours as she was in the dark hours of the night and particularly this morning "she [is] not seeking refreshment or help from any source . . . ." To describe Edna's new sense of herself, Chopin uses such words as "blindly following . . . alien hands . . . [which] freed her soul of responsibility."

This is a Sunday morning, and Chopin's Sabbath tableau includes once again the symbolic young lovers, strolling toward the wharf and also the lady in black. Edna, having passed through a night saying things to herself and to Léonce she has never said before, thinking things she has never thought before, and certainly doing things she has never done before, does something else this morning which she has never done before: she tells a little Negro girl who is sweeping the galleries to go and awaken Robert and tell him that she has decided to go to the Chênière, the nearby island where Sunday mass is held; moreover, Edna adds an afterthought of urgency: she says that the young girl should "tell him to hurry," and her impulsive decision to include an injunction to Robert contains three parallel phrases: "She had never. . . . She had never. . . . She had never . . . ." All this must have seemed frighteningly revolutionary to women (and men) readers of 1899; revolt was a fearsome thing for those who had the abundance of leisure to read "novels," themselves things of "folly," according to many male intellectuals. Female independence was threatening; any modicum of liberty allowed to women was a dangerous risk. But Edna's defiance of her husband was clearly no whim that surfaced and disappeared during a night that Robert Lebrun mischievously termed as being "enchanted." Edna Pontellier is just as firmly assertive this morning as she was when she was lying in the hammock, and she is putting her new-found sense of liberty to a test. She commands Robert's presence, and he comes to her. Her future is dim and still vague, obscured by a present that is overpowering in its potential, but Edna is happy as she starts out on this small voyage to Sunday mass and on a much larger voyage out toward the fulfillment of her womanhood.

In addition to the collection of summer vacationers on the wharf, including the lovers and the lady in black, double-edged symbols of Edna's obscure new destiny as an independent woman, Chopin includes a new character in her Sunday tableau—a young Spanish girl, Mariequita. Mariequita is a pretty girl, and she and Robert speak Spanish briefly, a language that no one else understands. Edna notices the girl's feet: Mariequita is barefoot, her feet are broad, and there is "sand and slime between her brown toes."

The girl is a flirt, openly "making 'eyes' at Robert," and tossing saucy comments to the man in charge of the boatload of passengers.

Although no one else understands what Robert and Mariequita are saying, Chopin reveals their conversation to us. Mariequita wants to know more about Robert's relationship with Edna; the fact that Edna is married is of no consequence to the young Spanish girl—marriage is no barrier to sexual satisfaction between two lovers, but she wants to know because she is interested in Robert herself: is Robert the lover of Mrs. Pontellier? Robert does not answer her directly; he teases and hushes her with a light jest. Meanwhile, Edna is dreamily intoxicated by the fierce new tenacity she feels within herself. As the boat's sails swell and become full-blown, Edna feels "borne away"; she feels "chains . . . loosening," and she feels "free to drift whithersoever *she* chose to set her sails" (emphasis mine). Her horizons are no longer limited. As the Sunday morning air strikes Edna's face, she is aware that she has been confined too long by social convention and marital muzzles.

Robert's spur-of-the-moment suggestion to Edna that they go to Grand Terre the next day excites Edna's new taste for boldness. She likes the idea of going and of being "alone there with Robert." Chopin stresses the physical satisfaction that Edna hopes will be hers when she imagines herself and Robert "in the sun, listening to the ocean roar and watching the slimy lizards writhe in and out among the ruins of the old fort." It is the seductive earthiness of the adventure that excites her, the pounding power of the ocean that fills her sense of adventure, and there is also a sexual suggestion when Chopin mentions the lizards writhing among the "ruins" of an old fort—symbolically, Edna's old fortress of middle-class security that she has been locked in until now. Neither Léonce nor even Robert fully comprehends this new woman; Robert asks if Edna won't be afraid of crossing the sea in a canoe, and Edna's "no " is sure and assertive. This causes Robert to promise her other trips, at night; then he slips into his jester's role, teasing her again about the "Gulf spirit" and warning her that it will whisper to her where hidden treasures can be found. Spontaneously, Edna matches Robert's imaginative caprices, saying extravagantly that she will squander any pirate gold they might find and throw it to the four winds, just "for the fun of seeing the golden specks fly." Edna is rich already; she has unearthed her own hidden treasure—herself, and the sureness of herself; it is exciting to see her laughing so freely and fancifully about imaginary hidden treasures.

Significantly, the oppressiveness of the church service becomes so restrictive and stifling that Edna is forced to leave the service. The ritual of the circumscribed dogma filling the tiny enclosure begins to suffocate Edna's new, bursting spirit. To be imprisoned so soon after she has experienced a breath of freedom is impossible for her. Robert solicitiously follows her out of the church and instinctively, perhaps, takes her where she can hear "the voice of the sea." She takes a drink from a rusty cistern and is "greatly revived"; this is Chopin's symbolic mass for Edna—a baptism with water that is holy not because it is divinely sanctified but because it comes from the earth and is naturally cool and refreshing to Edna's *physical* body, as well as to her spiritual body.

At Madame Antoine's, where Robert takes Edna, notice the freedom which Edna feels when she decides to loosen and remove her clothes, how responsive she is to the feel of the sheets and to the odor of laurel in the air; there is a sensuousness within her as she stretches her body to its full length. Edna is discovering the pleasure of physical self-awareness, how delicious her own body can feel. This is part of the "ponderous weight of wisdom" that Chopin spoke of earlier. Edna is claiming, as well as discovering, her own sensuality: "she saw for the first time, the fine, firm quality and texture of her flesh."

After she sleeps long and soundly and awakens late in the afternoon, her first words to Robert strike him as somewhat fey, but they are symbolically full of great significance: "How many years have I slept?" Robert's playful joking about her sleeping one hundred years seems romantically the right kind of response from this young man who has, summer after summer, assumed the role of a knight errant, attending some fair lady at his mother's summer resort. But Edna's question, if exaggerated, is weighty. She has metaphorically been asleep a very long time. And as she awakens from her late afternoon nap, she is also just beginning to awaken to the reality of an identity crisis. Of course, at this moment it is no crisis—that will come later—but the immediacy of her new identity is of concern and that concern now is with her resolve to commit herself fully to the new identity that she conceives is possible for her—whatever that illusive, unformed, unimaginable identity might be.

Among Edna's many thoughts, she considers whether or not Léonce will be "uneasy," but note that this is only a "consideration" for her; it is not a concern that he might be worried about her. We must realize that Edna no longer fears a possible reproach from him for her "folly," as Léonce will no doubt declare her actions to be.

When Robert and Edna sit down to eat at Madame Antoine's, Robert notices the "relish" with which Edna eats; she is discovering new and satisfying sensations in even such commonplace acts as eating. Her appetite for food and, more important, her appetite for living has been whetted and sharpened. She allows herself the freedom to sit under the orange trees, watch the shadows lengthen, and listen to the Creole tales and fancies of Madame Antoine until "the night came on." She is severing herself, freeing herself to absorb what is offered to her—the food, the cooling air from the sea, and the compelling, storytelling voice of Madame Antoine. These moments are not dictated by "habit" or directed by a mindless adherence to duty or by any other consideration, save one: herself. Feeling freed from a past of repression, Edna allows herself to linger fully in the luxuriousness of this moment.

This long Sunday afternoon has not been satisfying for the rest of Edna's family. Adèle Ratignolle, however, Edna's mother-woman confidante, has been able to coddle and pacify the younger of Edna's children, as well as Edna's husband, who has gone off to discuss the latest happenings of the cotton exchange. Now that Edna has returned, Adèle admits to suffering from the heat, and she refuses to remain even for a moment with her friend, even to hear about Edna's afternoon adventures. Monsieur Ratignolle is "alone, and he detested above all things to be left alone." The contrast between Edna's new sense of herself and her role as a wife and mother is in bold contrast to Adèle's life, governed wholly by domestic duties and demands; she must take charge of and take care of a multitude of mother-woman things—food, children, and a husband. She satisfies herself by being useful to them; she knows of no other possible pleasure for herself. Her value lies in her devotion to her utility—to the man she married and to their children.

When Robert leaves Edna finally, after both children are in bed, Edna asks him with the wonder of a child who realizes that something very special has happened, if *he* realizes that they have been together "the whole livelong day." His answer is serious, despite his surface joking: "all but the hundred years when you were sleeping," and when he leaves, Chopin tells us that he goes not to join the others, but that he walks alone toward the Gulf. This afternoon has touched Robert also.

Alone, Edna breathes deeply and her sense of solitude swells; she allows her mind to billow backward over the long day's length, trying to discover "wherein" this summer has become suddenly different from "every other summer of her life." Softly, she sings a song to herself that Robert sang earlier, the refrain returning after each verse, "*si tu savais*": "if you only knew . . . ." There is little doubt that she is falling in love with her fresh sense of freedom, in love with the sense of adventure she has discovered in life and in herself, and in love with Robert.

Chapters 15-16

Time passes—we cannot be sure how long—and Chopin begins this chapter with startling news: Edna comes to dinner and is told simultaneously by several guests that Robert has decided to go to Mexico. What has happened between the two of them since we left them on that Sunday evening and this moment we can measure only by Edna's genuine confusion. For example, they spent the entire morning together, and Robert did not mention Mexico. His leaving Grand Isle so rashly seems unreal, and as Edna sits across from him at dinner, she allows him—and everyone else—to see her undisguised bewilderment. Robert looks both embarrassed and uneasy when Edna asks "of everybody in general" when he is going. When she learns that he intends to leave this very evening, her voice rises in astonishment at the utter impossibility of such an unexpected exodus. Even Robert's voice begins to rise, Chopin tells us, as he defensively explains that he has said "all along" that he was going to Mexico. Only the two high-pitched voices are haranguing, and yet Madame Lebrun must finally knock on the table with her knife handle and declare that her table is becoming a bedlam.

It is an awkward scene as Robert is forced to admit that his decision was made only this afternoon. As he explains his actions to Edna, Chopin describes him as feeling as though he is "defending himself against a swarm of stinging insects"; explaining his leaving to the other guests, Robert is characterized as feeling like a "criminal in a court of justice." Edna senses that his answers are too lofty and that he is posturing; we feel this too. It is as though Robert is trying to make his decision to go to Mexico seem like a mature decision made after long months of weighing and mulling over the alternatives and advantages—instead of the hasty escape from Grand Isle that Edna half-fears and half-believes that it may be.

Later, Adèle Ratignolle's mother-woman instincts try to comfort Edna; what Adèle feared at the beginning of the summer has happened: Edna has fallen in love with Robert Lebrun. Adèle assures Edna that Robert was wrong to say nothing about his leaving until only moments before he was due to leave, but she thinks that Edna should, for manners' sake, join her and the others in seeing Robert off; otherwise, it won't "look friendly." Here, she reveals how thoroughly imprisoned and confined she is in her prescribed role as a perfect and proper mother, wife, and woman. Adèle cautions Edna not to expose her emotions, especially her wounded feelings toward Robert; even if Edna's heart is broken, she should camouflage her shattered dreams and submissively join the rest of the guests. Edna's swollen pride, however, refuses to yield to her friend's pleadings, and it is Robert who finally seeks out Edna, instead of the traditional frantic female pursuing the departing male.

Bluntly, Edna asks Robert how long he will be gone; she admits that she is unhappy and doesn't understand him or his silence. Edna plays no games. Her love for Robert has no coy edges; she admits to having daydreamed of seeing him often in New Orleans after the summer was over. Robert half-confesses to having had the same hopes, then breaks off, assuming the manners of a gentleman, extending his hand, and addressing her as "Mrs. Pontellier." Edna cannot, or will not, conceal her hurt and disappointment; clinging to his hand, she asks him to at least write to her, and he promises to do so. Then he is gone. Edna struggles to keep from crying, from lapsing into silly, adolescent feelings of desertion. She realizes all too well what has happened; she allowed herself to take Robert's presence for granted, just as she allowed herself to joyously take for granted her newly discovered feelings of independence and the knowledge that she was in love with young Robert Lebrun. There is, however, nothing to be done now. Robert will be gone in a few minutes.

Edna's suffering and pain in this scene is another of her awakenings; when she opened herself to the possibility of passion for a man, she should also have included the possibility of great pain. It seems a simple enough equation, but Edna was still a naïve woman, even though she was twenty eight years old when she fell in love for the first time. Yet once she accepted the profound delights of love, she should also have realized the possibility of profound pain as being the probable denouement of love between a married woman and a single man in the restricted, patriarchal southern society of 1899. Edna, however, is an innocent and she committed emotional adultery without forethought and without guilt because of her loveless marriage.

In contrast, Robert—a role-oriented and role-defined Creole—cannot break his community's mores. We sense that he has fallen in love with Edna, but that he is unwilling to risk an affair with her—out of respect for her and out of respect for a code which forbids it. Thus he flees to Mexico rather than confront his feelings for her; he refuses to resolve or cope with what seems to be an unsolvable dilemma. Throughout this summer, he has been Edna's teacher; he opened her soul to spiritual and physical delights, but when he realized that he was falling in love with his married, adoring pupil, he could not deal with his desire for her. His long-time fantasy of going to Mexico and finding success and happiness abruptly became an instantaneous destination for him. To remain in Grand Isle and become Edna's lover would make him a cad; to exit to Mexico is the way of a coward, yet he sees no alternative for himself. He is too weak to stay, and his weakness accentuates Edna's emotional heroism. Seemingly, she would be willing to risk everything; Robert cannot commit himself to such a decision.

After Robert's departure, Chopin tells us that Edna spent much time in a "diversion which afforded her the only pleasurable moments she knew"—that is, swimming in the sea. Edna belongs to no "community" here, in the way that Adèle belongs to her community of mother-women. Without Robert's companionship, Edna feels her closest kinship with the sea, especially now that she has learned to swim. Remember that the sea once offered her the soothing company of its solitude. Now she returns to it.

The Creole community misses Robert's vivacious presence; they naturally assume that Edna does also. Certainly Léonce is aware that his wife greatly misses her young friend. Yet no one guesses the extent to which Edna is pained by Robert's absence.

Chopin speaks of Edna's unconsciously looking for him, seeking out others to talk about him, and gazing at old photographs of Robert in Madame Lebrun's sewing room, taken when he was a young boy. One photograph in particular amuses her—a picture of Robert, looking "full of fire, ambition and great intentions." It is a positive sign of Edna's growing maturity that she is able to smile at that picture. Despite her pain of missing him, she knows full well that she is infatuated with a man who is sorely lacking "fire, ambition and great intentions." Robert is, by nature, gentle, sensuous, and a dreamer; it was these qualities that first attracted Edna to him. And because he is basically a gentle young man, his abrupt severing of their relationship is all the more painful.

We now encounter a passage in the novel that probably shocked Chopin's readers far more than the notion of Edna's romantic need for an "affair." We learn that Edna and Adèle Ratignolle once had a rather heated argument during which Edna told her mother-woman confidante that she "would give [up her] money, I would give my life for my children, but I wouldn't give myself"—that is, Edna would *not* sacrifice day after day of living an empty, unfulfilled life for her children's sake—"or for anyone." She would, if ever such a drastic choice were necessary, sacrifice her life so that her children might live, but she would *never* live an empty life, devoted solely to her children, dedicated to them, doing everything for *their* sakes. She could never define herself in terms of them, nor would she use their lives as a surrogate for her own life.

Surely this was the fullest declaration of independence uttered by a heroine in a novel that Chopin's readers had ever encountered. Many novels prior to *The Awakening* had contained episodes in which married heroines left their husbands for another man, or had an affair with a young lover, but here was a woman who defied the whole concept of the family unit. Edna would give her life, if necessary, for her children, but she would not give up *herself* and continue living a life dedicated to anyone—save herself and what *she* considered essential for herself. This is as shockingly revolutionary to Adèle Ratignolle as it must have been to Chopin's readers and early critics. The whole masculine-conceived, family-oriented universe is being suddenly defied by young Edna Pontellier. Edna is protesting against a woman's living vicariously through the lives of her husband, her children, or anyone else. Edna demands full responsibility for herself—and to herself. She refuses to dedicate herself to a role that she does not fashion, define, and fulfill.

Chapters 17-19

Within two weeks, the Pontelliers are reestablished in their large house in New Orleans. Seemingly, they are the happy master and mistress of the charming, many-columned, broad verandaed home, and Chopin details for us its dazzling white exterior, contrasting it with the serenity of the inner furnishings—the soft carpets, the damask draperies, the cut glass, the silver, and the rich paintings—all presents from Mr. Pontellier to Edna, "the envy of many women whose husbands were less generous than Mr. Pontellier." Mr. Pontellier takes great pride while walking through his house, surveying its sumptuous details. "He greatly valued his possessions," Chopin states, and we recall a sentence near the beginning of the novel when he irritably commented on his wife's sun-bronzed body. He scolded that she was "burnt beyond recognition . . . looking at his wife as one looks at a valuable piece of personal property which has suffered some damage." Léonce Pontellier esteems "his possessions, chiefly because they [are] *his*" (emphasis mine). Among his possessions, he obviously and unthinkingly includes his wife because he lives in an era when he and his men friends conceive of their wives in terms of their being personal possessions.

The lazy summer days of the Gulf resort seem remote as Chopin describes the Tuesdays which are Edna's official "reception days," when "a constant stream" (an ironic image here) of lady callers alight from carriages or stoll up to the front door, greet the mulatto houseboy, who holds a tiny silver tray for their calling cards, and are offered liqueur, coffee, or chocolate before they are finally allowed to greet the mistress of this elegant mansion: "Mrs. Léonce Pontellier, attired in a handsome reception gown." This role has occupied and embodied Edna's existence ever since she became Mrs. Pontellier, six years ago. Certain evenings are designated for the opera, and others are for plays; days are scheduled very much alike—Mr. Pontellier leaving between nine and ten o'clock and returning between six and seven in the evenings, and dinner is always at half past seven.

It is on one of these Tuesdays when Léonce returns home and notices, much as he might detect an unexpected crack in an expensive china bowl, that his wife is not wearing a reception gown; she is wearing an ordinary house dress. Léonce comments that no doubt she is overly tired after her many callers, and Edna confirms that there were indeed many callers—at least there were many cards in the silver tray when she returned. Deliberately, she does not say from where she had returned. Edna has broken a long-established pattern: she was not a "hostess" today.

Léonce is almost, but not quite, angry with her. He is busy adding condiments to his soup, scolding her softly: "people don't do such things"—unless they have a good excuse. Edna has no excuse, nor did she leave any explanation for her callers, nor does she offer any to Leonce.

Mr. Pontellier explains to his wife, much as he would to an absent-minded maid or a socially backward daughter that they both must observe "*les convenances*" (the conventions). That his chiding is done in French is an added affront of smug male superiority, as is his cranky complaining about the tastelessness of the soup, as though he were a culinary authority. He requests that the silver tray of cards be brought to him; social callers musn't be snubbed—especially the monied ones, he comments, as he discovers that a certain Mrs. Belthrop found his wife not at home this afternoon. He tries to humor Edna and make her realize that these niceties *are* important, and he insists that she must apologize to a certain caller and that she must avoid another. Just as he has *his* business duties, Edna has *her* social duties, which are an important extension of his business world.

Mr. Pontellier's critical evaluations continue and include each of the food courses, all of which he finds fault with. "Cooks are only human," he says, implying that hired help must be constantly kept on guard lest they become lazy. He adds that hired help, if not watched carefully, will soon "run things their own way." The phrase is intense with significance. Mrs. Pontellier's refusing to perform the social pattern of her Tuesdays, as she has for six years, is an example of someone deciding to do "things their own way." And while Edna cannot literally be considered an employee of Mr. Pontellier, he certainly considers her a functionary in the house. His comment is purposely pointed. Of course, he rewards Edna generously for performing her duties, but that means that she is duty-bound to repeat on each Tuesday a succession of mindless greetings and chatter to insure and further the Pontelliers' social status. Edna is symbolically and, in fact, a costly, performing puppetlike possession of Mr. Pontellier. Their marriage ceremony decreed it, he identifies her as such, and he expects *her* to do likewise. As a reward, he bestows every possible material thing of value upon her so that she will further enhance him and be satisfied with being defined as "Mrs. Léonce Pontellier." She is envied. He knows it, and other people know it, and being envied is of much importance to Mr. Pontellier.

There were times, Chopin tells us, when Edna attempted to plan a menu or when she studied cookbooks, trying to please her husband's highly critical expectations, but those days are over. Tonight, after Edna finishes dinner, she goes to her room and stands in front of an open window. At this point in the novel, one can't even imagine Edna's standing in front of a *closed* window; she has finally felt the satisfaction of independent judgments and actions, and the open window is symbolic of the free flowing, fresh air of freedom. Edna is not terribly unhappy tonight; she is frustrated. She recognizes the mystery of the night beyond the window. It revives old memories, but she is not soothed by them. She paces, she tears a tiny handkerchief to ribbons, then flings her wedding ring onto the carpet, and stamps the heel of her shoe upon it as though she could crush it. The strength of the tiny gold band, however, mocks her frustration and causes her to grab up a glass vase and fling it onto the tiles of the hearth. The crash and clatter are welcome sounds of destruction—until a well-trained maid hurries in and begins cleaning up the mess. When the maid returns the ring to Edna, she slips it on, slipping uncomfortably once again into the tightly restricted role of being Mrs. Léonce Pontellier.

The following morning, the Pontelliers quarrel briefly about new fixtures for the library. Edna thinks that her husband is excessively extravagant for wanting to buy them; he regrets that she doesn't feel like selecting them. Cautioning her to rest and take care of herself, he takes his leave and Edna is left alone. The world beyond the Pontellier veranda is fragrant with flowers and noisy with street vendors and young children. Edna, however, feels alienated from them, alienated from everything and everyone around her. Chopin has built up a good deal of tension and suspense.

Edna is about to do something. Her frustration will not allow her to return to a world where she ignorantly and innocently half-lived for six years as her husband's charming hostess and wife and the dutiful mother of his children.

Edna leaves the house, and as she walks we learn that "she [is] still under the spell of her infatuation." She has tried to forget Robert, but has been unsuccessful. As she did on Grand Isle, Edna has decided to seek out Adèle Ratignolle and try to talk about her problems. The two women are confidantes, even though the Ratignolles are certainly less well off, materially and socially, than the Pontelliers. They live above their drug store, prosperous though its trade is, in an apartment, commodious though it might be. In addition, Adèle does not have a "receiving day"; she has, instead, once every two weeks, *soirees musicales*, evenings of musical entertainment which are very popular and considered a privilege to be invited to.

The mother-woman is unsurprisingly busy, sorting the family laundry; she says that it is really the maid's work, but she enjoys doing it, yet stops to chat with Edna. Once again, Chopin contrasts the two women. The domestic harmony that Edna sees is pleasing but she does not and cannot belong to that world. Edna can never find full, true contentment folding laundry, preparing meals, and listening with honest interest to her husband's dinner talk. That world is colorless, boring, and confining to Edna. It contains no measure of exhilaration and nothing of what Edna suddenly voices in her inner thoughts as "the taste of life's delirium." Chopin comments that "Edna vaguely wondered what she meant by 'life's delirium.' "

Chopin's readers were also probably puzzled by that phrase. Modern readers, however, do not find the term puzzling at all; it seems antiquated in its articulation perhaps, but we do not "vaguely wonder" about the meaning of the term. We realize that Edna is beginning to demand for herself no more or no less than the right to experience the fullness of her emotional spectrum. The solidarity of the Ratignolles' life-style is too mechanical and unimaginative; it is constructed on routine and precludes all possibility of unbounded pleasure and passion, as well as violent pain. Edna finds no consolation in Adèle's maternal security and happiness. Adèle has traded her identity and her independence to attain serenity and security.

Adèle's life is centered on her utilitarianism, just as Léonce's world is centered on material possessions and social position. A free existence for a woman—devoid of her being equated with husband, children, and household chores—was unheard of in 1899, unless one were an "artist." And this seems to be at least a possibility for Edna. She lives in New Orleans, a city filled with writers, painters, and artistic types; Edna is beginning to envision that perhaps this life-style is her only alternative. The position of being sovereign of the Pontellier mansion that Léonce offers to her is repugnant. Léonce places Edna on a pedestal, yet at the same time he shackles her there. Edna wants to break these chains. It is a dangerous, nebulous ideal that Edna desires; years later, a modern Greek writer, Nikos Kazantsakis, articulated precisely the yearnings of this frustrated Victorian woman in his novel *Zorba the Greek*. The hero, speaking to a rather prudish young Englishman, tells his friend that one "must, sometimes, cut the rope [of rationality]; a man needs a little madness in his life." Zorba, of course, would (like Léonce Pontellier) deny such freedom to a woman. But not Chopin. She created a heroine who, like Zorba, wanted "a little madness" in her life, something besides the dull and conventional and stifling role that was forced on her by generations of men and by their submissive wives, as well. Edna is beginning to distrust the value of permanence and is beginning to trust the value of her instincts. She was awakened on Grand Isle to feel that there was a possiblity for her to be more than a wife and more than a mother; she is not sure *what*, but she is certain of the possibility.

Unfortunately, Léonce Pontellier is not aware of this change within his wife. He expected her to begin once again the patterned ritual of their New Orleans social life once they returned to the city for the winter. Edna cannot; she is struggling with her deliverance from that role, and she feels within her a force superior to Léonce's drive for power and position and also superior to Adèle's happy security within the four walls of Monsieur Ratignolle's home.

It was childish to stamp on her wedding ring; it was childish to smash a vase. Edna realizes that she was acting exactly like a frustrated child. Yet Léonce conceives of his wife as childlike; he assumes that she will accept docility and dependence as her natural lot. Ironically, she behaved exactly like Léonce's child-wife, the person whom she desperately tries *not* to be. And in order "to do as she liked and to *feel* as she liked" (emphasis mine), Edna realizes that she must control her emotions, as well as her actions. As long as she is smashing vases and raging, she is denying herself moments of self-declared and self-defined control. She can complain as loudly as she wishes, but unless she begins to act upon her own convictions, she will be doomed to the futile, cliched role of being yet another woman moaning about the injustice of the world and blaming men for her misery. Her violence was spontaneous, but it ultimately solved nothing. It left her as powerless as before. But she will *not* be bought or compromised by the promise of new library furnishings or the threats of social disapproval.

Thus Edna decides to completely abandon her "Tuesdays at home"—an act of social revolution that was unheard of in the Pontelliers' New Orleans social circle. Nor does Edna explain her decision—just as she refuses to return the visits of her lady callers.

Mr. Pontellier is at first bewildered, then shocked, and is finally angered that his wife means to exchange the role of being "head of a household" for being a painter in an atelier. Her lack of logic confuses him, but it does not confuse or even frighten Edna. For the moment, she *feels* like painting; "perhaps I shan't always feel like it," she says, knowing and admitting to Léonce that she is "not a painter." She does not know *why* she is doing what she is doing, but it is what she *must* do. Edna is hearing and responding to the beat of what Thoreau calls "a different drummer," and she is following it without being overly concerned about her final destination. A man in her time could have been able to do the same thing and no one would have questioned his gambling with life. Nor would they have been shocked by his admission that his ultimate goals were undefined; after all, Robert was able to pack up and suddenly leave for Mexico, and the only consternation concerned his sudden departure—not his actual leaving. Such things are possible—if one is a man. Edna wants that same choice for herself; it is her only hope of release from years of habitual submission.

When she was on Grand Isle, swimming in the sea, listening to its soothing music of freedom, feeling it surround her—all this intoxicated her. It relieved her from the heavy weight of nineteenth-century New Orleans convention. Her exultation unlocked her; Edna is shedding a fictional self that Léonce and even she herself created for her, dressed her in, and taught her to perform as.

Léonce allows her this "whim"; like a restless child, his wife will tire of dabbling in painting and dawdling in obscure, transient "folly"; he is sure of this. He could not be more mistaken. Edna knows that she is no great painter; she never intends to turn out great masterpieces of art. She simply needs to paint at the present and, most important, she needs *not* to entertain boring streams of women callers every Tuesday.

Edna works, then, with great energy—"without accomplishing anything"—but as she draws and paints, she sings to herself the refrain that Robert sang after they had spent the day on the island of Chênière Caminada. The memory of the rippling water and the flapping sails are sensual memories, preludes to her body's remembering "a subtle current of desire." This is not simple romantic revery; this is richly sexual, a yearning to have the desire consummated. Chopin is boldly stating that a woman experiences the same sexual excitement and needs that a man does when she is aroused by certain smells and certain sounds and memories. The memories of the brief hours spent with Robert exude the heat of an aphrodisiac for Edna, a concept considered unhealthy and akin to heresy in Chopin's time.

Edna's desires must, of necessity, remain unsatisfied, but she accepts the inevitable—for the present. She knows that she can recreate and rekindle the fire within herself, even if she cannot satisfy it. This is part of the breadth of the emotional spectrum that Edna claims for herself in exchange for her former role as the wife and possession of the well-to-do Léonce Pontellier.

Chapters 20-24

Although Edna is not completely satisfied with being an "artist," she continues to paint; being a painter frees her to a great extent, and it causes her to seek out another woman who is also an artist, a character from the past—old Mademoiselle Reisz, the pianist who played the powerfully passionate music the night Edna discovered that she could actually swim; it was also on that night that she discovered the courage to defy her husband's demands that she obey something as insignificant as "coming to bed" because of the possibility of being "devoured by mosquitoes." Edna cannot easily locate the old woman's address, but her impetuous decision to find the old woman becomes a challenge for Edna. She follows suggestions from strangers, is led to new neighborhoods, hears disagreeable gossip from those who claim to have known her, but Mademoiselle Reisz herself remains illusive until Edna remembers that if anyone would know the whereabouts of the eccentric musician, it would probably be her summer landlady, Madame Lebrun, now living in New Orleans for the winter months.

Ironically, it is while Edna is on this capricious, independent adventure that she hears a quarrel within the Lebrun house before the door is opened. A black servant is demanding of Victor, Robert's brother, that *she* be allowed to open the door; it is her duty. This is sharply symbolic. Chopin is contrasting Edna's new independence with the actions of a servile, submissive black servant; it is inserted inobtrusively, yet very naturally, into the scene, as Chopin quietly denounces pride in what is ultimately an abject role.

It is Victor, Robert's handsome, nineteen-year-old brother, who greets Edna with undisguised delight, and he allows Edna to sit on the side porch instead of "properly" guiding her into the parlor. Impetuously, he begins to tell the handsome older woman about a romantic escapade he had the night before when he followed the flirtatious lead of a girl who was taken by his good looks. This is obviously something he would never tell his mother, but he feels—after the summer that he observed Edna on Grand Isle—that Edna is "different," even if she is older than he is, and a wife and a mother.

Edna indulges Victor's imaginative, male bravado-embroidered storytelling until Madame Lebrun enters. The family, she learns, has received two letters from Robert, letters which Victor declares to be of little value and glibly recites the contents of. Futilely, of course, Edna had hoped for some greeting to her; instead, Robert simply asks that his mother remember him affectionately to "all his friends."

Edna's mood darkens briefly, but because the Lebruns know old Mademoiselle Reisz' address, Edna leaves the Lebrun house in good spirits. Not only Madame Lebrun notices how "handsome" Edna looks, but Edna's beauty has not escaped Victor; "ravishing" is how he describes her, commenting that ". . . she doesn't seem like the same woman."

Mademoiselle Reisz also comments on Edna's handsome, healthy looks. She prides herself on a candor that she can afford because of her old age and "artistic" eccentricity. Edna, however, is also direct—because she *chooses* to be. When the old pianist says that she feared that Edna would not come to see her in New Orleans, she is told candidly that Edna herself has not been sure whether or not she likes the woman—a frankness that pleases the old woman. She therefore quickly reveals the fact that she has had a letter from Robert, written in Mexico City. But she refuses to let Edna read the letter, even though she says that it contains nothing but questions about, and recollections of, Edna. In particular, Robert asks Mademoiselle Reisz to play the Polish composer Chopin's "Impromptu" for Edna, should Edna pay a call on Mademoiselle Reisz. According to Mademoiselle Reisz, Robert wants to know, afterward, how the music affects Edna.

The old woman is teasing Edna. We sense that she is trying to measure Edna's passion for young Robert, trying to determine whether or not Edna is merely a dilettantish, frivolous, bored wife of the well-to-do Mr. Pontellier. She is trying to decide whether or not Edna is merely dabbling in painting and pretending passion for a young man who is living in an exotic, faraway country. Therefore, she does not play merely the Chopin "Impromptu"; she combines it with one of Wagner's love themes, hoping that her background mood music will expose the truth of Edna's emotions as she reads Robert's letter. The music, the deep shadows in the little room, the night air, and Mademoiselle Reisz' music all cause Edna to begin sobbing—something she has not done since a night long ago on Grand Isle.

Léonce Pontellier decides to call up his old friend Doctor Mandelet, a "semiretired physician . . . . [who had] a reputation for wisdom rather than skill," and it must have given Chopin much secret delight to write an entire chapter, short though it is, devoted to "man talk" about women. Mr. Pontellier boasts of his own manly good health and his healthy Creole genes—in contrast to his wife who, while not sick, is "not like herself." The two men agree that women are moody, delicate creatures, not to be fully understood. Of course, however, Mr. Pontellier assures the old doctor that Edna's *heredity* has nothing to do with her problems. He *chose* her from "sound old Presbyterian Kentucky stock"; Chopin's satire is especially keen here. In particular, Mr. Pontellier is puzzled about Edna's notions that she has recently acquired "concerning the eternal rights of women." This also causes the old doctor some concern as he lifts "his shaggy eyebrows," protrudes "his thick nether lip," and taps "the arms of his chair . . . ." Chopin's portrait is magnificent. Léonce continues: Edna isn't interested in attending her younger sister's wedding; she says that "a wedding is one of the most lamentable spectacles on earth." The doctor nods; Edna is another woman "going through a phase." He assures Mr. Pontellier that "the mood will pass . . . it will pass; have patience." Secretly, the old doctor wonders if another man might be involved in Edna's personality change, but he knows better than insult Mr. Pontellier with such a question.

The introduction of Edna's father into the narrative is unexpected; he was mentioned at the beginning of the novel, when we learned that he had once had a Mississippi plantation before he settled in the bluegrass country of Kentucky, and we recall that he was not merely opposed to Edna's marriage to Léonce, a Catholic Creole, but that he was "violently opposed." Edna is "not warmly or deeply attached" to her father, but most of their antagonism seems to have faded; she welcomes his coming to New Orleans as a distraction from her own indecision about what she must ultimately do with her life.

Adèle Ratignolle, Edna's confidante, urges Edna to encourage Léonce to spend more time at home and less time at his men's club. Edna does not understand how this would solve anything; "What should I do if he stayed home? We wouldn't have anything to say to each other," she counters. And frequently while reading this novel, one needs to go back almost a century and imagine the readers of this novel and the critics who were suddenly confronted with such intimate, honest declarations as this. It is little wonder that they were puzzled, shocked, and offended. Yet Chopin is not being racy. She is simply allowing Edna to speak openly about the emptiness of her marriage. Almost a hundred years later, the problems of such marital voids are the subject of many monthly articles in magazines in the supermarkets and drugstores, but in Chopin's day, such indiscretions were considered, if not sinful, at least a defect on the part of a negligent, willful wife. It was a wife's duty to keep her marriage harmonious—at any cost—sincerely, as well as superficially. Edna will not permit any of this mindless convention, especially now that she realizes what thoroughly different people she and Léonce are.

Her moments of anguish may be painful, but she plumbs them and exhausts them, and she does not harbor them morbidly or romantically. And when they are finished, she opens herself to new experiences, just as she does in this chapter when she and her father share rare moments of excitement and thrills at the racetrack. Doctor Mandelet is particularly struck by Edna's radiance when he sees her; there is none of the mysterious moodiness that Léonce was worried about. Yet the old doctor is not pleased to learn that Edna encountered Alcée Arobin, a man we heard about earlier, in Chapter 8, when tongues clucked about his affair with the consul's wife at Biloxi. The old doctor fears that a rich (and bored—if Léonce's assessment can be relied on) wife might be an easy target for the notorious heartbreaker; in addition, the doctor notices that Edna has a new "animal" vitality; Léonce Pontellier's wife seems "palpitant with the forces of life. . . . [like] some beautiful sleek animal waking up in the sun"—an even more dangerous ingredient in the possibility that she and Arobin find one another attractive, fascinating, and each with ample time to spend together.

Chopin ends the chapter with four stories, one told by each of her principal characters; each of the characters has been warmed by wine, made comfortable by each other's company, and each reminisces about particularly telling episodes. Mr. Pontellier's story is about himself and is humorous and mischievous; the Colonel's likewise concerns himself, although more solemnly; and the doctor's tale concerns an "old, ever new" story about a woman, lured briefly away from her husband, but returning sensibly after a few days. Edna's tale is quite different. She tells about a pair of young lovers who drift away in a canoe into the southern night, "drifting into the unknown," never to be heard of again. She tells it with such purity and passion that everyone present is moved; its aftermath is strangely akin to the way the summer vacationers on Grand Isle felt after old Mademoiselle Reisz played Chopin's powerful piano music.

The leave-taking of Edna's father is not pleasant. He insists that Edna attend her sister's wedding, and she refuses to do so; he threatens that neither of her sisters will probably speak to her, and he is certain that the bride-to-be will not accept "any excuse." It is at this point that Chopin inserts one of her stylistic gems; still speaking about the outrage of Edna's father, Chopin notes that he assumes that Edna has given an excuse as to why she isn't coming back to Kentucky; the old Colonel is "forgetting that Edna had offered none." This has been characteristic of Edna ever since she decided to have no more "Tuesdays at home." She offers no excuses; Edna is straightforward and frank in her reactions. For that reason, she is often terribly disarming, but she refuses to let herself be compromised by coercion or convention.

Edna's husband, in turn, treats the old Colonel with excessive courtesy; he himself will attend the wedding, hoping that his presence, his "money and love will atone" for what he, we assume, considers to be his childish wife's "mood." Edna's father is as direct as his daughter; he advises Léonce to use authority and coercion on Edna. According to him, they're the "only way to manage a wife"—a subject that has long been just beneath the surface of this novel.

Mr. Pontellier's leaving, which we have been alerted to for some time, occurs shortly after Edna's father departs. While she is packing Léonce's clothing, Edna fears briefly that she may be lonely, but she feels a "radiant peace" when she is at last alone in the house. Even the children are gone, we are told; Léonce's mother has taken them, fearful of her daughter-in-law's lack of maternal indulgence and anxious for their young company, anxious to keep alive in them the Creole ways and temperament.

When Chopin describes Edna's feelings and actions after Leonce leaves, it is as though she were describing the inner thoughts of a person who has just been released from prison. Edna, after "a big, genuine sigh of relief," tours the house, sitting in various chairs and lounges; the house, without Leonce, is like a new acquaintance. She immediately brings in big bouquets of bright flowers and plays with the children's small dog. Edna fills her solitude with the satisfaction she feels within herself. We feel that there is a sense of beginning over, of a new awakening. Edna is enjoying, for the first time, talking with the cook and dining alone, comfortably, in a peignoir. Even the dog seems to be aware of the change within Edna, who is delighted and astonished by her new joy. As the chapter ends, Edna has a long refreshing bath and washes herself clean of old frustrations, of Léonce's interference, and her father's demands. She is "determined to start anew . . . now that her time was completely her own. . . . a sense of restfulness invaded her, such as she had not known before."

Chapters 25-32

This section contains many of the novel's most revealing revelations about Edna Pontellier. Following Léonce's departure and her own initial exuberance, Edna becomes restless and moody—filled not with despair, but with boredom, with a sense that "life was passing [her] by." She is a woman who has recently been awakened by romance and love and has declared her independence to paint, but her "art" is not enough to fill her long days; she is aware that she has no real artistic ambitions and that she is not driven by a need for accomplishment.

She fills this void by going again and again to the races; she knows horses and likes the thrill of gambling, the excitement and tenseness of the crowd, and the nostalgic memories of Kentucky horses and paddocks. She is as knowledgeable as most of the men at the track about horses, and she knows it. It is this aura of unusual knowledge and power, in addition to Edna's high-colored handsomeness, that arouses the interest of Alcée Arobin when they attend the races by coincidence together, in the company of one of Edna's friends, a Mrs. Highcamp. Arobin catches "the contagion of excitement," Chopin comments, and is drawn to Edna "like a magnet."

Edna is not unaware of this fact, and she does not flirt with Arobin. On the contrary, it is Arobin, the "young man of fashion" who flirts coquettishly with Edna. Edna's conduct is remarkably cool and contained, even though she feels a fever burning within her. After their first day at the races, and after Arobin has driven her home, she is unusually hungry. She munches on some Gruyere cheese and sips from a bottle of beer, while she pokes "at the wood embers on the hearth"; this is as symbolic to Edna as it is to us. Arobin has stirred the embers of passion within Edna, embers from the summer that were kindled within Edna by Robert Lebrun. There is a restlessness within Edna that wants a release from the bounds of the Pontellier garden and from the four walls of her painting atelier. For this reason, Edna decides to allow herself to go to the races with Arobin alone, to invite him for dinner, and to linger afterward. Yet she cannot allow herself to become another of Arobin's conquests, even though his intimate, confessional tone does tempt her.

When Edna is finally alone, she ponders the possibility of having an affair with Arobin—but on her terms. Chopin is not so blunt as this, but then she could not be in her time. Edna cold-bloodedly considers the consequences of having an affair with this "young man of fashion," and it is significant that it is not herself that she worries about. She doesn't worry about her feelings or even her reputation; it would be easy for her, for "Arobin was absolutely nothing to her." Nor does Edna consider Léonce. It is Robert whom she thinks about; her love for him disturbs her, and an affair with Arobin would seem cheap, a little like adultery. She did not marry Léonce because of love, but she does love Robert, and she cannot reconcile these feelings with the temptation to satisfy her physical craving for a sexual affair with young Arobin. She has sent him away, saying that she no longer likes him, but she is sure that she is as much a narcotic to him as he is to her. Her passion is a need she no longer fears fulfilling, but if she chooses to fill its demands, she must be the one to do the choosing.

Later, after Arobin's polite, elaborate note of apology for acting overly bold so soon after they met, the matter of his kissing her hand seems trivial. Of course, he may see her art studio. Edna is convinced that electric though his charm may be, Arobin is no threat to her. Arobin responds on cue, Chopin tells us "with all his disarming naïveté." He is aware that beneath Edna's maturity is raw passion—and he is correct. Chopin tells us that Arobin, despite his rather silly subservience and wide-eyed adoration, pleased the "animalism that stirred impatiently within" Edna.

Feeling a need to talk with someone, it is to old Mademoiselle Reisz that Edna now turns; Edna feels a freedom with her that she can express with few other people. Nothing shocks the old pianist. She is not embarrassed that Edna finds her ailing, her neck wrapped in flannel and that Edna did not ask for an invitation. Nor is Edna embarrassed to drink from the old woman's brandy "as a man would have done." There are no ridiculous, "lady-like" preludes to Edna's reason for coming; she announces immediately that she is moving out of Léonce's house and into a small four-room house around the corner from Léonce. She wants—and needs—a house of her own. Once uttered aloud, however, the fact of Edna's leaving Léonce's house seems too severe, but old Mademoiselle Reisz will not let Edna make any feeble excuses—such as the Pontelliers' house being too large, the servants too much trouble, etc. She makes Edna state aloud that Léonce's house is not *hers*; it is his. Edna says that she has a little money of her own, the promise of more, and she does want a place of her own in addition to a "feeling of freedom and independence." That afternoon, over a roaring fire in the old lady's stove, over chocolate, Edna resolves "never again to belong to another than herself." This is one half of this section's climax; the other half concerns another letter that Mademoiselle Reisz has received from Robert Lebrun. Even though the old lady knows that it is painful for Edna to read letters that Robert has written to someone else, she shares them with Edna. She is convinced that Robert is in love with Edna and that he is trying to forget her; that is the reason he left so abruptly for Mexico and why he has not written Edna, something he would have done had he considered Edna merely a casual "friend." Mademoiselle Reisz is sure that Robert saw the social consequences, as well as the futility, of his falling in love with Edna. Thus the old woman gives Edna the letter, one that is unlike any of his other ones. In this letter, Robert writes that he is returning to New Orleans—very soon.

The old woman then forces Edna to admit aloud what she has admitted to no one else: that she is indeed in love with Robert Lebrun and that a woman cannot say *why* she loves whomever it is that she loves. Moreover, she does *not* select the man she falls in love with; love is unreasonable because of its very nature. Edna does not know what she will do when Robert returns. For the present, the mere fact that he is returning is enough. Irrationally, generously, she orders a huge box of bonbons for the children in Iberville. Likewise, her exuberance causes her to write to Léonce; because of Robert's welcome news, Edna is able to break the news of her impending move in a letter to her husband, including her plans for a large "farewell dinner." Edna believes that her letter is charming, and Chopin assures us that it is; it is "brilliant and brimming with cheerfulness."

That night Edna allows herself to be kissed, by firelight, by Arobin; "it was the first kiss of her life to which her nature had really responded." She is as intoxicated as a child before Christmas who cannot wait to open the packages. She allows Arobin's charms to be a surrogate for Robert, for what she imagines will happen when Robert returns. Passion, like an effervescence, builds within Edna.

She is choking with the emotions of anticipation, and she allows Arobin to touch her. She follows her instincts instead of thinking about them. But she does not wholly abandon her rationality. When she kisses Arobin, she *decides* to kiss him, "[clasping] his head, [holding] his lips to hers." The promise of Robert's anticipated passion is tumultuous. Edna satisfies her craving, and even Arobin is probably aware that Edna's thoughts are not about him, for he told her earlier in the evening that he felt as though her thoughts were "wandering, as if they were not here with me." He was far more accurate than he would ever have believed, or than his ego would have allowed him to believe.

Inserted into this short scene is an observation made by old Mademoiselle Reisz; touching Edna's shoulder blades, she explained to her that she was feeling to see if "the little bird would soar above the level plain of tradition and prejudice." Such a bird would need "strong wings," she said, adding that it was a "sad spectacle to see the weaklings bruised, exhausted, fluttering back to earth." The old woman senses Edna's strong determination to become something more than Léonce Pontellier's "property," but the old woman cannot imagine how a married woman and a mother of two young children can successfully cope—even in New Orleans—merely because she is in love with a man other than her husband.

Irresponsibility, perhaps, is the first feeling which troubles Edna after Arobin leaves. She can be sure of Léonce's reproach, were he to find out about her kissing Arobin; but as we have seen, Léonce has reproached Edna before. Robert's reproach—that can be matched and overcome by love and understanding. Significantly, Edna feels no shame nor remorse for letting Arobin kiss her and for her taking his head and kissing him deeply. It was a kiss of passion that she shared with Arobin, not a kiss of love—and that makes a vast difference to Edna. She needed Arobin's kiss of passion and regrets that it could not have been, simultaneously, a kiss of love, but it was not. It was only that: a kiss of passion—no more or no less—and Edna felt better afterward: ". . . as if a mist had been lifted from her eyes, enabling her to look upon and comprehend the significance of life." Passion is a part of life, and Edna has satisfied passion. Life is not just love—beautiful, lovely romantic love. Life is a "monster made up of beauty and brutality"—for women, as well as for men.

Chopin must have enjoyed creating the character of Arobin, the

Casanova. She makes him thoroughly charming, certainly handsome, kind, well-mannered, but, without caricature, she makes him a man who is rather shallow, who satisfies himself on the sighs and bodies of married women until they become uninteresting and a new prospect appears before him. His "conquest" of Edna contains all the little things that might cause him to believe that Edna is yet another lonely, idle rich wife who is so captivated by him that she dares convention to make love with him—for awhile—until he replaces her with another. Edna's unusually lively conversation with him, the fever burning in her cheeks and eyes at the races, her going to the races with him alone, their sitting beside the fire together, her responsiveness to his boyish frankness and boastings, her allowing him to kiss her hand, and then her boldly taking his head to kiss him—all these things have convinced him that *he* has "stolen her heart" and that when he appears next, he will find her "indulging in sentimental tears."

Arobin could not be more surprised than he is the next day when he finds Edna high atop a ladder, a kerchief knotted around her head, her sleeves rolled to her elbows, looking "splendid and robust," helping a housemaid prepare to take down and pack "everything which she had acquired aside from her husband's bounty." Arobin implores Edna to come down, anxious that she will fall and hurt herself. But Edna refuses. She can barely wait to move to the "pigeon house," as she calls it. There is no recourse for the confused Arobin, since he is a proper gentleman, than to offer to climb up on the ladder himself and unhook the paintings. Edna lets him do this; the offer is convenient. She even makes him don one of her dust caps, which sends the housemaid into "contortions of mirth." The short scene is a brief masterpiece of male-female reversal, filled with the joy of poetic revenge and justice.

Chopin took great care to create interest and suspense about Edna's making one last, grand gesture—a magnificent farewell dinner party. It would be visual, social proof, accompanied by approval and joy, that Edna was "moving out," an artist on her own, maintaining her own life-style and her affairs in what she humorously called the pigeon house. Not surprisingly, however, the party is not the grand affair which Edna fantasized about. We know that Edna has sundered most of her New Orleans social relationships and that she has abandoned her "Tuesdays at home"; logically, New Orleans' social world will not be rocked. The party, as it turns out, is a comfortable group of ten people. Yet Edna has furnished even this small number of people with grandeur and sumptuous magnificance, including a group of hired mandolin players to serenade her guests softly and discretely at a distance from the dining room.

Chopin herself is present, discretely, slipping in brief comments about the guests and making us aware that this is a rather odd assemblage of people. For example, we have never heard of the Merrimans until now; we learn that Mr. Merriman is "something of a shallow-pate" and that, because he laughs at other people's witticisms, he is "extremely popular." Arobin is there, of course, overindulging in flattery for his hostess, and there is also Mrs. Highcamp, a fellow enthusiast of the races. Old Mademoiselle Reisz is wearing fresh violets in her hair, and she is seated, because of her diminutive size, atop a number of plump cushions. Monsieur Ratignolle is alone (his wife fears that she will soon begin labor pains). The aging Miss Mayblunt inspects her food and the other guests through lorgnettes and is said to be intellectual. There is also a "gentleman by the name of Gouvernail . . . of whom nothing special could be said"—in short, a motley lot. Representing the Lebrun family is young and handsome Victor Lebrun, who unexpectedly becomes the center of attention at the party and the reason for the party's coming to a quick conclusion.

Edna, of course, looks magnificant as the hostess in a dazzling golden satin gown, with a fall of flesh-colored lace at the shoulders and a cluster of diamonds atop her forehead. Chopin comments on her regal bearing, her sense of being "alone"; Edna, it seems, stands alone, outside the assemblage of her party and is aware that one person is missing—the person she desires most to be there: Robert. Her love for Robert overpowers her precisely when it should not. The party—if it is to be a true celebration of her independence demands that she retain—despite any mishap—a regal air and command as a hostess, but as it turns out, she cannot bear the sight of the handsome Victor, slightly drunk, garbed and garlanded by Mrs. Highcamp as (in Gouvernail's murmured words) ". . . the image of Desire." She cannot bear the sight of him as the embodiment of pagan desire, and neither can she bear to have him begin to sing the "*si tu savais*" (if you only knew) refrain of the song which Robert once sang to her, the song she sings softly to herself as a rhapsodic and romantic comfort.

The party's tableau, with Victor as its focus, is shattered almost in slow motion. The wine has lulled the party into semi-drowsiness and no one is unduly alarmed when Edna cries out for Victor to stop his song, nor when she accidentally shatters her wine glass and its contents across Arobin's legs, nor when she rushes to Victor and places her hand over his mouth. The guests make charming small talk and, like the mandolin players, slowly steal away, and Edna is lost amid a "profound stillness."

The "little bird" that Mademoiselle Reisz spoke of earlier is emotionally—and perhaps physically—exhausted. Her nervous energy caused her to do a good deal of preparation for the party herself. But, for the most part, Edna's exhaustion is due to the coinciding of the monumental decision to move out of her husband's house and the unexpected news that Robert Lebrun is returning to New Orleans. Arobin, of course, thinks that it was his overwhelming charm which is preying upon her sensibilities; her virtue is battling a fierce love for him. Edna lets him think whatever he pleases; she does not concern herself unduly with Arobin. For example, he has filled her pigeon house with large bouquets of fresh flowers and, with old Celestine's help, distributed them everywhere as a surprise for Edna. Edna does not even comment on the flowers. She sits and rests her head on a table and asks Arobin to leave. Instead, he comes to her and smoothes her hair, his hand caressing her bare shoulders, kissing her lightly there, and continuing to caress her until "she had become supple to his gentle, seductive entreaties." Once again, he imagines that it is he and his touch that are causing Edna's anguish. He imagines that he is irresistible and that if he is patient, he can have any woman he chooses. Edna, however, allows him to caress her because she lets herself enjoy what he is a master of.

Emotionally, Edna knows that Arobin is nothing to her. With her head on her arm, her eyes closed, Arobin is simply a stimulus to ease and arouse and please her; her nerves are tense and his touch is tender. Besides, Edna is confident that if Arobin were to become too aggressive, she could tell him to leave and he would do so. She can handle young Arobin—if she chooses to. As noted, she allows him to caress her because her body enjoys—and needs—being touched and soothed. Arobin leaves, feeling triumphant that he has aroused Edna's passion; little does he fully realize that Edna let herself be aroused by his anonymous, trained touch. With her eyes closed, Edna was scarcely aware of Arobin himself. Her thoughts were with Robert Lebrun.

Léonce Pontellier proves to be far more clever than one might have imagined. When he realizes that his wife seriously means to move out of their house, he invents a ruse of their having their already grand mansion remodeled. The idea is certainly original and certainly ingenious. It is also a surprise when we discover that he does not worry about Edna's moving out causing a personal scandal. On the contrary, Léonce is alarmed about what people might think concerning their "finances." The idea that others might gossip about Edna's moving out being a prelude to Léonce's joining her in the pigeon house almost undoes him. Thus he hires a well-known architect and, within days, the Pontellier house is cluttered with packers, movers, and carpenters—all in an effort to disguise any hint of instability in the Pontellier *fortune.* Léonce's entire concern is with financial scandal; his "unqualified disapproval and remonstrance" are related to the possibility that Edna's latest "whim" might do "incalculable mischief to his business prospects." Chopin's satire on Pontellier's material vanity is superb when she tells us about a brief notice in one of the daily papers (inserted, we can be sure, by Léonce himself) about the possibility that the Pontelliers might spend the summer abroad. Chopin, in her own small way, repays in kind the many years of male laughter over the vanity of women. To be sure, she tips her hand by not suppressing her impulse to include an exclamation point, but who can blame her for summing up Léonce's reaction with ". . . Mr. Pontellier had saved appearances!"

Edna is satisfied with her small house so completely that she soon feels ready to leave it and go see her children, and the week that she spends there is described by Chopin in detail; the paragraphs are full of the "local color" that her critics—prior to the publication of *The Awakening*—were so quick to praise her for. Edna listens to her little boys' tales of mule riding, fishing, picking pecans, and hauling chips. Even Edna herself enjoys going with them to see the pigs and the cows and also the black servants—laying the cane, thrashing the pecan tree, and catching fish in the back lake. Edna thoroughly enjoys being with the children, answering their questions about the new house—where everyone will sleep and where their favorite toys are. For the entire week, Chopin tells us, Edna gave "all of herself" to her children—unreservedly and happily. And when she has to leave, it is with a sense of regret. All the way home, "their presence lingered with her like the memory of a delicious song." But once Edna returns to New Orleans, her thoughts are not on her children.

This joyous scene of Edna with her children and of her leaving them and returning to New Orleans helps us understand what Edna meant when she told her friend Adèle Ratignolle that she would die for her children, but that she would not give up a life of her own in exchange for a daily devotion to them. Edna loves her children; of that there is no doubt, but she cannot make her family the focus of her life. She admires Adèle's beautiful embodiment of the mother-woman role, but she herself cannot compromise herself for the stifling demands of the role. Edna does not want a predefined role, and her options seem to be either a mother-woman like Adèle or an eccentric, living only for her art, like old Mademoiselle Reisz. Like her children, Edna's art can richly consume her time, but Edna has no ambition to be a great artist. She doesn't want to be a "dedicated artist," in the same way that she defies being a "dedicated mother" and, especially, a "dedicated wife." The allegiance to the world of "art" is ultimately as unacceptable as the world of "mother, wife, and housekeeper." When Edna decides to move out of the big house into a house of her own, she has no role model to follow. She is aware of the solitude that accompanies her decisions and actions. She has no man to talk with that might offer understanding or direction, nor does she have any other woman—save Adèle and Mademoiselle Reisz—to share her feelings with. Chopin's ending Chapter 32 with the simple sentence "She was again alone" is a clear, direct summing up of Edna's predicament. She is very much alone. Not only now, but ever since her first moments of her awakening, solitude has accompanied her growth. On Grand Isle, she especially felt the embodiment of this solitude in the sea. For that reason, she was supremely happy when she learned to swim in it and no longer had to fear it and have a "hand nearby"; she could freely share in its abundant solitude.

Chapters 33-39

Robert Lebrun's actual return to New Orleans is as surprising to us as it is to Edna. During Edna's dinner party, Victor mentioned nothing about his brother's leaving his job in Mexico; Madame Lebrun has said nothing definite to Edna, nor has Adèle Ratignolle. We know from his letter that Robert plans to return, but we are as shocked as Edna is when she is sitting alone in Mademoiselle Reisz' apartment one evening, waiting for her to come home, and Robert suddenly opens the door.

Coincidentally, one of the reasons that Edna has come to see Mademoiselle Reisz is to talk about Robert. Even though Robert has been gone for almost a year, he has not written to Edna—not even once. As a result, he has become somewhat of a fantasy lover to Edna. She has no certain hope for his returning permanently to New Orleans, so she has filled her stray moments by romantically imagining his returning for a brief visit. Always in her fantasies, Robert has come to her and declared his love for her; or else, in another fantasy, he has accidentally revealed his love for her. Either way, his love for Edna has matched her deep love for him.

Now, however, he is suddenly, physically, before her, and the situation evokes a phrase that Edna used not long ago to describe life; she called it a "monster of beauty and brutality." Reality has come crashing down upon fantasy; the rendezvous she fantasized has occurred and it is the antithesis of how Edna hoped it would be. Robert is as handsome as ever, but he is ill at ease and awkward. When he sits on the piano stool, one of his arms crashes discordantly across the piano keys. The noise is brutal, as is his confession that he has been in New Orleans for two days. Edna's movements in this scene are mechanical, awkward, and unsteady. She has been caught completely off-guard; this is not the way it should have happened. She came to Mademoiselle Reisz' apartment for peace and some solace after a boring, irritating morning, and Robert (her fantasy of peace) has broken her quiet revery.

In the midst of this sudden "brutality" of life, the shattering of all her romantic daydreams, there is also beauty, however, for in spite of Robert's not writing to her, Edna finds in his eyes the tenderness she saw long ago on Grand Isle. Now she finds "added warmth and entreaty," qualities that were not there before. In his eyes, she sees the warmth that kept alive her love for him, the love she sensed was shared between them. Here is the proof—in his eyes.

Yet even this discovery becomes ultimately painful because Robert refuses to acknowledge his feelings for her. Instead, he speaks about settling in with his old firm and, ambiguously, excuses his not writing by saying that there "have been so many things . . . ." Robert has obviously asked a great many questions about Edna. He knows, for example, that the Pontelliers might spend the summer abroad and that Edna has moved into her small house. He seems as shy as Edna is bold. He dares not to do what she has done—that is, face herself and life, with all its "beauty and brutality" and cope with, if not solve, life's problems. Robert has committed himself to the role of becoming a proper New Orleans gentleman and businessman, as Adèle Ratignolle and Mademoiselle Reisz have committed themselves to their prescribed roles. Edna cannot bear the fraudulence she finds in Robert. When she says that his letters would not have been "of any interest" to Edna, the lie is too painful and too insulting. ". . . it isn't the truth," Edna says, and prepares to go. She has waited too long, anticipated too much, fantasized too freely, and now when she is confronted with the man she loves most, she cannot and will not listen to lies or excuses. She has become a fervent disciple of a new integrity and she will not abide hypocrisy, especially from Robert.

When Robert insists on accompanying her home, she allows him to do so because, after all, Edna is human. She loves him and she has missed him. He begs to stay a bit if Edna will "let" him. The tension between them is broken, and Edna is able to laugh and relax and put her hand on his shoulder and tell him that he is beginning to seem like the old Robert she once knew.

This intimate mood is broken almost immediately, however, when Robert finds a picture of Arobin and is jealous that Edna has it. Edna is neither ashamed nor embarrassed by the picture. Arobin is nothing to her; we know that. Edna tried to make a sketch of Arobin, and he brought the photograph, hoping that it might help her sketching. The photograph is no "lover's gift," no memento. Edna tells Robert no more or no less than the truth: she finds Arobin's head worth drawing, he is a friend of hers, and of late she's come to know him better. Robert calls Edna "cruel" for being so blunt. Edna is not cruel; quite simply, she can play games no longer. Robert grew up playing games; the Creoles all play games. When Edna met Robert, he was playing the role of a knight in search for a fair lady to serve during the summer. In fact, everyone Edna knows plays role games—speaking and acting predictably—and no one questions the role or varies from its prescribed actions. Yet Edna was "awakened," and she questioned her role as wife and mother; afterward, she began to try and fashion a life that would be uniquely hers—something no one she knows has ever done before. Where it will end, she cannot imagine, but she will not compromise—not now, not even with Robert, the man she loves. If Edna is cruel, it is because she has recognized and accepted the fact that life is beautiful and that it is also cruel. If Robert is ever to mature, he too must make his own odyssey, searching for his own truths as thoroughly as Edna has done.

A certain coolness comes between Edna and Robert; Chopin terms it "a certain degree of ceremony." Edna is not able to penetrate Robert's reserve and his reluctance to admit his emotional feelings toward her. He admits to forgetting "nothing at Grand Isle," but this statement is cautious and non-commital. In contrast, Edna says that being with Robert "never tires" her. He does not comment on this. During the dinner and afterward, Edna is patient with Robert's aloofness until she notices a strikingly embroidered tobacco pouch that Robert lays upon the table. She admires the needlework, and when Robert reveals that the pouch was given to him by a Mexican girl, Edna become uncharacteristically jealous. Her questions are uncharacteristically indirect and bitter, and Robert's answers are taunting and ambiguous; behind all of Edna's questions is one single, unasked question: did you love the Mexican girl who gave you the tobacco pouch?

As Robert is pocketing the pouch, Arobin enters. The scene is already bristling with intensity, and Arobin's entrance multiplies that tenseness. When Arobin discovers Robert with Edna, he and Edna perform an impromptu charade of camaraderie, ridiculing Robert's romantic luck with women. Robert's demeanor is seemingly unruffled; he shakes hands with both Edna and Arobin, asks to be remembered to Mr. Pontellier, and leaves. His mentioning Mr. Pontellier is only proper good manners, of course, but it is Robert's subtle way of reminding Edna and Arobin that Edna is a *married* woman.

The morning's sunlight cheers Edna; after the previous night's confusion and brooding, Edna feels that she was foolish to have been so introspective and jealous. Robert loves her; she was certain of that yesterday and she is just as certain of that today. It is only a matter of time before Robert's reserve is broken—for two reasons: first, because he does love her; and second, because of her passion for him. Edna is convinced that Robert knows that she loves him; soon, he will also realize that she desires him, that he has awakened sexual passion within her. She confronts the possibility of his remaining cool and distant for awhile, but she can live with that possibility. The important thing now is that he *has* returned, that he lives in New Orleans, and is not almost a continent away. Time will awaken Robert; Edna can wait.

Because of her decision to allow Robert his freedom to adjust once again to the business of living in New Orleans and to adjust to the new circumstances of her freedom, Edna is able to deal decisively with the morning's mail. To her son who asks for bonbons, she promises treats; to Léonce, Edna is diplomatic and friendly, though evasive; she has made no plans to go abroad. In fact, she has made no plans whatsoever. She is absolutely open to whatever Fate offers.

Edna burns Arobin's love note; his professed concern for her is of no consequence. She does allow him, however, to fill her empty hours when days go by and Robert does not call or even send a note. Arobin is allowed to be a surrogate. He possesses a sense of danger and romance and fulfills her need for male companionship. Arobin, meanwhile, preys on Edna's "latent sensuality." And whereas earlier, she often went to bed despondent because Robert had not called, at least now, when Arobin fills her evenings, there is no despondency when she falls alseep, but neither is there a freshness and joy when she awakens in the morning.

Thus Edna lives on the periphery of hope, longing to see Robert and compromising for Arobin's ready, romantic companionship. For that reason, she often goes alone to a small enclosed garden cafe, where she can be alone, can read quietly, and dream idly of Robert. Yet, quite by accident, Robert walks into the garden one day and interrupts her reverie. They are awkward, apologetic, and then distant. Edna attempts to explain why all of her questions to him must seem "unwomanly": she has changed. She says what she thinks now, and she asks questions, and she is prepared to face the consequences. Robert is obviously attracted to her, but he is cautious before this new woman he has discovered. He follows her home, although she does not ask him to do so, and he stays, sitting in the shadows while she goes to bathe her face. When she returns, he leans down and kisses her.

It is Edna, however, who satisfies her passion first, putting her hand to his face and pressing her cheek against his. They kiss and he confesses to having wanted to kiss her many times. It was his love for her that drove him away from Grand Isle. He had no other choice.

Edna tries to explain that it makes no difference to her if she is married to Léonce Pontellier. She jokes that Léonce is generous; perhaps he might "give" her to Robert, an offer she finds absurd. No one can "give her away." Edna already *is* free. She belongs to no one except herself. When Robert mentions wanting her to be his wife, she is affronted; she scoffs at "religion, loyalty, everything . . . ." Kissing Robert on the eyes, the cheeks, and the lips, she chides him for imagining that someone must "set her free" in order for them to be able to make love.

At that moment a message is delivered, and fate interrupts their passionate avowals. Long ago, Edna promised Adèle to help her when her labor pains began; now Edna must go to her friend. The two lovers kiss goodbye, and Edna feels that Robert's passion matches her own. She promises him that *nothing* is of consequence now—except their love for each other. She leaves him precisely when he needs her most. Robert is weak; he needs Edna's strength. He fully realizes how thoroughly he loves this married woman who promises herself, who promises to defy all convention for him.

Witnessing Adèle in the throes of childbirth is painful for Edna. The physical pain she sees is symbolic of the psychological pain she feels is inherent in motherhood. This scene of birth is ugly and bloody and preludes, for Edna, Adèle's never-ending bondage to a child who will overpower her will and identity. And Adèle will allow it to happen. Edna cannot. The scene causes Edna to remember her own painful scenes of childbirth and her "awakening to find a little new life she had been given." But Edna has awakened now, as an adult, and found a new little life that she herself has created—and this new life is liberating. It does not limit; being a mother limits one, and the pain Edna sees before her is not as painful as the fact that once one has decided to become a mother-woman, one gives up everything for the children. Despite the torture that Edna sees Adèle enduring, torture and pain which Edna finds repulsive, Edna stays—in revolt and as a witness against nature for its cruel demands. She stays so long, in fact, that Adèle is able to whisper, exhaustedly, that Edna should "think of the children. . . . think of the children! Remember them!" Adèle, even in her great pain, is thinking of Edna, afraid that Edna is about to abandon her husband and children in exchange for a romantic whim. She appeals to what she, as a mother, holds most sacred: the children, even as she suffers the pains of birth.

For Adèle, this new baby is new evidence of her worth as a mother-woman; for Edna, it is yet another burden; it is a reminder of a woman's powerlessness, of how her liberty is checked by men, family, and society.

When Edna is free at last of the confines of the Ratignolle's apartment, she feels dazed; the trauma of seeing her friend give birth has unnerved her. Even Doctor Mandelet thinks it was cruel for Adèle to insist that Edna witness the childbirth scene in order that she might recall that she too had once given birth, that she too had brought forth children from her body, and that they were, by definition, physical extensions of herself. They grew within her body and despite their being severed, they are still part of her flesh and blood.

The object lesson was not wholly lost on Edna. Before she left for Adèle's house, she was convinced that no one would, or could, or should, demand that she do anything she did not wish to do. Now she is not sure. She *is* sure that Léonce cannot force her to go abroad, but she is unable to say, unreservedly, that no one has the right to force her to do anything that she does not wish to do "except children, perhaps . . . ." Her thoughts are incoherent.

Yet of one thing she is sure; she has awakened to new visions and new perspectives and new possibilities, and she can never return to a life of dreaming and illusions or of being Mrs. Léonce Pontellier. Motherhood, in contrast, has become nebulous; *her* life should come first; she should be able to live her life her way—regardless of whom she must "trample upon," and yet, ultimately, she realizes that she cannot "trample upon the little lives."

We have never seen Edna, for any length of time, exhibit maternal feelings. Her children and her love for them have been vague and on the periphery of this novel, except for the week spent at their grandmother's home. Yet witnessing Adèle give birth has made Edna realize anew that her children were created within her own body and that a mother must, ultimately, be responsible for them.

At the same time, she can envision no greater bliss than that which she shared with Robert—their embracing, their kissing and expressing their love for one another. He almost gave himself to her. She resolves to think of the children tomorrow. She will awaken Robert's passion again tonight with her kisses and arouse him with her caresses. There will be time to think of the children tomorrow. Tonight she will awaken Robert and claim him.

But Robert is not waiting for her. He has left a note saying goodbye. He leaves her because he loves her. She has been willing to sacrifice everything—even the little ones—for him, but he is afraid to risk anything.

The final chapter of the novel is set once again on Grand Isle. Robert's brother, Victor, is patching up one of the cottages and the feisty, flirtatious Mariequita is sitting in the sun watching him, handing him nails and dangling her legs. Victor has talked for an hour of nothing but the fabulous party at Edna's; he has described in exaggerated detail the party, embroidering his memories with romantic fancy, especially his memory of Edna, resplendent in sparkling diamonds. Both young people are struck dumb with amazement when Edna suddenly appears and begins to chatter about hearing the hammering and being glad to know that the loose planking is being mended, complaining how dreary and deserted everything looks. She has come to rest, she says; any little corner will do. She is alone and simply needs to get away and rest.

The young people continue to chat and argue, while Edna walks toward the beach; she does not hear them. The sun is hot and she lets its heat penetrate her. Edna has reached a crisis, one which she must solve alone. She has no man she can relate to; Robert is gone. Léonce does not matter. She has no woman she can relate to: Adele's role of mother-woman is as oppressive and limited as old Mademoiselle Reisz's role as an artist. Edna's priorities demand that she cannot compromise her newly awakened life for anyone. All of her friends have safe, well-defined niches, but those niches have walls; the old-fashioned, rosy ideals of marriage and motherhood are rank to Edna. The absurdity of condemning herself to such tyranny is too much to ask.

As she enters the sea, she cuts cleanly through the waves and begins to swim out farther than any woman has ever done before.

Here, there are no goals, no roles, no boundaries; there is only the solitude that whispered to her long ago. There is a freshness in the sea that is denied her in the Pontellier house; as a wife and mother, she would stagnate, losing all self-confidence and direction; thus she chooses to swim out to her death. Already, of course, metaphorically she has swum out further than any woman has done when she risked enticing Robert to a romance that would preclude her roles of wife and mother. Edna knows what she is rejecting. Never again will she be bound into a role that she does not choose for herself.

She hears the sea and its murmurs; they seem to be "inviting the soul to wander in abysses of solitude." Edna's solitude is her own companion. Robert, especially, has abandoned her. Above, a bird with a broken wing, beats the air, fluttering, circling, until it reels down the water." Mademoiselle Reisz warned Edna once, using the symbol of a little bird, about having the strength and courage to be able to fly if one were to "soar above the level plain and prejudice . . . ." At that time, the old woman felt Edna's shoulder blades to see if Edna's "wings were strong." It was a sad spectacle, she said, to see the weaklings "bruised, exhausted, fluttering back to earth."

Yet the bird Edna watches does not fall to the earth; it falls into the sea. And Edna does not die "bruised" and "fluttering." She enters the water naked, swimming where "the waves . . . invited her." There is no sense of melodrama and hysteria here. Edna lets the sea "caress her, enfold her" in its "soft, close embrace." These are words of love and passion. Edna listens to its voice, and she understands its depths of solitude. She knows that this is no shallow haven of simple calm. This is a deep, restless sea of change and currents. She is not afraid, even though her arms and legs are tiring. No one can claim her now; she can give herself to the sea. And she does, freely joining her solitude with its own solitude. She had to choose and decide whether or not life was worth being lived on terms other than her own, and she decided that it was not. She confronted life's most fundamental philosophical question. That act was an "awakening" in itself. She acts in revolt against the tyranny she finds in social myths that would limit her growth as a free woman. She cannot find meanings in the family unit as it exists and to accept the sacred connotations that generations have given to it would be living fraudulently. The quality of short experience that Edna finds swimming out to her death is measureless, compared to the endless years of robot-like role playing which she would be condemned to were she to return to Léonce Pontellier and her family. Edna's awakening on Grand Isle gives her no alternative. Swimming out to her death gives Edna a sense of dignity that the choice is hers. She has grasped the full reality of the hollow life that would be hers if she condemned herself to living "for the little ones." By choosing death, she frees herself from continuing an existence that would be miserably mechanical. She cuts off all hope for herself by choosing death, but she can conceive of no real hope otherwise. Freedom is more important, even in these few short minutes that she swims out. It is a strange, new clarity that Edna possesses. Her last thoughts are of her youth, the time prior to her awakening. She returns to this state of purity, free of a world that would encase her and consume her. Edna's strokes in the sea are "long, sweeping"; they are not "frantic beatings." We must, of necessity, imagine her as happy and free at last.

QUESTIONS FOR REVIEW

1. What is Grand Isle? Where is it, geographically, in relation to New Orleans?

2. How much older is Mr. Pontellier than Edna? How long have they been married, and what is the significance of their age difference?

3. Describe Edna's physical appearance and her character at the beginning of the novel.

4. What are the circumstances of Edna's first "awakening"? Would you describe Edna's "awakening" as happy or unhappy? Explain.

5. Describe Robert Lebrun's charm early in the novel. Why does he finally decide to leave Edna?

6. Characterize the Creole women, in contrast to Edna.

7. Why does Robert decide to go to Mexico?

8. Mademoiselle Reisz's life-style is one of the choices Edna considers after her "awakening." Describe this particular life-style.

9. What kind of a mother is Edna? What kind of a hostess is she for her husband?

10. Is Chopin sympathetic to Alcée Arobin? Why or why not?

11. What is Mr. Pontellier's reaction to Edna's announcement that she is moving into the pigeon house?

12. Describe Edna's relationship with Arobin.

13. Briefly comment on the conclusion and the consequences of Edna's grand party.

14. How does Edna finally come to view life? How is this viewpoint different from her viewpoint at the beginning of the novel? Explain the term "life's delirium."

15. How does Adèle's childbirth scene affect Edna?

16. What importance does Chopin assign to the sea in this novel?

17. In your own words, paraphrase Edna's reasons for committing suicide. Do you agree or disagree with her? Explain.

SELECTED BIBLIOGRAPHY

BERTHOFF, WARNER. *The Ferment of Realism: American Literature 1884-1919.* New York: Free Press, 1965.

BUTCHER, PHILIP. "Two Early Southern Realists in Revival," *College Language Association Journal*, 14 (1970), 91-95.

EATON, CLEMENT. "Breaking a Path for the Liberation of Women in the South," *Georgia Review*, 28 (Summer, 1974), 187-99.

EBLE, KENNETH. "A Forgotten Novel: Kate Chopin's *The Awakening*," *Western Humanities Review*, X (Summer 1956), 261-69.

FLETCHER, MARIE. "Kate Chopin's Other Novel," *Southern Literary Journal*, 1 (August 1966), 60-74.

______. "The Southern Women in the Fiction of Kate Chopin," Louisiana Historical Quarterly, 7 (Spring, 1966), 117-32.

MAY, JOHN R. "Local Color in *The Awakening*," *Southern Review*, 6 (1970) 1031-40.

LEARY, LEWIS. "Introduction," *The Awakening and Other Stories*. New York: Holt, Rinehart and Winston, Inc., 1970.

______. "Kate Chopin and Walt Whitman," *Walt Whitman Review*, XVI (December 1970), 120-21.

______. "Kate Chopin, Liberationist?" *Southern Literary Journal*, III (Fall 1970), 138-44.

MILLINER, GLADYS W. "The Tragic Imperative: *The Awakening* and *The Bell Jar*," *Mary Wollstonecraft Newsletter*, II (December 1973), 21-26.

OBERBECK, S.K. "St. Louis Woman," *Newsweek*, LXXV (February 23, 1970), 103-04.

POTTER, RICHARD H. "Kate Chopin and Her Critics: An Annotated Checklist," *Missouri Historical Society Bulletin*, XXVI (July 1970), 306-17.

RINGO, DONALD A. "Romantic Imagery in Kate Chopin's *The Awakening*," *American Literature*, 43 (January 1972), 580-88.

ROCKS, JAMES E. "Kate Chopin's Ironic Vision," *Louisiana Review*, I (Winter 1972), 110-20.

ROSEN, KENNETH M. "Kate Chopin's *The Awakening*: Ambiguity as Art," *Journal of American Studies*, 5 (August 1971), 197-200.

SCHUYLER, WILLIAM. "Kate Chopin," *The Writer*, VIII (August 1894), 115-17.

SEYERSTED, PER. *Kate Chopin: A Critical Biography*. Baton Rouge: Louisiana State University Press, 1969.

SKAGGS, MERRILL M. *The Folk of Southern Fiction.* Athens: University of Georgia Press, 1972.

SPANGLER, GEORGE. "Kate Chopin's *The Awakening*: A Partial Dissent." *Novel*, 3 (1970), 249-55.

SULLIVAN, RUTH AND STEWART SMITH. "Narrative Stance in Kate Chopin's *The Awakening*," Studies in *American Fiction*, I (1973), 62-75.

WILSON, EDMUND. *Patriotic Gore: Studies in the Literature of the American Civil War.* New York: Oxford University Press, 1962.

WOLFF, CYNTHIA. "Thanatos and Eros: Kate Chopin's *The Awakening*," *American Quarterly*, XXV (October 1973), 449-71.

ZIFF, LARZER. *The American 1890s: Life and Times of a Lost Generation.* New York: The Viking Press, 1966.

ZLOTNICK, JOAN. "A Woman's Will: Kate Chopin on Selfhood, Wifehood, and Motherhood," *Markham Review*, III (October 1968), 1-5.

NOTES

NOTES

NOTES

NOTES

NOTES

NOTES

A CONNECTICUT YANKEE IN KING ARTHUR'S COURT

NOTES

including

- *Life of the Author*
- *Introduction to the Novel*
- *A Brief Plot Summary*
- *List of Major Characters*
- *Summaries and Critical Commentaries*
- *Twain's Method of Characterization*
- *Questions for Review*
- *Selected Bibliography*

by

L. David Allen, Ph.D.
University of Nebraska

and

James L. Roberts, Ph.D.
Department of English
University of Nebraska

INCORPORATED

LINCOLN, NEBRASKA 68501

Editor

Gary Carey, M.A.
University of Colorado

Consulting Editor

James L. Roberts, Ph.D.
Department of English
University of Nebraska

ISBN 0-8220-0324-4
© Copyright 1982
by
C. K. Hillegass
All Rights Reserved
Printed in U.S.A.

1990 Printing

The Cliffs Notes logo, the names "Cliffs" and "Cliffs Notes," and the black and yellow diagonal-stripe cover design are all registered trademarks belonging to Cliffs Notes, Inc., and may not be used in whole or in part without written permission.

Cliffs Notes, Inc. Lincoln, Nebraska

CONTENTS

A CONNECTICUT YANKEE IN KING ARTHUR'S COURT NOTES

LIFE OF THE AUTHOR

As one of America's first and foremost realists and humorists, Mark Twain, the pen name of Samuel Langhorne Clemens, usually wrote about his own personal experiences and things he knew about from firsthand experience. Two of his best-known novels typify this trait: in his *Adventures of Tom Sawyer*, Twain immortalized the sleepy little town of Hannibal, Missouri (the fictional St. Petersburg), as well as the steamboats which passed through it daily; likewise, in *Adventures of Huckleberry Finn* (both written before *A Connecticut Yankee*), the various characters are based on types which Twain encountered both in his hometown and while working as a riverboat pilot on the Mississippi River; and even though *A Connecticut Yankee* is not based on personal experience (it is set in sixth-century England), Twain uses many of the same techniques that he used in his *Prince and the Pauper*. In that novel, for example, two young boys gradually lose their innocence; in *A Connecticut Yankee*, Hank Morgan wakes up in a land of innocence–Camelot.

Mark Twain's father was a lawyer by profession, but he was never quite successful, and so he dabbled in land speculation, hoping to become wealthy someday. He was, however, a highly intelligent man who was a stern disciplinarian. Twain's mother, a southern belle in her youth, had a natural sense of humor, and was known to be particularly fond of animals and unfortunate human beings. Although his family was not wealthy, Twain apparently had a happy childhood. Twain's father died when Twain was twelve years old and, for the next ten years, Twain was an apprentice printer, both in Hannibal and in New York City. Hoping to find his fortune, he conceived a wild scheme of getting rich in South America. On a riverboat to New Orleans, however, he met a famous riverboat pilot who promised to teach him the trade for five hundred dollars. After completing his training, Twain was a riverboat pilot for four years and, during this time, he became familiar with all of the towns along the Mississippi River.

When the Civil War began, Twain's allegiance tended to be somewhat southern due to his regional heritage, but his brother Orion convinced him to go west on an expedition, a trip which became the subject of a later work *Roughing It*. Even though some of his letters and accounts of traveling had been published earlier, Twain actually launched his literary career with the short story "The Notorious Jumping Frog of Calaveras County," published in 1865.

Because of the acclaim of *Roughing It*, Twain gave up his career as a journalist-reporter and began writing seriously. His fame as a writer was immediate; one of his first efforts, *Innocents Abroad*, became an immediate best seller, and it is still one of his most popular works. The satire that Twain uses to expose the so-called sophistication of the Old World, in contrast to the old-fashioned Yankee common sense, is similar to that found some years later in *A Connecticut Yankee*, when Hank Morgan confronts nobility and knighthood. But it was the Mississippi River and the values of the people who lived along its length that have made Twain one of America's best and favorite storytellers. The humor which he found there, along with its way of life, has continued to fascinate readers and to embody an almost mythic sense of what it meant to be a young American in the latter part of the nineteenth century.

After Twain turned fifty, however, his fortunes reversed themselves; his health began to fail and he faced bankruptcy; in addition, his wife became a semi-invalid, one daughter developed epilepsy, and his oldest daughter died of meningitis. Yet Twain survived. He became a critic and an essayist, and he became more popular as a satirist than as a humorist. The body of work which he left behind is immense and varied – poetry, sketches, journalistic pieces, political essays, novels, and short stories – all a testament to the diverse talent and energy which used the folklore of frontier America to create authentic American masterpieces of enduring value.

INTRODUCTION TO THE NOVEL

There are two approaches to *A Connecticut Yankee*: there are the numerous polemic digressions on such weighty subjects as social criticism on slavery, on the injustices of the Church and the nobility, on the absurdity of hereditary preferments, on the ridiculousness of knighthood, and on the existence of unjust laws. However, conjointly, we also have a very fanciful story (bordering on science fiction) which delights the reader with its inventiveness.

A Connecticut Yankee, interestingly, has frequently been referred to as Twain's most "magnificent failure." Of course, the novel is not a failure, but what has troubled many critics is the fact that the novel contains at least two major concerns and these concerns, at times, seem to contradict each other.

The first basic contradiction occurs when Hank Morgan, a representative of Nineteenth-Century Progress, is thrown back into the sixth century, where he is supposed to use his Yankee ingenuity and inventiveness to remove the barbaric ignorance and superstitions of that inhumane and unjust world. He is supposed to enlighten and improve these "innocent" people through the use of his modern skills and the inventions and political views of his time, but, finally, he not only fails, but he destroys, in large measure, a beautiful civilization (Camelot) that existed so peacefully and idyllically before his arrival.

The second contradiction occurs upon Morgan's return to the nineteenth century. In the final chapter, we hear him ranting and raving; his deathbed wish is to be permitted to return to his Camelot, his "lost land," his home, and his friends; he wants to be allowed to return to "all that is dear . . . all that makes life worth the living." His last wish is to rejoin his wife, Sandy, and their child, Hello-Central. When he thinks that he holds her, he thinks that all is well: "All is peace, and I am happy again."

Consequently, every judgment against Camelot, every harsh statement concerning the conditions of Camelot, every condemnation rendered against the entire feudal society of sixth-century England and all other objections are contradicted by Hank Morgan's nostalgic longings to return to that happy and innocent land.

We have, therefore, two different views throughout the novel; we have Twain's own condemnations of certain aspects of feudal England, and we have Hank Morgan's nostalgic longing for the beauty of a pure, simple, and innocent society. This is illustrated throughout the novel in many ways. There are long polemic digressions against knight-errantry, and alongside these digressions, Twain details the positive, chivalric nobility of Sir Launcelot. We hear other condemnations against the concept of monarchy, including the idea that when two people are dressed alike, no one can tell the difference between a commoner and a royal personage. In contradiction, Hank Morgan constantly reiterates the fact that no matter what one may do, one cannot disguise the fact that King Arthur has royal blood and a spirit that cannot be humbled or brought to yoke. Many more examples such as these inform the entire novel. Thus, it is for these reasons that the novel is often referred to as a "magnificent failure"–that is, Twain's social criticism is brilliant and pointed; Hank Morgan's view of Camelot, however, does not agree with the criticisms which Twain levels against Camelot and its institutions.

The subject matter of *A Connecticut Yankee* appealed to Twain because it was an age controlled by nobility and royalty, a subject which Twain enjoyed deriding. But in most of his novel, Twain was always fascinated by the concept of an innocent people dwelling in an innocent society. Furthermore, the subject matter of *A Connecticut Yankee* allowed Twain to specifically utilize his vast knowledge of history and biography, two subjects which occupied much of Twain's reading time; in addition, writing this novel allowed Twain the opportunity to meditate on the injustices inherent in human nature (or "the damned human race" as it was so termed in his later work, *The Mysterious Stranger*). The subject matter of this novel also allowed Twain to indulge in one of his favorite pastimes–using a language different from that used by either the common people or the educated people; the idioms and dialects of *Tom Sawyer* and *Huck Finn* and the archaic language of *The Prince and the Pauper* and *A Connecticut Yankee* are all illustrations of Twain's penchant for utilizing different sorts of language.

A BRIEF PLOT SUMMARY

A Connecticut Yankee in King Arthur's Court is a "framed story." That is, the first chapter tells how a tourist in England, presumably Mark Twain, meets a stranger who tells him part of his story and then gives him a manuscript that tells the rest of his strange tale. In the last chapter, the tourist has finished reading the manuscript and searches out the stranger, only to find him dying and calling out for the wife and daughter whom he had lived with in sixth-century England.

In the first chapter, this stranger (we later learn that his name is Hank Morgan, but he is usually referred to in the novel as The Boss) tells the tourist that he was something of a jack-of-all-trades who had a particular aptitude for making and inventing things mechanical. He is from Hartford, Connecticut, where he had been head superintendent in a munitions factory until, in a fight with one of the workers, he was hit in the head with a crowbar. When he awakened, he was sitting in the grass under a tree. A man in old-fashioned armor took him prisoner, and they rode off to what Hank Morgan believed would probably be an insane asylum. At this point in the story, this stranger begins to feel very sleepy, so he gives the tourist the manuscript detailing his adventures, which he has written from the journals that he kept.

The first chapter of the manuscript (the introductory chapter is technically a prologue) begins with the knight and Hank Morgan riding through a quiet countryside that Morgan does not recognize. After a time, they arrive in a small, wretched town and pass through the gates of a huge castle; they then enter into a great paved court.

Trying to find out what asylum this is, Hank Morgan talks with a young man who tells him that the year is 528 and that the day is June 19; Morgan has been captured by Sir Kay the Seneschal, and he will be exhibited before the court. Then he will be sent to the dungeons to either rot or be ransomed.

At the feast around the Round Table, Sir Kay's turn to tell of his adventures finally arrives, but he is interrupted by Merlin, who tells the story of how King Arthur got his sword from the Lady of the Lake; he puts the entire crowd to sleep. When Sir Kay does tell his story, he exaggerates immensely. Then Arthur sentences Morgan to die at noon on the 21st. Morgan is stripped of his "enchanted" clothes and is hauled off to the dungeons.

When Clarence (the boy to whom he had talked) comes to visit him, Morgan tells the boy to take a message to the court; he says that he is a magician more powerful than Merlin. The message has some effect, but Merlin ultimately scoffs at the claims of this "magician" because the so-called spell that Morgan says that he will cast is not specified. By this time, Morgan has remembered that there will be an eclipse of the sun at noon on the 21st, so Morgan sends Clarence back to tell the court that he will blot out the sun – if he must.

Shortly thereafter, Morgan is hauled out to the courtyard and chained to a stake. A monk is praying for him when, suddenly, he stops, and Morgan notices that the solar eclipse is just beginning. He realizes that when he asked Clarence what day it was, Clarence gave him the incorrect day. Thus Morgan puts his knowledge of the eclipse to good use, thereby gaining his freedom and a position as "perpetual minister and executive" to the king, as well as liberal funding, if he will "let" the sun shine again. He keeps the king and the knights in suspense for a time, ostensibly to make sure that the king meant what he said; then, when he notices that the eclipse is total, he announces that his spell will now begin to pass away.

This "miracle" makes Morgan a man of great interest to the people of the kingdom, and when Merlin begins spreading rumors about him, Morgan blows up Merlin's tower, using explosives which he and Clarence have made. This "miracle" solidifies Morgan's position in the country.

At one of the frequent tournaments held in Camelot, Sir Dinadan (who tells many bad jokes) is being drubbed by Sir Gareth, and The Boss (as Morgan is now called) says that he hopes that he (Sir Dinadan) dies. By the time these ambiguous words are uttered, however, Sir Gareth has crashed into Sir Sagramor le Desirous, and Sir Sagramor thinks that Morgan's derogatory wish was meant for him. Sagramor therefore challenges Morgan, The Boss, to a bout after he, Sagramor, returns from questing after the Holy Grail. The king and others urge The Boss to also undertake a quest so that he will be more worthy of taking on Sir Sagramor. Morgan puts off this journey for some time, though, so that he can make some changes in the kingdom – such changes as providing some schools, factories, military academies, telephones, and telegraph lines; all these changes are done quietly, of course, so that they will not be too noticeable immediately.

Finally, Morgan can put off his quest no longer. The king decides that Morgan will accompany the Demoiselle Alisande la Carteloise to free her mistress and forty-four princesses held captive by three giants with one eye each.

Along the way, Morgan, The Boss, discovers many things; first, he learns that armor is very uncomfortable to ride in and also to sleep in. Then he and the Demoiselle have a meal with several freemen, one of whom is willing to think about change; as a result, he is sent back to Camelot for Clarence to put into training. A little later, The Boss terrifies six armed knights by stoking up a head of smoke with his pipe as they charge at him; the knights halt, amazed, and are willing to surrender. That evening, the evening of the second day out from Camelot, they come upon the castle ruled by Morgan le Fay. Although the wicked le Fay has a quick temper and is willing to kill anyone who crosses her even slightly, she becomes very deferential when she learns that her visitor is The Boss. She allows him his way even after he frees a man accused of killing a deer on the royal preserve and even though he frees nearly all of the prisoners in her dungeons. She casually stabs for a young boy, but she refrains from throwing his grandmother, who curses her for that deed, into the dungeons.

Several days later, Sandy (the name which Morgan has given his traveling companion) informs The Boss that they are coming upon an ogre's castle. The Boss, however, can see only a pigsty filled with pigs, but Sandy assures him that it *is* a castle and that those *are* princesses (and not pigs) who must be freed. Rather than argue with her, The Boss agrees that this castle must surely be enchanted–but enchanted for his eyes only. Thus, he rides down and buys the pigs from the swineherds. He and Sandy then drive the pigs to a nearby castle, where the "princesses" will wait to be reclaimed by their kin or friends.

When The Boss and Sandy meet a band of pilgrims heading toward the Valley of Holiness, they also decide to travel in that direction. On the way, they meet one of The Boss's "sign board knights," knights who are advertising various products which The Boss wants to introduce into England. But it is not long before they learn that there is a problem in the Valley of Holiness that requires one of the Boss's spells to set right, so he sends a knight back to Camelot with a note to Clarence for supplies and helpers.

The problem in the Valley of Holiness is that the holy well, believed to be the product of a miracle in an earlier day, has gone dry. The Boss examines it and finds that a section of the wall has been broken. While he waits for his supplies and aides to arrive from Camelot, he insists that professional courtesy requires him to wait until Merlin gives up before he takes over. Merlin does finally admit that he has failed to fill the well, but he gives up just as two of The Boss's helpers arrive; when they do, they quickly repair the hole in the well's wall, and then they prepare to make a spectacle of the restoration of water to the well. The "miracle," of course, is a success, and The Boss's reputation is reaffirmed.

A short time later, however, another magician arrives, and for the moment, he eclipses The Boss's reputation. All is not lost, however. Using a telephone that has just been installed in one of the abandoned caves in the Valley, The Boss predicts that the king and his retinue will be in the Valley of Holiness in two days; the other magician insists that the king will be traveling in the other direction. When the king does arrive on time, the other magician is discredited.

While the king is there, he dispenses justice, he oversees the choosing of officers for the standing army (a process that The Boss is unhappy with), and he allows those who are ill to attempt to heal themselves by touching him. After this business is taken care of, The Boss and the king set out to travel into the countryside in disguise. The Boss wants to find out, firsthand, what the conditions of the country are, and the king thinks that it might be a lark to go along. Thus, the two set out.

The Boss and the king have a number of problems on their journey because the king simply will not, or cannot, act like a peasant; indeed, The Boss manages to save them from being killed several times, once by using a dynamite bomb to blow up a group of charging knights.

During one incident, they help a woman who is dying of smallpox, leaving just before her sons, who had been imprisoned by the local lord, escape and arrive home. As The Boss and the king move through the night, they see the glow of a fire in the distance, and they discover the corpses of a number of men who have been hanged. Near morning, they come to a hut, and they finally convince the woman who greets them to give them some hospitality. After they have slept, she feeds them, and they learn that the lord of that area has been killed and that all the freemen in the neighborhood have been out all night looking for whoever is responsible for the murder. The Boss notices that his host and hostess are terribly nervous, and he guesses that they are probably related to the boys who are responsible for the lord's death. Therefore, he goes out with his host, Marco, and they agree that they will say nothing about key suspects who escaped. Instead, they walk through the village talking to people. The Boss invites a number of them to dinner that Sunday, and he insists on paying for everything; thus a sumptuous spread is prepared at the store.

The Boss's purpose in gathering these people for a meal is to find out what they think about wages and about the relationship between wages and purchasing power; he wants to convince them that his way of thinking is better than theirs, but all he manages to do is make them suspicious of him. Then, before he can cover up his error and ease their suspicions, the king begins talking about agricultural matters in such a way that makes these people think that he is mad. As a result, the men set upon the king and The Boss. Although the king and The Boss are winning the fight, they notice that their hosts have left. Suspecting that they have gone for help to aid their neighbors, the king and The Boss flee.

They are finally captured, however, but before these villagers can beat them, as they intend to do, the king and The Boss are rescued by an earl named Grip. Although Grip feeds them, gives them a room for the night, and lends them horses to ride to the next town, once they are there, he has them bound and sold as slaves.

They are then driven to London, along with a number of other slaves. Along the way, they see several instances of the cruelty of the laws and the difficulties of the life of the common people. After a time, The Boss manages to steal a metal clasp with a long pin from a prospective slave buyer; he uses this as a lock pick, and he is able to free himself. Before he can escape, however, the slave master comes in. The Boss tries to catch him, but he scuffles with the wrong man, and both of them are arrested. In the morning, in court, The Boss tells the judge a story that effects his immediate release, and he uses a telephone to call Clarence in Camelot so that knights can be sent to the rescue.

In the meantime, he learns that the slaves had killed the slave-master in the night and that all of them are to be hanged. He tries to make some contacts with people he knows, but in doing so, he is captured and put in with the other slaves; the jailer tells him that they are all to be hanged in the middle of the afternoon.

At a climactic moment when three of the slaves have been hanged, and the blindfold has been put on the king, suddenly five hundred of Camelot's finest knights ride up on bicycles. They take charge of the situation and rescue the king and The Boss.

Just after they return to Camelot, The Boss learns that he must enter the tournament lists and must joust against Sir Sagramor.

Instead of conventional weapons, however, The Boss uses a lasso and ropes Sir Sagramor and yanks several other knights off their horses. After Merlin steals the rope, Sir Sagramor challenges The Boss again; this time, The Boss uses a revolver which he has made and shoots him. When one of the other knights challenges him, The Boss challenges all of them together, and he shoots nine of them before the rest turn and flee.

After this, The Boss has his own way for a time, and he makes many changes in England, revealing some of the earlier changes which he quietly accomplished. He also marries Sandy, and they have a child whom Sandy names Hello-Central. When Hello-Central falls ill, The Boss spends a great deal of time with her and, on the advice of doctors, he takes her to the seaside. She falls ill again while they are visiting a kingdom on the French coast. About a month later, after she is fully recovered, The Boss goes to England to see what has happened to the boat which they had sent to bring them supplies; they are worried, for it should have returned at least three weeks earlier. Once in England, The Boss learns that all of the changes which he had made have now fallen under an Interdict of the Catholic Church.

The Boss then makes his way to Camelot. He and Clarence make plans for a final battle against most of England, with only fifty-two of the people whom they trained as helpers. Working from Merlin's cave, they kill twenty-five thousand knights, using electric fencing, Gatling guns, and an ingeniously diverted stream. When The Boss goes out to see if they can give aid to any of those who still survive, one of the wounded enemies stabs him. Luckily, however, the wound is only slight. Yet all is far from being peaceful yet, for Merlin enters the cave in the guise of an old woman and casts a spell on The Boss that makes him sleep for thirteen hundred years. Thus the novel ends with the tourist's reaching The Boss's room just as The Boss dies, calling for Sandy and Hello-Central.

LIST OF MAJOR CHARACTERS

Mark Twain

Samuel Langhorne Clemens, the author of *A Connecticut Yankee in King Arthur's Court*; he is the tourist to whom Hank Morgan tells part of his story and to whom Morgan gives the manuscript that chronicles his adventures in sixth-century England.

Hank Morgan

The Connecticut Yankee in King Arthur's court. Using his nineteenth-century knowhow, he becomes known as a "magician" in sixth-century England; he tries to bring about many changes in the way of life in that century. Throughout most of the book, he is referred to as The Boss.

Sir Kay the Seneschal

The knight who captures Morgan when he first appears in the sixth century.

Clarence

A page whom Morgan meets when he first arrives in Camelot; he becomes Morgan's first recruit and his second-in-command in Morgan's attempts to change Arthurian England.

Arthur

King of Britain, the ruler in Camelot, and The Boss's companion during an incognito visit among the lower classes of England.

Merlin

Supposedly the mightiest magician of the times, he is bested several times by The Boss; it is he who puts The Boss under a spell that causes him to sleep from the sixth century to the nineteenth century.

Guenever

Queen of England; she is Arthur's wife, although she is much more romantically interested in Sir Launcelot.

Sir Launcelot

He is the most prominent knight of the Round Table, and he is the main cause, along with Guenever, of the Interdict that overtakes England late in the novel.

Sir Sagramor le Desirous

Another knight of the Round Table; he challenges The Boss because of a supposed slight; he is finally shot by The Boss.

Sandy

She is more formally known as the Demoiselle Alisande la Carteloise; she comes to Camelot with a tale about her mistress being held captive by three ogres. King Arthur decides that The Boss will accompany her to set this matter right. Morgan later comes to admire her a great deal and, eventually, he marries her.

Morgan le Fay

Arthur's sister and King Urien's wife; she is the real ruler of their small kingdom, but she is deferential to The Boss, since his reputation as a magician preceded him to her castle.

Marco

He is a charcoal burner; the king and The Boss stay with him and his wife on their incognito tour of the realm; after a while, Marco and his wife become alarmed by the behavior of the king and The Boss, and they go after help against these two strangers.

Dowley

The blacksmith in the village near where the Marcos live; he is a primary target of The Boss's attempts to bring the villagers' thinking about economic matters into line with his.

Grip, an Earl

An important man in the neighborhood where the Marcos live; he and his men rescue the king and the Boss from the villagers, but they sell them into slavery the next day.

Hello-Central

The daughter of The Boss and Sandy; she is given her unusual name when Sandy hears The Boss repeat it frequently in his sleep; she believes that it is the name of one of Morgan's old girlfriends.

Sir Mordred

A nephew of King Arthur. He is the primary cause of the Interdict that wipes out the progress which The Boss has brought to England because he uses the fighting between the king's party and Launcelot's party in the battle over the queen to try and take power himself.

Sir Meliagraunce

A knight wounded in Morgan's last battle; he stabs Morgan, and this allows Merlin to put a spell on Morgan that causes him to sleep thirteen hundred years.

SUMMARIES AND COMMENTARIES

A WORD OF EXPLANATION

Summary

"A Word of Explanation," together with a "Final P. S. by M. T." at the end of the novel, establishes a "frame" for the story of Hank Morgan's adventures in Arthurian England. The narrator in this introductory chapter tells us how he came to hear parts of this story and that he read the rest of the story in a manuscript.

It happened that he was taking a tour through Warwick Castle when he met another man, who began walking with him and began telling him tales about such people as Sir Launcelot of the Lake, Sir Galahad, and other knights of the Round Table. In the course of the tour and the conversation, this man introduces to the narrator the idea of the transpositions of epochs and of bodies. He also mentions that it was he who put a bullet hole in the armor of Sir Sagramor le Desirous. This strange man disappears, however, before the narrator can ask him further questions about any of these subjects.

That evening, the narrator reads a tale from Sir Thomas Malory's famous book, *Le Morte Darthur*; the tale he reads concerns how Sir Launcelot rescues Sir Kay and conquers three other knights in the process. As he finishes the tale, a knock is heard at the door: it is the stranger. After drinking four Scotch whiskeys, this man, whom the narrator met earlier in the day, tells his story.

He is, he says, an American from Hartford, Connecticut, and he is "a Yankee of Yankees." He learned blacksmithing from his father, horse doctoring from his uncle, and all manner of mechanical arts from a job which he had in a factory. Because of his skill in making and inventing things mechanical, he soon became head superintendent of the factory and supervised several thousand men. One day, however, an unfortunate accident occurred; while he was in a fight with one of his fellow employees, he was knocked unconscious with a crowbar.

When he came to, he was sitting in the grass under an oak tree, and then a man in "old-time iron armor from head to heel, with a helmet on his head the shape of a nail keg with slits in it" rode up and challenged him. Not understanding what was going on, the man from Connecticut, the stranger, told the man in armor to get "back to your circus." The knight backed off and lowered his lance, and the stranger climbed the tree. After some argument, the stranger agreed to go with the knight, even though he believed that the man was probably an escapee from a lunatic asylum.

At this point, the stranger seems to be drifting off to sleep, but before he does so, he gives the narrator a manuscript of his adventures, tales which he has written down from journals which he kept. As he leaves the stranger, who is falling asleep, the narrator begins to examine the manuscript; it is written on old, yellowed parchment over "traces of a penmanship which was older and dimmer still – Latin words and sentences: fragments from old monkish legends, evidently." Filled with curiosity, he begins to read.

Commentary

Twain uses the age-old literary device of a "frame" to enclose his story; the use of this device adds a certain degree of credibility to a story which will ultimately be seen as a type of utopia in reverse. Here, there will be a constant double vision of Camelot throughout the narrative. Hank Morgan will try to change everything which he sees, and he will try to bring this medieval civilization up to the "standards" of the nineteenth century, and yet, at the same time, the medieval civilization is presented in idyllic images of innocent people playing charming games, surrounded by an elegant landscape which is colored by pageantry of all types.

In the opening frame, the narrator is touring the ancient Warwick Castle, and when the guide mentions a mysterious hole in one piece of ancient armor and suggests that it must have been done maliciously at a much later date in history, a mysterious stranger announces that he was there when the hole was made. In the opening scene of this novel, then, we have information about the final disposition of Sir Sagramor le Desirous, information which will not fully appear until Chapter 39. But our imagination is caught and our interest in this mystery is sparked. We will not know anything further until many more chapters later, but obviously Twain had his basic plot worked out at the beginning of the frame. Later, the mysterious stranger comes to the narrator's room in the Warwick Arms Hotel with the manuscript; it is aged, written on yellow paper and supposedly it was written thirteen hundred years ago; in addition to the manuscript's seeming to be very old, note that the handwriting looks strained. These facts all add to the suspense, and they also give further "credence" to the story inside the frame.

Whereas many of Twain's other great novels deal with the Mississippi River or the Mississippi River Valley or some other subject matter which he knew well, in this particular novel, *A Connecticut Yankee in King Arthur's Court*, Twain sets his narrative far back in time so as to compare and contrast certain aspects of a long-dead civilization with a modern, industrial one. Hank Morgan, the central character whom Twain chooses for his hero, is perfectly suited for this "transposition of epochs" for several reasons. First, like so many of Twain's narrators, Morgan is one of Twain's innocent people – that is, like Huck Finn, Morgan reports pretty much what he sees. But more important, before his transposition, Morgan has been trained in all sorts of practical matters. The combination of his being associated with both a blacksmith and a horse doctor will serve him well in sixth-century England. More important, his knowledge of "guns, revolvers, cannons, boilers, engines [and] all sorts of labor-saving machinery" will be of the utmost use to him. Furthermore, he can seemingly invent anything; therefore, he is both an inventor and inventive.

The blow on the head that Hank Morgan received in the fight then leaves everything in doubt as to whether or not he was actually back in the sixth century, or whether or not he has dreamed all of these fanciful thoughts. Certainly in the Post Script section, Hank (or The Boss, as he will be called) longs to return not to the nineteenth century but to the sixth century. Thus, in the final analysis, whatever criticism that The Boss makes of Camelot and its civilization, we must remember that at the end of the novel, when Morgan is sick and his mind is rambling, he would prefer Camelot and that century to the one in which he is now living.

Twain's own comments about his Connecticut Yankee help us better understand his intention in writing this novel; he wrote to the illustrator: "This Yankee of mine . . . is a perfect ignoramus; he is boss of a machine shop, he can build a locomotive or a Colt's revolver, he can put up and run a telegraph line, but he's an ignoramus nevertheless." By this, Twain meant that the Yankee was not a person of intellect, but that he was a person of Yankee ingenuity. An intellectual in sixth-century England would not have survived; indeed, it would take an inventive and ingenious person to survive such an incredible, unbelievable time transposition.

CHAPTERS 1 and 2

Summary

As they ride along, the narrator of "A Word of Explanation" notices the quiet of the countryside and the lack of people and wagons. When they meet a young girl, he is surprised that she is calm; seemingly, the man in armor causes no alarm within her; nor does she seem unusually interested in him. But when she sees the narrator, her hands fly up. She is startled and astonished by his appearance. He cannot imagine why *he* would cause such fright and curiosity.

The two men ride on, then, and the town they come to, finally, is a wretched place. The streets are narrow and crooked, the dogs and hogs roam at will, and there is a pervasive stench about the place.

The townsmen have unkempt hair, most of the people wear knee-length robes of coarse tow-linen, and many of them wear iron collars; the children are mostly naked. And again, it is the narrator who draws the astonished stares, not the man in armor.

Suddenly, they hear military music, and soon a noble company in rich clothing rides through the town, paying no attention to the people or the animals. The narrator and his captor follow this procession to a huge castle and into the great paved court.

The narrator – we later learn that his name is Hank Morgan – tries to find out what kind of "asylum" he has come to, and he concludes that the first person whom he talks to is one of the "patients." The second person whom he meets refuses to talk, but he points to "an airy slim boy in shrimp-colored tights." This lad comes up to him and tells him that he is wanted. As they walk, the boy tells Hank that the year is 528, that all the people whom they see are not "patients"; they are in their right minds, and this is King Arthur's court into which he has been brought. The boy also tells him that the day is June 19. From his memory, Hank dredges up the fact that at noon of June 21, 528, there is supposed to be a complete eclipse of the sun. He determines to use this as a test of whether or not he is somehow in the year 528 or in his own year of 1879.

That settled, he decides to make the best of his situation and to find out what he can about it; he also decides that if this really is the sixth century, he is going to take charge and make some changes. Accordingly, he names the boy Clarence. Hank then asks the name of his captor. He is told that the knight is "Sir Kay the Seneschal, foster brother to our liege the king." Clarence also tells Hank that he will be thrown into a dungeon until his friends ransom him, or until he rots, whichever comes first. Before that, however, Hank hears that Sir Kay will show him off to the court and tell the tale of his capture, exaggerating the details.

As they wait for Sir Kay's turn to speak, Hank looks about the place. It is immense and built of ancient stones. There is little ornamentation, except for a few tapestries showing scenes of battle and of men in armor. In the middle of the hall is the Round Table, as large as a circus ring. Around this huge oaken table are "men dressed in such various and splendid colors." They are eating and drinking prodigiously, and one of their diversions is to throw a bone to the dogs surrounding the table and then watch them fight for it. Hank judges that the "speech and behavior of these people [is] gracious and courtly" most of the time, but that "they [are] a childlike and innocent lot," for they believe every lie that someone tells.

He also discovers that he is not the only prisoner waiting to be exhibited and that the others are in much worse shape than he is; most have been severely hacked up and are in great pain, although not a sound of distress is heard from them. He reasons that they must have treated others in like manner; thus, their punishment is something they could expect and prepare for; it is, in other words, a matter of training rather than of philosophy.

Commentary

Chapter 1 begins the narrative proper of the novel. For centuries, Camelot has been the idyllic dream of romantic perfection (even in the twentieth century, one of the most popular Broadway musicals is entitled *Camelot*), thus the fact that Hank Morgan has never heard of Camelot shows him to be grounded in reality and practicality; nothing of the sentimental or romantic will affect him.

Yet part of the dual vision of the novel occurs immediately. Hank's opening description of the landscape suggests that he is affected by the quiet and lovely beauty of the area; thus, the hard-nosed, practical Yankee is placed in an innocent, idyllic land: "It was a soft, reposeful summer landscape, as lovely as a dream, and . . . the air was full of the smell of flowers and the buzzing of insects, and the twittering of birds. . . ." This kind of countryside could belong anywhere in Twain's novels that deal with an innocent person entering into another land; it is very much like Huck Finn's Jackson Island and many other places in Twain's fiction. But Morgan's practicality brings him quickly out of this romantic idyll.

The double view of Camelot and its inhabitants is presented in Chapter 2, and it continues in one form or another throughout the novel. Hank Morgan sees the knights and the royalty as being childish but charming: "As a rule the speech and behavior of these people were gracious and courtly . . . and . . .they were a childlike and innocent lot; telling lies of the stateliest pattern with the most gentle and winning naivete. . . ." Thus, throughout the novel, Hank is charmed by the very people that he is desperately trying to change. Ultimately, Hank Morgan will try to destroy the innocent habits of Camelot, but, ironically, he will, in turn, be destroyed by his own plans. The manner in which these gentle people tell lies in stately patterns is later correlated with the manner in which modern diplomats also tell stately lies in gentle patterns. Thus, the centuries have not changed people in high diplomatic positions very much.

CHAPTERS 3-5

Summary

Around the Round Table, the various knights tell the tales of their prowess at arms. As he watches and listens, Hank decides that there is something lofty, sweet, and manly about these men, but also that they are simplehearted and lacking in brainpower.

Sir Kay is brought to the fore when six prisoners come forward and, to the disbelief of most present, announce that they have been conquered by him. Sir Kay then tells the tale of how they were captured by Sir Launcelot (the tale that the frame narrator read in Malory), as well as other tales of Sir Launcelot's adventures, exaggerating the whole time.

At that point, Merlin – a very old, white-bearded man – stands "upon unsteady legs, and feebly swaying his ancient head [surveys] the company with his watery and wandering eye." Clarence groans and tells Hank that Merlin is about to tell the tale that he always tells when he has gotten drunk. Merlin does, putting most of the court to sleep in the process. His story is about how King Arthur got his sword from the Lady of the Lake.

Sir Dinadan is the first to awaken after Merlin's tale, and he amuses himself by tying metal mugs to a dog's tail. This arouses the other dogs, who chase the first; the noise then awakens all the knights, and they all have a good laugh. After that excitement dies down, Sir Dinadan strings together a number of jokes that Hank has already heard about thirteen centuries later; they were old even in the sixth century.

After this, Sir Kay gets up to tell of his feat at arms. Hank says, "He spoke of me all the time in the blandest way as 'this prodigious giant,' and 'this horrible sky-towering monster,' and 'this tusked and taloned man-devouring ogre,' and everybody took in all this bosh in the naivest way." The other facts of the encounter are likewise stretched. After this tale, Arthur sentences Hank to die at noon on the 21st. There is a discussion of what to do about Hank's enchanted clothes; when Merlin has the sense to suggest that they strip him, they do so immediately. Hank is embarrassed, but everyone else discusses his physique with no hesitation or concern.

Finally, Hank is carried off to the dungeon, but he is so tired that he falls asleep almost as soon as they leave him to himself in the cell. When he awakens, he is sure that everything that has happened to him is a dream. Just then, however, Clarence comes to visit him, which dispels the notion.

After he finally gets it through his head that this is no dream, Hank asks Clarence to help him escape; Clarence, however, thinks that such a feat is impossible because there are so many guards. In addition, Merlin has put a spell on the dungeons, and no one in the kingdom would think of helping anyone escape. Hank, hard-headed Yankee that he is, hoots at the idea of a magic spell, but that gives him an idea: he tells Clarence that he is a magician himself. Furthermore, he claims to be a much more powerful magician than Merlin, and he sends Clarence to let the court know that there will be trouble if anything happens to him.

While Clarence is gone, Hank worries about whether or not it will occur to the boy that a magician wouldn't have to send a boy with this message. (It doesn't.) He also decides to use the eclipse as his piece of magic.

When Clarence returns, he reports that the message had an effect, but that Merlin scoffed because the disaster was not named. Thus Hank sends Clarence back with the message that he will blot out the sun if he must.

Commentary

In Chapter 3, we are introduced to many of the "Knights of the Round Table." We must remember that when Hank Morgan carried his manuscript to the "frame narrator" that the frame narrator was reading from Sir Thomas Malory's *Le Morte Darthur*; Twain himself was exceptionally fond of this old volume and used certain episodes from Malory's book.

The dual perspective of Camelot and its royalty continues in Chapter 3 when Hank Morgan observes: "There was something very engaging about these great simplehearted creatures, something attractive and lovable. There did not seem to be brains enough in the entire nursery, so to speak, to bait a fishhook with." But these are the charming, innocent, and lofty people whom he loves, and yet he will be determined to destroy large numbers (25,000) of them later in order to have his own way–that is, in order to force civilization on them.

Chapter 3 also introduces Merlin, who will function as the antagonist to Hank Morgan. They will be not just rival magicians, but they will also be rivals in all ways.

Chapter 4 emphasizes the childish aspects of the knights–the games that amuse them are games that children still play today–games such as tying a can on the tail of a dog and then laughing to see the dog run, frightened of its own tail. Furthermore, Hank Morgan has to also listen to some dull, flat jokes that he has already heard thirteen hundred years later, only to discover that they were dull and flat in the sixth century also. In both the jokes and in the tales that the knights narrate, there is so much gross exaggeration in them that Hank Morgan finds it incredible that anyone would believe the stories. Yet it is part of the charm of the innocents that they would believe anything that is told to them.

At the end of Chapter 4, Hank Morgan's clothes are removed, at the suggestion of Merlin, and they all comment upon his physique. He is extremely embarrassed both by his nakedness and even more by the language that the ladies use to describe his various naked parts. Later, we discover that essentially Hank Morgan is not just a Yankee, but a Yankee prude. He chides the court for its foul speech, he feels (later) that it is improper to ride through the countryside alone with Sandy, and even though he is fully clothed underneath his armor, he feels that it is indecent to remove his armor in front of her.

One of the great ironies of the novel is found in Chapter 5. One of Hank Morgan's desires is to rid the country of superstitions. Yet, in order to gain control, he will use superstition to frighten the people into acknowledging his magical powers. Thus, Hank will use his practical Yankee knowledge of eclipses in order to perform his first miracle; the contrast between the practical and the miraculous is one of the comic devices which Twain uses throughout the novel.

CHAPTERS 6-8

Summary

Hank feels rather proud of himself and is almost impatient for the next day so that he can be "the center of all the nation's wonder and reverence." All such feelings vanish, however, when the men at arms come to get him, telling him that the stake is ready and that the execution has been moved up a day. Clarence joins him on the way to the courtyard and proudly announces that he is responsible for getting the king to change the date.

Hank is chained to the stake, and a monk begins to pray over him. Suddenly he stops, looking into the sky. Hank follows his gaze and notices that the eclipse has begun. He makes good use of the situation, telling those gathered that he will allow the darkness to proceed for a time. If the king agrees in good faith to make him the king's "perpetual minister and executive" and pay him one percent of any new revenues which he creates, Hank will allow the sun to shine again. The king agrees to the terms and orders Hank freed and clothed in rich clothing. Finally, when Hank notices that the eclipse is total and that the sun will soon peak beyond the moon, he says, "Let the enchantment dissolve and pass harmless away," much to the relief of those present.

In his new role as second in command to the king, Hank is given fine clothing and a choice suite in the castle. As he accustoms himself to his new quarters, he notices things that are lacking—bells, speaking tubes, chromo pictures, gas, candles, books, pens, paper, ink, glass, sugar, tea, coffee, tobacco, and many other things common to the nineteenth century.

In the meantime, the people of the kingdom are immensely interested in him. The eclipse frightened the whole kingdom, and everybody wants to see the magician who caused it. They flock in from all over the country to see him. It is clear that while they are there, they would like to see another miracle performed so they can carry the tale back to their villages.

The news that Merlin is busy spreading the idea that this "upstart" is a humbug causes Hank to decide that he will do something else. He has Merlin thrown into prison and then begins the preparations for having Merlin's tower blown to pieces by fire from heaven. Working with Clarence, he makes a great deal of blasting powder and constructs a lightning rod. They run wires from the lightning rod to caches of powder hidden throughout the tower. Then they wait until the weather is right.

At the first sign that there will be a storm, the event is announced to the people, and Hank has Merlin brought to him. He gives Merlin a chance to stop what is to take place, but Merlin cannot. So Hank, judging matters closely, waves his hand in the air three times, and the lightning strikes the lightning rod. There is a crash, fire spews forth, and the stones of the tower leap into the air. It is an effective miracle.

Hank, who is now known as The Boss, muses over the situation in which he finds himself. He has colossal power, and he plans to make some changes in the social and religious attitudes of the people so that they are more in line with what he thinks is right.

Commentary

After the great miracle, Hank could have demanded a title of nobility, but since he will later use all of his powers to destroy the concept of a privileged class of nobility, he refuses to ask for one; instead, he is extremely pleased with his newly invested title: he is *The Boss*, and known by this title, he will be admired and feared all over the kingdom. Ironically, The Boss wants to destroy the aristocracy, yet he fully enjoys the powers that he now has and plans to use them for his own advantages in the same way that the aristocracy uses their special privileges.

Furthermore, The Boss is filled with a need to be theatrical. Many of his actions are designed so as to bring a sense of applause to his own person; that is, he always seeks after the proper effect when he is performing a miracle. In Chapter 7, he makes sure that there are large numbers of people present to see his announced miracle of blowing up Merlin's castle. This act serves another purpose. In addition to bringing glory to The Boss, it discredits Merlin and, therefore, it allows The Boss to relax his guard.

In Chapter 8, Twain makes his first critique of the Roman Catholic Church. Later, he will continue his attacks on the Church in greater measure, but here he contents himself with commenting on how the Church has made common men into "worms"; thus, since the nation is composed largely of common men, the Church is responsible for making England "a nation of worms." He also questions here the duplicity of the church's helping to establish the concept about the "divinity of kings" and the "divine right of things." This only allows the aristocracy to treat the commoners in any way that the aristocracy so pleases. The Boss is determined to make the country into a republic where every man shall have an equal vote.

CHAPTERS 9 and 10

Summary

Tournaments are frequent events at Camelot, and The Boss usually attends them in order to see if there are any improvements that he can make. Indeed, he has such an interest in improvements that his first official act is to open a patent office. As this particular tournament takes place, he sets a priest in his Department of Public Morals and Agriculture to work toward learning to become a reporter, since he also wants to begin a newspaper.

During the course of the tournament, Sir Dinadan comes over and begins regaling The Boss with the same old jokes. This is cut short when Sir Dinadan is called out to fight Sir Gareth. Sir Gareth is giving him a good drubbing, and The Boss involuntarily says, "I hope to gracious he's killed!" Unfortunately, by the time he actually says these words, Sir Gareth has crashed into Sir Sagramor le Desirous, and Sir Sagramor thinks that the words were meant for him. He takes offense, and he names a date several years in the future – after he returns from searching for the Holy Grail – when he will demand satisfaction from The Boss.

In the four years following his fateful exclamation at the tournament, The Boss has the beginnings of nineteenth-century industrial civilization well underway in sixth-century England. His previous efforts have grown and spread. He has begun a military and a naval academy, and he has started stringing wires for both telegraphs and telephones, going across country and stringing the wires at night to avoid detection and to keep the Church from knowing what he is doing.

Indeed, in spite of all the changes which he has started, the country seems much the same as it was when he arrived in sixth-century

England. The main, obvious change is that revenues have quadrupled, while being spread about more equitably.

He can, therefore, take time out from his labors to undertake the quest that the king and many others think that he must undertake in order to honorably meet Sir Sagramor in the challenge match.

Commentary

In Chapters 9 and 10, The Boss has been in control for some undetermined length of time. Twain does not bother unduly with chronological details. At one tournament, Sir Sagramor, misunderstanding a comment, challenges The Boss to a duel; thus, throughout the novel, this duel is to be constantly remembered, and in Chapter 10, in order for The Boss to become "noble enough" to meet Sir Sagramor, he is encouraged to go on a quest. This prepares us for The Boss's first excursion into the rural parts of the kingdom.

CHAPTERS 11-15

Summary

People arrive in Camelot regularly with tales of captured princesses. These tales are accepted without question, and knights vie with one another for the honor of going out to "right the wrongs."

One day, a young lady with a tale about how her mistress and forty-four other "young and beautiful girls, pretty much all of them princesses," are held captive by "three stupendous brothers, each with four arms and one eye." King Arthur decides that this is *the* quest for The Boss – whether he wants it or not.

The Boss questions the young lady, whose name is Demoiselle Alisande la Carteloise. Finally, after confusing the girl and getting few answers that satisfy him, he gives up his questioning in disgust. He is appalled by the impropriety of this young woman's riding with him on his quest, but she *must* since she cannot give him any directions to follow.

Before The Boss leaves, he is given much good advice about how to handle himself, and, after a good breakfast, he is helped into his armor and carried out and set on his horse, things that he could not have managed himself.

The ride through the countryside is quite pleasant – until the sun has been up for several hours. The Boss begins to sweat, and he cannot get at his handkerchief to wipe the sweat away. Finally, he gives up, has Sandy (he has quickly given Alisande a nickname) take off his helmet, and lets her pour water into his suit of armor. But he now has a new problem: he cannot get back onto his horse by himself; therefore, they must wait until someone shows up who is willing to lift him up.

As night comes on, they find shelter from a storm. But still The Boss must keep his armor on because he can't take it off himself. In addition, he cannot ask Sandy to help him because having her help would make him feel as though he were undressing in public (even though he is well clothed inside the armor). He does not spend a good night, although his companion evidently does.

In the morning, they move on – Sandy on the horse and The Boss on foot – and before long, they come upon a group of freemen who are flattered by the idea that these two would want to share their food. As they eat, The Boss tries to stir up some sentiment for changing the form of government. For the most part, he gets no positive response of any kind, but one of the men does respond tentatively. The Boss thus writes a note to Clarence, and he sends this man to Camelot for training.

The Boss pays three pennies – an extravagant price – for his breakfast; the farmers then help him on his horse, and he and Sandy continue on their way. The next day, about mid-afternoon, they come across half a dozen knights, and Sandy fears that The Boss's life is in danger. The Boss, however, looks on this as an opportunity. He lights his pipe, and by the time that the knightly company has charged toward them, he has a good cloud of smoke coming through the bars of his helmet.

This breaks the charge, and the knights come to a halt several hundred yards away. The Boss is puzzled by this, until Sandy informs him that they are waiting to yield themselves to him. Sandy also takes care of the yielding, charging them "to appear at Arthur's court within two days and yield themselves, with horses and harnesses, and be my knights henceforth, and subject to my command." This impresses The Boss; he thinks that she handles it much better than *he* could have; his opinion of her is rising constantly.

As they ride on, The Boss asks Sandy about these knights. She tells him, at great length, all she knows. He, however, cannot follow the tales, and he falls asleep in the middle of Sandy's ramblings. He lectures Sandy about how to tell a story; she listens to him patiently, and then she goes on to tell the story her way.

As the day ends, Sandy's story is still unfinished, but they are approaching a large and impressive castle.

Commentary

One of Twain's most frequently used narrative techniques involves the innocent narrator taking a journey and encountering various adventures. In *Life on the Mississippi, Roughing It, Huck Finn, Innocents Abroad, The Prince and the Pauper*, and many other works, the concept of the narrator on a journey prevails. Here, we have the nineteenth-century Yankee traveling through sixth-century England, and his adventures are in the form of a series of contrasts. They are interesting reversals of Cervantes's *Don Quixote*, a novel that Twain greatly admired. In *Don Quixote*, the traveler was a knight who protected the innocent. Here, The Boss is a commoner who is *opposed* to knights. But one adventure is common to both stories: the story of the bewitched pigs is found in both works.

At first, when The Boss meets Sandy (Demoiselle Alisande la Carteloise), he is impatient with her, and he is also shocked that she will accompany him on his journey; it does not seem proper or decent for the two of them to travel together – alone. Thus, beginning with their meeting and their subsequent travels, we have a contrast between civilization and primitive innocence. In their first meeting, The Boss is professional, curt, businesslike, and skeptical. He wants written proof of her identity, a map, or directions to the so-called bewitched palace. He even calls her "innocent and idiotic" when she cannot understand why he would want all of the troublesome information that he is asking for, and she is incapable of understanding why he would even doubt her word. Therefore, until they are later married, The Boss continues to be patronizing and prudish; in contrast, Sandy is patient and loving.

In Chapter 12, when the two of them set out on their adventures, the contrast between the city and the lovely countryside is emphasized, especially in the opening paragraph where they "left the world behind and entered into the solemn great deeps and rich gloom of the forest. . . ." The quietness and peacefulness is reminiscent of Huck and Jim's trip down the Mississippi when no one is bothering them.

The irony is that in this lovely, peaceful solitude which The Boss so enjoys, he plans to start building huge, smoky factories filled with laboring people who must drudge through life. This is correlated by the fact that The Boss feels trapped in his suit of armor, and yet he would take these free and innocent people and trap them in the huge nineteenth-century factories–a trap much worse than the armor which he is now wearing.

The Boss's meeting with some "freemen" in Chapter 13 prompts some of his views on the Catholic Church and the ruling aristocracy. Here in Camelot, the majority of the people are ruled by only a half dozen people, and these people don't even seem to care because the Church has brainwashed them into believing that they are inferior and that they must be content with their place in life, a place assigned to them, according to the Church, by God Himself. Thus, they remain in servitude because of the alignment of the Church with the aristocracy.

CHAPTERS 16-18

Summary

Before The Boss and Sandy reach the castle, they come upon a knight who is wearing one of The Boss's signboards advertising soap. They chat for awhile, and this knight informs them that the castle belongs to Morgan le Fay, who is King Arthur's sister and King Uriens's wife.

The Boss encourages the knight, gives him a new advertising idea, and sends him on his way. Then they enter the castle and are taken before Morgan le Fay, her husband, and her son, Sir Uwaine le Blanchemains. While they are talking, a page trips and falls against her knee; she slips a knife into him without a thought and keeps on talking.

In the course of the conversation, The Boss forgets the relationship between the king and his sister and makes a complimentary remark about Arthur. Morgan le Fay orders them hauled to the dungeons, but the order is quickly withdrawn when Sandy informs her that this man is *The Boss*.

After prayers, they have dinner in a huge banquet hall, with over a hundred guests present. There is music, a great deal of food, and plentiful quantities of wine and mead.

About midnight, an old woman enters the hall and curses the queen for the murder of her grandson (the page whom the queen had stuck a knife into). The queen immediately orders her taken to the stake. Sandy, however, speaks for The Boss, telling Morgan le Fay to either cancel that order or The Boss will cause the castle to crumble around them. The queen cancels the order. So that she won't feel too humiliated, The Boss allows her to hang the musicians, who had played rather wretchedly.

The Boss would dearly love to go to bed, but Morgan le Fay insists that he must see her dungeons, especially the man who is on the rack. This man is accused of killing a deer on the royal preserves. The Boss tries to point out that an anonymous accusation is not proper, but le Fay will not accept that excuse. In the meantime, the man on the rack is tortured as they try to get him to confess. After watching for a moment, The Boss decides that the man must be turned loose, and Morgan concedes to The Boss's request.

As The Boss talks to the man, he learns–after word has been given that the man will not die–that the man did, indeed, kill the deer. He would not confess, however, because that would mean that his property would be confiscated, leaving his wife and child with nothing.

The Boss makes arrangements to send this man to Camelot for training and, afterward, sends him home. Then, because he did not like the executioner's actions, and because the priest had complained about him, The Boss makes the executioner the new leader of the new band that will play for the queen.

Before he and Sandy leave, The Boss asks to see the queen's dungeons. There, in small cells cut out of rock, are people, many of whom have been there so long that no one knows why they were put in the dungeons in the first place; indeed, the common practice in the kingdom is to throw them down there and forget about them.

The Boss orders forty-seven of the prisoners freed; the only person whom he leaves there is a lord who had killed a kinsman of Morgan le Fay.

Commentary

In earlier chapters, the knights have been seen as innocent and delightful children playing games and enjoying life. Now, however, when The Boss puts them between advertising sandwich-boards, they become truly ridiculous. The signs that the knights carry introduce another modern concept–advertising. This particular knight is advertising soap, and the advertising campaign is going so successfully that the workers in The Boss's soap factories are being overworked. Were we to be logical–a fallacy in reading a book such as this–we would have to point out that the advertising campaign could *not* work since no one except the clergy could read, thereby rendering the campaign unsuccessful. In fact, on this particular point, in Chapter 25 ("The Competitive Examination"), the young men who have been born of royal birth consider it an insult to be asked if they can read or write–that is a trivial task reserved for lowly clerks, and nobility should not be bothered by such trivia.

The entire idea of introducing both soap and advertising was done with the "several wholesome purposes in view toward the civilizing and uplifting of his nation." The irony here, as elsewhere, is that The Boss views civilization only in terms of material progress. This is one of the reasons that Twain refers to him as an "ignoramus."

In his meeting with Morgan le Fay, The Boss is again exposed to contradictory reactions in the same person. He has heard that she hates her brother, King Arthur, and that she is a vicious sorceress. Yet when he meets her, he is charmed by her "manner of pretty graces and graciousness." But when a page slips and falls upon her, she kills him with a dagger without a blink of an eye. From this act of atrocity, she immediately goes to her prayers. The Boss is mystified by this course of events, but he realizes that the Church has such a hold on the people that while the aristocracy can kill commoners at will, they must obey the call of the Church, which has the power to forgive them for their actions.

In Chapter 17, Twain is having some more of his good-natured fun. The Boss, after having freed the old grandmother, feels that Morgan le Fay needs someone to murder, so The Boss gives her permission to hang the band leader, the composer, and the entire band because they played so badly the night before. This is The Boss being arbitrarily cruel, and this is Mark Twain suggesting that bad artists who impose their bad art upon the public should be strung up; interestingly, later in the novel, when the press is prepared to publish books, Sir Dinadan publishes a book of his jokes, which is so bad that The Boss has him hanged because of the bad jokes.

In Chapter 18, Twain strikes out against the Church. Once The Boss is in total control, he will try to abolish the established Church–"my idea is to have it [religion] cut up into forty free sects, so that they will police each other, as had been the case in the United States in my time. Concentration of power in a political machine; it was invented for that; it is nursed, cradled, preserved for that; it is an enemy to human liberty." In this regard, one should note that many great writers and thinkers have seen a strong centralized church as being more of a political force than a spiritual force. Significantly, later in the novel, the Church *does* assert its political strength, and it proves to be more effective than The Boss's scientific realism.

Also in Chapter 18, Twain reiterates an idea that was the basis of an earlier novel, *The Prince and the Pauper*. In that novel, the prince and the pauper exchange clothes and no one can tell which is the prince and which is the pauper–except by the clothes which they wear. In this chapter, a man was imprisoned for saying that he believed that "if you were to strip the nation naked and send a stranger through the crowd, he couldn't tell the king from a quack doctor, nor a duke from a hotel clerk." Later on, we will see a verification of this idea when the king dresses as a peasant and goes unrecognized among his people.

CHAPTERS 19 and 20

Summary

The next morning, The Boss and Sandy take to the road again, and Sandy begins once more her tale of the knights, the story that she left unfinished when they reached Morgan le Fay's castle.

After they cover about ten miles in three hours, they stop for a long lunchbreak. While they are there, Sir Madok de la Montaine, another of The Boss's advertising knights, comes upon them. He is cursing and swearing, for another knight has played a practical joke on him, sending him across fields and through swamps for a chance to sell his wares to five of the people whom The Boss just released from Morgan le Fay's dungeons. He vows that he will avenge this insult.

Toward noon, two days later, Sandy informs The Boss that they are approaching an ogre's castle. When she points it out to him, all he can see is a pigsty filled with pigs. Finally, to keep her happy – she is sure that it is a castle and that the pigs are princesses – he tells her that it must be enchanted to his sight, but he agrees to "rescue" the princesses. He does so by buying the pigs from the three swineherds, paying more than the market value. Then they drive the pigs to a castle about ten miles farther on. They have a great deal of difficulty keeping the "princesses" together, and when they arrive at the castle, servants have to be sent out to find several of the "princesses."

Commentary

Sandy's story in Chapter 19 does very little for the novel except slow it down and bore the reader. Twain's editor would have done well to have cut this chapter severely.

In Chapter 20, focusing on the rescue of the princesses who have been turned into pigs by some evil sorcerer or sorceress, we have a scene that is evocative of scenes from Cervantes's novel, where Don Quixote will often be blinded and see things from a different reality than other people do. In a reverse sort of way, The Boss *pretends* that his sight is bad, and to pacify Sandy, he pretends that he sees things as she does. But whereas Don Quixote was a madman and an idealist in a nation of sane people, The Boss is a sane man of practicality in a nation of fools and children.

CHAPTERS 21-23

Summary

The next day, The Boss and Sandy leave the pigs in the castle – whose it is they never discover – and they set out again. Shortly thereafter, they meet a band of pilgrims who are headed toward the Valley of Holiness – a place where the holiness of the monks and the prayers of a holy abbot once brought forth a stream of water in a desert. Some time later, the monks persuaded the abbot to build a bath, and they bathed in it; this caused the well to dry up. Once the bath was destroyed, however, the stream sprang forth again.

In the afternoon, The Boss and Sandy overtake another, less cheerful group, a procession of slaves being herded by a slavemaster who goads them along with his whip. The Boss would like to free them all immediately, but he feels that he cannot change things too quickly.

The following morning, they meet another of the salesmen-knights, who tells them that business has been fine and that the well at the Valley of Holiness has dried up again. The monks have sent to Camelot to see if The Boss would come; if he could not, Merlin was invited. Merlin has been there for three days, working on the problem. On hearing this news, The Boss writes an order for materials and assistance, and he sends this knight off to Camelot, urging him to go swiftly. He plans to continue on to the Valley of Holiness.

The Boss and Sandy reach the monastery by nightfall, and the abbot rejoices that The Boss has come. Indeed, the abbot urges him to begin work immediately, but The Boss demurs, saying that it would not be right for him to do anything until Merlin has admitted defeat. Yet, even though The Boss will not take charge, the monastery is much cheered by his arrival, and for the first time in the week and a half since the well dried up, there is a good deal of food and drink and merriment that night.

The next day, The Boss examines the fountain, which is an ordinary well, dug and walled up in the ordinary way. He suspects that the well has sprung a leak; so he has the monks lower him into the well; there, he finds a huge hole in the wall of the well, and he begins to plan his campaign to restore the well. His first point is to suggest how difficult it will be to do so; it is good for business.

He talks with Sandy about the hermits, and afterward, they visit the various hermits during the afternoon. One of them rapidly bows to his feet almost continuously; later, The Boss uses him to supply the power to run a sewing machine that produces shirts.

About noon on Saturday, Merlin makes his last great effort. When that fails, he predicts that no one will *ever* be able to make the fountain flow again. The abbot is most upset, but The Boss suggests that there is still a chance that he might be able to do something.

That evening, the two men sent by Clarence in response to The Boss's request arrive with the equipment which The Boss needs–

"tools, pump, lead pipe, Greek fire, sheaves of big rockets, Roman candles, colored fire sprays, electric apparatus, and a lot of sundries." Toward midnight, after a nap, they go out to the well, and by sunrise they have the well repaired and everything in place for the miracle. By noon, the water in the well has risen to its customary level. They build a platform, arrange the Greek fire at the corners, prepare the rockets, and fence off the area around the platform.

The performance begins at 10:30 with the arrival of the abbot's procession; masses of people have come to see what will happen. Finally, The Boss stands up and begins to pronounce long, strange words in German, lighting a Greek fire at the end of each name. Finally, he pronounces the name of the spirit that has shut off the water supply and sets off the hogshead of rockets. By the glare of the rockets, the crowd sees the water gushing forth from the chapel.

Commentary

In Chapter 21, The Boss meets a group of pilgrims, and he is surprised to see that the procession includes people from all occupations, professions, and social ranks. Twain is obviously echoing here the pilgrims of Chaucer's famous *Canterbury Tales.* In this tale, the only way that people of different social classes and different occupations could be found in each other's company was by their making a religious pilgrimage. Also, Chaucer's group of pilgrims were very much like these pilgrims; that is, they are a "pleasant, friendly, sociable herd; pious, happy, merry, and full of unconscious coarseness and innocent indecencies." The prude in the Yankee emerges, and he is offended by the vulgarity which he hears. The description of the pilgrims, then, continues Twain's double vision of the people of this country – innocent, yet indecent by nineteenth-century standards.

In contrast to the pilgrims, the treatment of the group of slaves anticipates Chapter 34, where The Boss and King Arthur will be captured and made slaves themselves. Thus, here, while The Boss wants to do away with slavery, the abolition must wait until King Arthur himself has felt the yoke of slavery.

While religion often comes under criticism in this novel, the most sustained criticism on religion occurs in these chapters, during The Boss's visit to the Valley of Holiness. In other parts of the novel, Twain constantly attacks the authoritarianism of the Roman Catholic

Church, but here, his views are more concentrated; he sees the Church as being undemocratic, despotic, and absolutist. He also sees it as being hypocritical in its complete support of the aristocracy. Furthermore, the Church even aids the nobility in pillaging from the peasants and other commoners, but mainly, it fosters ignorance and superstitions. At the end of the novel, the Church is able to play upon the superstitions of the people in Chapter 41 ("Interdict") in order to regain control of the country and to eject The Boss from his position of authority.

The first aspect to come under attack is the absurdity found in making a pilgrimage to worship hermits, many of whom will ultimately become saints. For Twain, a hermit (and also a saint) is, by definition, an abnormal person – a weirdo. That people would come and worship such strange, bizarre people is totally confusing to The Boss. The rationale behind worshipping someone who lives on nuts and berries and goes naked is beyond his Yankee common sense. Living the life of a hermit – that is, living in pure asceticism – contributes nothing to material progress or to the betterment of humanity, and rather than being worshipped, these strange creatures should be ridiculed. Thus, to illustrate his denunciation of this type of asceticism, The Boss is extremely critical of the hermit who sits on a pillar sixty feet high and spends the entire day "bowing his body ceaselessly and rapidly almost to his feet." Because of his large pillar, this hermit will later be known as St. Stylite. The practical Connecticut Yankee sees this movement as being wasted power; thus, he creates a method of attaching a power take-off to the hermit which will, by his incessant motions, create enough power to run a sewing machine which will, in turn, produce *"genuine St. Stylite"* shirts. At least something practical is attained because of the hermit's useless, and heretofore non-productive, bowing. Other hermits are shown doing equally useless things, and yet being worshipped for doing them.

Twain also pokes good-natured fun by some sly or indecent observations – such as the monastery being on one hill and the nunnery (or convent) on the other hill, and in between the two lies the home for foundlings, implying that the latter place is filled with the children of the monks and nuns.

The Boss's desire for theatricality is shown again in the miracle which he performs in the Valley of Holiness. After he has used his

Yankee practicality to patch up the hole in the well, he then has hordes of people gather for the "miracle," which is accompanied by "Greek fires" and "Roman candles"–names given to fireworks, but, one should note, *pagan* names used to celebrate a Christian miracle. The people are awed, and The Boss, greatly to his satisfaction, is elevated in the sight of everyone present. Ironically, The Boss has once again used superstition to gain control over superstitious people whom he wants to educate *not* to be superstitious.

CHAPTERS 24-26

Summary

After this miracle, The Boss's reputation is great in the Valley of Holiness, so he decides to suggest that a bath be built. He assures the abbot that it will not dry up the water again and that an error had been made the previous time, when it was believed that the bath had been the cause of the fountain's failure. The abbot agrees, and when the bath is finished, he is the first to try it out.

A heavy cold and a touch of rheumatism ensue and leave The Boss weak. Later, while walking about the valley to get his strength back, he discovers a cave that had been abandoned by a hermit. He looks inside and finds one of his telephone linemen putting in a phone. He uses the opportunity to call Clarence and find out what is happening back in Camelot. One thing that he learns is that the king and the queen, with a large party of nobles, have just set out toward the Valley of Holiness. He also learns that the king has started raising a standing army, one of his suggestions to the king, although he had wanted to oversee its development.

When he returns to the monastery, another magician has arrived; his specialty is announcing what great people around the globe are doing. The Boss tests him by asking what Arthur is doing; the new magician says that Arthur is presently asleep, but that the next day, Arthur and the court will ride to the north–away from the Valley of Holiness–for two days. The Boss contradicts him, telling him that the king and his party will be in this very valley by evening two days hence.

The new magician, however, seems to sway the crowd, for they make no preparations for the king's arrival. Thus, The Boss uses the telephone to check on the king's progress and manages to gather together something of a crowd to go out and greet the king. When the abbot and the monks discover that Arthur is indeed arriving, they dash out to greet him, although they take the time to–in Twain's words–ride the rival magician out on a rail.

In Chapter 25, we see that King Arthur always takes care of business matters wherever he is. The Commission charged with examining candidates for posts in the army arrives with the king, and the examination of officer candidates takes place. The Commission and the king insist that the main qualifications that an officer must have is a noble lineage that extends at least four generations into the past. Thus, The Boss's candidate, who has been trained at his "West Point," is denied a post, even though The Boss leads him through a series of questions that shows that he does know military matters thoroughly. Another candidate is given a post because he has the requisite lineage, even though The Boss shows that he knows *nothing* about military matters.

Later, The Boss proposes to the king that he form a regiment to be considered the king's own, formed of officers only, that can do as it pleases during battles. The other regiments would have to follow orders and do the dirty work of fighting.

In Chapter 26, we learn that The Boss is planning to go about the countryside as a "petty freeman" in order to find out what things are like on that level of society. When he tells the king about his plan, Arthur decides that he will come along.

In the meantime, however, the king must take care of "the king's evil business," a time when all those who are genuinely ill (they are screened) can come forward, touch the king, and receive a small piece of gold–or, now, one of The Boss's new nickles. In this process, many are cured because of their faith that they will be cured.

It is a long and tedious process, but the tedium is relieved by the sound of a boy's hawking the first edition of the Camelot *Weekly Hosannah and Literary Volcano*. The Boss gets a copy through the window and spends his time looking through it rather critically. His judgment, however, is that it is a pretty fair first effort, although he sees some things which he wants changed. It is passed about from hand to hand, and the people are amazed.

Commentary

In Chapter 24, The Boss again uses his Yankee ingenuity and practicality to discredit another magician. By the use of the telephone wire that he finds in a hermit's cave during one of his walks, he finds out from Clarence that King Arthur and his court are on the way to the Valley of Holiness. Thus, when the rival magician has everyone entranced by his ability to tell what people in faraway places are doing at any given moment, The Boss, who *does* know what Arthur is doing, uses this information to trap the charlatan. Once again, however, The Boss is playing upon the superstitions of the people while also asserting that he is trying to educate the people *not* to be superstitious. Ironically, none of these simple people can see through the hoax of the rival magician; they reject him only when The Boss's prediction comes true; they are truly a fickle group, ready to quickly change their allegiances. Thus, at the end, all of The Boss's teachings will be lost on everyone except those whom he has trained since birth.

In Chapter 25, Twain is able to make further comments on the injustices caused by the Church and its collaboration with the aristocracy. This is shown in the scene where the young girl loses all of her property to the bishop (also a member of the nobility) because of *le droit du seigneur* (the rights due to the lord of the manor).

Furthermore, The Boss thinks that ability, talent, and intelligence should be the key qualities in choosing commissioned officers to defend the country. Thus, he is totally depressed and defeated when he discovers that lineage is more important than intelligence and ability. As a result, the defense of the country will lie in the hands of the nobility simply because they *are* nobility–not because they are capable of defending the country.

Twain uses this episode to bring his narrative to a halt and to offer his own personal polemic on royalty and democracy. In one of his most famous statements, he writes: "Men write many fine and plausible arguments in support of monarchy, but the fact remains that where every man in a state has a vote, brutal laws are impossible." The Boss also feels that the people in this kingdom have been debased so long by the brutality of the monarchy that they are poor material for a democracy. Furthermore, he believes that the masterminds of history who have moved civilization forward have come from its masses–"not from its privileged class"; therefore, the following is a self-proven fact: "even the best governed and most free and most enlightened monarchy is still behind the best conditions attainable by its people." These thoughts of The Boss, spoken here in a polemic digression, do not always coincide with the depiction of the characters of Camelot. The individual person, such as King Arthur, is depicted as being a royal man of good character and fine appearance. Thus, Twain has his double focus–in his polemics, he attacks certain institutions, but in his narrative, he depicts aspects of these institutions or individuals as being fine and noble.

Chapter 26 does very little to move the plot forward except to let us know that The Boss announces his intention to tour England as a common peasant. Additionally, The Boss's first newspaper is presented to us, and the comedy of this newspaper lies in how crudely it is printed, but no one can read it anyway, and it is passed around merely as a curiosity piece.

CHAPTERS 27-30

Summary

Late that night, The Boss cuts the king's hair, trims his beard, and dresses him in a long robe and sandals. In this costume, they can pass as poor freemen, and they slip away from the monastery just before dawn.

The first problem occurs when some of the nobility pass by; the king is not ready to take the humble attitude that is necessary, and he does not do a very good job of it. Fortunately, his behavior elicits nothing more than scowls.

The next day, the king produces a dirk (a dagger), which he bought from a smuggler at the inn where they had stayed; it is illegal for members of the lower class to possess such weapons, and The Boss must talk quickly to persuade the king to throw the dirk away.

As they walk along, the king is perplexed that The Boss does not know what, in particular, will happen tomorrow. The Boss must explain that his special kind of prophecy is the kind that can more easily see 1300 years into the future than it can see into the next day; the king is satisfied with this explanation.

In the meantime, every time a knight passes by, The Boss must restrain the king, for the sight fires the king's martial spirit. During one such encounter, The Boss takes a stroke of a whip that is meant for the king, and at another, he has to use a bomb to save them from the charge of a group of knights whom the king challenges.

By the morning of the fourth day, The Boss has decided that the king must be drilled in "proper behavior" so that he will not disclose his true identity when they meet people or when they enter a dwelling. First, The Boss discusses the way the king walks, how he stands, and how he looks at people, plus the way he talks, addresses people, and how he treats his companion – in effect, The Boss tries to remold the king's entire pattern of behavior. He also tries to tell the king something about the life of the people who they are pretending to be, but this means little or nothing to the king, since it is not at all like life as *he* has experienced it. Although they work long and hard at remaking the king's new "image," and although the king gains some ability to approximate the appropriate actions, he never truly succeeds because he cannot understand the spiritual state of the lower classes.

In the middle of the afternoon, they arrive at a hut that seems deserted. They enter it cautiously, finding a woman on the floor. She tells them to go quickly, since this place is cursed by God and by the Church. They decide to care for the woman, and here, the king takes an active part, even though the woman is suffering from smallpox. Her husband is dead, as is one of her daughters. The king brings the remaining daughter down from the loft, and she dies in her mother's arms. The Boss and the king learn that this family had a good life, more or less, until this year. Then their sons were arrested for a crime that they hurried to report. As a result, the harvesting of the family's crop suffered, and they were fined for not providing the full complement of workers for harvesting their lord's crops. In addition, the Church condemned them because the woman spoke blasphemous words under the pressures which she suffered. Now, she can only wait and hope to die.

By midnight, the woman is dead. As the king and The Boss leave the hut, they hear voices, and they quickly conceal themselves, learning that it is the three sons who have come home.

The king finally figures out that these boys have escaped, and he feels that he must do something about recapturing them. The Boss, of course, has entirely different feelings about the matter, and he works hard to convince the king to forget about it.

Only the fact that they see a fire in the distance is effective in turning the king's thoughts to other matters. The Boss and the king continue to move through the forest, and they come across a man hanging from a tree, and then they discover two other bodies. In the space of the next mile, they discover six more bodies dangling from branches.

Finally, they come upon a house and manage to convince the woman that they are travelers who have lost their way during the night and are badly in need of hospitality. She gives them a place to sleep and feeds them when they awaken late in the afternoon. While they eat, she tells them that the manor house of Abblasoure has been burned and the master killed. Men have been out all night hunting the men who, it is thought, are responsible for this crime.

The king announces that he has seen three possible suspects; he is sure that his hosts will be eager to go out and spread the news. The Boss then notices some concern on the faces of the couple, so he volunteers to go out with the charcoal burner in whose house they have rested. Questioning the man, The Boss realizes the possibility that the charcoal burner is related, in some way, to these young men and the burning of the manor house. He also learns that no one in the community would want to see them hanged; indeed, he learns that the man of the house had no desire to be out the night before and went out only because staying home would have been considered suspicious. For himself, he is happy that the lord got his just deserts.

Commentary

In Chapters 27 through 30, we have a large segment of the novel dealing with the wanderings of King Arthur and The Boss, dressed as peasants and encountering various adventures, most of which are created so as to show King Arthur how much injustice prevails throughout his kingdom.

In Chapter 27, The Boss tries to make the king look like a peasant by dressing him in peasant's clothes and cutting his hair in the same manner as that of a peasant. As Twain often advocated, it is the dress that often makes the man; undress two people and you cannot tell the royal one from the plain one. Here, we have Twain's double focus again. In Twain's polemic, we have his views about dress stated overtly, but when The Boss tries to make the king act like a peasant, the king's nobility cannot be concealed. Thus, we have the contrast between Twain's view and Twain's presentation.

Chapter 28 continues to emphasize the fact that the king has such a royal bearing that he must be drilled again and again to overcome this fact. The main trouble is that the king cannot mentally understand the sufferings and the "spiritlessness" of the lower classes.

The purpose of Chapter 29 is to show the basic humanity of the king. In spite of the threat to his own life–he might catch smallpox and die himself–the king is nevertheless determined to help the poor suffering woman even though she ironically blames her present problems on the Church and the king, totally unaware that the complaint is made to the king himself.

In Chapter 30, even though King Arthur knows that the old woman's sons are innocent, yet the mere fact that they have escaped from the dungeon of one of the nobility means that they have to capture the innocent men and return them to the nobility for punishment. The Boss is again mystified concerning the amount of loyalty that there is to other members of the royalty. The nobility was able "to imprison these men, without proof, and starve their kindred, [and it] was not harm, for they were merely peasants and subject to the will and pleasure of their lord . . . but for these [innocent] men to break out of unjust captivity was insult and outrage."

When The Boss goes out with the charcoal burner, he discovers that the man *had* to participate in a hunt for his friends or else he would be under suspicion himself. Yet even he is glad that the evil lord is dead. This prompts Twain to assert again the value of the common man for "a man *is* a man. . . . Whole ages of abuse and oppression cannot crush the manhood clear out of him. . . ." Then The Boss decides that this is the type of material that he will use when he gradually establishes his republic.

CHAPTERS 31-34

Summary

After this confession has been made and The Boss accepts it completely, the two men walk toward the hamlet, talking. In the village, The Boss makes the acquaintance of a number of people and learns what he can about the matter of wages here. One of the things that he discovers is that the new coins which he introduced are being used widely.

As they talk to various people, The Boss invites a number of them to come to Marco's (the charcoal burner) on Sunday for dinner. Lest Marco become too upset, he insists that he will pay for the whole thing, and he makes a lavish provision for the dinner. He also has Marco buy new clothing for himself and his wife, saying that it is a gift from Jones (the king), who is too shy to say anything himself.

Sunday is a beautiful day, and the guests arrive at the Marco's about noon. They gather under a huge tree outside and spend a good deal of time talking and becoming better acquainted. Dowley, the blacksmith, has been doing well, and he is in an expansive mood, telling about how he has worked his way up in the world and how he can now afford to give his family such luxuries as fresh meat on the table twice a month and salt meat eight times more.

About this time, as The Boss had planned, the Marcos bring out a number of chairs, some other furniture, and a great variety of provisions. In addition, the storekeeper's son arrives with the bill, which The Boss treats casually, even though it seems like a horrible sum to all those present. He pays it easily, and the blacksmith is crushed by this show of wealth.

The Boss now thinks that he has these men at a psychological advantage, so he begins a discussion about wages and buying power. He tries to get them to see that wages are important only in relationship to what can be bought with those wages, that a man with high wages and a man with low wages are equally well off if they can both buy the same amount of goods with what they earn. He fails totally.

Then, partly out of frustration at his failure to make these people see his point, he turns to the idea of a freeman being able to work where he wishes, for the wages he chooses. In his efforts to make a point against Dowley, the blacksmith, his comments suggest that he could now turn Dowley in for violating the law; very suddenly, all the people at the gathering are very quiet and suspicious. Thus, he tries to win back their trust and to show them that they have nothing to fear from him. At that moment, however, the king rejoins them after his nap and begins talking about agriculture. He quickly convinces the men that he is crazy, and they charge them. The Boss and the king have the better of the fight, but The Boss soon realizes that their hosts have left, undoubtedly to fetch help.

As they are chased, they throw the pursuers off their trail, and they use a stream to cover their tracks and then climb a tree, using a bough that was hanging over the water. They are, however, found when one of their pursuers climbs the tree by mistake. Yet they still manage to hold out until they are smoked out of their tree. When they land on the ground, they are immediately set upon, and a fight ensues.

They are "apparently rescued" when a gentleman and his retinue come upon the scene. They are given horses, fed, and housed at an inn, and told to ride ahead to the next town, where they will be safe. When they arrive, they come across a troop of slaves which The Boss had first seen on his way to the Valley of Holiness. They soon become a part of this band of slaves, however, for Lord Grip, their apparent rescuer, has them bound and sold. Although the king rages, it makes no difference.

Commentary

Chapters 31 and 32 are interludes which have nothing or very little to do with the plot. That is, the supposed purpose of this section is to expose the king to the customs of his subjects, but these chapters neither move the plot forward, nor do they serve to inform the king about his subjects.

The most amusing thing about the chapters is the manner in which The Boss wants to play the bountiful host and impress these rather lowly people. No matter how much power, he has, The Boss still wants to be theatrical and attract attention to himself. Of course, it is also human nature to want to put a braggart in his place, as The Boss does with Dowley, who brags about having meat twice a month and having all sorts of luxuries just before the Marcos bring out the plentiful bounty that The Boss has provided.

In Chapter 33, which again does not move the plot forward and thus is another digression, we see The Boss attempting to explain the economic theory that wages are important only in so far as what they will buy. He is a complete failure at this, and resenting the fact that the peasants don't see his point, he childishly begins to get revenge on them.

In order to show them how illogical they are, he creates another analogy about the absurdity of the pillory, and at the end of this analogy, he has placed all of the peasants in a position of being placed in the pillory. Rather than making a logical point, The Boss has only turned the peasants against him, and thus, at the first opportunity, they will use their fear to betray him.

In Chapter 34, this opportunity soon presents itself. When King Arthur makes his absurd remarks concerning agriculture, the superstitious men are going to use this opportunity to seize the "mad man" and "the one [who] would betray us." All these events are leading up to the enslavement of The Boss and the king. The comedy of the situation is that The Boss brings a higher price than the king does at the slave market, and both men are annoyed that they are sold for so little, for they both believe that they should have brought a far higher price. Since King Arthur cannot prove himself to be a freeman, and he and The Boss are sold into slavery, they find themselves upon the slave block; thus, Twain hopes that everyone will realize the "hellish" horror of slavery. The king's enslavement will, however, cause him later to abolish the entire concept of slavery.

CHAPTERS 35-38

Summary

The king is upset that the price he brought was only seven dollars, and he complains incessantly. In point of fact, his style of conduct is at odds with his apparent condition, and this discrepancy is responsible for his low price and for the fact that he becomes a difficult slave to sell. Yet, despite even the conditions of his tramping around the country and of being beaten regularly (even the king's body is battered), nothing seems to reduce his spirits.

At one point in their travels, The Boss and the king are caught in a snowstorm, and although the slave master keeps them going to keep warm, they are nearly exhausted. At this point, a woman runs up to them, begging for protection from the pursuing mob, which wants to burn her. The slave master turns her over to them, then he gathers the troops of slaves around the fire to keep them warm and protect his investment.

Finally, they reach London. There, they see a young woman about to be put to death for stealing a small piece of cloth so that she might sell it and thus be able to feed her baby daughter. She has been reduced to these circumstances because her husband had been impressed as a sailor, and she knew nothing about it. Before she is hanged, a priest speaks forcefully about the injustice of the situation, and he promises her that her child will be cared for.

In London, The Boss spots newspaper boys, so he knows that Clarence is working swiftly. He also notices that wires for either the telephone or the telegraph have been strung in the city; thus, he begins making plans to escape. At first, these plans are quite extravagant, particularly in the matter of what he will do to the slave master.

The opportunity for escape arrives when a man comes for a third time to haggle about the price of The Boss. This man's outer garment is fastened in the front with a metal contraption containing a long pin, and as he bargains with the slave master, The Boss manages to loosen one of these clasps. Using this pin as a lock pick, he frees himself. Just as he is about to free the king, however, the slave master comes in. Yet he does not notice anything unusual, and so he leaves. At this point, the king urges The Boss to fetch the slave master back. He dashes out and tackles the figure whom he sees retreating from the building, and a fierce scuffle ensues. This brings the watchmen, and they take the two combatants into custody; only then does The Boss discover that he tackled the wrong man.

When he is taken to court the next morning, The Boss relates a tale about being a slave belonging to Earl Grip, who had been sent into London to fetch a physician when the Earl became suddenly ill; he had been running as fast as he could when he happened to run into this man, who seized him by the throat and began beating him. The Boss is quickly released, and he returns to the slave quarters and finds them all gone. He learns that the slaves had revolted in the night and had killed the slave master. All the slaves have been condemned to die in the next day or so.

The Boss quickly buys some new clothing and arranges a disguise of sorts. Then he finds the telephone office, where he forces the attendant to put in a call to Camelot and to ask for Clarence. After a time, Clarence is reached. They decide that a mighty force of knights will be the best way to handle the situation; Clarence assures him that they will leave in half an hour.

After he leaves the telephone office, The Boss decides to try and make contact with people he knows. However, he is over-confident and walks, literally, into the shackles of the law and is put into prison with the other slaves. There, he learns that they are to be hanged in the middle of that afternoon, before the knights can get from Camelot to London.

About four in the afternoon, the slaves are taken out to be hanged; it is a superb day. The king creates a diversion when he leaps up and proclaims himself to be Arthur, King of Britain. Of course, the crowd does not believe a word he says; instead, they are amused, and they call for him to speak, but he will not.

Three slaves are hanged in short order, and the blindfold is then put on the king. Suddenly, five hundred knights in mail come riding up on *bicycles*, led by Sir Launcelot. The knights swarm upon the scaffold, tossing the sheriffs and others off, and freeing the king and The Boss. Clarence has also come along, and he explains how he has had the knights drilling for a long time; they have just been waiting for a chance to show off their newly acquired skills.

Commentary

Again in Chapter 35, we are given Twain's double focus. Even though Twain says that only clothes can determine royalty from nobility, yet The Boss is constantly impressed with the spirit and bearing of the king because no amount of slavery or abuse can break his royal spirit.

Even though there is the implication that The Boss could arrange for their freedom, he deliberately chooses to keep the king in slavery until the king realizes the horrors of slavery; then, hopefully, he will, of his own accord, want to abolish it. In addition, even though The Boss is indignant and horrified by the various injustices that he has encountered so far, King Arthur has shown no particular concern for the various injustices and cruelties that they have encountered, and it is not until they are both made slaves that King Arthur personally feels the marks of injustice and vows to abolish at least that social crime from his realm.

Chapter 35 also shows Twain's penchant to sink suddenly into the most maudlin bathos. In this chapter, for example, we witness the burning of a woman at the stake during a snowstorm with her two daughters clinging to her and slaves being forced to gather around her to absorb the warmth from her burning body in order to keep from perishing of the bitter cold; in addition, Twain includes a scene in which a young nursing mother is hanged for stealing a small bit of cloth. The late nineteenth-century reading public, one should remember, was the same public that adored attending melodramas at the theater, but today when we make fun of the typical nineteenth-century "mellerdrammer," we also find such scenes as the above to be almost embarrassingly sentimental. More important, however, in these events, we are not told how the king responds to them, or if they have any effect at all upon him.

In Chapter 36, we see that The Boss could have escaped earlier, but he waited until the king had recanted his position concerning slavery; then The Boss merely uses his Yankee ingenuity to pick the locks, and no one is smart enough to understand how he did it.

In Chapter 37, King Arthur is exposed to the dreadful conditions of English prisons, but we still do not know what effect it has upon him. The change in the time of the death sentence parallels the change in The Boss's death sentence at the beginning of the novel when the eclipse appeared a day earlier. Thus, in terms of plot, we await now to see how Twain handles this change. Actually, Twain's handling of this episode is a type of the cheapest melodrama to be found in first-class literature. In the use of the knights' being dressed in armor and riding to the rescue on bicycles, the readers' plausibility is stretched outlandishly, and the entire execution is handled in such a slipshod fashion that it has no place in an otherwise serious book. If one did not know Twain's penchant for the melodramatic atmosphere and for the sentimental effect, one could almost make out a case that he was satirizing works of melodrama, but unfortunately, Twain did not make such fine distinctions.

CHAPTER 39 and the FINAL P.S. BY M. T.

Summary

Just a few days after his return to Camelot, The Boss must fight Sir Sagramor le Desirous to give satisfaction for the supposed malediction several years earlier. In this tournament, a new rule takes effect: each combatant can use any weapon which he chooses.

Merlin, of course, is on the side of Sir Sagramor, working to make him invisible to his opponent although visible to everyone else. Indeed, all of the knights are siding with Sir Sagramor, since The Boss has made known his anti-knighthood feelings. He is alone with his servants at his end of the field.

The two combatants meet in front of the king's stand. Sir Sagramor is in full battle regalia and is seated upon a huge, magnificent horse. The Boss is in tights and riding a medium-sized, quick horse.

The tournament begins, and the two opponents charge at each other. The Boss uses the agility of his horse to evade Sir Sagramor's lance; he does this several times, until Sir Sagramor loses his temper, and the fight turns into a game of tag. Finally, The Boss takes out a lasso; he ropes Sir Sagramor and yanks him from his saddle.

Several other knights challenge The Boss, as is their right, and each of them, including Sir Launcelot, meets the same fate. After this bout, however, Merlin manages to steal the lasso. When the bugle is blown again for yet another joust, Sir Sagramor rides out, and The Boss pretends to find him by the sound of his horse's hooves. Sir Sagramor tells The Boss that he is a dead man and that The Boss will die on Sir Sagramor's sword. When the king suggests that The Boss borrow a weapon to replace the missing rope, Sir Sagramor denies him this right.

Sir Sagramor charges, but The Boss remains unmoving. When Sir Sagramor is some fifteen paces away, The Boss pulls out a pistol, which he has made, and he shoots Sir Sagramor, killing him. The crowd is amazed, for there is no apparent reason for the man to be dead. No one else steps forward to challenge The Boss, so he challenges them all. Five hundred knights mount and charge, and when they get close enough, The Boss pulls out both of his guns and begins to shoot; nine knights fall – and then, suddenly the others stop, they stare, and they turn in flight.

In the ensuing three years, The Boss reveals the mines and factories and workshops that he had started but had kept hidden. He also continues to challenge any and all knights who wish to face him – alone or *en masse*. He has no takers.

Many changes have taken place in these three years. Books begin to be printed, railroads begin running, and steam and electricity become available throughout the country; machines that run on these modes of power have been introduced, telephones and telegraph lines are everywhere, steamboats are plying the Thames, and a navy has been formed. The Boss is ready to try to overthrow the Catholic Church and to introduce universal suffrage.

The Boss has also married Sandy, and they have a child–a daughter–named Hello-Central. Just as things are going entirely his way, however, The Boss's daughter, Hello-Central, becomes very ill. The Boss decides to halt all of his plans of progress in order to take care of her, and when the doctors suggest that sea air is necessary to bring her back to health, he takes a man-of-war and a party of two-hundred and sixty men and goes cruising. After two weeks of sailing, they land on the French coast, decide to stay for awhile, and send the ship back for supplies.

Shortly after the ship has sailed, Hello-Central takes a turn for the worse, and The Boss's attention is taken up with caring for her. One should note here that The Boss married Sandy for the sake of appearance. She, however, turned out to be a fine wife and an excellent mother. She chose the name "Hello-Central" because The Boss cried it out in his dreams (his girlfriend back in Hartford had been a telephone operator); Sandy, of course, thought it was the name of a lost girlfriend.

After two and a half weeks, Hello-Central recovers, but the ship, which was supposed to be gone only three or four days, has not returned. After another two weeks without a ship, The Boss returns to England to find out what has happened. When he arrives, everything is shut down. The Church has struck back; an Interdict is in effect.

In disguise, The Boss sets out for Camelot alone. When he reaches it, the gate is wide open, and everything is silent. The Boss finds Clarence alone in his quarters, and the electric lights have been replaced by rag lamps. The whole business, Clarence tells The Boss, was caused by Launcelot and Guenever. Launcelot manipulated the stock market to undo a number of knights, including Sir Agravane and Sir Mordred, nephews of the king. As a result, twelve knights laid an ambush for Launcelot, but he killed all but Mordred. As a result of this, the country became divided; some supported the king in his grievance, while others supported Sir Launcelot.

Then the king proposed to purify the queen by fire, but Launcelot and his men came to the rescue. This, of course, intensified the lines of battle. A truce between the parties was arranged, except for

Sir Gawaine, whose brothers had been slain in the fighting. He told Launcelot to expect an attack. Launcelot left for another stronghold, and Gawaine followed, luring the king with him. Unfortunately, Arthur left Mordred in charge, and Mordred used the opportunity to try to make his position permanent.

Again, a truce was arranged, but that was broken when a knight slashed at a live snake (an adder) at the treaty conference, causing a riot to break out. The king is now dead, Guenever is a nun, and the terms of the Interdict include The Boss. Indeed, he learns that the doctors who ministered to Hello-Central and who told him that sea air was needed were servants of the Church. Thus, The Boss and Clarence make plans for a last-ditch effort to hold off the forces arrayed against them. They have fifty-two boys who are faithful; all of the others whom they had trained reverted to their former superstitious ways when the Interdict was announced. Clarence has prepared a cave, fitting it with a dynamo, wires, and other similar supplies. In addition, if the end seems to be approaching, Clarence and the faithful will blow up all the factories and other institutions which The Boss has had built, so that these cannot be used against them; in addition, they have planted explosives in strategic places.

In front of the cave, they have rigged electric wire fences, and they have Gatling guns arranged to cover the entrance of the cave and the area beyond it. They also have torpedoes. Everything is ready, and so The Boss decides that they should take the offensive. He and Clarence declare the country to be a Republic, abolishing the monarchy, the nobility, and the Church. Then they head for the cave.

The first thing which they do when they reach the cave is to vacate the factories. Then they wait.

It takes a week, but a large part of England, nobility and common men alike, begins to gather near the cave. As more and more people reach the area, the boys become uneasy about the fact that they might have to kill their own people, along with the gentry. The Boss points out to them, however, that the nobility will lead the charge; they will be the only ones who are on the receiving end of what they plan to do. This reassures the boys.

Finally, the knights charge. They hit the spot where the torpedoes have been set, and they are blown to bits. At the same time, an order is given and the factories are blown up.

Then, while they wait to see what will happen next, The Boss sends engineers to divert a stream within their lines in a way that it can also be used against their attackers if needed. Then, when nothing more happens for a time, he prepares a message to "the insurgent chivalry of England," offering them their lives if they will surrender and acknowledge the Republic, but Clarence shows him that it cannot be sent to them.

During the night, the knights approached the fortified cave. As the knights crept forward, the electrified wire fries them. In their armor, the knights passed the current along to whomever touched them, so that when the mass attack occured, all of the men who touched the fences or who touched men who had touched the fences were killed. Still, however, others crept forward, not yet having reached this point. When a large enough number of them were between the ditch and the fences, The Boss ordered the stream diverted into the ditch. The Gatling guns cut down many of the attackers, and the rest were drowned as they try to escape. In all, The Boss estimates that they kill twenty-five thousand of England's knights. He believes that they are now the masters of England.

The Boss proposes that they go out and help the wounded, if possible, and they do so, even though Clarence objects. The first man whom they try to help is Sir Meligraunce; he stabs The Boss, as The Boss leans over to help him. The wound is not serious; however, Merlin slips into the cave in the guise of an old woman and puts a spell on The Boss that will make him sleep for thirteen centuries. Clarence, unfortunately, wakes up in time to see only the end of the spell and cannot stop him. Merlin, however, gloats about what he has done, brushes up against one of the wire fences, and dies.

As a last tribute to The Boss, they find a place in the cave where no one can bother his body, and they place this manuscript with it.

Then the original narrator, the one introduced in "A Word of Explanation," finishes reading this manuscript at dawn. He goes to the room of the stranger and finds him delirious, calling out for Sandy and Hello-Central. Gradually, his mutterings become more and more incoherent. As the end nears, he starts up and says, " 'A bugle? . . . It is the king! The drawbridge, there! Man the battlements! – turn out the–' "

"He was getting up his last 'effect'; but he never finished it."

Commentary

Chapter 39 begins The Boss's onslaught on the entire concept of knighthood, and it also reveals his monomania to destroy all of the institutions of Camelot – not just knight-errantry – but the nobility and the Church, as well. Chapter 39 also presents The Boss's attack against the knights. First, he takes the pageantry and makes fun of it by being dressed in tights rather than in armor. Then he rides a small, fast horse with great flexibility instead of using a huge, powerful steed. Instead of attacking, as was the proper form, he subverts the entire system by dodging rather than charging, and by using a lasso rather than a lance. The undignified manner in which he downs Sir Sagramor further shows the absurdity of the entire duel or joust.

After The Boss has made a farce out of the joust by roping several more knights, and after he has been deprived of his lasso, he has to face Sir Sagramor without a weapon, a most unknightly attitude on the part of Sir Sagramor; thus, Twain inserts another undermining of the nobility of knighthood. The scene where The Boss pulls out his recently made pistol and kills Sir Sagramor, then, explains the bullet hole that was in the armor in Warwick Castle in the opening section entitled "A Word of Explanation."

The final blow to knight-errantry lies in the absurd challenge that The Boss makes to all five hundred of the knights. As they charge, and he starts shooting with both guns, we have an absurd, imaginative picture of the Western cowboy firing into the overdressed and plumed knights, and when nine of these men are killed, the others immediately make a cowardly retreat, which reveals the final indignation of knighthood. In short, knighthood is made to seem utterly and absolutely ridiculous. An entire way of life is destroyed: "The victory is perfect – no other will venture against me – knight-errantry is dead."

Thus, with Chapter 39 and until the end of the novel, the book takes an amazing turn. In Chapter 40, for example, during the lapse of three years, The Boss is well onto his way of destroying the nobility and the Catholic Church and offering in its place democracy and universal sufferage "given to men and women alike."

Then, in Chapters 40 and 41, The Boss discovers that he has been tricked by the Church to take a voyage out of the country, thus allowing the Church to announce the Interdict. The indication, therefore, is that the Church is opposed to the advancement of civilization, and as Twain has pointed out elsewhere, the Catholic Church has often resisted advances in civilization.

Chapter 42 again tests the reader's credulity. In The Boss's absence, so much has happened in that short period that it is impossible to respond to it. The sixth-century aristocracy was made into railroad conductors, the Round Table became a stock exchange, admirable people such as the noble Sir Launcelot, the most noble of the knights of the Round Table, began to manipulate the stock market. Very shortly, jealousy and greed broke out among the knights leading to England's being divided into two warring camps–Arthur's and Launcelot's. The lovely, idyllic Camelot exists no more; instead, the greedy materialistic nineteenth-century America is now rampant throughout the country.

The last stand is made in, ironically, Merlin's cave. Here, the preparations that have been made for warfare again exceed our imaginations. In the chapter entitled "The Battle of the Sand Belt" (Chapter 43), the entire forces of The Boss consist of the fifty-two youths that The Boss has been able to train from childhood. The others that he trained were too old to withstand the superstitions of the Interdict. Nevertheless, the scientific advancements of the nineteenth century are too powerful for the simple knights of the sixth century. They have no way of withstanding mines, electrified fences, or Gatling guns; consequently, we have a devastation and death of such magnitude that it can only be accounted for by the ingenious inventions of modern weaponry. The peaceful beauty of ancient Camelot has been destroyed by modern, destructive weapons, and at the end of the battle, "twenty-five thousand men lay dead around us." Yankee ingenuity has won over knighthood, and The Boss acknowledges that from his own men "the applause I got was very gratifying to me."

The victory, however, is a Pyrrhic victory. The dead bodies of the 25,000 slain knights form an insurmountable barrier around the cave, and they are trapped inside their magnificent victory. The bodies begin to rot and putrify and in the process, victory begins to poison the victors one by one.

In Chapter 44, it is Clarence, not The Boss, who sums up the predicament: "We had conquered; in turn we were conquered."

This same sentiment is repeated by Merlin: "Ye were conquerors; ye are conquered!" The Boss is put into a deep sleep, and in the final Post Script by Twain, we find Twain (or the original narrator) entering Hank Morgan's room to find him ranting, calling out for his lost land, his wife, and his child. Thus, in the final view, The Boss is defeated *not* by Merlin, but by the methods of nineteenth-century war, commerce, and destructive weapons. Ironically, in the end, The Boss is more interested in returning to his happy life in the beautiful and idyllic land of innocence that he destroyed than he is in returning to the nineteenth century.

CHARACTERIZATION IN *A CONNECTICUT YANKEE*

In traditional terms, there are no characters in *A Connecticut Yankee*: there is only Hank Morgan. The other characters who appear are only pawns who serve to reflect some quality of Hank Morgan's. For example, Clarence appears more than any other secondary character in the novel, and we know that Clarence grows physically from a young page ("he was hardly a paragraph") to a fully mature man in charge of all of the Yankee's operations, but we are aware of only his chronological development. Or else, Hank Morgan and King Arthur travel together for eleven chapters, but we never really get to know the king; he remains a distant, shadowy figure, completely undelineated.

Hank Morgan is an ingenious, inventive Connecticut Yankee, filled with practicality and common sense, believing in complete democracy, opposed to the Catholic Church, and possessing a disdain for royalty and nobility; he finds knight-errantry to be absurd and childish. Thus, we have Hank Morgan, champion of nineteenth-century democracy, commerce, industry, progress, and science, placed in a society that is controlled by heredity, aristocracy and a dictatorial church and infested with unjust laws, injustices, and inhumanity.

While acting as the champion of the modern, nineteenth-century view, Hank Morgan's main attitude is his desire to show off. His love of an effect, his eye for the stage value of a matter, and his wish to perform picturesquely are all directly related to his indignations and his prejudices.

Because he has a more advanced knowledge of technology and because he has been exposed to thirteen more centuries of advancement, and because he knows how to do ingenious things, such as make gun powder, build a locomotive, and set up a telephone line, Hank Morgan immediately assumes that he is a superior being: "Here I was – a giant among pygmies, a man among children, a master intelligence among intellectual moles; by all rational measurements the only actually great man in the whole British world." It is his belief that because he is technologically more knowledgeable than other men, he is superior as a human being; this leads Hank Morgan to attempt to change, improve, and "civilize" Camelot, but in the process, he destroys it.

While acting as the champion of the modern, nineteenth-century view, then, Hank Morgan becomes essentially an unscrupulous opportunist who is more concerned with bringing personal glory to himself and in controlling other people than he is in actually improving the lot of mankind in general. Beginning with his first "miracle," Morgan is intent that the center of all attention must be constantly focused upon him. Most of his actions are performed for the purpose of self-glorification and personal gain. For example, when he performs two of his great "miracles" – the blowing up of Merlin's castle and the restoring of the Fountain of Holiness (using Greek fires and Roman candles for the effects), he makes sure that there are large numbers of people there to appreciate him and his efforts. He craves attention and is always on the lookout for the "theatrical effects" that he can achieve in his performance.

Yet while disdaining superstitions, especially the many superstitions that the Church has burdened the common people with, Hank Morgan constantly uses the superstitions of the common people to gain power for himself. In this way, he does not differ significantly from the Church – which he disdains. Ultimately, the long tradition of the Church and its control upon the superstitions of the people defeat Hank Morgan when it announces its Interdict. At this time, the people whom Hank has trained revert back to their religious and superstitious ways; ironically, they have seen Hank Morgan's scientific inventions *not* as science but as some new sort of *magic*. Thus, Hank Morgan's power is gained through superstition, and he is also defeated by superstition.

It should be stated, however, that Hank Morgan possesses real humanitarian concerns. He does not understand fundamental nature sufficiently to be able to respond to the real needs of the people of Camelot, but he believes that if he technologically provides a better soap that the people will become a cleaner people spiritually. However, one doesn't clean the *inner* soul of a people by washing the outer layers of the skin. While Hank Morgan is opposed to all types of injustice (all precedence given to heredity, to nobility, to a dictatorial church, and to all non-humanistic matters), yet he is not sufficiently educated to appreciate that the souls of people need to be changed gradually. And even though Hank Morgan is an advocate of progress, a man whose views, attitudes, and intentions are to be admired, yet his personal flaws–prudery, lack of insight, and desire for self-glory–cause him to become the "evil invader" of the innocent and idyllic land of Camelot. This, in turn, was responsible for Twain's later saying of Hank Morgan: "This Yankee of mine has neither the refinement nor the weakness of a college education; he is a perfect ignoramus; he is the boss of a machine shop; he can build a locomotive or a Colt's revolver, he can put up a telegraph line, but he's an ignoramus, nevertheless."

QUESTIONS FOR REVIEW

1. What is the function of the use of the "frame" around the story of Hank Morgan?

2. Discuss the two opposing views of knighthood that are presented in the novel.

3. What is Hank Morgan's view of the nobility, of the Catholic Church, and of aristocratic preferment?

4. How does Hank Morgan use his technological knowledge to gain power?

5. How well does power set with Hank? That is, does he use his power for the betterment of the people or for the glory of Hank Morgan?

6. What features of Camelot does Hank Morgan find attractive? Why does he try to change these aspects?

7. What is Hank Morgan's views on superstition? Does he ever use superstition for his own advantage? Explain.

8. How does Hank's nineteenth-century prudery affect his views about Camelot?

9. Which aspect of the novel do you consider more important–the social criticism, or the science fiction fantasy?

10. Discuss Hank Morgan's total failure to modernize Camelot in terms of his inventions, his attention to human needs, and his own prejudices.

SELECTED BIBLIOGRAPHY

PRINCIPAL WORKS

The Celebrated Jumping Frog of Calaveras County, and Other Sketches, 1867.

Innocents Abroad, 1869.

Roughing It, 1872.

The Adventures of Tom Sawyer, 1876.

A Tramp Abroad, 1880.

The Prince and the Pauper, 1882.

Life on the Mississippi, 1883.

Adventures of Huckleberry Finn, 1885.

A Connecticut Yankee in King Arthur's Court, 1889.

The Tragedy of Pudd'nhead Wilson and the Comedy of Those Extraordinary Twins, 1894.

The Man That Corrupted Hadleyburg and Other Stories and Essays, 1900.

The Mysterious Stranger, 1916.

BIOGRAPHICAL MATERIAL

BROOKS, VAN WYCK. *The Ordeal of Mark Twain.* New York: E. P. Dutton, 1920. Rev. ed., 1933. An influential study suggesting that the moralistic pressure of family, friends, and American culture affected Mark Twain's genius.

DE VOTO, BERNARD. *Mark Twain's America.* Boston: Little, Brown, 1932. This book gained notoriety for its heavy attack on Van Wyck Brooks's book listed above.

FERGUSON, DELANCEY. *Mark Twain: Man and Legend.* Indianapolis: Bobbs-Merrill, 1943. An excellent biography.

HOWELLS, WILLIAM DEAN. *My Mark Twain: Reminiscences and Criticisms.* Edited by Marilyn A. Baldwin. Baton Rouge: Louisiana State University Press, 1967. An affectionate memorial by an old, loyal friend.

WAGENKNECHT, EDWARD. *Mark Twain: The Man and His Work.* 3rd ed. Norman: University of Oklahoma Press, 1967. Originally published in 1935, this study is still one of the best.

CRITICAL WRITINGS

BELLAMY, GLADYS CARMEN. *Mark Twain as a Literary Artist.* Norman: University of Oklahoma Press, 1950. An early, full-length study of Mark Twain.

BLAIR, WALTER. *Mark Twain and Huck Finn.* Berkeley: University of California Press, 1960.

BRANCH, EDGAR MARQUESS. *The Literary Apprenticeship of Mark Twain: With Selections from His Apprentice Writing.* Urbana: University of Illinois Press, 1950. An account of Twain's early career.

CARDWELL, GUY A., ed. *Discussions of Mark Twain.* Boston: D.C. Heath, 1963. A collection of critical material.

COX, JAMES M. *Mark Twain: The Fate of Humor.* Princeton, N. J.: Princeton University Press, 1966. The author's thesis is that Twain's work was successful in his comic writings and unsuccessful in his serious writings.

DE VOTO, BERNARD. *Mark Twain at Work.* Cambridge, Mass.: Harvard University Press, 1942. The volume contains three long essays about Twain.

LEARY, LEWIS. *Mark Twain.* Minneapolis: University of Minnesota Press, 1960. No. 5 in the "Pamphlets on American Writers" series.

LONG, E. HUDSON. *Mark Twain Handbook.* New York: Hendricks House, 1957. A summary of Twain's life, background, ideas, and reputation.

MARX, LEO. "Mr. Eliot, Mr. Trilling, and Huckleberry Finn," *American Scholar*, XXII (Autumn, 1953), 423-40.

ROURKE, CONSTANCE. *American Humor: A Study of the National Character.* New York: Harcourt, Brace & Company, Inc., 1931, pp. 209-20.

SALOMON, ROGER B. *Twain and the Image of History.* New Haven, Conn.: Yale University Press, 1961. The book covers Twain's historical ideas and writings.

SCOTT, ARTHUR, L., ed. *Mark Twain: Selected Criticism.* Dallas: Southern Methodist University Press, 1955.

SMITH, HENRY NASH, ed. *Mark Twain.* Englewood Cliffs, N.J.: Prentice-Hall, 1963. A collection of critical essays.

STONE, ALBERT E., JR. *The Innocent Eye: Childhood in Mark Twain's Imagination.* New Haven: Yale University Press, 1961.

DAISY MILLER & TURN OF THE SCREW

NOTES

including

- *Introduction*
- *Life and Background*
- *List of Characters for each novel*
- *General Plot Summaries for each novel*
- *Summaries and Commentaries for each novel*
- *Critical Notes*
- *Questions for Review*
- *Selected Bibliography*

by
James L. Roberts, Ph.D.
Department of English
University of Nebraska

INCORPORATED
LINCOLN, NEBRASKA 68501

Editor

Gary Carey, M.A.
University of Colorado

Consulting Editor

James L. Roberts, Ph.D.
Department of English
University of Nebraska

ISBN 0-8220-0355-4
© Copyright 1965
by
C. K. Hillegass
All Rights Reserved
Printed in U.S.A.

1990 Printing

The Cliffs Notes logo, the names "Cliffs" and "Cliffs Notes," and the black and yellow diagonal-stripe cover design are all registered trademarks belonging to Cliffs Notes, Inc., and may not be used in whole or in part without written permission.

Cliffs Notes, Inc. Lincoln, Nebraska

CONTENTS

INTRODUCTION

AUTHOR'S LIFE AND BACKGROUND

Henry James was a true cosmopolite. He was a citizen of the world and moved freely in and out of drawing rooms in Europe, England, and America. He was perhaps more at home in Europe than he was in America, but the roots of his life belong to the American continent. Thus, with few exceptions, most of his works deal with some type of confrontation between an American and a European.

Henry James was born in New York in 1843. His father, Henry James, Sr., had inherited a considerable sum of money and spent his time in leisured pursuit of theology and philosophy. The father often wrote essays and treatises on aspects of religion and philosophy and developed a certain degree of mysticism. Among the guests in the James household were some of the most famous minds of the mid-nineteenth century. Henry James was able to hear his father converse with people like Ralph Waldo Emerson, Bronson Alcott, and George Ripley. The father was insistent that his children learn to approach life with the broadest possible outlook.

In the strictest sense of the word, Henry James had no formal education. As a youth, he had private tutors. Then in his twelfth year, his father took the entire family to Europe, where they moved freely from Switzerland to France to Germany in pursuit of stimulating conversation and intellectual ideas. The world of Europe left an everlasting impression on young Henry James. He was ultimately to return and make his home in Europe.

When the family returned from Europe, the elder James decided to settle in New England. He chose Cambridge because this was the center of American intellectual thought. Many of the writers of Cambridge, Boston, and nearby Concord, where Emerson and Thoreau lived, were often visitors in the James household. It was in Boston that James met the first great influence on his literary career. He established a close friendship with William Dean Howells, who as editor of one of America's leading magazines, was able to help James in his early efforts to write and publish.

In Boston, Henry James enrolled briefly in the Harvard Law School but soon withdrew to devote himself to writing. His older brother, William James, the most famous philosopher and psychologist America had yet produced, was also a student at Harvard, where he remained after graduation to become one of the most eminent lecturers in America.

By the late 1860's, James had done some reviewing and had sold one work of fiction to the *Atlantic Monthly*. He also went to Europe on his own, to see the continent as an adult. He returned again to Cambridge and New York in the hope of continuing his literary career, but he gradually came to the realization that Europe was more suitable for his writings. Thus, in 1876, when he was in his thirty-third year, James made the momentous decision to take up residence abroad. With the exception of short trips to various parts of the world, he lived the rest of his life in and near London. Until 1915, he retained his American citizenship, but when World War I broke out, he became a naturalized citizen of England in protest over America's failure to enter the war against Germany.

James' life and background were ideally suited for the development of his artistic temperament. Even though he was not extremely wealthy, he did have sufficient independent means to allow him to live a leisured life. His father's house provided all the intellectual stimulation he needed. The visitors were the most prominent artists of the day, and James was able to follow the latest literary trends. In his travels, he moved in the best society of two continents and came into contact with a large variety of ideas.

With such a life, it is natural that James' novels are concerned with a society of people who are interested in subtle ideas and subtle refinements. There are no really poor people in his novels. He wrote about people who had enough money to allow them to develop and cultivate their higher natures. His novels develop with a deliberate slowness and conscientious refinement. Many critics and readers resent the deliberate withholding of information and the slow development found in the Jamesian novel, but James' life was lived with a high degree of leisure and refinement. And finally, James was the first American qualified to develop the theme of the American in Europe. By the time he made his decision to settle in Europe, he had made several trips there and had lived and attended school in several parts of Europe. Thus, the subject matter of most of James' works is concerned with an American of some degree of innocence meeting or becoming involved with some European of experience.

In spite of his decision to live abroad, James remained essentially American in his sympathies. His greatest characters (or central characters) are almost always Americans. But at the same time, some of his most unpleasant characters are also Americans. But the important thing is that the characters who change, mature, and achieve an element of greatness are almost always Americans.

THE REALISM OF HENRY JAMES

Henry James has had a tremendous influence on the development of the novel. Part of this influence has been through the type of realism that he employs. On the other hand, the most frequent criticism against James has been that he is not realistic enough. Many critics have objected that James does not write about life, that his novels are filled with people whom one would never meet in this world. One critic (H. L. Mencken) suggested that James needed a good whiff of the Chicago stockyards so as to get a little life into his novels. Others have suggested that James' world is too narrow and incomplete to warrant classification as a realistic depiction of life.

Actually James' realism is of a special sort. By the early definitions, James is not a realist. The early definitions stated that the novelist should accurately depict life and that the novel should "hold up a mirror to life"; in other words, the realist was supposed to make an almost scientific record of life.

But James was not concerned with all aspects of life. There is nothing of the ugly, the vulgar, the common, or the pornographic in

James. He was not concerned with poverty or with the middle class who had to struggle for a living. Instead, he was interested in depicting a class of people who could afford to devote themselves to the refinements of life.

What then is James' special brand of realism? When we refer to James' realism, we mean James' fidelity to his own material. To best appreciate his novels and his realism, we must enter into James' special world. It is as though we ascended a ladder and arrived at another world. Once we have arrived at this special world and once we accept it, then we see that James is very realistic. That is, in terms of his world, he never violates his character's essential nature. Thus, James' realism, in the truest sense, means being faithful to his character. In other words, characters from other novels often do things or commit acts that don't seem to blend in with their essential nature. But the acts of the Jamesian character are always understandable in terms of that character's true nature.

James explained his own realism in terms of its opposition to romanticism. For James the realistic represents those things which, sooner or later, in one way or another, everyone will encounter. But the romantic stands for those things which, with all the efforts and all the wealth and facilities of the world, we can never know directly. Thus, it is conceivable that one can experience the same things that the characters are experiencing in a James novel: but one can never actually encounter the events narrated in the romantic novel.

When James, therefore, creates a certain type of character early in the novel, this character will act in a consistent manner throughout the entire book. This is being realistic. The character will never do anything that is not logical and acceptable to his realistic nature, or to our conception of what that character should do.

Writing about realism in later years, James maintained that he was more interested in a faithful rendition of a character in any given situation than in depicting all aspects of life. Accordingly, when he has once drawn Winterborne's or Daisy Miller's character in one situation, the reader can anticipate how that person will act in any other given situation. Likewise, the governess' actions, even in view of possible unrealistic apparitions, are always consistent. We are always able logically to understand all the actions of any character. Thus James' realism would never allow the characters to perform actions which would be inconsistent with their true natures.

STRUCTURE

Almost all of James' novels are structured in the same way. There must be a center–something toward which all the lines point and which "supremely matters." This is essentially James' own explanation of his structure. The thing that "supremely matters" is the central idea of the novel or that idea around which the novel functions. In *Daisy Miller,* the thing that "supremely matters" is Winterborne's attempt to discover how innocent Daisy really is. That is, could she possibly be a mistress of the art of deception and in truth be essentially an improper girl, or is she simply responding so innocently and spontaneously to life that she ignores all the rules of decorum. Thus, every scene is structured to illustrate something more about Daisy's personality. Likewise, in *The Turn of the Screw,* the thing that "supremely matters" is the innocence of the young children. Consequently, every scene and every action is designed to further illuminate this question. We are constantly pondering the relative innocence or evil of the young children.

James' creative process is also important to understanding the structure of his works. He begins his novels with a situation and a character. Many writers–like Nathaniel Hawthorne–would begin with an idea or theme in mind and then would create a situation and characters to illuminate the basic idea, but James' technique is just the opposite. He created a certain situation, and then he would place his characters in it. James would then, in effect, sit back and simply observe what would happen when a character was confronted with this new situation. Often, James said, he had no particular ending in mind when he began a novel. Instead, he would let the character and situation determine the outcome. This allowed him more freedom and allowed him the opportunity of "getting to know" his character by observing him in a series of scenes.

Thus, the central situation in *Daisy Miller* is the arrival in Europe of a charming young girl who feels restricted by the formalized rules of behavior in Europe. Owing to her failure to observe certain social restrictions, she is considered improper by many people. But others recognize that her actions are a part of her free American ways and maintain that she is innocent. Consequently, Daisy is placed in various situations where we can observe her actions and determine to what degree she is innocent and spontaneous.

The central situation in *The Turn of the Screw* involves the governess' view of her charges. Consequently, certain situations are created so that we may watch the governess react to the innocence or evil of her pupils.

We have said that all lines must point toward the thing that supremely matters, but these lines do not follow a straight course. This is not the way James structures his novels. Everything in the novel is aimed at the central situation, but he moves toward the center by exploring all the related matters. In other words, the structure could be best described by a series of circles around the center. Each circle is an event which illuminates the center, but highlights only a part of it. Each circle then is often a discussion by several different people. For example, one character observes something and then goes to another person to discuss his observation. Then two other characters might discuss the same event. By the end of the various discussions, James has investigated all of the psychological implications inherent in this particular situation. This would represent one circle. Then, we go to another event or situation, which will be fully discussed before proceeding to the next. Thus by the end of the novel, James has probed and examined every moral, ethical, and psychological aspect of the central situation, and the reader has heard the views of many people on the same subject.

Consequently, the structure of James' novels are circular in approach to the central subject, but every circle in some way illuminates the thing that supremely matters. Every incident functions to tell us more about a character or situation. There is nothing that is superfluous or extraneous.

DAISY MILLER

LIST OF CHARACTERS

Daisy Miller

A young, exceptionally pretty, young lady from the United States who shocks the more formalized European society by her spontaneous acts.

Mrs. Miller

Daisy's mother, who seems to sanction most of Daisy's erratic actions.

Winterborne

The narrator of the story and an acquaintance of Daisy Miller.

Mrs. Costello

Winterborne's aunt, who acts as his confidante; she thoroughly disapproves of Daisy Miller.

Mrs. Walker

A mutual friend of both Winterborne and Daisy Miller who later severs her relationship with Daisy.

Mr. Giovanelli

A handsome young Italian whom Daisy picks up in Rome.

GENERAL PLOT SUMMARY

In a Swiss resort, Winterborne meets a pretty young American girl who seems to have no qualms about talking to strangers. During the course of their conversation, she mentions her desire to visit the castle across the lake. Winterborne declares that he would be delighted to accompany her.

A few days later, Daisy introduces him to her mother, and Winterborne fears that Mrs. Miller will deeply disapprove of his invitation. Instead, Mrs. Miller readily agrees as long as she does not have to go along. That night Daisy suggests a boat ride on the lake. Even though it would be improper, Daisy insists, but she suddenly changes her mind on learning that her brother is in bed. Winterborne is perplexed and confused by her actions.

Winterborne is aware that it was highly indiscreet for Daisy to go with him to the castle, but he is so charmed and pleased by her spontaneity and gaiety that he is willing to overlook everything else. Furthermore, he is convinced she was acting with perfect innocence.

Winterborne wants to introduce Daisy to his aunt, a Mrs. Costello, but this elderly lady has heard enough about the young American girl to think her common and vulgar, and consequently, refuses to meet her.

During the visit to the castle, Daisy learns that Winterborne has to leave the next day. After teasing him about being under the influence of some woman, she makes him promise to visit her in Rome that winter.

Some months later, Winterborne does go to Rome and immediately hears that Miss Daisy Miller is being "talked about." She is accused of picking up strange men and being seen with them in indiscreet places. At the house of a mutual friend, Mrs. Walker, Daisy meets and teases Winterborne again. Soon she mentions that she is going for a walk in order to meet a Mr. Giovanelli. Mrs. Walker is shocked and tries to tell Daisy how improper it would be to be seen walking the streets. Daisy solves this by asking Winterborne to accompany her.

After Daisy meets her companion, the three of them stroll about for a while. In a few minutes, Mrs. Walker drives up in her carriage and tries to convince Daisy to come with her. She lets the girl know how improper it is to be seen walking along the street with a man. Daisy thinks that if what she is doing is improper, then she is completely improper and asks the others to forget about her.

Later, at a party given by Mrs. Walker, Daisy offends her hostess by coming very late with her Italian friend. When Daisy leaves,

Mrs. Walker snubs her and later tells Winterborne that Daisy will never again be allowed at her home.

For some time, Winterborne hears additional stories about Daisy, but he still maintains that she is an innocent but impetuous girl. He even tries to warn her about her indiscretions, but she is unconcerned. Winterborne continues to believe in Daisy's innocence until he passes by the Colosseum late one night. He enters to observe the arena and accidentally sees Daisy with her Italian friend. Then he realizes that she is not a young lady that a gentleman need be respectful to.

Winterborne advises Daisy to leave immediately, and he questions the Italian's intentions in bringing her there so late. A few days after this, Daisy catches the Roman fever, which causes her death. Three times during a period of consciousness, Daisy sent Winterborne a message which he could only interpret at a later date. He realized that Daisy was a very innocent girl who would have welcomed someone's esteem.

Note to the reader: Henry James revised almost all of his work for a final edition. Therefore, sometimes *Daisy Miller* appears with four sections, as is found in the following analysis. But it is just as possible to find it divided in only two sections. In this division, Section I combines the first two sections, that is, the episodes which take place in Switzerland, and Section II handles the Italian episodes.

SUMMARIES AND COMMENTARIES

SECTION 1

Summary

In the town of Vevey, Switzerland, a young gentleman named Winterborne has stopped to visit his aunt. But because she is "now shut up in her room smelling camphor," he has a large amount of free time. The town of Vevey is, in the summer time, so filled with Americans that one could almost consider it an American resort.

Winterborne usually spends most of his time in Geneva, where it is rumored that he is studying, but in the summer he always pays this visit to his aunt.

While Winterborne is sitting in a cafe drinking a cup of coffee, a child about nine or ten comes up to him and asks for a lump of sugar. Winterborne grants the request but admonishes the boy that sugar is not good for the teeth. The boy responds that he has virtually no teeth anyway. The boy is an American and maintains that the trouble with his teeth results from the dreadful European hotels and climate. What he really misses is some good American candy. Everything that is American seems better to the boy than anything European.

While Winterborne is talking with the young boy, they notice a pretty girl approach. The boy announces that it is his sister and Winterborne observes that American girls are indeed pretty. The young lady approaches and begins to reprimand young Randolph for various things. As she talks with her brother, Winterborne observes that she is a very charming creature who seems to have a lot of confidence in life.

He offers a passing remark to her and then wonders if he has been too forward. In Geneva, "a young man wasn't at liberty to speak to a young unmarried lady save under certain rarely-occurring conditions." But Winterborne tries to make another remark: he asks her if they are planning to go to Italy. After a few more remarks, he is able to determine that the young lady is "really not in the least embarrassed." In fact, she seems perfectly relaxed and composed.

After a brief conversation, Winterborne observes her more closely. She possesses remarkable and expressive features, but there is a "want of finish." Her conversation is quite pleasant, and she tells Winterborne that she comes from New York State. He addresses the young boy by asking for his name. The boy blurts out that he is Randolph C. Miller and wants to tell his sister's name. She tells him to be quiet until the man asks for it. Winterborne assures her that he would like to know her name. Randolph explains that his sister uses the name of Daisy Miller, but that her real name is Annie P. Miller. Winterborne also learns that their father lives in Schenectady, New York, is very rich, and doesn't like Europe.

Miss Daisy Miller explains that they should get some tutor to travel with them who could teach young Randolph, but they haven't been able to find anyone. "She addressed her new acquaintance as if she had known him a long time." She tells Winterborne that the only thing she doesn't like about Europe is the lack of society, especially gentlemen society. Schenectady and New York City had plenty of society which she enjoyed, but here in Europe, she has been unable to discover any.

Winterborne hears all of this with a certain amount of shocked amazement. "He had never yet heard a young girl express herself in just this fashion." He wonders if she is a great flirt or simply the essence of innocence. He finally decides that she is a pretty American flirt.

Daisy soon points to a nearby castle and wonders if Winterborne has seen it. She wants to go, but her mother doesn't feel up to it. Winterborne offers his assistance. He will be glad to escort Miss Miller and her mother to the castle, but Daisy thinks that her mother wouldn't like to go. Suddenly Winterborne realizes that Daisy is willing to go with him alone. When Eugenio appears, she explains to Winterborne that he is their courier and then, addressing Eugenio, says that Mr. Winterborne has promised to take her to the castle. Winterborne feels that there has been a breach of discretion and he offers to introduce Daisy Miller to his aunt, who will vouch for his character. But Daisy doesn't seem concerned. She leaves telling him that they will soon arrange a trip to the castle.

Commentary

In this story, James uses something he calls a "central intelligence" to narrate the story. This means simply that the story is about Daisy Miller, but we see Daisy through the eyes of Winterborne. Thus, Winterborne is the central intelligence (sometimes called the sentient center). In order to utilize this technique, James must set up the qualities of his narrator. Thus Winterborne is an

American who has lived most of his life in Europe. He is, therefore, more European than he is American. Being American, he will be more understanding of Daisy Miller's behavior; but at the same time, being reared in Europe, he will also be fully aware of the unconventionality of her behavior. Throughout the story, then, we will observe Daisy Miller indirectly through Winterborne's eyes.

A principal concern in most of James' fiction is the contrast of the American society and values with those found in Europe. In fact, *Daisy Miller* is one of the first works ever to investigate this particular theme. Appropriately, the novel opens in a Swiss inn which is frequented by Americans.

An early contrast is suggested by the actions of young Randolph. He is more forward than the European youths would be, and he has no qualms about approaching a stranger. When Daisy Miller does the same, we are prepared to accept this as a part of the American character. Young Randolph is also quite frank: he tells Winterborne with all sincerity that American men are better than European men. The statement was not meant as a specific compliment to Winterborne, but serves as one anyway.

It is with the appearance of Daisy Miller herself that the contrast between the two cultures or two systems of values is expanded. Daisy approaches with the confidence of a person accustomed to a certain amount of independence. Thus, two of the American qualities are those of confidence and independence. Even young Randolph has more freedom than do his European counterparts. As Daisy Miller says: "There's one boy here, but he always goes around with a teacher. They won't let him play." In contrast, young Randolph seems to have more freedom than he needs.

Some critics have superficially criticized this story as being too absurd to read in this modern age when there is naturally more freedom than was found in the nineteenth century. But even though we don't understand much of the restrictions, James is very careful to set up certain norms of behavior from which the character deviates. For example, Winterborne ponders the actions that are allowed a man in Geneva and wonders how far he can go with the American girl. His perplexity, his confusion, and his failure to understand certain qualities in Daisy Miller intimate the normal code of behavior expected of young ladies. Thus, it is quite clear to any reader just how much Daisy is exceeding the bounds of propriety.

The reader should be aware of another of James' techniques. It is James' habit to let the reader gradually learn more and more about a character. We have a brief scene in which Daisy Miller is presented, then we have a brief scene where Winterborne contemplates the meaning of the girl's behavior. Gradually then, we arrive at a conclusion about her as Winterborne investigates more and more aspects of her character. Essentially by the end of this first section, we have most of her characteristics outlined for us. The remaining three sections will simply develop these basic traits.

What then is Daisy Miller? She has a want of finish, but still radiates with a charm and innocence. Her pert little face gives no trace of irony or mockery. She responds to things with sincerity and is perfectly frank in talking about her desire for the company of gentlemen. She is not bashful even when she should be. She does not understand that she cannot do the same things in Europe that she did in Schenectady, New York. Even her language is not of the most refined type. Daisy possesses a mixture of qualities that tend to confuse poor Winterborne. He even feels that perhaps he has become morally muddled. But finally, in spite of all of Daisy Miller's innocence, he decides that she is a flirt—"a pretty American flirt." What Winterborne does not understand is that according to Daisy Miller's viewpoint, there is nothing wrong with being a flirt. In fact, in America, it is expected that a girl be something of a flirt. It all depends on how far the flirtation was carried.

At the end of the section, Eugenio seems to disapprove of the arrangements Daisy Miller has made with Winterborne, and the narrator is quick to let the courier know that he is also aware of the impropriety of the entire situation. But he is so charmed and perplexed by this unusual girl that he will allow to escape him any chance to find out more about her.

SECTION 2

Summary

Winterborne has promised too much in saying he would introduce Daisy Miller to his aunt. The aunt, Mrs. Costello, is very aloof and aristocratic, and she does not approve of the Millers. She cannot accept them because they are so common. She has heard particularly unfavorable things about the young Miss Miller. Winterborne tries to explain that Daisy is really quite innocent but has not yet learned all of the educated ways of the world. When he tells his aunt that he is going to take Daisy Miller to the castle, Mrs. Costello is "honestly shocked."

When Winterborne next meets Daisy, he is concerned about his aunt's refusal to meet her. Daisy promptly tells him that she has been looking for his aunt. She has heard a great deal about Mrs. Costello from the chambermaids and is quite anxious to become acquainted with her. Winterborne tries to cover for his aunt by saying that she is often confined to her room with headaches. Upon further questioning, Daisy suddenly realizes that the aunt doesn't want to know her. Then Winterborne feels like admitting that his aunt is a "proud, rude woman and . . . that they needn't mind her."

Mrs. Miller appears and Daisy introduces Winterborne. Soon Daisy mentions that she is going to visit the castle with Mr. Winterborne. When Mrs. Miller says nothing, he assumes "that she deeply disapproved of the projected excursion." He has even taken it as a matter of course that she would accompany them. But Mrs. Miller simply says that the two should go alone.

Suddenly, Daisy suggests that they go for a row on the lake. Even Mrs. Miller thinks this would not be good, but Daisy insists. The courier appears and it is obvious that he is shocked when he learns that Miss Miller (or any young lady) would actually go out alone at night with a gentleman. Then just as suddenly, Daisy changes her mind, leaving Winterborne extremely perplexed and puzzled by her actions.

Two days later, he takes Daisy on the boat. She is extremely relaxed and yet animated. Her responses to the castle are refreshing. The day is proving to be exceptional for Winterborne until he mentions that he has to leave the next day. Immediately, Daisy tells him that he is horrid. To his bewilderment, she attributes his departure to the demands of some possessive woman. She then promises to quit "teasing" him if he will promise to come see her in Rome. Winterborne says that it is an easy promise to make because he has already accepted an invitation to visit his aunt when she goes to Rome.

That evening, Winterborne tells his aunt that he went with Daisy Miller to visit the castle. When she finds out that they went alone, she is thankful that she refused to be introduced to Miss Miller.

Commentary

Mrs. Costello is introduced as a contrast to Daisy Miller. The aunt represents the aristocratic and noble lady who emphasizes adherence to proper conduct, decorum, and all the correct forms of behavior. Her reaction to any situation would be reserved and formal, whereas Daisy's would be simple and spontaneous. For Mrs. Costello, Daisy's conduct is that of a vulgar and common person. Through the aunt's views, we are better able to realize that some of Daisy's actions are improper or in bad taste.

Mrs. Costello also serves as the *confidante* to Winterborne. James uses the confidante to help present certain aspects of the story. As in the case of Mrs. Costello, the confidante is usually separated from the main action of the story. Mrs. Costello never meets Daisy Miller, but she hears enough about her in order to express her views rather forcefully. Furthermore, she is called the confidante because the main character (Winterborne) can come to her and discuss his problems and express his views with confidence. In other words, by discussing his views with Mrs. Costello, Winterborne is better able to define his exact position.

Note that Daisy Miller is not as insensitive as at first appears. She is able to tell immediately that Mrs. Costello has refused to see her and is somewhat disturbed by the slight, but she is too involved with experiencing and enjoying life to allow this refusal to affect her response to life.

Winterborne's reaction to his aunt's refusal is also significant. Essentially, he agrees with his aunt about Daisy's deportment, but in Daisy's presence, he is captured by her charms. Thus, his views combine those of the American and those of the European. He is, furthermore, the formal man who is attracted by Daisy's spontaneity.

When Daisy attempts to introduce Winterborne to her mother, she explains that her mother doesn't like to be introduced to people and is especially shy about meeting Daisy's gentlemen friends. In contrast, a European mother would *insist* upon being introduced to a daughter's friends. Thus, we have another insight into Daisy's free behavior; she is acting with her mother's accord. Moreover, a European mother would never allow her daughter to go to the castle alone, whereas Mrs. Miller tells Daisy that it would be better if she went alone. Note, however, that even Winterborne thinks Mrs. Miller would deeply disapprove of the excursion. Here, then, we are dealing with Americans who function under a more liberal set of rules and under less formal conditions than do the Europeans.

Daisy's request to Winterborne that they go for a boat ride at night again shows her spontaneous but perplexing nature. Daisy does not allow the restrictions of social forms to inhibit her from doing something she really wants to do. Her desire to take the boat ride is a type of foreshadowing of what will later occur in Rome. Throughout the scene, it is obvious that Winterborne analyzed Daisy correctly when he thought her a flirt. She does openly flirt with Winterborne, but it is still an innocent flirtation. As Winterborne emphasizes, Daisy is not bad; she just doesn't care for all the limitations society has placed on her freedom.

After the trip to the castle, Winterborne is more confused than ever about Daisy's behavior. She is a mixture of innocence and crudity. He finds her reactions to the castle charming and spontaneous, but her "teasing" is not in the best taste. In spite of this however, he recognizes her astuteness in surmising his reasons for leaving.

Our last view of Daisy in this section comes from Mrs. Costello. When she finds out that Daisy actually did go to the castle, she is horrified and glad that she refused to meet the girl. We have seen that the excursion in itself was an innocent affair and that nothing improper or immoral happened; consequently, we are perhaps partly prepared to criticize the set of values which condemns Daisy's behavior as improper. The question is how far can a young lady disregard the conventions of society and still retain her reputation.

SECTION 3

Summary

That winter in Rome, Winterborne speculates to his aunt about the propriety of calling on the Millers. After what happened in Switzerland, Mrs. Costello can't understand why he would want to keep up the acquaintance. Furthermore, Daisy Miller has been compromising herself by "picking up half a dozen...regular fortune-hunters." Daisy's mother apparently isn't concerned. In general, Mrs. Costello thinks that the Millers are "very dreadful people." Winterborne adds that they are ignorant but also very innocent. "Depend upon it they are not bad." Mrs. Costello still maintains they are hopelessly vulgar and should be avoided.

Winterborne is a little amazed that Daisy Miller has picked up so many acquaintances because he had hoped that he had made an impression on her. The next day he calls on an old friend and during his visit the Millers arrive. Daisy immediately reprimands him for not coming to see her. She then turns to talk with the hostess, Mrs. Walker, and tells her how mean Winterborne was for leaving her in Switzerland. She then asks Mrs. Walker if she can bring a friend (a Mr. Giovanelli) to her party. In answer, Mrs. Walker tells Mrs. Miller that she would be glad to see a family friend, but Mrs. Miller explains that she doesn't know the man. Daisy apparently picked him up somewhere. Mrs. Walker doesn't know what to do and says feebly that Daisy can bring the gentleman.

As the Millers are leaving, Daisy reveals that she is going for a walk in order to meet Mr. Giovanelli. Mrs. Walker is shocked and tells Daisy it is not safe. Daisy thinks it is, and then Mrs. Walker has to explain that it is not proper. Daisy doesn't want to do something improper and therefore asks Winterborne if he will accompany her. She then leaves with him.

While they walk, Daisy begins to tease Winterborne for not having come immediately to visit her. She tells him how much she is enjoying the society in Rome. As they approach the Pincian Gardens, Winterborne tells her that he is not going to help her find Mr. Giovanelli and that he plans to remain with her. Daisy ignores this and when Winterborne asks if she really means to speak to that man in public, Daisy doesn't understand him. He asserts his feeling that it is necessary to remain with her. Daisy again doesn't understand his meaning and tells him she never allows a gentleman to interfere with her. Winterborne advises her to listen to the right gentlemen and as they approach Mr. Giovanelli, he tells her that her new acquaintance is not the right one.

Daisy introduces the two gentlemen with perfect ease. Winterborne notices that Mr. Giovanelli is not a gentleman. He is a clever imitation but anyone with discrimination could see that he is, however, an imitation. As they walk, Daisy continues to perplex Winterborne. She is not the type one could simply dismiss as a "lawless woman"; on the other hand she certainly does not conduct herself as a young lady should.

After a few minutes, Winterborne notices Mrs. Walker in a nearby carriage motioning to him. When he goes to her, she tells him it is a pity to let Daisy Miller ruin herself. She plans to take Daisy into the carriage with her and then deposit her at home with Mrs. Miller, She calls to Daisy, who comes readily. Mrs. Walker asks her to get in, but Daisy refuses. Mrs. Walker reminds her that she is too young to ruin her reputation and that she is being talked about. Daisy is surprised and wants to know what Mrs. Walker means. She tells Daisy to get into the carriage and she will explain. Suddenly, Daisy says that she thinks she would prefer *not* to know what Mrs. Walker means. She wonders if Winterborne thinks she should get into the carriage in order to save her reputation, and Winterborne tells her directly that he thinks she should get in. Daisy then tells them that if it is improper for her to walk, then she is completely improper and they must give her up entirely. She bids them goodby and leaves.

At Mrs. Walker's request, Winterborne enters her carriage and rides with her. She tells him that Miss Miller has gone too far. Winterborne still maintains that she meant no harm and her only fault is that "she is very uncultivated." Mrs. Walker then begs Winterborne not to flirt with Daisy anymore, but he tells her that he still likes Miss Miller extremely and assures Mrs. Walker that his attentions will not evoke any scandal.

When Mrs. Walker lets Winterborne out, he notices Daisy and her companion seated some distance away in a very intimate manner. He observes her a few minutes and then walks toward his aunt's residence.

Commentary

This section opens with Winterborne hearing from Mrs. Costello that Daisy Miller is still compromising herself. Thus, we get from the aunt the distant view of Daisy before we meet her again. Winterborne still maintains that she is ignorant or innocent, but that she is not really bad.

When Daisy meets Winterborne again, she acts as though they are very old and intimate friends. In other words, she does flirt with him. Of more importance is her desire and request to bring Mr. Giovanelli to Mrs. Walker's party. If Daisy thought she were doing anything improper, she would not have made the request. But the point is that Daisy is indeed innocent. She has met someone and has responded to that person. Now she wishes to bring that person to a party. It seems a natural reaction and if it is improper, then Daisy thinks the restrictions of society are unnatural.

Furthermore, when Daisy wants to go for a walk, she sees nothing wrong about this. When Mrs. Walker objects, Daisy says she doesn't want to do anything improper, but then she proceeds to do just that. She asks Winterborne to go with her because she is more interested in living than she is in the proper forms of behavior.

While Daisy is the spontaneous person, her friend Mr. Giovanelli is aware of all the proper forms of behavior and decorum. He is extremely urbane and is able to cover his disappointment and seem even more charming in proportion to how much he is disappointed. This demeanor is just the opposite from that of Daisy Miller, who allows people to know her feelings immediately. Furthermore, Mr. Giovanelli represents the imitation of a gentleman. This again reflects on Daisy, who cannot tell the real thing from the imitation.

During the walk with Daisy and Mr. Giovanelli, Winterborne is still unable to tell what type of person Daisy actually is. She was an "inscrutable combination of audacity and innocence." She showed no awareness of shame or improper conduct and responded gaily to any event.

Mrs. Walker's intervention indicates that Daisy is certainly more concerned with life than she is in the proper forms. She knows that what she is doing is innocent and she sees no reason why she should deny herself pleasure simply to satisfy the whims of an established convention. Perhaps no sentence characterizes Daisy as well as does her comment that she does not want to know what Mrs. Walker would tell her. In other words, Daisy would rather not hear something that is unpleasant. She builds her life on enjoyment and appreciation rather than adherence to staid and set rules. She is, furthermore, quite direct and honest in saying that if she is improper for walking in public with a man, then she is completely improper and should be given up. In other words, Daisy would like people to respond to her and quit judging her. She is not immoral, but prefers to live life rather than abide by rules which seem designed to deny life.

Finally, even Winterborne questions the rules which condemn Daisy's actions. He has been with her while she was committing something improper and found her charming and innocent. Consequently, why should an innocent girl be censured for her actions? As Winterborne says to Mrs. Walker: "I suspect...that you and I have lived too long at Geneva." He means, of course, that they are too much influenced by Europeans' emphasis on proper decorum and have forgotten the spontaniety with which Americans approach life.

SECTION 4

Summary

For the next two days, Winterborne calls on the Millers but does not find them at home. The third day was Mrs. Walker's party, which Winterborne attended. Mrs. Miller arrived by herself and told Mrs. Walker that she left Daisy *alone* with Mr. Giovanelli. Daisy had pushed Mrs. Miller out the door because she wanted to practice some singing with her new friend. Mrs. Walker is shocked and feels Daisy is intentionally being improper.

At eleven, Daisy comes bustling in with Mr. Giovanelli and gaily chats with everyone. With charming vivacity she tells Mrs. Walker that Mr. Giovanelli sings quite well. During the party, her companion conducts himself according to all the *proper* forms of behavior, while Daisy gaily chats with everyone. When she approaches Winterborne, she mentions how strange Mrs. Walker's behavior was the day before. Daisy thinks it would have been highly improper to desert Mr. Giovanelli. Winterborne explains that it was wrong for Mr. Giovanelli to ask her to walk because he "would never have proposed to a young lady of this country to walk about the streets with him." Daisy's response is that she is glad she is not a young lady of this country, for they must have a bad time of it. Winterborne tells her that her "habits are those of a flirt" and Daisy explains that all "nice girls are flirts." But she doesn't like to flirt with Winterborne because he is so stiff.

Winterborne continues to explain that Daisy's actions in public are being talked about and her reputation is in danger. Daisy responds by saying that at least Mr. Giovanelli doesn't say such unpleasant things to her. The gentleman in question arrives and offers Daisy some tea, which she accepts, observing that she prefers weak tea to good advice.

When Daisy goes to bid her hostess goodnight, Mrs. Walker intentionally turns her back and leaves Daisy "to depart with what grace she might." Winterborne observes the entire scene and sees Daisy turn "very pale." When Winterborne tells Mrs. Walker how cruel it was, she responds that Daisy will never again enter her drawing room.

After this, Winterborne often calls at the Millers and always finds Mr. Giovanelli there. Daisy is never upset and can converse as brightly with two men as with one. Winterborne is convinced from these visits that Daisy is very much interested in her Italian friend.

With his aunt, Winterborne admits that Daisy's actions are strange, since the young lady apparently does not want to marry and he cannot believe that Mr. Giovanelli expects it. Furthermore, Winterborne has made inquiries about "the little Italian," and discovered him to be an undistinguished lawyer.

Constantly hearing more about Daisy's many indiscretions, Winterborne decides to try approaching Mrs. Miller. Hearing one day that Daisy is riding through town alone with Mr. Giovanelli, he goes to visit Mrs. Miller. But the mother is so unconcerned that he considered his attempt futile.

Some days later, Winterborne meets Daisy and her companion in the Palace of the Caesars. Daisy thinks Winterborne is annoyed at her because she goes around so much with Mr. Giovanelli. He explains that he is not as annoyed as others are and that the others will show it by being disagreeable. She wonders why Winterborne allows people to be unkind to her. He says that he has tried to defend her by telling everyone that Daisy's mother considers her to be engaged. At first Daisy declares that she is engaged and immediately says that she is not. She then leaves with her companion.

A week later, Winterborne is returning from a party and decides to stroll into the Colosseum to see it in the moonlight. As he draws near, he hears voices, one of which he recognizes as belonging to Miss Daisy Miller. He stops and observes her and Mr. Giovanelli. Suddenly, he realizes that Daisy is "a young lady whom a gentleman need no longer be at pains to respect." As he is leaving, he hears Daisy cry out that Mr. Winterborne is cutting her.

Winterborne goes to her and reminds her of the danger of the Roman fever. He then wonders why Mr. Giovanelli countenanced such an imprudent action. The Italian explains that he told Miss

Miller it would be an indiscretion, but she insisted upon seeing the Colosseum by moonlight. Winterborne advises them to leave immediately.

As Giovanelli goes for the carriage, Daisy asks Winterborne if he still thinks of her as engaged. He tells her "it makes very little difference whether" she is engaged or not. As Daisy leaves, she seems changed and says that she does not care whether she catches the fever or not.

A few days later Winterborne hears that Daisy is sick. He goes to call at the hotel and learns that Miss Miller is seriously ill. The mother comes to him and gives him a message from Daisy. He hears that when she gained consciousness, she wanted her mother to be sure and tell Mr. Winterborne that she was not engaged. She also asked him to remember their visit to the castle in Switzerland.

A week after this, Daisy dies. At the funeral, Winterborne meets Mr. Giovanelli, who speaks of Daisy in the best terms and concludes by saying she was the most innocent person. He admits that she would have never married him, but he still admired her tremendously.

The following summer when he is visiting his aunt, Winterborne speaks of the injustice he had done to Daisy. He tells Mrs. Costello that Daisy sent him messages from her deathbed that he now understands. She would have appreciated someone's esteem. Winterborne thinks that he has indeed lived "too long in foreign parts."

Commentary

The entire last section recounts Daisy's rapid decline through showing several more of her indiscretions. We hear immediately that Daisy is alone in the apartment with Mr. Giovanelli and that she sent her mother on ahead so that she could be alone with the man. We do not know Daisy's motivations for this indiscretion, but she is certainly open about it. When she arrives at the party, she innocently tells that she remained alone in order to practice some songs. If Daisy had any concept or thought of impropriety, she would not have been so free to discuss it at the party.

Daisy apparently lives for the worth of the human being and for human relationships. In other words, she thought it would have been more improper for her to desert Mr. Giovanelli than to be seen walking with him. Simply because the ladies of Italy do not walk is no reason for Daisy to be denied this simple pleasure. As she said, she sees no reason why she should change her habits to conform to the ladies of Italy, when their habits deny most of the simple pleasure in life.

Daisy is, however, sensitive to rebuffs from others. When Mrs. Walker turns her back on Daisy, Winterborne notices that the young lady is deeply hurt. She has never been treated so rudely before and is temporarily at a loss of know how to interpret it.

As Winterborne continues to see Daisy, he realizes more and more that she is a person who likes her freedom and who likes to respond to any aspect of life without restrictions. When Winterborne visits the Millers, he is constantly aware of Daisy's "inexhaustible good humour." He knows that she prefers to have a good time to being thought of as absolutely proper. She seems to work always with an inner knowledge that she is innocent and, with innocence, one should not have to worry about one's reputation. As Daisy tells Winterborne, she prefers tea to advice, and would rather be with people who say agreeable things to her than with those who say disagreeable things.

What disappoints Winterborne is the fact that Daisy represents so much that is pretty, innocent, spontaneous, and good, but all of these qualities are being misdirected. So much that is admirable is being made ugly.

Winterborne is, of course, stultified when he attempts to speak with Mrs. Miller. Here is a mother the like of which he has never before encountered. She seems totally indifferent to her daughter's behavior. Consequently, Daisy's actions must be in accord with some new type of American behavior.

Finally, even Winterborne is shocked with Daisy. When he discovers her alone at night with Mr. Giovanelli in the Colosseum, he too admits that she need no longer be treated with respect. But this final indiscretion is paid for severely. Because of this night Daisy contracts the Roman fever and is soon dead. It is as though her final act of imprudence is equated with her death.

It is only after Daisy's death that Winterborne realizes she would have enjoyed someone's esteem. But the person to esteem her would have had to be a person who realized that she was essentially innocent and only searching for some simple but enjoyable experiences in life.

The final emphasis of the story is again on Daisy's innocence. Mr. Giovanelli maintains that she was the most wonderful and innocent person he had ever met. It is an innocence that is American and this same quality when not tempered with the proper forms of behavior will often be interpreted incorrectly. Thus, Winterborne feels that he has lived too long in Europe.

MEANING THROUGH SOCIAL CONTRASTS

Henry James was the first novelist to write on the theme of the American versus the European with any degree of success. Almost all of his major novels may be approached as a study of the social theme of the American in Europe, in which James contrasts the active life of the American with the mannered life of the European aristocray or he contrasts the free open nature of the American with the more formalized and stiff rules found in Europe. Embodied in this contrast is the moral theme in which the innocence of the American is contrasted with the knowledge and experience (and evil) of the European. *Daisy Miller* is one of James' earliest works involving this theme. All the comments presented here are not found in this work, but for the sake of James' entire theory, it is useful to see how he took some of the basic aspects found in *Daisy Miller* and used them consistently throughout his fiction.

In its most general terms, that is, in terms which will apply to almost any Jamesian novel, the contrasts as seen as follows:

THE AMERICAN		THE EUROPEAN
innocence	vs.	knowledge or experience
utility	vs.	form and ceremony
spontaneity	vs.	ritual
action	vs.	inaction
nature	vs.	art
natural	vs.	artificial
honesty	vs.	evil

The above list could be extended to include other virtues or qualities, but this list, or even half this list, will suffice to demonstrate James' theme or idea in the use of this American-European contrast.

The reader should also remember that James uses these ideas with a great deal of flexibility. It does not always hold that every European will have exactly these qualities or that every American will. Indeed, some of the more admirable characters are Europeans who possess many of these qualities and in turn lack others. Because a European might possess urbanity and knowledge and experience does not necessarily mean that he is artificial and evil. And quite the contrary, many Americans come with natural spontaneity and are not necessarily honest and admirable.

In *Daisy Miller,* James is more concerned with the difference in behavior than he is with the specific person. But generally, the character who represents the American is, of course, Daisy Miller herself. The representative of the European attitude in the worst sense of the word is Mrs. Costello, and to a lesser degree Mrs. Walker and Winterborne. Of course, all of these "Europeans" were actually born in America, but they have lived their entire lives in Europe and have adopted the European mode of viewing life.

One of the great differences that is emphasized is the difference between the American's spontaneity and the European's insistence upon form and ceremony. Daisy likes to react to any situation according to her own desires. Even though people tell her that certain things are improper, Daisy likes to do what she thinks is free and right. On the contrary, Mrs. Walker would never act in any manner except that approved by all society. The American than acts spontaneously, while the Europeans have formalized certain rituals so that they will never have to confront an unknown situation. Thus, there is a sense of sincerity in the American's actions; whereas the European is more characterized by a sense of extreme urbanity. Throughout the novel, we never see Daisy perform any action but that which is natural and open.

The American's sense of spontaneity, sincerity, and action leads him into natural actions. He seems to represent nature itself. On the other hand, the European's emphasis on form, ceremony, ritual, and urbanity seems to suggest the artificial. It represents art as an entity opposing nature.

Ultimately, these qualities lead to the opposition of honesty versus evil. This question is not investigated in *Daisy Miller,* but in terms of James' final position, it might be wise to know his final stand. When all American qualities are replaced by all of the European, we find that form and ritual supplant honesty. The ideal person is one who can retain all of the American's innocence and honesty, and yet gain the European's experience and knowledge.

THE TURN OF THE SCREW

LIST OF CHARACTERS

The Governess

Narrator of the story, who is appointed as governess of Miles and Flora with the instructions that she never bother her employer, the children's uncle.

Flora and Miles

The two children who, as orphans, are placed in the governess' charge by their uncle.

Mrs. Grose

The housekeeper and confidante to the governess.

Peter Quint

Former personal servant to the employer of the governess and familiar companion to Miles. He has been dead a year.

Miss Jessel

The children's former governess, who died the year before.

GENERAL PLOT SUMMARY

In an old house on a Christmas Eve, the subject of ghosts is brought up. A man named Douglas tells of his sister's governess, who had reported seeing apparitions some years ago; in fact, she had recorded her experience in a manuscript that he promises to send for. Upon further questioning, it is learned that the governess was hired to take care of two young pupils who had been left under the care of an uncle. When this man hired the governess, he gave her implicit instructions that she was to cope with any problem and never bother him.

The governess' story opens on the day she arrives at her new position. Her charges—Miles and Flora—are perfect little children who would apparently never cause anyone any trouble. She grows very fond of them in spite of the fact that little Miles has been discharged from his school. In discussing this occurrence, the governess and Mrs. Grose, the housekeeper, decide that little Miles was just too good for a regular school.

The governess loves her position and her children, and secretly wishes that her handsome employer could see how well she is doing. Shortly after this, she notices the form of a strange man at some distance. She wonders if the large country house harbors some secret. But some time later, she sees the same face outside the dining room window. When she describes this face to Mrs. Grose, she hears that it was that of Peter Quint, an ex-servant who has been dead for about a year.

Next the governess encounters another apparition in the form of a lady. Upon further consultation with Mrs. Grose, it is determined that this was the children's former governess, Miss Jessel, who died mysteriously about a year ago. When the present governess presses Mrs. Grose for additional information, she learns that Peter Quint and Miss Jessel had been intimate with each other and, furthermore, that both had been too familiar with the children.

After more appearances, the governess decides that the figures are returning to see the children. She then begins to wonder if the children know of the presence of the apparitions. Upon observing the children's behavior, she decides that they must be aware of the presence of these figures. She notes that once in the middle of the night little Miles is out walking on the lawn. Also, little Flora often gets up in the night and looks out the window.

Coming back early one day from church, the governess finds Miss Jessel in the schoolroom. During the confrontation, the governess feels that the former teacher wants to get Flora and make the little girl suffer with her. She is now determined to break her arrangement with her employer and write to him to come down.

Walking by the lake that day, she sees the figure of Miss Jessel again and directs little Flora's attention to it. But the little girl can see nothing. Furthermore, the housekeeper, who is along, can see nothing. Mrs. Grose takes little Flora and goes back to the house. The next day the housekeeper comes to the governess and tells of the awful language young Flora used and reasons that the girl must be in contact with some evil person in order to use such language.

The governess has little Flora taken away and that night as she is talking with little Miles, the figure of Peter Quint appears at the window. When the governess confronts little Miles with this apparition, the boy collapses and the governess notes that he is dead.

SUMMARIES AND COMMENTARIES

"PROLOGUE"

Summary

A group of visitors are gathered around a fireplace discussing the possible horror of a ghost appearing to a young, innocent child. A man named Douglas wonders if *one* child "gives the effect another turn of the screw," what would a story involving a ghostly visitation to two children do? Everyone wants to hear his story, but Douglas explains that he must send for a manuscript. The story he wants to relate was narrated by a governess who has been dead twenty years. She was once his sister's governess and Douglas has heard the story firsthand.

When the group has heard more about the governess, everyone wonders if she was in love. Douglas admits that she was and that the beauty of her love was that she saw the man she loved only twice. He was her employer and had hired her on the condition that she never trouble him, "never appeal nor complain nor write about anything," and that she was to handle all problems herself. In other words, she was to take complete charge of the two children to be placed under her authority.

Commentary

In this introductory section—note that James does not call it a prologue—we are given just the bare essentials of the story. It will be left for the manuscript, that is, the governess, to tell the main story. The only outside or objective facts we have in the entire narrative come from this section. But at the same time, we must be aware that these come from Douglas, who is accused of having been in love with the governess, and thus his view may be colored.

SECTION 1

Summary

After having come to an agreement with the uncle of the two children and fully understanding that he does not wish to be bothered in any way with the upbringing of his wards, the governess takes a carriage to the great country house. Here she meets the first of her two pupils. Young Flora, a child of eight, is "so charming as to make it a great fortune to have to do with her." She is the most beautiful child the governess has ever seen.

On the way to the great country house, the governess had brooded over her future relationship with the housekeeper, but upon meeting Mrs. Grose, it is obvious that they would have an excellent understanding.

The governess is so charmed by young Flora that she takes the first possible opportunity to question Mrs. Grose about young Miles, her second pupil. She learns that the little boy, who is two years older that his sister, is as charming and delightful as Flora. He is to arrive in two days from his boarding school.

Commentary

The reader should remember constantly that the governess is now narrating the story and that all impressions and descriptions come from her viewpoint. Thus, to the governess, young Flora appears as the most charming young girl she has ever seen. We should now go back and speculate about the possible relationship between the governess and her employer. As the governess tells Mrs. Grose: "I was carried away in London!" As the simple daughter of a country parson, the young girl has been impressed by the elegance and free manner of her employer. Thus, some critics would suggest that the governess' view of the young girl is simply a subconscious desire to see everything connected with her employer as beautiful and wonderful. Other critics suggest that James is here establishing the beauty and innocence of the young girl, which will later be used in various ways.

It is likewise important to note that the governess and Mrs. Grose become immediate friends and agree basically on most things. This rapport will allow the governess to convince Mrs. Grose later of the possibility of ghosts.

SECTION 2

Summary

Shortly before young Miles is to arrive home from school, the governess receives a letter from her employer. It contains an unopened letter from the headmaster of Miles' school and a cursory note from her employer requesting her to open the letter and attend to all details. Above all, she is not to trouble him.

After reading the letter, the governess searches out Mrs. Grose and reports that Miles has been dismissed from his school. She inquires if young Miles is "really bad," and is assured by Mrs. Grose that young Miles is incapable of injuring anyone, even though he is a lively young boy.

At her next meeting with Mrs. Grose, the governess inquires about her predecessor. She hears that the earlier governess was not careful in all things, and after leaving the last time on her vacation, was suddenly taken ill and died. Mrs. Grose knows no more particulars, and the governess must be content with this incomplete report.

Commentary

The first strange element is now introduced into the story. Miles, we find out, has been suspended from his school and will not be allowed to return. This dismissal immediately brings to the forefront the possibility of his being a bad boy. "Is he really bad?" the governess asks, and the idea is given further significance by the later use of words "contaminate" and "corrupt."

The idea of death is also introduced here as the governess discovers that her predecessor left with the intentions of returning and then was taken ill and died. The cause of her death is left unexplained, thereby adding a note of mystery to it.

SECTION 3

Summary

As soon as the governess sees young Miles, she thinks him to possess the same exceptional qualities, with the "same positive fragrance of purity" that characterize young Flora. She soon lets Mrs. Grose know that Miles' dismissal must have been a cruel charge. Furthermore, she has decided to ignore the letter and will not even write to the boy's uncle about the incident.

In the first weeks of her duties, the children are wonderful; "they were of a gentleness so extraordinary." But in spite of the pleasure the governess has in the presence of the two children, she still treasures her free time, which falls late in the afternoon, between daylight and darkness. She often strolls through the grounds and meditates on the beauty of her surroundings. Sometimes, she thinks that it would be charming to suddenly meet someone on the path who would stand before her "and smile and approve." In fact, she wishes her employer could know how much she enjoys the place and how well she is executing her duties.

One evening during her stroll, she does perceive the figure of a strange man on top of one of the old towers of the house. He appears rather indistinct, but she is aware that he keeps his eyes on her. She feels rather disturbed without knowing why.

Commentary

The innocence of both children is further emphasized in this section. The governess perhaps makes her first mistake in refusing to investigate the causes of Miles' dismissal. The mystery connected with this suspension will later allow the governess to attribute a duplicity to Miles' actions. The governess' refusal to investigate stems from her overzealous desire to exercise complete control over her wards and to view them in her own way.

Note how carefully James sets up the machinery for the governess' first sight of the "ghosts." Her free time falls at dusk, and at this time she usually likes to wander around alone. Furthermore, on her walks, she wishes that her employer could see her in this environment and would commend her upon her excellent performance with the children. In other words, it seems obvious that the governess is attracted or infatuated by her employer. Whether or not this infatuation is strong enough or psychotic enough to allow the governess to "create" the ghosts must be determined by each individual reader. Many critics have suggested that the ghosts are only creations of the governess' imagination, evoked to compel her employer to come to the country house. Whatever the circumstances, the governess' wish to meet someone on her walks is soon fulfilled, since she sees in the distance some strange figure standing and observing her.

SECTIONS 4, 5

Summary

After seeing the person (or apparition), the governess wonders if there was a "secret at Bly" (Bly is the name of the country house). She spends a good portion of the succeeding days thinking about this encounter. The shock has "sharpened all" her senses, and she fears that she might become too nervous to keep her wits about her.

The children occupy most of her day, and she continues to discover new and exciting things about them. The only obscurity which persists is the boy's conduct at school which had brought about his dismissal. The governess finds him to be an angel and decides that he was too good for the public school. Even though things are not well at the governess' own home, she has no complaints about her work.

One Sunday as the group is preparing to go to church, the governess returns to the dining room to retrieve her gloves from the table. Inside the room she notices the strange weird face of a man staring in at her in a hard and deep manner. Suddenly she realizes that the man has "come for someone else." This thought gives her courage, and she goes immediately to the outside. Once there she finds nothing, but looking through the window, she sees Mrs. Grose, who upon seeing the governess outside the glass, turns pale from fright.

In a moment, Mrs. Grose appears outside the house and tells the governess how white she is. The governess explains that just a moment before she saw the figure of a man standing on the outside looking in. She reports having seen him one time before. It is settled that the man is no gentleman, in fact the governess calls him "a horror." She refuses to go to church with the others because she is afraid—not for herself but for the children.

When Mrs. Grose asks for a description of the stranger, the governess is able to give a rather minute and detailed account of him. His red hair, his thin but good features, and his clothes remind her of some actor who is imitating some other person. Even though he was dressed in clothes a gentleman would wear, he was indeed no gentleman. Mrs. Grose immediately seems to recognize the person described and explains that the man was dressed in the master's clothes. He is Peter Quint, who was once the master's personal valet and who wore the master's clothes. When the governess wonders what happened to the ex-valet, she is told that he died.

Commentary

Section 4 opens with the mystery of some secret at Bly. This secret is built up in the governess' mind and she thinks about it until later she sees the figure at the window. Again, the climate combines to help add mystery to the appearance. The figure appears on a cold, gray day. There are several ways of approaching the appearance of Peter Quint. Some critics maintain that the ghost is a product of the governess' imagination, and she sees him only because she has been brooding on the subject for so long that her mind actually creates a figure. This point is supported by the fact that the governess knows the type of clothes that her employer wears and has constantly desired another view of him; thus in her imagination, she has created a person looking handsome but, as in dreams, appearing rather horrible also. This person then is in some ways the dream fulfillment and exists only in the governess' imagination.

The other point of view is that the governess could not give such an exact description if she had not actually seen the ghost. In this view, the governess is seen as a pure and innocent person who is the guardian of the pure and innocent children. In these two sections, great pains have been taken to emphasize once again the natural purity and sweetness of the two children. Therefore, the ghost could be symbolic of evil approaching upon innocence and the struggle such an encounter must involve.

Thus, through the use of ambiguity, James has left room for more than one view of the situation. There are even a few critics who maintain that this story is nothing more than a pure, chilling ghost story and has no meaning beyond this reading.

SECTIONS 6, 7

Summary

Mrs. Grose accepted what the governess had to say about the appearance of the stranger without questioning anything. The governess knows what she herself is capable of to shelter her pupils, and she tells the housekeeper that the apparition was looking for little Miles. She cannot explain how she knows this, but she is sure of it. She suddenly remembers that neither of the pupils has even mentioned Peter Quint's name to her. Mrs. Grose states that Quint often took great liberities with the child. In fact, she adds, he was too free with everyone. The governess then wants to know if everyone knew that Quint was admittedly bad. Mrs. Grose knew about him, but the master suspected nothing; and she never presumed to inform, since the master didn't take well to people who bore tales and bothered him. And actually, she was afraid of what Peter Quint could do. The governess is shocked because she thinks that one would be more afraid of what effect this evil person might have on the innocent life of the young boy than of what the master or Quint would do.

During the next week, Mrs. Grose and the governess talk incessantly of the appearance of this sinister figure. The governess learns that he had fallen on ice while coming home drunk from a tavern and was later found dead. Through it all, the governess discovers that she has more strength than ever and is more determined to protect her pupils from any danger.

Soon after, the governess and little Flora are out by the lake when a figure appears standing on the opposite side, observing them. The governess watches to see if little Flora will take notice of the figure. She is certain that the girl sees it and only pretends to be oblivious to it.

As soon as possible, the governess finds Mrs. Grose and explains that the children know of the presence of these other beings. Mrs. Grose is horrified and wants to know why the governess has come to such a conclusion. The governess explains that she was with Flora on the bank when Miss Jessel, Flora's previous governess, who died last year, appeared on the other side. Mrs. Grose is horrified and can't believe it. She wants to know how the governess was able to determine that it was Miss Jessel. The governess explains that by the way Miss Jessel looked so intently at little Flora and by the grand beauty and lady-like presence but at the same time an infamous quality that exuded from her. Then Mrs. Grose admits that Miss Jessel, in spite of her position, was familiar with Peter Quint. It is suggested that when she left her position, she couldn't return, but Mrs. Grose doesn't know exactly what Miss Jessel died of.

Suddenly, the governess realizes that she can't shield or protect the young children because she fears that they are already lost.

Commentary

In the discussion with Mrs. Grose, the governess discovers that the housekeeper knew Peter Quint was evil, but she was afraid to tell the master because he did not like to be bothered by details and complaints and he was impatient with people who bore tales against their fellow workers. Consequently, the governess is again reminded that she is in complete charge of her pupils and will not be able to go to the master with any complaint.

With the appearance of Miss Jessel, James is rounding out his story. The male ghost appears for the boy, and the female apparently returns for the young girl. The governess finds herself trapped in the middle.

We should be aware in this section that not as much credence is given to the appearance of Miss Jessel. There is even a bit of doubt in the mind of good Mrs. Grose. It is almost as though the governess' mind has brooded on the subject until she creates the appearance of Miss Jessel. There is not the direct description which will allow Mrs. Grose to positively identify the former governess, and the details given could apply to almost any governess.

Another level of meaning is added here. The governess thinks that the apparitions are returning to capture or corrupt the children. As long as she thinks this, then she is ready to fight diligently in order to protect the children. Her fears are made more real when she learns that both Peter Quint and Miss Jessel were immoral people. She is already afraid that the mere presence of these people in real life might have had a corrupting influence on the children. Thus, in their spectral appearance, they want to continue the corruption began in life.

The most horrifying thing for the governess is the conviction that the children know of the presence of the ghosts and pretend not to know it. Here we must begin to wonder if the governess is not letting her imagination carry her away. Even if the ghosts do appear, it is quite plausible that little Flora did not notice the figure which was, indeed, at some distance. But if the ghosts are real, then we must admire the governess, who is determined to protect her wards against the evil influence.

SECTIONS 8, 9, 10

Summary

At a later time, the governess has a talk with the housekeeper, when they agree that the governess couldn't make up the story because she had given such a perfect description, even to the last detail, of the two characters. In the meantime, the governess has devoted herself to her pupils, who have been more than charming —they have been perfect.

The governess cannot forget that Miles was discharged from his school. Therefore, one day she decides to question Mrs. Grose about him. She wonders if he has ever been bad. Mrs. Grose responds that she could not like a boy that did not sometimes show signs of typical badness. Upon being pressed further, she does admit that once Miles was very bad to her. Mrs. Grose had suggested that the young boy was stepping beyond his position by having so much to do with Quint, and the young child reminded her that she was also a servant and no better than Quint. Furthermore, he lied to her about how much time he actually did spend with Peter Quint.

It is brought out that the previous year, young Miles spent an exceptionally large amount of time with Quint, and during this time Flora was alone with Miss Jessel. Thus, the governess thinks it is quite possible that the young children knew what was taking place between Quint and Jessel.

The governess decides to do nothing but wait and see what should happen. She waits a long time before another incident occurs. One night, she wakes up at about one o'clock, and taking her candle, goes to the stairs. Halfway down the staircase, she sees the figure of Peter Quint standing at one of the landings. She faces him directly until he retreats into the darkness. She feels that he knew her just as well as she knew him. After he has disappeared, she returns to her room. She knows that she left the candle burning and now it is out. Immediately she notices that little Flora is at the window. When she questions the child suspiciously, little Flora says that she awakened and felt that the governess had gone and she was watching to see if the governess was outside walking. The young woman wonders if she saw anyone, but little Flora innocently answers that she saw no one. When the governess tries to trap the girl by asking why she pulled the curtain over the bed to conceal her absence, little Flora simply says that she didn't want to frighten the governess. Everything seemed perfectly natural to her.

For many days after this, the governess again goes to the staircase, but never again sees Quint. Once on one of her walks, she sees the back of a woman's figure bent over as though in heavy mourning.

One night the governess awakens to find that little Flora is again missing from her bed. This time she notices that the young girl is seemingly talking to someone outside the window. Rather than confront the girl directly, the governess decides to go to Miles' room and then changes her mind because this act could be awkward. Instead, she goes to a room above, where she can view all the actions. As she peers out the window, the thing that most strikes her is the figure of poor little Miles out on the lawn by himself.

Commentary

In this story dealing with the ghostly element, we are obliged to examine the governess' fortitude. If the ghosts are real, how does she have the courage and perseverance to meet them time and time again. After all, she is a rather helpless female, and even the love that she had earlier felt for the children is not modified by her belief that they are in the confidence of the ghosts. Only a more noble urge to rescue them from the evil influence could justify the governess' actions.

Thus, can we view the entire tale as the conflict between good and evil with the governess representing the forces of good while the so-called ghosts represent something of the evil nature of the world from which the governess wishes to protect the children, while finding it impossible to do so. In this section, the innocence of the children is again emphasized. But then, if the children are actually innocent, what the governess is committing is perhaps the most neurotic and horrible of all perversions. That is, she is compromising the innocence of the children by insisting upon the actual appearance of the ghosts.

Again, the subject of Miles' dismissal from the school comes up. The mistake that the governess made was not in learning the exact nature of his dismissal. Thus she is able to conjecture about the possible reasons. She goes to Mrs. Grose and elicits information about Miles' past behavior. The housekeeper reveals that Miles had once been bad in protecting Peter Quint. But then the realistic reader would expect any boy to prefer the rough companionship of a man to that of acting the role of the gentleman at so young an age.

In these chapters, the reader should note how the governess suggests certain meanings to Mrs. Grose, who then accepts the suggestion as fact. This aspect lends credence to the view that the governess imagines much of what happens and then convinces the more simple Mrs. Grose.

A large portion of these chapters is devoted to relating additional meetings with apparitions. By now, the reader should be aware that the governess meets these figures at a time or place where it would be impossible for anyone else to confirm the phenomena. Thus, there is an ambiguity about each appearance.

The last appearance of Miss Jessel was made for the benefit of little Flora, that is according to the governess. She is convinced that Flora is talking with a strange presence and goes to investigate. During her investigation, she notices young Miles walking out on the lawn. From this observation, she will draw many conclusions, but the reader should be aware that she did *not* see either Miles or Flora in direct communication with the apparitions.

SECTIONS 11, 12

Summary

After the recent incidents, the governess keeps close watch on her charges. She feels as though she could not withstand the pressure of these days if it were not for the comfort of Mrs. Grose, who apparently believes the governess' story without reservation. Even though Mrs. Grose is a good woman, she is lacking in imagination and thus could not comprehend fully the extent of the implications involved in the present danger. Thus, the governess has to explain the meaning of last night's escapades.

As soon as she saw Miles in the yard, the governess went to the terrace, where Miles was able to see her. He came directly to her. Using the direct approach, she asked the reason for his being out on the lawn so late at night. Little Miles told her he did it so she would think him bad. His simple and sweet explanation was followed immediately by a genuine kiss.

Miles explained how he had arranged the matter with Flora. His sister was to get up and look out the window. In this way the governess would be aroused and would then see him.

After completing her narration of the preceding night to Mrs. Grose, the governess suggests that the children talk to Quint and Miss Jessel all the time. She realizes that neither pupil has even made an allusion to their old friends. She concludes that her pupils belong to them and not to her.

Mrs. Grose is shocked and wonders why "Quint and that woman" continue to return. "What can they now do?" she asks. The governess explains that they return simply "for the love of all the evil that, in those dreadful days, the pair put into them." And unless something is done, the children will be destroyed. Mrs. Grose wants the governess to write immediately to the children's uncle and have him come down to solve the situation. The governess is horrified at this suggestion and reminds Mrs. Grose that the master does not like to be bothered and that he might think the story to be some "fine machinery [she] had set in motion to attract his attention to her slighted charms." So she tells Mrs. Grose that the master is *not* to be disturbed. In fact, she would leave immediately if he were informed of the present difficulties.

Commentary

These chapters are devoted partially to exploring the relationship between the governess and Mrs. Grose. We find out that Mrs. Grose is a good-natured woman who is lacking in imagination, insight, and intuition. Accordingly, she accepts the governess' interpretation of any event. She is too amiable and simple to question the governess' view. Every conclusion that is made about the predicament comes from the governess. Mrs. Grose merely acquiesces.

The most significant revelation found in this section is the governess' attitude toward her employer and her apprehension that he might regard the entire story as a contrivance on her part to attract him. When we step back from the immediate events, we must realize that if the ghostly appearance were in actuality true, then the governess should definitely inform her master. Her refusal to do so indicates that even she partially recognizes that the ghosts could be emanations of her warped imagination. Certainly if they were real, she should acknowledge that she alone does not possess the power to contend with them. In this situation, Mrs. Grose is definitely correct in thinking the master must be informed. The governess' refusal to agree must arouse suspicion as to her motivations.

SECTIONS 13, 14, 15

Summary

In the ensuing days, the governess often thinks that her pupils are conspiring against her, and she wonders when they would openly admit that they know about Miss Jessel and Peter Quint. Sometimes she wants to cry out: "They're here, they're here, you little wretches ...and you can't deny it now." But her charges do deny it with all of their sweetness and obedience.

For many days, the governess spends as much time as possible in the presence of the children. As she tells Mrs. Grose, she feels safe as long as she also has the gift of seeing the ghosts. She believes that she must constantly observe, since it has not yet been definitely proved that the children have really seen the ghosts. But at the same time, she is unable to reject the idea that whatever she saw, "Miles and Flora saw *more*."

Often in the classroom, Flora and Miles write letters to their uncle requesting him to come for a visit, but the governess never allows these to be sent. She explains that the letters are "charming literary exercises."

While walking to church one Sunday, Miles surprises the governess by asking when he will be allowed to go back to school. He does not consider it good for a little boy to be always in the company of a lady, even though that lady is ideal. He wants to know what his uncle has done about his return to school and thinks that he should write to his uncle soon if something is not done.

The manner in which little Miles insists upon returning to school shocks the governess so much that she is not able to attend the church services. Instead, she returns to Bly. Upon entering the schoolroom, she finds herself in the presence of Miss Jessel, who is seated at the governess' desk as though she has more right to be there than did the present governess. Drawing upon all of her strength, the governess addresses the intruder directly, saying: "You terrible, miserable woman." In an instant, she has "cleared the air" and she is alone in the room with the sense that she must stay at Bly and fight against this evil influence.

Commentary

In Section 13, the governess strikes a note of contradiction. She first admits that it's not yet definitely proved that the children are aware of the ghosts, and then a moment later, expresses the fear that Miles and Flora see more (that is, more of the ghosts and more of the hidden meaning) than she does.

The subject of the uncle's appearance is further developed in these sections. First, there are the letters the children write but which are never sent. Then comes Miles' demand that his uncle be consulted about his schooling. As much as the governess wants her employer to be pleased with her and to come to Bly, she is still frightened of the possibility that he actually will appear.

It is, therefore, while under the pressure of Miles' demand and the subconscious desire to see her employer that the governess once again sees the ghost of Miss Jessel. This time, the ghost appropriately appears in the schoolroom, which suggests there is a connection between Miles' demand for more schooling and the appearance of Miss Jessel in the schoolroom.

Again the reader should note that the apparition appears to the governess when the house is completely deserted. Thus, she is again the only one who sees the ghost. Furthermore, she sees it when her mind is most troubled by difficult problems that she must solve or else break her agreement with her employer.

The conversation between Miles and the governess about his schooling rings with enough ambiguity to allow the governess to think that little boy is being extremely astute and that he is implying deeper and more threatening meaning. Yet a careful reading of the conversation shows that there is nothing more ambiguous than the actual desire of a young boy to return to normal schooling.

SECTIONS 16, 17

Summary

When the others return from church, they make no mention of the governess' absence. At teatime, the governess questions Mrs. Grose and discovers it was little Miles' idea that nothing be said. The governess tells how she returned to meet "a friend" (Miss Jessel) and to talk with her. She informs Mrs. Grose that Miss Jessel "suffers the torments...of the lost. Of the damned." The governess claims that her predecessor confessed this and also stated that she wants little Flora to share the torments with her.

After this discovery, the governess decides that she must write to the uncle and insist he come down and assume responsibility for the entire predicament. In addition, she now concludes that little Miles must have been expelled from his school for wickedness.

That night, the governess begins the letter to her employer. Leaving her room for a moment, she walks to little Miles' door. Even though it is late in the night, he calls for her to come in. She discovers that he is lying awake worrying about "this queer business" of theirs. The governess thinks he means the business about the ghosts, but little Miles quickly adds that he means this business about how he is being brought up. He emphasizes again his desire to return to a normal school, and the governess tells him that she has already written his uncle. She then implores him to let her help him. In answer to her plea, there comes a big gush of wind through the window. Little Miles shrieks and when the governess recovers her composure, she notices that the candle is out. Little Miles confesses that he blew it out.

Commentary

By teatime, the governess is able to approach Mrs. Grose and tell her that "it's now all out" between her and Miles. She then describes her meeting with Miss Jessel. It is important here to note the discrepancies between the presentation of the meeting in the last chapter and governess' narration of it to Mrs. Grose. In the actual meeting, the apparition disappeared immediately after the governess spoke to it. But in her explanation to Mrs. Grose, the governess maintains Miss Jessel said she suffers torments and that she has come back to get little Flora to share in her suffering.

This divergence could be a clue to the interpretation of the novel. The governess could be seen as the exceptionally intuitive and perceptive person who can fathom the meaning of any situation by her sensitive awareness. Or else, she is deliberately creating a situation which will allow her to write her employer. It could be argued that she has slowly been developing her case and slowly convincing Mrs. Grose so that when the employer arrives, Mrs. Grose will be able to confirm the fantastic story.

Furthermore, the governess finally convinces Mrs. Grose that Miles must have been expelled for *wickedness,* since he has no other flaw or fault that could warrant expulsion. Thus, we can see now the governess' motivation in not investigating the real reasons for Miles' dismissal. She is now able to use it for her own machinations.

If the governess is absorbed with her bizarre plot, it becomes even more natural and remarkable that little Miles should want to leave. He must feel—as he does emphasize—the strangeness of his position with the governess. After the interview in his room, he becomes even more sensitive and taut over their peculiar relationship. We should be aware that James is now building for little Miles' death at the end of the story, a death that will result from the governess' weird behavior.

SECTIONS 18, 19, 20

Summary

The next day, the governess tells Mrs. Grose that the letter to the master is written, but she fails to mention that she has not yet mailed it. That day, Miles is exceptionally kind to the governess. He even volunteers to play the piano for her. Suddenly the governess asks where Flora is. Little Miles does not know, so she assumes that Flora is with Mrs. Grose. To her consternation, she discovers that the good housekeeper has not seen Flora.

Then, the governess understands that Flora is with that woman. Also, little Miles is probably with Quint; and all the time he was being nice to the governess, he was simply covering up so that Flora could escape. Together with Mrs. Grose, the young woman goes straight to the lake in search of little Flora. The governess is convinced that the children are in communication with that awful pair and, moreover, "they say things, that, if we heard them, would simply appall us."

On arriving at the lake, they discover that Flora has apparently taken the boat and gone to the other side. Mrs. Grose is dumbfounded that such a small girl could manage a boat alone, but the governess reminds her that Flora is not alone—that woman is with her.

They walk around the lake and find Flora, who meets them with her sweet gaiety. When the child asks where Miles is, the governess in turn asks little Flora, "Where is Miss Jessel?" Immediately upon hearing this question, Mrs. Grose utters a loud sound, which causes the governess to look up and see the figure of Miss Jessel standing on the other side of the lake. She points out this figure for both Mrs. Grose and little Flora, but the young pupil keeps her eyes glued on the governess. Mrs. Grose is unable to see anything in spite of the governess' explicit directions. After a few moments, Mrs. Grose addresses little Flora and tells her then there is no one there. "It's all a mere mistake and a worry and a joke." She wants to take little Flora home as fast as possible.

Suddenly, the young girl cries out that she did not see anyone and never has. She wants to be taken away from the governess, who has been so cruel and frightening. Mrs. Grose takes the child and returns to the house. The governess is left alone to realize that the apparition appears only to the children and to herself. This will make it more difficult for her now. When she returns to the house, she finds that little Flora's things have been removed from the room.

Commentary

Here we have the revealing chapters concerning the appearance of the ghosts. Previously, the ghosts have appeared only when the governess is alone, but now Miss Jessel appears while Mrs. Grose is present. But the good housekeeper is unable to see the apparition. Consequently, the reader may now doubt seriously that the visitation has any existence except in the mind of the governess. The question arises as to whether she actually sees them. We know that the mind can convince itself that such things happen.

Another approach is to accept the governess' view that one must possess a certain amount of perception before one can discover the presence of the evil ghosts. But if we accept this view, we must also see the children as possessed of superhuman cunning and ingenuity. And note that little Flora seems distraught by the accusations made by the governess.

SECTIONS 21, 22

Summary

Early the next morning, Mrs. Grose comes to the governess' room and tells her that little Flora was "so markedly feverish that an illness was perhaps at hand." All of Flora's fears are directed against the governess. She is afraid of seeing her again, and pleads to be spared the sight of the governess.

The governess asks if Flora still persists in saying that she has seen nothing. She believes that those creatures have made the child so clever that now little Flora can go to her uncle and make the governess "out to him the lowest creature—!" The governess believes that it is best for Mrs. Grose to take the child away from the region, and in that way, she might be saved. Then the young woman will devote herself to saving little Miles.

The governess suddenly wonders if Mrs. Grose has seen something that makes her believe. The housekeeper tells her that she has seen nothing but has heard a great deal. Little Flora has used terrible language and awful words that could only be learned from some very evil source. Thereupon the governess considers herself justified in the belief that little Flora learned such words from the corrupt Miss Jessel. In answer to the governess' direct question as to whether Mrs. Grose now believes in the ghosts, the housekeeper concedes that she does.

It is then agreed that Mrs. Grose will take little Flora to London. She is warned that the master will know something because of the governess' letter. Mrs. Grose then tells the governess that the letter has disappeared. Both assume that Miles has stolen it and perhaps this was the offense he committed which brought about his expulsion. The governess hopes that in being alone with her, the boy will confess and then be saved.

The next day, Miles cannot understand how his sister was taken ill so suddenly. But he seems to accept the fact that she was sent away to keep from becoming worse because of the bad influence around Bly.

Commentary

The fact that little Flora is seriously ill suggests again the very innocence of the girl. However much she might be able to pretend on some subjects, it would be quite difficult to feign a feverish sickness. In other words, she must be deeply repulsed by the behavior of the governess. The reader should note how concerned the governess is with the possibility that the employer will hear everything from Flora, who will make the governess out to be "the lowest creature." Most of her actions are designed to influence or impress her employer. In the ensuing days, she hopes to bring Miles to her side and then she will be able to convince the master of the rightness of her actions.

Mrs. Grose is convinced of Flora's evilness simply because the little girl has used some bad words. The child's behavior is easily explainable when we consider that Miles, while away at the school, must have picked up some bad words and could have passed them on to Flora. But for the genteel Mrs. Grose who is, in fact, rather old, these words sound horrible and wicked when spoken by the child, and on this proof, she is willing to accept the premises that the girl could only learn them from an evil influence.

Little Flora's illness acts as a method of foreshadowing and preparing for Miles' reaction in the final sections. If the suggestion of the appearance of a ghost makes Flora ill, then in the next sections, the governess' actions could be too much for the nerves of the young boy.

SECTIONS 23, 24

Summary

After Flora is gone, Miles joins the governess, and they talk about how they are alone. The governess explains that she stayed to be with and help Miles. She reminds him that she is willing to do anything for him, and he promises that he will tell her anything she wants to know. First, she asks him if he took the letter she had written to his uncle. The boy readily admits that he took it and opened it in order to see what she had written about him. He further admits that he found out nothing and burned the letter.

The governess asks him if he stole letters at his school or did he take other things. Miles explains that he said certain bad things to his friends, who must have said the same things to other friends until it all got back to the masters. Just as the governess is about to insist on knowing what he said, she sees the apparition of Peter Quint at the window. She hears Miles ask if it is Miss Jessel, but she forces him to admit that it is Peter Quint who is at the window. He turns suddenly around to look and falls in her arms. The governess clutches him, but instead of a triumph, she discovers that she is holding Miles' dead body.

Commentary

Somewhere little Miles had learned some naughty or evil words. It is quite possible that he had earlier learned them from his association with Peter Quint. He repeated these words at school and when others in turn repeated them, little Miles was expelled from school. Furthermore, this accounts for little Flora's learning the awful words she used to describe the governess. During this interview with Miles, the governess thinks that she sees Peter Quint at the window. Miles' first question is to ask if she sees Miss Jessel. This question seems to attest to his innocence. In other words, he must have learned from Flora (even though it is thought by Mrs. Grose that the brother and sister had not seen each other) that the governess thinks she had seen Miss Jessel. Otherwise, the young boy would not have immediately thought that the apparition seen by the governess was Miss Jessel. It is upon the mention that the apparition is a male that the young Miles associates it with Peter Quint. But whereas the fright of a ghost had caused little Flora to become ill, it is the instrument of little Miles' death.

The last section lends great support to regarding the story as a psychological study of the governess' mind. If the ghost were real or if little Miles were in communication with the ghost, the only way to account for his death is to admit that the ghosts and their evil ways have conquered the young boy. But it seems more reasonable to assume that the ghost was visible only to the governess, and through her psychotic imagination, she simply frightened the young boy to death.

THE MEANING OF *THE TURN OF THE SCREW*

There is no story in literature which has produced such a variety of interpretations. The forgoing commentaries are accordingly based upon certain facts which could be taken in more ways than one, but lean essentially toward a psychological interpretation of the story. No understanding of this story is complete then without the knowledge of certain central critical articles written about it.

The reader interested in various approaches should consult the following important articles:

For the Freudian, or psychological, interpretation, see:

Edna Kenton, "Henry James to the Ruminant Reader: *The Turn of the Screw," The Arts* (November, 1924), pp. 245-55.

Edmund Wilson, "The Ambiguity of Henry James," *Hound and Horn,* VII (April-June, 1934), 385-406.

For an interpretation in which the governess is seen as an instrument fighting against evil as represented by the ghosts, see:

Robert Heilman, "The Turn of the Screw as Poem," *The University of Kansas City Review, XIV (Summer, 1948). 277-89.*

These articles (plus others) are collected in *A Casebook on Henry James's "The Turn of the Screw,"* edited by Gerald Willen.

SPECIAL PROBLEMS AND INTERESTS

CENTRAL INTELLIGENCE AND POINT-OF-VIEW

One of James' contributions to the art of fiction is in his use of point-of-view. By point-of-view is meant the angle from which the story is told. For example, previous to James' novels, much of the fiction of the day was being written from the author's viewpoint, that is, the author was telling the story and he was directing the reader's response to the story. Much of the fiction of the nineteenth century had the author as the storyteller, and the author would create scenes in which certain characters would be involved, but all of the scenes would not necessarily have the same characters in them.

James' fiction differs in his treatment of point-of-view. He was interested in establishing a central person about whom the story revolved, or else a central person who could observe and report the action. Usually, the reader would have to see all the action of the story through this character's eyes. Thus, while the central character in Daisy Miller is Daisy herself, we see her through the eyes of the "central intelligence," that is, through the eyes of Winterborne. Sometimes the central character will also be the central intelligence, as happens in *The Turn of the Screw*. In James' fiction we respond to events as the "central intelligence" would respond to them.

Furthermore, every scene in a James work has the central character present or else is a scene in which some aspect of the central character is being discussed by the central intelligence. So if Daisy is not present, the discussion is about some aspect of Daisy's character.

CONFIDANT

James wrote fiction in an era before the modern technique of the "stream-of-consciousness" was established. In the modern technique, the author feels free to go inside the mind of the character. But in James' time, this was not yet an established technique. Since James as a novelist wanted to remain outside the novel – that is, wanted to present his characters with as much objectivity and realism as possible – he created the use of a confidant.

The confidant is a person of great sensibility or sensitivity to whom the main character reveals his or her innermost thoughts (as long as they are within the bounds of propriety). The confidant is essentially a listener and in some cases an adviser. This technique of having a confidant to whom the main character can talk serves a double function. First of all, it allows the reader to see what the main character is thinking, and second, it gives a more rounded view of the action. For example, after something has happened to the main character, the confidant hears about it and in the discussion of the event, we, the readers, see and understand the various subtle implications of this situation more clearly.

The confidant is also a person who is usually somewhat removed from the central action. For example, Mrs. Costello never meets Daisy Miller but she serves as a listener to Winterborne and offers her own view about Daisy. Likewise, Mrs. Grose in *The Turn of the Screw* has never seen any of the apparitions, but she serves as the person to whom the governess expresses her doubts and fears. Thus, essentially the confidant observes the action from a distance, comments on this action, and is usually a person of some exceptional qualities who allows the main character to respond more deeply and subtly to certain situations.

FORESHADOWING

James is a very careful artist who uses rather often and freely the technique of foreshadowing a later action. This means that he has given hints in the early parts of the novel about some important thing that is going to happen later in the story. Thus, a touch of realism is added to the novel because so many things have foreshadowed the main action that the reader should not be surprised to discover the action at the end.

For example, in *Daisy Miller* we are given very early in the novel hints of Daisy's spontaneous and impetuous nature. Thus it is not surprising to find that she carries this characteristic to its logical extreme. Furthermore, we hear several times about the danger of catching the Roman fever, so when Daisy does become sick, we have been prepared for this by earlier allusions to the illness. In *The Turn of the Screw,* there is every type of indication that sooner or later the governess will confront the children with the presence of one of the apparitions. When she confronts Flora with the presence of Miss Jessel, the little girl becomes sick. As a result, we are prepared to accept the fact that Miles will die from his exposure to the apparition of Peter Quint. Thus, James uses foreshadowing to prepare the reader for the climactic events of the story.

QUESTIONS

DAISY MILLER

1. Why does James shift his setting from Switzerland to Italy?

2. What is the purpose of having a narrator who comes from America but has lived so long in Europe?

3. In addition to functioning as Winterborne's confidante, what other purpose does Mrs. Costello serve?

4. If Daisy's actions in going to the castle with Winterborne were innocent, why does he assume that her actions with Mr. Giovanelli are improper?

5. What is gained by having Daisy die at the end of the story?

6. Does Winterborne learn anything from his associations with Daisy?

7. Why does Mrs. Walker try to save Daisy and then later snub her?

8. What does Mr. Giovanelli expect from his relationship with Daisy?

9. Describe Daisy's system of values.

10. How innocent is Daisy of the fact that she is being improper?

THE TURN OF THE SCREW

1. What motivates the governess to accept such an unusual position?

2. Describe the circumstances surrounding each appearance of an apparition.

3. How does Mrs. Grose come to believe in the presence of the ghosts?

4. Why does James emphasize so strongly the sweetness and innocence of the children?

5. Why does the governess fail to investigate Miles' expulsion from school?

6. What is gained by having the governess relate the story?

7. How do you account for little Flora's illness at the end of the story?

8. What does the governess think of her employer?

9. Is it important that this was the governess' first position?

10. How responsible is the governess for the fate of the children?

SELECTED BIBLIOGRAPHY

Beach, J. W. *The Method of Henry James.* rev. ed. Philadelphia: Saifer, 1962.

Bewley, Marius. *The Complex Fate.* London: Chatto and Windus, 1952.

Dupee, F. W. (editor). *The Question of Henry James.* New York: Henry Holt and Company, 1945.

Edel, Leon. *The Modern Psychological Novel.* New York: Grove Press, 1959.

______. *The Untried Years.* Philadelphia: Lippincott, 1962.

James, Henry. *Autobiography.* New York: Criterion Books, 1956.

Lubbock, Percy (editor). *The Letters of Henry James,* Two Volumes. New York: Charles Scribner's Sons, 1920.

McCarthy, Harold T. *Henry James: The Creative Process.* Toronto: A. S. Barnes and Co., 1955.

Matthiesen, F. O. and Murdock, Kenneth (editors). *The Notebooks of Henry James.* New York: Oxford University Press, 1947.

Matthiesen, F. O. and Murdock, Kenneth (editors). *The Major Phase.* London, New York: Oxford University Press, 1944.

NOTES

NOTES

NOTES

EMILY DICKINSON: SELECTED POEMS

NOTES

including

- *Life and Background*
- *Introduction*
- *The Texts of Dickinson's Poems and Letters*
- *Dickinson's Poetic Methods*
- *The Poems*
    - Nature: Scene and Meaning
    - Poetry, Art, and Imagination
    - Friendship, Love, and Society
    - Death, Immortality, and Religion
- *Brief Comments on Forty Additional Poems*
- *Questions for Review and Writing*
- *Selected Bibliography*
- *Index of First Lines*

by
Mordecai Marcus, Ph.D.
Department of English
University of Nebraska

INCORPORATED
LINCOLN, NEBRASKA 68501

Editor

Gary Carey, M.A.
University of Colorado

Consulting Editor

James L. Roberts, Ph.D.
Department of English
University of Nebraska

ISBN 0-8220-0432-1
© Copyright 1982
by
C. K. Hillegass
All Rights Reserved
Printed in U.S.A.

1990 Printing

The Cliffs Notes logo, the names "Cliffs" and "Cliffs Notes," and the black and yellow diagonal-stripe cover design are all registered trademarks belonging to Cliffs Notes, Inc., and may not be used in whole or in part without written permission.

Cliffs Notes, Inc. Lincoln, Nebraska

CONTENTS

EMILY DICKINSON NOTES

LIFE OF THE AUTHOR

Emily Dickinson was born in Amherst, Massachusetts, on December 10, 1830, and died there some fifty-five years later on May 15, 1886. With the exception of a few visits to Boston, Philadelphia, and Washington, D.C., and some nine months at school at South Hadley, Massachusetts, she spent her whole life in Amherst, most of it in the large meadow-surrounded house called the Dickinson Homestead, across the street from a cemetery. From 1840 to 1855, she lived with her family in a house on North Pleasant Street, after which they returned to the Homestead. She never married, and she lived in comfortable dependence on her well-to-do father and his estate, though she did more than her share of household chores while creating a large body of poems and letters.

Amherst, a farm-based community, grew in her lifetime from about 2,700 to about 4,200 inhabitants. It was the seat of Amherst College, a citadel of Protestant orthodoxy, and later of Massachusetts Agricultural and Mechanical College (now University of Massachusetts). Though somewhat isolated, Amherst had a good private academy, a rich but mixed cultural tradition of reading the Bible, Shakespeare, and the classics; and, as the nineteenth century progressed, contemporary American authors and a large amount of popular and sentimental literature became current there. Social life was confined largely to church affairs, college receptions, agricultural shows, and such private socializing as walking, carriage riding, and discussing books. Newspapers and magazines from Springfield and Boston brought current literature and opinion, serious and ephemeral, to the more literate. The Dickinson clan were old Yankee stock, tolerant of such religious dissidence as Unitarianism and Roman Catholicism, but deeply rooted in the orthodox Protestant tradition as it lived on in their own Congregational church (and the Presbyterian church), still actively Calvinistic and requiring public profession of faith for membership. Waves of religious enthusiasm and conversion swept through Amherst, especially during Emily Dickinson's early years, and gathered up her friends and members of her family, but never her.

Little is known of Emily Dickinson's earliest years. She spent four years at a primary school and then attended Amherst Academy from 1840 to 1847, somewhat irregularly because of poor health. She wrote imaginatively for school publications but none of these writings survive. Her intense letters to friends and classmates show a variety of tones, especially in her reluctance to embrace Christ and join the church and in her anticipations and fears about the prospect of a married life. The world, as she understood the idea, was more dear to her than the renunciations which conversion seemed to require, and quite possibly she sensed something false or soft-minded in the professions of others. In a period of rigorous living conditions, without the benefits of modern medicine, life spans were shorter than ours, and Dickinson suffered the early deaths of many acquaintances and dear friends. She witnessed several deaths, doubtlessly impressed and shocked by the Puritan doctrine that looked for signs of election and salvation in the demeanor of the dying and especially in their willingness to die.

During this period, she was fond of, or attached to, two older men, Leonard Humphrey (1824-50), the young principal of Amherst Academy, and Benjamin Franklin Newton (1821-53), a law student in her father's office. Newton, a Unitarian and something of an Emersonian, discussed literature, ideas, and religion with her, and praised her early poetic efforts. After he left her father's office and moved to Worcester, he married and soon died of tuberculosis. Dickinson evidently felt a warm, sisterly affection for him, and on learning of his death, she worried about the state and future of his soul. It was a kind of worry which she would continue to experience throughout the rest of her life about the many people whom she cared for. Romantic inclinations towards Humphrey and Newton seem extremely unlikely for Dickinson, but these men are probably related to the descriptions of several losses in her early poems. In the fall of 1847, Dickinson began the first of a two-year program at Mount Holyoke Female Seminary in South Hadley, where she did not yield to continued pressures to give up the secular world for Christ and join the church. A good student and fond of her classmates and teachers, she suffered homesickness and poor health, and she did not return for the second year.

Her immediate family were probably the most important people in Dickinson's life. Her father, Edward Dickinson (1803-74), a graduate of Yale law college, was a successful lawyer and Amherst's chief citizen by virtue of his imposing personality, his connection with Amherst College (its treasurer), his two terms in the state legislature, his one term in the United States Congress, and his leadership in civic endeavors. A man of unbending demeanor and rectitude, he appears to have had a softer side that he struggled to conceal. It came out in incidents of pleasure in nature, kindliness to people, and the embarrassed desire for more intimacy with his children than he ever allowed himself. He joined the church at the age of fifty. Dickinson expressed her distress over his death in many poems and letters. In some sense, she may have lived in his shadow, but she went her own way and saw him with a critical as well as with a tender eye. He probably appears in some of her poems about deprivation and about explosive behavior. It is unlikely that he made any explicit attempts to keep either of his daughters from marrying, although he probably did communicate a sense of his need for their presence and support.

A clear picture of Dickinson's mother, Emily Norcross Dickinson (1804-82), is difficult to formulate. She seems to have been dignified, conventional, reasonably intelligent, and probably subservient to her husband. She suffered periods of poor health, probably of emotional origin, and her health was shattered by her husband's death. Dickinson and her sister, Lavinia, cared for her as an invalid for the last four years of her life, during which Dickinson's affection for her greatly increased. Dickinson's declaration to T. W. Higginson, her chief literary correspondent, that she "never had a mother" is poetically exaggerated.

Dickinson's sister and brother, Lavinia (1833-99) and William Austin, known always as Austin, (1829-95), were close to her all her life. Lavinia was a vivacious, pretty, and clever girl, but not particularly intellectual, although she had a reputation for having a sharp tongue. She seems to have rejected several offers of marriage, possibly in order to remain Dickinson's lifelong companion. Fiercely protective of her elder sister, she probably tried to shield the ever more reclusive Dickinson, and she may have understood Dickinson's need to have time and privacy for her poems. More imaginative and intellectual than his father, Austin had an artistic side and was interested in new ideas. After finishing law school and marrying, he succumbed to his father's pressures for him not to leave Amherst for

Chicago, became his father's law partner, and settled for life in a house across the street from the Dickinson home. Partly because of Dickinson's influence, he married Susan Gilbert, who had long been a close friend of Dickinson's. The marriage was unhappy, and its increasing tensions were probably visible to those in the house across the street.

Dickinson's relationship with her sister-in-law is very revealing and is relevant to these Notes. It was in the early 1850s that Susan Gilbert, (later Dickinson) (1830-1913), an orphan, came to live with relatives in Amherst and became Dickinson's dearest friend. They shared books, ideas, and friends. After a stormy courtship, Susan married Austin in 1856. A woman of attractiveness, intelligence, powerful social demeanor, and a stinging tongue, Susan became the social leader of Amherst. Her relationship with Dickinson remained highly ambivalent, Dickinson suffering from Susan's sarcasm mixed with her tenderness and also from Susan's pressures to make her submit to conventional religion. Dickinson wrote warm and revealing letters and poems to Susan but seems to have become quite disillusioned with her, though her fondness for Austin and Susan's three children and her sympathy for her brother kept her bonds with Susan partly whole. The death of Gilbert Dickinson (1875-83), Austin and Susan's youngest child, was a terrible blow to Dickinson.

During the 1850s, Dickinson made the most of her few travels outside Amherst, visiting Boston, Washington, and Philadelphia, but she was becoming more reclusive; she stopped attending church services (she had been a keen observer and often sarcastic commentator on sermons), and she spent much of her time writing poems. Towards the end of the decade, Dickinson seemed to be approaching several emotional crises. In her early twenties, she had experienced some normal social attentions from young men, but probably none of them constituted what one could call courtship. In 1858, 1861, and 1862 (these dates are approximate), she wrote draft copies of three fervent letters to someone whom she addressed as "Master," while calling herself "Daisy." The letters are anguished descriptions of a guilty, rejected, and subservient love. Quite possibly, these letters were never sent. They are the strongest available evidence that a desperate and impossible love was the chief source of her crises, although there is no proof of it.

Among the many candidates advanced as Dickinson's secret love, two men have been singled out as being most likely: the

Reverend Charles Wadsworth (1814-82) of Philadelphia and San Francisco, and Samuel Bowles (1826-78), editor of the Springfield *Republican* and a lifelong friend of the Edward and Austin Dickinson families. Charles Wadsworth was a successful orthodox preacher–sober but imaginative, rigorous yet tender. Dickinson probably heard him preach in Philadelphia in 1855. He visited her in Amherst and of his correspondence with Dickinson, only a short letter from him to her survives, revealing a pastoral concern for an unspecified distress. After his death, Dickinson wrote of him in various endearing terms, calling him her "dearest earthly friend." Happily married and the father of several children, Wadsworth must have been completely unaware of any romantic attachment which Dickinson may have felt for him. The fact that Wadsworth's San Francisco church was called Calvary and that many of Dickinson's love poems employ religious allusions have suggested but do not prove that she was romantically infatuated with Wadsworth.

Samuel Bowles is a more likely candidate for the person addressed in Dickinson's so-called Master letters. An extremely handsome and worldly man, Bowles numbered many women among his friends, much to his wife's pain. A frequent visitor at the Dickinsons, he may have tempted Emily to plead with him for recognition of her poetic ability, a recognition which he was quite unable to give. Emily Dickinson's letters to him bear significant similarities to the Master letters, and she sent him many poems, including "Title divine–is mine!" (1072); this one was accompanied with a note, which may imply that in her imagination he was her husband. Various details of the lives and travels of both Wadsworth and Bowles fit selectively into Dickinson's comments on separations and losses which she suffered, but others do not. Possibly Dickinson worshipped in her imagination a composite of these two men or a version of someone else who cannot be identified. Her emotional crises of the early 1860s may also stem from her fear about the condition of her eyes (which, in turn, may have been of emotional origin), fears for her sanity in connection with these difficulties and with family instabilities, or a combination of love-desperation with all of these frustrations. She may also have been desperate because no one could recognize her poetic gifts. Her increasing reclusiveness and her continually wearing white dresses may be chiefly related to the idea that in spirit she was married to someone; this may suggest that in addition to all these conflicts, there was a need for time and privacy for her writing and an increasing conviction that she derived more satisfaction from living in the world of her poems than in ordinary society. In any case, her poetic productivity from 1861 to about 1866 continued at an astonishing rate. The figure of an unattainable lover looms large in her poems, but it is probably a mistake to think that a frustrated love was the chief cause of her becoming a poet. Nevertheless, one must grant that her writing served as an emotional catharsis and as a healing therapy for her, which contributes to its appeal.

Emily Dickinson's chief attempt to establish contact with the literary world and gain recognition for her poems began in 1862 when she wrote a letter to Thomas Wentworth Higginson (1823-1911) and sent him the first of many packets of poems. Dickinson was responding to advice that Higginson had offered to young writers in the *Atlantic Monthly.* Higginson was a minister, editor, writer, soldier, and a champion of liberal causes. Emily Dickinson's correspondence with him, which continued almost until her death, is the most important part of her correspondence, and Higginson, who visited her in 1870 and 1873, has left the most detailed reports on her conversation that we have. Higginson recognized in Dickinson a sensitive, gifted, and imaginative person, but he could not see her work as poetry; he described it as beautiful thoughts and words, and he cautioned her against early publication, trying to steer her towards conventional form and expression, and trying to draw her into society. She pretended to accept all his criticism and to plead for a continued tutor-mentor relationship, but she seems to have recognized all his limitations and to have drawn sustenance from his personal, rather than from his literary support. Higginson probably appears in a number of Dickinson's poems about the relationship of artist and audience. After Dickinson's death, Higginson helped edit her poems, and their popular success greatly advanced his opinion of them.

During Emily Dickinson's lifetime, only seven of her poems appeared in print – all unsigned and all altered and damaged by editors. She had probably agreed to only a few of these publications. Five of these poems appeared in Bowles's *Springfield Republican.* One appeared in 1878 in the anonymous anthology *A Masque of Poets*, surely as a result of the persuasion of Dickinson's only other important literary friend, Helen Hunt Jackson (1830-85), who, as Helen Fiske, had been among Dickinson's childhood friends in Amherst. After the death of her first husband, Helen Hunt, later Jackson, became a successful poet and novelist (famous for *Ramona*, 1884). In the 1870s, she wrote to and visited Dickinson, became convinced of her greatness as a poet, and tried to persuade her to publish. Her only success, however, was to persuade Dickinson to contribute "Success is counted sweetest" (67) to *A Masque of Poets*, but she told Dickinson that she was a great poet, and Dickinson's correspondence shows a warm affection for her.

The other important relationship of Emily Dickinson's later years was her reciprocated love for Judge Otis P. Lord (1812-84), a friend of her father's, who became Dickinson's close friend after he was widowed in 1877. Dickinson's letters to him are fervent with bashful love. He seems to have proposed, and she seems to have refused in the name of her persisting sense that fulfillment would have overwhelmed her. Lord's death in 1884 seems to have shocked Dickinson into a rapid physical decline. According to some writers, he appears in a few of her late poems.

After her withdrawal from the world in the early 1860s, Dickinson's life revolved around her correspondence, her poetry, and her household duties. She remained a faithful daughter and sister, and in her own terms, she was a faithful friend to many to whom she related chiefly through letters. Her later reclusiveness may have approached a certain pathological state, as evidenced by her turning friends away and sometimes conversing and listening to music through only slightly opened doors. But Dickinson constantly insisted that she did not suffer from her isolation and that she felt deeply fulfilled and in intimate contact with the world. Her correspondence with Higginson probably convinced her that her poems would find no significant or sympathetic audience during her lifetime, for though she protested to Higginson that she did not want publication, it is evident that she wanted to make her relatives proud of her work after she died, and her combination of pride and resignation probably stemmed from her awareness of her great gift and her frustration that so many people were as mystified by her poems as by her talk. Many of the poems give eloquent testimony that she longed for an audience. As luck would have it, her poems survived. But their struggle for adequate publication, understanding, and recognition almost parallels her inner life in its complexity.

INTRODUCTION

Enormously popular since the early piecemeal publication of her poems, Emily Dickinson has enjoyed an ever-increasing critical reputation, and she is now widely regarded as one of America's best poets. These Notes focus on clarification of some eighty-five of her poems, chosen and emphasized largely according to the frequency of their appearance in eight standard anthologies, where the average number of her poems is fifty. These poems also seem to offer an excellent representation of her themes and power. In a final section to these Notes, additional poems are commented on briefly.

In face of the difficulty of many of her poems and the bafflingly diffuse and contradictory general impression made by her work and personality, Dickinson's popularity is a great tribute to her genius. Her poems are often difficult because of their unusual compression, unconventional grammar, their strange diction and strained figures of speech, and their often generalized symbolism and allegory. She took up baffling and varied attitudes towards a great many questions about life and death, and she expressed these in a great variety of tones. The speaker in these individual poems is often hard to identify. In many poems, she preferred to conceal the specific causes and nature of her deepest feelings, especially experiences of suffering, and her subjects flow so much into one another in language and conception that often it is difficult to tell if she is writing about people or God, nature or society, spirit or art. One often suspects that many such subjects are being treated simultaneously. Furthermore, her condensed style and monotonous rhythms make sustained reading of her work difficult. The flagging attention that results can contribute to misperception and hasty judgment. Nevertheless, since her poems are mutually illuminating, the reader may face the choice of trying to learn much from a generous selection or trying to concentrate on the essentials of a smaller number.

Fortunately, common sense and expert guidance can offer new insights into this maze. Usually, biographical information is useful in interpreting a poet according to the degree of strangeness in the situations and states of mind which the poet portrays. It is true that Emily Dickinson's themes are universal, but her particular vantage points tend to be very personal; she rebuilt her world *inside* the products of her poetic imagination. This is why some knowledge of her life and her cast of mind is essential for illuminating much of her work. Such knowledge, however, must always be used with caution and tact, for otherwise it can lead to quick judgments, simplifications, and distortions. Understanding of her work is helped even more by recognizing some of her fundamental *patterns* of subject matter and treatment, particularly her contrasting attitudes and the ways in which her subjects blend into one another. Such patterns may – and for the Dickinson expert must – include material from her life and letters, but this approach requires a continual awareness that, like her poems, her letters were written for specific effects *on* their readers (they were often drafted), and they are often even more vague than her poems on parallel subjects. The Dickinson devotee will eventually emerge with a multi-faceted and large-scale conception of her poetic personality. Fortunately, a smaller-scale and yet rich conception is possible for readers who immerse themselves in only fifty or a hundred of her poems. One of the joys of such reading, very particular to Emily Dickinson, is that the effort to keep such a conception flexible will bring added pleasure with fresh visits to her work.

Nothing, however, will help quite as much as careful reading of her own words, sentences, stanzas, and whole poems. Particular attention should be given to grasping the sense of her whole sentences, filling in missing elements, straightening out inverted word order, and expanding the sense of telescoped phrases and metaphors. Perhaps most important for understanding Emily Dickinson is the testing of one's conceptions of the tone or tones of individual poems and relating them to other poems and to one's own emotional ideas and feelings.

Scholarly aids are generously available but not equally reliable. Outdated and wrong-headed materials are sometimes recommended, but the wise beginning student should disregard these resources until he or she has a firmer foundation to build on. For a full understanding of Emily Dickinson, a reading of her complete poems and letters is essential. For a more than generous sample of her best poetry, *Final Harvest* is outstanding. The early biographies by Bianchi, Pollitt, and Taggard should be avoided. The biographies by Whicher, Chase, and particularly the biography by Johnson give accounts reliable up to a point. The biography of Sewall outdates all of these in its thoroughness and use of new materials, but it is cumbersome in its bulk and organization. Excellent critical books and articles abound but are frequently one-sided. Often after one has immersed himself or herself in Emily Dickinson thoroughly, one's own intellectual and emotional responses and implications are as genuine and accurate as the scholars' evaluations.

THE TEXTS OF DICKINSON'S POEMS AND LETTERS

After Emily Dickinson died, she left behind several drawersful of poems in various states of completion: fair copies, semi-final drafts, and rough drafts, all strangely punctuated and capitalized. Her handwriting is difficult, and many manuscripts list alternate choices for words, lines, and stanzas. In the 1890s, T. W. Higginson and Mabel Loomis Todd began publishing some of her poems in *First Series* (1890), *Second Series* (1891), and, by Mrs. Todd alone, *Third Series* (1896); these volumes included 449 poems. In order to create popular public acceptance, they often corrected grammar, conventionalized punctuation, improved rhymes, omitted stanzas, and supplied titles. In succeeding decades, Martha Dickinson Bianchi and A. L. Hampson edited several more small volumes and then collected many of the remaining poems into *The Poems of Emily Dickinson*, 1937. They took fewer liberties with the texts, but they misread many words in the manuscripts. In 1945, Millicent Todd Bingham issued her completion of her mother, M. L. Todd's, editing of another 668 poems, under the title *Bolts of Melody*, a carefully edited but also repunctuated text. (To repunctuate Dickinson is often to re-interpret her poems.) In 1955, Thomas H. Johnson edited from all known manuscripts *The Poems of Emily Dickinson, Including Variant Readings*. This edition, known as the Johnson text, attempted to report the manuscripts with complete accuracy and arranged the poems according to their dates of composition, as estimated by Emily Dickinson's changing handwriting, which helped establish Dickinson's yearly rates of composition. This volume also supplied poem numbers which are now almost universally used with first lines to identify each poem. This edition contains 1775 poems and fragments. When faced with textual variants, Johnson chose words and lines listed first, but he reported all the others in footnotes. In 1960, Johnson simplified the variorum edition into a single volume, reader's edition, *The Complete Poems of Emily Dickinson*, recently reissued in a reduced-type paperback edition. The single volume edition occasionally departs from the textual choices of the variorum. In 1961, Johnson issued *Final Harvest*, a selection of 575 poems. Early printings of the one-volume edition and of *Final Harvest* contain a number of misprints. As for Dickinson's letters, a body of work which many critics believe to be as valuable as her poetry because of its imagery and ideas, two editions of selections from Emily Dickinson's letters appeared under M. L. Todd's editorship in 1894 and 1931. In 1958, T. H. Johnson gathered all known letters into the three-volume *The Letters of Emily Dickinson*. A number of the best known early critical essays on Emily Dickinson, including those by Conrad Aiken, Allen Tate, and Yvor Winters, quote from the sometimes mangled pre-Johnson texts. Most contemporary anthologies employ the Johnson texts, but the earlier editions still reside on library shelves and two selections of Emily Dickinson's poems that remain in print, edited respectively by R. N. Linscott and J. M. Brinnin, use pre-Johnson texts either wholly or substantially, sometimes misleadingly for the reader.

DICKINSON'S IDEAS

Emily Dickinson's major ideas are readily available to us in her poems and letters, but on first reading, they form complicated and often contradictory patterns. This is not surprising; her world was insular and small, and she was highly introspective. In addition, her work has its roots in the culture and society of her times, but though these can be explored extensively and many parallels can be established between her statements and various literary and religious documents, the poems create more mutual illumination than does Emily Dickinson's background itself. Orthodox Protestantism in its Calvinistic guise was the major underpinning of nineteenth-century Amherst society, though it was undergoing shocks and assaults. This New England faith, often called Puritanism, was based on the idea of man as being sinful and unregenerate and completely at the mercy of a loving but arbitrary God. Salvation was by predestined election (it lay entirely in the will of God), but acceptance of God's will, and renunciation of the world for Christ, were paramount for proof of piety and peace of soul. Worldly success and religious faith were taken as signs of salvation but not as its causes. In Dickinson's time, this faith was wearing thin, and material success had long replaced deep piety as the real standard for recognizing the elect. This thinning out of faith helped create the ideas of New England Unitarianism and Transcendentalism. Unitarianism having watered down the emotional components of religion, the transcendentalism of Ralph Waldo Emerson and others elevated man's spirituality, self-development, and union with the stream of nature to the level of the divine, without ever quite denying the Godhead. The Puritans had seen God's will everywhere in the signs of nature. In Emerson's footsteps, Whitman, Thoreau, and certainly Emily Dickinson tended to see man's spirit manifested or symbolized in nature, though Dickinson often saw only the human mind reading its feelings into nature. Dickinson was aware of and troubled by the admitted and surreptitious breakdown of faith in her time, and she was dubious of all measures to shore it up. She drew sustenance from new ideas, but sometimes found them shallow. She rejected old ideas, but found in them much emotional correspondence to her own set of mind.

For Dickinson, the crucial religious question was the survival of the soul after death. She rejected absolutely the idea of man's innate depravity; she favored the Emersonian partial reversal of Puritanism that conceived greatness of soul as the source of immortality. The God of the Bible was alternately real, mythical, and unlikely to her. She could neither accept nor reject His assurance of a life beyond death, and her doubts pushed her faintly in the direction of transcendental naturalism or towards mere terror of dissolution. She declares, alternately, faith and doubt with equal vehemence, surely as much because of her own struggles with the idea of and need for fulfillment as because of any intellectual battlement. Her sarcastic comments on the God of the Bible are not necessarily jocular. She was independent minded, but she did not shift her stance in her letters to suit her recipients, nor in her poems presumably, to suit her moods; she was interested primarily in her poetic momentum.

In some sense, Dickinson is almost always a religious poet – if her concerns with human perception, suffering, growth, and fulfillment as directed towards something permanent can be called religious concerns. These concerns are as important for her as are death and immortality, and though they have doctrinal and literary sources, they come chiefly from her observations and reflections on life.

Dickinson's reading was comparatively wide, and she knew both the essays and poems of Emerson, as well as Shakespeare, the Bible, the works of George Eliot, Hawthorne, the Brownings, and other earlier and contemporary classics. She alludes often to the Bible, and her combination of dense metaphors with everyday reality sometimes resembles Shakespeare's. However, both the Emersonian cast of her mind, which we will note in several poems, and her darker Puritan strain, were as much a part of the general atmosphere of her culture as of its specific beliefs and its reading matter. Dickinson's literary culture overlaps her religious culture, but the parallels they provide to her work are usually more incidental than revealing.

Although she prided herself on her indifference to broader social concerns, Dickinson does comment occasionally on the social landscape, particularly as it catches her satirical eye. Nature appears widely in her work – as a scene of great liveliness and beauty, as the embodiment of the processes of the universe which may resemble the actions of God and the shape of the human mind, and as an endless source of metaphors and symbols for all of her subjects. Nature, for her, is usually bright and dark mystery, only occasionally illuminated by flashes of pantheism and sometimes darkened by hopeless fatality. Her treatment of nature blends into all of her subjects.

The tradition of classifying Dickinson's poems into thematic groupings for analysis and comparison has been unjustly criticized. As we have remarked, it can contribute to simplification and distortion, but it is more illuminating than approaching the poems by categories of technique or periods in her life, and the danger of simplification can be easily met by a persistent testing of her poems against categories; that is, one can always consider the possibility that they have been misplaced or need to be viewed as part of several categories. For these Notes, we have grouped her poems under five major headings, aware that a few major poems may escape such a classification: (1) Nature: Scene and Meaning; (2) Poetry, Art, and Imagination; (3) Friendship, Love, and Society; (4) Suffering and Growth; and (5) Death, Immortality, and Religion.

DICKINSON'S POETIC METHODS

A glance through Dickinson's poems reveals their characteristic external forms as easily as a quick look through Whitman's poems shows us his strikingly different forms. Most of Emily Dickinson's poems are written in short stanzas, mostly quatrains, with short lines, usually rhyming only on the second and fourth lines. Other stanzas employ triplets or pairs of couplets, and a few poems employ longer, looser, and more complicated stanzas. Iambic rhythms dominate, but they are varied and loosened, speeded and slowed, in many ways. A large number of Dickinson's rhymes are what we call partial, slant, or off-rhymes, some of these so faint as to be barely recognizable. She was obviously aware that she was violating convention here, but she stubbornly stuck to her ways. These stanza forms and, to a lesser extent, her poetic rhymes took their chief source from the standard Protestant hymns of her day, largely from those of Isaac Watts.

Dickinson evidently found a convenient mold for her thoughts in these forms, and her use of partial rhyme may have helped her to compose swiftly and to focus on selection of words and metaphors. It is possible that her slant rhymes reflect her emotional tensions (fracture would be a stronger word for it), but most critical attempts to establish clear-cut correlations between types of rhyme and particular moods in her poems are relatively unsuccessful. Nevertheless, these slant rhymes seem consistent with the improvisatory and brooding quality of her mind.

The relative simplicity and monotony of her verse forms contribute to the difficulty of reading Dickinson in large quantities at single sittings, but one never fails to sense and remember her unique poetic genius. Her stanza forms and rhythmical nuances continuously contribute brilliantly to her effects. For example, Dickinson's poems often burst with images and metaphors drawn from many diverse sources. Nature is paramount. Other sources include domestic activities, industry and warfare, and law and economy. Her images sometimes create natural or social scenes but are more likely to create psychological landscapes, generalized scenes, or allegorical scenes. She is like a deep, mysterious mine where one can find many examples of how she blends symbolism and allegory. (Symbolism is the use of real scenes and actions to suggest universal ideas and emotions in addition to the scenes. Allegory is the use of scenes and actions whose structuring is so artificial and unreal that the reader comes to see that they stand for people, scenes, and ideas recognizably different from the representation itself.) This blending of symbolism and allegory in Dickinson's poems is another reason for some readers' difficulty when they encounter her many poems for the first time; yet, Emily Dickinson's evocative powers are paramount: she is always a challenge to the reader.

Besides the great conciseness of language we have already stressed, the most striking signature of Dickinson's style is her blending of the homely and exalted, the trivial and the precious, in her images, metaphors, and scenes. The chief effect that she achieves here is to increase our scrutiny of small-scale things and focus on the texture and significance of large ones. It also serves to permeate her physical world with questions of value. Dickinson's sense of humor and her skepticism help communicate the urgencies of her doubts and need to find faith. Her metaphors are also sometimes telescoped; that is, they incorporate elements so condensed or disparate that they must be elongated, drawn out like a telescope, to reveal the full structure of a picture or an idea.

Dickinson herself told Higginson that the speaker in her poems is *not* herself but a supposed person, thereby anticipating the perhaps too popular modern idea that poems are always spoken by a fictitious person. This provides a very healthy caution for interpreting Dickinson, but this idea should not keep us from using our knowledge of her life and thought to interpret her poems. Of equal importance is the variety of tones throughout her poems, a variety related to the problem of identifying her speakers. The chief tonal problem is distinguishing between ironic and non-ironic voices. Her ironies can be very obvious or very subtle. Clues to irony are often found in the structure of a poem's statements where doubts and reversals reveal earlier ironies. The likelihood that Dickinson was deliberately posing in many of her poems complicates the problem of tone – but her poses are not necessarily sentimental. Awareness of her shifting of masks can help us resist our doubts that she is serious when she adopts a view we dislike. We also need to recognize her possibly fierce ironies when she is denouncing beliefs which we hold precious or when she is reacting in ways we disapprove of. Again, the poems sometimes seem puzzling, yet after a rereading, they are often suddenly illuminating. To paraphrase Dickinson, scrutiny of this problem keeps the mind nimble. Probably she wanted to keep her own and her readers' minds as nimble as possible.

THE POEMS

Nature: Scene and Meaning

Since Emily Dickinson was a child of rural nineteenth-century New England, it is not surprising that the natural scenes and figurative language drawn from it loom very large throughout her work. She had read in the poetry of Wordsworth, Bryant, and Emerson—all products of a Romantic movement that looked for meaning, imagery, and spiritual refreshment in nature. Her roots in a Puritanism that saw God manifested everywhere in nature contributed to her pursuit of personal significance in nature. The New England countryside of her time was still largely untrammeled, and she was fascinated by its changing seasons and their correspondence to her own inner moods. Although her direct observations were confined to meadows, forests, hills, flowers, and a fairly small range of little creatures, these provided material highly suitable to her personal vision and impressive symbols for her inner conflicts. Unlike the major English and American Romantic poets, her view of nature as beneficent is balanced by a feeling that the essence of nature is baffling, elusive, and perhaps destructive.

Her nature poems divide into those that are chiefly presentations of scenes appreciated for their liveliness and beauty, and those in which aspects of nature are scrutinized for keys to the meaning of the universe and human life. The distinction is somewhat artificial but still useful, for it will encourage consideration of both the deeper significances in the more scenic poems and of the pictorial elements in the more philosophical poems. As we have noted, nature images and metaphors permeate Dickinson's poems on other subjects and some of those poems may be more concerned with nature than at first appears.

"It sifts from Leaden Sieves" (311) shows Dickinson combining metaphor and imagery to create a winter scene of great beauty. The poem does not name the falling snow which it describes, thereby increasing a sense of entranced wonder. The "leaden sieves" that stand for an overcast sky also contribute to the poem's initially somewhat sad mood, a mood that is quickly changed by the addition of images that suggest a healing process. The following five lines show everything in the scene becoming peacefully smooth. With the third stanza, the observer's eyes have dropped from sky, horizon, and distant landscape to neighboring fences and fields. The fence becoming lost in fleeces parallels the image of wool, and the image of "celestial vail" (meaning *veil*) skillfully provides a transition between the two stanzas and brings a heavenly beauty to what had been the dissolution of harvested fields. Perhaps it also implies something blessed about the memorial which it makes to those harvests. The idea of snow providing a monument to the living things of summer adds a gentle irony to the poem, for snow is traditionally a symbol of both death and impermanence. In the last stanza, the observer takes delight in a close-up thing, the queenly appearance of fence posts, and then, in a tone of combined relief and wonder, the poem suggests that the lovely winter scene has really had no external source, but has simply arrived by a kind of inner or outer miracle. Our analysis can provide a basis for further symbolic interpretation of the poem.

An apparently more cheerful scene appears in the popular "I'll tell you how the Sun rose" (318). This poem divides evenly into two metaphorical descriptions—of a sunrise and a sunset on the same day. The speaker assumes the guise of a little girl urgently running with news of nature, delighted with the imaginativeness of her perception and phrasing, and pretending bafflement about the details and meaning of the sunset. The sun's rising is described as if it were donning ribbons, which is paralleled by hills untying their bonnets. The ribbons are thin strips of colored clouds which are common at sunrise, and which, as it gets lighter, might seem to appear in various and changing colors "a ribbon at a time." The news "running like squirrels" creates excitement in the scene, for squirrels do become active when the sun rises. The sound of the bobolinks prompts the speaker to address herself softly, holding in her excitement. At midpoint, the poem skips over the whole day, as if the speaker had remained in a trance. She claims to be unable to describe the sunset. Not surprisingly, the images for the sunset are more metaphorical than those for the sunrise. The entire scene is presented in terms of little school children climbing a stile (steps over a hedge). They go over the horizon into a different field, where a "dominie" (an archaic term for schoolmaster or minister) shepherds them away. The yellow children are the waning shafts of light and the purple stile is the darkening clouds at sunset. Sunset clouds are a traditional symbol of a barred gateway into another mysterious world of space and time, or into heaven. Dickinson has gently domesticated what may be a fearful element in the scene.

In several of her most popular nature portraits, Dickinson focuses on small creatures. Two such poems, "A narrow Fellow in the Grass" (986) and "A Bird came down the Walk" (328), may at first seem quite different in scene and tone, but close scrutiny reveals similarities. In "A narrow Fellow in the Grass" (986), as in "It sifts from Leaden Sieves," Dickinson does not name her subject, probably in order to create a mood of surprise or wonder in the reader, paralleling the speaker's reactions. "A narrow fellow," of course, is a snake. The use of "fellow" for the snake combines a colloquial familiarity with a sense of something presumptuously foreign to the speaker's habitat. The first two stanzas paint a very vivid picture of the smooth movement and semi-invisibility of a snake in deep grass. If one does not meet him (as if by introduction or full vision), one gets the shock of seeing grass divide evenly as a signal of his unseen approach. Surprise is continued by the snake's proceeding in a similarly semi-magical way. After this eight-line introduction, the poem slows down for the next eight lines as the speaker reflects on the snake's preference for cool, moist terrain, where perhaps she ventured when younger, or from which a snake once ventured into territory closer to her. We call Dickinson's speaker "her" despite the curious and significant reference to herself as a boy. Dickinson uses a male persona in a few other poems. Here, she is probably thinking of herself as a boy to stress her desire for the freedom of movement which her society denied to girls. Reflecting now on an earlier encounter with a similar snake, Dickinson describes the snake as a whiplash to emphasize its complete disguise when it lies still, a description that pairs neatly with the snake's concealed comb-like appearance in the second stanza. When she tried to pick up the whiplash and it had disappeared, she apparently was not overly surprised. Her desire to secure the whiplash is a faint echo of the tying of the worm with a string in "In Winter in my Room" (1670).

After the reflective interlude of the middle eight lines, Dickinson makes some general conclusions in the last eight lines. The reference to creatures as being nature's "people" is similar to the personification of "fellow," but it lacks its touch of disdain. She is moved to cordiality by other creatures because they recognize her and, in so doing, they have at least one human quality. But the snake belongs to a distinctly alien order. Even if she is accompanied when she meets one, she always experiences an emotional shock that grips her body to its innermost parts. The famous phrase "zero at the bone" converts a number into a metaphor for frightful and cold nothingness. The snake has come to stand for an evil or aggressive quality in nature – a messenger of fear where she would prefer to greet the familiar, the warm, and the reassuring. However, there seems to be ambivalence in her attitude; her vivid and carefully accurate, though fanciful, observation of the snake implies some admiration for the beauty and wonderful agility of the strange animal. The combination of such homely details and diction as "fellow," "comb," "boggy," "whiplash," and "wrinkled" with such formal terms as "notice," "secure," "transport," and "cordiality" gives the poem a particularly American and Dickinsonian flavor. One cannot imagine a Wordsworth or a Tennyson using anything but consistently formal diction for such description, and the American poets Bryant and Longfellow would have made such a sight an occasion for both a formal description and a positive moral. This poem is both descriptive and philosophical, and it runs counter to the tradition of poems that claim to see good intentions in nature.

The almost equally popular "A Bird came down the Walk" (328) is more cheerful than "A narrow Fellow" and more descriptive, but it also deals with man's alienation from nature. In the snake poem, the speaker is threatened by an emanation of nature. Here, she unsuccessfully tries to cross the barrier between man and nature as it is embodied in a less threatening creature. The first two stanzas show the bird at home in nature, aggressive towards the worm which it eats and politely indifferent to the beetle. The description of the angleworm as being a fellow eaten raw simultaneously humanizes the little creature and places it in a diminutive animal world. The speaker is enjoying her secret spying, which adds to the tension of the scene, a tension that becomes more explicit in the third stanza's description of the bird's frightened uneasiness. Its natural habitat is being invaded, and the speaker appreciates the bird's increased beauty under stress, a stress which is implied by the metaphors of its eyes being like beads and its head being like velvet.

In the fourth stanza, tension is divided between the speaker, who, rather than the bird, now seems to be in danger, and the bird who is about to flee. This device shows the speaker identifying with the bird, a sign of her desire for an intimacy that the bird will reject. The last six lines use metaphors for the bird that counter the humanizing touches of the opening stanzas, and they also counter the somewhat alienated tone of the middle stanza with more aesthetic images of the bird's power, ease, and union with nature. The bird departs into an ocean of air where all of creation is seamless. Probably the ambiguous quality in the speaker's experience is intended to contrast with the atmosphere of relaxed, almost cosmic, unity of these closing lines. Written in primarily iambic rhythm, the poem communicates its uneasy tone partly through its subtle metrical variation, chiefly reversal of accent, and through its cacophonous sounds – all largely in the first three stanzas. In the last two stanzas, the rhythms become smoother and the sounds more euphonious, in imitation of the bird's smooth merging with nature.

Mixed feelings of a different kind are striking in "The Wind begun to knead the Grass" (824), one of the finest of Dickinson's many poems about storms with (and occasionally without) rain. Not until the end of this poem do we realize that the speaker is probably safely inside a house and looking out of a door or a window at a developing storm. The details of the scene are presented in a series of vigorous personifications and metaphors. In the first eight lines, the wind is rising and sweeping across the land. Its force makes some of the grass stand up high and some lie down. The analogy to women kneading and tossing dough creates aesthetic detachment. The description of leaves unhooking themselves and dust scooping itself animates the landscape and conveys a sense of excitement about the release of power. The speaker is excited both by this manifestation of strength and by her safe situation, where no road for escape is needed. The human element enters very briefly with the "quickened wagons" that imply both fear and the vigor of fleeing people. Lightning is a giant bird whose head and toe stand for its jagged sweep (these details are clearer and more consistent in Dickinson's second version of the poem, which accompanies the first version in the *Complete Poems* and in the variorum edition). Birds putting up bars to nests humanizes their actions and parallels the behavior of people. All the images of flight thus far, including the description of the landscape, build up a tension which begins to ease with the description of the drop of giant rain, but the tension is maintained by the repeated "thens" and by the metaphor of hands holding up a dam, until these hands part and the rain comes. This passage creates the feeling of a breathless participation in the scene by the speaker, as if she herself were holding back the torrent. When the released waters "wreck" the sky (it has become a structure paralleling her dwelling), she is safe inside her father's house looking at a tree that has been split by lightning. It seems to please the speaker to see nature as both alien and familiar, wild and domestic. She enjoys watching the release of power in nature and can empathize with it while she remains in the safety of her home. The understatement of the last two lines suggests that she accepts her protected situation as a natural aspect of her life.

The very popular "A Route of Evanescence" (1463) often puzzles readers until they learn that Dickinson referred to it as "My hummingbird." Several critics have been interested in it as a possible revision of the earlier and not very accomplished "Within my Garden, rides a Bird" (500). "A Route of Evanescence" appears to be more purely descriptive than the snake and bird poems which we have discussed, but some readers have found philosophical elements in it. For analysis, the poem can be divided into three parts. The first four lines describe a hummingbird in flight. The first line presents a paradox – the route or path of the hummingbird is made of evanescence because the bird's speed denies its substantiality; bird and route have become identical. In the second line, the bird's whirring wings are a revolving wheel, a more definite image and therefore easier for us to apprehend, even though the bird is still seen as a blur. The third line employs synesthesia – the description of one sense in terms of another. Here the emerald of the bird's back and wings is a resonating sound, probably to give a sense of vibration. The fourth line is close to synesthesia in representing the bird's ruby-colored throat as "a rush of cochineal," a fusion of kinesis and sight. The fifth and sixth lines describe the bird's gathering nectar from the flowers from the blossom's own point of view. The blossoms are personified, and we sense an identification between speaker and flower. In the last two lines, the speaker comments on the whole experience. Tunis, in North Africa, is approximately 8,000 miles from New England. A morning's ride from there would be incredibly swift. The poet is implying by such an accomplishment that the bird is completely at home in nature and serenely confident of its power. These last two lines probably allude to a passage in Shakespeare's *The Tempest* in which a message from Naples to Tunis (a mere 400 miles was huge in the ancient world) could not be expected "unless the sun were post."

In the popular "I taste a liquor never brewed" (214), Emily Dickinson describes an intoxicated unity of self and nature without the alienation that haunts some of her other nature poems. Unlike most of the nature poems that we have discussed, this one describes not a scene but a state of mind. In the first line, the poet shows that the experience is just beginning by her use of the word "taste," which implies a sensation not yet dominant. The grammar of the second line is puzzling. The tankards may be places for real alcohol, or they may be her drinking vessels, in which case the pearl would refer to the preciousness or rarity of the experience. As soon as we read the poem's third and fourth lines, we see that a liquor never brewed must be a spiritual and not a physical substance, and her rejection of what comes from vats on the Rhine, a distant and romantic place, shows her reveling in the superiority of her home surroundings, no matter how small their compass. In the second and third stanzas, she is drunk on the essence of summer days, which seem endless. The formal diction of "inebriate" and "debauchee" light-heartedly spiritualizes the intoxication. Dickinson creates her scene of endless summer in a very few images, the image of "Molten blue" and the relatively simple images of bees, flowers, and butterflies being sufficient. The word "molten" gives us simultaneously the sense of a fluid sky along with a feeling of dissolving into this sky, and it is also a symbol for the spiritual liquor being drunk. This simplification imparts to the speaker's reveling a childlike quality in keeping with the poem's quick transformation of the sensuous into the spiritual. The third stanza suggests that no one can own the things of nature, and that when butterflies have had their fill of nectar, the speaker will go on drinking from nature's spiritual abundance. Her continued drinking indicates her insatiability but may also imply the triumph of her imagination over the decline of summer. In the last stanza, she has ascended into heaven, perhaps by the way of sunbeams, and heavenly angels come to the windows of paradise to see this spiritual drunkard leaning against the sun for rest. For the variorum edition, Thomas Johnson accepted a much different and tamer variant for the last two lines, but he restored the famous sun-tippler in *Complete Poems* and in *Final Harvest*. This poem has been compared to Emerson's "Bacchus," and one critic has suggested that Dickinson is parodying Emerson's poem. The comparison is interesting, but the poems are quite different in tone, the Emerson poem communicating an intense pathos much more reminiscent of Emily Dickinson in her poems which deal with her dark contemplations of the mysteries of the cosmic process.

Emily Dickinson's more philosophical nature poems tend to reflect darker moods than do her more descriptive poems and are often denser and harder to interpret. The nature scenes in these poems often are so deeply internalized in the speaker that a few critics deny the reality of their physical scenes and insist that the poems deal exclusively with states of mind. Our observation of the blending of idea with scene in the nature poems which we have already discussed cautions us against such an extreme view. It is more accurate to say that the philosophical nature poems look outward and inward with equal intensity.

In "What mystery pervades a well!" (1400), nature is seen as a large-scale abstraction. Although it is more expository than most of Dickinson's philosophical nature poems, it still maintains a balance between abstraction, metaphor, and scene. The imagery is centered on a well whose strange and frightening depths the speaker contemplates until her mind moves on to larger vistas of nature and finally, quite probably, to a contemplation of death. In the first two stanzas, we are made aware of the close and familiar aspects of a well and of its mystery. The metaphor of a neighbor from another world contained in a jar typifies Dickinson's combination of the familiar and the mysterious. In the second stanza, the homely lid of glass becomes terrifying when converted into "an abyss's face," one of Dickinson's most brilliant uses of a metaphor to represent an abstraction. The third and fourth stanzas show nature at home with itself, suggested by the grass's and the sedge's familiarity with wells and with the sea. In the last two stanzas, Dickinson grows more abstract and yet she preserves considerable drama through the personification of nature, the actions of those that study it, and the frightening results. She is skeptical about the real knowledge of those who most frequently talk of nature, evidently referring to transcendental philosophers and analytical scientists. Such people are pompous fools because they do not realize that nature's mysteries are ultimately unknowable. If they had ever looked at nature closely they would have become baffled and probably frightened by her and would not so glibly use her name.

The haunted house and the ghost bring up the question of death's relation to nature, which is further explored in the last stanza. There are possibly two different, but not necessarily contradictory, ideas here. Perhaps in the last two lines Dickinson is saying that the more an individual knows about a complicated subject such as nature, paradoxically the less he knows because he becomes aware that there is so much more to know and that there is so much that it is impossible to know. But it is more likely that Dickinson is suggesting that the closer a person comes to death, which is an aspect of nature, the fewer resources he has left to understand it because of waning powers of mind and body. Dickinson implies that to know nature fully is to be dead, which seems to be a more regrettable state than the pitiable state of ignorance.

Turning to Dickinson's more descriptive philosophical poems of nature, we start with the genial and popular "These are the days when Birds come back" (130), written in about 1859, a few years before the full flowering of her genius. The days when birds come back make up Indian summer, an event of great beauty in rural New England. As an early critic of this poem noted, birds do *not* return during Indian summer, and bees continue to gather nectar whenever they can. The scene, however, remains convincing, for we all have witnessed the persistence of some birds in early autumn, and we can understand the speaker's identification with bees, whose supposed skepticism is part of her mood. The poem dramatizes the speaker's unwillingness to see the year die, along with her acceptance of that death and an affirmation of a rebirth in nature. The bird's backward look symbolizes the speaker's yearning for the vanished summer. The sophistries of June are its false arguments that it will last forever – a feeling that Dickinson yields to in "I taste a liquor never brewed." The blue and gold mistake represents bright skies and changing leaves as false signs of persisting vitality.

The third stanza begins a transition with the speaker starting to resist the fraud that she would like to believe in. The seeds of the fourth stanza bear witness (a religious term) that the year's cycle is indeed running down, but these seeds also promise rebirth. The altered air emphasizes the reality of autumn, and the personified timid leaf partly stands for the apprehensive speaker and her fear of mortality. These two stanzas show her beginning to believe in a rebirth despite the atmosphere of decline, and this ambiguity is maintained in the last two stanzas. The supreme moment of Indian summer is called a last communion. The haze describes the literal atmosphere of such a scene and also suggests the speaker's sense of two seasons dissolving into each other and herself dissolving into the scene. These last two stanzas form a prayer in which she is asking to join in what she sees as nature's sacred celebration of the end of summer – she wants to be part of the sad joy of the time. The emblems and consecrated bread and wine are the apparatus of the Christian communion, but the poem presents them as part of the scene: seeds that will flower, and sap that will rise again, although the immortal wine is more an emotional condition in the speaker than an image. If we stress the Christian analogies, we can interpret the poem as an affirmation of conventional immortality, but it is more likely that it celebrates the immortality of the cycle of life while indulging in a bittersweet pathos about the beauty of the season's and life's decline.

Dickinson's novel stanza and rhyme pattern contribute to her effects. Except for the first, the stanzas all employ a rhymed couplet plus a shortened line which rhyme in pairs. The variation in the first stanza is effective; here, the first and third lines use a partial rhyme echoed at the end of the second stanza, and in the second line there is vowel rhyme (assonance) in "resume" and "June." This interlocking parallels the stop-and-go action of the bird's return, the backward look, and the colorful mistake. The metrical and rhyme patterns emphasize the hesitancy and yearning at each stanza's end. "Sophistries of June" and "blue and gold mistake" show Dickinson turning physical phenomena into metaphorical abstractions. The gentle personification of leaves prepares for the conversion of natural elements into religious symbols in the last stanza. We have seen the Dickinson persona in the form of a child in several other poems but never as strikingly. Here, the child guise suggests that the speaker is trying to hold onto faith. In her sterner poems about seasonal change, the childlike stance is absent.

Although "Of Bronze—and Blaze" (290) is not based on seasonal change, it provides material for an interesting contrast to "These are the days." Apparently written only two years after that poem, this one employs a completely different tone in its treatment of human mortality. The pre-variorum editions of Dickinson give the word "daisies" in place of "beetles" in the poem's last line in accordance with a manuscript variant. This grammatically difficult poem begins with a description of the aurora borealis, or northern lights, frequently visible in New England. Only the first two lines, however, present the physical occurrence. The rest of the poem elaborates on its meanings and their significance for the speaker's life. The northern lights are a display of awe-inspiring beauty, and watching them, the speaker is struck by their completely self-contained quality. The third line can mean "it forms an adequate conception of itself or the universe," or "forms" can be read as taking the object "unconcern" in the sixth line, in which case an understood "which" must be inserted before "infects my simple spirit." The sense of the lines is that this beauty in nature shows the sovereign universe to be indifferent to everything except itself or the processes that create it. Dickinson describes its influence on herself as infectious. Its contagious excitement is not proper or healthy for people because it makes them elevate themselves beyond the human sphere. The speaker's strutting on her stem proclaims her lofty pretensions and her revolt from ordinary organic life. She disdains the sustenance of oxygen because she wants to live superior to all human limitations, displaying an arrogance like that which the universe flaunts in these blazing lights.

The splendors mentioned in the second stanza are probably the poet's creations. As "menagerie" (Dickinson is turning this noun into an adjective), her creations have variety and charm but they are severely limited. The northern lights are beyond all competition because they manifest the coldly self-contained power and beauty of the universe itself. The fact that the lights are described as both unconcerned and arrogant suggests that arrogance is a quality which humans feel and project but which the universe does not need. That this show will entertain the centuries means that it will go on forever, while the poet dies and becomes dust. The grass is dishonored because it is nourished by the poet's lowly body. Thoughtless beetles crossing her grave illustrate the unworthiness of her dust and imply that death is extinction. The word "competeless" stresses the inability of the artist to even approximate the magnificence of the general creation.

Unlike "These are the days," this poem shows Emily Dickinson alienated from the natural processes that symbolize immortality. The poem need not, however, be read as wholly pessimistic. The speaker criticizes herself for imitating the arrogance of the cosmos, but she also seems to be reveling in the energy that she acquires from making such an imitation. In the second stanza, she seems to be both affirming the value of her own artistic creations and taking pleasure in the superiority of the universe to herself. On the psychological level, she is perhaps preparing herself for a turn towards conventional religious faith or towards that celebration of the poet's supremacy that we will see in several poems about the poet and artist. These different possibilities suggest the numerous and powerful thrusts of Emily Dickinson's mind in various directions.

In several of Dickinson's best poems, the elevating and the destructive qualities of nature balance one another. Perhaps the best known of these is the widely anthologized "There's a certain Slant of light" (258). As are several of Dickinson's best philosophical poems, this one is also related to a moment of seasonal change. The scene is further along in the year than that of "These are the days," and the poetic artist is more mature (although the poem was written only about two years later). With the exception of its last two lines, this poem presents few difficulties in its word choice or grammar. Nevertheless, it shows so much intensity and strangeness of feeling that when most students first read it, they are usually puzzled.

The physical substance of the scene appears only in the first two lines of its opening stanzas and in its concluding stanzas. The landscape seems to be a meadowland, perhaps with trees and hills, for one gets a sense of expanse and looming objects. On winter afternoons, the sunlight is diminished because the northern hemisphere is inclined away from the sun, making the days shorter and the sun's rays less direct. Also, there is often a cloud cover. The first stanza stresses the heaviness of the atmosphere. Beyond this initial observation, a discussion of the poem should begin with an examination of the parallels and differences among its four stanzas. Their most obvious similarity is the presence of interrelated paradoxes in the first three stanzas, which are echoed by the paradoxical tone of the last stanza.

In the first stanza, cathedral tunes that oppress join a mood of depression to the elevating thought of cathedrals, and in the second stanza, this paradox is concisely suggested by "Heavenly Hurt," which connects bliss with pain. This mixed feeling in the third stanza is called the "Seal Despair," seal referring to the stamped impressure or wax attachment of a king or a government on a document, which guarantees its authenticity, and perhaps referring also to the biblical seals that open to admit the saved into paradise. In the third stanza, "imperial affliction" further reinforces this paradox. This phrase continues the imagery of royalty begun by "seal," and also "affliction" is a typical Bible term for suffering that requires the healing of God.

In the second stanza, "it" refers to the slant of light with its hidden message, but in the third stanza, "it" refers only to that message, which has now become internalized in the speaker. In the last stanza, "it" is once more the slant of light, now perceived as mysterious. The landscape, symbolic of human perception, listens; and shadows, probably symbols of darkened understanding, hold their breath in anticipation of understanding the meaning of the winter light. When the light goes, its going resembles either the fading of consciousness in the eyes of dying persons, or the look in the eyes of personified death itself. Because these last two lines are so condensed, it is difficult to choose between these two interpretations. Although the light seems to symbolize death at the end of the poem, its association with cathedrals in the first stanza modifies this symbolism. The imagery of the opening lines and the tone of the poem as a whole suggest that this strange, pale, and somber light can give to the human spirit a feeling of exultation even while it is portending death.

The second stanza tells us that this winter light inflicts a spiritual wound, and the third stanza explains that this suffering cannot be taught, given consolation, or even explanation. The implication is that such suffering is precious as well as painful. Perhaps it is also implied that the soul belongs to and will find itself most truly in heaven. However, these final stanzas seem to be more concerned with the deepening of human sensibility on earth. Thus, it is likely that the "seal despair" passage is saying that we become aware of our spirituality and experience the beauty of the world most intensely when we realize that mortality creates this spirituality and beauty.

The style of this poem is representative of Dickinson in a meditative mood. The sense impressions employ synesthesia (light and sound are given weight). The "heavenly hurt," "seal despair," and "imperial affliction" turn abstractions for emotions into semi-pictorial metaphors and thereby give a physical feeling to purely internal experiences. The last stanza returns to the physical world but assigns to its personified landscape the feelings of a person who is observing such a scene.

"As imperceptibly as Grief" (1540) is often compared to "There's a certain Slant of light" as another poem in which seasonal change becomes a symbol of inner change. The relationship of inner and outer here, however, is somewhat different. "There's a certain Slant" begins with a moment of arrest that signals the nature and meaning of winter. This poem tells us that summer has passed but insists that this passing occurred so slowly that it did not seem like the betrayal that it really was. The comparison to the slow fading of grief also implies a failure of awareness on the speaker's part. The second and third lines begin a description of a transitional period, and their claim that the speaker felt no betrayal shows that she has had to struggle against such a feeling. The next eight lines create a personified scene of late summer or early autumn. The distilled quiet allows time for contemplation. The "twilight long begun" suggests that the speaker is getting used to the coming season and is aware that change was occurring before she truly noticed it. These lines reinforce the poem's initial description of a slow lapse and also convey the idea that foreknowledge of decline is part of the human condition. The personification of the polite but coldly determined guest who insists on leaving no matter how earnestly she is asked to stay is convincing on the realistic level. On the level of analogy, the courtesy probably corresponds to the restrained beauty of the season, and the cold determination corresponds to the inevitability of the year's cycle.

The movement from identification with sequestered nature to nature as a departing figure communicates the involvement of humans in the seasonal life cycle. The last four lines shift the metaphor and relax the tension. Summer leaves by secret means. The missing wing and keel suggest a mysterious fluidity—greater than that of air or water. Summer escapes into the beautiful, which is a repository of creation that promises to send more beauty into the world. The balanced picture of the departing guest has prepared us for this low-key conclusion.

A similar but more difficult poem is "Further in Summer than the Birds" (1068). This poem's imagery and syntax are very concentrated, and a line-by-line analysis is helpful in understanding it, although Emily Dickinson lends some assistance by describing the poem as "my cricket" in one of her letters. The phrase "further in summer than the birds" indicates that the time of year is late summer when noisy insects proliferate, rather than early summer when bird-song is predominant. The crickets are pathetic in the spectator's eyes because they are small and doomed, unlike the birds who will winter over or go south. Their concealment in the grass concentrates the poet's attention on their song and helps her to consider them "a minor nation." As do Catholics, they celebrate a Mass – an enactment of a sacrifice with a promise of resurrection.

The second stanza continues to stress the insects' invisibility, again with sound replacing sight. An ordinance is the sign of a change in a phase of a religious ritual. There are changes in the crickets' mass, but they are too continuous and subtle to be perceived. The grace which the crickets seek or celebrate is gradual because it is part of the life process that they are rehearsing in their pulsing rhythm. In the seventh line, "pensive custom" is a more definite personification of the insects than the implicit personification of the earlier lines because it suggests a willed rather than an automatic action. This provides for a smooth transition to the enlargement of loneliness, because this idea clearly applies more to the speaker than to the crickets – if it doesn't apply exclusively to her – for the apparently thoughtless crickets have the companionship of their nation, whereas the contemplative speaker seems to be observing them in isolation. She is looking ahead to the loneliness of winter when she will not have even the companionship of nature and its small creatures.

In the word "antiquest," Dickinson invents a comparative form for the adjective "antique" – meaning "most antique." The crickets' mass seems most antique; that is – primeval, ancient, rooted in the very foundation of the world or of nature – at what is for Dickinson the moment of life's greatest intensity, noon. Other poems and passages of her letters reveal that noon often represented for her immortality or perfection. Also the juxtaposition of "noon" and "burning low" in these lines suggests the double nature of autumn; it is a season characterized by the brightness of high noon, but it is also the season where everything is "burning low" or "running down." The "spectral Canticle" is a ghostly religious song. Throughout the first three stanzas, the extensive use of *m*'s and *n*'s emphasizes the drowsiness of the late summer scene; these humming sounds are pensive, and like the crickets' song, they also "typify" repose – sleep and death.

The final stanza, as in other Dickinson poems on similar themes, moves from meditation back towards the physical scene. Its first line says that the grace or beauty of the world remains undiminished. "Furrow on the glow" is one of Dickinson's strangest figures of speech. A furrow is a physical depression or cleavage, usually made by plowing or shoveling earth. The glow is the general beauty of nature. She is creating with her fused image of earth and light a metaphorical picture to repeat the idea that this beauty is undiminished. The Druids were ancient pagan priests and prophets who sometimes practiced human sacrifice. A "druidic difference" would mean that this aspect of nature prophesies a coming magical and mysterious change, but this prospect of change enhances rather than mars nature. Also, there is an implication in these lines that nature and its small creatures are sacrificing themselves so that spring will come again with all of its abundance. Probably the simplest explanation of the "enhancement" is that it is due to our increased awareness of natural beauty, or of life itself, when we reflect on its coming disappearance, an idea which we have found in other Dickinson nature poems.

Despite their relative brevity, Dickinson's philosophical nature poems are often quite rich in meaning and connotation, and they can be re-read and re-experienced from many angles. This is certainly true for one of the shortest of her nature poems, "Presentiment – is that long Shadow – on the lawn" (764). Although there are personifications in this poem, the scene is real and resembles those in Dickinson's poems about seasonal change. In the long and slow-moving first line, the speaker is in a contemplative mood and sees the shadow of night move across a lawn – usually a place of domestic familiarity and comfort. Thought and experience seem to have occurred to her simultaneously. The formal word "indicative" and the generalized image of setting suns suggest the universality of her fear of the coming darkness and implicitly link darkness with death. The second two lines personify both the shadow of night and the grass. The darkness announces its approach with a formal detachment that resembles that of the quest in "As imperceptibly as Grief." The startled grass symbolizes the speaker's inner self as the darkness looms up suddenly. The tone of these lines is similar to the mood suggested by the listening landscape in "There's a certain Slant." The conclusion of the poem is deliberately abrupt, creating a dramatic tension between it and the slow contemplation of the first two lines. The speaker seems to be displaying cool resolve in the face of her shock, but we know nothing of the content of her thoughts. As do most of Dickinson's philosophical nature poems, this one shows the poet confronting mystery and fright with a combination of detachment and involvement.

Poetry, Art, and Imagination

A close examination of Emily Dickinson's letters and poems reveals many of her ideas, however brief, about poetry and on art in general, although most of her comments on art seem to apply chiefly to poetry. Many of her poems about poetic art are cast in allegorical terms that require guesswork and parallels from other of her poems for their interpretation. Although we are mostly concerned with the meaning and value of these poems, it is interesting and useful to note that the views which they express about aesthetics can fit into many significant theories about literature. For example, if one uses M. H. Abrams's convenient four-fold division of theories of literature: imitative (the poet re-creates reality); expressive (the poet expresses his inner feelings); pragmatic or affective (the poet seeks to move his audience); objective (the poet tries to construct self-contained works of art) – one finds comments and poems by Emily Dickinson that support all of these theories. She sees poems as artifacts giving permanence to the fading world and the mortal poet. She sees the poet achieving relief, personal identity, and communication through poetry. She sees the poet as a seer, yet she despairs of the poet's power to capture the final mysteries. She sees poetry as being able to open new visions and the heart of its hearers to perspectives and ideas which they otherwise miss. She distinguishes between the false and the genuine in poetry, and she chides herself for sometimes failing to make the distinction in her own work. Perhaps her chief emphasis is on the poet's building a world and gaining relief from his expressions, but it is easiest to discuss her relevant poems by moving from those treating the poet's relationship to audience and world to those treating the poet's inner world.

A number of Emily Dickinson's poems about poetry relating the poet to an audience probably have their genesis in her own frustrations and uncertainties about the publication of her own work. "This is my letter to the World" (441), written about 1862, the year of Emily Dickinson's greatest productivity, looks forward to the destiny of her poems after her death. The world that never wrote to her is her whole potential audience, or perhaps centrally its literary guardians, who will not recognize her talent or aspirations. She gives nature credit for her art and material in a half-apologetic manner, as if she were merely the carrier of nature's message. The fact that this message is committed to people who will come after her transfers the precariousness of her achievement to its future observers, as if they were somehow responsible for its neglect while she was alive. The plea that she be judged tenderly for nature's sake combines an insistence on imitation of nature as the basis of her art with a special plea for tenderness towards her own fragility or sensitivity; but poetry should be judged by how well the poet achieves his or her intention and not by the poem alone, as Emily Dickinson surely knew. This particular poem's generalization about her isolation—and its apologetic tone—tend towards the sentimental, but one can detect some desperation underneath the softness.

"If I shouldn't be alive" (182), an earlier poem than "This is my letter," is a firmer and more powerful statement of a similar idea, thematically richer and with a different twist. Here, the poet-speaker anticipates being cut off from the splendid presence of nature by death. The time of robins is the spring, a season of joyous rebirth, and the robin-as-singer is a fellow poet. The robin's red cravat is a witty, half-personifying touch, giving the bird something of that nervy artifice that sustained Dickinson. The memorial crumb serves to remind us of the poet's own slim spiritual nourishment by those who might have recognized and sustained her, as well as of the small needs of robins. Although the second stanza continues the conditional mood, it moves more decisively into the time when the poet will be dead; hence, it anticipates those brilliant later poems in which Emily Dickinson's speaker is dying or speaks from beyond the grave. The speaker's being fast asleep combines a note of relief with sadness at the loss of all feeling, leaving a striking shock effect for the climactic last two lines. If she is fast asleep, her efforts to speak through that sleep show the spirit at war with death—rebellious against the arrest of the voice with which she brought nature to expression and drew close to it. The image of the granite lip combines the sense of body as mere earth with body as the energy of life. Possibly, granite also suggests the potential power of her expression or even the strength of her unrecognized poems. The parallels to other Emily Dickinson poems about robins as poets, effortful expression as poetry, and poetry as a challenge to death support this interpretation. The consistency, rich suggestiveness, and emotional complexity of this poem mark it as a superior effort in what may, on a first reading, seem to be merely a casual vein.

"Essential Oils—are wrung" (675) is an equally personal but more allegorical comment on poems as a personal challenge to death. It is the same length as "This is my letter" and "If I shouldn't be alive," but its highly compressed images and action make it a richer poem. The central symbol here is attar (perfume) of roses, expanded to refer to some undefined essence of rose that will lie in a lady's drawer after her death. Surely this image represents Emily Dickinson's poems accumulating in her drawers, as they quite literally did, and finding an audience after her death, as they fortunately did. The wringing of the rose – "expressed" means pressed out or squeezed – combines the creative force of nature as represented by the sun, with the special suffering that sensitive and artistic souls undergo. The first stanza emphasizes creative suffering, and the second stanza emphasizes its marvelous result, but both stanzas combine the sense of suffering and creation. The general *rose* may represent ordinary nature or ordinary humanity, or perhaps merely the idea of natural beauty as opposed to its essence. The marvelous generality of this reference leads us gently but firmly from the attar of roses as an allegorical symbol to all beauty as a symbol of accomplishment. The poem is chiefly allegorical, therefore, but this transition and the stress on the dead lady give it a strange combination of allegorical mystery and concrete reality. The reference to decay reminds us of the physical fate of all things natural – that is, here she evokes a decay challenged by art. The essence of roses – the art as poetry that the lady has created out of nature through effort and suffering – makes nature *bloom* again, or live even more *vividly*, for those who read the poems. The lady lying in ceaseless rosemary may, at first, suggest a contrast between her dead body and the nature that continues around her, but when we recall that rosemary is the flower of remembrance and was often placed in coffins ("There's rosemary, that's for remembrance – pray you, love, remember," says Shakespeare's Ophelia, suggesting even more connotations for Emily Dickinson's line), we may see this phrase as suggesting a special immortality for the lady poet. Although the stress here is on creation through suffering, an aura of triumph and assurance permeates the poem.

"I died for Beauty – but was scarce" (449) should remind us that Emily Dickinson said that John Keats was one of her favorite poets, and it is likely that the poem is partly a simplification and variation on the theme, or at least echoes the conclusion, of his "Ode on a Grecian Urn": "Beauty is truth, truth beauty – that is all/ Ye know on earth, and all ye need to know." The poem's speaker looks back from death to life and laments the cessation of speech – quite probably representing poetic communication. Here, however, rather than our finding a wistful, desperate, or self-assured struggle for posthumous expression, we discover a dignified and almost peaceful resignation. The emphasis here on beauty, truth, and lips correlates to themes about poetry elsewhere in Emily Dickinson, just as the covering up of names on tombstones correlates to her concerns about surviving because of the immortality of her poems. The strangely abrupt use of "adjusted" for the dead suggests a struggle against and a resignation to death. The mutual tenderness of the two buried figures shows lonely souls longing for company, and the use of "failed" for the more normal "died" suggests that the defeat of their art and thought contributed to their deaths, which we are to see as sacrifices. These terms also reflect Emily Dickinson's sense that the novel authenticity of her poems kept people from appreciating them. The mind-teasing problem of equating truth and beauty is perhaps as great in Emily Dickinson's poetry as it is in Keats's poem. One simple interpretation would be that accuracy, penetration, and ordering of vision, at least for the artist, create beauty, and that such efforts are painful almost to the point of self-sacrifice. The kinsmen in the last stanza seem comfortable and cheered by each other, though still separated, but the stilling of their lips by moss and the covering of their names suggest Emily Dickinson's feelings that her struggles for beauty and truth were unavailing in their accessibility—if not in their quality. Nevertheless, the resignation of the poem maintains a fine dignity, and the poem as a whole creates a charming variation on Emily Dickinson's treatments of voices from beyond death and of survival through poetry. Of course, this poem need not be interpreted as a comment on Emily Dickinson's situation as a poet. One can read it merely as a fantasy about the light which death throws on the life struggles of sensitive souls and on the question of their rewards for their struggles, but correlation with other poems supports our interpretation and enriches the suggestiveness of the details.

"Publication—is the Auction" (709) is Emily Dickinson's best-known statement of her feelings about publication, but the poem should be read as a partial and complicated version of her attitudes. The unusual stress on publication as auction (rather than mere sale) may reflect resentment that poets must compete by adjusting their gifts and vision to public taste to earn profitable attention. Poverty would justify such a shaping of skills for the market, but that would strain the poet's integrity. This interpretation, however, may be excessively biographical because of its stress on Emily Dickinson's need for artistic independence, but it is also possible that she was chiefly rationalizing her fear of seeking a public and attributing a white innocence to the seclusion which her fears compelled, or it may be that she is only emphasizing the unworldly purity of art. The poet's garret stands for a worldly poverty which she never experienced, but it does accurately symbolize her isolation. The idea of not investing purity continues the economic metaphor and gives the poem something of a snobbish tone. The two "hims" of the third stanza may refer to God and the poet *or* they may refer to the poet in two guises – as an inspired person and as a craftsman. (It is possible that the poet here is analogous to God becoming man.) The last six lines, switching to a scornful second person, suggest that the poet as human spirit is even more precious than the beauty of nature or the words of God and that reducing his words to a commercial level is blasphemy. The insistent and somewhat wooden trochaic rhythm of the poem enhances and enriches its scorn and determination, but it also communicates some uncertainty about the viewpoint, as if Emily Dickinson were protesting too much. Nevertheless, the curiously mixed diction of the poem, combining commercial, religious, and aesthetic terms gives dignified pride to its anger.

When Emily Dickinson writes about the relationship of poet and audience more distinctly from the viewpoint of the living and with the poet's elevated status in mind, her assertions tend to be less ambiguous, her tone either reverent or triumphant, and her eyes almost equally on what the poet communicates as on the fact of communication. Such poems include "This was a Poet – It is That" (448), "I reckon – when I count at all" (569), and "A Word made Flesh is seldom" (1651). "This was a Poet – It is That" (448), an almost explosively joyous poem, probably celebrates the triumph of some other poet, the speaker basking in reflected glory. The poem combines an analysis of the poet's methods, her visionary power, and her achievement of permanence. The amazing sense and "attar so immense" stress how novelty and compressed expression give new significance to transient beauty and thereby create both envy and surprise about one's own limited vision. The idea that poetry helps us see the familiar freshly by presenting it strangely or with novelty is at least as old as Aristotle's *Poetics*. The third stanza stresses the pictorial quality of poems, as one might expect from an image-maker like Dickinson – no matter how generalized her own picturing. The somewhat puzzling notion that the poet entitles others to poverty may be an ironic pun on "entitling," as giving others a low status, but more likely it means that they can endure their own poverty because they can *borrow* the poet's riches, although both meanings may be intended. The last stanza seems to refer back to the poet a little cryptically and not to those who suffer poverty. The poet's portion is so deep and permanent that he is unconscious of it and will feel no resentment about how much others take from him. Of course, poets are usually pleased and not even unconsciously resentful at lending their vision, so one assumes that Emily Dickinson's overstatement is designed to suggest some strangely personal apprehension about feeding on the spirit of poets – possibly a serious or playful concern with an emotional parasitism in herself, or even in those who will not recognize her ability.

"I reckon – when I count at all" (569) echoes themes from "This was a Poet" but is even more extravagant. Here, the subject is poets in general, who head her list of precious things – before nature and heaven. She then decides that since the work of poets includes nature and heaven, she can dispense with them. Poets are *all* – insofar as their work contains the body of nature and heaven and, by implication, all of experience. Unlike "natural" summers, the summers of poets do not fade, and their suns are brighter than the sun itself. So far, interpretation is easy; in contrast, the last five lines of this poem are more condensed and difficult. The "further heaven" probably means the heaven beyond life – as opposed to the earthly one that poets create or capture. The line "Be Beautiful as they prepare" probably means turning out to be as beautiful as the one that poets create for their worshippers (readers). The last two lines would then mean that it is impossible to imagine a real heaven that could match the heaven that poets have already given us. Emily Dickinson here gives the poet or the poetic imagination a status greater than God's. This extravagance can be attributed to her need for reassurance about the richness of her own narrow living space or of her own creations, or a combination of the two. An equally extravagant poem in which the poet is made superior to God is "This is a Blossom of the Brain" (945); here, poetry is given traits like Emily Dickinson's own shyness, the vitality of nature, and the promise of reproducing its own kind. The mystery of the poetic process and the rare recognition given to it echo Emily Dickinson's feelings about her neglect and isolation as a poet and imply that poets receive more than enough compensation for this neglect by the world. More playful and perhaps less desperate than "I reckon—when I count," this poem may be taken as a deliberate extravaganza or a serious assertion of Emily Dickinson's feelings about art as a religion and her participation in it.

In "A Word made Flesh is seldom" (1651), a Bible text is woven into another assertion of the poet's godlike nature. Here, the first stanza seems to imply that the Christ of the Bible is difficult to know but that something like Him is more available elsewhere and that the private act of securing it gives us joy suitable to our personal identities. That something else seems to be the *word* as spoken by the whole-spirited poet, which is as immortal as God. The speaking of this word seems to satisfy both speaker and audience. If God could dwell among us as flesh, his condescension would need to be extraordinary to match that of the poet. This poem exists only in a transcript, and its original punctuation is perhaps distorted, for it seems to require a question mark at the end, which would make it imply that language brings spirit into flesh more than Christ did.

In several poems, Emily Dickinson stresses the inner world of poetry as the source of joy, identity, and growth. One of the best of these poems is "I dwell in Possibility" (657), perhaps not immediately recognizable as a poem about poetry. Although possibility might refer to an openness to all experience, the contrast of this dwelling place with prose, the emphasis on an interior world which shuts out ordinary visitors so it may welcome others, and the idea of a captured and concentrated paradise virtually guarantees that the subject is the poetic imagination transforming the world and creating objects of satisfaction to the speaker. The windows and doors allow everything the poet needs to enter, while holding out the eyes and presence of intruders. Gambrels, which are slanting roof cones, are transferred from this house of the imagination to the house of the sky, which represents nature or the universe, suggesting the mergence of the poet's inner and outer worlds. The second stanza shows the speaker having the best of both worlds without suffering exposure, which well suits the assured and almost arrogant tone. Once exclusions are firmly established, the tone relaxes, and the slight harshness of the first two stanzas gives over to tenderness in the last stanza, where the parallelism of visitors and occupation allows a secure relaxation. The tender paradox of a wide spread to narrow hands welcomes the paradise of nature and imagination into the poet's spirit and work and emphasizes how greatness of spirit makes a small space infinitely large. A remarkable example of Emily Dickinson's fusion of the concrete with the abstract, and the large with the small, this poem also bears the peculiar signature of her pride in withdrawal, though its boastfulness does not identify the poet with God, as in the two poems just discussed.

A similar but less boastful poem is the very beautiful but rarely anthologized "Alone, I cannot be" (298), where the emphasis is entirely on the arrival of visionary messengers to a self that does not seem to need to ward off intrusions. The fact that these visitors are "recordless" associates the poem with the evanescence of poetry more than with its permanence, as does another interesting variant on the theme of imagination capturing reality, the brilliant but also infrequently anthologized "The Tint I cannot take—is best" (627), which shows some familiar traits of Emily Dickinson's view of the poetic imagination but also severely reverses some of them. Here, the emphasis is on the impossibility of art's capturing the essence of precious experience, especially of nature and of spiritual triumphs. The poem echoes the fleeing grandeur of such experiences but implies that unsuccessful attempts to capture them create something of their preciousness. Rather than asserting that heaven will scarcely equal these experiences or the expression of them, as in "I reckon—when I count at all," this poem's conclusion insists that only beyond death will we capture or experience them in all their essence. Still, the arrogance assigned to the dying attributes greatness of soul to the imaginative person. This poem may have a repressed note of anger, perhaps the other side of the inflated joy with which Emily Dickinson often treats the poet's recreation of his world.

Poetic creation is also viewed sadly in "The Missing All—prevented Me" (985), one of those poems whose subject seems quite indeterminate. Perhaps "the missing all" is a beloved person, a solid religious faith, an acceptable society, or a high status in the social world. In any case, its absence turns the poet's head downward to total concentration on her work—surely her poems. The ironic comments on such unlikely things as the world tearing loose or the sun going out emphasize the scope of her loss and the importance of the effort which she makes to compensate for it. The pretended indifference to the world expressed in the conclusion makes the poetic process all-important but also somehow tragic. The world created by the imagination is not characterized here – as in "I dwell in Possibility" and other poems – and the poem ends with a regretful grandeur.

Although many of the poems discussed here comment on the poet's craft, other poems make it their central subject. "We play at Paste" (320) can be viewed as a comment on spiritual or personal growth, but it is probably chiefly concerned with the growth of a poet's craftsmanship. The poem provides a fine illustration of the allegorical method in a short poem. "Paste" refers to artificial jewelry. Adults do not play with or at the process of making artificial jewelry as a preparation for making real jewelry, nor do they usually regard themselves with scorn when they look back at artificial playthings and adornments. The scene as presented and the strong emotions associated with it are not realistic as given. Thus the paste, the real pearl, and the maker's hands are not ordinary symbols. Rather, they are allegorical symbols (or images or emblems). If the speaker, distancing herself slightly and making herself one of a group by the use of "we," drops an artificial – that is, inauthentic – creation and judges herself ill for making it, objects of art – poems for Emily Dickinson – seem the most likely subject. In the second stanza, she gains the equilibrium of maturity and looks back to see that her earlier creations prepared her for the later and more genuine ones. "New hands" emphasizes the growth of creative skill and perhaps extends the change from artistry to the whole person. The emphasis on tactics, and several sound effects in the second stanza, especially the echoing hard *k* sounds, again emphasize the effort and precision of craftsmanship. (Alliteration is particularly effective in the first stanza.) This emphasis gives the poem a feeling of crisp restraint, almost an amused detachment, quite unlike the exaltation in poems that celebrate the poet as visionary.

Poems somewhat more specific about the poet's tactics include "Tell all the Truth but tell it slant" (1129), "The thought beneath so slight a film" (210), and "A Spider sewed at Night" (1138), but they tend to be more superficial and less developed, however immediately charming. "Tell all the Truth but tell it slant" (1129) immediately reminds us of all the indirections in Emily Dickinson's poems: her condensations, vague references, allegorical puzzles, and perhaps even her slant rhymes. The idea of artistic success lying in circuit – that is, in complication and suggestiveness – goes well with the stress on amazing sense and jarring paradoxes which we have seen her express elsewhere. But the notion that truth is too much for our infirm delight is puzzling. On the very personal level for Emily Dickinson's mind, "infirm delight" would correspond to her fear of experience and her preference for anticipation over fulfillment. For her, truth's surprise had to remain in the world of imagination. However, superb surprise sounds more delightful than frightening. Lightning indeed is a threat because of its physical danger, and its accompanying thunder is scary, but it isn't clear how dazzling truth can blind us – unless it is the deepest of spiritual truths. We can, however, simplify these lines to mean that raw experience needs artistic elaboration to give it depth and to enable us to contemplate it. The contemplation theme is reasonably convincing but the poem coheres poorly and uses an awed and apologetic tone to cajole us into disregarding its faults. A similar idea is more lucid in the epigrammatic "The thought beneath so slight a film" (210) because here the idea of obscurity is connected to the necessity of great effort for good artistic perception, which links this poem to her praise for "amazing sense" and makes her shyness before the beautiful but frightening mountains symbolic of universal experiences.

In "A Spider sewed at Night" (1138), Emily Dickinson seems to delight in the spider's isolation, determination, and structural success. The short-line rhyming triplets imitate the spider's almost automatic thrusts. The poem says that no one quite knows what the spider is making, but his own knowledge satisfies him. He has built so well that his structures appear permanent. But the poem is strangely open-ended. Without the wistfulness or apology of other poems on art, and with a more distanced boastfulness, this poem leaves the possibility that the spider's web will be quickly swept away. If so, his triumph was entirely in his own mind, and we know nothing of its ultimate significance. Perhaps the spider's constructive process is an analogue for Emily Dickinson's own power as a poet, which promises a kind of permanence which the spider can't achieve. The "ruff of dame" could be a mere decoration for Emily Dickinson herself, and the "shroud of gnome" could refer to Emily Dickinson's signing herself "your gnome" to Higginson – possibly as an answer to his complaints about her gnomic (condensed to the point of obscurity) expression. Such negative connotations would stand in opposition to the poem's assertations about trying to build something immortal. Whatever ironies this poem contains may have been unconscious or slyly intended. It is a fine example of how an Emily Dickinson poem that is lucid on the surface can be looked at from various angles and given nuances or even about-faces of interpretation.

A few other poems on art and poetry deserve brief treatment here. In "I cannot dance upon my Toes" (326), ballet seems to be a metaphor for poetry. Her poor training stands for her unconventional expression, her inability to follow established forms, and her acknowledgment that she cannot express what she wants contradicts the exuberance of other poems and matches the sense of limitation in yet others. Here, the full house of her spirit doesn't seem to display the fairest visitors, but that is probably because an insensitive audience wants a flashy performance. She probably wrote this poem as a secret reply to Higginson's complaints about the awkwardness of her poems. In "It dropped so low–in my Regard" (747), Emily Dickinson is probably echoing themes of "We play at Paste." From what seems an even more mature perspective, she now looks at an earlier creation and criticizes herself for not seeing how unworthy of her best it was. "To hear an Oriole sing" (526) may be chiefly about problems of perception, but it can also be interpreted as a comment on poetry in which Emily Dickinson takes an outside perspective on the innerness of man's response to successful art. The commonness or divinity of the singing depends on the sensitivity of the audience. Reference to the tune's being in the tree may be a covert comment on the conventions of art as opposed to the force of the inspired poet. Perhaps Emily Dickinson is revolting against the dead ear of someone who found her singing flat. In "I would not paint–a picture" (505), Emily Dickinson pretends that her delight in art is more that of an observer than a creator, but as an observer she is filled with life by poetry and art. Perhaps it substitutes differently for the missing all. But as she concludes by pretending to reject her role as poet, she reveals that, for her, the creation and the enjoyment of poetry are fused, or it may be that she merely–for the time being–wishes that the joy of creation could match and merge with the joy of appreciation.

Friendship, Love, and Society

In an enigmatic four-line poem beginning "That Love is all there is" (1765), Emily Dickinson implies that love is impossible to define and that it transcends the need for definition. She seems to be suggesting that we can recognize love either because it fits our souls perfectly or because we can endure the suffering which it brings. She does not present these alternatives; rather, her lines make these alternate interpretations possible. Such ambiguity permeates her love poems, in which fulfillment is often accompanied by loss. With the exception of the Master letters, whose intended recipient we cannot identify, and her later letters to Judge Otis P. Lord, we have nothing by Dickinson which we could call love letters. However, her early correspondence with Susan Gilbert reveals an awareness that the fulfillment of love might be disappointing. Later in life, Emily Dickinson wrote to Samuel Bowles: "My Friends are my 'estate,' " and still later she declared that letters feel to her like immortality because they contain the mind "without corporeal friend." These statements reinforce our sense that perhaps she preferred an imagined consummation of love to any physical reality, and that she sometimes treasured friendship held at a distance more than the actual presence of friends. However, such psychological speculation should be used carefully in interpreting her poems.

There is a blend of love and friendship in a few of Dickinson's poems. Many of her elegies for family members and friends express love and yet do not lament lost loves. Several poems which are addressed to girlfriends have a romantic tinge, but these are not very good. However, there are some poems about dear people who seem to be regarded more as beloved friends than as objects of romantic ardor. In Dickinson's love poems proper, it is possible to distinguish between romantically passionate poems and poems in which there is a curious physical detachment. In this second type, the beloved person sometimes seems so exalted that it is difficult for the reader to see the beloved as an object of desire to the poem's speaker. But the bulk of Dickinson's love poems are certainly not cold, detached, and ethereal. Circumstances and fears may have kept her from physical fulfillment, but the images and actions of many of her love poems are determinedly passionate.

Three popular Dickinson poems about lost friends are similar in length and style. These are "My life closed twice before its close" (1732), "I never lost as much but twice" (49), and "Elysium is as far as to" (1760). Like the first two of Dickinson's poems about poetry that we examined in the preceding section, the first two of these poems are petulant and urgent in tone. "My life closed twice" is less colloquial and concrete than the other two, but equally witty. This poem exists only in a transcript, so we have no idea when it was written. Although heaven and hell are mentioned, and although some critics see the parting as deaths, the parting is probably not the result of death. Probably the subject is the departure of dear friends who are expected to be long lost or forever absent. The reference to life's closing shows Dickinson's turning a statement about a death-like feeling into a metaphor. Something closing before the final close suggests both an overwhelming extinction of the senses and a general collapse, as if the speaker could feel nothing but her ecstasy and grief. She seems to be folding up like a flower. The immortality that may reveal another experience as inexpressible as these two emotions lies beyond death. Life can bring to her no more profound an experience, and her tone is exultant at having encountered something ultimate in life. The description of parting as being both "heaven" and "hell" is brilliantly witty; parting increases the value of the departing person because parting makes us suffer terribly. The idea that suffering and friendship produce an experience almost more rewarding than we can hope to find in heaven parallels Dickinson's celebration of art.

"I never lost as much but twice" (49) is a fine example of Dickinson's jocular blasphemy combined with a quite serious theme. We could place this poem under the headings of death and religion as easily as under friendship. The fact that earlier losses were *in* (literally *to*) the sod surely refers to the death of friends. The contrast of such losses to a present loss by the use of "but . . . that" indicates that this loss is not to death, but it is just as bad and perhaps harder to explain and accept. The descending angels must have brought new friends. The reference to these friends as "store" suggests that they are a treasure and prepares us for the outburst against God as being both a burglar and a banker. The witty placing of "Father!" after these terms strengthens the accusation that God is playing by unfair rules, and the last line shows an abrupt and stubborn resentment against God's cheating. The manuscript of this poem can be dated at about 1858, a number of years after the deaths of Leonard Humphrey and

Benjamin Newton, and yet it is possible that Dickinson is looking back at their deaths and comparing them to the present departure or faithlessness of a friend or a beloved man.

"Elysium is as far as to" (1760), evidently written quite late in Dickinson's life, is a more general poem than the two just discussed, but, rather curiously, it has a stronger sense of physical scene and of the presence of people than either of them. It is true that neither a specific room nor people are described, and that the room may be a symbol of a condition of life, but possibly the very generality of the situation has allowed Dickinson to create more of a scene than she usually attempts. This poem is more complicated than it may at first appear, and it echoes themes from "My life closed twice." "Elysium" is a Latin word for *heaven*. The heaven described is a state of emotional elevation resulting from anticipation of a friend's achieving great happiness, a happiness intensified by the risk of doom. The fortitude of soul may belong to the speaker of the poem as well as to the friend. If this is true, Dickinson is being made happy both by her admiration of her friend's fortitude and by the joy of sharing such endurance with her friend. Similarly, the anticipated arrival may refer to the friend's awaiting his or her fate, or to the speaker's awaiting the arrival and the fate of the friend. The fine restraint of the poem's conclusion, which reinforces the sense of a hushed atmosphere, implies a favorable outcome for the situation, but it is difficult to tell if it directs our attention more to the friend or to the speaker. The combination of such Latinate terms as *Elysium* and *fortitude* with such Anglo-Saxon words as *doom* and *door*, a striking trait of Dickinson's style, adds to the forcefulness and verbal music of this poem.

Fears of love that Emily Dickinson may have felt do not make her much different from the rest of us. Exactly what combination of character and circumstances kept her from a romantic union we will never know. Many of her poems relating to passion and love reflect intense anxiety, but we should not stress their possible abnormality any further than the clarification of these poems requires. This allows us to recognize the unusual in her feelings and possible experiences while still being able to relate them to our own feelings. First, we will consider her poems that are burdened with anxiety, next go on to those in which anxiety is mixed with renunciation, and finally look at those in which the choice of love creates some kind of spiritual union or faith, either on earth or in heaven. But we should remember that these categories often overlap.

"In Winter in my Room" (1670) is surely Dickinson's most explicit treatment of her fear and mixed feelings about love and sex—if we dare to call a poem so purely symbolic a fantasy explicit. The poem exists only in a transcript, and so it cannot be assigned even approximately to a period of Dickinson's life, but it very possibly is a product of her earlier mature years, her early thirties. There do not seem to be reasonable alternatives to the view that the worm-turned-snake is the male sexual organ moving toward a state of excitement and making a claim on the sexuality and life of the speaker. Psychoanalytic theory and speculation about the sexual knowledge of reclusive virgins are no more helpful than is common sense in making this interpretation. Traditionally, snakes are symbols of evil invading an Eden, and snakes in Emily Dickinson's poems sometimes represent a puzzling fearfulness in nature, just as Eden often represents a pure innocence which might be spoiled by the intrusion of a lover. Such symbolism does not contradict the sexual symbolism. Rather, viewing the snake as a symbol of evil, in addition to seeing it as a sexual symbol, helps us to see how ambivalent is the speaker's attitude toward the snake—to see how she relates to it with a mixture of feelings, with mingled fear, attraction, and revulsion. In the first stanza, the speaker appears almost childlike, and the worm-snake is a minor threat that she can control. In the second stanza, the creature appears in a changed and terrifying guise. The transformation seems unexpected, but the snake bears a sign (the old string) that he is the creature that she once tried to control. In the third stanza, she admits to the fear and insincerity that make her call the snake "fair." But her attraction cannot be denied. The statement that the snake fathomed her thoughts implies admiration for its power, and the description of its rhythmic movements reveals more admiration than repulsion. The rhythmic projection of the snake may refer even to the speaker's mental processes, as well as to the snake's actual motion. The last stanza clearly distinguishes between her two encounters with the worm-snake. At the second meeting, she gives no thought to controlling or pacifying him; she runs until she evades him, but the fact that she had hoped to hold him off by her staring somehow mutes the terror, possibly by implying an unconscious recognition of what the snake stands for and of how valid are its claims. It is difficult to say just why the concluding statement, "this was a dream," seems essential to the poem. Without it, we would easily recognize the fantasy element. Certainly the next-to-the-last line—"I set me down"—is too unassertive for a conclusion. Possibly the last line is both an acknowledgment of the unconscious source of the fantasy and an insistence on its being taken very seriously. Perhaps Dickinson is saying here that dreams can't lie.

The much debated poem "I started Early–Took my Dog" (520) has been more popular than "In Winter in my Room." Many critics take it to be about death or about threatening nature, but we prefer to side with those who think it is about fearful anticipations of love or passion. The coy tone of the poet suggests that she may be taking refuge from a symbolic experience involving combined sexual attraction and threat by adopting a child-like attitude. In the first two stanzas, the speaker visits the sea of experience, accompanied by her protective dog. Dogs in Dickinson's poems are often symbols of the self, partly stemming from her many years of companionship with her setter, Carlo. The mermaids in their mysterious beauty may symbolize the repression of the speaker's femininity, in which case the more helpful frigates may represent an urge to accept herself as she is. The speaker's calling herself "Mouse" reveals her timidity. In the third stanza, the threatening sea merges with the threat of a man who may be able to move her emotionally and, hence, prepares her for flight. The climbing of the sea up over her protective clothing (apron, belt, and bodice are particularly domestic) becomes almost explicitly sexual when linked with the image of dew being eaten. A drop of dew which becomes part of the sea would lose its identity. This image recalls images of pleasurable engulfment in other Dickinson poems, but here it is clearly threatening. The speaker flees and the man-sea pursues. Silver heel and shoe filled with pearl add aesthetic charm to the sexual threat. The last stanza shows the pursuing sea-lover disregarding the social surroundings. The town is probably a symbol of the social conventions that reinforced Dickinson's own timidity and gave her something to fall back on when she was overwhelmed by fears. The mighty look of the sea resembles the explicitly acknowledged power of the snake in "In Winter in my Room"; and, as in that poem, this one ends with a kind of stand-off, as if the threatening world of love and passion were recognized by the poet and carefully distanced. As we have noted, other interpretations of this poem are quite arguable, partly because the tone of the poem is so ambivalent. But the mixture of fear and attraction with a defensive playfulness seems to support our view. The poem is built with great care, but its artifice may make its effect less powerful and revealing than the effect obtained from the starker symbolism of "In Winter in my Room."

Dickinson's poems about the renunciation of a proffered love tempt readers and critics to seek biographical interpretations. Many early critics took these poems too literally; they assumed them to be reports of scenes in which Emily Dickinson refused the love offers of a married man, while offering him assurances of her peculiar faith and her hope for reunion after death. Such interpretations probably do not reflect the reality behind these poems. In all likelihood the poems present fantasies which would have emotionally satisfied Dickinson more than her actual lonely renunciation did. These fantasies provide dramatic plots for cathartic poems.

"I cannot live with You" (640) is probably her most popular poem of this kind. This painful and tense poem is grammatically difficult and deserves more space than we can give it. Careful study of its images, progression, and grammar would be a valuable exercise in understanding Dickinson's poetic techniques. The speaker addresses a beloved man from whom she is permanently separated in life. To live with him would be life, she says, implying that she is dead without him. Paradoxically, the only life together possible for them will be when they are in the grave. Two stanzas representing the dead as broken chinaware poignantly and reluctantly praise death over the apparent wholeness of life. In the third stanza, the speaker imagines death scenes in which she would prefer to comfort her dying lover rather than to die with him. She is also reluctant to die with him because that would give her the horrible shock of seeing her lover eclipse Jesus and dim heaven itself. The lover is like God, and love is superior to heaven (just as Dickinson can find the artist's heaven superior to God's). For two stanzas, beginning with "They'd judge Us—How," the speaker's attention moves to the unconventional nature of her love. People, perhaps representing God, would condemn the lovers for breaking some social or ethical tradition. Perhaps the lover is married, a minister, or both, or perhaps the service of heaven is a more general stewardship. The speaker's desperation now threatens the poem's coherence. The fact that the lover saturates her sight (echoing the eclipse of Jesus' face) makes her not care about heaven and its values. Furthermore (perhaps), his being lost (damned) would make her glad to give up her salvation in order to share his fate, and were he saved, any possible separation would be, for her, the same thing as hell. The last stanza does not connect logically to what precedes it. The poem seems to return to the world of the living, and it seems to be saying that the lovers' complicated prospects and perhaps their shocking unconventionality make the future so uncertain that they can depend on only the small sustenance of their present narrow communication and tortured hopes. The short lines and abruptly rocking movement of the poem echo their struggles.

"My Life had stood – a Loaded Gun" (754) is an even more difficult poem, ending with what is probably the most difficult stanza in any of Dickinson's major poems. Defiantly joyous in tone – at least on the surface – until its almost tragic final stanza, this poem presents an allegory about the pursuit of personal identity and fulfillment through love, and yet it is quite possible that the joy of the poem conceals a satire directed back against the speaker, a satire which may be the chief clue to the meaning of the last stanza. The life of the person as a loaded gun probably stands for all of her potential as a person, perhaps creatively as well as sexually. Her being claimed by the owner suggests subservience to a lover as the only way to achieve selfhood – a stereotype of woman's position in society. Her powers are released by the owner-lover, and the landscape of the world rewards her by acknowledging her expression of his power. The Vesuvian face suggests the speaker's sexual release being read into the landscape, and perhaps also the joy on the face of the lover, who remains curiously uncharacterized throughout the poem. The nighttime scene in which the speaker-as-gun takes more pleasure in protecting the owner than in sleeping with him (the grammar makes it possible to conclude that she has not slept with him, or to conclude that she enjoys protecting him more than sharing his bed) gives to the sexual element a strange ambiguity, because she seems equally joyous at resuming her daytime role of releasing destruction. Just what she kills is difficult to say, but the yellow eye and emphatic thumb are sinister enough to suggest that the speaker is aware of something demeaning in her dependent, destructive, and self-denigrating role. The poem's joy, or pretended joy, dissolves in the last stanza. The speaker thinks that she may outlive the owner-lover, but she knows that in some sense she cannot. These lines appear to contradict one another completely. The qualification that the speaker-gun has "but the power to kill" undercuts the earlier celebration of her power.

Evidently her celebrating that power as something good is a delusion. The power to kill, then, does not give identity, and its satisfactions are misleading. The last line presents an absolute paradox. The speaker-gun's inability to die will make the owner-lover outlive her. The paradox can be resolved by assuming that *die* may have a special meaning. Quite possibly to die means to realize some kind of consummation or identity, including the sexual – to achieve the self by a discharge of energy more real than the act of totally serving another. If this is the case, the speaker-gun has never really lived and so the owner-lover must outlive her. Of course the specific fantasies that lie behind the poem are unrecoverable. The poem has been interpreted as a comment on the speaker's relationship with God or on her activity as a poet. Individual beliefs about psychological and sexual motives and symbols can influence the interpretation of this poem. Our interpretation of "In Winter in my Room" and "I started Early – took my Dog" may reinforce our view of this poem.

Although "There came a Day at Summer's full" (322) contains some painful elements, the kinds of fantasies that we have just examined receive a much more gentle, exuberant, and joyful treatment in it. The resignation seen in "I cannot live with You" here turns into a prelude to a triumph beyond death for a love that could not succeed on earth. This poem presents a more visual scene than both "I cannot live with You" and "My Life had stood – a Loaded Gun," but it is still clearly an allegorical scene, and there is no reason to assume that Emily Dickinson ever had an experience like the one it presents. The action occurs on the day of the summer solstice, usually June 21st, the longest day of the year, when the promise of spring, symbolically, if not literally, becomes the fullness of summer. The first two stanzas stress the spiritual triumph of this day for the speaker, which overshadows the fullness of nature and places her and her lover in a world entirely apart from it. She seems to be expressing surprise that nature carries on in its usual way without paying any attention to her great experience. Love is so intrinsic to their companionship that speaking of their love would be a kind of profanation, just as the idea that priestly garbs are essential to sacraments is a profanation. (Nature is brushed aside, and love substitutes both for it and for religion.) The lovers, excluding the world, become their own church and hold their own communion, an act which will prepare them for heaven. However, they are destined to part, but their parting will intensify their relationship. Still maintaining silence, they exchange crucifixes, which seem to substitute for wedding rings, perhaps guaranteeing union through suffering. Their betrothal–depending on how we interpret the grammar of the last stanza–will overcome the grave and give them a marriage in heaven. Probably these lines are saying that their suffering is the sufficient troth that will ensure their marriage. The last line can be read as modifying "marriage," or as describing their general troth and suffering. In this poem, the element of conflict and suffering is held in balance with, or made subservient to, the triumphs of love. The lovers' rapt attention to each other and their disregard of the world contribute to the poem's tone of affirmation. The conflicts dramatized in this poem lack the ambiguity of "I started Early–Took my Dog" and "My Life had stood–a Loaded Gun," where the sexual elements probably puzzled even the author-speaker. Dickinson seems to confront her longings more straightforwardly when she sees them as simple matters of separation.

In "If you were coming in the Fall" (511), Dickinson treats love-separation and hope for earthly or heavenly reunion in an even more straightforward manner. The poem's domestic images show Dickinson using the everyday and trivial to describe strong emotions, but these images also serve to suggest that the speaker is used to her situation. It is a part of her daily life, and she is able to take a detached, but not quite flippant, attitude towards it. The stress on geography implies a physical separation–she never sees the beloved. The image of a fly and the image of time as balls of yarn–these show that she is occupied by routine tasks while she is thinking about the beloved. In the third and fourth stanzas, she grows extravagant, imagining how easy it would be to wait out centuries, or to pass through death, if either would bring her the lover. The counting by hand and the tossed rind (which represents the act of dying) continue the domestic images, not only unifying the poem but reducing the vastness of time and death to something controllable. The last stanza says that since she has no idea how long she must wait for him, she is goaded like a person around whom a bee hovers. The goblin nature of the bee lends mystery and ambivalence to whatever she must suffer to be with her lover. The poem employs four parallel stanzas before its concluding fifth stanza, but rather than creating monotony these build up a pleasant suspense that is given a concentrated expression in the end, where one also senses a concentration of restiveness. This effective conclusion is quite different from the endings of the poems just discussed, and it helps to demonstrate that Dickinson uses a variety of tones and methods in her treatment of similar material.

We move now to a number of love poems in which the reality of consummation, in addition to the choice of a beloved, is more explicit and emphatic, but we should remember that disappointment, renunciation, and irony against the self may always lurk beneath the surface. "Mine—by the Right of the White Election!" (528), which is very popular with readers and anthologists, almost seems a concentration of the conclusions of her love poems. Gaining extraordinary emphasis from its lack of a main verb (which would logically appear in an implied statement such as "He is . . ."), its insistent parallelism, and its concentrated metaphors, this poem declares that a beloved person is the speaker's possession, although he is now physically absent and will be closer—if that is possible—only after death. "White Election" may refer to Emily Dickinson's typically white garb and to her sexual innocence. The prison is her isolation that cannot hide her dedication. "Vision" and "Veto," which critics sometimes use as caption descriptions of Dickinson's view of love, or even of her poetry as a whole, suggest the presence of love in the spirit intensified by the forbidding of its physical presence. Only the "grave's repeal" will give permanent confirmation to what she already somehow possesses. Although this poem has considerable appeal because of its exuberance and technical virtuosity, its somewhat hysterical tone may lessen its effectiveness. The poet's frenetic attitude may influence even our perception of the poem's central purpose, which is to celebrate the possession of a beloved person, by leading us to suspect that considerable doubt may lie behind its overly emphatic affirmation. The poem can also be interpreted as an affirmation of the speaker's assurance of God's choice of her for salvation ("white election"). We prefer our interpretation largely because the phrase "Vision and . . . Veto" echoes Dickinson's sense of an enforced separation from a beloved person.

Possession of an infinitely worshipped person is presented in a different manner in "Of all the Souls that stand create" (664). The subterfuge of life which we put behind at death may refer to the physical elusiveness of the beloved person, to the artificiality of social life, or to both. The notion of separating the before and the after, and the description of life as a process of shifting sands, suggest the greater reality and stability of the afterlife. The concentrated last four lines show an overlapping of the physical and the spiritual. Life is presented as being mistlike in that it obscures real values. One beloved person, a mere atom in all creation, will stand out from every other human being, but will be visible only as a spirit. The speaker rejoices in her preference as if it were an indication of her own superiority. Unlike many of her religiously oriented love poems, this one does no violence to Christian doctrine in its view of life, death, and love. This conventional set of mind contributes to the poem's detachment, for although other of her love poems insist that reunion will occur only in heaven, they still reflect a strong sense of concrete physical presence. Because this poem is so detached, as a result of its being intellectually demonstrative rather than personally dramatic, some readers may find the beloved figure somewhat vague and fatherly.

That Dickinson's hopes for becoming close to a lover fluctuated dramatically at times can be demonstrated by moving from "Of all the Souls that stand create" to two such different poems as "Wild Nights–Wild Nights!" (249) and "The Soul selects her own Society" (303), both among her best and most popular poems. In "Wild Nights–Wild Nights!" Dickinson expresses passionate longing for a loving physical intimacy with the specific person she is addressing. The scene is presented metaphorically and its water images remind us of details in "I started Early–Took my Dog" and "There came a Day at Summer's full." In "Wild Nights–Wild Nights!" she desires a fulfillment that in those poems is feared or looked forward to only after death. Here, the first stanza anticipates nights to be spent with a beloved. Both wildness and luxury are part of a shared, overflowing passion. In the second stanza, these nights become a reality, and the concentrated imagery shows that the wildness stands both for passion and for the threat to it from the socially forbidding world. She imagines herself, at the same time, at sea with love and in a protective harbor, and no longer does she need to traverse the sea of separation and prohibition. Sea and port paradoxically seem to merge. In the final stanza, this merging is suggested by "rowing in Eden," where the combination of sea and port corresponds to the physical reality of harbors, except for their exclusion of storms, and where "Eden" implies the attainment of paradise in this world, rather than after death. At this point, the sea as a place for mooring represents the beloved. The last line acknowledges again that Dickinson is describing a fantasy, not a reality, but in it there is a sigh of relief – assisted by the rhyme that echoes back to the first stanza – rather than a cry of desperation. The speaker as a mooring ship suggests a woman nestling against the body of a man and into his life. It is also a fitting symbol for the end of a quest. The suggestions of masculinity in this poem's speaker may reveal in Dickinson an urge to be active in creating a situation that she usually anticipates more passively.

The rarely anthologized but magnificent poem, "I had not minded – Walls" (398), which was added as an appendix to *Final Harvest* after its first edition, makes yet another interesting contrast to "Wild Nights – Wild Nights!" In this poem the emphasis is on the inaccessibility of a beloved person held at an impossible distance by the laws of society, which laws make a barrier that the speaker says she would find easy to penetrate if it were merely physical and as large as the universe. Perhaps in Dickinson's mind this was the same distance that her imagination joyously traversed in "Wild Nights – Wild Nights!"

"The Soul selects her own Society" (303) is a difficult poem that has been variously interpreted. It seems to stand midway between the yearning of "There came a Day at Summer's full," where fulfillment is hoped for in heaven, and the scene of almost-fulfilled desires in "Wild Nights." Here, Dickinson appears to assert that in some special and mysterious way she is always in the company of one person whom her soul has chosen as its only needed companion. The poem is written not in the usual first person of her love poems, but in a detached and meditative third person, until the last stanza where the speaker appears and comments on the third person figure of the first two stanzas. The "Soul" of the first line may at first appear to represent any person, but close examination shows that it is Dickinson herself, or the speaker of the poem, seen from a distance. Also "Society" at first may appear to be a large group of people, but in reality it is one person. "Divine Majority" paradoxically implies that one person or better yet – two people – have become more important than anyone else. The third line is probably a declaration that no others are present, but since Dickinson proposed the word "obtrude" as an alternative to "present," the line may be an imperative telling other people to stay away. In the second stanza, the soul, or essential self, sees people arriving in chariots, an elevated way of describing carriages (perhaps hinting at heavenly as well as at kingly status), but she indicates that she would not be moved even if an emperor asked for her attention. These figures may stand for people in general or for prospective suitors. In the last stanza, the switch to first person shows Dickinson quietly reveling in the strength of her renunciation. The ample nation is everyone available to her. The chosen one is the beloved whose spirit she lives with or has perhaps taken into herself by the power of imagination. "Valves of her attention" gives the soul the power of concentration. The soul has almost denied everything else in life to lock itself into its strange relationship with the chosen "one." "Stone" represents its complete rejection of the rest of the world. The alternating short-long lengths of the poem's lines, culminating in the two-syllable lines of the last stanza, parallels this closing down of attention and strengthens our sense of a painful but glorious triumph in the concluding lines. Unusually rich in sound effects, including alliteration, rhyme, and modulation of vowels, this is one of Dickinson's greatest successes in poetic technique. Some critics believe that the subject of this poem is the union of the soul with the muse or with God, rather than with a lover.

The idea of a spiritual union with a beloved person is more explicit in several other Dickinson poems, but none is as brilliant as "The Soul selects." Because in several of these poems Dickinson, or her speaker, refers to herself as wife or bride, these poems are sometimes called "the marriage group." However, they are not necessarily any more joyous than "The Soul selects." Probably "I'm 'wife'–I've finished that" (199) is the most revealing of these "marriage " poems. (We did not include "There came a Day" and "Mine–by the Right" here because they are about an anticipated rather than a fulfilled union.) This slow-paced poem has an eerie and detached tone. The placing of quotation marks around "wife" and "woman" suggests that these are chiefly social concepts related to status, or it may indicate that the speaker is changing the meaning of those concepts to suit herself. She regards her earlier pre-marriage state with scorn, implying that she has found her own safety without having gone through a conventional marriage. The soft eclipse of her imagined or spiritual marriage blurs the harsh light of what preceded it, although "eclipse" may also refer to the loss of individuality. The use of "folks" in her contrast between heaven and earth implies that her accomplishment has been easy to will or that it resembles the wish-fulfillment of a dream. Having exchanged pain for comfort, she seems astonished that it could be willed so easily. The paired question and assertion of the last two lines suggests a certain numbness reinforcing the implication that the whole process has been painful and reinforcing the poem's aura of unreality. The poet's attitude toward her triumph is ambiguous; she seems uncertain about its nature, and yet she is reluctant to explore her state further, as if through further questioning she might lose everything.

We find an even more intense mixture of feelings in another "marriage" poem, "Title divine – is mine!" (1072), one of Dickinson's most complex and ambiguous poems. Like other poems that we assign to the category of love, this one has also been interpreted as being about God, or poetry, or the achievement of selfhood. In our view, this poem, like "The Soul selects" and "I'm 'wife' – I've finished that," deals primarily with the fantasy of a spiritual marriage to a man from whom the speaker is physically separated. This time, however, she seems quite aware that the suffering is greater than the rewards, and that, in fact, the whole thing is a bitter delusion. The title of wife is divine for two reasons – because society considers it to be, and because it brings elevation. Possibly "divine" also indicates that this marriage exists only spiritually. The missing sign refers to the physical and social reality of marriage. "Acute degree" and "Empress of Calvary" are both paradoxical. The acuteness is the sharp angle of pain. "Calvary" is an elevating suffering, but still the worst suffering imaginable. She has gone through this marriage without the fearfully ecstatic loss of self that other women experience, but her loss is more terrible. In one day she has been born through love, has been made bride, and therefore been bridled like a horse, and has been shrouded, in the sense that her peculiar marriage is a kind of living death. Such a victory is triply ironic. She tries to pronounce the words of love and elevation proper to a real wife, but asks if her way – probably referring to her whole bitter poem – has caught the right tone. On the biographical level, perhaps this poem shows Dickinson's combination of doubts and affirmations about real marriage as much as it shows her anguish over her own ambivalent idea of a spiritual marriage.

Two lesser marriage poems, "She rose to His Requirement" (732) and "A Wife – at Daybreak I shall be" (461) are harder to interpret within the pattern of Dickinson's love poems. "She rose to His Requirement" (732) appears to describe an actual marriage in which a woman gives up the casual play of girlhood for the honorable status of wife. This new state, however, seems to be a considerable disappointment. The woman perhaps has not found the riches of fulfillment that she had expected. However, she allows herself no mention of her disappointments. The comparison of what she does not mention to both pearl and weed suggests that in the depths of the woman's soul there are both secret rewards and secret sufferings. Knowledge of these depths is assigned to the sea rather than to the woman, but the sea seems to be a symbol for part of the woman. This symbolic splitting of woman and sea implies that the woman has detached herself from her husband, and reaps, or faces, special rewards and punishments by herself. Very probably an attempt to look objectively at the rewards and losses of those real-life marriages in which Dickinson did not share, this poem may also contain parallels to her own condition as imagined wife and as poet.

"A Wife—at Daybreak I shall be" (461) places an anxious and almost desperate emphasis on that split between girlhood and the married state that has been a subject of other poems that we have discussed. The chronology here is somewhat overlapping, suggesting an anxious thrust towards a fulfilling future. The speaker alternates between expecting to move from girlhood to marriage and asserting that she has done so. In the second stanza, she repeats the pattern, this time rushing up the stairs of childhood towards her marriage. Now, however, the marriage seems to be in eternity or heaven. The poem may represent a suicidal impulse, or a blending of the idea of spiritual marriage with the idea of a union in heaven. In any case, the poem's repetitive method does not create the complexity of feeling of Dickinson's better and more dramatic poems about an imagined or future marriage.

The infrequently anthologized "I'm ceded—I've stopped being Theirs" (508) makes an interesting connection between the marriage poems and the poems about growth and personal identity. Here, there is no mention of marriage, but the speaker's progression from shallow girlhood, where she gained identity from her family and their values, to her fully realized potentiality in which she hears her true and self-given name, reveals striking parallels to the marriage poems. Her whole existence becomes full, and she is crowned. She has moved from a low rank to the highest imaginable rank. The implied doubts of "I'm 'wife,' I've finished that," the isolation of "The Soul selects," and the irony of "Title divine" are entirely absent from this poem. Probably the condition of a crowned queen here represents that being a poet gives her the feeling that she is a whole person. Thus we see illustrated one of the many thematic overlappings between her love poems and her poems on other subjects.

We have grouped Emily Dickinson's poems on social themes with her love poems partly because both types of her poetry stress her evaluation of people whom she observed. For many poets, society provides a context for their treatment of love, or perhaps a clear delineation of a world from which they withdraw into love. Dickinson's social satire criticizes all kinds of shallowness from which she fled to thoughts of love. Although early critics of Dickinson emphasized her neglect of the social scene, later critics have scrutinized her work to find every conceivable treatment of social themes. We confine ourselves here to mostly a few widely anthologized poems relating to society.

The very popular "I'm Nobody! Who are you!" (288), on the surface, may seem a slight performance, but it is not a superficial poem. On the biographical level, the poem perhaps reflects Dickinson's resentment of shallow writers who gain undeserved attention. Or she may be satirizing the character and situation of people who loom large in the eyes of society – people whom we call "somebodys." Taking assurance from the company of a fellow nobody, the speaker pretends to be worried that they will be held up to public shame for their failure to compete for attention. However, the sudden transition to a denunciation of "somebodys" suggests that if one gains notice as a nobody, it makes one into a kind of somebody. Clearly she prefers a position of invisibility, where she can take her own measure. The somebodys sit in the middle of bogs, a nasty representation of society, and the somebodys bellow to people who will admire them for their names alone. The poet seems to be mildly congratulating herself that unlike the vulgar and pretentious somebodys, she is shy and sensitive. The poem is jocular, amusing, and surely a bit defensive, and its psychology and satire are keen.

Turning her attention more critically to a more specific human type in "What Soft – Cherubic Creatures" (401), Dickinson produces one of her most popular and admired poems, although its unusual compression and its concentrated biblical allusions create difficulties for many readers. The poem is a portrait of excessively genteel women whose claims to status are based entirely on the externals of behavior, dress, and manners. Irony pervades the poem. The softness and cherubic nature of the ladies represents their pretended gentleness and false sweetness (with perhaps a hint at obesity). But the third and fourth lines show us that these women are detached from the real world around them and perhaps they even revel in this detachment. "Plush" describes the softness of upholstery material. The word is an adjective here converted into a noun for a cloth substance too soft to provoke anyone to assault it. Dimity is a dainty white cotton cloth and "dimity convictions" transfers the frailness and pretended innocence of the women's clothing to the women's beliefs. Perhaps we are to see them displaying their false values at religious services or in condescending acts of charity. Their convictions seem limited to a refined horror of ordinary human nature, perhaps in themselves as well as in others. The poem extends this shame about human nature to a shame about Christ, who was quite willing to put on human flesh. The antecedent of "It's" is human nature. The fisherman's degree, we think, refers not, as some critics suggest, to Peter, Christ's disciple, who was a fisherman, but to Christ himself, who, when He associated with fishermen, was a fisher of men. The last two lines state that the women's attitudes would make redemption (the Redeemer) ashamed of them and presumably deny them salvation. The switch from "soft" to "brittle" in reference to the women, that has troubled some critics, is easily explained as a shift from social demeanor to frail values, but also both of these adjectives suggest values that will not endure.

In "She dealt her pretty words like Blades" (479), Dickinson turns her attention to a single lady—perhaps one whom we can imagine imitating the softness of cherubic creatures until the lady has sufficient privacy to reveal a vindictive cutting edge. (Or it may be that she is a different but equally shallow human type.) The aggression here seems the reverse of the repression in some gentlewomen. Probably Dickinson wrote this poem with her sister-in-law, Susan, in mind. The pretty and glittering words suggest the pleasure which a clever woman takes in her speech while being at least partly aware of how much her words hurt those whom she is addressing. The poem's claim that the woman does not believe that she hurts must describe a rationalization in the woman. Since the woman proudly sees herself as being like steel, she judges what she says to people as being properly corrective. Despite her implied denial, she realizes quite well the hurt she gives, but she adds to her original attack by scorning her victims for not exhibiting pain gracefully. The poem is very cleverly built. The first stanza is spoken in detached anger by an observer or a victim. The second stanza imitates the viewpoint of the vicious woman. The third stanza passes a cool judgment on the whole affair, first defending the victim's sensitivity and painful response, and then describing those defenses which finally lead hurt people to withdraw into a protective death-like state. The tone of the last two lines is somewhat jocular. In them, the speaker, drawing upon her own experience, claims a knowledge of suffering so keen that it is like death – a suffering which the attacker refuses to see.

The very popular "Much Madness is divinest Sense" (435) expresses just such a strong feeling of personal suffering, and it leaves the picture and nature of the cruel behavior which it attacks so generalized that one may not immediately notice its social satire. If we wish to make a biographical interpretation, we can note the relationship of its ideas of divinity and a majority to those of "The Soul selects her own Society," where a divine majority of two requires the shutting out of the ordinary majority. In this poem, the discerning eye represents the person who sees that going her own way and choosing her own values may lead to the intensest life, whereas choosing what the world calls sense may produce emptiness, or waste, or pretension, all of which are madness to a sensitive person. The fourth and fifth lines protest against the majority's dictating standards for personal values and conduct, as well as for the rest of society's organization. As she moves from personal situation to social dictatorship, the poet expresses an increasingly mocking anger. The last three lines imply the instruments, social ostracism or even the asylum or prison, which the majority uses to hold people in line. The last line confirms our earlier sense that the concealed speaker feels imprisoned. The poem is brilliantly constructed, with the first three lines illustrating the daring of independent souls, the last three lines showing how they are restricted, and the middle two lines providing the transition from the personal to the social level. This poem ritualizes the internalization of social bondage.

There are three interesting and brief glances at social situations in the poems, "The Popular Heart is a Cannon first" (1226), "The

Show is not the Show" (1206), and "This quiet Dust was Gentlemen and Ladies" (813). "The Popular Heart is a Cannon first" seems to describe the celebration of a national holiday, possibly the Fourth of July, when patriotic types fire off cannons, march with drums, and get drunk. It may, however, be chiefly about the drilling of militia soldiers. The second stanza satirizes their sinking into a drunken stupor, and their lying in ditches and jail and ridicules their activities as an improper memorial for historical events.

"The Show is not the Show" (1206) presents more objectively the kind of social criticism shown in "I'm Nobody! Who are You?" Attendance at a public entertainment brings out the showiness or pretense of those who attend more than it reveals anything spectacular in the event. In lines three and four, she seems to be saying that her neighbors are like zoo creatures to her, and the last two lines imply that her view of them is fair because her neighbors are probably making a similar judgment of her.

"This quiet Dust was Gentlemen and Ladies" (813) was a popular Dickinson poem several decades ago, when in the public eye her superficial wit sometimes eclipsed her deeper insights. It makes, perhaps, a gentle companion piece for "What Soft—Cherubic Creatures." Here, the poem looks back at both young and old who were socially pretentious and given to shallow pursuits. Instead of the shocking contrast of dead people and continuing nature that we find in many Dickinson poems on death, this one attributes a certain superficiality or pointlessness to the cycle of nature. The poem itself expresses comic relief, perhaps as if the speaker were glad not to be troubled about either social pursuits or death. It is also possible that the poet in a neutral or slightly elegaic tone is saying not much more than that the cycle of nature resembles the cycle of man.

What may be Dickinson's most popular poem on a social theme, "I like to see it lap the Miles" (585), is devoid of both people and an explicit social scene. However, its satirical treatment of the invasion of her quarter of the world by a mechanical monster that seems to have delighted everyone else but her can be seen as a satire on the advance of industrial society. The poem domesticates a railroad train by presenting it as a horse. The idea of speed is satirized by making the train into a licking animal, while the impersonality of the train's fueling is converted into feeding. In the second and third stanzas, the train-as-horse takes on somewhat disagreeable human qualities as it enjoys its conquest of the landscape while making a racket that the speaker finds horrid. In the last stanza it reaches its goal, and the conjunction of "docile and omnipotent" shows it as both under man's control and potentially breaking loose – or perhaps lending its omnipotence to the humans who have created it. The speaker seems to sigh with relief at the end, perhaps reflecting Dickinson's difficulty in dealing with social subjects.

Quite possibly, Dickinson could not apply her talents to social subjects with much force because they did not arouse in her the kinds of emotion which she struggles to express and control in her best love poems. However, such triumphs of satire as "What Soft – Cherubic Creatures" and "She dealt her pretty words like Blades" are partly inspired by angers that resemble the tensions in her love poems.

Suffering and Growth

Emily Dickinson's poems often express joy about art, imagination, nature, and human relationships, but her poetic world is also permeated with suffering and the struggle to evade, face, overcome, and wrest meaning from it. Many of her poems about poetry, love, and nature that we have discussed also treat suffering. Suffering is involved in the creative process, it is central to unfulfilled love, and it is part of her ambivalent response to the mysteries of time and nature. Suffering also plays a major role in her poems about death and immortality, just as death often appears in poems that concentrate on suffering. Her poems on this subject can be divided into three groups: those focusing on deprivation as a cause of suffering, those in which anguish leads to disintegration, and those in which suffering – or painful struggles – bring compensatory rewards or spiritual growth.

When Emily Dickinson's poems focus on the fact of and progress of suffering, she rarely describes its causes. Looking back at the love poem "I cannot live with You" (640) and the socially satirical "She dealt her pretty words like Blades" (479), we find passages about specific suffering, but this is not their central subject. However, the evidence that she experienced love-deprivation suggests that it lies behind many of her poems about suffering – poems such as "Renunciation – is a piercing Virtue" (745) and "I dreaded that first Robin so"

(348). In "Renunciation – is a piercing Virtue" (745), Emily Dickinson seems to be writing about abandoning the hope of possessing a beloved person. However, she is more abstract here than in her poems where a lover is visible, and she is not clear about the final meaning of her painful experience. The first four lines present renunciation as both elevating and agonizing. The alternating line length gives the poem a slow, hesitating movement, like the struggles of a mind in torment. The speaker hopes that her renunciation will be rewarded and the use of "Not now" for "but not now" emphasizes her effort. The eyes that are sunrise resemble the face that would put out Jesus' eyes in "I cannot live with You," but this passage is more painful, for the force of "piercing" carries over to the description of eyes being put out and suggests a blinding not so much of the beloved person as of the speaker. She is drawing back, she claims, from the sacrilege of valuing something more than she values God, a person who is like the sunrise. In the last seven lines, the speaker is struggling to develop and express her ideas. She chooses something which she does not want in order to justify herself – not to others (such as God) but to *herself*, and this striving for justification is done less for the present moment than for some future time. "Larger function" means a clearer scheme or idea about existence – one which explains the meaning of mortality – in which her present, selfish desires will appear small. When she is dead, she will finally understand the limitations of her present vision. At the conclusion of the poem, she is still staggering in pain, and the whole poem shows that she has only partial faith in the piercing virtue of renunciation. Her all-encompassing suffering remains a mystery.

The image of piercing which we have just examined resembles Emily Dickinson's typical image of Calvary, which appears in "I dreaded that first Robin so" (348), where the speaker's description of herself as Queen of Calvary suggests a suffering stemming from forbidden love. But this can only be speculation, and Emily Dickinson seems to take pleasure in making a lengthy parade of unspecified sufferings. Her dread of the first robin shows that her bereavement occurred before spring came, or that it was endurable during winter. Now she fears that the contrast of spring's beauty and vitality with her sorrow will intensify her pain. The poem refers repeatedly to her earlier anticipations. She feared that the bird's song and the blooming flowers would torture her by contrast to her situation. Her thoughts of the grass and bees are a bit different, however, for she says that she would want to hide in the grass, and though she implies that the bees liveliness would be a threat, her reference to their "dim countries" is envious. Her having rehearsed her anticipations helped her face spring's arrival. The last two stanzas are somewhat lighter in tone. The failures of creatures and flowers to stay away gives her some pleasure, for she now makes of them her own mournful parade. The image of Queen of Calvary is a deliberate self-dramatization. The creatures and flowers, she insists, are indifferent to her pain, but she is able to project enough sympathy into them to make the experience almost rewarding. She seems aware of the posing dramatized in her lifting childish plumes. The poem expresses anger against nature's indifference to her suffering, but it may also implicitly criticize her self-pity.

Among Emily Dickinson's less popular poems are several about childhood deprivation. Here she is explicit about the sources of suffering, but the poems are less forceful than her general treatments of suffering, and their anger against the people they criticize is weaker than the anger in "What Soft – Cherubic Creatures" and "She dealt her pretty words like Blades." In "It would have starved a Gnat" (612), Emily Dickinson seems to be charging that when she was a child her family denied her spiritual nourishment and recognition. The pervasive metaphor of a starving insect, plus repetition and parallelism, gives special force to the poem. Something as tiny as a gnat would have starved upon what she was fed as a child, food representing emotional sustenance. The phrase "live so small" converts the idea of spiritual nourishment into the idea of a self compelled to remain unobtrusive, undemanding, and unindividual. The image of hunger as a claw shows the natural strength of the child's needs, and the analogy to a leech and a dragon, using Emily Dickinson's typical yoking of the large and the small, dramatizes the painful tenacity of hunger. In the third stanza, she is explicit about the denial of individuality, and she adds a twist to the gnat comparison by showing that the tiny insect's freedom gives it a strength (and implied size) which is denied to her. The envy of the gnat's self-destructiveness, as it beats out its trapped life against the windowpane, suggests a suicidal urge in the speaker, and the poem ends on an unfortunate note of self-pity.

In "I had been hungry, all the Years" (579), Emily Dickinson shows one possible result of the kind of upbringing which she described (probably an autobiographical exaggeration) in "It would have starved a Gnat." Here, the symbolic meaning of food remains indeterminate. The first two stanzas contrast food seen through windows which the speaker passed with the spare sustenance which she could expect at home. The third stanza implies that she has been dining less at home than with the birds, who probably represent the world of imagination and art as well as the world of nature. She finally finds herself inside another dwelling where she is offered an abundance of food and drink. This image probably represents a warmth of society denied to her at home. Her character, however, has been formed by deprivation, and her description of herself as ill and rustic, and therefore out of place amidst grandeur, shows her feelings of inferiority or insecurity. However, the pleasure she has taken in sharing crumbs with birds suggests that there is something distinctive and valuable in her character. In the last stanza she finds the world of social abundance to be artificial and not capable of delivering the kind of food which she needs, and so she rejects it. However, she is probably aware that it is an exaggeration to say that her hunger disappears when food becomes available. Several critics have said that the yearning here is for affection and sexual experience, but no matter what the underlying desires, Emily Dickinson is expressing a strange and touching preference for a withdrawn way of life; this is a variation on the fervent rejection of society in poems such as "I dwell in Possibility" and in a few of her love poems.

In the rarely anthologized "A loss of something ever felt I" (959), a deep sense of deprivation and alienation is expressed rather gently. In the first two stanzas, Emily Dickinson recalls a childhood feeling that she had lost something precious and undefinable, and that no one knew of her loss. She lived very much apart even as she associated with people. In the last two stanzas, she describes her situation with a tender and accepting sadness that implies a forgiveness for those who have hurt her. The "delinquent palaces" are the ideal conditions or loving relationships which she never found, but her calling them, rather than herself, "delinquent" suggests that they, and not she, are responsible for the failure. The speculation in the last stanza is a further clue to the psychology of her deprivation. If she is searching for the kingdom of heaven, she wants something that was never available to her in childhood or adulthood. This contradicts her implied accusations against others and indicates both that she forgives those who hurt her and recognizes that her expectations were impossibly high. In everyday terms, the mental formula would be: why should I blame you for not giving me what really isn't available on this earth?—a formula which can contain much repressed anger.

Among Emily Dickinson's poems in which anguish goes on indefinitely, or is transformed into protective numbness, are two fine epigrammatic poems. In treating this subject, Emily Dickinson rarely hints at the causes of suffering, apparently preferring to keep personal motives hidden, and she concentrates on the self-contained nature of the pain. However, close examination sometimes reveals possible causes of the suffering.

"Pain—has an Element of Blank" (650) deals with a self-contained and timeless suffering, mental rather than physical. The personification of pain makes it identical with the sufferer's life. The blank quality serves to blot out the origin of the pain and the complications that pain brings. The second stanza insists that such suffering is aware only of its continuation. Just as the sufferer's life has become pain, so time has become pain. Its present is an infinity which remains exactly like the past. This infinity, and the past which it reaches back to, are aware only of an indefinite future of suffering. The description of the suffering self as being enlightened is ironic, for although this enlightenment is the only light in the darkness, it is still characterized by suffering.

"The heart asks Pleasure—first" (536) appears to be simple, but close study reveals complexities. The first of its eight lines deals with the desire for pleasure, and the remaining seven lines treat pain and the desire for its relief. This proportion may at first suggest that pleasure is being sought as a relief from pain, but this idea is unlikely. The rapid shift from a desire for pleasure to a pursuit of relief combines with the slightly childlike voice of the poem to show that the hope for pleasure in life quickly yields to the universal fact of pain, after which a pursuit of relief becomes life's center. Such relief is pursued in four stages. To ask for an excuse from pain means either to dismiss it or to leave it behind, like a child asking to be excused from a duty. Anodynes (medicines that relieve pain) are a metaphor for activities that lessen suffering. The hesitant slowness of the phrase "deaden suffering" conveys the cramped nature of such ease. The cumulative "and then" phrases imitate a child's recital of a series of desired things. The child has doubts about the procedure being described and the adult speaker knows that it will fail. The hope that sleep will relieve pain resembles advice given to unhappy children. The Inquisitor stands for God, who creates a world of suffering but won't allow us to die until He is ready. He is being compared to the torturers of the medieval Inquisition, although it is also possible that the Inquisitor represents a sense of guilt on the part of the speaker.

"The heart asks Pleasure–first" takes a passive stance towards suffering, but it also criticizes a world that makes people suffer. Such attitudes are shown more subtly in "After great pain, a formal feeling comes" (341), Emily Dickinson's most popular poem about suffering, and one of her greatest poems. As are the two poems just discussed, it is told in the third person, but it seems very personal. The speaker watches her suffering protagonist from a distance and uses symbols to intensify the psychic splitting through the images of the nerves, heart, and feet. The pain must be psychological, for there is no real damage to the body and no pursuit of healing. The "formal feeling" suggests the protagonist's withdrawal from the world, a withdrawal which implies a criticism of those who have made her suffer. A funeral goes on inside her, with the nerves acting both as mourners and as a tombstone. Reference to the stiff heart, whose sense of time has been destroyed, continues the feeling of arrest. Since Emily Dickinson capitalizes words almost arbitrarily, one cannot know for certain if "He" refers to Christ. The grammatical reference is more continuous if "He" refers to the heart itself, although it may refer to both Christ *and* the heart. The heart feels so dead and alienated from itself that it asks if it is really the one that suffered, and also if the crushing blow came recently or centuries earlier. Time feels dissolved–as if the sufferer has always been just as she is now.

In the second stanza, the protagonist is sufficiently alive and desirous of relief to walk around. She walks in a circle as an expression of frustration and because she has nowhere to go, but her feet are unfeeling. Her path, and her feet as well, are like wood–that is, they are insensitive to what is beneath and around them. Almost from its beginning, the poem has been dramatizing a state of emotional shock that serves as a protection against pain. As the second stanza ends, this stance becomes explicit, the feet and the walking now standing for the whole suffering self which grows contented with its hardened condition. "Quartz contentment" is one of Emily Dickinson's most brilliant metaphors, combining heaviness, density, and earthiness with the idea of contentment, which is usually thought to be mellow and soft. "The hour of lead" is another brilliant metaphor, in which time, scene, and body fuse into something heavy, dull, immovable. As does "quartz contentment," this figure of speech implies that such protection requires a terrible sacrifice. The last eight lines suggest that such suffering may prove fatal, but if it does not, it will be remembered in the same way in which people who are freezing to death remember the painful process leading to their final moment. In reality, however, they could not remember the moment of letting go which precedes death unless they were rescued soon after they slipped into unconsciousness. Perhaps Emily Dickinson is depicting the feeling that rescue, for her, is unlikely, or she may be voicing a call for rescue. But a sense of terrible alienation from the human world, analogous to the loneliness of people freezing to death, pervades the poem. The last line is particularly effective in its combining of shock, growing insensitivity, and final relief, which parallels the overall structure of the poem. The varied line lengths, the frequent heavy pauses within the lines, and the mixture of slant and full rhymes all contribute to the poem's formal slowness. This labored movement of the lines reinforces the thematic movement of the poem from pain to a final, dull resignation.

Although most critics think that "I felt a Funeral, in my Brain" (280) is about death, we see it as a dramatization of mental anguish leading to psychic disintegration and a final sinking into a protective numbness like that portrayed in "After great pain." But the poem is difficult to interpret. In "After great pain," the funeral elements are subordinate to a scene of mental suffering. In this poem, the whole psychological drama is described as if it were a funeral. This funeral is a symbol of an intense suffering that threatens to destroy the speaker's life but at last destroys only her present, unbearable consciousness. The poem offers no hints about the causes of her suffering, although her self-torment seems stronger than in "After great pain." The fourth line is especially difficult, for the phrase "breaking through," in regard to mental phenomena, usually refers to something becoming clear, an interpretation which does not fit the rest of the poem. If "sense" is taken as paralleling the "plank in reason" which later breaks, then "breaking through" can mean to collapse or shatter. The formal and treading mourners probably represent self-accusations strong enough to drive the speaker towards madness. But she is slow in getting there. The service continues, the coffin-like box symbolizing the death of the accused self that can no longer endure torment. Now the whole universe is like a church, with its heavens a bell. Unable to escape from her terrifying consciousness, she feels as if only she and the universe exist. All sounds pour into her silence. This is a condition close to madness, a loss of self that comes when one's relationship to people and nature feels broken, and individuality becomes a burden. At last, the desired numbness arrives. Reason, the ability to think and know, breaks down, and she plunges into an abyss. The worlds she strikes as she descends are her past experiences, both those she would want to hold onto and those that burden her with pain. Then she loses consciousness and is presumably at some kind of peace. The poem's regular rhythms work well with their insistent ritual, and the repeated trochaic words "treading–treading" and "beating–beating" oppose the iambic meter, adding a rocking quality.

Many images and motifs from "After great pain" and "I felt a Funeral" appear in varying guises in the less popular but brilliant "It was not Death, for I stood up" (510). The first two stanzas describe a terrible experience which is composed of neither death nor night, frost nor fire, but which we soon learn has qualities of them all. The bells are like those in "I felt a Funeral." The frost resembles the freezing in "After great pain," and the standing figures resemble the funereal ones in both those poems. Next, the speaker likens herself to corpses ready for burial, paralleling the deathlike images of those poems. In the third stanza, she describes a figure robbed of its individuality and forced to fit a frame–perhaps the standards of others. The mention of midnight contrasts the fullness of noon (a fullness of terror rather than of joy) to the midnight of social- and self-denial. In the fifth stanza, she compares her situation to a deserted and sterile landscape, where the earth's vitality is being cancelled. In the last stanza, she switches the simile and shows herself at sea–a desolated and freezing sea. Her condition here is worse than despair, for despair implies that hope and salvation were once available and now have been lost. She has no hope; her terrible feeling extends backwards as well as forward into emptiness. But although the self is oppressed and at the mercy of warring emotions and torments, the experience seems distanced. The ritualization of how the world persecutes her, the symbolizing of her suffering by landscape and seascape, and the analytical ordering of the material suggest some control over a suffering which she describes as irremediable.

"Twas like a Maelstrom, with a notch" (414) is an interesting variation on Emily Dickinson's treatment of destruction's threat. This poem employs neither the third person of "After great pain" nor the first person of "I felt a Funeral" and "It was not death"; instead, it is told in the second person, which seems to imply involvement in, and yet distance from, an experience that almost destroyed the speaker. The speaker appears threatened by psychic disintegration, although a few critics believe that the subject is the terror of death. For analysis, the poem can be divided into three parallel parts, plus a conclusion: the first two stanzas; the second two stanzas; the fifth stanza and the first two lines of the last stanza; and then the final two lines. In each of the three major sections, the speaker – who addresses herself with a generalizing "you" – is brought to the brink of destruction and then is suddenly spared. In the first section, her torturer is a murderous device designed to spill boiling water, or to pull her by the hem of her gown into a cauldron. The experience, however, turns out to be a nightmare from which she awakens. In the second section, the torturer is a goblin or a fiend who measures the time until it can seize her and tear her to pieces with its beastlike paws. She reacts stiffly and numbly – as in other poems – until God forces the satanic torturer to release her. God seems to act by whim – just barely remembering a task that ought to greatly concern him. In the third section, the torturer is a judicial process which leads her out to execution. The "luxury of doubt" in which she had been imprisoned is luxurious because it, at least, offers some hope of freedom from a miserable condition. But the prison from which she has been led cannot be the same thing as the forces that have been threatening to destroy her. Probably the prison is experienced as a realm of conflict, and the torturer-executioner who appears in three different guises is the possibility that her conflicts will drive her mad and kill her by making her completely self-alienated. In the last section, she is offered not freedom but a reprieve, implying that the whole process may start again. That is why she cannot tell if 1) being destroyed and leaving her suffering behind, or 2) going on with a life which faces constant threat, causes the greater anguish. This poem probably treats the same kind of alienation, lovelessness, and self-accusation found in "After great pain" and "I felt a Funeral."

"I read my sentence–steadily" (412) illustrates how difficult it can be to pin down Emily Dickinson's themes and tones. The poem fits the category of suffering for several reasons: it provides a bridge between Emily Dickinson's poems about suffering and those about the fear of death; it contains anxiety and threat resembling that of several poems just discussed; and its stoicism relates it to poems in which suffering is creative. Although the sentence delivered to the poem's speaker appears to be death, this interpretation creates difficulties. First, few of us have any clear idea of when we will die. Second, the poem's mockery of the judicial formula accompanying a death sentence is hard to connect to anything except a criminal's execution. Third, the soul's increasing familiarity with the inevitability of death and its tranquility do not go well with the anticipation of a definite time of death. The apparent pun on "matter" in the final line is troublesome, for if the word refers to the body as well as to the trial, the first meaning contradicts the indication that death is passing her by for the time being. These problems can be partly solved by seeing the drama as being dreamlike. In this view, the sentence to a specific time and manner of death may symbolize death's inevitability, and the temporal confusion at the end may represent the double-time of a dream, in which one lives on past an event and then continues to expect it to reoccur. The crime of the speaker would be merely having been born, and the mocking would be directed against an inexplicably cruel God. This interpretation is reasonable but makes it hard to account for the speaker's understated stoicism.

An alternate view is that the sentence is to a living-death–its date immediate, its manner her present suffering, and its shame the result of her feelings of unworthiness. Her scorn of the jury's piety suggests her anger at the notion that mercy could mitigate her suffering and shame. Knowing that all she has left is death, she comforts herself with the thought that its final stroke will not be novel. She and death need no public show of familiarity–she because of her pride and stoicism, and he because his power makes a display unnecessary and demeaning. They are equally cheerful and cold. This interpretation may not seem plausible on an initial reading of the poem; however, it accounts for more of the details than does a more conventional interpretation.

As we have seen, several of Emily Dickinson's poems about poetry and art reflect her belief that suffering is necessary for creativity. Poems on love and on nature suggest that suffering will lead to a fulfillment for love or that the fatality which man feels in nature elevates him and sharpens his sensibilities. Similar ideas appear in many poems about immortality. Emily Dickinson's ideas about the creative power of suffering resemble Ralph Waldo Emerson's doctrine of compensation, succinctly stated by him in a poem and an essay, each called "Compensation." According to this view, every apparent evil has a corresponding good, and good is never brought to birth without evil. A version of this idea appears in Emily Dickinson's four-line poem "A Death blow is a Life blow to Some" (816), whose concise paradox puzzles some readers. The "death blow" in this poem is not death literally. If the subject were salvation beyond death, the poem would have no drama. Emily Dickinson is writing about a select group of people whom she observes and who represent part of herself. She is struck by their transformation. The death blow is an assault of suffering, mental or physical, which forces them to rally all of their strength and vitality until they are changed. The first two lines present the basic observation. The second two lines look back at what would have gone on with a living death. Their suffering, therefore, becomes a matter of great good luck. Good and evil are held in balance.

Emily Dickinson takes a more limited view of suffering's benefits in "I like a look of Agony" (241). The speaker is an observer, but the anger of the poem suggests that she may see something of herself in the suffering of other people. She is a person who has been disgusted by artificiality and, therefore, she treasures the genuine. The first line is a deliberate challenge to conventionality. She is willing to praise what people hate in order to express her disgust with the sham that can go with everyday values. People who are truly convulsed are not acting. Several critics take the poem's subject to be death. We disagree – despite the obvious allusion to the crucifixion in the last two lines. The poem seems designed to show mounting anger. The second stanza rushes impetuously from the idea of terrible suffering to the absolute of death, as if the speaker were demanding that we face the worst consequences of suffering – death, in order to achieve authenticity.

Emily Dickinson's most famous poem about compensation, "Success is counted sweetest" (67), is more complicated and less cheerful.

It proceeds by inductive logic to show how painful situations create knowledge and experience not otherwise available. The poem opens with a generalization about people who never succeed. They treasure the idea of success more than do others. Next, the idea is given additional physical force by the declaration that only people in great thirst understand the nature of what they need. The use of "comprehend" about a physical substance creates a metaphor for spiritual satisfaction. Having briefly introduced people who are learning through deprivation, Emily Dickinson goes on to the longer description of a person dying on a battlefield. The word "host," referring to an armed troop, gives the scene an artificial elevation intensified by the royal color purple. These victorious, or seemingly victorious, people understand the nature of victory much less than does a person who has been denied it and lies dying. His ear is forbidden because it must strain to hear and will soon not hear at all. Pain lends clarity to the perception of victory. The bursting of strains near the moment of death emphasizes the greatness of sacrifice. This is a harsh poem. It asks for agreement with an almost cruel doctrine, although its harshness is often overlooked because of its crisp pictorial quality and its pretended cheerfulness. On the biographical level, it can be seen as a celebration of the virtues and rewards of Emily Dickinson's renunciatory way of life, and as an attack on those around her who achieved wordly success.

Emily Dickinson sometimes writes in a more genial and less harsh manner about suffering as a stimulus to growth. Two examples of this approach are the rarely anthologized "Revolution is the Pod" (1082) and "Growth of Man – like Growth of Nature" (750). Most of the few critical comments on "Revolution is the Pod" take its subject to be the revitalization of liberty. This is quite reasonable, although in the bulk of her poems and letters, Dickinson gives almost no attention to politics. However, the stress on individual in the first stanza suggests the possibility that Emily Dickinson is thinking about personal renewal as much as social renewal. Also, most of her nature metaphors that represent human activities are about individual growth. In any case, this exuberant poem begins by celebrating liberation and creation, both important values to a poet who chafed against restrictions and ordered her life through her writing. The second stanza continues the central metaphor of a seed-pod and a flower for society and self, and it offers the painful caution that they must undergo death and decay if, as the third stanza says, they are not to remain torpid. The function of revolution, then, like suffering, is to test and revive whatever may have become dead without our knowing it.

"Growth of Man – like Growth of Nature" (750) is a slower moving and more personal poem. It declares that personal growth is entirely dependent on inner forces. External circumstances may reveal its genuineness but they do not create it. The poem praises determination, personal faith, and courage in the face of opposition. The audience that looks on but can offer no help, described in the last stanza, is disembodied, even for Emily Dickinson's mental world. Surely it is a sign that she often felt that she could receive no help from the outside and must find her own way. Nevertheless, the poem seems to distort reality, although its quietness makes this quality unobtrusive.

Although the difficult "This Consciousness that is aware" (822) deals with death, it is at least equally concerned with discovery of personal identity through the suffering that accompanies dying. The poem opens by dramatizing the sense of mortality which people often feel when they contrast their individual time-bound lives to the world passing by them. Word order in the second stanza is inverted. The speaker anticipates moving between experience and death – that is, from experience into death by means of the experiment of dying. Dying is an experiment because it will test us, and allow us, and no one else, to know if our qualities are high enough to make us survive beyond death. The last stanza offers a summary that makes the death experience an analogy for other means of gaining self-knowledge in life. Neither boastful nor fearful, this poem accepts the necessity of painful testing.

"My Cocoon tightens – Colors tease" (1099) is both a lighter and a sadder treatment of the pursuit of growth. Several critics take its subject to be immortality. Its metaphor of the self as a butterfly, desiring both power and freedom, makes us think that it is about the struggle for personal growth. In the first stanza, the speaker is restricted but is faintly hopeful, and she contrasts her present limitations with her inner capacity. In the second stanza, she expresses a yearning for freedom and for the power to survey nature and feel at home with it. These personal qualities and this symbolic landscape represent life and its experiences as much, or more, than the achieving of paradise. In the last stanza, the speaker's hope for growth changes into a state of bafflement. She cannot read in herself, or nature, the formula which will allow her to make the right transformation, and she remains both puzzled and aspiring.

The rarely anthologized "Dare you see a Soul *at the White Heat?*" (365) is an unconstrained celebration of growth through suffering, though a few critics think that the poem is about love or the speaker's relationship to God. Addressed to the reader, the poem invites us to see a soul being transformed inside a furnace. When this soul is able to stand the suffering of fire, it will emerge white hot. The purified ore stands for transformed personal identity. At line nine, the poem divides into a second part. Here, the speaking voice is that of someone who has undergone such a transformation and can joyously affirm the availability of a change like its own for anyone willing to undergo it. The blacksmith's forge is described as a symbol, providing a metaphor within a metaphor. Just as small villages always have a blacksmith, so every soul has in it the possibility of passing through the fires of rebirth. The last four lines return to the poem's initial exuberance, and as the speaker sees the changed souls rising from their forges, she is thinking once more of her own triumph.

"The Brain—is wider than the Sky" (632) has puzzled and troubled many readers, probably because its surface statements fly so boldly in the face of accepted ideas about man's relationship to God. The three stanzas make parallel statements, but there is a significant variation in the third. The first stanza declares, with a deliberate defiance of ordinary perception, that the small human brain is larger than the wide sky, and that it can contain both the sky and all of the self. Emily Dickinson seems to be asserting that imagination or spirit can encompass, or perhaps give, the sky all of its meaning. The second stanza repeats the theme but lends it a fresh power through the metaphor of sponges absorbing buckets, which may suggest the poet's internalization of reality. The third stanza tries to outdo the earlier ones in overstatement. The "just" comparing the weight of the brain and of God is designed to show that the speaker is not boasting, but that she has taken a precise measure and can present her findings with offhand assurance. This stanza seems to claim for the human spirit equal status with the creative force in the universe, although possibly Emily Dickinson is merely suggesting that all human knowledge comes from God. Emily Dickinson's ideas here may resemble her most extravagant claims for the poet and the human imagination. We have placed the poem with those on growth because its exuberance conveys a sense of relief, accomplishment, and self-assertion.

Death, Immortality, and Religion

Even a modest selection of Emily Dickinson's poems reveals that death is her principal subject; in fact, because the topic is related to many of her other concerns, it is difficult to say how many of her poems concentrate on death. But over half of them, at least partly, and about a third centrally, feature it. Most of these poems also touch on the subject of religion, although she did write about religion without mentioning death. Other nineteenth-century poets, Keats and Whitman are good examples, were also death-haunted, but few as much as Emily Dickinson. Life in a small New England town in Dickinson's time contained a high mortality rate for young people; as a result, there were frequent death-scenes in homes, and this factor contributed to her preoccupation with death, as well as her withdrawal from the world, her anguish over her lack of romantic love, and her doubts about fulfillment beyond the grave. Years ago, Emily Dickinson's interest in death was often criticized as being morbid, but in our time readers tend to be impressed by her sensitive and imaginative handling of this painful subject.

Her poems centering on death and religion can be divided into four categories: those focusing on death as possible extinction, those dramatizing the question of whether the soul survives death, those asserting a firm faith in immortality, and those directly treating God's concern with people's lives and destinies.

The very popular "I heard a Fly buzz–when I died" (465) is often seen as representative of Emily Dickinson's style and attitudes. The first line is as arresting an opening as one could imagine. By describing the moment of her death, the speaker lets us know that she has already died. In the first stanza, the death-room's stillness contrasts with a fly's buzz that the dying person hears, and the tension pervading the scene is likened to the pauses within a storm. The second stanza focuses on the concerned onlookers, whose strained eyes and gathered breath emphasize their concentration in the face of a sacred event: the arrival of the "King," who is death. In the third stanza, attention shifts back to the speaker, who has been observing her own death with all the strength of her remaining senses. Her final willing of her keepsakes is a psychological event, not something she speaks. Already growing detached from her surroundings, she is no longer interested in material possessions; instead, she leaves behind whatever of herself people can treasure and remember. She is getting ready to guide herself towards death. But the buzzing fly intervenes at the last instant; the phrase "and then" indicates that this is a casual event, as if the ordinary course of life were in no way being interrupted by her death. The fly's "blue buzz" is one of the most famous pieces of synesthesia in Emily Dickinson's poems. This image represents the fusing of color and sound by the dying person's diminishing senses. The uncertainty of the fly's darting motions parallels her state of mind. Flying between the light and her, it seems to both signal the moment of death and represent the world that she is leaving. The last two lines show the speaker's confusion of her eyes and the windows of the room – a psychologically acute observation because the windows' failure is the failure of her own eyes that she does not want to admit. She is both distancing fear and revealing her detachment from life.

Critics have disagreed about the symbolic fly, some claiming that it symbolizes the precious world being left behind and others insisting that it stands for the decay and corruption associated with death. Although we favor the first of these, a compromise is possible. The fly may be loathsome, but it can also signify vitality. The synesthetic description of the fly helps depict the messy reality of dying, an event that one might hope to find more uplifting. The poem portrays a typical nineteenth-century death-scene, with the onlookers studying the dying countenance for signs of the soul's fate beyond death, but otherwise the poem seems to avoid the question of immortality.

In "This World is not Conclusion" (501), Emily Dickinson dramatizes a conflict between faith in immortality and severe doubt. Her earliest editors omitted the last eight lines of the poem, distorting its meaning and creating a flat conclusion. The complete poem can be divided into two parts: the first twelve lines and the final eight lines. It starts by emphatically affirming that there is a world beyond death which we cannot see but which we still can understand intuitively, as we do music. Lines four through eight introduce conflict.

Immortality is attractive but puzzling. Even wise people must pass through the riddle of death without knowing where they are going. The ungrammatical "don't" combined with the elevated diction of "philosophy" and "sagacity" suggests the petulance of a little girl. In the next four lines, the speaker struggles to assert faith. Puzzled scholars are less admirable than those who have stood up for their beliefs and suffered Christlike deaths. The speaker wants to be like them. Her faith now appears in the form of a bird who is searching for reasons to believe. But available evidence proves as irrelevant as twigs and as indefinite as the directions shown by a spinning weathervane. The desperation of a bird aimlessly looking for its way is analagous to the behavior of preachers whose gestures and hallelujahs cannot point the way to faith. These last two lines suggest that the narcotic which these preachers offer cannot still their *own* doubts, in addition to the doubts of others.

In "I know that He exists" (338), Emily Dickinson, like Herman Melville's Captain Ahab in *Moby-Dick*, shoots darts of anger against an absent or betraying God. This poem also has a major division and moves from affirmation to extreme doubt. However, its overall tone differs from that of "This World is not Conclusion." The latter poem shows a tension between childlike struggles for faith and the too easy faith of conventional believers, and Emily Dickinson's anger, therefore, is directed against her own puzzlement and the double-dealing of religious leaders. It is a frenetic satire that contains a cry of anguish. In the first-person "I know that He exists" (338), the speaker confronts the challenge of death and refers to God with chillingly direct anger. Both poems, however, are ironic. Here, the first stanza declares a firm belief in God's existence, although she can neither hear nor see him. The second stanza explains that he remains hidden in order to make death a blissful ambush, where happiness comes as a surprise. The deliberately excessive joy and the exclamation mark are signs of emerging irony. She has been describing a pleasant game of hide and seek, but she now anticipates that the game may prove deadly and that the fun could turn to terror if death's stare is revealed as being something murderous that brings neither God nor immortality. Should this prove so, the amusing game will become a vicious joke, showing God to be a merciless trickster who enjoys watching people's foolish anticipations. Once this dramatic irony is visible, one can see that the first stanza's characterization of God's rareness and man's grossness is ironic. As a vicious trickster, his rareness is a fraud, and if man's lowliness is not rewarded by God, it is merely a sign that people deserve to be cheated. The rhythms of this poem imitate both its deliberativeness and uneasy anticipation. It is as close to blasphemy as Emily Dickinson ever comes in her poems on death, but it does not express an absolute doubt. Rather, it raises the possibility that God may not grant the immortality that we long for.

The borderline between Emily Dickinson's poems in which immortality is painfully doubted and those in which it is merely a question cannot be clearly established, and she often balances between these positions. For example, "Those–dying then" (1551) takes a pragmatic attitude towards the usefulness of faith. Evidently written three or four years before Emily Dickinson's death, this poem reflects on the firm faith of the early nineteenth century, when people were sure that death took them to God's right hand. The amputation of that hand represents the cruel loss of men's faith. The second stanza asserts that without faith people's behavior becomes shallow and petty, and she concludes by declaring that an "ignis fatuus,"–Latin for *false fire*–is better than no illumination–no spiritual guidance or moral anchor. In plain prose, Emily Dickinson's idea seems a bit fatuous. But the poem is effective because it dramatizes, largely through its metaphors of amputation and illumination, the strength that comes with convictions, and contrasts it with an insipid lack of dignity.

The tenderly satirical portrait of a dead woman in "How many times these low feet staggered" (187) skirts the problem of immortality. As in many of her poems about death, the imagery focuses on the stark immobility of the dead, emphasizing their distance from the living. The central scene is a room where a body is laid out for burial, but the speaker's mind ranges back and forth in time. In the first stanza, she looks back at the burdens of life of the dead housewife and then metaphorically describes her stillness. The contrast in her feelings is between relief that the woman is free from her burdens and the present horror of her death. In the second stanza, the speaker asks her listeners or companions to approach the corpse and compare its former, fevered life to its present coolness: the once nimbly active fingers are now stone-like. In the last stanza, attention shifts from the corpse to the room, and the emotion of the speaker complicates. The dull flies and spotted windowpane show that the housewife can no longer keep her house clean. The flies suggest the unclean oppression of death, and the dull sun is a symbol for her extinguished life. By citing the fearless cobweb, the speaker pretends to criticize the dead woman, beginning an irony intensified by a deliberately unjust accusation of indolence—as if the housewife remained dead in order to avoid work. In the last line of the poem, the body is in its grave; this final detail adds a typical Dickinsonian pathos.

"Safe in their Alabaster Chambers" (216) is a similarly constructed but more difficult poem. After Emily Dickinson's sister-in-law, Susan, criticized the second stanza of its first version, Emily Dickinson wrote a different stanza and, later, yet another variant for it. The reader now has the pleasure (or problem) of deciding which second stanza best completes the poem, although one can make a composite version containing all three stanzas, which is what Emily Dickinson's early editors did. We will interpret it as a three-stanza poem. As with "How many times these low feet staggered," its most striking technique is the contrast between the immobility of the dead and the life continuing around them. The tone, however, is solemn rather than partially playful, although slight touches of satire are possible. The first stanza presents a generalized picture of the dead in their graves. The description of the hard whiteness of alabaster monuments or mausoleums begins the poem's stress on the insentience of the dead. Day moves above them but they sleep on, incapable of feeling the softness of coffin linings or the hardness of burial stone. They are "meek members of the resurrection" in that they passively wait for whatever their future may be, although this detail implies that they may eventually awaken in heaven.

In what we will consider the second stanza, the scene widens to the vista of nature surrounding burial grounds. Here, the vigor and cheerfulness of bees and birds emphasizes the stillness and deafness of the dead. The birds are not aware of death, and the former wisdom of the dead, which contrasts to ignorant nature, has perished. In what is our third stanza, Emily Dickinson shifts her scene to the vast surrounding universe, where planets sweep grandly through the heavens. The touch of personification in these lines intensifies the contrast between the continuing universe and the arrested dead. The dropping of diadems stands for the fall of kings, and the reference to Doges, the rulers of medieval Venice, adds an exotic note. The soundless fall of these rulers reminds us again of the dead's insentience and makes the process of cosmic time seem smooth. The disc (enclosing a wide winter landscape) into which fresh snow falls is a simile for this political change and suggests that while such activity is as inevitable as the seasons, it is irrelevant to the dead. This stanza also adds a touch of pathos in that it implies that the dead are equally irrelevant to the world, from whose excitement and variety they are completely cut off. Resurrection has not been mentioned again, and the poem ends on a note of silent awe.

Conflict between doubt and faith looms large in "The last Night that She lived" (1100), perhaps Emily Dickinson's most powerful death scene. The poem is written in second-person plural to emphasize the physical presence and the shared emotions of the witnesses at a death-bed. The past tense shows that the experience has been completed and its details have been intensely remembered. That the night of death is common indicates both that the world goes on despite death and that this persisting commonness in the face of death is offensive to the observers. Nature looks different to the witnesses because they have to face nature's destructiveness and indifference. They see everything with increased sharpness because death makes the world mysterious and precious. After the first two stanzas, the poem devotes four stanzas to contrasts between the situation and the mental state of the dying woman and those of the onlookers. Moving in and out of the death room as a nervous response to their powerlessness, the onlookers become resentful that others may live while this dear woman must die. The jealousy for her is not an envy of her death; it is a jealous defense of her right to live. As the fifth stanza ends, the tense moment of death arrives. The oppressive atmosphere and the spiritually shaken witnesses are made vividly real by the force of the metaphors "narrow time" and "jostled souls." At the moment of death, the dying woman is willing to die – a sign of salvation for the New England Puritan mind and a contrast to the unwillingness of the onlookers to let her die.

The simile of a reed bending to water gives to the woman a fragile beauty and suggests her acceptance of a natural process. In the last stanza the onlookers approach the corpse to arrange it, with formal awe and restrained tenderness. The condensed last two lines gain much of their effect by withholding an expected expression of relief. Instead of going back to life as it was, or affirming their faith in the immortality of a Christian who was willing to die, they move into a time of leisure in which they must strive to "regulate" their beliefs—that is, they must strive to dispel their doubts. The subtle irony of "awful leisure" mocks the condition of still being alive, suggesting that the dead person is more fortunate than the living because she is now relieved of all struggle for faith.

"Because I could not stop for Death" (712) is Emily Dickinson's most anthologized and discussed poem. It deserves such attention, although it is difficult to know how much its problematic nature contributes to this interest. We will briefly summarize the major interpretations before, rather than after, analyzing the poem. Some critics believe that the poem shows death escorting the female speaker to an assured paradise. Others believe that death comes in the form of a deceiver, perhaps even a rapist, to carry her off to destruction. Still others think that the poem leaves the question of her destination open. As does "I heard a Fly buzz—when I died," this poem gains initial force by having its protagonist speak from beyond death. Here, however, dying has largely preceded the action, and its physical aspects are only hinted at. The first stanza presents an apparently cheerful view of a grim subject. Death is kindly. He comes in a vehicle connoting respect or courtship, and he is accompanied by immortality—or at least its promise. The word "stop" can mean to stop by for a person, but it also can mean stopping one's daily activities. With this pun in mind, death's kindness may be seen as ironical, suggesting his grim determination to take the woman despite her occupation with life. Her being alone—or almost alone—with death helps characterize him as a suitor. Death knows no haste because he always has enough power and time. The speaker now acknowledges that she has put her labor and leisure aside; she has given up her claims on life and seems pleased with her exchange of life for death's civility, a civility appropriate for a suitor but an ironic quality of a force that has no need for rudeness.

The third stanza creates a sense of motion and of the separation between the living and the dead. Children go on with life's conflicts and games, which are now irrelevant to the dead woman. The vitality of nature which is embodied in the grain and the sun is also irrelevant to her state; it makes a frightening contrast. However, in the fourth stanza, she becomes troubled by her separation from nature and by what seems to be a physical threat. She realizes that the sun is passing them rather than they the sun, suggesting both that she has lost the power of independent movement, and that time is leaving her behind. Her dress and her scarf are made of frail materials and the wet chill of evening, symbolizing the coldness of death, assaults her. Some critics believe that she wears the white robes of the bride of Christ and is headed towards a celestial marriage. In the fifth stanza, the body is deposited in the grave, whose representation as a swelling in the ground portends its sinking. The flatness of its roof and its low roof-supports reinforce the atmosphere of dissolution and may symbolize the swiftness with which the dead are forgotten. The last stanza implies that the carriage with driver and guest are still traveling. If it is centuries since the body was deposited, then the soul is moving on without the body. That first day felt longer than the succeeding centuries because during it, she experienced the shock of death. Even then, she knew that the destination was eternity, but the poem does not tell if that eternity is filled with anything more than the blankness into which her senses are dissolving. Emily Dickinson may intend paradise to be the woman's destination, but the conclusion withholds a description of what immortality may be like. The presence of immortality in the carriage may be part of a mocking game or it may indicate some kind of real promise. Since interpretation of some of the details is problematic, readers must decide for themselves what the poem's dominant tone is.

The borderline between Emily Dickinson's treatment of death as having an uncertain outcome and her affirmation of immortality cannot be clearly defined. The epigrammatic "The Bustle in a House" (1078) makes a more definite affirmation of immortality than the poems just discussed, but its tone is still grim. If we wanted to make a narrative sequence of two of Emily Dickinson's poems about death, we could place this one after "The last Night that She lived." "The Bustle in a House" at first appears to be an objective description of a household following the death of a dear person. It is only the morning after, but already there is the bustle of everyday activity. The word "bustle" implies a brisk busyness, a return to the normality and the order shattered by the departure of the dying. Industry is ironically joined to solemnity, but rather than mocking industry, Emily Dickinson shows how such busyness is an attempt to subdue grief. The second stanza makes a bold reversal, whereby the domestic activities – which the first stanza implies are physical – become a sweeping up not of house but of heart. Unlike household things, heart and love are not put away temporarily. They are put away until we join the dead in eternity. The last line affirms the existence of immortality, but the emphasis on the distance in time (for the dead) also stresses death's mystery. Viewed as the morning after "The last Night that She lived," this poem depicts everyday activity as a ritualization of the struggle for belief. Such a continuity also helps bring out the wistfulness of "The Bustle in a House." Few of Emily Dickinson's poems illustrate so concisely her mixing of the commonplace and the elevated, and her deft sense of everyday psychology.

"A Clock stopped" (287) mixes the domestic and the elevated in order to communicate the pain of losing dear people and also to suggest the distance of the dead from the living. The poem is an allegory in which a clock represents a person who has just died. The first stanza contrasts the all-important "clock," a once-living human being, with a trivial mechanical clock. This prepares us for the angry remark that men's skills can do nothing to bring back the dead. Geneva is the home of the most famous clockmakers and also the place where Calvinist Christianity was born. The reference to a puppet reveals that this is a cuckoo clock with dancing figures. This image of the puppet suggests the triviality of the mere body, as opposed to the soul that has fled. The second stanza rehearses the process of dying. The clock is a trinket because the dying body is a mere plaything of natural processes. A painful death strikes rapidly, and instead of remaining a creature of time, the "clock-person" enters the timeless and perfect realm of eternity, symbolized here, as in other Emily Dickinson poems, by noon. In the third stanza, the poem's speaker becomes sardonic about the powerlessness of doctors, and possibly ministers, to revive the dead, and then turns with a strange detachment to the owner – friend, relative, lover – who begs the dead to return.

But whatever is left of vitality in the aspects of the dead person refuses to exert itself. The residues of time that this "clock-person" incorporates suddenly expand into the decades that separate it from the living; these decades are the time between the present and the shopman's death, when he will join the "clock-person" in eternity. The arrogance of the decades belongs to the dead because they have achieved the perfect noon of eternity and can look with scorn at merely finite concerns.

In the early poem "Just lost, when I was saved!" (160), Emily Dickinson expresses joyful assurance of immortality by dramatizing her regret about a return to life after she – or an imagined speaker – almost died and received many vivid and thrilling hints about a world beyond death. Each of the first three lines makes a pronouncement about the false joy of being saved from a death which is actually desirable. Her real joy lay in her brief contact with eternity. When she recovers her life, she hears the realm of eternity express disappointment, for it shared her true joy in her having almost arrived there. The second stanza reveals her awe of the realm which she skirted, the adventure being represented in metaphors of sailing, sea, and shore. As a "pale reporter," she is weak from illness and able to give only a vague description of what lies beyond the seals of heaven. In the third and fourth stanzas, she declares in chanted prayer that when next she approaches eternity she wants to stay and witness in detail everything which she has only glimpsed. The last three lines are a celebration of the timelessness of eternity. She uses the image of the ponderous movements of vast amounts of earthly time to emphasize that her happy eternity lasts even longer – it lasts forever.

"Those not live yet" (1454) may be Emily Dickinson's strongest single affirmation of immortality, but it has found little favor with anthologists, probably because of its dense grammar. The writing is elliptical to an extreme, suggesting almost a strained trance in the speaker, as if she could barely express what has become for her the most important thing. The first two lines assert that people are not yet alive if they do not believe that they will live for a second time – that is, after death. The next two lines turn the adverb "again" into a noun and declare that the notion of immortality as an "again" is based on a false separation of life and an afterlife. The truth, rather, is that life is part of a single continuity. The next three lines analogize death to a connection between two parts of the same reality. The ship that strikes against the sea's bottom when passing through a channel will make its way over that brief grounding and enter a continuation of the same sea. This sea is consciousness, and death is merely a painful hesitation as we move from one phase of the sea to the next. The last three lines contain an image of the realm beyond the present life as being pure consciousness without the costume of the body, and the word "disc" suggests timeless expanse as well as a mutuality between consciousness and all existence.

"Behind Me – dips Eternity" (721) strives for an equally strong affirmation of immortality, but it reveals more pain than "Those not live yet" and perhaps some doubt. In the first stanza, the speaker is trapped in life between the immeasurable past and the immeasurable future. Death is represented as the dark of early morning which will turn into the light of paradise. The second stanza celebrates immortality as the realm of God's timelessness. Rather than celebrating the trinity, Emily Dickinson first insists on God's single perpetual being, which diversifies itself in divine duplicates. This difficult passage probably means that each person's achievement of immortality makes him part of God. The phrase "they say" and the chant-like insistence of the first two stanzas suggest a person trying to convince herself of these truths. The pain expressed in the final stanza illuminates this uncertainty. The miracle behind her is the endless scope of time. The miracle before her is the promise of resurrection, and the miracle between is the quality of her own being – probably what God has given her of Himself – that guarantees that she will live again. However, the last three lines portray her life as a living hell, presumably of conflict, denial, and alienation. If this is the case, we can see why she is yearning for an immortal life. But she still fears that her present "midnight" neither promises nor deserves to be changed in heaven. These doubts, of course, are only implications. The poem is primarily an indirect prayer that her hopes may be fulfilled.

It is hard to locate a developing pattern in Emily Dickinson's poems on death, immortality, and religious questions. Clearly, Emily Dickinson wanted to believe in God and immortality, and she often thought that life and the universe would make little sense without them. Possibly her faith increased in her middle and later years; certainly one can cite certain poems, including "Those not live yet," as signs of an inner conversion. However, serious expressions of doubt persist, apparently to the very end.

Emily Dickinson treats religious faith directly in the epigrammatic " 'Faith' is a fine invention" (185), whose four lines paradoxically maintain that faith is an acceptable invention when it is based on concrete perception, which suggests that it is merely a way of claiming that orderly or pleasing things follow a principle. When we can see no reason for faith, she next declares, it would be good to have tools to uncover real evidence. Here, she finds it hard to believe in the unseen, although many of her best poems struggle for just such belief. Although "Drowning is not so pitiful" (1718) is a poem about death, it has a kind of naked and sarcastic skepticism which emphasizes the general problem of faith. The poem's directness and intensity lead one to suspect that its basis is personal suffering and a fear for the loss of self, despite its insistence on death as the central challenge to faith. Its first four lines describe a drowning person desperately clinging to life. In the next four lines, the process of drowning is horrible, and the horror is partly attributed to a fear of God. The last four lines bitingly imply that people are not telling the truth when they affirm their faith that they will see God and be happy after death. These lines make God seem cruel. Emily Dickinson's uncharacteristic lack of charity suggests that she is thinking of mankind's tendency as a whole, rather than of specific dying people.

Emily Dickinson sent "The Bible is an antique Volume" (1545) to her twenty-two year-old nephew, Ned, when he was ill. At this time, she was about fifty-two and had only four more years to live. The poem might be less surprising if it were a product of Emily Dickinson's earlier years, although perhaps she was remembering some of her own reactions to the Bible during her youth. The first three lines echo standard explanations of the Bible's origin as holy doctrine, and the mocking tone implies skepticism. It then quickly summarizes and domesticates scenes and characters from the Bible as if they were everyday examples of virtue and sin. Lines nine through twelve are the core of the criticism, for they express anger against the preaching of self-righteous teachers. In conclusion, she pleads for literature with more color and presumably with more varied material and less narrow values. The poem may be a complaint against a Puritan interpretation of the Bible and against Puritan skepticism about secular literature. On the other hand, it may merely be a playful expression of a fanciful and joking mood.

Given the variety of Emily Dickinson's attitudes and moods, it is easy to select evidence to "prove" that she held certain views. But such patterns can be dogmatic and distorting. Emily Dickinson's final thoughts on many subjects are hard to know. With this caution in mind, we can glance at the trenchant "Apparently with no surprise" (1624), also written within a few years of Emily Dickinson's death. The flower here may seem to stand for merely natural things, but the emphatic personification implies that God's way of afflicting the lowly flowers resembles his treatment of man. The happy flower does not expect a blow and feels no surprise when it is struck, but this is only "apparently." Perhaps it does suffer. The image of frost beheading the flower implies an abrupt and unthinking brutality. The personification of Frost as an assassin contradicts the notion of its acting accidentally. Nature in the guise of the sun takes no notice of the cruelty, and God seems to approve of the natural process. This implies that God and natural process are identical, and that they are either indifferent, or cruel, to living things, including man. The subtleties and implications of this poem illustrate the difficulties that the skeptical mind encounters in dealing with a universe in which God's presence is not easily demonstrated. The poem is strangely, and magnificently, detached and cold. It makes an interesting contrast to Emily Dickinson's more personal expressions of doubt and to her strongest affirmations of faith.

BRIEF COMMENTS ON FORTY ADDITIONAL POEMS

To conclude, we offer one-sentence comments on forty poems not analyzed or mentioned in these Notes. Since we have already suggested a variety of thematic patterns among Dickinson's poems, we are avoiding classification of these additional poems, leaving the reader free to relate them to Dickinson's themes. They are arranged here in alphabetical order. These brief comments do not attempt definitive or assured interpretations, nor do they mention alternate views.

"A Light exists in Spring" (812): A special light on the landscape during spring conveys a feeling of urgency and vitality, and its departure leaves the viewer with a sense of restive deprivation. "A Word made Flesh is seldom" (1651): The speaker wishes that the experience of expressing one's feelings adequately, which is like the act of God taking on flesh, could come more frequently. "A *Wounded* Deer – leaps highest" (165): Various kinds of suffering produce apparently joyful compensations which take the form of defenses against real pain. "Ample make this Bed" (829): Instructions for the correct frame of mind about burying people are given in a sinister manner, suggesting uncertainty about the destiny of the dead. "As the Starved Maelstrom laps the Navies" (872): The speaker compares her aggressive desire to consume something exotic, probably a beloved person, with the behavior of starved creatures.

"Civilization – spurns – the Leopard!" (492): A leopard, symbolizing the poet-speaker, was oppressed and rejected by her conventional society and deserves pity for her inability to live according to her natural desires. "Death is the supple Suitor" (1445): Death takes the form of a dishonest lover and woos his victims to a secret and silent realm. "Did the Harebell loose her girdle" (213): As an allegory drawn from nature may suggest, after women yield their virginity to estimable men, the promised rewards and the stature of the men will probably be diminished. "God is a distant – stately Lover" (357): The Christian idea that God needed to become Christ in order to win men over is satirically compared and contrasted to Miles Standish's use of John Alden to carry his marriage suit to Priscilla, in Longfellow's narrative poem *The Courtship of Miles Standish.* " 'Heavenly Father' – take to thee" (1461): We pray that God will receive us in heaven despite our sins, but such a prayer neglects the likelihood that the creator made us sinful.

"He fumbles at your Soul" (315): The power of a magnificently eloquent speaker (or minister or writer) to transform his audience's feelings is compared to music, thunderbolts, and forest winds. "He preached upon 'Breadth' till it argued him narrow" (1207): A liberal minister makes such exaggerated claims for his broad-mindedness and grasp of truth that he reveals insincerity, lack of faith, and pretentiousness. " 'Hope' is the thing with feathers" (254): Hope has various characteristics of a courageous bird, the most important being its total self-reliance or sourcelessness. "How happy is the little Stone" (1510): In its complete independence and security, a small stone provides a model for man's spiritual self-sufficiency. "I breathed enough to take the Trick" (272): The speaker learned to function adequately when she had a supportive environment, but now that she lives with deprivation she manages to survive by sheer nerve.

"I can wade Grief" (252): The speaker finds pain easier to endure and more creative than joy, for she has learned that unchallenging circumstances weaken people, whereas heavy burdens strengthen them. "I found the words to every thought" (581): The speaker is taking both pain and pleasure in illustrating her feeling that she can find no words for her most valuable experience, possibly some sense of personal or cosmic wholeness. "I got so I could take his name" (293): The speaker rehearses her agonizing and slow adjustment to a forcible separation from a beloved man and continues to address prayers about her situation to a deity who seems unlikely to care about her suffering. "I've seen a Dying Eye" (547): The speaker remembers watching a dying person whose slowly closing eyes revealed nothing of whatever happy future they could see. "Of God we ask one favor" (1601): People ask God to forgive their sins even if their only sense of sin is awareness of God's accusation, and they are thereby compelled to criticize an earthly happiness which they would like to have perpetuated in heaven.

"One dignity delays for all" (98): Everyone, no matter how low, can look forward to dying as something that will elevate him to a high rank, presumably a spiritual existence in heaven. "One need not be a Chamber–to be Haunted" (670): Psychological or spiritual threats inside people are greater dangers than threat of ghosts or of physical aggression, though most people take the opposite view. "Myself was formed–a Carpenter" (488): The speaker's earnest and elevated view of her destiny as a carpenter suggests that she is talking about the way in which someone belittles her sacred poetic gift by wanting her to subdue it to convention. "Not with a Club, the Heart is broken" (1304): The speaker externalizes an inner drama of self-accusation to show the crushing power of shame in human life. "Pain–has an Element of Blank" (650): A major ingredient of pain, presumably a pain permeating all of one's being, is its loss of any time-sense about its own engulfment.

"She lay as if at play" (369): The body of a recently dead girl shows such vivid signs of its recent vitality that it is hard not to believe that she is merely asleep and will soon awaken. "Some keep the Sabbath going to Church" (324): The speaker indirectly offers various reasons why she finds more vividness and joy in performing Sunday worship in a natural setting near her home than she would in celebrating it by attending church services. "Split the Lark–and you'll find the Music" (861): Addressing a dear person who seems to doubt the speaker's absolute devotion, she insists that exposing the torment inside her would prove her sincerity. "The Admirations–and Contempts–of time" (906): When we are on the verge of dying, we can see that the true meaning of time is that it shows the conditions of mortality and immortality to be fused together through the power of God. "The Bat is dun, with wrinkled Wings" (1575): The unpleasant but relatively harmless physical aspects of bats are puzzling, but we should assume that God acts with goodwill in making such a strange creature.

"The Brain, within its Groove" (56): The human brain, standing for the individual personality or for psychic wholeness, functions smoothly unless some part of it breaks down, in which case the damage to the whole is almost irreversible. "The Lamp burns sure–within" (233): The human spirit is like a lamp tended and fed by outside forces, but if these forces fail it, it can miraculously go on just as it previously did. "The Malay–took the Pearl" (452): The speaker compares her timid self to a primitive person who is able to achieve satisfactions that frighten her but who has little of her appreciation for such achievements. "The soul has Bandaged moments" (512): The soul, a person much like the poet, goes through periods of bitter self-condemnation and then of joyful release, but when she returns to the oppressed state, things are worse than ever. "The Soul's Superior instants" (306): During its best moments, the sensitive soul revels in its detachment from everything and in its complete self-sufficiency; such realizations are identical with the sense of immortality.

"There is a pain–so utter" (599): Some kinds of engulfing pain protect the sufferer from distintegration by making him numb to the causes and nature of the pain. "Three times–we parted–breath–and I" (598): The speaker was three times threatened with the complete destruction of her spirit, but after giving up hope of outside help she was saved by an inner transformation or rebirth. "To fight aloud, is very brave" (126): The speaker celebrates the act of enduring spiritual suffering, and she is sure that people who practice the former will be elevated in heaven. "To hang our head–ostensibly" (105): The fact that many people pretend to have faith and humility that they discover they do not really feel is evidence that a person being addressed by this poem does not really believe in his frail arguments for some articles of faith. "What Inn is this" (115): Having arrived in the realm of death, the speaker is satirically curious about a lack of vitality in its residents and caretakers, for she had expected to find miraculous resurrection.

QUESTIONS FOR REVIEW AND WRITING

1. Why is a good general knowledge of Emily Dickinson's life useful for interpreting her poems?
2. How can knowledge of Emily Dickinson's life be misused in interpreting her poems?
3. Compare and contrast "We play at Paste" (320) and "Essential Oils–are wrung" (675).
4. Discuss the use of abstractions as vivid metaphors in "I dwell in Possibility" (657).
5. Compare and contrast the use of animals as symbols in Dickinson's love poems.
6. Discuss the relationship between deprivation and fulfillment in Dickinson's love poems.
7. Compare and contrast Dickinson's joyful and melancholy responses to nature.
8. Discuss the use of metaphors in Dickinson's nature scenes.
9. Discuss Dickinson's various tones, from ecstatic to anguished, in showing how rebirth can come from suffering.
10. Discuss the figure of the speaker as a little girl in Dickinson's poems.
11. Offer detailed arguments for the varying interpretations of "Because I could not stop for Death" (712).
12. Compare and contrast the changes of mood dramatized in "This world is not Conclusion" (501) and "I know that He exists" (338).
13. Discuss the figure of death as a lover in Dickinson's poems.
14. Compare and contrast Dickinson's first-person and third-person death scenes.
15. Discuss in detail your reasons for disagreeing with any whole interpretation of a poem made in these Notes.

SELECTED BIBLIOGRAPHY

ANDERSON, CHARLES R. *Emily Dickinson's Poetry: Stairway of Surprise.* New York: Holt, Rinehart, and Winston, 1960. Careful analysis of over one hundred poems.

BLAKE, CAESAR R. AND CARLTON F. WELLS, EDS. *The Recognition of Emily Dickinson: Selected Criticism Since 1890.* Ann Arbor:

University of Michigan Press, 1964. Collection of critical reviews, essays, and excerpts from books, arranged chronologically. Especially valuable for early critical views of Dickinson.

CHASE, RICHARD. *Emily Dickinson.* New York: William Sloane Associates, 1951. Competent critical biography based on pre-Johnson texts. Very qualified admiration for poems.

CODY, JOHN. *After Great Pain: The Inner Life of Emily Dickinson.* Cambridge, Mass.: Harvard University Press, 1971. Highly speculative psychoanalytic study interrelating life and poems.

DAVIS, THOMAS F., ED. *14 By Dickinson.* Chicago: Scott, Foresman, 1964. Collection of explications of fourteen well known poems.

GELPI, ALBERT J. *Emily Dickinson: The Mind of the Poet.* Cambridge, Mass.: Harvard University Press, 1965. Excellent study of Dickinson's major ideas, their sources, and interrelations.

GRIFFITH, CLARK. *The Long Shadow: Emily Dickinson's Tragic Poetry.* Princeton University Press, 1964. Largely psychological treatment of Dickinson's most anguished poems as her greatest accomplishment. Exaggerates her skepticism.

JOHNSON, THOMAS H. *Emily Dickinson: An Interpretive Biography.* Cambridge, Mass.: Harvard University Press, 1955. First critical biography based on Johnson text.

LEYDA, JAY. *The Years and Hours of Emily Dickinson.* New Haven: Yale University Press, 1960. 2 vols. Huge compilation of documents bearing on Dickinson's life; partly duplicates edition of her letters.

LINDBERG-SEYERSTED, BRITA. *The Voice of the Poet: Aspects of Style in the Poetry of Emily Dickinson.* Cambridge, Mass.: Harvard University Press, 1968. Systematic study of Dickinson's language habits, including prosody.

PICKARD, JOHN. *Emily Dickinson: An Introduction and Interpretation.* New York: Holt, Rinehart, and Winston, 1968. Probably the best brief general introduction.

ROSENBAUM, S. P. *A Concordance to the Poems of Emily Dickinson.* Ithaca, New York: Cornell University Press, 1964. Computer assisted concordance to variorum edition of poems. Invaluable for locating individual poems and for studying Dickinson's use of specific words.

SEWALL, RICHARD B. *The Life of Emily Dickinson,* 2 vols. New York: Farrar, Straus and Giroux, 1974. A biography. Hugely inclusive of facts and carefully non-dogmatic in its interpretation.

__________. *Emily Dickinson: A Collection of Critical Essays.* Englewood Cliffs: Prentice Hall, 1963. Excellent collection of critical essays and excerpts from books.

WARD, THEODORA. *The Capsule of the Mind: Chapters in the Life of Emily Dickinson.* Cambridge, Mass.: Harvard University Press, 1961. Interrelated essays on key stages of Dickinson's inner life; sharp insights without technical psychological vocabulary.

WEISBUCH, ROBERT. *Emily Dickinson's Poetry.* Chicago: University of Chicago Press, 1975. Fine study of how Dickinson's representational and symbolic techniques relate to problems of interpretation.

WHICHER, GEORGE F. *This Was a Poet: A Critical Biography of Emily Dickinson.* New York: Charles Scribner's Sons, 1939. The pioneering scholarly biography. Still useful for critical insights and commentary on background of Dickinson's ideas.

INDEX OF FIRST LINES

NOTES

NOTES

ADVENTURES OF HUCKLEBERRY FINN

NOTES

including

- *Life and Background*
- *General Plot Summary*
- *List of Characters*
- *Note on Chapter Titles*
- *Summaries and Commentaries*
- *Character Analyses*
- *Review Questions*
- *Selected Bibliography*

by
James L. Roberts, Ph.D.
Department of English
University of Nebraska

NEW EDITION

LINCOLN, NEBRASKA 68501

Editor

Gary Carey, M.A.
University of Colorado

Consulting Editor

James L. Roberts, Ph.D.
Department of English
University of Nebraska

ISBN 0-8220-0606-5
© Copyright 1971
by
C. K. Hillegass
All Rights Reserved
Printed in U.S.A.

1990 Printing

The Cliffs Notes logo, the names "Cliffs" and "Cliffs Notes," and the black and yellow diagonal-stripe cover design are all registered trademarks belonging to Cliffs Notes, Inc., and may not be used in whole or in part without written permission.

Cliffs Notes, Inc. Lincoln, Nebraska

CONTENTS

Huckleberry Finn Notes

LIFE AND BACKGROUND

As one of America's first and foremost realists and humorists, Mark Twain, the pen name of Samuel Langhorne Clemens, usually wrote about his own personal experiences and things he knew about from firsthand experience. The various characters in *Adventures of Huckleberry Finn* are based on types which Twain encountered both in his home town and while working as a riverboat pilot on the Mississippi River.

Twain was born in the little town of Florida, Missouri, on November 30, 1835, shortly after his family had moved there from Tennessee. When he was about four, the family moved again, this time to Hannibal, Missouri, a small town of about five hundred people, situated on the Mississippi River about eighty miles from St. Louis. Hannibal was dusty and quiet with large forests nearby which Twain knew as a child and which he uses in *Huck Finn* when Pap kidnaps Huck and hides out in the great forest. The steamboats which passed daily were the fascination of the town and became the subject matter of Twain's *Life on the Mississippi*. The town of Hannibal is immortalized as St. Petersburg in Twain's *The Adventures of Tom Sawyer*.

Twain's father was a lawyer by profession, but was only mildly successful. He was, however, a highly intelligent man who was a stern disciplinarian. Twain's mother, a southern belle in her youth, had a natural sense of humor, was emotional, and was known to be particularly fond of animals and unfortunate human beings. Although the family was not wealthy, Twain apparently had a happy childhood. Twain's father died when Twain was twelve years old and, for the next ten years, Twain was an apprentice printer and then a printer both in Hannibal and in New York City. Hoping to find his fortune, he conceived a wild scheme of making a fortune in South America. On a riverboat to

New Orleans, he met a famous riverboat pilot who promised to teach him the trade for five hundred dollars. After completing his training, Twain was a riverboat pilot for four years and, during this time, he became familiar with all of the towns along the Mississippi River which play such an important part in *Huck Finn,* and he also became acquainted with every type of character which inhabits his various novels, especially *Huck Finn.*

When the Civil War began, Twain's allegiance tended to be somewhat southern due to his southern heritage, but his brother Orion convinced him to go west on an expedition, a trip which became the subject matter of a later work, *Roughing It.* Even though some of his letters and accounts of traveling had been published, Twain actually launched his literary career with the short story "The Celebrated Jumping Frog of Calaveras County," published in 1865. This story brought him national attention, and he devoted the major portion of the rest of his life to literary endeavors. He died in 1910.

GENERAL PLOT SUMMARY

Huck Finn decides to tell his own story since the reader has already heard about him through a novel called *The Adventures of Tom Sawyer.* As the son of the town drunkard, Huck has had difficulty living with the Widow Douglas and her sister, Miss Watson, since both want to civilize him. He prefers the easy and free manner of living wild. When his father discovers that Huck has some money, Huck is kidnapped and held prisoner in a shack across the river. His father beats him so brutally that Huck decides that he must escape or else his father will kill him some day. He creates a plan whereby it will appear that he has been murdered and then he goes to Jackson's Island to hide.

On the island he discovers Jim, Miss Watson's runaway slave, and Huck promises to keep Jim's secret. Huck discovers that some men are coming to the island to search for Jim, and the two escape by floating down the Mississippi River on a raft they had earlier discovered. They plan to go to the Ohio River and travel north into free states. On the river, they feel free and easy as they travel during the night and hide during the day. One night, in a storm, they float past Cairo and, since the raft can't go upstream, they search for a canoe. Before they find one, a steamship runs into the raft.

Huck climbs ashore and finds himself being challenged by the Grangerford men who are having a feud with the Shepherdsons. Huck tells them that he is George Jackson and that he fell overboard off a steamboat. He stays with them until he witnesses the deaths of many people in an outbreak of the feud. In the meantime, Jim has been discovered and they return to the raft and escape from the feuding.

Down the river, two scoundrels make their way to the raft and call themselves a duke and a king. At one town along the river, the king and the duke put on a trumped-up show and gull the townspeople out of a large sum of money. Continuing down the river, the king and the duke discover that a Peter Wilks has just died and left a large sum of money to two brothers in England who are expected any day. The king and the duke imitate the brothers in order to rob the Wilks family of its inheritance. Huck, however, is sympathetic to one of the nieces and foils their plan. As they escape and head down the river, the king and the duke are desperate for money, so they sell Jim to Silas Phelps for ransom money.

Huck hides the raft and goes to the Phelps farm where he is immediately mistaken for Tom Sawyer, who is supposed to arrive the same day. Huck goes out to meet Tom and they decide that Huck will remain Tom, and Tom will pretend to be his brother Sid. After many fantastic and ridiculous plans are put into effect to free Jim, at the moment of escape Tom is shot in the leg and Jim has to give up his chance for freedom to help nurse Tom. After the episode, however, it is discovered that Jim was already freed by his owner, Miss Watson, just before she died. Huck decides to head out for new territory because he does not like civilized society.

LIST OF CHARACTERS

Huckleberry Finn

Son of the town drunkard and narrator of the novel.

Tom Sawyer

Huck's respectable friend who delights in fantastic schemes.

Widow Douglas

Huck's unofficial guardian who wants to civilize him.

Miss Watson

The widow's hypocritical sister who pretends to be very pious.

Jim

Miss Watson's slave whom she plans to sell down the river.

Aunt Polly

Tom's aunt who is also his guardian.

Jo Harper, Ben Rogers, and **Tommy Barnes**

Members of Tom Sawyer's gang.

Pap

Huck's brutal, drunken father.

Judge Thatcher

The kindly judge who invests money for Huck.

Mrs. Loftus

A town lady whom Huck visits dressed as a girl.

Jake Packard, Bill, and **Jim Turner**

Cutthroats whom Huck discovers on a ship that is sinking.

The Grangerfords

The family who adopts Huck for a while and who are feuding with the Shepherdsons.

The duke and the king

The two scoundrels who take over the raft for a while.

Boggs

An offensive drunkard in a small Arkansas town who is shot down in cold blood.

Colonel Sherburn

The man who shoots Boggs and who later turns away the mob by ridiculing them.

Buck Harkness

The man who tries to lead the mob against Colonel Sherburn.

Peter Wilks

A well-to-do businessman with relatives in England. He has recently died and the family is waiting for the arrival of his two brothers from England.

William and Harvey Wilks

The two brothers who arrive after the duke and king pretend to be them.

Mary Jane, Susan, and Joanna

Peter Wilks' nieces.

Dr. Robinson and Levi Bell

Two townspeople who see through the guise of the duke and the king.

Silas Phelps

The man who buys Jim for the ransom money.

Aunt Sally Phelps

Silas' wife, also Tom Sawyer's aunt.

NOTE ON CHAPTER TITLES

In the original edition of the novel, Twain did not give titles to the individual chapters. In later editions, however, he did include titles to the various chapters. The following list presents the title he assigned to each chapter:

Chapter I	I DISCOVER MOSES AND THE BULRUSHERS
Chapter II	OUR GANG'S DARK OATH
Chapter III	WE AMBUSCADE THE A-RABS
Chapter IV	THE HAIR-BALL ORACLE
Chapter V	PAP STARTS IN ON A NEW LIFE
Chapter VI	PAP STRUGGLES WITH THE DEATH ANGEL
Chapter VII	I FOOL PAP AND GET AWAY
Chapter VIII	I SPARE MISS WATSON'S JIM

SUMMARIES AND COMMENTARIES

"TWAIN'S INTRODUCTORY NOTE"

Although Twain wrote this novel from 1876 through 1883, he set the time back in the era of slavery about "forty to fifty years" earlier. In between the actual time of the novel and the composition, the Civil War had theoretically freed the slaves, but the status of the Negro had not been improved and they were still kept in a subservient position.

Twain warns his readers that they will be persecuted if they attempt "to find a motive . . . or a moral" in the novel. This ironic statement, then, calls attention to the fact that there is definitely a serious intent to this novel which was missing in the earlier *The Adventures of Tom Sawyer.* While both books deal with the escapades of youths, and while both books capture something of the lost world of the young adolescent, the latter book can be read on a much deeper level.

Even though *Huck Finn* can profitably be read by younger persons, the greatness and the depth of the novel can only be fully appreciated and understood by the perceptive adult. Only the mature reader can completely recognize the complexity of this work of art, the profound social message, the verisimilitude of characterization, the psychological depths, and the moral values found individually throughout the various chapters.

In these introductory remarks, Twain makes it clear that he is imitating several different types of dialect—even though to an unfamiliar ear, it is sometimes difficult to distinguish between them. However, one has only to read the dialect found in other "local color" writers to recognize the greatness of Twain's use of dialect. The dialect used by Johnson Jones Hooper or Joel Chandler Harris, for example, has become almost impossible to read. Yet Twain was so careful and yet so accurate that his dialect lends piquancy to the novel and does not interfere with reading.

Twain's use of dialect has also contributed to the reputation of the novel, helping to evoke comments such as Ernest Hemingway's that this novel is the beginning of American literature. The novel, with its precise location, its subject matter of slavery and freedom, its rather definite time, and its unique array of frontier people place it as a uniquely American work of art.

CHAPTER I

Summary

Huck Finn reminds the readers that he has already appeared in a book about Tom Sawyer called *The Adventures of Tom Sawyer.* This book was "made by Mr. Mark Twain, and he told the truth, mainly. There was things which he stretched, but mainly he told the truth." He reminds us that at the end of that book, he and Tom had found six thousand dollars apiece. Since then, the Widow Douglas has been trying to civilize Huck, and Judge Thatcher has invested the money for him, bringing a dollar a day in interest.

The widow's sister, Miss Watson, also lives in the house, and she is forever picking at Huck, trying to make him do things her way. Unlike the Widow Douglas, who is kind and patient with Huck, Miss Watson is sharp and nagging. Her insistent interference makes Huck resent home life and its restraints. They won't even let him smoke.

Huck is so disgusted with home life that he accidentally kills a spider, and he knows that this act is bound to bring bad luck to him. However, as he sits and smokes, he hears Tom Sawyer's secret call. Huck puts out the light, slides to the ground, and finds Tom waiting for him among the trees.

Commentary

The opening sentence of the novel connects Huck with his appearance in *The Adventures of Tom Sawyer.* But as Huck says, "it ain't no matter" if the reader has not read the earlier work. In other words, Twain is letting us know that this is not a serial continuation—this novel is a complete work of art in its own right, is self-contained, and is not dependent upon other works.

Furthermore, Huck himself is going to be the narrator of this book and, thus, the reader will see all the events as Huck reports them. This choice of a narrator will provide the reader with much of the basic humor. That is, Huck, as narrator, reports things directly and never comments much on them. He is not aware of many of the incongruous items which he reports, and his failure to see the incongruity contributes to our reading pleasure. For example, in this chapter he runs away, but Tom Sawyer tells him that if he will "go back to the widow and be respectable," then he can become one of Tom's gang of robbers. The contradiction between the terms "respectable" and "robber" is beyond Huck's comprehension, but is immediately funny to the reader. This type of straightforward reporting, and failure to see the incongruous elements while reporting factually, is the basis of much of Twain's humor.

Of the many themes which run throughout the novel, several are introduced in this first chapter. First, Huck mentions that the Widow Douglas wanted to "sivilize" him. In contrast, Huck wants to escape and be "free and satisfied." The conflict between society and the individual becomes a controlling theme as the novel develops, and is investigated on several different levels. Furthermore, the novel ends with Huck planning "to light out" for a different territory because Aunt Sally plans to "sivilize" him. In between these opening and closing remarks, Huck encounters varying aspects, attitudes, and restrictions of society and learns to prefer his own individual freedom. This idea will receive its dramatic climax when Huck decides to oppose the dictates of society and "go to hell" for the sake of his friendship with Jim.

The restriction of living with the Widow Douglas also introduces the idea of Huck's quest for freedom which will later be correlated with Jim's quest of freedom from slavery. This theme will also function on many levels as Huck and Jim begin their trip down the river in search of freedom.

In conjunction with the restrictive effects of civilization is Twain's subtle satire on the traditional concepts of religion. Huck sees Miss Watson's traditional view of "a pearly gate" concept of heaven as being essentially boring and restrictive. The Widow Douglas' view is somewhat more appealing, but Huck would prefer to go to a more exciting place. The concept of religion, in general, throughout the novel is attacked by Twain in various guises. Basically, a society which required its property (its slaves) to become practicing Christians is a contradiction of the tenets of Christianity. Slaves were sometimes referred to, ironically, as "baptized property." For Twain, the concept of slavery and the pious religious concepts of the southerners were the height of contradictory absurdity.

Another theme introduced in this first chapter is that of Huck's birth and rebirth. When he feels stifled or deadened by society, he escapes to become reborn again. And throughout the novel, Huck loses his identity, assumes different names (even Tom Sawyer's), arranges his own murder, and then, in turn, is reborn with new or different values.

Furthermore, each time that Huck escapes from some situation, the theme of his loneliness and isolation is often touched upon. In this first chapter, he says that "I felt so lonesome I most wished I was dead." Man's feeling of loneliness and isolation is a recurrent theme in the total works of Twain. In this novel, it is expressed by Huck's encounter with the vastness of the frontier, with the magnitude of the Mississippi River and with the formidable forests which surrounded the settlements.

This feeling of loneliness is also correlated with the superstitions which permeate the novel. Confronted with the vastness of their isolation, Huck, Jim, and other characters put great reliance on superstitions of one sort or another. These superstitions develop into an important motif as the novel develops. In this first chapter, Huck is horrified by the implications inherent in accidentally flipping a spider into a candle and immediately makes the proper signs to ward off any bad luck.

Finally, Twain's careful craftsmanship is fully illustrated in the seemingly casual manner in which he introduces most of his major themes in his first chapter. In the hands of a lesser author, the introduction of such a variety of thematic material could possibly become contrived or artificial, yet Twain presents each theme as an integral part of the narrative structure of this short, first chapter.

CHAPTERS II AND III

Summary

As Huck joins Tom Sawyer in the garden, he accidentally trips over a root and alerts Miss Watson's slave, Jim, to the fact that something unusual is happening. Jim sits down on the ground between Tom and Huck, and he would have discovered them if he had not gone to sleep. Tom then plays a trick on Jim—a trick which multiplies in size as Jim tells the story after he awakes. With each telling, the story becomes more fanciful until Jim becomes the most envied Negro in the village.

Tom and Huck meet some other boys, and Tom wants to organize a band of robbers. From the various "pirate-books and robber-books" that Tom has read, he binds the members of his gang together with a beautiful oath and then makes plans to "stop stages and carriages on the road, with masks on, and kill the people and take their watches and money." Tom also wants to kidnap people and then hold them for ransom, but nobody knows what a ransom is. It is almost daylight before Huck creeps back through his window with his new clothes "all greased up and clayey. . . ."

After receiving a scolding from Miss Watson, Huck is also instructed in religion by the old maid, but he can't make any sense out of her type of sermonizing. About this time, a drowned body has been found and many people think it is Huck's pap, but Huck knows that he couldn't be that lucky. Unfortunately, he knows that his father would show up again some day even though he hasn't been around for over a year.

For about a month, the boys play robbers until Huck and all the other boys resign, for, by then, they have neither robbed nor killed anyone "but only just pretended." The romantic Tom argues with the realistic Huck about the value of make-believe and the importance of magicians, "genies," and the like. Huck tests the theory of genies by getting an old lamp, rubbing it for hours, and making elaborate plans for the genie. But when no genies appear, he loses faith in it and also questions Tom Sawyer's assertions.

Commentary

Chapters II and III introduce the characters of Tom Sawyer and Jim, both of whom will function prominently in the rest of the novel. Jim is introduced as Miss Watson's Negro. Such a seemingly innocent fact carries in Twain a certain importance. In other words, why couldn't Jim belong to the Widow Douglas? Twain is continuing his subtle distinction between these two women. Miss Watson's religion is based upon a more superficial and restrictive system than is the Widow Douglas'. In contrast, the Widow Douglas would "talk about Providence in a way to make a boy's mouth water," whereas Miss Watson would then "take hold and knock it all down again." Thus, with the Widow Douglas being more of a humanist in her religion, it is more fitting for the narrow-minded, restrictive Miss Watson to *own* a slave. Also, Huck's offering of Miss Watson—and not the Widow Douglas—as a person to be killed if he violates the oath to the band of robbers is a further indication of the contrast between Huck's system of values and that of the old maid.

The introduction of Tom functions as a contrast to Huck Finn. The extravagant plans and games which Tom introduces contrast to the sensible, practical, and functional plans which Huck institutes. This contrast is seen in Huck's escape from Pap, and in all of his schemes along the river, and is finally brought to a climax when Tom reappears at the Phelps plantation and instigates his fantastic escape schemes.

In contrast to the personality of Huck, Tom Sawyer represents a type of conformity to society. He *does* leave five cents on the table for the candles which they "steal," whereas Huck will always "borrow" what he needs to complete any scheme and will usually justify it in some manner or another. This small fact lends credence to Huck's view that Tom Sawyer could not possibly help free a slave (at the end of the novel) because of Tom's respectability and conformity to the views of society.

Tom's oaths, his schemes, and his escapades are based upon books about romantic adventures which he has read. Whereas Huck is involved in real life, Tom functions only when he is imitating something which he has read in a book. Furthermore, both here and at the end of the novel, Twain is ridiculing various aspects of romantic fiction which were very popular during that time. All of Tom's plans are satiric takeoffs on such fiction as *The Arabian Nights,* Alexander Dumas' *The Count of Monte Cristo,* or Cervantes' *Don Quixote* and many more novels of fantastic adventures. Mainly, however, these fictional adventures function as a contrast to the realistic and believable experiences of Huck Finn.

The Mississippi River, which will take on increasing symbolic importance as the novel progresses, is introduced as being "awful still and grand." Ultimately, the river will become the controlling image and main structural device, but already this early in the novel, Twain suggests its power and grandeur.

Jim's adherence to superstition, particularly with witches and devils in Chapter II, continues the superstition motif of the first chapter. Throughout the novel, Jim will often attribute their misfortunes to some type of bad luck sign, especially the snake bite in a subsequent chapter.

Through Huck Finn, Twain continues his gentle satire against religion. Twain himself had undergone serious contemplations about the nature of religion and the implications of religious faith, which receive their fullest expression in *The Mysterious Stranger,* published posthumously in 1916. Here, however, his satire is mild and is directed at religious sentimentality and superficiality. Huck's attempts to pray in order to get some fish hooks can hardly be viewed as a bitter attack on religion.

Huck's literal belief both in praying for fish hooks and in finding a genie in an old lamp illustrates again his literal mindedness. This literal mindedness is a quality which will allow Huck to recognize Jim's basic qualities later on. That is, Huck accepts everything at face value and is not influenced by the values of society, as is Tom Sawyer. Huck's reliance upon the face value of an object then allows him to formulate his own system of values.

CHAPTERS IV AND V

Summary

After three or four months, during which time he attends school and learns to read and write, Huck sees some signs which suggest that his pap is back in town. Fearing his pap, he goes to Judge Thatcher and asks if there is any money from the investments. The judge tells him the amount, and Huck wants to give it to the judge. Leaving the judge confused, Huck goes to have Jim consult his hair-ball to discover Huck's fortune. Huck's fears of his father's return are justified because that night when he went to his room, "there set pap, his own self!"

Pap stands before Huck looking vicious and mean. He curses Huck out for trying to get some education, for wearing nice clothes, and for the possibility that someday he might want to get some religion. He will not tolerate the idea of his son improving himself and trying to be better than his own father. He forces Huck to give him the dollar which he had gotten from Judge Thatcher and goes to get some whiskey with it. He tries to bully Judge Thatcher into giving him the rest of Huck's money, but the judge refuses. He then goes to court to get custody of Huck, and even though the Widow Douglas and the judge oppose it, a new judge gives the custody of the boy to his father. Pap promises to reform with the aid of the new judge, but the improvement is short lived. Soon Pap trades his new coat for a jug of whiskey, gets drunk, rolls off the porch, and breaks his left arm in two places. The new judge gives up on Pap.

Commentary

The superstition motif is continued in Chapter IV and leads to Huck's fears that Pap is coming back. Spilling the salt leads to the discovery of the "cross in the left boot-heel" which Huck associates with his pap. Huck's fears impel him to rely upon Jim's knowledge of the occult. Beneath this scene is the gentle ridicule of superstition and magic; yet, Huck's fears are realized when he discovers his pap in the room at night.

When he first suspects that Pap has returned, Huck's immediate action is to try to give all his money to Judge Thatcher so that he won't be persecuted by his father. This is our first realization of Huck's perception and his shrewdness; that is, he knows that his pap will leave him alone if he has no money and since he dreads an encounter with his pap, he tries to give away the money so that he won't have to lie. This is not to imply that Huck objects to lying, but, in this case, it is the easiest course to follow because then he can convince his father that he has no money. Furthermore, Huck knows, as we later find out, that legally, a father has a right to any of his son's possessions. So, in one sense, Huck may be protecting his investment since he trusts the judge but not his own father.

Huck's willingness to part with such a large sum of money indicates his reliance upon other values and upon his own ability. Later, small sums seem much more important than such large abstract sums. This also suggests that Huck has not yet developed society's acquisitiveness.

In the depiction of Huck's pap, we have one of a series of superior characterizations of a minor character. Throughout the novel, Twain is able to depict so many of the secondary characters with such skill that they become memorable characters.

The introduction of Pap and his characterization indicate that Pap is a part of that society from which Huck wishes to escape. In contrast to Miss Watson's hypocrisy, Pap represents the brutality and severity of civilization which threaten to destroy Huck. Later we find that civilization is not as concerned over Huck's suffering at the hands of his pap as it is over discovering and rescuing Huck's dead body.

Unlike the American dream in which the parents desire something better for their children, Pap reprimands Huck for being able to read and write and climaxes his reprimand by asserting "First you know you'll get religion, too." More important is the reverse irony here. On a basic level, Pap is wrong because all children should learn to read and write, but, in the larger sense, we, the readers, do not want Huck to get educated in terms of the values of a society which advocates slavery, and we do not want him to adopt the type of religion which Miss Watson practices. Thus, on one level, Pap is wrong, but on a greater level, unknown to him, he is right.

The appearance of Pap prepares us for Huck's need to escape from a society which forces a son to obey such a thoroughly corrupt and evil person as Pap. The lack of understanding in the "new judge" when he refuses to "take a child away from its father" is another example of how society follows the old stereotyped concepts without considering the individual factors in the case. Only when the new judge sees personally the hypocrisy of Pap does he realize his error.

CHAPTERS VI AND VII

Summary

Huck is now determined to continue with his schooling, partly to spite his pap, who thrashes Huck every time he can catch him. When Pap hangs around the Widow Douglas' house too much, she threatens him. To get even with her, he kidnaps Huck and takes him across the river to a cabin in the woods where he keeps Huck locked up every time he leaves. Soon Huck gets used to living in the woods and has no desire to return to the widow and "sivilization."

The worse thing about living in the woods is that Pap beats Huck quite frequently and sometimes leaves him locked up in the cabin for as long as three days. Once when Pap returns from town, he is so drunk that he almost kills Huck. It is then that Huck decides that he has to find some way to escape—to avoid being killed.

The next day Huck discovers a canoe which he hides in the underbrush. When Pap catches some logs, he immediately leaves for town in order to sell them. Huck takes out a saw that he had hid, finishes sawing a hole in the wall, and then loads his canoe with provisions. He then shoots a wild pig, smashes the door of the cabin and scatters the pig's blood all over the place. He pulls out some of his own hair and sticks it on the back of the bloody axe, thereby giving the impression that he has been murdered. He then goes to the canoe and waits until dark. After a nap, he heads across the river for Jackson's Island, barely escaping detection from Pap, who is returning home.

Commentary

We see that in Pap's mind, money and education are juxtaposed, and since Pap has neither, he doesn't want Huck to have either. His frantic activities show him as a person to be avoided and Huck now intentionally goes to school "to spite pap."

It is a bizarre situation which Twain is presenting here when a father has to kidnap his own son. The entire relationship between Huck and his pap is endowed with the most extreme behavior on the part of Pap, and since Huck associates his own father with the evils of civilization, then the brutality of Pap becomes vaguely correlated in his mind with the brutality of civilization.

This father-son relationship stands as a contrast later on when Jim says that he will "steal" his own daughter if he can't free her in any other way. But Jim's comments are the result of his love and concern for his daughter. By this broad sweeping contrast between Huck and Pap and between Jim and his daughter, Twain is making a broad comment on the nature of parental love which cuts through the stereotyped view that *naturally* a white father would care more for his child than would a black father.

Huck's adaptability is again emphasized in this chapter. Earlier, in Chapter IV, Huck had reached a point where he "was getting sort of used to the widow's ways, too, and they warn't so raspy on me." Then after two months of living with Pap in the wilderness, he became so adjusted that he "didn't see how I'd ever got to like it so well at the widow's. . . ." Thus, one of Huck's major attributes is his ability to adapt to any situation and to live in a variety of different surroundings, including the comfort of the raft later on.

In Chapter VI, Huck definitely seems to prefer the freedom of the wilderness to the restrictions of society. However, his freedom is modified by the presence of Pap, and the very safety of his life is often threatened by Pap's actions. Huck is mature enough to recognize the danger and only when he becomes convinced that Pap represents an immediate threat to his life does he decide upon the necessity of an escape.

Furthermore, Pap's actions toward him are a violation of Huck's belief that everyone should be kind to everyone else. His concept of freedom, then, is modified only when he feels that his life is endangered and that Pap does not "feel right and kind toward . . . others," which Huck uses as a basis for his own actions. The freedom is also modified by Huck's feelings of loneliness and isolation, particularly when Pap leaves him locked up.

Pap's drunken tirade against the "prowling, thieving, infernal, white-shirted free niger. . . ." fully illustrates a basic concept about prejudice. The lower and the more incompetent the dregs of humanity are, the oftener they preach subservience so as to protect their own inadequacies.

The final actions in Chapter VI convince Huck of the necessity of putting his escape plan into action immediately. Throughout his plans to escape, he is more concerned for his life than he is about anything else. He makes no attempt to inform people that he is alive so that his six thousand dollars will be protected—in fact, he knows that even if he were to try secretly to protect it that his pap might find out. Huck prefers simply to disappear and begin a new life, especially since, as we have seen, material comforts connected with great wealth are not important to Huck.

Huck's plan for escape is one of simple common sense combined with shrewdness and imagination. Ironically, he wishes that Tom Sawyer were there to give the plan the "fancy touches," but the reader knows that Huck is totally wrong. If Tom were there, the entire plan would probably fail or would soon be exposed as a trick even if Huck escaped. Tom's plans always carry a large dose of romantic falseness and absurdity. Thus, ultimately, Huck's plan here, based upon common sense, necessity, and shrewd judgment contrasts to Tom's pretentious and ridiculous plans at the Phelps' plantation. Again this is Twain's insistence that common sense and natural actions are to be valued above romantic pretensions. The plans also illustrate clearly that Huck will be able to take care of himself in the *larger* world, and suggests, by contrast, that Tom Sawyer, left to his own artificial ingenuity, would soon perish.

CHAPTERS VIII AND IX

Summary

The next day, Huck knows that his plan was a success when he sees a ferryboat filled with the important people of the town searching for his body. A cannon which is fired to make the body come to the surface almost kills Huck, and a loaf of bread which is supposed to lead them to the body floats to Huck's hiding place and he eats it for his breakfast.

After they leave, Huck is left alone on the island for three days and nights and begins to get lonesome. On the third day, he discovers the remains of a camp fire. Huck is frightened and paddles over to the Illinois shore, but fearing discovery from some travelers, he returns and keeps watch over the place where he discovered the ashes. Soon, Miss Watson's Jim appears and

Huck is awfully glad to see him. Thinking Huck is dead, Jim is frightened by Huck's "ghost." Huck tells him that he isn't dead, and they talk about their adventures. Jim confesses to Huck that he has run away because Miss Watson was about to sell him down south. Huck promises not to tell on Jim, even though "people would call me a low down Ablitionist and despise me for keeping mum. . . ."

During the next few days, Jim and Huck move their supplies to a cavern at the top of the hill on Jackson's Island. They spend their days collecting various things on the river that have floated loose because of the rising river water. Among the choice possessions they find is a large raft twelve feet wide and fifteen or sixteen feet long.

One night, they see a two-story frame house float by. They catch up with it and climb aboard to see if they can find any useful articles. While there, they discover a dead man who had been shot in the back. Jim quickly throws some rags over the corpse so that Huck won't have to see this gruesome sight. They load their canoe with all the worthwhile stuff in the cabin and head back to Jackson's Island.

Commentary

With Chapter VIII, Twain introduces another of his larger themes, that of death and rebirth. In terms of the entire novel, Huck symbolically dies in this chapter to be born again with a new set of values. The rebirth begins immediately when Huck encounters Jim, the runaway slave. Having died to the society from which he is escaping, Huck has spent three days in total isolation and loneliness—"by-and-by it got sort of lonesome." Thus, the encounter with Jim represents Huck's need for some sort of human companionship.

The need for human contact is pitted against Huck's past values as Jim confesses that he has run off. Huck knows that people (society) would "call me a low down Ablitionist and despise me for keeping mum," but he decides to keep his word to Jim in spite of the dictates of society. Had Huck not escaped from society, from Pap, and possibly death at the hands of Pap, then Huck's reaction to Jim's escape might have been different. This acceptance of Jim foreshadows Huck's later set of values when he totally defies society for the sake of his friendship with Jim.

Huck's rebirth is, therefore, first seen in his decision to help Jim and is set against the background of the society from which he is escaping. The irony is that when Huck was kidnapped by his father, the Widow Douglas made a nominal attempt to rescue Huck, but not until the boy is thought to be dead is there a full scale effort to rescue his body. Twain's satire on American values is obvious; society is more concerned about a dead body than it is in the welfare of living people. And, as we find out in Chapter XI, there is a three-hundred-dollar reward for the capture of Jim, but only two hundred dollars are offered for the capture of Huck's murderer.

These two chapters also continue Twain's contrast between the natural, or practical, sense of Huck set against superstitions of varying sorts. First, there are the actions of the seemingly educated people of town – Judge Thatcher, Tom Sawyer, Aunt Polly, Sid, the captain, etc. – who superstitiously load up bread with quicksilver which, ironically, feeds Huck and who shoot cannons over the water which, ironically, almost kills Huck.

The superstitions receive greater credence since they are seen against Huck's practical and natural actions of hiding his canoe, concealing his traps, preparing a camp under cover, and in escaping detection. It is also very natural and practical the way he is able to discover whose campfire he stumbles across. Then, Huck's first appearance causes Jim to think that he has seen a real ghost.

The practical, or natural, sense and superstitions are brought together in Jim's predictions. In almost all of Jim's superstitious utterings, there is embedded very practical, common sense knowledge. For example, Jim watches the actions of the birds and predicts the weather, which is good frontier practicality. Man can often predict certain natural events by observing the actions of the animals. Furthermore, in Jim's predictions about wealth, he leaves so much leeway that there is a practical sense about his views in that they could come true in many different ways. Jim also points out that no one needs to know any good luck signs because no one wants to prevent good luck.

Jim and Huck do share one trait in common—both are literal minded. Like Huck, who tried to pray for fish hooks, Jim thinks that if he gives money away he will "git his money back a hund'd times." Also, he considers himself rich now that he owns himself.

In Chapter VIII, Jim introduces his plan to escape by getting to the Illinois side of the river and later going up the Ohio River to free territory. Illinois, which was just across the river from slave territory, was historically not sympathetic to runaway slaves, and often they were returned by professional bounty hunters. Therefore, the more practical plan would be to go up the Ohio River to a state sympathetic to freeing the slave.

In Chapter IX, Jim and Huck establish a rather good place to live, and this serenity will not be interrupted until Huck discovers the plan of the townsmen to come looking on Jackson's Island for the runaway slave. From their base they are able to capture various items which float down the river. The frame house with the dead body in it attests to the fact that Twain had already planned on the death of Pap at this stage in the novel, but he will not reveal this fact until the last chapter of the novel.

CHAPTERS X AND XI

Summary

After breakfast, Huck wants to talk about the dead man, but Jim refuses to do so, saying that it might bring them bad luck. The bad luck comes in terms of a practical joke which Huck plays on Jim. He kills a rattlesnake and curls it up at the foot of Jim's bed, thinking it will be fun to watch Jim's reaction when he sees it. But the rattlesnake's mate crawls up around the dead one and when Jim returns, the mate bites him. Huck realizes that it happens because he was "such a fool as to not remember that wherever you leave a dead snake its mate always comes there and curls around it." Huck quickly throws the two snakes away before Jim can discover what happened. Jim is sick for four days and nights before he recovers. After a few days, Huck becomes restless and wants to know what is going on in town. Jim advises him to dress up like a girl in some of the clothes that they salvaged from the floating house. He heads out for the shore and, in town, he finds a house of a woman who is a newcomer. He decides to talk with this woman, trying hard to remember that he is a girl.

Huck identifies himself as Sarah Williams and, as he talks with the lady, he learns of the gossip and rumors connected with the separate disappearances of Huck and Jim. Although the lady has lived in the town only two weeks, she is already well informed in regard to the different theories of the supposed murder of Huck and the disappearance of Jim. The two murder suspects are Jim and Pap. Some people think that Pap did it in order to get Huck's money without bothering with a lawsuit. Others think that Jim did it, since he ran away the same night that Huck disappeared. There is a three-hundred dollar reward offered for Jim and a two-hundred dollar reward for Pap.

When Huck hears the lady say that she has seen smoke on Jackson's Island and that her husband is going over to see if he could capture Jim, Huck becomes so anxious that he forgets that he is a girl. Using several basic tests, the lady soon discovers that Huck is a boy. Huck then admits that he is in disguise and invents another story about his escape from a hard master and his flight to Goshen. He is promptly informed, however, that this is not Goshen; it is St. Petersburg. He convinces her that someone has played a trick on him and leaves as soon as possible.

After Huck leaves, he goes as quickly as possible back to Jackson's Island, starts a fire in the old camp site, then goes to find Jim. When he comes upon Jim, he tells him to get ready quickly because "They're after us!" Since their raft is already loaded, it takes only a few minutes to leave, and they glide along the shady side of the island until they have passed the foot of the island.

Commentary

Chapter X presents the climax of the theme of superstition when Jim is bitten by the rattlesnake. This is the first time that Huck has done something which shows that he is not using common sense. He knows that the mate to a dead snake always comes and curls around the dead one, and yet he left the dead snake there anyway. This lapse from common sense causes Jim to get bitten.

On another level, the episode with the snake bite shows Huck performing a Tom Sawyer-type of trick. Huck will pull only one more trick on Jim and then will develop into a more mature person. His deep regret at pulling this trick on Jim indicates the beginning of a deep relationship. We can assume that Tom Sawyer would not have the deep regret that Huck does.

Ultimately, whenever something bad happens later in the novel, Jim will blame it on the bad luck caused by the rattlesnake, which then involves Huck more intricately because the bad luck was caused by Huck himself. The superstition motif is brought to a climax because the remedies which Jim uses have the therapeutic effect of making Jim drunk enough so that he won't feel the pain.

The superstition theme is used at the beginning of the chapter so that Jim will not have to tell Huck that he saw Pap dead in the floating cabin. Jim's refusal to talk about the death carries several implications. First, the news is not revealed until the last page of the novel, thus attesting to the fact that Twain had planned ahead to the ending of his novel. Second, Jim's refusal might be selfish in that if Pap is dead, one more obstacle is removed from Huck's need to flee society, thus leaving Jim stranded in his flight. But, more important, as we later discover,

Jim feels so devoted to his own children that he assumes that this would be a terrible tragedy for Huck and therefore wants to spare Huck any feelings of grief. The implied comparison between Jim's love for his family and the brutality in Pap's relation to Huck will be later developed and will be one of the values by which Huck learns of Jim's humanity and love for others.

At the end of Chapter X, Huck is preparing to make his first journey to shore. The need to know whether Jim's escape was successful prompts the trip ashore and becomes the first of many subsequent adventures which pit the life on the raft against the life of society on the shore. Chapter XI also represents the end of the idyllic existence that Jim and Huck have been enjoying on the island.

Huck's trip ashore dressed as a girl is one of the classic excerpts from the novel and has often appeared separately. Thematically, this is another identity for Huck, and it is also the beginning of many different types of identities he will assume throughout their long journey.

Also introduced in this chapter is Huck's ability to invent stories. While Huck is fantastic, shrewd, and imaginative in creating a believable story which will conceal his real identity, he is also unable to remember the story which he tells and often has to resort to another ruse or shrewd trick in order to find out what he said earlier. As he says in a later chapter (XXXII), he seldom has a particular plan in mind, but, instead, he goes along "trusting to Providence to put the right words in my mouth when the time come." In other words, Huck relies upon his native ability, whereas Tom Sawyer has to have some ridiculous or fantastic plan.

While Huck is able to create believable stories, he is unable to fool the shrewd country woman. The tricks which she uses to reveal his identity as a boy have become classic. But while she traps Huck in his disguise, he is able to construct another story which gets him out of difficulty.

At the end of Chapter XI, Huck, having discovered that some men are going to Jackson's Island to look for Jim, returns as quickly as possible to the island and tells Jim: "Git up and hump yourself, Jim! There ain't a minute to lose. They're after us!" However they are *not* after *them,* only Jim. But by this time Huck has so completely identified with Jim and Jim's plight that he accepts Jim's struggle as his own. This, then, leads to his later acceptance of Jim as superior to the values of a society which would enslave him.

Chapter XI ends the first part of the novel and, with the next chapter, we enter into the second section, the experiences along the Mississippi River.

CHAPTERS XII AND XIII

Summary

It is almost one o'clock before they get below the island. At daybreak they tie the raft to a tow-head on the Illinois side which is covered with trees and bushes so that they are protected from sight. Here they can watch the steamboats go by. Huck tells Jim about the conversation with the lady in the cabin and how he built the fire to make the men stay there to catch Jim when he returned.

Jim builds a tent in the middle of the raft for protection from the weather. He and Huck also make an extra steering oar for emergencies. For five nights they travel down the river, lying on their backs and looking at the stars. Every night, Huck slips ashore for provisions. Five nights below St. Louis, they encounter a big storm and they board a wrecked steamboat, even though Jim tries to dissuade Huck from boarding it.

Once on the steamboat, they see a light down the "texas-hall" and overhear a conversation between two robbers, Jake Packard and Bill, who are about to murder an accomplice, Jim Turner, because he threatened to inform on them. At this point, Huck has to crawl into a stateroom on the upper side to keep from being detected. The thieves accidentally follow him into the room but Huck is able to hide from them. Packard argues that instead of murdering Turner they should take their boat ashore and leave Jim Turner on the wreck which will break up in two hours and wash down the river. Huck goes back to tell Jim and to set the robbers' boat adrift so that the men cannot get away. At this point, Jim reveals that the raft has broken loose in the storm, and they are also stranded.

Huck and Jim look for and find the boat (skiff) that the robbers arrived in. Just as they are about to board the skiff, Packard and Bill appear, arguing about the money which they left in Jim Turner's pocket. They decide to go back and get it. Huck and Jim then jump into the boat, cut the rope and escape, leaving all three cutthroats stranded on the foundering boat.

Before they are able to notify anyone about the wrecked boat, a summer storm comes up and a flash of lightning reveals their raft floating ahead of them. They recapture it, and Jim guides the raft while Huck follows in the skiff until they see the lights of a village on a hillside. Huck startles the sleeping watchman of a ferryboat and relates one of his stories designed to force the watchman to rescue the people on the wrecked boat. Artfully giving the impression that the niece of the richest man in town is on the boat, Huck influences the watchmen to rescue the cutthroats.

In a few minutes, the wreck comes floating along. It is so deep in the water that Huck knows that no one could still be alive, but he paddles around it and hollers. After hearing no sound, Huck gives up and goes to catch up with Jim. By now, it is daylight and they pull to shore and sleep "like dead people."

Commentary

Chapter XII begins the second major part of the novel and covers the various adventures down the Mississippi River until Jim is sold back into slavery. This chapter begins the odyssey down the river, which immediately takes upon a mythic quality as Huck notes the contentment found by escaping from society: "It was kind of solemn, drifting down the big still river, laying on our backs looking up at the stars. . . ."

The first significant adventure involves the wreck of the *Walter Scott* which Jim and Huck discover one night. The name of the wreck is one of Twain's subtle uses of satire since he apparently thought Walter Scott's novels, and any romantic novels, were something of a wreck which foundered when they tried to sail.

With this adventure and others like it, Huck constantly wishes that Tom Sawyer were along because this is much closer to life than were the Sunday School picnic raids which Tom used to organize. But Huck doesn't fully realize the inherent danger he is in when he embarks upon this adventure.

The purpose of boarding the vessel is to see if they can rescue anything of value from the wreck. Discovering the cutthroats and murderers on board, Huck is almost trapped since the raft has floated away, but is saved only by the greed of the men who return to get Jim Turner's "loot" before leaving him to his destiny.

Huck's first thought after escaping is to save Jim Turner (a murderer) from being murdered by the other two cutthroats, showing again Huck's sympathy for human beings. Even after he escapes, he conceives of the clever plan of sending the man with the ferry in order to try and save all three of the cutthroats from death. His sympathy with even the worse dregs of society allows Huck to respond to all classes of people and prepares us for his total acceptance of Jim.

Having attempted to save them, Huck ironically and erroneously thinks that the Widow Douglas would be proud of him for protecting the lives of these cutthroats because "helping . . . rapscallions and dead beats is the kind the widow and good people takes the most interest in."

Chapter XIII also shows again Huck's ingenuity in creating a story which serves his purpose. He hears the old ferryman speak jealously of the wealth of someone named Hornback and then Huck creates a story about Hornback's niece being trapped on the sinking boat—a story which immediately causes the ferryman to attempt a rescue mission.

CHAPTER XIV

Summary

When Huck and Jim awaken, they examine the loot which the robbers took from the wreck and find all sorts of valuable things, along with many books which Huck reads to Jim. The books contain tales of kings and dukes and earls and their many adventures in life. The only figure familiar to Jim is "King Sollermum," who was not a good person, in Jim's opinion, because King Solomon would have divided a child into two parts. Huck tries to explain the story of King Solomon to Jim, but Jim will not change his opinion. Furthermore, the entire concept of anyone speaking a language different from English is also astonishing to Jim who thinks that if a Frenchman is a man then he should speak like a man.

Commentary

Chapter XIV functions as a kind of interlude in which Huck and Jim enjoy some of the rewards (such as the cigars) which they got from the wrecked *Walter Scott.* If later in the novel, Huck seems to possess too much knowledge of history and other matters for a person of about fourteen years, we must remember that they rescue "lots of books" from the wreck and that Huck spends much of his leisure time reading them to himself and Jim. Since we have already seen Huck's practical and shrewd knowledge in operation, there is no reason to conclude that he cannot equally master "book" knowledge.

Furthermore, his reading about history and the discussion of the "dolphin" (dauphin) prepares us for the appearance and story of the "king" in Chapter XIX. Historically, there were persistent rumors, known even on the frontier, that the Dauphin, Louis

Charles (born 1785) had escaped execution and had fled to the new world. At the time of the novel, then, he would be about fifty-five years old, instead of seventy, which is the age of the "king."

This chapter also obliquely presents some more of Twain's satire against religion. For a person like Jim, who is in bondage or slavery, the stories of Christianity and of the Bible have little meaning to him and are often incomprehensible. As noted earlier, the concept of forcing slaves (property) to become practicing Christians is a violation of the concept of Christianity.

CHAPTERS XV AND XVI

Summary

In three more nights, Huck and Jim expect to reach Cairo, where they will sell the raft and catch a steamboat up the Ohio River. On the second night, however, there is so much fog that Huck takes the canoe and tries to find a place for them to tie up. Because of the swift current, the raft floats by and Huck cannot find Jim and the raft. He searches until he is exhausted and then falls asleep.

When he awakens, he sees the raft close by, filled with leaves and all sorts of trash, and Jim is asleep from worry and exhaustion. Huck slips onto the raft and when Jim finally wakes up, Huck tries to make him think that they have never been separated and that Jim dreamed everything that happened to them. When he has Jim almost convinced that it was all a dream, he asks Jim to interpret the dream—which Jim does; next, Huck asks him to interpret all the trash and branches on the raft. Then Jim realizes the truth and tells Huck that trash is "people . . . dat puts dirt on de head er dey fren's en makes 'em ashamed." Huck apologizes to Jim and vows to himself that he will never play a trick on Jim again.

Jim knows that they must be close to Cairo and therefore close to freedom, and he begins to talk about his freedom in a jubilant manner. Suddenly Huck's conscience begins to trouble him because he knows that he is helping someone else's property to escape. But then Jim says that if the owner of his children will not sell Jim his children, then he will get an abolitionist to help steal them. This is almost more than Huck can stand, and he knows suddenly that he is doing an awful thing in helping Jim to escape, and he resolves to slip ashore and tell. As he takes a canoe to go tell, Jim calls out that he will never forget what a good friend Huck has been to him.

When Huck meets some men looking for some runaway slaves, he cannot bring himself to betray Jim. Instead, he creates a story about his father on the raft having smallpox, and the men become frightened and give Huck money with instructions that he should never let it be known that his father has smallpox when he is seeking help. After the men leave, Huck feels again that he has done wrong, but it is too much bother to do right.

Later, Huck and Jim try to find out if they have passed Cairo, and when they see the clear water of the Ohio, they know that they have already passed the town. They go to the canoe so as to paddle back upstream, but the canoe has disappeared. As they continue downstream, a steamboat approaches them and, before they can get out of its way, the boat smashes directly into the raft. Jim goes overboard on one side and Huck on the other. Huck stays underwater until the thirty-foot wheel has passed over him. Soon the boat is churning along upstream again, but Huck cannot find Jim. He goes ashore alone, where he finds dogs barking in front of a large house.

Commentary

In these two chapters, Twain reached a crucial point in his narrative which was difficult to resolve. Somewhere along this point (probably toward the end of Chapter XVI), Twain put the manuscript aside and did not begin writing on it again for about two years.

After having Jim and Huck pass Cairo and the mouth of the Ohio River, Twain's original plan for Jim to escape up the Ohio

River must have been abandoned; but if this is so, it undercuts the larger theme of Jim's quest for freedom because the farther down the Mississippi they travel, the deeper they travel into slave territory. But, apparently, Twain was more concerned with the type of freedom represented by Huck and Jim on the raft, as contrasted to the imprisonment, the cruelty, and inhumanity represented by Huck's many encounters on the land.

In Chapter XV, when Jim and Huck get separated by the currents, Huck's loneliness is emphasized so as to stress the importance of his and Jim's relationship. Huck, however, still has some of his youthfulness about him and decides to fool Jim. The trick he plays on Jim is the last juvenile thing that Huck does until Tom Sawyer appears in the final part of the novel.

When Huck plays this trick on Jim, he fails to recognize the fullness of Jim's devotion to him. After Jim's classic definition of what is "trash," Huck understands the fullness of Jim's humanity and vows to play no more tricks on him. This recognition and Huck's resolve to "humble myself to a nigger" attest to his maturing and to his accepting the innate value of the human being. Furthermore, one of Huck's basic attributes is that he treats everyone kindly. Throughout the novel, he cannot stand the idea of even scoundrels having something mean done to them.

In Chapter XVI, after Huck's changing view of Jim, he has to pit his own values against those of society and those of his own conscience. When Huck hears that Jim is jubilant at the thought of escape, and also that Jim plans to steal, if necessary, his own children out of slavery, he is horrified at such audacity and shocked at his own part in such an "immoral" undertaking.

Huck's shock and his troubled conscience must be viewed historically in terms of his going against church, society, and state as he helps the runaway slave. Huck is not old enough or experienced enough to recognize the importance of his own values and the falseness of those of society. Thus, his conflict here is a sincere one in which he is deeply troubled over his actions.

The irony reaches cosmic proportions when a man has to try to buy his children and, if he can't buy them, he must steal them – "children that belonged to a man I didn't even know, a man that hadn't ever done me no harm." Here the lesser sin of "stealing" is placed against the greater sin of enslaving a race. The horror of this situation causes Huck to decide to reveal Jim's presence – an act which, according to society, would elevate Huck's moral position.

The thought of telling on Jim is juxtaposed to the encounter with the bounty hunters who are out to capture some runaway slaves. At the crucial moment, Huck cannot bring himself to inform on Jim, thus showing that his innate sense of right exceeds that of society.

The larger irony of the situation lies in Huck's thinking that he is committing a great sin by protecting Jim – while at the same time we see the slave hunters who are hunting down humans but will not help a theoretically sick man. Huck's ingenuity is seen both in the story which he tells the men and, more directly, in his knowledge that the men, being selfish and narrow, will not help him. This illustrates that Huck has more than the ingenuity to create a story – that he has a profound knowledge of human nature which allows him to create stories which play upon the selfishness and pettiness of the slave hunters.

The men think they remove their moral obligation by giving Huck some money. Thus, we have a contrast between their refusal to commit themselves to helping another human being and Huck's commitment to protect Jim. As the men leave to track down the slaves, Huck is troubled in his conscience, but we must assume that the men are not bothered by their duplicity and selfishness as they go back to hunting slaves and feeling that they have discharged their responsibilities by giving a sum of money. Few scenes in the novel capture the essential inhumanity of society as well as does this powerful scene.

At the end of Chapter XVI, both Huck and Jim recognize by the clear water in the Mississippi that they have passed the mouth of the Ohio River. Again, Jim blames this piece of bad luck on the rattlesnake.

Twain has the canoe lost in this chapter so that they can't go back and paddle up the Ohio River. Realistically, then, they must wait until they can find a canoe so as to return to the mouth of the river. This is the excuse for continuing down the Mississippi River—a river which Twain was familiar with—rather than going up the Ohio—a river which Twain did not know. The destruction of the raft at the end of the chapter is another indication that Twain was puzzled over how to continue his story, and it is at this point that critics have projected that Twain laid aside his manuscript for two years.

CHAPTERS XVII AND XVIII

Summary

At the house, Huck is forced to identify himself. He tells the man confronting him that he is George Jackson and that he fell overboard from a passing steamboat. He invents another fantastic story which the people believe. This house belongs to a wealthy landowner, whose youngest child is Buck, about Huck's age. The two boys share a bedroom together and soon become good friends.

The house is furnished in a manner that impresses Huck, but of special interest to him are the crayon drawings made by Emmeline Grangerford, who died when she was fourteen. Most of the drawings are of rather morbid subjects. Her attempts at poetry about dead people are also rated high by her relatives and by Huck. On the whole, Huck is very content to be here since there is so much good food.

While living with the Grangerfords, Huck is impressed by their manners and mode of living. Every member of the family has a Negro servant, including Huck. The only other aristocratic family is named Shepherdson and, one day while Huck and Buck are walking, Buck jumps behind a bush and shoots at young

Harney Shepherdson. Huck is confused, and Buck explains that the two families are having a feud. Since Huck has never heard of a feud, Buck has to explain that it is a type of quarrel in which everyone on one side wants to kill everyone on the other side until "by and by everybody's killed off, and there ain't no more feud." This particular feud has been going on for thirty years and everyone has forgotten how it started.

One day when Huck is delivering a message for Miss Sophia Grangerford, his servant takes him down to the river. There he discovers Jim in hiding. Jim has been collecting material and preparing the raft for the day when he and Huck can continue their journey.

With the knowledge that Miss Sophia has run off with Harney Shepherdson, the feud breaks out with more intensity. So many Grangerfords and Shepherdsons are killed that Huck is sorry that he ever came on shore. He escapes as quickly as possible, rejoins Jim, and they continue their journey down the river.

Commentary

These two chapters dealing with the Grangerford and Shepherdson feud allow Twain to satirize many aspects of American culture. In general, Twain is against such feuds, which were still known to exist in parts of the country. Twain reveals the senseless brutality and the needless manslaughter involved in such an arbitrary concept of honor. For Twain, such a feud goes counter to common sense and anything that violated common sense was abhorrent to Twain.

The feud itself has overtones of a Romeo and Juliet story placed in the Kentucky wilderness. It has gone on so long that the people do not even know why they are fighting; yet, embedded in the bloody feud are many artificial concepts of honor and behavior. For example, Mr. Grangerford tells Buck that he shouldn't shoot from behind a bush but should step out in the road to kill a Shepherdson.

Huck's reaction to this needless slaughter is finally one of sickness and revulsion for such a waste of human life. Huck's practicality here, then, is important because it allows him to see through the superficial concepts which keep the feud alive and to evaluate it according to his common sense.

In terms of the larger thematic patterns, we see Huck again using his shrewdness on shore as he creates yet another new identity for himself. When he forgets his name, he has to be shrewd enough to conceive a plan whereby Buck Grangerford will spell his name. Huck has such an understanding of people that he easily gulls a boy the same age, one who loves to show off his knowledge of spelling, into spelling Huck's assumed name. Thus Huck is able to rediscover his new identity.

Huck's literal mindedness is emphasized again in this section as he fails to catch the point of the joke about Moses and the candle. This same literal minded quality will allow him to evaluate the impractical waste of human life in the feud. This same quality also allows Huck to report directly about other aspects of the Grangerford life, and his direct reporting without evaluating underscores Twain's satire.

For example, Twain's satire against, and parody of, the type of sentimental poetry written during his day is seen in Huck's "appreciation" of Emmeline Grangerford's sickening verse. That Huck is impressed by this poetry ("If Emmeline Grangerford could make poetry like that before she was fourteen, there ain't no telling what she could a done by-and-by.") is part of Twain's technique of using Huck as a realistic reporter rather than one who evaluates for us. Yet, even Huck finally becomes "soured on her a little" because of her predilection for death and morbidity. (Historically, Twain is satirizing specifically the poetry of Julia A. Moore who called herself "the Sweet Singer of Michigan"; Twain called her the "Queen and Empress of the Hogwash Guild.")

Huck's description of the Grangerford house emphasizes all the taudry, cheap objects which decorate the house. All of this satire is against those who have a predilection for morbid works of art, sentimental poetry, and bad taste in almost everything.

As long as Huck hears about the feud in vague terms, he is not terribly concerned about it. But once he becomes involved and observes the brutality of Buck's death, his horror surpasses direct expression. It is only by contrast with the return to the river that Huck can express his disapproval of such senseless brutality: "It made me so sick I most fell out of the tree. I ain't agoing to tell *all* that happened—it would make me sick again if I was to do that. I wished I hadn't ever come ashore that night. . . ." The contrast between the horror of events on shore and the freedom of the raft is a comment upon the inhumanity of society in general.

Back on the raft, Huck feels "free and safe once more." Part of the irony is that in contrast to the small, confined raft, "other places do feel so cramped up and smothery, but a raft don't. You feel mighty free and easy and comfortable on a raft." By this oblique statement, Huck arrives at a metaphysical evaluation of the contrast between the idyllic life of peace and brotherhood of himself and Jim as opposed to the inhumanity of the feud and the values of society.

CHAPTERS XIX AND XX

Summary

Two or three days and nights slide by as they travel by night and hide by day. One morning about daybreak, Huck finds a canoe, crosses to the main shore, and paddles up a creek looking for berries. Suddenly he hears two men being pursued by dogs and other men are following the dogs. When the pursued men beg Huck to save them, he quickly tells them the best way to throw the dogs off their scent.

One man is seventy and bald; the other is about thirty. They are not acquainted but both were run out of the town because of their efforts to defraud the citizens by cheating, quackery, and other fraudulent schemes. Once on the raft, the youngest claims to be the rightful Duke of Bridgewater. After Huck and Jim hear his sad story, they begin to treat him with respect. The older man then tells them that he is the lost Dauphin of France. Huck, however, is not deceived and knows that the two are nothing more than "humbugs and frauds."

They question Huck about the presence of Jim on the raft and are temporarily satisfied when Huck assures them that a runaway slave would never run south. Huck then invents another fantastic story to protect both Jim and himself.

The two frauds soon appropriate both beds in the wigwam, leaving Jim and Huck out in the rain. By this time, even Jim doesn't want any more kings and dukes to appear. The two frauds pool their resources and decide to rehearse a Shakespearian presentation of *Romeo and Juliet,* letting the seventy-year-old king play the part of Juliet. When the raft stops for provisions near a small town, the king wanders into a camp meeting where he pretends to be a reformed pirate in need of money to go back and reform the other pirates. By this ruse, he is able to collect eighty-seven dollars and seventy cents.

Meanwhile, the duke goes to a printing office where he cheats the owner out of nine dollars and, at the same time, prints a handbill describing Jim as a runaway slave from forty miles below New Orleans. If anyone questions them, they will simply say that they are returning Jim for the reward.

Commentary

By this time in the novel, all thought of returning to Cairo and going up the Ohio River is set aside. Now Twain emphasizes the peaceful, calm, and quiet qualities of the river which will function as a contrast to the difficulty Huck and Jim have with the duke and king later on.

The appearance of two men being pursued immediately evokes sympathy from Huck, and he is anxious to help. He is also shrewd enough to give them the best method of covering up their escape.

The traveling confidence man, or fraud, is common to many types of frontier literature, but Twain, by individualizing these two "types," makes them into fully realized characters. These people have to possess a certain degree of cleverness in order to dupe people so successfully. Their success is often based upon their ability to analyze the society which they are going to defraud and thus take advantage of it because that society, through its ignorance, allows itself to be defrauded.

The stories of the king (Dauphin) and the duke have been prepared for by Huck's earlier reading in history. After the duke receives special treatment because of his impressive story, the king tells an even bigger lie in order to receive preferential treatment. At first, we are led to believe that Huck believes these stories, but by the end of the chapter, his shrewdness surpasses his literal mindedness. He sees through their ruse: "It didn't take me long to make up my mind that these liars warn't no kings nor dukes, at all, but just low-down humbugs and frauds."

It is necessary for Huck to have this insight since it allows him to realize that they would sell Jim at the first opportune moment. Thus he temporarily protects Jim with another shrewd story, one which both the king and duke seem to believe. Therefore, Huck's shrewdness exceeds both the king's and duke's since he sees through their facade and is able to make his own story credible. Huck's insight also suggests his knowledge of human nature, a knowledge which has the practical purpose of protecting both himself and Jim.

The absurdity of the plan to present *Romeo and Juliet* is another comment upon the stupidity of their audience. Throughout these scenes, Twain's point is that the gullibility of the average person allows such rogues to function. However, historically speaking, the parts of women were still played by young boys so that the audience would not expect a real lady; nevertheless, Juliet was *never* played by a seventy-year-old, bald-headed man;

only the most credulous audience would accept such an absurdity.

A stock situation in frontier humor is a rogue who goes to a revival meeting, confesses to any type of sin, pretends to reform, takes up a collection, and then flees with the money. (For example, see Johnson J. Hooper's "Simon Suggs Attends a Camp-Meeting.") Twain, however, takes this basic situation and turns it into sophisticated art. The basis of the humor is again the gullibility of the audience and also the king's knowledge that the audience takes a vicarious delight in hearing about evil. The more evil a person, the more delightful is his reform. Since the audience is so gullible, Huck does not take a moral stand, the emphasis again being that such an audience deserves to be defrauded.

The episode with the handbill suggests something of the cleverness and shrewdness of the duke. We realize that both of these rogues are clever enough to live by their wits. By the end of the chapter, however, even Jim has recognized that they are scoundrels and hopes that he and Huck don't meet any more "kings" and "dukes" on their trip.

CHAPTERS XXI, XXII, AND XXIII

Summary

The king and the duke begin to rehearse for the Shakespearean production which they will present in some town along the river. When they arrive in a small Arkansas town, there is already a circus there. The duke distributes his advertisements of the show throughout the town.

While Huck is lounging around the town, a person named Boggs comes in from the country "for his little old monthly drunk." Everybody laughs at him as he proclaims drunkenly that he is there to "kill old Colonel Sherburn." While the townspeople are assuring Huck that Boggs is harmless, they are also sending for Boggs' daughter to take care of him. However, before she arrives, Boggs continues to insult Colonel Sherburn, who appears with a gun and shoots Boggs down in cold blood just as the daughter arrives.

Led by a man named Buck Harkness, a mob gathers, gets drunk, and then goes to Colonel Sherburn's house to lynch the murderer. The colonel calls them cowards and taunts them by saying that if any lynching is to be done, it will be done in the dark with a *man*, not half a man, as a leader. At the end of Colonel Sherburn's speech, the crowd "broke all apart and went tearing off every which way."

Huck, intent on seeing the circus, dives under the tent and marvels at the color and action of it all. Later, since only twelve people attend the Shakespearean performance, the duke and the king change to a performance where ladies and children are not admitted, thus assuring themselves of a good turnout.

The show is, of course, a fraud and a cheat, but those seeing it the first night do not admit being taken in and advise their neighbors to see the second performance. The third night, both audiences return, ready to tar and feather the king and the duke, but the two con men catch on to the audience's intent and escape to the raft after having cheated the town out of four hundred and sixty-five dollars.

Commentary

The Shakespearean production is in the best of the frontier humor tradition where bits and pieces of fractured Shakespeare were carelessly put together. The ability to do even this suggests something of their cleverness. In fact, the entire episode reveals them to be so clever that Huck recognizes how dangerous they are and knows that he must be extremely careful so as to protect Jim.

Basically, the circus in the town helps them put over their schemes. We should note that throughout the entire proceeding, Huck remains the observer and not a participant. In other words, he retains a moral neutrality which will change only in the Wilks episode. The importance of his moral neutrality is that the audience, being so gullible, deserves to be defrauded by these scoundrels.

After the Shakespearean program flops, the rogues conceive of the plan to attract an audience by presenting a show where "Ladies and Children" are not admitted, knowing that man's propensity for the vulgar will draw a large audience. The show, "The King's Camelopard or The Royal Nonesuch," is based upon vulgar, obscene, and coarse humor, essentially degrading in its nature, and the large crowd that gathers is Twain's method of saying that man is base and depraved.

The ultimate cleverness of the rogues is illustrated in the fact that they know that the town plans to punish them, but they are always one step ahead of the townspeople. The amount of money, $465.00, becomes important in the next episode when they add most of that amount to the Wilks hoard.

These chapters also show Twain's undisguised contempt for certain aspects of frontier life and, more important, his dislike for "the damned human race," the title of a later work by Twain. The description of the town in Chapter XXI and of the bums who hang about the street shows Twain's dislike for shiftless, worthless men who live in a place where there is mud in the streets, where the livestock run freely, and where houses are run down, etc.

His contempt for man is fully illustrated in the Sherburn-Boggs episode which was based on a real event. Twain's contempt for mob action, and mobs in general, recurs in other of his works. Twain does not condone Sherburn's shooting down Boggs in cold blood. His point, however, is that one powerful man is stronger than any mob. Sherburn's contempt for the townspeople is also Twain's contempt for "the damned human race": "The average man's a coward," Sherburn maintains and then proves his statement by his actions. Further proof is that the mob has to get drunk before it can attempt to act.

The circus episode in Chapter XXII again shows Huck's literal mindedness and his tendency to report things factually. The comedy of this situation depends entirely upon Huck's narrative point of view in that he thinks that the ringmaster—and not he—was the person most deceived.

Huck's description of kings and rulers is highly comic on an intellectual basis. Some critics have complained that the fourteen-year-old Huck could not possibly know this much about history, and their complaint carries some value. However, Huck did find "a lot of books" in the floating cabin and he has been reading from the books on their trip down the river. The intellectual comedy results from the utter and grand confusion of history with fiction and in the manner in which Huck juxtaposes historical persons, incidents, and events which are centuries apart with occurrences from fictional narratives. The general point of the satire is that all kings or rulers or politicians are "mighty ornery" and "you couldn't tell them [the king and the duke] from the real kind."

At the end of the chapter, Jim tells his story of how he treated his daughter, 'Lizabeth. The purpose of the story is to further humanize Jim and to make us sympathize with him. In contrast to the manner in which Huck's pap treated him, we see a deeper love and humanity in Jim's relationship with his daughter. Furthermore, it forces Huck into another important recognition: "I do believe he cared just as much for his people as white folks does for their'n. It don't seem natural, but I reckon it's so." This recognition is another step toward Huck's total acceptance of Jim as an equal human being.

CHAPTER XXIV

Summary

Back on the raft and safe from the mob, the duke dresses Jim as a sick Arab so that he will not have to remain tied up all day when the others want to leave him. Then they all dress up in some "store bought" clothes, and the king tells Huck to paddle toward a steamboat. On the way, they meet a young country fellow who mistakes the king for a Mr. Wilks from England, whose brother, Peter Wilks, has just died leaving his two brothers a fortune. The king inquires into various details about Peter Wilks' family, about his financial holdings, and about other people who live in the town.

The young man, who is going to South America, is free with his information, telling the king all sorts of things about the town and its people. Later, the king has Huck paddle him to another town and then sends Huck to fetch the duke. Since Peter Wilks had another brother who was deaf and dumb, the king instructs the duke to pretend to be deaf and dumb, and then the two hail a steamboat and get off at the town posing as Peter Wilks' brothers. When Huck understands their plans, he feels that "it was enough to make a body ashamed of the human race."

Commentary

Chapters XXIV through XXX deal with the Wilks episode. In general, the entire episode satirizes the absolute gullibility of the human race and becomes one of Twain's most damning comments on the subject. His point is that only through the sentimentalizing and the gullibility of the general public can such rogues function. He also depicts the degree to which man wants to be deceived for sentimental reasons rather than face brutal reality.

In the revival scene, Huck was merely amused at how people deceive themselves, but in this episode, Twain shows his contempt for the "damned human race" which is about to create a grave injustice by so willingly embracing the effusive rogues. Ultimately we too must criticize the townspeople—almost as much as we do the rogues.

In this scene, Huck shifts from being an amused observer to becoming morally involved in the events. Huck's comment at the end of Chapter XXIV, "Well, if ever I struck anything like it, I'm a nigger. It was enough to make a body ashamed of the human race," indicates that Huck is learning to make moral evaluations. Earlier, the people gypped by the rogues were not worthy of Huck's concern. The Wilks girls, however, are honest, grief-stricken people who are about to be exploited, thus removing the rogues' actions from the realm of simple fraud and sinking it to the level of immoral exploitation. Huck's commitment here to a moral stand leads ultimately to his final commitment to Jim.

Huck's expression, damning the actions of the king and the duke, involves his saying "I'm a nigger." When he says this, he apparently does not consider Jim's friendship. Huck, unfortunately, still views Negroes as "niggers" and, therefore, as subhuman. Because he uses the phrase – "I'm a nigger" – to express the impossible, we realize that he has not, and perhaps cannot, divorce himself completely from the standards of society.

Furthermore, at the beginning of Chapter XXIV, the inhumanity of tying up Jim all day shows a basic lack of regard for Jim's personal worth. Huck, being physically afraid of the rogues, can do nothing about this situation.

In the beginning of the episode, the technique which the king uses to pump the young boy of all the information he can get is an excellent example of the ability of the rogue to capitalize on any situation. Huck is so literal minded that he cannot understand the king's purpose; he is confused and, therefore, reports the episode without any comment. Only when he understands the king's purpose does he make his first moral comment upon the immorality of the scheme.

CHAPTERS XXV AND XXVI

Summary

The king and the duke put on an impressive act beside the coffin of Mr. Wilks and have most of the town sobbing in sympathy. Using the names acquired from their young informant to prove acquaintance with the leading citizens of the town, the duke and the king make their case so plausible that no questions are asked. The king does all the talking, while the duke poses as the deaf mute brother.

The hoax is successful for a while. The nieces of Peter Wilks show his will to the king. The dwelling house and three thousand dollars are bequeathed to the girls and the remainder of the wealth, a considerable amount, goes to the brothers of Mr. Wilks. When the impostors count the money in the cellar, it is four hundred and fifteen dollars short. They make up the deficit and, as a magnanimous gesture, present the money to the girls. All the townspeople are impressed except one. Dr. Robinson, a close friend of the late Peter Wilks, sees through the deception and tries to get the girls to listen to him. But the girls continue to trust their bogus uncles and even turn their money over to them for investment.

At breakfast the next morning, the hare-lip, Joanna, asks Huck so many questions that he almost gives away the secret. Her older sisters, however, make her quit heckling Huck. Since the girls are so nice to him, Huck's conscience begins to bother him and, that evening, he spies on the king and the duke as they hide the money in a mattress. Huck removes it to his bedroom and lies awake all night guarding it, intending to restore it to the Wilks girls as soon as possible.

Commentary

Twain is known to sometime laspe into bad taste; for example, the episode in Chapter XXIII about the King's Cameleopard was reportedly tamed down for publication. In this episode, the use of a "hare-lip" is in bad taste. Any comedy at the expense of physical deformity is always considered in bad taste.

Greed will function as the denouement of the king and the duke. The king's greed for everything will ultimately be the cause of their failure. Ironically, most of the money they defrauded the town of Bricksville out of is added to the Wilks money. First, their cleverness is illustrated by the fact that they needed to add enough money to make it $3000.00 since that is what it should be. Thus, ironically, the girls ultimately profit from the rogues' effort to cheat them out of their inheritance.

This chapter also shows what Twain meant by people acting as a herd. One sensible person, Dr. Robinson, is ignored by the crowd, which is completely taken in by the artifice of the king and the duke.

In Chapter XXVI, Huck thinks he is about to be trapped by the hare-lip and involves himself in a series of lies. His fear, however, is unwarranted since the hare-lip is only bantering with Huck because she knows Huck is the typical fourteen-year-old who likes to exaggerate. She never doubts the idea that he comes from England, only that he is exaggerating in some of his stories about England.

Of great significance in Chapter XXVI is Huck's commitment to help the Wilks girls. Earlier, as noted above, Huck's refusal to hinder the king and the duke was based upon the corruptness of society. As an outcast from society, Huck, in protecting Jim, has already violated many rules of society. However, we have seen in many episodes that he instinctively responds to the individual and his needs. Since he admires and respects Mary Jane and since he knows that she is about to be cheated out of her inheritance, he is drawn morally into the episode and determines at great danger to himself to save their inheritance. Ironically, money, which is not terribly important to Huck, becomes a motivating factor in his decision to help the ladies since he knows what their plight would be if left penniless in a frontier town.

Huck's basic knowledge of human nature is again illustrated when he knows that he can't tell Mary Jane the entire truth because she is so honest that she would give it away by her looks and actions. Thus, again, he has to create a story and a plan which will take this fact into consideration.

CHAPTERS XXVII AND XXVIII

Summary

When Huck tries to leave the house with the money, he finds that he is locked inside. Fearing discovery, he shoves the bag of money under the coffin lid. He spends an uncomfortable night and has no opportunity to retrieve the money before the funeral.

The house is filled with people for the funeral sermon. When the undertaker finally screws the lid on the coffin, Huck is not sure whether the money is still inside or not. The next day, the king and the duke begin selling the Wilks property, including the slaves, claiming that it is necessary to return immediately to England, taking their nieces with them. The girls are overjoyed at the prospect.

On auction day, the king and the duke discover that the money is missing and they call Huck to account for it. Huck shifts the blame on the slaves, already sold, as he realizes that the sale is not valid and that the Negroes will be back in a week or two.

Huck encounters Mary Jane, weeping because of the separation of the slaves. Huck blurts out that the slaves will soon be returned and reunited. He makes Mary Jane promise to leave town for four days if he tells her why he knows that the slaves will be returned. When she promises, he reveals the entire hoax to her. She wishes to have the imposters tarred and feathered at once, but Huck reminds her of her promise to go away. He shortens the time to one day, asking her to put a candle in the window at eleven o'clock that night. If he does not come, she will know that he and the nameless other person whom he is shielding are gone; the spurious uncles can then be arrested and jailed. His purpose in sending her away is to keep her from betraying the secret through facial expressions.

Mary Jane promises to stand by Huck in case he should not escape. He advises her to use the "Royal Nonesuch" as proof of the rascality of the pair. He also writes a statement saying that he put the money in the coffin, but he makes her promise not to read it until she is on the way to the neighbor's home. She promises to pray for Huck. He explains her absence to the family by saying that she has gone to help a sick friend. While the sale is in progress, two more claimants of Peter Wilks' property arrive by steamboat.

Commentary

When *Huck Finn* first appeared, the book received some violent criticism for "violating" the taste and sensibility of the reading public. One of the scenes most often objected to was this one depicting the funeral. Critics found no humor in this "side-splitting account of a funeral, enlivened by a 'sick melodeum,' a 'long-legged undertaker,' and a rat episode in the cellar" (See *Life,* V, February 26, 1885). However, for the more sophisticated audience of today, Twain's description has become a classic. It is the first significant American satire on the sentimentality of funeral customs, ridiculing undertakers and all other aspects of burial customs.

The separation of families by the sale of slaves shows Huck's and Mary Jane's sense of humanity. The response is to the humanity of the Negroes and to the needless suffering. This response again prepares us for Huck's defense of Jim.

Huck's ability to lie successfully serves him well when he is confronted by the king and the duke about the stolen money. Without this ability, Huck's life would be in serious danger and he would be subjected to the brutality of the king and the duke. His conscience is not bothered by this lie because of the necessity of it. But in Chapter XXVIII, when he has to lie to Mary Jane, he considers for a moment the value of telling the truth: ". . . I'm blest if it don't look to me like the truth is better, and actuly *safer,* than a lie." But for Mary Jane's protection, he has to tell another lie. Furthermore, Huck's lying and his plan partly involve getting rid of the king and the duke so that he and Jim can continue on their odyssey without being hampered by others.

CHAPTERS XXIX AND XXX

Summary

The new set of Wilks brothers confront the king and duke, but when the handwriting of all four claimants is compared with that of letters written from England by Harvey Wilks, there are no satisfactory results. Then an argument arises about the tattoo marks on the dead man's chest, and it becomes necessary to exhume his body to find out. When the gold is discovered in the coffin, there is so much excitement that Huck is able to break loose from his captor and make a dash for the raft. Although he sees Mary Jane's candle in the window, he cannot stop until he rejoins Jim on the raft.

At first, Huck is happy to be back on the raft and to be free of the king and the duke, but soon he and Jim hear the rogues catching up with them in a canoe. Huck pacifies the king and duke by telling them that the man who had hold of him let him go and told him to run. The king and the duke argue with each other about the presence of the gold in the coffin, each blaming the other for planning to steal it later. Soon, however, the rogues make up their quarrel and become "thick as thieves" again.

Commentary

In Chapter XXIX, Twain uses an established comic technique – the confused identity of two sets of characters. This technique goes back to classical times. Thus in this chapter, we have a series of *tests* and the tests are conceived of in such a way as to provide humor and suspense. The suspense builds as each ruse devised to reveal the real identity of the people involved is thwarted in one manner or another. For example, the real William can't write because he has broken his right arm. Twain's magnificent narrative ability sustains the suspense.

It is ironic that when Huck is called upon to tell what he knows, Dr. Robinson tells him to sit down because he has had no practice in the art of lying. Of course, this is the first time that

Huck has had to lie to such an intelligent and honest man, and also the first time that he has had to lie when there was no practical reason for the lie.

The narrative plot is brought to its climax by the necessity of digging up the body to determine if there is a tattoo which would establish the real identity of the contesting uncles. This, therefore, reveals the presence of the gold and, while the townspeople are staring at the gold, Huck is able to make his escape.

At the end of Chapter XXIX, Huck's excitement and relief over escaping from the rogues and returning to Jim suggests the importance which he places on his relationship with Jim. But this relief is short-lived since the king and the duke escape their captors at the same time that Huck is fleeing.

In Chapter XXX, the scoundrels argue between themselves, each refusing to take the blame for the failure. In a rare insight, the duke reminds the king that they would have done the same thing to escape that Huck did. Thus, after the rogues' treachery with the Wilks, Twain tries to lessen their villainy somewhat so that we view them as believable characters rather than symbols of pure evil.

CHAPTER XXXI

Summary

For days and days, the king and the duke dare not let Huck and Jim stop at any town for fear of being detected. But when they consider themselves out of danger, they begin their old tricks of swindling again, but with small success. When they begin whispering to each other and talking confidentially, Huck and Jim become uneasy. One day the king goes ashore and sells Jim as a runaway slave for forty dollars. He then squanders the money without sharing it with the duke. Huck is indignant, claiming that Jim was *his* property and could not be sold without his permission. Huck then has a struggle with his conscience about returning Jim to Miss Watson, but his love for Jim is more important. Huck tears up the letter that he has written to Miss Watson, decides that he is willing to "go to hell" for Jim, and goes to search for Jim – determined to free him. He discovers that Jim is at the Phelps plantation not far away.

Commentary

Every detail and every scene has been leading up to this climactic chapter. By this time, both Huck and Jim are thoroughly fed up with the king and the duke, but are still afraid, physically and otherwise, of them. Jim is, after all, still a runaway slave and there are several indications that the king and the duke are aware of this.

The final calumny of the king and duke is selling Jim back into slavery. Even though Huck has known them to be the worse sort of scoundrels, his innocence does not allow him to foresee this ultimate treachery – to "make him a slave again . . . for forty dirty dollars." The horror for Huck lies partly in the reiterated fact that he is not overly concerned with money (he left $6000 in order to escape from Pap); to sell a human being such as Jim for "forty dirty dollars" is beyond Huck's understanding.

With the sale of Jim, Huck faces isolation and loneliness. Now, Huck is forced to come to terms with his own values, as opposed to the values of a society which would harbor such people as the rogues who sell Jim for forty dollars and the society which would buy him for that amount. Now he realizes the intrinsic worth of Jim as a human being and not as a piece of property to be bantered about at a sale.

In evaluating his position and coming to terms with this moral dilemma, Huck at first feels that his own behavior is at fault because he has helped a slave escape and that, consequently, he is being punished for this crime. He decides that "here was the plain hand of Providence slapping me in the face and letting me know my wickedness was being watched. . . ." Yet Huck cannot reconcile his own sense of personal wickedness with the needless torture of Jim.

Huck's attempt to pray is ironic and is a takeoff on *Hamlet*'s Claudius. But, unlike Claudius who can't pray because of his evil doings, Huck can't pray because his values are right, even though he can't realize that fact.

Accepting, as he has all along, that society is right and he is wrong, he can only ironically conclude that he is evil and, if his nature is aligned to evil, he might as well continue to live a life of wickedness. Thus, in deciding that he will "go to hell," he arrives at his momentous moral decision and decides that he will free Jim.

Huck's decision to "go to hell" is doubly ironic since we have seen Huck's higher moral sense in all the preceding scenes. Only in terms of the values of society has Huck done something wrong and, thus, we condemn society and embrace Huck's decision, even though he does not recognize his own moral superiority.

Immediately afterward, Huck encounters the duke and recognizes again their duplicity and fraudulence. At this time, however, Huck has no interest in making the rogues suffer for their action–his only concern is recovering Jim.

With the end of this chapter, in terms of formal structure, the second part of the novel–the experiences on the Mississippi River–comes to an end since the rest of the novel will take place on the Phelps plantation.

CHAPTERS XXXII AND XXXIII

Summary

When Huck arrives at the Phelps plantation, he hears the dim hum of a spinning wheel and a moment later is surrounded by dogs of all breeds and sizes. A Negro woman disperses them, and a white woman, followed by several small children, runs out and welcomes Huck, identifying herself as his Aunt Sally. Huck is at a loss to know who she is until Mr. Phelps appears and his wife introduces Huck as Tom Sawyer. To Huck, this is "like being born again" for he is now on familiar ground and can fabricate all kinds of stories about the Sawyer family.

On the way to town in a wagon, supposedly to bring back his baggage, Huck encounters Tom Sawyer. Tom has just alighted from a steamboat and thinks that he is seeing a ghost when the supposedly dead Huck appears. Huck confides his secret about Jim to Tom, who agrees to help the runaway slave gain freedom. Huck is astounded that Tom Sawyer would agree to such a horrible thing.

Tom puts on an act upon arrival, giving his name as William Thompson, from Ohio, looking for Mr. Archibald Nichols. He is told that Mr. Nichols lives three miles down the road, but that Tom must stay and eat with the family. Accepting the invitation, Tom at first offends Aunt Sally by kissing her but later is forgiven when he introduces himself as Sid Sawyer who had begged to come because Tom did.

After a meal large enough for seven families, the subject of the King's Cameleopard comes up. Huck and Tom try to warn the king and the duke that they are to be run out of town, but it is too late. The fraudulent two are tarred and feathered and ridden out of town on a rail.

Commentary

The basis of many of Huck's plans is found in his remark: "I went right along, not fixing up any particular plan, but just trusting to Providence to put the right words in my mouth when the time come." This practice has served Huck well so far in all the encounters throughout the book and now serves as a significant contrast to Tom Sawyer's elaborately contrived plots.

One objection which could be raised to this last section is the extreme coincidence in Jim's being sold to Tom Sawyer's aunt and uncle and the arrival of Huck Finn at the same time that

Tom Sawyer is expected and thus being taken for Tom. This coincidence tests severely the credulity of the reader.

Huck's story about the boat blowing out a cylinder-head evokes the often criticized remark of Huck's in answering if any one was hurt: "No'm. Killed a nigger." Huck has apparently come to terms only with Jim and does not apply his new values to the entire black race. It is also worth noting that Aunt Sally, for all of her pious religion, apparently accepts the same view as does society about the fate of the Negroes.

The entire farcical tone of this last section is set by Aunt Sally herself as she has Huck hide from Uncle Silas. Because Aunt Sally delights in playing practical jokes, these types of pranks will be played on Aunt Sally herself and will characterize the tone of this last section.

The idea of death and rebirth is again utilized as Huck receives another new identity – this time as Tom Sawyer. The comic implication is that when he does meet Tom Sawyer, he is taken for a ghost. The explanation of his deeds seem insignificant in terms of the plans which Tom Sawyer plots. We should also compare Tom's surprize at seeing Huck with the lack of surprize in a later scene when Aunt Polly expresses no surprize, an apparent lapse on Twain's part.

When Huck tells Tom Sawyer that he plans to steal Jim out of bondage, Tom almost reveals that Jim is already free, a fact which is not revealed until the close of the novel, but one which the reader should keep in mind throughout all of the involved attempts to steal Jim. Furthermore, since Huck has always associated Tom with respectability, he is shocked that Tom is going to help steal Jim: "I'm bound to say Tom Sawyer fell, considerable, in my estimation. Only I couldn't believe it. Tom Sawyer a *nigger stealer!*" The point is that Huck is reconciled to being a wicked being, but Tom has always stood for moral correctness and social acceptance. Even in the first chapters, Tom requires a nickle to be left as payment when they "steal" a candle. However, in the total view, Tom is still the representative of socially correct behavior since he is *not* stealing Jim because Jim is already free.

The essential humanity that we saw in Huck is again illustrated when he sees the king and the duke tarred and feathered. In spite of the dirty trick which these scoundrels played on him, Huck is responsive to their suffering. Twain uses this scene as a comment against the "damned human race" by having Huck say: "It was a dreadful thing to see. Human beings *can* be awful cruel to one another." However, one objection to this last part is that Huck, basically sensitive to the sufferings of others, allows Jim to suffer insensitively while effecting the plan for Jim's escape. In contrast, however, it has been argued that Jim allows these tricks and indignities to be perpetrated against him.

CHAPTERS XXXIV, XXXV, AND XXXVI

Summary

Tom Sawyer discovers that Jim is a prisoner in a hut behind the house. The two boys discuss plans of freeing their friend, but Tom finds Huck's plan too simple. Tom favors something more elaborate than stealing the key, unlocking the door of the hut, and taking Jim down the river on a raft. The boys must dig Jim out using the complicated methods of adventure tales. The Negro in charge of Jim is made to believe that witches are haunting him when Jim unwittingly speaks words of recognition to Huck and Tom.

Tom's dark, deep-laid plans include digging a tunnel, sawing off the leg of the bed to which Jim is chained, using a rope-ladder, having Jim break out a window that is flimsily secured, and a variety of other invented difficulties. Tom cites examples from his reading, proving how the job should be done. Huck is overwhelmed by Tom's erudition and superior grasp of the subject. Willingly, Huck steals a sheet, a shirt, and some case-knives for use in the great liberation of Jim. The boys have to make haste because Mr. Phelps will soon hear from New Orleans that Jim did not come from there and will probably learn the truth.

Digging with case-knives proves so slow and laborious that Tom finally consents to use picks and pretend that they are case-knives. Dog-tired, he is unable to climb the lightning rod to the second story and yields to Huck's suggestion to "let on" that the stairway is a lightning rod. The boys in various ways acquire and smuggle in such articles as a pewter spoon, a chopped-up brass candlestick, and three tin plates to assist in the great plan of escape, in addition to the rope ladder and the white shirt on which Jim is to record his experiences in blood. Tom says that this is the best fun he has ever had in his life. Jim's Negro keeper, Nat, is to deliver the witch-pie, containing a rope ladder made of a sheet torn in strips.

Commentary

In the presence of Tom Sawyer, Huck becomes less self-sufficient. He loses that sense of independence which he possessed on the raft and in earlier episodes. He is, however, still shrewd enough to know that any plan which he might suggest would not be good enough for Tom Sawyer. In showing the contrast between Huck's plan and Tom's plan, Twain is continuing the contrast between Huck's natural common sense as opposed to the bookish artificiality of Tom's absurd plans based upon romantic fiction. Throughout these chapters, Twain is ridiculing the then-current popularity of romantic fiction whose pages were filled with daring escapes and thrilling adventures.

Huck's main conflict in these chapters is that of having to choose and follow the absurd plans of Tom Sawyer, which were conceived for their "style" and "artistic value," rather than following his own innate sense of what was practical. As Tom continues to allow Jim to suffer in order to effect his ridiculous plan, we see again that the respectable element of society is often oblivious to the suffering of the human being.

Tom's respectability is emphasized mainly to make the above contrast. For example, Tom forces Huck to pay a dime for the watermelon he stole, but at the same time he has no human feeling for Jim's suffering. His respectability becomes more cruel when we realize that Jim's freedom has already been given to him, yet Tom Sawyer's plans keep Jim in bondage, thereby making Tom Sawyer directly responsible not for the freeing of Jim but for the enslavement of Jim. Thus, for the sake of romantic style, Tom keeps a free man in prison simply to satisfy his own sense of personal achievement. With this view in mind, these episodes lose a great deal of the humor inherent in the escapades.

The use of superstition is continued, but now it loses much of its humor. For example, Tom and Huck have convinced the slave Nat that he sees witches and, by this ruse, they are able to carry out many of their plans. But while they are convincing Nat that there are no dogs in Jim's cabin, Jim is suffering from having bitten into the corn-pone with the concealed candlestick which "most mashed his teeth out." Humor ceases to be funny when it involves actual physical pain, but Tom Sawyer is not concerned with the suffering of others as long as his plan is done with style. Additionally, however, Tom is not later concerned with even his *own* suffering because of the gun shot; the plan was carried out with such style that nothing else matters.

CHAPTERS XXXVII, XXXVIII, AND XXXIX

Summary

Soon, Aunt Sally begins to miss things that have disappeared, including a shirt, a spoon, and six candles. One servant adds a sheet to the list of missing articles and another reports a brass candlestick. Uncle Silas sheepishly produces a spoon from his pocket, where, without his knowledge, Tom has put it. The boys have to acquire another spoon and are able to do so right under Aunt Sally's nose. They drop it in her apron pocket, and Jim takes it out, as prearranged. So confused does she become eventually that she cannot remember her original number of sheets, shirts, and spoons.

Making pens out of candlesticks and saws out of case-knives proves slow and tedious, and it takes Huck and Tom three weeks to collect rats, snakes, spiders, shirts, spoons, and other equipment necessary for the freeing of Jim in grand style. The Phelps household is in constant turmoil, as the rats and snakes get loose and frighten the occupants, especially Aunt Sally. Jim, who has to endure the spiders, rats, and delays says that if he ever gets out this time, he will never be a prisoner again, not for any salary. He is supposed to produce captive's tears with an onion and to write on the shirt with blood drawn when the rats bite him. An anonymous letter, Tom's idea, warns the family and their friends that a *"desprate gang of cutthroats from over in the Ingean Territory"* is going to steal Jim that night.

Commentary

If we could forget the serious implications of keeping Jim imprisoned, then these chapters involving the preparations for the escape could be seen as in the best tradition of the frontier tall tale, filled with all sorts of exaggerations. The only alleviating factor in the perverse cruelty to Jim is the fact that Jim allows these things to be done—and even participates in some of the antics. We must remember that Jim knows and trusts both Huck and Tom and, therefore, consents to the antics even though he could at any time effect his own escape.

With these thoughts in mind, one can read these chapters for their preposterous scheme with all the gaudy details. In other words, the intellectual implications are somewhat obscured by the very fantastic nature of Tom's plans. The rendering of the frontier, religious household, filled with snakes, rats, spiders, and frogs, is a comic scene which overrides many of the intellectual objections.

Yet, the very comic aspect of these schemes is somewhat modified by the horror which they cause other people. Aunt Sally is, after all, a kind and generous person in most ways, and her undue fears and painful experiences cause these episodes to lose some of their comic value. For Tom Sawyer, his plans and his own satisfactions overrule any consideration for others and, for this reason, Tom must be seen as a rather self-centered boy who subjects not just Jim—but anyone—to cruel tricks for his own sense of personal gratification. Furthermore, Tom's letter, which threatens a raid by outlaws, was more serious than he realizes since a raid by outlaws is a real threat to people living on the edge of the frontier.

These chapters also illuminate the characters of Aunt Sally, dictatorial but generous of heart, and Uncle Silas, hen-pecked but good natured. It is only when we take the larger view that we see that both, in spite of their pious religious mouthings, are still anxious to get the reward for Jim and, this failing, they will sell him on the open market. Their view, then, is the same as society's view. It becomes even more paradoxical when we realize that these "good Christians" are very concerned with teaching Christianity to Jim before they sell him.

CHAPTERS XL AND XLI

Summary

On the night of Jim's escape, Huck and Tom get up at half-past eleven and begin eating a lunch they stole. Tom sends Huck to the basement to get some butter, and Huck is caught by Aunt Sally and sent into the "setting-room." There he sees fifteen farmers with guns, all prepared for the desperate men from the Indian Territory. As soon as Huck can slip away, he joins Tom and Jim in the hut, and the three escape, as planned, through the hole. Tom gets caught on a splinter, which snaps and makes a noise. In a moment, bullets and dogs pursue them. The three get away, but not before Tom is shot in the leg.

Tom is proud of his wound and insists on bandaging it himself. Huck and Jim consult, however, and agree that Tom must have a doctor. Huck is to go for one, and Jim is to hide in the woods until the doctor is gone again.

After Huck tells the doctor a convincing story, the doctor takes Huck's canoe and goes to tend to Tom. Huck is discovered by Uncle Silas, and he hears how worried Aunt Sally is over them. When they get back to the plantation, there are many exaggerated versions of what really happened. Aunt Sally tells Huck that she is not going to lock the doors but relies upon him not to run away again. Because of her kindness to him, Huck stays in his room that night.

Commentary

High melodrama takes over in the lurid account of the liberation of Jim, replete with blood hounds, gun-toting men, an escape through a secret tunnel in the presence of the posse, and a wild gunshot which wounds Tom. Thus Tom's foolishness and devotion to "style" leads to real danger, one that could have cost Jim his life. Tom is punished by being shot, but his wound will later be a source of great pleasure when he wears the bullet around his neck.

With Tom wounded and the "mixed-up en splendid" plan completed, Huck takes over and returns to his practical planning. To effect the plan to help Tom, Jim has to lose his freedom again. His sacrifice restores the innate dignity to him that he was deprived of during the wild schemes of Tom Sawyer. Jim's anxiety over Tom and his willingness to risk his hard-earned freedom—and even his life—to procure a doctor for the wounded Tom shows Jim's unselfishness and basic response to humanity in contrast to the selfishness of Tom and his desire for a successful, stylistic escape.

In getting the doctor, Huck ignores Tom's instructions and makes up a simple, believable story in order to get the doctor to come to Tom. Ironically, had Huck followed Tom's advice, Tom would probably have died of the gunshot wound. No longer under the influence of Tom Sawyer, Huck reverts to the type of behavior which characterized him during the earlier parts of the novel. And finally, after all of the trouble which Tom Sawyer has caused Aunt Sally, Huck's compassion for her reaffirms his superiority to Tom Sawyer.

CHAPTER XLII AND CHAPTER THE LAST

Summary

When Tom is brought home the next morning on a mattress, he is delirious. Jim is at once captured and chained again in the cabin, with a guard on duty at all times. The doctor intervenes in Jim's behalf, however, and explains how unselfish Jim's conduct has been.

Aunt Sally concentrates on nursing Tom back to health. When he regains consciousness, he explains to her the whole elaborate procedure for freeing Jim, the "nonnamous" letter and how much fun it all was. She has never heard of the likes and can hardly believe that these "little rapscallions" are responsible for it all. She promises to punish Tom when he is well enough. Tom sits up in bed and makes the startling announcement that Jim was already set free two months ago by Miss Watson's will. The whole escapade was planned for adventure only. At this point, Aunt Polly arrives from St. Petersburg and greets her sister, Aunt Sally. The identity of Tom, posing as Sid, and Huck, pretending to be Tom, is at last revealed.

Jim is out of chains in no time and Tom gives him forty dollars for being such a patient prisoner. Jim finally reveals that the dead man in the floating house was Pap. Tom is proud of his wound and wears the bullet around his neck. Huck, however, feels that it is time for him to head out for new territory because Aunt Sally wants to adopt him and "sivilize" him and he can't stand that again.

Commentary

These final two chapters resolve the fantastic mistaken identity and clear matters up for Jim. Huck is able once again to reclaim his own name and become his real self once more.

In Chapter XLII, Jim is about to be killed as an example to other Negroes who try to run off; what saves him, however, is man's fear of destroying someone else's property and thus being financially in debt for the lynching. Yet, the doctor attests to the goodness of Jim and, instead of killing him, the good, decent Phelps merely locks him up and keeps him "on bread and water, and loaded down with chains. . . ."

When Tom hears that Jim is again imprisoned, he reveals that Jim has been free all this time. This revelation is partly due to his disappointment that his fantastic scheme to free Jim did not work. This revelation, however, is totally unmotivated. There is no indication earlier in the novel that someone like Miss Watson could undergo such a transformation as to actually free Jim. Instead, her type and her society represent everything that Jim and Huck were trying to escape from. But most critics tend to overlook some of these flaws as Twain's attempt to bring the novel to a rapid ending. With this revelation, Huck can finally understand why someone like Tom Sawyer could actually help "set a nigger free." Huck now realizes the hypocrisy of Tom's actions and now that he has his own name back, he recaptures some of those qualities which were suppressed when he assumed Tom's name.

In the last chapter, Twain returns to Jim's superstitions. Jim had predicted earlier that he would be rich and, now that he owns himself, he feels that he is now a rich man. In contrast, however, Huck feels that his pap has probably drunk up all of the money that Huck had. This fear necessitates Jim's revealing that Pap is dead. The mere fact that when Huck learns this and says nothing, nor shows any regret, indicates his lack of concern over the welfare of his worthless pap.

The novel ends as it began. In the second paragraph of Chapter I, Huck feared that the Widow Douglas would try to "sivilize" him and, at the end of the novel, he feels the need to escape again because this time Aunt Sally wants to adopt him and "sivilize" him. And throughout the novel, we have seen that Huck functions as a much nobler person when he is not confined by the hypocrisy of civilization.

CHARACTER ANALYSES

HUCK FINN

Huck Finn is one of America's best-loved fictional characters. Critically, he has been the subject of numerous studies and interpretations, many of them so unique as to make Huck unrecognizable.

Since Huck is the narrator of a book filled with humor, it is highly significant that we recognize that Huck himself has no sense of humor; in fact, he is almost totally literal minded. For example, he can see no humor in the age-old joke about where Moses was when the lights went out. It is inconceivable to him that the drunk riding the horse at the circus is really a highly trained acrobat. For a while, he literally believes a genie can be made to appear by rubbing an old lamp.

Since Huck is so completely literal minded, he therefore makes a superb narrator in that he tells or reports everything he sees or hears with straightforward accuracy. He never exaggerates or embroiders on anything he narrates and, therefore, we can always trust Huck's account or narration of any event to be realistic.

Huck possesses most of the qualities which are necessary for life on the frontier. He is always practical and natural, exhibiting good common sense except in such rare episodes as the snake episode. Furthermore, Huck is extremely adaptable. He can learn to tolerate living with the Widow Douglas and then can quickly transform his ways to that of living in the wilderness, or on a raft, or in the "so-called" elegance of the Grangerfords. Huck's adaptability, then, allows him to function well in different types of situations.

Huck is also very shrewd and possesses a good inventive ability. On the frontier, a man had to be shrewd to survive many situations. Thus, Huck is shrewd enough to be able to determine what motivates such people as the "bounty hunters" and then is inventive enough to create a story which is so credible that he and Jim are left alone.

Huck is also a person who responds sympathetically to other human beings. He tries to save the cutthroats on the *Walter Scott*, he saves the king and the duke from a posse and later even feels sorry for them when they are tarred and feathered, and he responds deeply to the plight of the Wilks girls. This is the same quality which allows him to appreciate and love Jim.

Huck's sympathy for other human beings, his shrewdness and ingenuity, his basic intelligence, his good common sense and his basic practicality—these are among the qualities which make Huck Finn one of the great characters in American fiction.

JIM

Along with Huck, Jim is the other major figure in the novel. One of his primary functions is to act as a gauge for Huck's development. In other words, while Huck knows Jim in St. Petersburg, it is not until Jackson's Island and the trip down the river that Huck learns to appreciate Jim's great worth as a human being.

At first, Jim is seen only as a person who is filled with superstitions, but once on the island, we discover that many of his superstitions are based upon good common sense, practicality, and a knowledge of natural surroundings. Gradually, on the trip down the river, we begin to see many other fine attributes such as his unselfish and towering love for his family, his dedication and love for Huck and, later, even his love for Tom Sawyer.

Jim's willingness to sacrifice himself for others and take on Huck's duties as they float down the river causes Huck to see Jim's basic worth. As he begins to accept Jim as a human being, he becomes aware of Jim's sense of love and humanity, his basic goodness, and his desire to help others. These qualities, then, force Huck into his decision to "go to hell" for Jim.

TOM SAWYER

In contrast to the individuality of Huck Finn and his rejection of the values of society, Tom Sawyer represents the values of the society from which Huck is escaping and also a conformity to those values. On a superficial level, it would appear that Tom Sawyer is the more imaginative of the two, but Tom's oaths, his schemes, and his escapades are based upon books about romantic adventures which he has read. Whereas Huck has the ability and shrewdness to function outside of society, Tom Sawyer would founder. Huck is involved in real life and Tom functions only when he is imitating something which he has read in a book. Tom's plans are always extravagant, absurd, or ridiculous while Huck's are simple, practical and shrewd.

Tom's conformity is seen in such events as when he makes Huck leave a nickle on the table for the candles, or when he makes Huck pay for the watermelon. These small facts lend credence to Huck's view that Tom Sawyer could not possibly help free a slave in the last section of the novel because of Tom's respectability and conformity to the views of his society.

REVIEW QUESTIONS

1. Compare and contrast the characters and personalities of Tom Sawyer and Huck Finn.

2. Choose several episodes from along the Mississippi River and show how each contributes to Huck's education.

3. In writing a humorous book, why does Twain have a narrator who has no sense of humor?

4. Discuss the principal function of the river in this novel.

5. Discuss the role of superstition in this novel.

6. Many critics have objected to the episodes at the Phelps plantation. What could be some of the objections?

7. Lionel Trilling says that Jim is Huck's "true father." Defend or refute this statement.

8. Discuss the differences between the freedom of the raft and the restrictions of society on the shore.

9. If the purpose of the trip down the Mississippi is to gain freedom for Jim, why do they continue deeper and deeper into slave territory?

10. Huck has been accused of knowing more than a fourteen-year-old boy could possibly know. Citing specific material from the novel, discuss this statement.

SELECTED BIBLIOGRAPHY

BELLAMY, GLADYS CARMEN. *Mark Twain as a Literary Artist.* Norman: University of Oklahoma Press, 1950.

BLAIR, WALTER. *Mark Twain and Huck Finn.* Berkeley: University of California Press, 1960.

DEVOTO, BERNARD. *Mark Twain at Work.* Cambridge: Harvard University Press, 1942.

FERGUSON, DELANCEY. *Mark Twain: Man and Legend.* Indianapolis: The Bobbs-Merrill Company, 1943.

LEARY, LEWIS. *Mark Twain.* Minneapolis: University of Minnesota Press, 1959.

LONG, E. HUDSON. *Mark Twain Handbook.* New York: Hendricks House, 1957.

MARX, LEO. "Mr. Eliot, Mr. Trilling, and *Huckleberry Finn.*" *American Scholar,* XXII (Autumn, 1953), 423-40.

ROURKE, CONSTANCE. *American Humor: A Study of the National Character.* New York: Harcourt, Brace & Company, Inc. 1931, pp. 209-20.

SALOMON, ROGER B. *Twain and the Image of History.* New Haven: Yale University Press, 1961.

SCOTT, ARTHUR L., ed. *Mark Twain: Selected Criticism.* Dallas: Southern Methodist University Press, 1955.

STONE, ALBERT E., JR. *The Innocent Eye: Childhood in Mark Twain's Imagination.* New Haven: Yale University Press, 1961.

NOTES

LET CLIFFS NOTES HELP YOU GET BETTER ACQUAINTED WITH THESE AUTHORS

■ ISAAC ASIMOV ■ TENNESSEE WILLIAMS ■ PLATO ■ F. SCOTT FITZGERALD ■ SHAKESPEARE ■ CHARLES DICKENS ■ GEORGE ELIOT ■ JANE AUSTEN ■ WILLA CATHER ■ WALT WHITMAN ■ ARTHUR MILLER ■ SALINGER ■ MACHIAVELLI ■ FRANZ KAFKA ■ EDGAR ALLEN POE ■ EDITH WHARTON ■ THOMAS SINCLAIR ■ PERCY SHELLEY JONATHON SWIFT ■ EMILY BRONTE ■ KATE CHOPIN ■ DANIEL DEFOE ■ DANTE ■ HENRY JAMES ■ WILLIAM FAULKNER ■ JAMES FENIMORE COOPER ■ MARK TWAIN ■ CHARLOTTE BRONTE ■ EDWARD ALBEE ■ ERNEST HEMINGWAY ■ JOHN STEINBECK ■ STEPHEN CRANE ■ GEORGE BERNARD SHAW ■ THOMAS HARDY ■ NATHANIEL HAWTHORNE ■ JAMES JOYCE ■ DOSTOEVSKY

GET CLIFFS NOTES

Cliffs Notes are America's most widely used study aids for literature. More than 200 titles are available covering well-known poems, plays and novels. Each provides expert analysis and background of plot, characters and author, in a way which can make the most difficult assignments easier to understand.

Available at your bookseller or order from Cliffs Notes.

See back cover for complete title listing.

P.O. Box 80728
Lincoln, NE 68501

TWO CLASSICS FROM CLIFFS NOTES

Cliffs Notes on Greek Classics

Cliffs Notes on Roman Classics

These two publications are the definitive reference tools for students and teachers. Highly acclaimed by classical scholars, *Cliffs Notes on Greek Classics* and *Cliffs Notes on Roman Classics* aid in understanding the ideology, philosophy and literary influence of ancient civilization.

You'll find *Greek Classics* and *Roman Classics* at your local bookstore. Or to order your copies, simply return the coupon.

- Review plot summaries and characters of classical plays and epics
- Find term paper ideas and essay topics
- Check facts, dates, spelling and pronunciation
- Identify major literary movements
- Recognize literary allusions to people and events

Yes! I want to add these classics to my library.

	Quantity
Cliffs Notes on *Greek Classics* ISBN 0566-2 ($6.95)	________
Cliffs Notes on *Roman Classics* ISBN 1152-2 ($5.95)	________
Total	$________

Name ________

Address ________

City ________

State ________ Zip ________

get the Cliffs Edge!

Cliffs NOTES

P.O. Box 80728, Lincoln, NE 68501

Send the coupon with your check to:
Cliffs Notes, P.O. Box 80728, Lincoln, NE 68501

Your Guides to Successful Test Preparation.

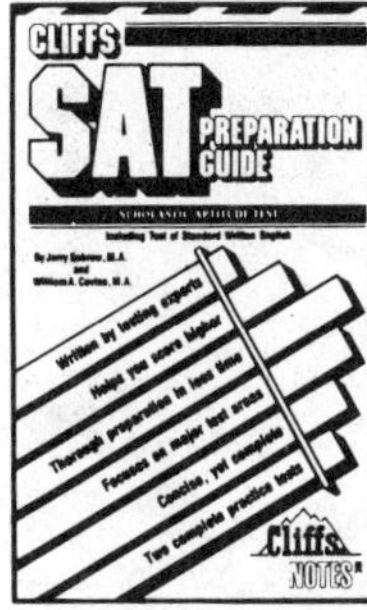

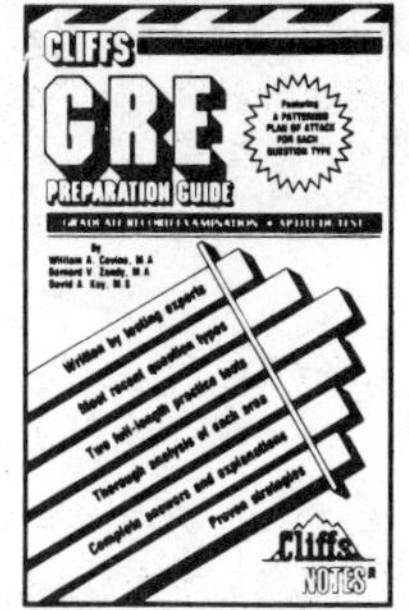

Cliffs Test Preparation Guides

Efficient preparation means better test scores. Go with the experts and use **Cliffs Test Preparation Guides.** They'll help you reach your goals because they're: • Complete • Concise • Functional • In-depth. They are focused on helping you know what to expect from each test. The test-taking techniques have been proven in classroom programs nationwide.

Recommended for individual use or as a part of formal test preparation programs.

TITLES		QTY.
2068-8	ENHANCED ACT ($5.95)	
2030-0	CBEST ($7.95)	
2040-8	CLAST ($8.95)	
1471-8	Essay Exam ($4.95)	
2031-9	ELM Review ($6.95)	
2060-2	GMAT ($5.95)	
2008-4	GRE ($6.95)	
2065-3	LSAT ($6.95)	
2033-5	MATH Review For Standardized Tests ($8.95)	
2017-3	NTE Core Battery ($14.95)	
2020-3	Memory Power for Exams ($4.95)	
2032-7	PPST ($7.95)	
2002-5	PSAT/NMSQT ($4.50)	
2000-9	SAT ($5.95)	
2042-4	TASP ($7.95)	
2018-1	TOEFL w/cassette ($14.95)	
2034-3	VERBAL Review for Standardized Tests ($7.95)	
2041-6	You Can Pass the GED ($9.95)	

Prices subject to change without notice.

Available at your local bookseller or order by sending the coupon with your check. **Cliffs Notes, P.O. Box 80728, Lincoln, NE 68501**

Name ____________________

Address ____________________

City ____________________

State __________ **Zip** __________

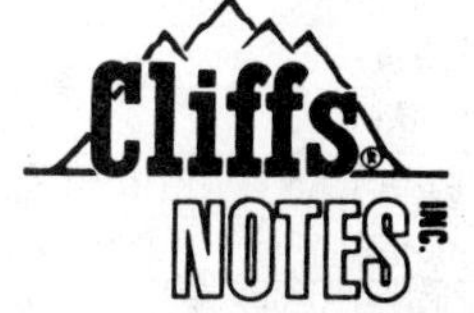

P.O. Box 80728
Lincoln, NE 68501

Here's a Great Way to Study Shakespeare and Chaucer.

Cliffs Complete Study Editions

These easy-to-use volumes contain everything that a student or teacher needs for an individual classic. Each attractively illustrated volume includes abundant biographical, historical and literary background information. A descriptive bibliography provides guidance in the selection of additional reading.

The inviting three-column arrangement offers the maximum in convenience to the reader. Shakespeare's plays are presented in a full, authoritative text with modern spelling. Each line of Chaucer's original poetry is followed by a literal translation in simple current English. Adjacent to the complete text, there is a running commentary that gives clear supplementary discussion. Obscure words and allusions are keyed by line number and clarified opposite to where they occur.

COMPLETE STUDY EDITIONS	QTY.
SHAKESPEARE	
Hamlet	
Julius Caesar	
King Henry IV, Part 1	
King Lear	
Macbeth	
The Merchant of Venice	
Othello	
Romeo and Juliet	
The Tempest	
Twelfth Night	
CHAUCER'S CANTERBURY TALES	
The Prologue	
The Wife of Bath	

Prices subject to change without notice.

$4.95 each

Available at your booksellers or send this form with your check or money order to Cliffs Notes.

Name ______________________

Address ______________________

City ______________________

State __________ Zip __________

P.O. Box 80728
Lincoln, NE 68501

Cliffs

Math Review and Verbal Review for Standardized Tests

Use your time efficiently with exactly the review material you need for standardized tests.

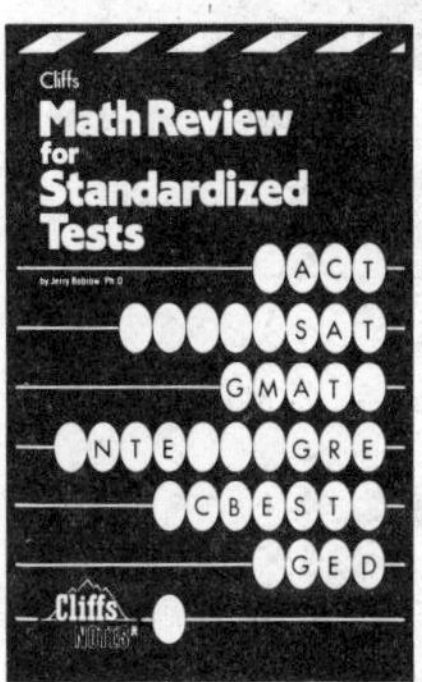

GMAT – SAT – NTE – GRE –
– State Teacher Credential Tests –
PSAT – CBEST – ACT – PPST – GED
and many more!

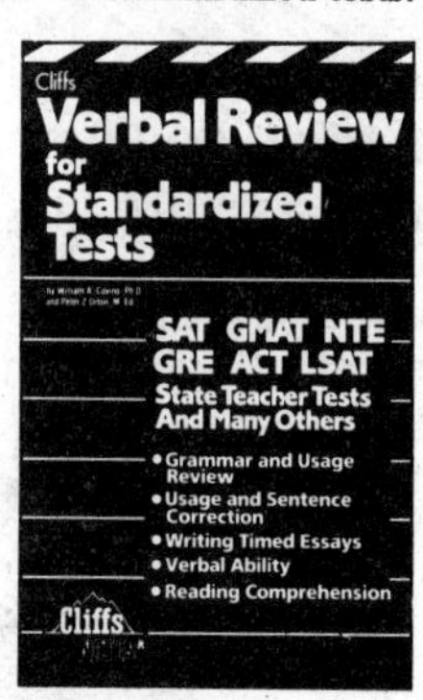

Math Review — 422 pages

- Provides insights and strategies for specific problem types, plus intensive review in the most needed basic skills in arithmetic, algebra, geometry and word problems.
- Includes hundreds of practice problems to reinforce learning at each step in a unique easy-to-use format.

Verbal Review — 375 pages

- Includes a grammar and usage review, dealing specifically with the concepts that exam-makers consistently use in test questions; exercises reinforce concept understanding at each step.
- Extensive practice and strategies in English usage, sentence correction, antonyms, analogies, sentence completion, reading comprehension and timed essay writing.

Cliffs Notes, Inc., P.O. Box 80728, Lincoln, NE 68501

Cliffs Math Review
for Standardized Tests $8.95 ________

Cliffs Verbal Review
for Standardized Tests $7.95 ________

• *Price subject to change without notice*

Cliffs NOTES

P.O. Box 80728
Lincoln, NE 68501

Name ____________________

Address ____________________

City ________ State ________ Zip ________

Make Your Best Score on these important tests...

Get Cliffs Test Preparation Guides

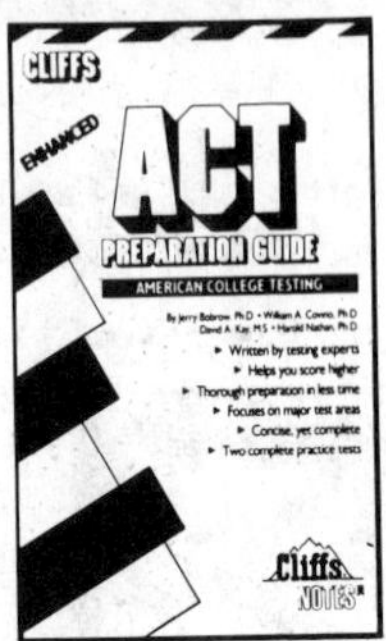

Full-length practice tests — explanatory answers — self-scoring charts let you analyze your performance.

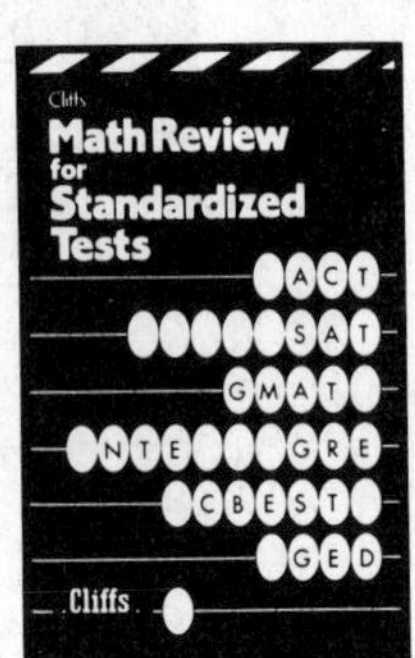

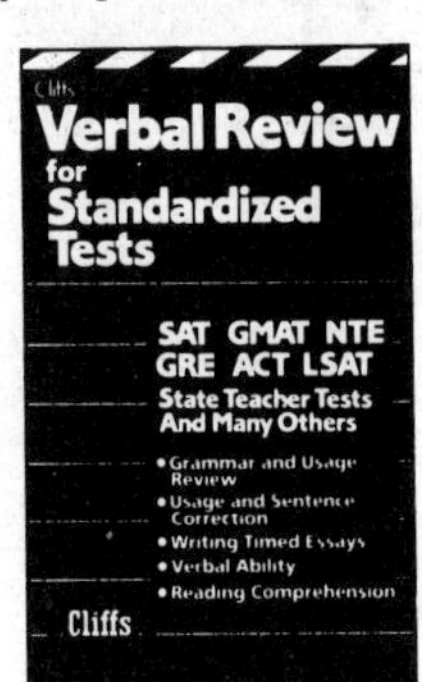

Needed by everyone taking standardized tests.

Available at your local bookseller or send in your check with the coupon below.
Cliffs Notes, Inc., P.O. Box 80728, Lincoln, NE 68501

TITLES	QTY.
Cliffs Enhanced ACT Preparation Guide ($5.95)	
Cliffs MATH Review for Standardized Tests ($8.95)	
Cliffs PSAT/NMSQT Preparation Guide ($4.50)	
Cliffs SAT Preparation Guide ($5.95)	
Cliffs VERBAL Review for Standardized Tests ($7.95)	

Prices Subject to change without notice.

Name ____________
Address ____________
City ____________
State ________ Zip ________

P.O. Box 80728
Lincoln, NE 68501

THE PORTRAIT OF A LADY

NOTES

including

- *Life and Background of the Author*
- *The Realism of Henry James*
- *Structure of the Novel*
- *General Plot Summary*
- *Summaries and Chapter Commentaries*
- *Meaning Through Social Contrasts*
- *Special Problems and Interests*
- *Character Analysis*
- *Questions for Review*

by
James L. Roberts, Ph.D.
Department of English
University of Nebraska

INCORPORATED
LINCOLN, NEBRASKA 68501

Editor

Gary Carey, M.A.
University of Colorado

Consulting Editor

James L. Roberts, Ph.D.
Department of English
University of Nebraska

ISBN 0-8220-1066-6
© Copyright 1965
by
C. K. Hillegass
All Rights Reserved
Printed in U.S.A.

1991 Printing

The Cliffs Notes logo, the names "Cliffs" and "Cliffs Notes," and the black and yellow diagonal-stripe cover design are all registered trademarks belonging to Cliffs Notes, Inc., and may not be used in whole or in part without written permission.

Cliffs Notes, Inc. Lincoln, Nebraska

CONTENTS

AUTHOR'S LIFE AND BACKGROUND

Henry James was a true cosmopolite. He was a citizen of the world and moved freely in and out of drawing rooms in Europe, England, and America. He was perhaps more at home in Europe than he was in America, but the roots of his life belong to the American continent. Thus, with few exceptions, most of his works deal with some type of confrontation between an American and a European.

Henry James was born in New York in 1843. His father, Henry James, Sr., had inherited a considerable sum of money and spent his time in leisured pursuit of theology and philosophy. The father often wrote essays and treatises on aspects of religion and philosophy and developed a certain degree of mysticism. Among the guests in the James household were some of the most famous minds of the mid-nineteenth century. Henry James was able to hear his father converse with people like Ralph Waldo Emerson, Bronson Alcott, and George Ripley. The father was insistent that his children learn to approach life with the broadest possible outlook.

In the strictest sense of the word, Henry James had no formal education. As a youth, he had private tutors. Then in his twelfth year, his father took the entire family to Europe, where they moved freely from Switzerland to France to Germany in pursuit of stimulating conversation and intellectual ideas. The world of Europe left an everlasting impression on young Henry James. He was ultimately to return and make his home in Europe.

When the family returned from Europe, the elder James decided to settle in New England. He chose Cambridge because this was the center of American intellectual thought. Many of the writers of Cambridge, Boston, and nearby Concord, where Emerson and Thoreau lived, were often visitors in the James household. It was in Boston that James met the first great influence on his literary career. He established a close friendship with William Dean Howells, who as editor of one of America's leading magazines, was able to help James in his early efforts to write and publish.

In Boston, Henry James enrolled briefly in the Harvard Law School but soon withdrew to devote himself to writing. His older brother, William James, the most famous philosopher and psychologist America had yet produced, was also a student at Harvard, where he remained after graduation to become one of the most eminent lecturers in America.

By the late 1860's, James had done some reviewing and had sold one work of fiction to the *Atlantic Monthly*. He also went to Europe on his own, to see the continent as an adult. He returned again to Cambridge and New York in the hope of continuing his literary career, but he gradually came to the realization that Europe was more suitable for his writings. Thus, in 1876, when he was in his thirty-third year, James made the momentous decision to take up residence abroad. With the exception of short trips to various parts of the world, he lived the rest of his life in and near London. Until 1915, he retained his American citizenship, but when World War I broke out, he became a naturalized citizen of England in protest over America's failure to enter the war against Germany.

James' life and background were ideally suited for the development of his artistic temperament. Even though he was not extremely wealthy, he did have sufficient independent means to allow him to live a leisured life. His father's house provided all the intellectual stimulation he needed. The visitors were the most prominent artists of the day, and James was able to follow the latest literary trends. In his travels, he moved in the best society of two continents and came into contact with a large variety of ideas.

With such a life, it is natural that James' novels are concerned with a society of people who are interested in subtle ideas and subtle refinements. There are no really poor people in his novels. He wrote about people who had enough money to allow them to develop and cultivate their higher natures. His novels develop with a deliberate slowness and conscientious refinement. Many critics and readers resent the deliberate withholding of information and the slow development found in the Jamesian novel, but James' life was lived with a high degree of leisure and refinement. And finally James was the first American qualified to develop the theme of the

American in Europe. By the time he made his decision to settle in Europe, he had made several trips there and had lived and attended school in several parts of Europe. Thus, the subject matter of most of James' works is concerned with an American of some degree of innocence meeting or becoming involved with some European of experience.

In spite of his decision to live abroad, James remained essentially American in his sympathies. His greatest characters (or central characters) are almost always Americans. But at the same time, some of his most unpleasant characters are also Americans. But the important thing is that the characters who change, mature, and achieve an element of greatness are almost always Americans.

THE REALISM OF HENRY JAMES

Henry James has had a tremendous influence on the development of the novel. Part of this influence has been through the type of realism that he employs. On the other hand, the most frequent criticism against James has been that he is not realistic enough. Many critics have objected that James does not write about life, that his novels are filled with people whom one would never meet in this world. One critic (H. L. Mencken) suggested that James needed a good whiff of the Chicago stockyards so as to get a little life into his novels. Others have suggested that James' world is too narrow and incomplete to warrant classification as a realistic depiction of life.

Actually, James' realism is of a special sort. By the early definitions, James is not a realist. The early definitions stated that the novelist should accurately depict life, and the novel should "hold up a mirror to life"; in other words, the early realist was supposed to make an almost scientific recording of life.

But James was not concerned with all aspects of life. There is nothing of the ugly, the vulgar, the common, or the pornographic in James. He was not concerned with poverty or with the middle class who had to struggle for a living. Instead, he was interested in depicting a class of people who could afford to devote themselves to the refinements of life.

What then is James' special brand of realism? When we refer to James' realism, we mean James' fidelity to his own material. To best appreciate his novels and his realism, we must enter into James' special world. It is as though we ascended a ladder and arrived at another world. Once we have arrived at this special world and once we accept it, then we see that James is very realistic. That is, in terms of his world, he never violates his character's essence. Thus, James' realism, in the truest sense, means being faithful to his character. In other words, characters from other novels often do things or commit acts that don't seem to blend in with their essential nature. But the acts of the Jamesian character are always understandable in terms of that character's true nature.

James explained his own realism in terms of its opposition to romanticism. For James the realistic represents those things which, sooner or later, in one way or another, everyone will encounter. But the romantic stands for those things which, with all the efforts and all the wealth and facilities of the world, we can never know directly. Thus, it is conceivable that one can experience the same things that the characters are experiencing in a James novel; but one can never actually encounter the events narrated in the romantic novel.

When James, therefore, creates a certain type of character early in the novel, this character will act in a consistent manner throughout the entire book. This is being realistic. The character will never do anything that is not logical and acceptable to his realistic nature, or to our conception of what that character should do.

In later years, James, in writing about realism, maintained that he was more interested in a faithful rendition of a character in any given situation than in depicting all aspects of life. Therefore, when he has once drawn Isabel Archer's character in one situation, the reader can anticipate how she will act in any other given situation. Her actions are not unexplainable. We are able to logically understand all of her actions. Thus James' realism would never allow the characters to perform actions which would be inconsistent with their true natures.

STRUCTURE

Almost all of James' novels are structured in the same way. There must be a center—something toward which all the lines point and which "supremely matters." This is essentially James' own explanation of his structure. The thing that "supremely matters" is the central idea of the novel or that idea around which the novel functions. In *The Portrait of a Lady,* the thing that "supremely matters" is for Isabel Archer to have the opportunity to develop *freely* to the limits of her own capacity. She is seen as a person who has great potential, but she does not have that freedom which would allow her to develop her own innate qualities. Therefore, almost all of the scenes and action of the novel are designed to hinder or to bring to completion this chance for Isabel to attain her full capacity.

James' creative process is also important to understanding the structure of his works. He begins his novels with a situation and a character. Many writers, like Nathaniel Hawthorne, would begin with an idea or theme in mind and then would create a situation and characters that would illuminate the basic idea, but James' technique is just the opposite. He created a certain situation, and then he would place his characters in it. James would then, in effect, sit back and simply observe what would happen when a character was confronted with this new situation. Often, James said, he had no particular ending in mind when he began a novel. Instead, he would let the character and situation determine the ending. This allowed him more freedom, and allowed him the opportunity of "getting to know" his character by observing him in a series of scenes.

Thus, the central situation in *The Portrait of a Lady* is the arrival of a charming young girl in Europe who is restricted by having no means to travel and be free. Many characters who meet her wonder what would happen if she were perfectly free to develop to her fullest. The thing that "supremely matters" is the full development of Isabel Archer. Thus, it must be arranged to secure money for her and then we will simply watch her to see which of the great men of Europe she will finally choose for a husband.

We have said that all lines must point toward the thing that supremely matters, but these lines do not follow a straight course. This is not the way James structures his novels. Everything in the novel is aimed at the central situation, but he moves toward the center by exploring all the related matters. In other words, the structure could be best described by a series of circles around the center. Each circle is an event which illuminates the center, but highlights only a part of it. Each circle then is often a discussion by several different people. For example, one character observes something and then goes to another person to discuss his observation. Then two other characters might discuss the same event. By the end of the various discussions, James has investigated all of the psychological implications inherent in this particular situation. This would represent one circle. Then, we go to another event or situation, which will be fully discussed before proceeding to the next. Thus by the end of the novel, James has probed and examined every moral, ethical, and psychological aspect of the central situation, and the reader has heard the views of many people on the same subject.

Consequently, the structure of James' novels are circular in approach to the central subject, but every circle in some way illuminates the thing that supremely matters. Every incident functions to tell us more about a character or the situation. There is nothing that is superfluous or extraneous.

LIST OF CHARACTERS

Isabel Archer

A young American girl of a free and independent nature who becomes an heiress.

Mrs. Touchett

Isabel's aunt, who brings Isabel to England and introduces her to European society.

Mr. Touchett

Isabel's uncle, who is a wealthy banker living in England.

Ralph Touchett
Isabel's cousin, who talks his father into making Isabel an heiress.

Lord Warburton
A very wealthy and important English nobleman who falls in love with Isabel.

Caspar Goodwood
Isabel's American suitor, who follows her to Europe to persuade her to marry him.

Henrietta Stackpole
An independent young lady who is Isabel's friend.

Madame Merle
Mrs. Touchett's friend, who becomes a confidante and close companion of Isabel's.

Gilbert Osmond
Madame Merle's friend who later marries Isabel.

Pansy Osmond
Gilbert Osmond's daughter, who develops a great admiration for Isabel.

Edward Rosier
A childhood acquaintance of Isabel's, who falls in love with Pansy Osmond.

Countess Gemini
Gilbert Osmond's sister, who is later instrumental in helping Isabel come to some realizations about Osmond.

Mr. Bantling
An Englishman who accompanies Henrietta Stackpole on many of her excursions throughout Europe.

GENERAL PLOT SUMMARY

Isabel Archer's aunt comes to America after the death of Isabel's father in order to take her niece to Europe. On her arrival in England, Isabel meets her cousin Ralph, her uncle, Mr. Touchett, and the great nobleman of the area, Lord Warburton, who immediately falls in love with her. After a short time, Warburton proposes to Isabel, but she turns him down, maintaining that she cherishes her freedom and independence too much to marry. A short time later, her journalist friend Henrietta Stackpole arrives in England and tells Isabel that her American suitor Caspar Goodwood has followed Isabel to England.

During a visit to London, Isabel encounters Caspar Goodwood, who tries to convince her that she should marry him. Again, Isabel says that she must have time to see the world and make a few independent judgments. She promises Goodwood that she will discuss the subject again in two years. He leaves, promising to remain in America for this time.

While in London, Isabel hears of the sickness of her uncle. She returns to his home, Gardencourt, where she finds him dying. She also finds another guest, Madame Merle, an old friend of Mrs. Touchett's. During the long days when the house is involved with sickness, Isabel and Madame Merle become good friends.

Ralph Touchett knows that his father plans to leave him a huge fortune, but he also knows that he is slowly dying himself and does not need much money. He therefore convinces his father to leave some of his fortune to Isabel.

After Mr. Touchett's death, Isabel becomes a great heiress. She continues to travel with her aunt and they go to Mrs. Touchett's home in Florence, Italy. Here, Madame Merle introduces Isabel to her old friend Gilbert Osmond. Madame Merle has already instructed Osmond to be nice to Isabel because she thinks that Gilbert should marry her.

After some time, Isabel believes that she is in love with Osmond. She maintains her independence by refusing to listen to any advice. Everyone is opposed to her marrying Osmond because all feel that he is a worthless fortune hunter.

Some years later, Isabel knows that she has made a mistake. Gilbert Osmond, now her husband, has tried to break Isabel's independent nature and has tried to make her obey his every wish. He wants Isabel to be as quiet and obedient as is his daughter. Pansy, the daughter, has been brought up in a convent and has been taught to obey her father in everything. Thus when the father disapproves of the young man that Pansy is in love with, she must submit to his wishes.

When Isabel receives a letter telling her that her cousin Ralph is dying, she wants to go to England to visit him. Osmond opposes the trip because it would not look proper. At this time, Isabel discovers that Pansy is actually the illegitimate child of Madame Merle and Gilbert Osmond. She then realizes that her friend Madame Merle tricked her into an imprudent marriage with Osmond, and with this knowledge Isabel leaves for England in spite of her husband's disapproval.

In England, she confesses the mistake she made in marrying Osmond, and Caspar Goodwood pleads with her to leave her husband. Isabel, however, feels that she cannot forsake the sacred bonds of marriage and feels that Pansy needs her help. She therefore decides to return to Osmond in spite of her dislike for him.

CHAPTERS 1 AND 2

Summary

One afternoon, Mr. Touchett and his son Ralph are entertaining Lord Warburton at tea. Mr. Touchett is infirm and remains in his chair. He and Ralph are busy advising Lord Warburton to interest himself in some woman. Lord Warburton says that he is not interested in marrying until he meets a really interesting woman. Mr. Touchett then warns him not to fall in love with Isabel Archer, Mrs. Touchett's niece, whom she is bringing back to England from America. Mrs. Touchett has wired that she is bringing a rather interesting and independent young niece, but the telegram revealed nothing more.

While the men are discussing Isabel, she happens to emerge from the house. She and her aunt have just arrived, and Isabel is getting her first glimpse of Gardencourt. Ralph goes to meet her, and Isabel explains that Mrs. Touchett went straight to her room and will come down for dinner. Ralph takes his cousin to meet Mr. Touchett and Lord Warburton. Mr. Touchett hopes that Isabel will remain with them for a long time, but Isabel says that his wife will have to arrange that. Mr. Touchett wonders if Isabel is the type of person who likes to have things arranged for her. Isabel tells him that she is, in fact, very fond of her liberty and treasures her independence. After observing Isabel in conversation for a few minutes, Lord Warburton tells Ralph that she is his idea of a very interesting woman.

Commentary

The first chapter presents the scene upon which Isabel Archer will encounter her first new experience. It is a part of James' technique to place his main character in an unfamiliar setting and then to observe the behavior of this character. We discover that Isabel is a person who, according to Mrs. Touchett's telegram, loves her independence. This quality will be one of her most discussed and most influential qualities throughout the novel.

The setting we encounter is that of Gardencourt. The novel opens and will close on this particular setting. It will initiate Isabel into her many adventures, and in the end will represent all the protection which she needs. It comes to represent the good, solid side of life that is also filled with much of the esthetic. There is a wholesome quality about it lacking in some of the other European houses. In other words, it is substantial and real, whereas Gilbert Osmond's house has a touch of the artificial and the contrived about it.

Like the novels of Jane Austen, many of James' works take the subject of marriage as their central idea. The thought of marriage comes up as Mr. Touchett ironically tells Lord Warburton that he is not to fall in love with Isabel Archer.

It will be a part of James' irony that he makes Isabel's cousin, Ralph Touchett, such a contrast to her. Ralph is sickly and dying, while Isabel is charged with life and activity.

It is often in the delicate shades of conversation that James gives the reader a hint of Isabel's nature. Thus through subtle innuendoes, we discover many small facts about the character. At the end of Chapter 2, we find out that Isabel likes things settled for her, *only* if they are settled as she likes them. She is very fond of her independence and doesn't like the intimation that her aunt has "adopted" her. James also uses one further technique. We often learn much about the major character from the comments and reactions of the people gathered around him. For example, to the average reader, Isabel is not notably impressive at this first meeting, but she does impress the other people. The chapter ends by Lord Warburton saying that here is his "idea of an interesting woman."

It is of additional interest that Isabel's concept of her independence comes up so early in the novel. It will be ironically reversed later in the novel. At the end of the story, she will be a virtual prisoner who has lost almost all of her independence and freedom. This concept will be fully developed as the novel progresses.

CHAPTERS 3 AND 4

Summary

Isabel's aunt has several peculiarities. For example, she long ago recognized the fact that she and her husband did not desire the same things in life; therefore, she decided to set up a house in Florence and pay wifely visits to her husband once a year. She also makes trips to America to keep in touch with some of her property there. Some years earlier, Mrs. Touchett quarreled with Mr. Archer, and they broke relations with each other. After Mr. Archer's death, she journeyed to Albany, New York, in order to inquire about her nieces. The two older sisters were married, but the youngest, Isabel, seemed to desire other things in life. Mrs. Touchett offered to take Isabel to live in Europe for a time.

Isabel's older sister, Mrs. Ludlow, was delighted to hear of Isabel's opportunity to visit Europe. She thought Isabel would have "a chance to develop." Isabel had always been the more intellectual of the three sisters. When young men came to visit, they always thought that they had to be exceptionally intelligent in order to converse with Isabel. There was, however, one named Caspar Goodwood who wished to marry Isabel. He traveled far just to see Isabel but received no encouragement.

Commentary

Chapter 3 fills in the background information and gives the reader more knowledge about Isabel. For example, in Isabel's first encounter with her aunt, we see that she was quite anxious to go to Europe, but she was just as anxious to retain her own freedom. She told Mrs. Touchett that it would not be possible to promise to do everything her aunt wanted her to do, but just the same, she "would promise almost anything."

James begins to introduce his theme more definitely in Chapter 4. Mrs. Ludlow told her husband that she wanted Isabel to go to Europe in order to have a "chance to develop." Thus, throughout the novel, we must watch to see just how much Isabel is capable of developing.

In his description, James suggests that Isabel is a rather intelligent and formidable person who reads considerably. However, Isabel would definitely prefer direct experience to that gained by reading. Consequently, she must be taken to Europe so as to be given the opportunity of experiencing various aspects of life firsthand.

The last part of Chapter 4 presents the character of Caspar Goodwood. As his name suggests, he is a high caliber person who does not weakly accept defeat. We should also note that he is a man who inspired Isabel "with a sentiment of high, of rare respect."

CHAPTER 5

Summary

Ralph Touchett had been educated in America and England. He was a small boy when his father came to England as a partner in a bank. Mr. Touchett has retained all of his American qualities, but Ralph grew up transformed into an Englishman. He has discovered that he is dying and has adjusted to this fact. He knows that he will not survive his father by many years, and he has resigned himself to the pleasures of life accessible to him.

When Ralph meets his mother before dinner, he asks her what she plans to do with Isabel. Mrs. Touchett tries to explain that Isabel has potential and she wants her to have the opportunity to see and learn more about the world. Isabel has only a limited amount of money, but has a great deal of imagination and independence. Ralph reveals to his mother that he is already interested in his cousin. He finds her to be quite exceptional and is interested in observing her adventures in Europe.

Later, Isabel asks Ralph to show her the pictures collected in Gardencourt. In their discussion, Isabel asks if the house doesn't have some famous ghost. Ralph explains that one must suffer a great deal before one can see the ghost. He hopes that she will never have to suffer, and Isabel admits that she is afraid of suffering. She tells him that she came to Europe to be as happy as possible and has every intention of devoting herself to that end.

Commentary

In the first part of this chapter, we find out that Mr. Touchett came to England some time ago, but has retained most of his American sympathies. He has, however, gotten along famously with the British. Ralph is, however, considerably less American than the father.

As so often happens in a James novel, a person such as Ralph, who is dying, will possess an extra sensitivity. He will be the person who will most directly understand and affect Isabel's destiny.

Ralph's first interest is to know what his mother plans to do with Isabel. Her motivations are many. Essentially, she wants to give Isabel the chance to see the world and to develop her capacities to a greater degree, but Jamesian characters seldom act without some extra motivations. Mrs. Touchett also admits that Isabel will "do her credit." She says that she likes to be well thought of and she thinks that an attractive niece will contribute to her general reputation.

An early and essential point of the novel is soon established. Isabel "seemed averse to being under pecuniary obligations." Consequently, Ralph will later conceive the idea of providing Isabel with enough money to allow her to be completely free so as to develop to her fullest potential.

In her conversation with Ralph, Isabel asks him if this old house doesn't have a ghost; she thinks that all famous old houses should have ghosts. Ralph tells her that before a person can see the ghost, that person has to suffer a lot, and he maintains that Isabel was not made to suffer. Thus, at the end of the novel, when Isabel returns to Gardencourt and feels the presence of someone else in her room, we may assume that she has then suffered enough so as to see the ghost.

CHAPTERS 6 AND 7

Summary

Isabel Archer is a person "of many theories; her imagination was remarkably active." She also possesses a fine perception and cares very much for knowledge. She is also determined to see the world as a place of brightness and free expansion, but "sometimes she went so far as to wish that she might find herself some day in a difficult position, so that she should have the pleasure of being as heroic as the occasion demanded." Among her friends is Henrietta

Stackpole, a lady journalist of advanced ideas and established reputation. Isabel admires her friend's "courage, energy, and good-humour."

Isabel soon develops a strong friendship with Mr. Touchett. In fact, she spends long hours talking with him. He even wishes that she would ask some favor of him so that he could show her how much he thinks of her. Mr. Touchett spends a good part of his time explaining the English to Isabel. What Isabel doesn't like about the English is that they have "everything settled beforehand"; she likes more "unexpectedness."

As Ralph begins to know Isabel better, he thinks more and more of her. She seems to be intelligent and generous. "She gave one an impression of having intentions of her own," and Ralph wants to be present when she executes them. Somewhat later, Lord Warburton returns to Gardencourt to spend a couple of days. One night, when Mrs. Touchett tells Isabel that it is time for them to retire, Isabel asks to remain downstairs with Ralph and Lord Warburton, but her aunt informs her it is improper. Isabel can't understand this and becomes somewhat annoyed at her aunt's insistence over such small matters of decorum. Upon parting, however, Isabel tells her aunt that she always wants to be told when she is taking "too much liberty." It is only by knowing, that she will be able to choose whether or not to do something.

Commentary

One of James' techniques is to constantly develop his character by revealing additional facts about the character or by placing the character in a new situation. At the beginning of Chapter 6, James writes about Isabel's remarkably active imagination. She has a large perception and she cares for so many important things. These are some of the qualities which make Isabel a rather exceptional person and which attract other people to her.

James' use of foreshadowing is here illustrated. Isabel imagines herself someday in a situation which is difficult. In fact, she "went so far as to wish that she might find herself some day in a difficult position, so that she should have the pleasure of being as heroic as the occasion demanded." Such statements as these prepare the reader for Isabel's final sacrifice at the end of the novel.

Isabel and Mr. Touchett become very close friends in these early sections. This friendship prepares the reader and Isabel to accept the inheritance that he leaves her. At one point Mr. Touchett "wished she would ask" something of him, but Isabel never did. Thus, he is easily persuaded by his son to leave Isabel a large portion of money upon his death.

These early chapters also often present Isabel in conversation with Ralph Touchett. This occurs so that Ralph will be able to see Isabel's gifts and will want to have a hand in developing them. He presents directly the problem of the novel. He views Isabel as "intelligent and generous" with a fine free nature. "But what was she going to do with herself?" She seems to Ralph destined for some unusual course in life and determined to execute some high intentions of her own. He hopes, therefore, that "whenever she executes them" that he will be there to see. Consequently, through the development of the friendship and through Ralph's understanding of Isabel's potential for development, he will later conceive of the idea of providing her with the financial means to accomplish her ends.

James places Isabel in a new situation at the end of the seventh chapter. Isabel is about to commit an indiscretion when she is stopped by her aunt. Isabel doesn't understand the reason, but tells her aunt that it is good to know what is accepted and not accepted. This knowledge will then allow Isabel the chance to choose. Thus, at the end of the novel, Isabel is faced with a choice after having all the sides clearly revealed to her. Little scenes like this one help, therefore, to prepare the reader for Isabel's final decision.

CHAPTERS 8 AND 9

Summary

Since Lord Warburton has invited Isabel to come to see his house, Isabel questions her uncle about him. From Ralph, she has heard that he is a man of very high social position and of great wealth. He is greatly admired and is somewhat of a radical. After she has found out a great deal about him, Isabel mentions that she would like to see him put to a test someday. Mr. Touchett tells her that Lord Warburton will never be a great martyr unless she makes him one. Isabel maintains that she will never make anyone be a martyr and hopes she will never have to be one herself.

At Lord Warburton's house, Isabel meets his two unmarried sisters, the Misses Molyneux. She discovers that they greatly admire their brother and could not conceive of ever disagreeing with him on any subject. Even though the two sisters are quite different from Isabel, they begin to feel a strong friendship for one another.

Lord Warburton takes Isabel for a walk and lets her know how charming he finds her. Isabel refuses to believe him and attempts to change the subject. Lord Warburton tells her that she strikes him as having great purposes and vast designs to execute. Isabel denies this and thinks that she only wants to see some more of the world and make a few independent judgments about it. Lord Warburton tells Isabel that he will come to see her again next week.

Commentary

Chapter 8 is devoted to developing the character of Lord Warburton, who comes to represent the ideal Englishman. He is a man of great wealth, position, and repute. He is also a man of perfect taste but rather liberal and sincere in his beliefs. The reader should also remember that later in the novel Gilbert Osmond thinks Lord Warburton would be an ideal husband for Pansy.

There is some of James' irony at the end of the chapter. Old Mr. Touchett thinks that Lord Warburton will never be a martyr unless Isabel makes him one. Isabel stoutly maintains that she will never make anyone a martyr; however, later Lord Warburton is in one sense a martyr to Isabel.

Chapter 9 continues to develop Lord Warburton's character. His two sisters are introduced so as to reflect on his good character and noble nature, revealing therefore what a perfect mate Isabel will soon refuse.

Lord Warburton's view of Isabel is also interesting. He thinks of her as having some "mysterious purposes—vast designs." He also sees her as a person who likes her independence. Therefore, in his marriage proposal, he will be offering her a chance to develop her independent nature and execute her mysterious purposes. He has no desire to change her nature in the way that Gilbert Osmond will try to change it.

CHAPTERS 10, 11, AND 12

Summary

After returning from her visit to Lord Warburton's, Isabel receives a letter from Henrietta Stackpole, who has come to Europe to do a series of articles on European life and wants to meet people. Isabel mentions the letter to her uncle, who immediately extends Henrietta an invitation. Ralph accompanies Isabel to meet Henrietta. He is told that Henrietta is the type who does not care what men think of her.

When Henrietta arrives, she tells Isabel that she already feels cramped in Europe. Later, she begins to write an article about Mr. Touchett and Gardencourt, and Isabel reminds her that it would not be in good taste. Henrietta doesn't understand, but defers to Isabel's wishes.

Henrietta finds it difficult to understand Ralph. When she is told that Ralph is a cosmopolite, she instinctively dislikes the word. She cannot understand a person who does nothing, and apparently Ralph spends his days doing absolutely nothing. She tries to pry into Ralph's mind and motivations until he has to admit that Henrietta is "too familiar." Isabel defends Henrietta, saying that it is Henrietta's vulgar quality that she finds appealing. There is something of "the people" in Henrietta and Ralph concedes that there is an odor of the future about Isabel's friend.

Henrietta and Mrs. Touchett could not agree on anything. Henrietta resents the fact that Mrs. Touchett has denied her American ties, and Mrs. Touchett finds Henrietta too vulgar and forward.

Henrietta later tells Isabel that she and Caspar Goodwood came over on the same ship and that he is now in England. Henrietta is worried that Isabel is changing too much and she wants Isabel to come to an understanding with Caspar Goodwood. She fears that Isabel is being too affected with European ways and manners. The next day, Isabel receives a letter from Caspar Goodwood telling her how much he admires her and how he followed her to Europe because of his devotion to her.

Isabel has just finished reading Caspar Goodwood's letter when Lord Warburton appears. As they stroll through the grounds, Lord Warburton takes the opportunity to tell Isabel how much he cares for her. He then proposes to her. Isabel is rather stunned and maintains that they do not know each other. Lord Warburton points out that he knows himself very well and knows that Isabel is the only person he will ever care for.

Isabel explains that she simply does not want to marry and that she certainly cannot accept his proposal now. He suggests that she consider it and write to him later. She promises to write very soon but warns him not to hope for a favorable answer.

Commentary

Chapter 10 is devoted to establishing the character of Henrietta Stackpole, who, as the name suggests, is a rather formidable person. James uses her as a confidante and also as a contrast to Isabel. We must see that Isabel is not so liberal as are some of her fellow Americans. We also see, by comparison, that Isabel has much more taste and fits into a situation better than most people.

Furthermore, by contrasting Isabel with Henrietta, we see that – in spite of their differences – Isabel still likes her. It is impossible for people like Madame Merle and Gilbert Osmond to see the good qualities that Henrietta possesses; instead they see only the loud, brassy, and objectional characteristics. Henrietta is aggressive, she has no sense of the private and she goes too far in her personal comments. But at the same time, she does possess a sincerity and honesty, an admirable candor and directness that are missing in most Europeans. Isabel, however, is capable of appreciating the good qualities in a variety of people.

Henrietta sums up so often the difference between the typical American and the typical European (or cosmopolite as Ralph is described). She says to him: "If you've got any charm it's quite unnatural. It's wholly acquired.... It's a charm that I don't appreciate...make yourself useful in some way, and then we'll talk about it." Thus, we see the American emphasizing the utilitarian aspect of life and stressing the natural in place of the acquired.

Chapter 11 continues the contrast between Henrietta and the European society. It also introduces Caspar Goodwood again. We find out that he has a "grand passion" for Isabel and according to Henrietta, there is "nothing so simplifying as a grand passion." Thus, at the end of the novel, when Caspar makes his last desperate plea to Isabel, we see that she is somewhat taken aback by this grand passion, even though she has undergone a series of complex relationships.

At the end of Chapter 11, one suitor has written to Isabel at Gardencourt requesting an interview. At the same time, in the next chapter, Isabel is going to receive a proposal from a new suitor.

Lord Warburton's proposal places Isabel in a new position. Thus is exemplified James' technique of allowing his main character to confront new experiences and observing how the character reacts to these new experiences. Certainly Lord Warburton's proposal is somewhat unexpected, and we see how Isabel receives it. Our opinion of Isabel is raised by her refusal. She does sincerely like Lord Warburton, but her reasoning now is that she does not wish to marry. We will later discover it is because she now treasures her liberty too much and thinks that by marrying Lord Warburton her course of life would be set out for her. It would be too easy.

CHAPTER 13

Summary

Wondering whether she might be a cold, hard, priggish person, Isabel decides to tell her uncle about Lord Warburton's proposal. Mr. Touchett's first question is whether she accepted. Upon learning that she plans to decline Lord Warburton's offer, he tells her that he has known about Lord Warburton's intentions because he received a letter stating them three days earlier. He then questions Isabel about her reasons for refusing such a grand person. She herself does not know her exact reasons except that she doesn't wish to marry anyone at the present moment.

Alone, she thinks about the "amount of diminished liberty" she would have as the wife of Lord Warburton. She then thinks of Caspar Goodwood and his letter and decides not to answer it. Instead, she writes Lord Warburton her refusal, stating that she is unable to see herself as his companion for a lifetime.

Henrietta Stackpole finds Ralph Touchett and asks for help. She wants Ralph to invite Caspar Goodwood to Gardencourt so that he can check Isabel's Europeanization. Ralph questions Henrietta about Caspar Goodwood and then agrees to issue an invitation, even though he thinks it not in good taste.

Two days later Ralph receives a note from Caspar Goodwood declining the invitation. Henrietta therefore suggests to Isabel that they make a journey to London to see the sights of that city. Ralph volunteers to go with them, and they plan to leave in a few days.

Commentary

The beginning of this chapter illustrates another of James' techniques. In the last chapter, Isabel received a proposal. This chapter devotes itself in part to a discussion of that event, thereby illustrating James' technique of recording an event and then exploring its implications. In this case, Isabel chooses Mr. Touchett as her confidant. Her choice, of course, makes it more acceptable for Mr. Touchett later to leave Isabel money. In other words, there is a close friendship developing between these two.

In the discussion, we find out more about Isabel's reasons for refusing Lord Warburton. Again, it is a matter of her liberty and a feeling that she has not yet seen enough of life. But the subject is not closed. It will be rounded out more in her next interview with Lord Warburton.

Moreover, Isabel's reasons are further elaborated by her letter to Lord Warburton, in which she says that she cannot picture herself as his wife.

Henrietta is used in this chapter to suggest that Isabel is altering. Of course, this is a part of Isabel's charm and attraction. She does not remain static, but is constantly undergoing a change. Henrietta's presumptuousness is seen in her request to Ralph that Caspar Goodwood be invited to Gardencourt. Goodwood's superior taste is demonstrated by his refusal.

CHAPTER 14

Summary

Before Isabel leaves for London, she receives another visit from Lord Warburton. Henrietta Stackpole is delighted to meet a real English lord and interrogates him about all aspects of his personal life. As soon as he can, he escapes from Henrietta and approaches Isabel. He questions Isabel about her refusal. She tries to explain that in marrying him, she would be attempting to escape from her fate. She feels that she would be gaining so much that she would then have no opportunity to confront her real destiny. For some reason, she fears that she cannot find happiness by avoiding the perils of life, and in marrying Lord Warburton, she would be trying to do that.

The conversation between Isabel and Lord Warburton is interrupted by the appearance of Miss Molyneux and Henrietta Stackpole. Henrietta wants to get some more information out of Lord Warburton and asks for an invitation to his house. He tells her to come anytime, but that she will have to come alone because Isabel won't come any more.

After the company leaves, Mrs. Touchett tells Isabel that she knows from her husband about Lord Warburton's proposal and Isabel's refusal. Mrs. Touchett is baffled and can't understand why Isabel told her uncle first. She wonders if Isabel expected something better when she refused Lord Warburton. Isabel tells her that her uncle didn't say anything like that.

Commentary

James, in his typical fashion, continues to examine a situation. Again, we return to the subject of Isabel's refusal of Lord Warburton's proposal. By the end of this chapter, James will have explored almost all possibilities. To review his technique: James has the proposal made; then we hear Isabel's first reaction. Next, she ponders the subject by herself. Then she consults with Mr. Touchett. There follows a letter, and in this chapter we have Isabel encountering Lord Warburton again and finally her discussion with her aunt, Mrs. Touchett. In each scene we find out more, and the subject is additionally refined.

Her reasons are further delineated. She feels that in marrying Lord Warburton, she would be giving up a chance to struggle with life. It would be too easy to settle down and become his wife. She would then miss the great challenges presented by confronting life. She thinks that she can't be happy by withdrawal, and in marrying Lord Warburton, she would be trying to escape her destiny.

She is convinced that she can never be happy in any extraordinary way—"not by turning away, by separating myself." Thus, she must face the chances and dangers of life. These are part of Isabel's admirable characteristics.

CHAPTERS 15 AND 16

Summary

Mrs. Touchett questions the propriety of Isabel's going to London with Henrietta and Ralph. But she implies that a girl who has refused a great proposal can perhaps afford to be unconventional.

In London, Ralph introduces Isabel and Henrietta to an old acquaintance, Mr. Bantling, who finds Henrietta amusing and delights in accompanying her. Left alone with Isabel, Ralph tells her that he has been informed of Lord Warburton's proposal. Ralph questions Isabel about her intentions and is fascinated with the idea of what Isabel could do with her life now that she has shown the independence to refuse such a magnificent proposal. Isabel justifies her refusal by saying that she loves the unexpected in life, and a marriage with Lord Warburton would have been too determined and definitely marked out in advance. She further explains that she wants to have more experience before resigning herself to marriage. She then refuses to dine with Ralph, on the grounds that she wants to be alone.

Alone in her room, she receives Caspar Goodwood's card and she consents to see him. She is greatly surprised and somewhat disappointed. She tells him that he should know when a person wants to be left alone. Goodwood reasserts his love for Isabel and expresses his fear that she will end up marrying some European. She tells him that she has already had that opportunity, and at present, she wants nothing but her own liberty and freedom. He assures her that in marrying him she would lose none of her independence. In fact, he wants to make her more independent. She tells him to leave her alone for two years and then perhaps she will again discuss the matter with him, but she refuses to make any definite commitments. She warns him that she "shall not be an easy victim" and that her love of her own liberty should be proof enough for him.

Commentary

In this chapter James continues to plumb the depths pertaining to Isabel's reasons for refusing Lord Warburton. Some readers think that James goes too far—that enough has been said about the subject. However, James' technique is to continue to refine any situation.

Ralph's conversation with Isabel is more disinterested than some of the other comments. He is delighted to sit back and watch just how far a person who has refused Lord Warburton can go. But then, in his interest to see how far—or in his desire to be amused at how far Isabel will go—he ceases to be the disinterested personality. He becomes involved in Isabel's destiny. It is, accordingly, Isabel's refusal of such a high honor that prompts Ralph to instigate the proceedings that lead to Isabel's becoming an heiress. As he says: "I shall have the thrill of seeing what a young lady does who won't marry Lord Warburton."

The appearance of Caspar Goodwood and his desire to marry Isabel help to round out our picture of Isabel. We see that she is not just a person who attracts one admirer. She is rapidly taking on the role of a woman to be universally admired.

Again, Isabel's refusal of Caspar Goodwood is based upon her desire for freedom and liberty. "It's my personal independence." Caspar, however, maintains that Isabel will gain freedom by marrying him. "It's to make you independent that I want to marry you." She then reminds Caspar to "remember what I have told you about my love of liberty." It is on this note that Caspar is willing to wait. Consequently, he is justifiably surprised to find out that Isabel is engaged to Gilbert Osmond. It is a point of irony that in her marriage to Gilbert she loses all of her freedom and if she had married Caspar, she might have retained it.

CHAPTERS 17 AND 18

Summary

Shortly after Caspar Goodwood's visit, Henrietta questions Isabel about the interview, only to be told that Goodwood is returning to America without having received any satisfaction from Isabel. Henrietta fears that Isabel is losing her sense of values and attempts to advise Isabel about her conduct. Isabel is forced to tell Henrietta that the affair is closed and requests Henrietta to leave her alone.

Ralph receives a telegram informing him that his father has taken a turn for the worse. When Isabel hears of this, she wants to return to Gardencourt with Ralph. Henrietta says that she has other plans and will not return. Alone with Ralph, Henrietta tells him that Isabel has sent Mr. Goodwood away.

At Gardencourt, Isabel enters the drawing room to find some lady playing the piano with a great deal of talent. She hears from the lady that Mr. Touchett is no better and that she is there to visit with Mrs. Touchett. She has already heard a lot about Isabel and introduces herself as Madame Merle, an old friend of Mrs. Touchett's. When Isabel later questions Ralph about Madame Merle, he tells her that she is the cleverest woman he has ever known. "She does everything beautifully. She's complete." From the nature of his comments, Isabel infers that Ralph does not like Madame Merle.

Ralph spends most of his time talking with his father. In one interview, he tells Mr. Touchett that Isabel has turned down another suitor while in London. Ralph then says he would like to see Isabel have the power to be completely independent. He wants to "put a little wind in her sails." He would like "to put it into her power to do some of the things she wants. She wants to see the world for instance." He would "like to put money in her purse." He wants her to be rich enough "to meet the requirements of her imagination," and he feels "Isabel has a great deal of imagination." He then proposes that Mr. Touchett amend his will to leave half the inheritance intended for his son to Isabel. He explains that he can't offer Isabel money, but she could accept it by means of such a legacy.

Mr. Touchett considers if the step might not be inadvisable. He wonders if it would be a favor to interfere so much in her life and to change her destiny so radically. He expresses the fear that Isabel might fall into the hands of a fortune hunter. Ralph, however, believes that Isabel will hardly become a victim of anyone. And furthermore, he will benefit by having "met the requirements of" his imagination.

Commentary

Part of Isabel's greatness is that she can see the best in most people. Thus, she remains on good terms with Henrietta Stackpole even when Henrietta does such things as arrange a meeting between Isabel and Caspar Goodwood. She does have to tell Henrietta not to interfere anymore.

Henrietta's intervention, however, allows Ralph to learn more about Isabel and to become more interested in her. He is now curious to observe just how far can a young person go who has turned down an English lord only to reject immediately thereafter a proposal from a rich American. This added interest will help him decide to make Isabel an heiress.

In Chapter 18, James introduces us to Madame Merle. In her first appearance, she is seen as a greatly accomplished woman with much charm and cleverness. Since she is alone, it is only natural that she spend a good portion of the day in Isabel's company. From

Ralph, Isabel learns that Madame Merle is an exceptional woman. She is about the only woman in Europe who can invite herself to many great houses for a visit. *But* Ralph's comments also imply some subtle criticism of Madame Merle. He suggests that a woman can be too perfect, too good or too clever. These early suggestions prepare the reader to view Madame Merle with some suspicion.

Much of Isabel and Ralph's relation with each other has been leading up to Ralph's proposal to his father that he make Isabel an heiress. He has seen her in enough situations so that his curiosity is aroused as to how far Isabel could go if she had the resources to meet the "requirements of her imagination." Ralph wants the money left to Isabel so that the fullness of her imagination can be developed, so that she can soar as high as she can, and so that she can rise to her fullest potential. All of these motives seem noble and good. Ralph seems to be acting for Isabel's benefit. But seldom in James are a character's motivations so simple. We must note that Ralph has very few interests in life and one of his most absorbing pastimes is observing Isabel. Thus, part of his motivation is selfish. He wishes to be amused by seeing what a person as grand as Isabel will do when she has complete freedom.

We must now look forward to the ultimate result of Ralph's good intentions. His intrusion into Isabel's life will prove to be the direct cause of her later tragedy. Often, in a James' novel, the meddling of one person will produce disastrous results. Furthermore, we should note here that Mr. Touchett has qualms about interfering in Isabel's life and he leaves the money because Ralph is rather insistent.

CHAPTERS 19 AND 20

Summary

Isabel's friendship for Madame Merle ripens very quickly during the days of Mr. Touchett's illness. She finds herself saying things to this lady more candidly than she has ever spoken to others. There was no doubt Madame Merle "had great merits—she was charming, sympathetic, intelligent, cultivated. More than this...she was rare, superior, and pre-eminent." She is, in general, the only woman whom Isabel thoroughly admires. Yet Isabel knows that Henrietta Stackpole would never like Madame Merle, but this realization does not alter Isabel's fondness for both people. If Madame Merle had a fault "it was that she was not natural."

Mrs. Touchett's view of Madame Merle helps influence Isabel's. Mrs. Touchett thinks that Madame Merle "is incapable of a mistake" and that she hasn't a fault. In their conversations, Madame Merle promises Isabel that she will someday tell about her life, but she has friends, especially an American named Gilbert Osmond, whom she wants Isabel to know. On one occasion, Isabel asked Madame Merle about Ralph and was told that Ralph did not like her, even though they have maintained cordial relations. She warns Isabel that perhaps someday Isabel will come to dislike her. Isabel declares that she will never dislike Madame Merle. Later, Madame Merle tells Isabel how ambitious she was when she was young. She admits that she is still "very ambitious." As they grow to know each other, Madame Merle comments on Isabel's excellences. There is only one drawback; she wishes Isabel had more money.

Madame Merle thinks it proper for her to leave, and some time after her departure, Isabel hears that Henrietta is going to Paris. Later the same day, she hears of her uncle's death.

Some weeks later in London, Madame Merle pays Mrs. Touchett a visit and learns that Mr. Touchett left Isabel a fortune. She thinks immediately what a clever girl Isabel must be for getting this wealth left to her.

Soon thereafter, Isabel journeys to Paris with her aunt. There she meets Edward Rosier, whom she had known as a child. She also sees Henrietta again and is told that Mr. Touchett made a mistake in leaving Isabel so much money. Henrietta is afraid that it might ruin Isabel.

Commentary

Chapter 19 is devoted to picturing Madame Merle. The reader must always keep in mind that Madame Merle is one of the most accomplished women in the world. It would, of course, take a woman as clever and as perfect as Madame Merle to deceive Isabel. Even here though, we are given a few insights into Madame Merle's true nature. She was not a natural person; she is the woman of acquired graces. She is, then, the European who has developed forms, rituals, and ceremonies to their highest degree of perfection. We do not learn the real truth about her until the end of the book. She uses her cultivated pose to cover up an essentially base nature. Therefore, when Mrs. Touchett says that Madame Merle does not have a fault, this is a comment on Madame Merle's external facade. Inwardly, one could say that she hasn't a virtue except her rare ability to appear always pleasant, charming, witty, etc.

Madame Merle also begins cleverly to interest Isabel in the character of Gilbert Osmond. She is too intelligent to push Isabel toward Gilbert; instead, she begins to plant some subtle hints about Osmond's talents this early in their relationship. We should also note that Madame Merle admits that she still has great ambitions. One of her unstated aspirations is to marry Pansy into an eminent family. To do this, she will need Isabel's money at her disposal. Thus, when she finds out that Isabel has refused Lord Warburton, she is pleased because she now knows that Isabel has different tastes and at the same time has some control over Lord Warburton.

In Paris, Isabel meets Edward Rosier. He will later play an important role in Pansy Osmond's life and consequently, will become a part of Isabel's life. She also meets Henrietta, who is apprehensive lest Isabel's inheritance be the cause of her ruin. Ironically Henrietta for one time is right.

CHAPTER 21

Summary

Mrs. Touchett, true to her nature, leaves Paris on the day that she had previously set for her departure. Accompanied by Isabel, she stops by the Mediterranean to see her son. Isabel takes the first available opportunity to ask Ralph if he knew that Mr. Touchett planned to leave her so much money. He reveals that he did know and told her it was left as a compliment on her "so beautifully existing." Isabel wonders if it was wise to leave her so much money and tells Ralph that Henrietta thinks it bad for her. Ralph tells her not to think so much about things but just to respond to them. He suggests that the money will allow her to "spread her wings [and] rise above the ground."

Commentary

With each chapter, Ralph is developing more and more into Isabel's private confidant. She turns to him to express delicately her most private thoughts. But she never exceeds the bounds of propriety. In this chapter, it becomes quite evident that Ralph thinks that Isabel will use her new wealth to develop her capacity to the fullest. This is all that Ralph asks of Isabel.

CHAPTERS 22 AND 23

Summary

About six months after Mr. Touchett's death, a gentleman named Gilbert Osmond is seated in his drawing room with two sisters from a convent and his young fifteen-year-old daughter, Pansy. The nuns have just brought Pansy from the convent where she had been in school for a long time. Gilbert Osmond is expressing his satisfaction with the manner in which his daughter has been educated. She has been taught to obey her father and all people of authority without question. In his view, she has the perfect education. "She's perfect. She has no faults." The sisters think that she is now prepared for the world.

Just as the sisters are about to leave, Madame Merle arrives for a visit. Pansy is about to accompany her father to see the sisters off when Madame Merle tells her to remain. Pansy faithfully obeys even though she is disappointed, and Madame Merle remarks that she has learned to obey quite well. When Gilbert Osmond returns, Madame Merle begins to discuss Pansy's education. Osmond suggests that Pansy leave the room so that they may discuss things more openly. After Pansy leaves, Madame Merle tells Gilbert Osmond that she wants him to make the acquaintance of Isabel

Archer. Following a discussion about Isabel, Madame Merle tells Osmond that she wants him to marry Isabel. She counts on Osmond to put forth an effort and to demonstrate his "adorable taste" to Isabel. As she is about to leave, Pansy returns. Madame Merle makes the observation to Osmond that Pansy does not like her and then she departs.

Since Madame Merle was visiting Mrs. Touchett, it was only natural that Osmond should come to the villa to see his old friend. And once there, he is bound to meet Isabel. Since Madame Merle has spoken so highly of Osmond and since Isabel thought so highly of Madame Merle, Isabel decided on their first meeting that it was better to get an impression of this gentleman than to try to produce one herself. At the end of his first visit, Osmond invites Isabel to visit his home with Madame Merle to see his collection of art objects.

After their first meeting, Madame Merle tells Isabel how charming she was. This irritates Isabel more than anything Madame Merle has ever done. She lets Madame Merle know that she is under no obligation to be charming to this man.

Isabel requests Ralph's opinion of Gilbert Osmond. She learns that Osmond has lived most of his life in Italy and probably has little money but possesses exquisite taste. He suggests that Isabel ask Madame Merle about Osmond because Madame Merle knows him better. He then speaks of Madame Merle with "exaggerated respect" and says that her only fault is that she is "indescribably blameless...the only woman...who never gives one a chance to criticize her." He continues by saying that "she's too good, too kind, too clever, too learned, too accomplished, too everything. She's too complete...." But at the same time, he recommends her as a companion for Isabel because she knows so much about the world and Isabel can learn so much from her.

Commentary

Chapter 22 is an abrupt shift from Isabel to a new character. We meet for the first time Gilbert Osmond and his daughter Pansy. Contrary to the typical James practice, the author here allows the reader to get an inside view of one of the characters before the main character comes to that insight. In other words, after this chapter, we know that Madame Merle plans to marry Isabel to Gilbert Osmond. Our future views of Madame Merle and Osmond are then colored by this fact. Furthermore, we see that there is a very close and suspicious relationship between Madame Merle and Gilbert Osmond—a relationship which will not become clear until the final pages of the novel.

In retrospect, we see that the type of person that Osmond likes is someone like his daughter Pansy—a person who has been taught to perform all the correct rituals and ceremonies with outward perfection but who obeys him with complete subservience. This will be what he expects of Isabel as a wife.

Osmond's tastes here are emphasized. His outstanding quality is that he possesses perfect taste. This quality will be instrumental in causing Isabel to fall in love with him. It is, of course, his only recommendation.

One element that will be emphasized throughout the novel is Pansy's dislike for Madame Merle. Realization of this will later make Isabel feel pity for Madame Merle in spite of all the treachery on Madame Merle's part.

More and more, Ralph is beginning to assume the role of Isabel's confidant. After meeting Osmond, she seeks out his opinion of the gentleman. The reader knows that Ralph's judgment of both Osmond and Madame Merle is the correct one, but even Ralph knows that Isabel must make her own judgments. In his praise of Madame Merle and Osmond, we should realize that both of these people are illusory, that their taste and their abilities are artificially contrived and false. Isabel, however, must learn this at a greater personal sacrifice.

CHAPTERS 24 AND 25

Summary

Isabel decides that no harm can come to her from a simple social visit to Gilbert Osmond's house. There, she meets his sister the Countess Gemini and his daughter Pansy. Osmond is very gracious and discusses his collection of art objects and his daughter with quiet admiration. Alone with Osmond, Isabel is asked her opinion of the Countess Gemini. Isabel does not, however, believe that she knows the lady well enough to express an opinion, but she has noted that there is no rapport between the brother and sister.

Isabel has difficulty placing Osmond in a class. He is unlike any person she has ever known. His kindness and charm almost overwhelm Isabel. He gives her a rather unflattering picture of himself, but Isabel's imagination fancies many missing elements.

While Isabel and Osmond are talking, Madame Merle is being reproached by the Countess Gemini for the little conspiracy she is executing. Madame Merle at first pretends ignorance of the Countess' meaning. The Countess, however, will not drop the subject and tells Madame Merle that the plan in operation would be bad for Isabel and that she might oppose it. Madame Merle warns the Countess not to interfere because both of them want Pansy to marry well, and in this aim, Isabel will be of immense value.

Commentary

The reader observes in these chapters how Isabel is slowly being trapped and deceived by the machinations of Osmond and Madame Merle. His discriminating taste and exquisite collection of art objects make Isabel think that Osmond is a superior person. "He resembled no one she had ever seen: most of the people she knew might be divided into groups of half a dozen specimens." But Osmond fits into no classification. Thus, Isabel's inability to classify him makes her see him in a different light. The reader knows that he is an evil type of person that Isabel has never confronted before.

Pansy is seen in this chapter as a perfect little person. She is like Osmond's collection of art objects. She fits into his life, not as an individual, but as something that will demonstrate his good taste.

Osmond has one effect on Isabel that convinces her that he is a superior person. No other person has ever made her think so precisely; no one has ever made her perception so refined. In his presence, Isabel feels that she is functioning as a superior person. Thus she allows her imagination to roam freely. When Osmond tells her that his life has been rather dull and useless, she assumes additional events and material, thus making him in her imagination much greater than he is in reality. Consequently, Isabel's own inventive faculty contributes to her tragic mistake in evaluating Osmond.

In the conversation between Madame Merle and the Countess Gemini, we see that there is a definite plan to trap Isabel. For all of her simplicity, the Countess Gemini is a more real and human person than either her brother or Madame Merle. It is ironic that the person with the tarnished reputation is the person who has the most human and sympathetic understanding of Isabel's predicament.

CHAPTERS 26, 27 AND 28

Summary

Gilbert Osmond calls so often at Mrs. Touchett's home that she becomes suspicious. She asks Madame Merle directly if Osmond is interested in Isabel. Madame Merle, of course, denies that Osmond is interested in Isabel but tells Mrs. Touchett that she will discreetly inquire of his intentions. She warns Mrs. Touchett not to mention anything about it to Isabel, since any discussion would inflame Isabel's imagination. Mrs. Touchett thinks that Osmond would like to marry Isabel just so he could use her money to provide a dowry for Pansy.

Osmond, however, continues his visits. Meanwhile, Henrietta arrives for a visit; she is planning a trip to Rome with Mr. Bantling. Isabel accedes to Ralph Touchett's proposal that they also go to Rome. When Isabel mentions the forthcoming trip to Osmond, he says that he would like to join the party, and Isabel promptly invites him to come along. Later, in an interview with Madam Merle, Osmond tells her that he is making progress with Isabel, for she asked him to go to Rome. He admits that Isabel has one fault – she has too many ideas – but this could, he feels, be easily corrected, since her ideas are all bad ones, and "they must be sacrificed."

In Rome, Isabel has a chance encounter with Lord Warburton, who is returning from a trip to the Middle East. He tells her that he wrote several letters to her but never mailed them. Isabel asks him not to renew his overtures if they are to remain friends. On the following Sunday, they are joined by Gilbert Osmond. As they walk in St. Peter's, Lord Warburton asks Ralph who the gentleman is. Ralph tells him that he is a nondescript American. They resign themselves to accept Isabel's course of action with regard to Osmond.

At the opera, Osmond questions Isabel about Lord Warburton. She tells him of Lord Warburton's high character and noble position. Two days later, Lord Warburton bids farewell to Isabel, saying that he is leaving Rome. Through some of the conversation, Osmond has inferred that Isabel received a proposal from Lord Warburton and rejected it.

Commentary

In her interview with Madame Merle, Mrs. Touchett comes to the direct center of the problem in saying that Osmond wants to marry Isabel for money. She is so direct that Madame Merle must be very careful to keep Mrs. Touchett from interfering. She even suggests that Isabel would make a good "stepmother" for Pansy so as to prepare the way for acceptance later on. Mrs. Touchett is deceived by Madame Merle into believing that this lady will investigate and report back to her. Mrs. Touchett is not aware at this point that Madame Merle has been instrumental in arranging the courtship.

We get the first hint as to what will happen to Isabel when Osmond complains that Isabel has too many ideas and that they must be sacrificed. This is exactly what will happen. Osmond will attempt to make Isabel into another simple, obedient Pansy—into a person who obeys him in everything and never has an idea of her own.

James has Lord Warburton appear in Rome in order to remind the reader how Isabel has affected this nobleman. But more important, this appearance allows Osmond to learn that Isabel has rejected the nobleman. Her rejection makes her all the more enticing and exciting to Osmond. Furthermore, he will later want Isabel to use her influence to promote a match between Lord Warburton and Pansy.

CHAPTERS 29, 30 AND 31

Summary

Shortly after Lord Warburton leaves, Isabel receives a note from her aunt inviting her for a visit to another part of Italy. Isabel accepts and bids Osmond good-bye. Osmond tells her that he approves of traveling and would do so himself if he had her means. Before she leaves, he tells her that he finds himself in love with her. Isabel is not offended by his declaration, even though he tries to explain that he has nothing to offer her except his love. She tells him that it is good that she is leaving Rome. He asks her to come back, for he has many more things to say to her. Since he is staying in Rome, he requests Isabel to visit his daughter. Isabel is glad to promise that.

Back at Florence, Isabel tells Madame Merle of her promise to visit Pansy. At first Madame Merle thinks she should go along, but Isabel prefers to go by herself. She tells Madame Merle that she thinks a great deal of her promises.

When Isabel meets Pansy again, she finds the young lady to be very quaint and charming. They discuss Osmond and Pansy tells how she lives just to please her father. Isabel agrees with her that it is very important to obey and please him.

After visiting with her aunt for a time, Isabel joins her sister in Switzerland and they spend several months in Paris. Then Isabel returns to Rome and suggests to Madame Merle that they tour the Middle East. Madame Merle consents and the two travel together. Returning from this trip, Isabel stays three weeks with Madame Merle and sees Gilbert Osmond every day. She then goes to her aunt's house for a visit, after a year of separation.

Commentary

Chapter 29 presents another development in Isabel's relationship with Gilbert Osmond. She receives his declaration of love with a certain degree of pleasure. When we compare her reaction to his love with her reaction to the love of Goodwood or Lord Warburton, we realize immediately that Isabel is gratified to hear the latest declaration. Furthermore, Osmond knows how to please. He emphasizes that he has nothing to offer except his own love and his own self. Thus, if she turned down Lord Warburton with all he possessed, Osmond knows that she would be more impressed with the simplicity of his declaration.

Isabel's interview with Pansy emphasizes how much value Isabel places on her own promises. Consequently, her promise to marry Osmond will be difficult to break once she gives it. This aspect of her nature helps prepare the reader for her final decision to return to Osmond in Rome rather than to remain apart from him.

Isabel, however, is deceived about Osmond when she thinks that "He'll never ask anything unreasonable." The reader should remember this statement when at the end of the novel, Osmond does make unreasonable demands on Pansy.

Chapter 31 serves in many ways as an interlude. Isabel avoids Gilbert Osmond's company for a long time. What she fails to be aware of is that she is spending some of this time in the company of Madame Merle and this is about the same as being courted by Osmond, since it is likewise Madame Merle's intention that Osmond marry Isabel. Isabel, however, comes to some additional recognitions about Madam Merle. She is now aware that Madame Merle "belonged to the old, old world, and Isabel never lost the impression that she was the product of a different moral or social clime from her own, that she had grown up under other stars." In other words, Madame Merle represents everything that is empty and useless in the forms and ceremonies of European society.

The end of this chapter presents a turning point in Isabel's life. After this, she will be engaged to Gilbert Osmond and will face a new series of problems.

CHAPTERS 32, 33, 34 AND 35

Summary

As soon as Caspar Goodwood hears that Isabel is engaged, he comes straight to Florence to see her. Isabel receives him in her aunt's house. He tells her frankly that he is disappointed and is selfish enough to wish her anything except marriage to another man. She wants to know if he told Henrietta. He tells her that Henrietta will find it out soon enough and will come herself to scold Isabel. Isabel knows that her friends do not like Mr. Osmond, but she says that she doesn't marry to please her friends. Goodwood wants to know something about Osmond. Isabel explains that he is a nobody without profession or reputation.

Goodwood inquires about what happened to Isabel's resolve not to marry, and she is unable to justify her change of opinion. And furthermore, she dislikes being placed in a position where she has to defend her decision. Therefore, she is delighted to hear that Goodwood will leave Florence the next day.

After Caspar Goodwood has left, Isabel decides it is time to inform her aunt of her engagement. Mrs. Touchett is not surprised, but she is vexed with Madame Merle. She tells Isabel that Madame Merle has not acted honorably in the entire matter. Isabel cannot understand what Madame Merle has to do with the situation. She refuses to believe it when Mrs. Touchett says that Madame Merle engineered the engagement or that Madame Merle could have prevented it. Isabel denies this. Her aunt, however, continues to be annoyed at Madame Merle. She maintains that she saw it coming and refused to act because she had trusted Madame Merle and now she feels betrayed. When Isabel persists in denying Madame Merle's influence, Mrs. Touchett says, "She can do anything; that's what I've always liked her for."

She wonders if Isabel would have listened to Ralph. Isabel admits that she would not have listened if Ralph abused Mr. Osmond; Mrs. Touchett, however, points out that Ralph never abuses anyone. Isabel tells her aunt that she refuses to defend Mr. Osmond – she does not feel it necessary.

Some days later Ralph arrives, but even if he disapproves of her engagement, Isabel is determined not to let it spoil her happiness. Ralph, however, does not speak of the matter for some time. One morning after she returns from a ride, Isabel finds Ralph half asleep in the garden. When she approaches he tells her that he was thinking of her. He apologizes for not having congratulated her on her engagement, but says he has been thinking of what to say. He fears that she is going to be put into a cage and he reminds her that she used to love her liberty. Isabel thinks that Ralph's criticism is a failure in trust. He explains that he trusts her but not Gilbert Osmond. Finally Ralph tells her that it is not the type of marriage he thought she would make. He is disappointed that she has settled for something so low. Furthermore, he can't get over the feeling that Osmond is "small...narrow, selfish. He takes himself so seriously." Finally Ralph tells Isabel that she was meant to do "something better than to keep guard over the sensibilities of a sterile dilettante." What hurts Ralph most is that Isabel really believes that she is right. "She was wrong, but she believed; she was deluded, but she was dismally consistent." When he tells Isabel that he feels sold out, especially because when one's in error, one's in trouble. Isabel tells him in anger that she will never complain of her trouble to him.

One day, while strolling with her, Osmond mentions to Isabel that their marriage is opposed by her friends. He bases his conclusion on the fact that he has not been congratulated. He feels that her family objects because he has no money and she is a great heiress.

When Pansy finds out that Isabel is to be her stepmother, she is delighted both because she sincerely likes Isabel and because she thinks Isabel well suited for her father. Later, the Countess Gemini anticipates that Isabel will help Osmond's family but she is afraid they will not be much credit to Isabel.

Commentary

These chapters, along with the others just preceding, show James' technique again. He has an event occur—this time it is Isabel's engagement to Gilbert Osmond. Then, he presents as many views of this subject as he can. We begin by observing Caspar Goodwood's bitter reactions. Then, we are acquainted with the reactions of Isabel's aunt to the event and how she censures not Isabel but Madame Merle. This is followed by Ralph's more objective and humane opinion of the engagement. He wishes nothing but for Isabel to find happiness and is disappointed solely because he thinks that Isabel will find only unhappiness. The next views are rather briefer – Osmond discloses his thoughts about the engagement and its reception by Isabel's family and friends; then we see Pansy's and the Countess Gemini's reactions. Thus, James' technique is here fully illustrated. An event occurs and then it is discussed by as many people as is possible. Each contribution leads the reader to a more refined and precise understanding of the situation.

In the discussion with Mrs. Touchett, we see that the aunt is astute enough to recognize the role played by Madame Merle. Isabel, however, believes so strongly in her own independent judgment that she cannot accept this fact. She denies that Madame Merle has acted with duplicity, but we, the readers, know that Mrs. Touchett is, in this case, correct.

In her interview with Ralph, Isabel is somewhat different. Again she prefers her own judgment to that of any one else's. She becomes angry when Ralph refers to Osmond as a sterile dilettante. She maintains that Ralph is not a disinterested person. What Isabel fails to comprehend is that a totally disinterested person would not care whether she married Osmond or not. But the subtlety here is that Ralph is partly disappointed because he had hoped to see Isabel do something more creditable than marry a "nobody" with no fortune and no position. He had thought that she could soar higher than Osmond. Isabel, however, contends that she marries to please only herself. This is her streak of absolute independence. Aside from this, one of her worst mistakes is in promising not to bother Ralph with her troubles in case her marriage turns out badly.

CHAPTERS 36, 37 AND 38

Summary

Some four years later, young Edward Rosier rings at Madame Merle's apartment. He has come to tell Madame Merle of his love for Pansy Osmond and his fear that Mr. Osmond does not think highly of him. He wonders if Madame Merle can intercede in his behalf. Madame Merle explains to him that Pansy's fate lies almost totally with her father and that Isabel could not help him, since she and her husband seldom agree on anything. She advises Rosier to let the matter rest for a while and she will make discreet inquiries.

Some time later at a party at the Osmond's, Rosier seeks out the company of Pansy. As soon as they are alone, he expresses his affection for Pansy. She does not repel Edward but admits that she likes him.

When Madame Merle arrives, she talks with Osmond about Mr. Rosier's intentions. Osmond lets it be known that he has better things in mind for Pansy. He tells Madame Merle that it doesn't matter if Pansy likes Mr. Rosier, because his daughter has been brought up to obey him. Madame Merle recommends that Rosier not be completely dismissed, since he might prove to be useful later on.

When Rosier appeals to Isabel for help, she responds that it is not in her power. A week later Rosier attempts to speak to Osmond but is rudely insulted and told that Pansy has no recollection of having declared her affections to Rosier. He intimates that Pansy has forgotten her suitor. The young man instantly seeks out Isabel and asks what Osmond has done to Pansy. Isabel reassures him that Pansy has not given him up.

At this moment, Isabel receives an unexpected visitor. It is Lord Warburton, who has just arrived from England. He tells Isabel that he has brought Ralph Touchett with him. Ralph has been steadily declining and is not expected to live too long. He came to Rome thinking that the southern climate would help prolong his life. Isabel promises to go to him as soon as possible. But first Isabel wants to introduce Pansy, who has already caught Lord Warburton's eye.

Meanwhile, Rosier has been talking with Pansy. She tells him that her father has forbidden her to marry Rosier or even to talk with him. But Pansy insists that she will not marry anyone else and will remain always in love with Edward. She says that she will ask Isabel to help them.

Commentary

There is a sudden advance in time with Chapter 36. Approximately four years have elapsed. The reader is informed indirectly that Isabel and her husband do not get along. Madame Merle speaks of them as always being in opposition to each other. Isabel says several times that her husband does nothing to accommodate her. She speaks of herself as powerless to oppose the wishes of Osmond and hints that he is quite unreasonable.

Rosier is introduced here so as to complicate the plot issues. Isabel's fate or purpose in life will now revolve in a large measure around the destiny of young Pansy Osmond, for whom she has a great affection. Thus, Pansy's love and desires will become uppermost in Isabel's actions.

Beginning with these sections, we see more directly into the selfish and corrupt motivations of Osmond. He states quite frankly that Pansy's feelings do not matter as long as she obeys him. He says that he educated her to obey him and that she is always to do what he decrees. Osmond is so self-centered that he ignores anyone's feelings except his own. He would destroy or sacrifice anything or anyone in order to fulfill his own wishes.

Lord Warburton returns with Ralph so as to further complicate issues. He is the great lord of wealth and prestige whom Osmond would like to have as Pansy's husband.

The reader should note here how even Rosier appeals to Madame Merle for help in his suit for Pansy. It seems that this grand lady still wields some influence—at least enough for a person like Rosier to think that she can still help him.

CHAPTER 39

Summary

When it came time for Isabel to marry, there had been a very quiet service with only her aunt and cousin invited. The Countess Gemini and Pansy Osmond were the only other people present. Henrietta let it be known that Isabel had taken a step that put a barrier between them. Immediately after the marriage Osmond attempted to make Isabel give up Henrietta, but Isabel refused to reject her old friend. Madame Merle became cool toward Mrs. Touchett after Isabel's aunt told her that her role in the match had been too dubious. Ralph felt excluded because he had spoken so honestly before the marriage and therefore has not seen his cousin for almost two years.

Ralph, however, saw through Gilbert Osmond. He knows that Osmond affects to disdain the world only because he wants the world to envy him. Osmond married Isabel just so he could use her money and have her "represent him." Everything Osmond does is a pose to impress society. In pretending to live only for intrinsic values, he actually lives exclusively for the world.

After Lord Warburton's visit to Isabel, he questions Ralph on his motives for coming to Rome. Ralph tells him that some years ago he stopped in Rome and realized that he caused trouble and felt obliged to leave. This time, however, he feels the need of remaining so as to protect Isabel in any way he can. Ralph explains that Isabel will never complain of her husband's unpleasantness, but he will be able to detect it.

Lord Warburton tells Ralph what a delightful girl he found Pansy to be. Ralph tells him how delighted Osmond would be to have Warburton marry his daughter. Ralph admonishes his friend not to be kind to Pansy just because she is near Isabel.

Commentary

James returns to Isabel's marriage and we find that her marrying Osmond has affected her relations with old friends. Furthermore, we are informed that Osmond wants Isabel to change and conform to all of his ways of thinking. Thus, since he does not like

Henrietta, he thinks that Isabel should give up her friend. But Isabel's independence will not permit her to abandon a true friend. Consequently, at the end of the novel, Isabel will not feel right in abandoning Pansy to the whims of Osmond and will consequently return to Rome.

Ralph's appearance in Rome will cause trouble and he knows it. But he thinks that there must be a crisis in Isabel's marriage and he is offering himself as a means to bring about that crisis.

Through Ralph's eyes, we see more into the character of Isabel's husband. We find out that Osmond is selfish and evil. He exists only for himself, and he attempts to make everything show him in a good light. He has no natural merits, and everything about him is an acquired pose in order to make the world think well of him. He is one of those people who like to give parties for the privilege of *not* inviting certain people. "His ambition was not to please the world, but to please himself by exciting the world's curiosity and then declining to satisfy it." In general, he represents all form and artifice with nothing of value to him.

CHAPTERS 40 AND 41

Summary

Since her marriage Madame Merle comes only seldom to Isabel's house. She has candidly explained that, since she had known Osmond before Isabel married him, she thought it best not to come too often. About a month after Lord Warburton's arrival, Isabel returns from a ride with Pansy to discover Madame Merle in private conversation with Osmond. What disturbs Isabel is that Madame Merle is standing and discussing something of an intimate nature with Osmond, who remains seated. When they see Isabel, both flush and Osmond leaves for a walk.

Madame Merle tells Isabel that Mr. Rosier comes to her often and talks about Pansy. Isabel knows that "poor Mr. Rosier" is in love with Pansy. Madame Merle explains that she washes her hands of the whole affair, but Isabel retorts that she can't because she is too interested. Madame Merle then questions Isabel about Lord Warburton's intentions. She learns that Lord Warburton is charmed with Pansy and wonders why Isabel has not told Osmond this. Isabel responds that she does not interfere. Madame Merle suggests that Lord Warburton will easily propose if Isabel will use her influence. Isabel is surprised to discover that Madame Merle knows of her earlier relationship with Lord Warburton.

That evening, Osmond discusses the same subject with Isabel. He finds out the Lord Warburton comes often to see Pansy. He wonders what Isabel thinks of it, and Isabel tells him that she is waiting to see what Osmond thinks because for once she wants to do something that will please her husband. Like Madame Merle, he lets her know that she can bring about the marriage at any time she desires it. Isabel discovers that he wants this marriage to take place and he desires it immensely. He tells her that he is depending on her to bring it about.

Commentary

There is a bit of irony working here. Isabel had herself rejected Lord Warburton in favor of Osmond. Now Osmond is showing how mean he is by demanding that Isabel use her influence with her former suitor in order to get him to marry Pansy. That both Madame Merle and Osmond desire this marriage so strongly and that Isabel had felt free to reject Lord Warburton's proposal is an ironic contrast to the values possessed by each person.

The fact that Osmond thinks that Isabel could bring about the marriage by using her influence puts Isabel in an awkward position. She is more interested in the desires of individuals such as Pansy and she will soon know that Pansy wants to marry only Mr. Rosier. Thus, Isabel will have to help Pansy or will have to fulfill the perverted desires of her husband.

CHAPTER 42

Summary

Osmond's demand upon Isabel causes her to review her life. She wonders if Lord Warburton is in fact interested in Pansy because he still harbors a love for her. This thought leads her to re-examine her marriage with Osmond. As with his comments about Lord Warburton, everything he touches turns to something ugly and unpleasant. She has developed a distinct distrust for her husband. Suffering for her has become an active condition.

She realized some time after their marriage that her husband objected to some of her ideas. He wanted her to change. She tried to conform to his wishes until she realized that he wanted her to change completely, totally. He wanted her to become a slave to him and to act as he wanted her to. Yet, she knew that she was a distinct individual and had to abide by her own nature. This caused her husband to hate her.

She now understands that her money has become a burden to her. She had hoped to use it to help her husband. But under "all his culture, his cleverness, his amenity, under his good-nature, his facility, his knowledge of life, his egotism lay hidden like a serpent in a bank of flowers." He has a sovereign contempt for almost everybody. For Osmond, life was "altogether a thing of forms, a conscious, calculated attitude. He was fond of the old, the consecrated, the transmitted." Her "real offence...was her having a mind of her own. Her mind was to be his—attached to his own like a small garden-plot." He even resented the fact that Isabel visited Ralph. Isabel believes the resentment stems from the fact that Ralph was "generous and her husband was not." Thus the question Isabel faces is what to do or what ought she to do when her husband hates her.

Commentary

This very important chapter presents an analysis of Isabel's relationship with her husband. Previous chapters have shown Isabel engaged in active matters with Osmond, and now James presents a close examination of the more intimate relationship. Osmond married Isabel because she was clever, witty, and charming and because she had a great deal of money. He expected her to change not just her ideas but her whole character, the way she felt, the way she judged. Since she cannot do this, her husband begins to hate her. In other words Osmond wants to destroy

Isabel and make her into a puppet who will simply serve as a complement to his own ego.

Essentially, the analysis within the chapter itself is self-sufficient and needs no other commentary. Accordingly, the reader should read the chapter carefully for all of the innuendoes and qualifications.

CHAPTER 43

Summary

At a dance party, Rosier approaches Isabel and asks about Pansy. He learns that Osmond has forbidden Pansy to associate or dance with him. Isabel has to send him away when she sees Pansy coming. Lord Warburton comes to Isabel and prefers to talk with her rather than to dance. She reminds him that some ten days ago he had said that he wanted to marry Pansy. She asks why he has done nothing. Lord Warburton responds that he wrote Osmond a letter this very morning; he has not sent it but will do so tomorrow.

When Lord Warburton sees Rosier, he wonders about him. Isabel reveals Rosier's intentions and that Osmond objects because Rosier is not important enough and does not have enough money. Isabel tacitly conveys to Lord Warburton that Pansy is in love with Mr. Rosier and that perhaps the best thing for Lord Warburton to do would be to let Pansy alone. She also realizes that Lord Warburton is not in love with Pansy. Thus later, she is able to tell Rosier that she is helping his cause.

Commentary

Apparently Isabel is not trying to induce Lord Warburton to marry Pansy. Her motives, however, are the best. She knows that such a marriage would please no one except Osmond and, moreover, she knows that it would make Pansy and Rosier very unhappy. The intrinsic happiness of Pansy is more important than the displeasure of Osmond. In the light of Isabel's actions here, we must note that she has finally decided to interfere. And her influence will be important.

CHAPTER 44

Summary

The Countess Gemini has not been a welcome visitor in her brother's home. But she has received an invitation and is preparing for a visit when she receives a call from Henrietta Stackpole. Henrietta asks the Countess for some information about Isabel, and explains that Osmond doesn't like her. The Countess has to admit that her brother doesn't like her either. The Countess tells Henrietta that she knows little about her brother's house, but has been informed that Lord Warburton is there and is making love to Isabel. Henrietta decides that she must leave on the next train to Rome.

Before leaving Florence, Henrietta meets Caspar Goodwood, who has come again to Europe because he has heard how unhappy Isabel is. He and Henrietta discuss Isabel's plight and decide to take the same train to Rome.

Commentary

The concern Isabel's friends have for her attests to her good nature and fine qualities. Osmond's dislike of these same people brings out his basic ill nature. James is slowly bringing most of the main characters together in Rome for a final round of confrontations.

CHAPTERS 45 AND 46

Summary

Isabel knows that her visits with Ralph are displeasing to her husband. "He wished her to have no freedom of mind, and he knew perfectly well that Ralph was an apostle of freedom." Yet Isabel knows that she has not yet directly opposed her husband; nor has he yet "formally forbidden her to call upon Ralph." Isabel is troubled by the thought that "if he should positively interpose, if he should put forth his authority, she would have to decide, and that wouldn't be easy."

On one of her visits to Ralph, Isabel asks him if Lord Warburton is in love. Ralph answers yes, but he means that Lord

Warburton is still in love with Isabel. Isabel informs Ralph that the best thing Lord Warburton can do is to is to leave Pansy alone, for she is in love with someone else. Ralph suggests to Isabel that her husband will perhaps suspect her of not pushing Lord Warburton enough and will attribute it to jealousy on Isabel's part.

Upon returning home, Isabel decides that she must approach Pansy on the subject. She discovers that "the only thing Pansy wanted in life was to marry Mr. Rosier." The girl tells Isabel that she won't encourage Lord Warburton and that this nobleman is aware of her feelings. She doesn't want her father to know because as long as he thinks Lord Warburton is interested in her, he "won't propose any one else."

Later, Osmond asks Isabel why Lord Warburton doesn't come any more to visit. Osmond thinks that Isabel has been plotting against him. He accuses her of "not being trustworthy." Isabel, wounded by this accusation, retorts that he "must want to make sure" of Lord Warburton very badly. This statement "recalled the fact that she had once held this coveted treasure in her hand and felt herself rich enough to let it fall." At this point, Lord Warburton enters and tells them that he has suddenly been recalled to England. He invites them to come to visit him. He thinks that Isabel and Pansy would enjoy the English countryside. Osmond excuses himself and goes to send Pansy to bid Lord Warburton good-bye. Alone, Lord Warburton admits to Isabel that Pansy doesn't care for him, and Isabel agrees with him that it is best that he leave.

That night, Osmond confronts Isabel and directs some more accusations at her. He charges her with "having prevented Pansy's marriage to Warburton." He then accuses her of having stopped Lord Warburton's letter. He is not, however, disappointed because this has proved to him that Pansy can aim high.

Commentary

James is building up his contrast between Isabel and Osmond. It becomes a perpetual battle of nerves between them. When he accuses Isabel of preventing the marriage, we must note that he is partially right. Isabel did let Lord Warburton know that Pansy did not love him, and she did suggest to Ralph that Lord Warburton should not force himself upon a poor girl who was in love with someone else. But in all of Isabel's actions, she was thinking of Pansy's feelings. Her every act was performed out of kindness for her stepdaughter; whereas Osmond would have forced the young girl into a marriage against her will.

The depth to which Osmond can sink is represented by his accusation that Isabel intercepted and destroyed Lord Warburton's letter. Furthermore, the zeal with which Osmond desires this union makes him a much smaller person, since Isabel had once felt high and noble enough to refuse Lord Warburton's proposal.

The reader should note that Ralph's sensitivity and perception enable him to foresee what will happen to Isabel, and he knows that Osmond will accuse Isabel of acting in opposition. All through the novel, Ralph has been able to see into the depth of any given situation.

James' emphasis on the European form and established ceremony assist Osmond to act admirably when Lord Warburton comes for a visit. Osmond has "the advantage of an acquired habit," so that his inner disappointment is not noticeable.

CHAPTERS 47 AND 48

Summary

Henrietta arrives in Rome and Isabel must get her a room in a hotel because Osmond objects to Henrietta so strongly. But at last Isabel can admit to someone how miserable she is. Henrietta wants Isabel to leave Osmond, but Isabel explains that she "can't publish" her mistake before the entire world.

Caspar Goodwood becomes a frequent visitor at Isabel's house. She asks him once if he would also visit Ralph, who was alone and ill. She explains that she can't go to him as often as she would like to. Henrietta also visits Ralph frequently. When he decides that he will return to England, Henrietta announces to him that she will accompany him in order to look after him. Meanwhile, Isabel has asked Caspar Goodwood if he would also travel with Ralph.

Before leaving, Henrietta again asks Isabel to leave Osmond before her "character gets spoiled." Isabel assures Henrietta that she won't change.

In bidding Ralph good-bye, Isabel tells him that if he should send for her she will come. He suggests that Osmond would not like that, and Isabel tells him that she would come anyway.

When Caspar comes to bid Isabel good-bye, he draws her apart from the company and tells her again how deeply he still loves her. He wonders whether he might pity her somewhat. She tells him that he can give a thought to it every once in a while.

Commentary

The arrival of her old friend, Henrietta, allows Isabel to openly express her thoughts about her mistake. But we see here that Isabel has too much pride to announce to the world that she has made a mistake, thus preparing us again for Isabel's later return to her husband in spite of her dislike of him. Henrietta's concern that Isabel's character will get spoiled is the main point of the novel at this point. Osmond has been attempting to change Isabel in any way that he can. The opposition between them comes from the fact that Isabel will not change.

In terms of plot, James is shifting his characters away from Rome. It will be necessary to have Ralph return to England so that Isabel will have to face the decision of opposing her husband's views by traveling to England. Ralph knows, too, that if he asks Isabel to come, it will mean that she will have to do so without her husband's consent.

CHAPTERS 49, 50 AND 51

Summary

Madame Merle returns to Rome a short time after Lord Warburton's departure. She immediately questions Isabel about Lord

Warburton's departure, and threatens to ask Pansy what Isabel said to her. Suddenly Isabel is aware that Madame Merle "was a powerful agent in her destiny." Her interest, Isabel realized, was the same as that of Osmond. Suddenly, Isabel asks her what she has to do with the matter. Madame Merle answers, "Everything." Thus, Mrs. Touchett was right: Madame Merle had married her.

Madame Merle visits Osmond and tells him how horrid she was that morning, but she receives no sympathy from him. She hears from him that her friendship has become tedious. Even though Madame Merle has worked solely for Osmond's benefit, he still finds her a bore. Thus she wonders if she "has been so vile for nothing." She warns Osmond not to destroy such a precious object as Isabel.

Later, Mr. Rosier comes to visit Isabel. He tells her that he has sold some of his art collection and is now considerably wealthier, but Isabel explains that Osmond still wants Pansy to marry a nobleman. Rosier meets the Countess Gemini, who becomes his sympathetic spokesman.

A week later, Pansy tells Isabel that she is being sent back to the convent. Osmond thinks that she needs some time for meditation and solitude.

Some time later, Isabel receives a letter from Gardencourt. Ralph Touchett is dying. She tells Osmond that she must go to him. Osmond responds that he doesn't believe that Ralph is dying and that there is no need for her to go. If she goes it will be "the most deliberate, the most calculated, opposition." Isabel is forced to tell her husband that his attitude is "malignant." Osmond explains that his only contentment in life comes from preserving appearances, especially maintaining the form of a successful marriage.

When the Countess hears that Osmond has forbidden Isabel to go to England, she feels it is time for her to speak. She tells Isabel that Osmond's first wife died childless and that Pansy is the daughter of Osmond and Madame Merle. They were lovers for six years, and when Pansy was born, she had to give up all claims to her. Furthermore, the Countess Gemini points out that Madame Merle brought Isabel and Osmond together so that Isabel could help Pansy. Upon hearing this disclosure, Isabel is determined to go to England.

Commentary

Madame Merle had said earlier that she had high ambitions. To fulfill these, it is necessary for her daughter Pansy to make a great marriage. Consequently, when Lord Warburton leaves without proposing, Madame Merle drops her pose for a while and shows her true nature to Isabel. But Isabel is so astounded by Madame Merle's actions that she fails to perceive the true nature of things. Thus, when the Countess Gemini tells Isabel about Pansy's parentage, Isabel, upon reflection, is able to credit the entire story. She realizes all the horror of her position. Not only did Madame Merle marry her to Osmond, but she also made Isabel's fortune available to her ex-lover.

Madame Merle, however, is not so evil as Osmond. We see in their interview that he lacks perception for other people. At least Madame Merle recognizes the fine and precious qualities that Isabel possesses. She warns Osmond not to destroy these. On the contrary, he is intent upon destroying Isabel's better attributes.

It becomes completely clear that Osmond lives solely for the sake of forms and appearance. He hates Isabel but wants to present to the world the appearance of a happily married couple. Anything that touches on the distasteful is for him repugnant. His sense of taste is thus corrupt and evil. It denies all human values in favor of superficial appearance. Consequently, he will send his daughter off to the convent for no logical reason except to satisfy some malignant purpose of his own.

The Countess Gemini has always disliked her brother. She has found Isabel attractive from the very first. Thus, this easily accounts for her revelation about her own brother. James carefully motivated this scene by having Osmond be especially unpleasant to his sister; therefore she now gets her revenge.

CHAPTER 52

Summary

Before leaving for England, Isabel makes one visit to see Pansy. At the convent she meets Madame Merle, who has just been with Pansy. She tries to explain her reasons, but Isabel is not interested.

Pansy is changed. She has had enough of the convent and would like to come out. She now knows that she must obey her father in anything or else there will be harsher consequences. She is frightened because Isabel is leaving and asks Isabel to come back and help her. Isabel promises not to desert her. As Isabel is leaving, Pansy mentions that Madame Merle was there to see her, saying that she doesn't like Madame Merle.

As Isabel departs, she meets Madame Merle again. This time Madame Merle tells her that it was Ralph who was responsible for her inheritance. Isabel simply tells Madame Merle that she never wants to see her again.

Commentary

After the interview with Pansy, Isabel knows that Pansy is now more her daughter than she is Madame Merle's. It is rather pathetic, that Pansy dislikes her true mother and is so attached to her stepmother. Knowing Pansy's plight, Isabel promises to come back to help the girl.

This chapter ends Madame Merle's association with Isabel. The older woman is now a rather lonely and forlorn person who must go to another land and begin over again.

CHAPTERS 53 AND 54

Summary

When Isabel arrives in London, Henrietta and Mr. Bantling are there to meet her. As soon as the two ladies are alone Henrietta asks if Osmond made a scene about Isabel's departure. Isabel replies that it wouldn't be called a scene. Henrietta objects to Isabel's promising Pansy to return and hopes that Isabel will reconsider and refuse to go back.

When Isabel arrives at Gardencourt, she finds out that there is no hope for Ralph. She also hears that Lord Warburton is to be married soon. Then Mrs. Touchett wants to ask Isabel only three questions. She wants to know if Isabel is sorry she didn't marry Lord Warburton. Isabel tells her no, but admits that her husband does not get along with her. Her aunt then inquires whether Isabel still likes Serena Merle. Isabel observes that she no longer does as she once did and – in reply to the third question – states that Madame Merle had made use of her.

When Isabel gets to see Ralph, she tries to thank him for all that he has done for her. Ralph, however, feels that he has ruined Isabel because of his generosity. Isabel then admits that Osmond married her for her money. She confesses how she has been punished for wanting to look at life independently. Ralph wants her to remain at Gardencourt, but Isabel will only stay so long as it seems right. She believes so strongly in doing what is right. Ralph reminds her that however much Osmond may hate her that she has also been loved and adored.

Commentary

Isabel returns at the end of the novel to the place (Gardencourt) that had been her starting point. Here she will gain the strength to do what she considers to be the right thing. Most important to her is to reveal everything as openly as she can to Ralph. She now knows fully how deeply he has loved her and how generous and forgiving he has been with his love. She then tells him about her suffering and the punishment she has received from life. She gains strength in knowing that Ralph sympathizes with her and does not rebuke her for anything. Thus in this final scene between Ralph and Isabel, each discovers that their lives have been enriched for having known each other.

CHAPTER 55

Summary

Ralph had told Isabel long ago that if she wanted to see the ghosts in Gardencourt, she must suffer greatly. During the night she senses the presence of something and upon leaving her room, learns that Ralph has just died.

Isabel remains at Gardencourt for a while so as to comfort her aunt and to recover her own strength. One day she receives two visitors. The first is Lord Warburton who again extends to her an invitation to visit his home. The second visitor is Caspar Goodwood. He tries to make Isabel see that it is foolish for her to return to her husband. He tells her that he knows everything and can see no reason for her to return to "that ghastly form" of a marriage. He tells Isabel that the world is wide and there are many places where they could live. "She had wanted help, and here was help; it had come in a rushing torrent." Goodwood takes her into his arms, and "his kiss was like white lightning, a flash that spread, and spread again, and stayed...." Isabel recovered herself and realized that her path was now very straight.

Two days later, Goodwood calls at Henrietta Stackpole's in London and learns that Isabel has left that morning for Rome.

Commentary

Why Isabel decides to return to Gilbert Osmond must be finally determined by each individual reader. There could be many reasons. Isabel is proud, and in her pride she cannot stand to admit her mistake to the entire world. As she told Henrietta, she cannot publish her error for the whole world to see. Furthermore, Isabel puts great emphasis on her promises. She had undertaken certain marriage vows and she cannot bring herself to break them. Likewise, she had promised Pansy Osmond to return. And finally, in her interview with Caspar Goodwood, Isabel sees the danger she would face if she does not go back. In this final scene, Isabel is afraid that if she does not return she would compromise herself and thus would be no better than Madame Merle or the Countess Gemini. In other words – given Isabel's nature – the only course open to her is to rejoin her husband.

MEANING THROUGH SOCIAL CONTRASTS: THE AMERICAN VERSUS THE EUROPEAN

Henry James was the first novelist to write on the theme of the American versus the European with any degree of success. Almost all of his major novels may be approached as a study of the social theme of the American in Europe, in which James contrasts the active life of the American with the mannered life of the European aristocracy. Embodied in this contrast is the moral theme in which the moral innocence of the American is contrasted with the knowledge and experience (and evil) of the European.

In its most general terms, that is, in terms which will apply to almost any Jamesian novel, the contrasts are seen as follows:

THE AMERICAN		THE EUROPEAN
innocence	vs.	knowledge or experience
utility	vs.	form and ceremony
spontaneity	vs.	ritual
sincerity	vs.	urbanity
action	vs.	inaction
nature	vs.	art
natural	vs.	artificial
honesty	vs.	evil

The above list could be extended to include other virtues or qualities, but this list, or even half this list, will suffice to demonstrate James' theme or idea in the use of this American-European contrast.

The reader should also remember that James uses these ideas with a great deal of flexibility. It does not always hold that every European will have exactly these qualities or that every American will. In fact, some of the more admirable characters are indeed Europeans who possess many of these qualities and in turn lack others. Because a European might possess urbanity and knowledge and experience does not necessarily mean that he is artificial and evil. And quite the contrary, many Americans come with natural spontaneity and are not necessarily honest and admirable. For example, Lord Warburton possesses urbanity and adheres to forms, ceremonies, and rituals, but he is nevertheless an admirable character. On the other hand, Henrietta Stackpole, who possesses a great amount of spontaneity, is at times rather overbearing and indiscreet.

In *The Portrait of a Lady,* the character who represents the American in the best sense of the word is, of course, Isabel Archer. The representative of the European in the worse sense of the word is Gilbert Osmond, and to a lesser degree Madame Merle. Of course, both of these people were actually born in America, but they have lived their entire lives in Europe and consider themselves European.

One of the great differences that is emphasized is the difference between the American's practicality and the European's insistence upon form and ceremony. Isabel likes to react to any situation according to her own desires. Early in the novel, Isabel's aunt tells her that it is not proper to remain with two gentlemen without a chaperon. Isabel likes to do what she thinks is right and not what other people tell her is right. But people like Osmond know ahead of time what type of form and ceremony they will employ in any given situation. The American then acts spontaneously, while the Europeans have formalized certain rituals so that they will never have to confront an unknown situation. Thus, there is a sense of sincerity in the American's actions; whereas the European is more characterized by a sense of extreme urbanity. Throughout the novel, we never see Madame Merle or Osmond perform a spontaneous act—they are the epitome of the perfect and correct form. Everything they do is calculated according to the effect it will have. Thus, there is something false in their reactions, while Isabel's reaction strikes one as honest and sincere.

Furthermore, the American is a person of action. The Europeans have been bred to view work as vulgar; they are people of inaction. Osmond has apparently never performed any useful task. He remains inactive while the American, such as Henrietta, can enter into any type of pursuit.

The American's sense of spontaneity, sincerity, and action leads him into natural actions. He seems to represent nature itself.

On the other hand, the European's emphasis on form, ceremony, ritual, and urbanity seems to suggest the artificial. It represents art as an entity opposing nature.

Finally, these qualities lead to the ultimate opposition of honesty versus evil. When all of the American's qualities are replaced by all of the European's we find that form and ritual are deemed more important than honesty. Thus, Osmond will insist upon Isabel's putting up the front of a happy marriage even though they detest each other. In other words, the form of the marriage must be maintained. James is not emphasizing that one should have all of one tendency and none of the other. The ideal person is the one who can retain all of the American's innocence and honesty, and yet gain the European's experience and knowledge. Lord Warburton is then great because he has the knowledge and experience; he has the form and ceremony and ritual. But he is not artificial, for he reacts to things with sincerity and naturalness. Isabel is great because she has retained all of her American qualities, but has learned a great deal about form and ritual and urbanity, and has also gained a tremendous amount of knowledge and experience without losing her native virtues.

SPECIAL PROBLEMS AND INTERESTS

Central Intelligence and Point-of-View

One of James' contributions to the art of fiction is in his use of point-of-view. By point-of-view is meant the angle from which the story is told. For example, previous to James' novel, much of the fiction of the day was being written from the author's viewpoint, that is, the author was telling the story and he was directing the reader's response to the story. Much of the fiction of the nineteenth century had the author as the storyteller, and the author would create scenes in which certain characters would be involved, but each scene would not necessarily have the same characters in them.

James' fiction differs in his treatment of point-of-view. He was interested in establishing a central person about whom the story revolved. Usually, the reader would have to see all the action of the story through this character's eyes. This central character was called at times the "central intelligence" and at times the "sentient center." Thus in James' fiction, we have the central character of the novel, and it is as though the central character were telling the story because we see or hear about all events through him. We the readers react to certain events as this central character would react to them.

Every scene in the novel, therefore, will be a scene which reveals something about the main character, and usually he is present in every scene. As the *central intelligence,* his sensibility is the dominant aspect of the novel. In *The Portrait Of A Lady,* Isabel Archer is, of course, the central character. Every scene is limited to showing her involved in some type of situation, and every scene confines itself to the interests of this central character.

Confidant

James wrote fiction in an era before the modern technique of the "stream-of-consciousness" was established. In the modern technique, the author feels free to go inside the mind of the character. But in James' time, this was not yet an established technique. Thus, since James as a novelist wanted to remain outside the novel—that is, wanted to present his characters with as much objectivity and realism as possible—he created the use of a confidant.

The confidant is a person of great sensibility to whom the main character reveals his or her innermost thoughts (as long as they are within the bounds of propriety). The confidant is essentially a listener and in some cases an adviser. This technique of having a confidant to whom the main character can talk serves a double function. First of all, it allows the reader to see what the main character is thinking, and secondly, it gives a more rounded view of the action. For example, after something has happened to the main character, the confidant hears about it and in their discussion of the event, we, the readers, see and understand the various subtle implications of this situation more clearly.

The confidant is also a person who is usually somewhat removed from the central action. For example, Ralph Touchett is not directly involved in the central action of the novel, except that he does instigate the action by being responsible for Isabel's inheritance. Henrietta Stackpole, another confidante, is even further removed from the central action.

Essentially, the confidant observes the action from a distance, comments on this action, and is a person of exceptional sensitivity and perception, who allows the main character to respond more deeply and subtly to certain situations.

Foreshadowing

James is a very careful artist who uses rather often and freely the technique of foreshadowing a later action. This means that he has given hints in the early parts of the novel about some important thing that is going to happen later in the story. Thus, a touch of realism is added to the novel because so many things have foreshadowed the main action that the reader should not be surprised to discover the action at the end.

For example, early in the novel there are many hints that too much independence will get a person in trouble. Accordingly, it is Isabel's absolute desire for independence that made her ignore the advice of others and rely solely upon her own judgment in marrying Osmond. Likewise, there are many hints that Isabel must suffer. Consequently, we are not surprised to find her suffering at the end of the novel. She is also a person who puts much emphasis on her promises and vows. So she must return to Osmond because of her marriage vows and her promise to Pansy. Thus, every action that is central to the novel has been prepared for by hints and many types of foreshadowing.

Contrast

Aside from the use of *Social Contrasts* (see previous section on this subject), James also used contrast in many other ways. There are many people surrounding Isabel. The contrast between Henrietta Stackpole and Madame Merle enables us to see how Isabel can attract different people to her. Through this contrast, we come to believe that Isabel has expansive qualities which allow her to react to varying types of people. Thus such differing people as Lord Warburton, Osmond, and Caspar Goodwood all find themselves in love with Isabel. This fact also attests to Isabel's charm and personality.

CHARACTER ANALYSES

Isabel Archer

Isabel is the central concern of the novel. She possesses all the attributes of James' typical American. She is innocent, but also intelligent. In contrast to the European such as Madame Merle, she does not possess a great amount of experience, but she does have the capacity to appreciate any new experience.

Isabel has an expansive personality. Ralph Touchett and others are attracted to Isabel because she apparently has a great capacity for growth. This quality allows her to react spontaneously to any new experience. Her response indicates a depth of perception missing from other people. It is a compliment to Isabel's combination of these qualities that she is able to attract so many divergent types of personalities to her. She excites the admiration of people as different as Madame Merle and Henrietta Stackpole, or as different as Gilbert Osmond and Ralph Touchett. Furthermore, men as divergent in personalities as Caspar Goodwood and Lord Warburton both fall in love with Isabel. Therefore, part of her greatness lies in her ability to attract all sorts of people to her.

Even though Isabel is not considered a great beauty, she is attractive enough to win attention. She possesses a natural charm and a sincerity that add to her looks.

Perhaps her most striking qualities are her desire for independence and her imagination. She believes strongly in her own opinion and cherishes the right to evaluate independently any person or situation.

This note of independence is struck in the first chapters of the novel. It is the trait which Ralph admires greatly. In conjunction with her independence, Isabel is also a very imaginative person. Ralph Touchett thinks that in order for Isabel to realize her imagination, she must be made financially independent. Thus, her inheritance gives her the freedom to allow her imagination to soar.

One of the first uses of her free imagination is in evaluating Gilbert Osmond. He told her that he had lived a dull life, but Isabel's imagination took flight to create for him a very interesting life. In her imagination, she filled in the vacant spots and saw him as a much more interesting person than he actually was.

It is ironic that Isabel's desire for complete independence causes her to marry Osmond. In her determination to follow only her own evaluation, she refused to listen to her many friends who cautioned her against such a marriage. Consequently, her highest quality also became her downfall.

Isabel also possesses a rather over-strong sense of pride. Even after she recognizes that she made a mistake in her marriage, she cannot admit this publicly. It took a great effort to confess her error to Ralph, and at the end of the novel, she has too much pride to confess her mistake to the whole world. Thus, partly for this reason, she returns to Rome to continue her life with Osmond.

Isabel, therefore, represents the innocent young American who is deceived by the superior cunning and deceit of Osmond and Madame Merle, who are representatives of the old order of European thinking. Isabel was capable of great potential and of great development—she had a large capacity for growth and for life. Her tragedy is in her mistaken judgment of Madame Merle and Gilbert Osmond. Once, however, she has recognized her error, she is determined to try to make the best of it.

Ralph Touchett

Ralph functions as the cosmopolite who has interested himself in Isabel's career. Upon first meeting her, he senses her potential capacity for development. He then devotes his life to observing Isabel's activities.

Ralph is well suited for his function in the novel. Knowing that he has only a few more years to live, he has developed a sensitivity which enables him to penetrate to the center of things. Owing to his sickness, he can remain relatively uninvolved and objective. But he is not completely disinterested. He feels that his last remaining years will be enriched by observing Isabel's activities. Thus, he is instrumental in placing a large fortune at her disposal. His act was performed in order to provide Isabel the opportunity to develop to her fullest capacity. But in actuality, it caused her to become a prisoner.

Ralph's objectivity and sincere love for Isabel also allow him to function as a confidant to her. He is able to discuss intimately with her various aspects of her career and thus give the reader a more rounded view of any situation.

Ralph, then, is a person of high intelligence and sensitivity who is able to perceive the essential aspects of any situation, and the reader has access to what he knows. Ralph knows that Osmond is a "sterile dilettante," but is unable to convince Isabel of this fact. Furthermore, he recognizes that some people, like Madame Merle, are too perfect. He remains, however, Isabel's closet friend and admirer and the person who brings about her first open break with Gilbert Osmond.

Madame Merle

Madame Merle is one of the most admired women in Europe. Everything she does is in perfect good taste. As Mrs. Touchett says, she hasn't a fault. But this means that Madame Merle has created a visible exterior to cover up her inner corruption. As the reader later learns. she has been an adultress, but she covered her licentious behavior with such good taste that the world is unaware of it.

Madame Merle had very great ambitions as a younger person. She has constantly been frustrated in her desires and has consequently developed certain forms and ceremonies to compensate for her failure. She plays the piano flawlessly; she is welcomed in most of the great houses of Europe; she is intelligent, witty, and charming; she is never given to excesses; and she never makes a blunder. She understands human nature and knows how to accomplish anything.

Given her nature, it is only natural that Isabel, innocent as she is, should fall prey to Madame Merle's more polished and experienced ways. In other words, Isabel is not an easy victim; her conqueror or superior must be a superior person.

Madame Merle's great flaw is her ambition. When she sees Isabel achieve something that she would have liked to possess, her true nature is revealed. Thus, it is her ambition to have Pansy make a superb marriage that leads Madame Merle to perpetrate her treachery against Isabel. Since Madame Merle has failed so miserably in life, she desires that her daughter should make a brilliant match. Her strong ambitions and firm pursuit of her goal finally make her an odious person. She is so determined to succeed that she goes beyond her usual good taste and decorum. This allows Isabel to see her for what she is. But even in her failure, Madame Merle recognizes that she has been "vile" for no apparent gain. Furthermore, we recognize that finally even Madame Merle's own daughter does not like her and quite the contrary, the daughter does like Isabel, whom Madame Merle had so horribly betrayed.

In the final analysis, Madame Merle, like Gilbert Osmond, represents the European personality that sacrifices all that is human and natural and sincere for something that represents the perfect form and ceremony. The acquired taste and rule become more important than real human relationships.

Gilbert Osmond

Gilbert Osmond is the epitome of everything that one finds objectionable in European society. He was, as a matter of fact, born in America, but since he was brought to Europe as a small child and has lived his entire life in Europe, we may consider him for all thematic purposes a European.

Osmond is a person who puts extreme value on the correct form and perfect ritual. He is a self-centered individual who thinks that the world should take note of his unusual attributes. Everything he does is calculated for its effect. He has never done anything without considering first what effect it will bear upon him. He is basically an indolent man who has the egoism to think that the world should come to him. If he is disdainful of most of the things in the world, it is because he desires them so strongly.

He is a man of perfect taste. But the reader should note that perfect taste can be carried too far. As with Madame Merle, everything is so contrived that the real person is concealed behind a mask of pretenses. Everything that he possesses is perfect. His objects of art, his house, his view, his daughter are all brought to absolute perfection. Thus, when he desires to marry Isabel, it is only because she will reflect what good taste he has. But when one devotes oneself entirely to creating an effect, there is naturally something artificial about the results.

Gilbert Osmond, then, has developed good taste so that he will be praised for it. It has been a project with him; it is acquired. On the contrary, Isabel has good taste but it is a naturally endowed quality. It stems from her personality; whereas Osmond's taste is studied and artificial.

It must be noted, however, that Osmond does not marry Isabel Archer solely for her money. Had Isabel not possessed talent, charm, intelligence, taste, and looks, her money would not have been sufficient cause to bring about the marriage. On the contrary, if Isabel had had every quality and attribute except money, Osmond would not have married her.

The evil of Osmond's nature comes from the fact that he calculates everything he does. That is, he does not take into consideration Isabel's independent personality. Quite the reverse, he finds this to be the most objectional part of her makeup. Thus, after the marriage, he deliberately sets about to undermine Isabel's individuality. He feels that his wife must conform to his every wish and desire. In other words, he wants a wife who will obey him with perfect obedience, as does his daughter. Consequently, he is determined to break Isabel's free and independent spirit. In attempting to do so, he is trying to destroy the finer capacity of her character. Thus, his desire to have everything, including his wife, revolve around him, shows his essential nature.

Finally, Osmond is not genuine. He prefers forms and ceremonies to real human relations. He does not love Isabel, but he wants her to obey him. He looks only to the appearance of things. He is, finally, the empty and evil man.

QUESTIONS

1. What qualities does Isabel possess which induce her to fall in love with Gilbert Osmond?

2. How does Henrietta Stackpole's function as a confidante differ from Ralph's function as confidant?

3. Why does Ralph talk his father into leaving Isabel a huge fortune?

4. How much of a disinterested spectator in Isabel's career is Ralph Touchett?

5. What qualities does Madame Merle possess which will enable her to deceive Isabel?

6. Why does Isabel refuse Lord Warburton's proposal?

7. How is Isabel's rejection of Lord Warburton important to Osmond's view of her?

8. Why does Isabel find it difficult to tell Ralph the exact nature of her marriage?

9. Why does Isabel return to Osmond at the end of the novel?

10. What accounts for Isabel's attraction to Pansy Osmond?

11. How much is Isabel responsible for Lord Warburton's refusing to propose to Pansy?

12. What has Isabel learned during the course of the novel?

NOTES

THE PRINCE AND THE PAUPER

NOTES

including

- *Life of the Author*
- *Introduction to the Novel*
- *General Plot Summary*
- *List of Characters*
- *Summaries and Commentaries*
- *Twain's Method of Characterization*
- *Questions for Review*
- *Selected Bibliography*

by
L. David Allen, Ph. D.
University of Nebraska

and

James L. Roberts, Ph.D.
Department of English
University of Nebraska

INCORPORATED
LINCOLN, NEBRASKA 68501

Editor

Gary Carey, M.A.
University of Colorado

Consulting Editor

James L. Roberts, Ph.D.
Department of English
University of Nebraska

ISBN 0-8220-1096-8
© Copyright 1980
by
C. K. Hillegass
All Rights Reserved
Printed in U.S.A.

1990 Printing

The Cliffs Notes logo, the names "Cliffs" and "Cliffs Notes," and the black and yellow diagonal-stripe cover design are all registered trademarks belonging to Cliffs Notes, Inc., and may not be used in whole or in part without written permission.

Cliffs Notes, Inc. Lincoln, Nebraska

CONTENTS

THE PRINCE AND THE PAUPER NOTES

LIFE OF THE AUTHOR

As one of America's first and foremost realists and humorists, Mark Twain (Samuel Langhorne Clemens, 1835-1910) usually wrote of things he knew about from firsthand experience. Two of his best-known novels typify this trait: in his *Adventures of Tom Sawyer,* Twain immortalized the sleepy little town of Hannibal, Missouri (the fictional St. Petersburg), as well as the steamboats which passed through it daily; likewise, in *Adventures of Huckleberry Finn* (written after *The Prince and the Pauper*), the various characters are based on types which Twain encountered both in his hometown and while working as a riverboat pilot on the Mississippi River. And even though *The Prince and the Pauper* is not based on personal experience (it is set in sixteenth-century England), Twain uses the experiences of two young boys gradually losing their innocence, as he did in both *Tom Sawyer* and *Huck Finn.*

Twain's father was a lawyer, but he was never quite successful, and so he dabbled in land speculation, hoping to become wealthy someday. He was, however, a highly intelligent man who was a stern disciplinarian. Twain's mother, a southern belle in her youth, had a natural sense of humor, was inclined to be overly emotional, and was particularly fond of animals and unfortunate human beings. Although his family was not wealthy, Twain apparently had a happy childhood. Twain's father died when Twain was twelve years old and, for the next ten years, Twain was an apprentice printer, both in Hannibal and in New York City. Hoping to find his fortune, he conceived a wild scheme of getting rich in South America. On a riverboat to New Orleans, however, he met a famous riverboat pilot who promised to teach him the trade for five hundred dollars. After completing his training, Twain was a riverboat pilot for four years and, during this time, he became familiar with all of the towns along the Mississippi River.

When the Civil War began, Twain's allegiance tended to be somewhat southern due to his regional heritage, but his brother Orion convinced him to go West on an expedition, a trip which became the subject of a later work, *Roughing It.* Even though some of his letters and accounts about traveling in frontier America had been published earlier, Twain actually launched his literary career with the short story "The Celebrated Jumping Frog of Calaveras County," published in 1865. Then, after the acclaim of *Roughing It,* Twain gave up his career as a journalist-reporter and begain writing seriously. His fame as an American writer was immediate, especially after the publication of *Innocents Abroad,* a book which is still one of his most popular works. The satire that Twain uses to expose the so-called sophistication of the Old World, in contrast to old-fashioned Yankee common sense, is similar to that found ten years later in *The Prince and the Pauper.* But it is his novels and stories concerning the Mississippi River and the values of the people who lived along its length that have made Twain one of America's best and favorite storytellers. The humor he found there, along with its way of life, has continued to fascinate readers and embodies an almost mythic sense of what it meant to be a young American in the latter part of the nineteenth century.

After Twain turned fifty, however, his fortunes reversed themselves; his health began to fail and he faced bankruptcy; in addition, his wife became a semi-invalid, one daughter developed epilepsy, and his oldest daughter died of meningitis. Yet Twain survived. He became a critic and essayist, and he became more popular as a satirist than as a humorist. The body of work he left behind is immense and varied—poetry, sketches, journalistic pieces, political essays, novels, and short stories—all a testament to the diverse talent and energy which used the folklore of frontier America to create authentic American masterpieces of enduring value.

INTRODUCTION TO THE NOVEL

The Prince and the Pauper, seemingly a simple novel, handles several divergent themes and ideas simultaneously. Foremost is the

the basic idea of the exchange of roles and lines between the prince and the pauper and the constant reference to their *twin* fates. Prior to meeting each other, both boys have dreams of living the life of the other. Both are, in a sense, innocents who learn a great deal about life as a result of their exchanging clothes and roles. Likewise, the dreams of each are shattered as a result of the exchange. Ironically, both live at first in an extremely *restricted* society. Like Huck Finn, who did not want to be "sivilized" and who rejected the confinements of society, Tom Canty has no freedom and is constantly beaten and restricted in his home environment. Likewise, the young prince is confined to his royal apartments and has little or no freedom—that is, he does not have the freedom that he believes a commoner has. The freedom that both young lads desire exists only in their dreams. Of Tom, Twain writes: "His old dreams had been so pleasant, but this reality was so dreary."

Another basic idea is, of course, Twain's satiric exposé of the concept that "clothes make the man": when the two lads exchange clothes, the prince immediately becomes the pauper and is thus treated like a pauper and, likewise, the pauper is treated like a prince merely because he is dressed in royal robes.

The subject matter of *The Prince and the Pauper*, like the subject matter of *A Connecticut Yankee in King Arthur's Court*, appealed to Twain because he was writing about an age controlled by nobility and royalty, political divisions which Twain enjoyed deriding; in addition, it was an age of great religious debate and distinction, yet it was filled with unchristian acts, just as it was also an age of enlightenment, where new laws and new concepts of justice were beginning to be popular. But, in this novel, Twain focuses particularly on the many social injustices which are exposed to the new king as he roams his land as a common pauper.

The subject matter specifically allowed Twain to utilize his vast knowledge of history and biography, two subjects which occupied much of Twain's reading time, and this novel also allowed him to meditate on the injustices inherent in human nature (or "the damned human race," as it was termed in his later work, *The Mysterious Stranger*). The subject matter also allowed Twain to indulge in one of his favorite pastimes—using a language different from that used by either the common people or the educated people; the idioms and dialects of *Tom Sawyer* and *Huck Finn* and the archaic language of

The Prince and the Pauper and *A Connecticut Yankee* are all illustrations of Twain's penchant for utilizing different sorts of language.

The Prince and the Pauper is also Twain's most elaborately plotted novel. Seemingly an insignificant incident, the whereabouts of the Great Seal of England, becomes the key to the real identity of the new king. Likewise, Tom's knowledge of Latin and his early role as a friend and counselor to the people of Offal Court influence his actions later as the surrogate king.

In his *Autobiography*, Twain wrote of this novel: "Edward VI and a little pauper exchange places by accident a day or so before Henry VIII's death. The prince wanders in rags and hardships and the pauper suffers the (to him) horrible miseries of princedom, up to the moment of crowning in Westminster Abbey, when proof is brought and the mistake rectified." From this bare sketch, Twain fleshed out the characters and created a masterpiece that has endured and delighted thousands of young readers and adults alike ever since its publication in 1882.

GENERAL PLOT SUMMARY

The Prince and the Pauper tells the tale of two boys who trade clothing one afternoon and, as a result, they trade lives as well. After many adventures, matters are set right again, with one of the boys resuming his rightful, royal position and the other boy accepting a position that recognizes his innate intelligence and goodheartedness.

One of these boys is the long-awaited male heir to the throne of England, Edward Tudor, son of Henry VIII. The other boy is Tom Canty, the unloved son of a beggar and thief. Coincidentally, Tom Canty and Edward Tudor were born in London on the same day.

Tom Canty's life in Offal Court, off Pudding Lane, is a hard life in one of London's poorest neighborhoods. He is forced by his father to go out begging daily, and he is beaten severely if he returns empty-handed. Father Andrew, however, provides him some respite from this life by telling him tales about the nobility, while instructing him in morality, reading, writing, and Latin. Treasuring these tales, which tell of a considerably better life, Tom Canty imaginatively relives them in his daydreams.

One day, Tom's daydreaming leads him out of the city of London, past the palaces of the rich, and finally to Westminster, where he actually sees Edward Tudor at play on the other side of a fence. Simultaneously, the prince notices Tom when he sees a soldier roughly pulling the young boy away from the fence; the prince rebukes the soldier and invites Tom into the palace. Each of the boys is fascinated by the other's life—Tom, by the luxury and the cleanliness that Edward has, and Edward, by the freedom that Tom has. To get a "feeling" of the other's life, they exchange clothing and discover that they look very much alike.

When the prince discovers a bruise on Tom's hand, he rushes out of the palace, paying no heed to the way he is dressed, to rebuke the guard. The guard, believing that the prince is the pauper, immediately puts him out of the gates, and thus the stage is set for Edward Tudor to experience the life of a commoner and for Tom Canty to live the life of a real-life prince.

Imperiously and angrily proclaiming that *he* is the Prince of Wales, Edward is mocked by the crowd around the royal gate, beaten, and has several dogs set upon him—all the while asserting that he *is* the son of the king. Chased back into London, Edward wanders around, not knowing where to go until he is finally collared by John Canty, Tom's father, and dragged off to Offal Court.

In the meantime, young Tom Canty has been left in the prince's royal apartment in the palace. At first, he enjoys the luxury of his surroundings, but he becomes increasingly apprehensive about what will happen to him if he is discovered in the prince's clothing. The Lady Jane Grey talks with him and becomes very confused about Tom's behavior; word quickly spreads that the prince is mad. Every time that Tom tries to say something to dispel this idea, it makes those around him only more convinced that the prince has indeed gone mad.

After talking with his "son," Henry VIII gives orders: first, he commands that the Duke of Norfolk be killed so that the prince can be immediately named heir apparent with no opposition. Second, he orders that all persons in the court say nothing about the prince's madness and that they ignore any indications of it. Finally, he orders his "son" to say no more about living in Offal Court and to try to regain his mental health. To this end, the Lord St. John and the Lord Hertford are to be his companions, to watch over him, and to remind him of what he is to do.

The first ceremony which Tom must undergo is dinner. Although he blunders frequently, his behavior is overlooked by those attending. Afterward, he finds a book dealing with the etiquette of the English court, and he begins the process of learning to cope in his new position. His next ordeal is a city dinner in London, toward which he and his entourage move in great splendor along the Thames River.

The scene then shifts momentarily to the Prince of Wales, who is now in the clutches of John Canty. He is brought to the filthy room where the Cantys live and is put on display to show the neighborhood his mad delusion that he is the Prince of Wales; later, he is beaten because he brought no money home.

Late that night, the Cantys are awakened by someone who has come to tell them that the man whom John Canty struck with his cudgel, while bringing his "son" home, has died. They all leave immediately, Canty keeping the prince in tow. The prince, however, manages to slip away from old Canty.

While Tom dines with the nobility and watches the pageantry of the dinner, the real prince stands outside the Guildhall, trying to get in, asserting that he is the true Prince of Wales. The mob jeers at him and would have thoroughly beaten him if Miles Hendon had not suddenly appeared and protected him. While the prince and Hendon are struggling with the crowd outside, and while the nobility is having a merry time inside the Guildhall, a messenger brings the news that Henry VIII is dead. Tom Canty is thus suddenly elevated from prince to king, and his first act is to free the Duke of Norfolk.

Hendon, meanwhile, leads the prince through the crowd toward his lodgings in an inn on London Bridge, then a city unto itself. John Canty, however, intercepts them and tries to take the prince, whom he still believes to be his son, but Hendon sends him away. In Hendon's rooms, the prince acts out his accustomed role and expects Hendon to serve him; Hendon does so, without a protest. As a reward for his help and kindness, Hendon is granted the right to sit in the presence of the king and is made a knight.

In the morning, Hendon leaves while the prince is still sleeping and goes out to buy new clothes for the boy. When he returns, however, the prince is gone, lured away by a boy who is later joined by a ruffian as they head toward Southwark. Although Hendon tries to follow, he loses the trail.

That same morning, Tom Canty is awakened, dressed, and fed; then the Lord Hertford takes him into the throne room, where he must sit through many tedious reports on affairs of state. Although Tom is learning to handle such situations, the Lord Hertford prevents him from making several blunders. In the afternoon, Tom makes good use of an interview with Humphrey Marlow, his "whipping-boy," to learn many of the things he needs to know; from this point on, Tom uses every opportunity to learn, and to remember, important royal matters.

The next two days are similar to the first, and Tom becomes more accustomed to what he must do. On the fourth day, however, the noise of a mob diverts Tom's attention. Looking out the window, he asks what the cause of this is and, after hearing about the trouble, he has the three condemned people brought before him. Questioning them shrewdly and disposing of their sentences decisively, he gains the admiration of all those present; his court also begins to wonder about the so-called rumors of his madness. With the new confidence that his actions have given him, Tom eats the state dinner, before all those who care to watch, without qualm and without error.

The prince, in the meantime, is lured into an old country barn by John Canty and Hugo, his accomplice. He falls asleep on a pile of straw, and when he awakens, he hears many tales of injustice at the hands of the law. Outraged, he declares such laws should be abolished. This, as well as his assertion that he is the King of England, earns him the mockery of the troop of vagabonds who have joined Canty and Hugo. Forced to travel with these vagabonds, the prince nevertheless refuses to take part in their escapades, and he finally manages to escape from Hugo's custody when he tells a man that Hugo is a thief. He then wanders alone across the countryside, driven away whenever he begs for food or rest, until at last he finds an empty barn. Sleeping that night next to a calf, the prince is awakened by two young children who believe his story about his royal claims and take him to their mother. The woman feeds him and sets him to doing a variety of household tasks. As he is working, however, he sees Canty and Hugo arriving in front of the house, so he runs off toward the woods. There, he makes his way until he reaches a hermit's hut. The hermit, who is genuinely mad, feeds the boy and cares for him, but when he hears that the boy is the King of

England, son of Henry VIII, he becomes consumed with revenge; he ties up the prince and is about to plunge a knife into him when Miles Hendon arrives at the door. The hermit manages to lead Hendon away, but, inadvertently, his absence allows John Canty and Hugo to take the prince with them.

Once again, Hugo tries to make the prince participate in begging and thieving; the prince, however, steadfastly refuses to have anything to do with such activities. Hugo therefore decides to put the prince into the hands of the law, which he accomplishes by snatching a bundle, thrusting it into the prince's arms, and dashing away. The appearance of guilt is enough for the crowd that gathers, and the burliest of them is about to beat the prince when Miles Hendon once again appears. To appease the crowd, Miles and the prince must go before the magistrate. The judge is kindly, and the sentence is short. Hendon then manages to convince the sheriff that the wisest course would be to free the boy, and the two leave, headed toward Hendon Hall, from which Miles has been absent for some ten years.

When they arrive there, Miles's brother Hugh and the Lady Edith, who once loved Miles, deny that Miles is still alive. In fact, Hugh Hendon has Miles arrested as an impostor, and the prince is taken to jail along with him. There, the prince discovers the filthy conditions of his country's prisons, and he hears more stories about the many injustices of English laws. Finally, Miles is sentenced to sit two hours in the pillory; he also takes twelve lashes because the prince once again tries to assert himself. When the two are released at last, they turn back toward London.

Coincidentally, as the prince is returning to London, Tom Canty is rapidly learning to be a king and is preparing for his coronation. On Coronation Day, he rides in a grand procession through London. Riding past Offal Court, he sees his mother, and he denies knowing her; immediately, however, he is stricken with remorse.

The ceremony begins; then, suddenly, just as the Archbishop of Canterbury is about to place the crown on Tom's head, the real prince steps forward and forbids it. Tom affirms the boy's claim. Several inconclusive tests are tried in order to determine the identity of the boys, and finally the location of the Great Seal of England is suggested. With some prompting from Tom, Edward Tudor tells the Lord St. John where the seal is to be found, thus establishing his true right to the throne of England.

When Miles Hendon, who has been separated from the prince, appears outside Westminster, he is arrested and brought before the newly crowned king. Having believed throughout their travels together that the boy was mad, Hendon cannot believe that his young friend, now on the throne, is the same person. To test him, he pulls up a chair and sits in his presence; Edward affirms Miles's right to do so, and he also affirms that he has made Hendon a knight and that, furthermore, Hendon is now a peer of England, Earl of Kent. Later, Tom Canty is made the "King's Ward," and his sisters and his mother are granted lifetime care at Christ's Hospital.

The last chapter ties up loose ends of the plot: Hugh Hendon, though not prosecuted, leaves England and goes to the Continent; the Lady Edith marries Miles; Edward amply rewards those who were kind to him, punishes those who were not, and makes reparations to those who suffered from the cruel injustice of English laws. Throughout his short life and reign, Edward Tudor always remembers his adventures and reigns more mercifully because of them.

LIST OF CHARACTERS

Edward Tudor, Prince of Wales

The main character, the prince referred to in the title of the novel. Having spent his entire life in the confines of the royal apartments, he has daydreamed about the freedom experienced by boys such as Tom Canty.

Tom Canty

The other main character of the novel; as a pauper's son, he has been brought up in one of the most disreputable parts of London and has spent much time daydreaming about living the life of royalty.

King Henry VIII

The loving father of Edward, Prince of Wales; he is anxious to see his son installed as the heir apparent before it is discovered that the prince is mad.

John Canty

The unloving and harsh father of Tom Canty; he keeps his son in tow solely so that young Tom can beg money for him.

Bet, Nan, and Mother Canty

The sisters and mother of Tom Canty, who try to protect him from John Canty's brutality.

Father Andrew

The good, retired priest who teaches Tom how to read and write and also teaches him a bit of Latin, a talent which he later uses at court.

The Lady Jane Grey, The Lady Elizabeth, and the Lady Mary

Half-sisters to Edward, Prince of Wales. At various times, they are kind or sarcastic to Tom Canty, who they believe to be the real prince.

The Lord Hertford and The Lord St. John

Two lords of the realm in charge of overseeing the welfare of the Prince of Wales.

Miles Hendon

A "diamond in the rough," so to speak; he is a good friend of young Edward Tudor, and he represents the best of Englishmen; he thinks that the young prince is ill, and because he feels sorry for him, he becomes his protector as they wander throughout the English countryside.

Hugo

A ruffian vagabond member of the troop which holds the prince captive; later, he is beaten by the prince in a contest of skill.

Hugh Hendon

Miles's brother who usurps Miles's rightful place in the family and also marries the woman Miles loves. He pretends not to recognize Miles, and he is responsible for Miles' and the young prince's being imprisoned.

Blake Andrews

The old retainer of Miles Hendon's father; he comes to jail and explains the various events that have transpired since Miles Hendon has been away.

Sir Humphrey Marlow (deceased)

An old friend of Miles's father. Miles hopes that the old fellow will help him regain his rightful position as a recognized member of the Hendon family.

Humphrey Marlow

A young boy who is hired to take the prince's whippings. He helps young Tom Canty adapt to his role as prince.

The Hermit

A mad old man who takes young Edward in and pretends to be kind to him; however, when he hears that Edward is the son of Henry VIII, the hermit is almost successful in killing the lad.

SUMMARIES AND COMMENTARIES

Chapter 1

Summary

The scene is London; the time is an autumn day, sometime between 1525 and 1550. On this particular day, two boys are born—Tom Canty and Edward Tudor. The Cantys are very poor and the baby is not wanted. The Tudors, on the other hand, are rich and powerful, and all of England celebrates the birth of this long-awaited child. There are bonfires, feasting, dancing, and parades which last throughout the day and on into the night. Edward Tudor lies in his crib in his silks and satins; Tom Canty lies in rags.

Commentary

The Prince and the Pauper is Twain's most carefully plotted novel, but unlike Twain's greater novels (such as *Huck Finn* and *Tom Sawyer*), where there is a great deal of character development, in this novel the characters are scarcely developed at all; instead, they are used largely as pawns to move the plot forward. Therefore, the main emphasis of the novel is not on character; it is on Twain's ingenious plot devices. In this first chapter, the plot begins with the birth of two boys—Tom Canty and Edward Tudor—on the same day in the same town: London, England. Twain immediately begins to contrast the two boys: one is very poor and unwanted, and the other is very rich and very much desired. As is typical of so many of Twain's novels (in particular, *Huck Finn* and *Tom Sawyer*), the main characters are young, innocent boys. Throughout the novel, Twain will continue the series of contrasts between the two boys which he sets in motion here.

Chapters 2 and 3

Summary

London is an ancient city; at the time of Twain's story, it is fifteen hundred years old and filled with a hundred thousand people—or maybe twice that number. The streets are narrow, crooked, and dirty, and in the part of town where the Cantys live, the streets are even more narrow, even more crooked, and are dirtier than most streets. The Cantys' house in Offal Court, out of Pudding Lane, is filled with the poorest of London's poor. The six members of the Canty family live in one room on the third floor of an old, decaying house. There is a bed for the parents, tucked in a corner, but "Tom, his grandmother, and his two sisters, Bet and Nan, were not restricted—they had all the floor to themselves, and might sleep where they chose." As a result, they sleep on some bundles of dirty hay which can be kicked back into a corner the following morning.

Tom Canty's father and grandmother are thieves and beggars—and are also often drunk and violent. They make the children beg, which the children do, but they will not steal. Life is hard; Pudding Lane and Offal Court are both drunken, brawling, riotous places, but young Tom Canty is largely unaware of how really bad his life is. He goes out in the morning and begs; if he returns empty-handed, he is roundly cursed, then beaten. Thus he begs enough to save himself from being beaten, but he spends most of his time listening to Father Andrew's old tales and legends. Father Andrew teaches Tom and his sisters "the right ways," and, in addition, he teaches Tom how to read and write and also some Latin. Father Andrew's tales fill Tom's mind and take away some of the pain of the beatings and hunger which the boy must endure, and they also feed Tom's desire to be clean—in body, mind, and spirit. For example, he sometimes pretends to be one of the princes in Father Andrew's tales, and he has come to gain a measure of stature among both the children and the adults who bring him their problems; they are quite often amazed by the wisdom with which he solves their troubles. Meanwhile, however, Tom harbors a deep, secret desire: to see a *real* prince.

One January day, Tom wanders through the city, aimlessly ambling farther and farther from home than ever before. Eventually, he finds himself outside the walls of London and on the Strand, where there is a scattering of the palaces of the rich. Aghast at what he sees, he walks into Charing Village, past the cardinal's palace and goes on toward Westminster, a vast building with colossal granite lions and other signs and symbols of English royalty. When he comes to the fence surrounding Westminster, he catches a glimpse of the sturdy, tanned, beautifully dressed Prince of Wales.

The noise of a soldier pulling Tom from the fence attracts the attention of the prince, who invites Tom into the royal grounds. The young prince takes Tom into a richly appointed apartment, treats him wonderfully, and feeds him all sorts of delicious treats. He asks many questions about Tom's life and is upset by what he hears, but he is fascinated by the races Tom tells him about and he is also interested in the other sports played in Offal Court. The prince is as curious about Tom's life as Tom is by what he has seen of the prince's life. Impulsively, the two boys decide to exchange clothing and they discover, afterward, how very much they look alike.

Discovering a bruise on Tom's hand, the prince dashes out to reprimand the guard, but Edward forgets that he is wearing Tom's rags and he is treated like an upstart and a beggar. Furthermore, he is immediately hustled off to London in the midst of a hooting and shouting crowd.

Commentary

Chapter 2 emphasizes the environment in which Tom Canty has been brought up. The name of the area—Offal Court—means "refuse" and "defecation" and is the home of London's most wretched and poor. In spite of his environment, however, Tom possesses a certain intelligence and sensitivity, and he attempts to escape from the miseries of his surroundings by unleashing his imagination and living in a world of fantasy, a world in which he pictures himself to be a part of the "charmed life of a petted prince in a regal palace." His dreams, in fact, cause him to try to be clean and to hope someday to be clothed in something other than the rags which he wears. This, of course, prepares us for the exchange he will later make with Edward, Prince of Wales. For example, in his dreams, Tom has imaginary Lord Chamberlains and other court officials to serve him, roles played by friends of his. This portends Chapter 32, "Coronation Day," a chapter which describes a procession in which Tom rides with a real Lord Chamberlain; as they pass Offal Court, Tom looks out and sees the boys who used to be his imaginary Lord Chamberlains. Small details such as this suggest the careful planning and plotting that went into the making of the novel. Likewise, in terms of the plot, Tom is taught by Father Andrew how to read and write Latin. This will later cause consternation among the officials of the court, since the real prince knows Latin, Greek, and French, while Tom Canty knows only Latin. Also in anticipation of later events in the novel, when Tom assumes the role of king, he is called upon to give advice to many people; already, we see that in this early chapter of the novel, because of his dreams and Father Andrew's moral tales, Tom is sought out by all sorts of people in Offal Court in order to give various types of advice which he is very successful at doing. Basically, then, Tom's dreams, his sensitivity, and his study of Latin all contribute toward making it somewhat feasible for him to be mistaken for a real prince.

In Chapter 3, it is Tom's dreaming which causes him to wander aimlessly through the city until he finds himself staring through a fence at a real, living prince. When Tom is abused by a soldier, the Prince of Wales rebukes the guard. Thus, our introduction to the Prince of Wales is through his protesting a simple injustice against a citizen of England. This prepares us for Edward Tudor's development into a good, humanitarian prince. In contrast to Tom Canty, whose dreams involve being a prince, the Prince of Wales dreams of the freedom to do all of the things that Tom does.

One of the main intellectual points of Twain's novel (and also a maxim that remained one of Twain's favorites throughout his career) is the notion that clothes do *not* determine a person's worth, his character, or his nature. As the Prince of Wales says to Tom, "Thou hast the same hair, the same eyes, the same voice and manner, the same form and stature, the same face and countenance that I bear. Fared we forth naked, there is none could say which was you and which the Prince of Wales." Consequently, for a joke, they exchange clothes.

In terms, then, of the plot, when the prince notices the bruise upon Tom's hand, he immediately goes out to rebuke the soldier. However, dressed as he is in the clothes of a pauper, he is mistaken for a pauper, reemphasizing Twain's point about the absurdity of evaluating a person merely by the nature of his clothes.

Also in terms of the plot, the prince, before leaving, quickly puts away "an article of national importance that lay upon the table." Plotwise, this insignificant action will ultimately become the means whereby the real prince is restored to his rightful position. Throughout the novel, this article—the Great Seal of England—is an item that plays an important role involving both Tom and the prince.

One line of narrative development that perhaps should be noted already is the fact that when the prince, dressed in rags, demands that he be treated as a prince and orders people to serve him, he is treated as a ruffian and as a knave. However, later in the novel, when he asserts himself less strongly, he is accorded better treatment. The prince utters the truth: "I am the Prince of Wales; my person is sacred; and thou shalt hang for laying thy hand upon me!"

Later on, Miles Hendon will consider such exclamations to be part of a "World of Dreams and Shadows."

Chapters 4 and 5

Summary

The prince is finally left alone by the rabble that has harried him into London, and he wanders aimlessly about, not knowing where he is until he comes to Christ's Hospital. There, he sees some children dressed as apprentices, playing in the yard. He talks to them and announces his claim that he is Edward, Prince of Wales; his actions at first amuse the boys, but then they begin to mock him. Angry and frustrated, he kicks one of the boys and threatens them all with the gallows, whereupon they beat him and set their dogs on him.

As night comes on, the bruised, battered, and muddied prince is confused and lost. However, he remembers Tom's story and begins to look for Offal Court. He also vows to provide learning for the children of Christ's Hospital, not just bread and shelter. Suddenly, John Canty collars him and drags him home—and again a crowd gathers to jeer as Edward claims to be the prince and demands to be taken immediately to the king. Everyone he has met outside the palace walls believes that he is mad—nothing more than a common beggar who has lost his wits.

Alone in his royal apartment, Tom awaits the prince's return. He admires his new finery in the mirror and practices a regal walk, saluting with his sword as he has seen one of the guards do. As he examines all of the ornaments in the apartment and seats himself in the soft chairs, he wonders what his friends would think of him now. Would they think him mad—or would they believe him? Then he suddenly begins to worry about the real prince's absence. He is also fearful about the terrible things that might happen to him if he is discovered. Might the nobles not, as he has heard, suddenly hang him? His fears rise, especially when the Lady Jane Grey enters, and he confesses that he is only Tom Canty of Offal Court; he begs that he might see the prince and get his rags back. When he continues to beg for mercy, she becomes frightened and flees. Tom then becomes more terrified than ever, and he is sure that the whole court will be upon him soon. However, word spreads throughout the palace that "the prince hath gone mad!" Quickly a royal proclamation forbids any mention of this, and all such talk stops immediately.

In the meantime, an entourage of nobles brings Tom to the king. Henry VIII, who is great and gross and sick, questions Tom about what has happened. When Tom realizes that he is standing before the king himself, he falls to his knees, believing that he is completely undone. The king acts as though Tom is Edward, however, and treats him kindly and with concern, thinking all the time that his son has gone mad.

Tom tries to tell the truth about his humble station, but his confessions only distress and confuse all who hear him and convince them that he is absolutely mad. His knowledge of Latin is proof enough for them that he *is* Edward, Prince of Wales, and this fact suggests the possibility that perhaps he may yet be cured.

Henry VIII orders that Edward be relieved of his studies so that he might have a better chance to recover. In addition, Henry insists that Edward be "installed in his princely dignity in due and ancient form" immediately, so as to forestall any questions about his madness. To achieve this, the king further orders that the Duke of Norfolk be "doomed" by morning. Tom tries to prevent this, but the king refuses to listen and sends Tom away. Tom feels trapped, as trapped as if he were shut up in a cage, and he feels terribly guilty about the impending death of the great Duke of Norfolk. He contrasts the pleasant pleasures of his dreams with the dreariness of this stark, fearful reality.

Commentary

These chapters, as a unit, present an obvious but rather interesting contrast. Chapter 4, for example, shows the prince dressed as a pauper confronting a cruel world that has no respect for him, and it ends with the prince being considered stark, raving mad. The following chapter presents the contrast of the pauper, Tom, in the role of the prince and, likewise, being considered mad—*royally* mad!

The prince's troubles in the real world are caused by the mere fact that he considers himself a prince, despite his being dressed as a pauper. The boys whom he approaches at Christ's Hospital treat him, at first, with laughter, until he insists the he *is* the prince; then he is treated with derision, and the more that he insists that he is the Prince of Wales, the more rude his treatment becomes until, ultimately, he is beaten, and dogs are set on him. The prince is finally discovered by John Canty, who believes the lad to be his own errant son, and even though old John considers his son to be mad, he still subjects him to a beating. Thus the real world that the Prince of Wales dreamed about is not at all like the world he imagined.

In contrast, Tom's dreams have all come true. He has, indeed, become a prince, a prince like the ones he dreamed about, but the reality of his situation is not nearly as pleasant as his dreams of old were. In particular, Tom is frightened that at any moment he will be discovered and punished for wearing the prince's royal clothing. Surprisingly, nothing that he does can convince the royal court that he is *not* the real prince, for he looks like the prince and he is dressed like the prince. And when the king asks Tom a question in Latin, Tom is able to respond to the question in Latin; this test proves that Tom is indeed the Prince of Wales; no pauper could possibly know Latin! Looking backward, we now see why Mark Twain had Father Andrew teach Tom some Latin. This "mad scene" is emphasized, satirically and ironically, by Twain because the heir to the throne of England is considered mad—and yet, in spite of his being "mad," it is decided that he must be installed as heir apparent immediately. In addition, Tom overhears that in order for him to be installed as heir apparent, the Duke of Norfolk must be put to death immediately. This injustice will soon be corrected, however, for as soon as Tom becomes King of England, his first act will be to countermand the order.

Chapters 6-9

Summary

Conducted into the principal apartment of the royal suite, Tom begins to receive instructions on the actions appropriate to a prince. In spite of his reluctance to sit while the great men of the realm are standing, he is told that it is fit and proper that they stand while he sits. When the Lord St. John requests a private audience with him, attended only by themselves and the Lord Hertford, Tom learns to make a gesture of dismissal.

The Lord St. John's message is brief and to the point: the king has commanded Edward to disguise all signs of his infirmity. He will cease to speak of his lowly birth, and he will make every effort to recover his former state of mind. Tom resignedly acquiesces.

He is then "reminded" of the city banquet that he is to attend, and at that moment the Lady Elizabeth (also called the Princess Elizabeth) and the Lady Jane Grey enter. The Lord St. John reminds Tom in a whisper to remember the king's command. Although Tom agrees, he almost breaks his pose while conversing with the two ladies. Several times, the tact of the Lady Elizabeth saves him, and several times the Lord St. John intercepts a difficult question and answers for him. Only once does Tom totally lose control and speak of his real father. He quickly catches himself, however, and apologizes. The two ladies finally leave and the Lord Guilford Dudley is announced; shortly, the Lord St. John and the Lord Hertford advise Tom to excuse himself, which he does, and is conducted into an inner apartment by Sir William Herbert, where Tom quickly learns that his every need will be handled by a servant. It seems that it is believed that he can do nothing at all for himself.

Once Tom is gone, the Lord St. John and the Lord Hertford discuss the matter of the prince's madness. The Lord St. John advances the possibility that the boy might not be Edward; Hertford scolds him for such thoughts but, nevertheless, after the Lord St. John leaves, the Lord Hertford considers the possibility that perhaps the lad is *not* the prince. Yet he finally sighs and declares, "Tush, he *must* be the prince! Will any he in all the land maintain there can be two, not of one blood and birth, so marvelously twinned? And even were it so, 'twere yet a stranger miracle that chance should cast the one into the other's place. Nay, 'tis folly, folly, folly!"

At noontime, Tom suffers through "the ordeal of being dressed for dinner." He is then conducted to the dining room, a room of ornate, stately grandeur. There, everything is done for him: a chaplain says grace for him; an earl fastens a napkin around his neck, and an official "taster" tastes everything before Tom tastes it—making sure that the food is not poisoned. This confuses Tom; why not use "a dog or a plumber," he wonders; but he concludes that "all the ways of royalty are strange." There are still other persons present to wait upon Tom, as he soon discovers, and among those whom Tom identifies are the Lord Chief Butler, the Lord Great Steward, and the Lord Head Cook. He also discovers to his amazement that he has three hundred and eighty-four *additional* servants to wait on him.

Everyone present in the dining room has been alerted that the prince is somewhat mad and that any strange behavior is to be ignored. Therefore, when Tom commits a blunder of dining etiquette, his attendants, rather than snicker, are most compassionate and ignore what seem to be "coarse" manners. Tom—because he knows of no other way—eats with his fingers, refuses to use the dainty napkin he is given, lest it become soiled, and inquires about the nature of such food as turnips and lettuce, both curiosities to him.

When dinner is finished, Tom fills his pockets with nuts and is about to leave when his nose begins to itch. Tom wonders momentarily if there might be an official "Nose Scratcher"; fearing that there might indeed be such a personage, he is afraid to scratch his nose, in spite of his discomfort.

When an elaborate finger bowl is presented to him, he takes it, drinks from it, and comments, "It hath a pretty flavor, but it wanteth strength." The servants grieve silently for their master's troubled mind. Meanwhile, Tom makes other unconscious blunders, then returns to his apartment, where he is finally left alone. Perusing the room, he finds some inviting books in a closet and among them is one about the etiquette of the English court. This is a prize, and he quickly curls up to read it.

Henry VIII awakens from a troublesome nap and is informed that the Lord Chancellor is waiting to see him. The Lord Chancellor's message is that, according to the king's command, the peers of the realm have agreed to the Duke of Norfolk's doom and now they await further instructions. The king would like to appear before them himself, but a sudden stab of pain forces him to reconsider. Nevertheless, he will put his seal upon the orders so that the Duke of Norfolk will be dead before another day is past.

There is a problem, however. No one can find the Great Seal of England. The Lord Hertford recalls that it had been given to the Prince of Wales, and he is immediately sent to fetch it. Unfortunately, since Tom has no idea of *what* it is, he thus doesn't know *where* it is. The king says not to trouble the poor mad child and dozes off. When he awakens, he discovers that the Lord Chancellor is still there; he tells him angrily to take care of the matter of the Duke of

Norfolk. To the Lord Chancellor's reply that he is still waiting for the Great Seal, Henry impatiently tells him to use the small Seal and not to return—until he brings him the head of the Duke of Norfolk.

At nine that evening, Tom goes into London to dine so that the city can see that he is not mad. The splendor he sees is absolutely magnificent. Great and richly decorated barges carry the royal entourage from Westminster, and the entire company—a troop of halberdiers, officers, knights, judges, and other dignitaries (English and foreign)—precedes the splendidly clothed Tom Canty, a young boy far more "familiar with rags and dirt and misery" than with all this ornate pageantry.

Commentary

These four chapters present Tom's rather traumatic adjustment to his sudden role as the Prince of Wales. All of his many blunders, however, are accounted for by the fact that he is believed to be mad. Furthermore, no one is to mention the fact that he is mad, but, nonetheless, the rumor spreads quickly and so far that even old Blake Andrews (in Chapter 27) mentions to Miles Hendon and to the true Prince of Wales that "the king is mad . . . [but] 'tis death to speak of it."

Twain, it should be pointed out, adheres to a certain degree of historical accuracy by having Edward's companions be the Lady (or the Princess) Elizabeth (later Queen Elizabeth I) and also the Lady Jane Grey. Both of these ladies help Tom through difficult situations—Elizabeth, in particular, being quick to note and make amends for Tom's blunders.

The fact that Twain emphasized in the first chapter that Tom Canty was a quick learner is illustrated again in Chapter 6, as Tom is able to learn his new role rather quickly; soon there are fewer and fewer "snags and sandbars," as Tom grows more and more at ease in his new surroundings.

Chapter 7 deals essentially with the various types of blunders that Tom, quite naturally, makes during his first day as prince and especially during his first "royal dinner." He does not know what a napkin is, for example, and has it sent away, fearing that he might soil it. In addition, he drinks from the finger bowl, and he evinces a growing distress with all of the servants who surround him. At the end of the meal, he greedily fills his pockets with nuts from the table. But it is not until the end of the novel that we discover that he uses the Great Seal of England to crack these nuts. In fact, he discovers the Great Seal because, in his daydreams of being a prince, he always wanted to wear a suit of armor. Here, Twain mentions "the greaves, the gauntlets, the plumed helmet" and other such pieces of armor, and it is while Tom is trying on these pieces that he finds the Great Seal.

Tom's ability to read and to learn quickly allows him to read the etiquette book about the English court and, by this means, he instructs himself on how to act in some of the situations which he will soon encounter.

In Chapter 8, the subject of the Great Seal of England is expanded upon. It is made clear that only the *true* Prince of Wales knows where this Great Seal is, and it is needed in order to make official the order commanding the Duke of Norfolk's death. Consquently, Tom's ignorance that his "nutcracker" is, in reality, the Great Seal temporarily delays Norfolk's death—a matter which Tom strongly objects to, anyway.

The main purpose of Chapter 9 seemingly has little to do with the plot of the novel; instead, it is a kind of "time out," during which Twain details the richness and pageantry of the royal court of England. In describing this scene, Twain strives for historical accuracy, and also he quotes from various sources that deal with precisely the kinds of actions that Tom must perform in an attempt to dispel the rampant rumors of his madness.

Chapters 10 and 11

Summary

"We left John Canty dragging the rightful prince into Offal Court, with a noisy and delighted mob at his heels." Twain aims for our compassion as the true prince struggles to get free, all the while raging against the cruel treatment by Tom Canty's father. The old man is ready to use his cudgel against the child when someone in the crowd stays Canty's hand. Canty is not to be stopped, however, and he delivers a severe blow to the bystander's head. The wounded man sinks to the ground, and the mob passes on. Finally they all arrive at Canty's den, and the prince sees Tom's mother and sisters—"animals habituated to harsh usage"; Tom's grandmother looks like "a withered hag with streaming grey hair and malignant eyes."

Prodded by Canty, the prince proclaims himself to be Edward, Prince of Wales. Tom's mother rushes to him, convinced that he is mad, and the prince tells her again that he is not her son: his father is King of England, whereupon she can do nothing but wail brokenheartedly. Tom's sister pleads with her father to be gentle with the boy, saying that rest will heal his madness. Canty, however, asks what the boy has managed to beg that day, and when the prince dismisses such "sordid matters," Canty and Tom's grandmother thoroughly beat him and send him to bed.

In the darkness, Tom's mother ponders what she has heard and the differences between her son and this mad boy: is he *really* her son? At last, she devises a test: Tom Canty habitually covers his eyes with his hands, palms outward, when confronted with sudden bright lights or noises. Thus she thrusts her candle into the prince's face and thumps loudly on the floor; the boy is startled, but he makes no gesture with his hands. She soothes the prince back to sleep, but she is left more confused than ever.

Just after the prince awakens, drowsily calling for his groom, the family hears several sharp raps on the door. They are informed that it was Father Andrew whom Canty struck in the crowd and, furthermore, that Father Andrew is now dying. Canty gathers the family together and hurries them out of the house and toward Southwark. The Canty family, however, is separated when they are caught up in the midst of revelers celebrating the Prince of Wale's procession into London. Canty, meanwhile, keeps his "son" in his grip until he is persuaded by a waterman to take a ceremonial drink with him. This requires Canty to use both hands, and Edward dives into the sea of legs and disappears.

Trying to get as far from John Canty as possible, Edward realizes that the young boy he exchanged clothes with has taken his place in the castle. He concludes that Tom Canty "had deliberately taken advantage of stupendous opportunity and become a usurper." He therefore determines that he will make his way to the Guildhall and announce himself. He also decides that the usurper will be "hanged, drawn, and quartered."

Meanwhile, the royal barge makes its way down the Thames River. There is music in the air, bonfires light the sky, artillery booms forth, and the crowd cheers loudly. For Tom, the pageantry is astonishing and wonderful, but to his two companions, the Princess Elizabeth and the Lady Jane Grey, it is commonplace.

Finally the barge docks, and Tom and his entourage walk to the Guildhall. There, too, the spectacle is grand and colorful, and Tom is seated at the highest table, while the guests, all richly dressed, are seated at lower tables, depending on their royal degree. After prayer and grace is given, Tom and the Princess Elizabeth drink from a large golden loving cup, which is then passed down the table, and the banquet begins.

Tom watches the dancing while the real prince stands at the gates of the Guildhall, proclaiming himself to be the Prince of Wales and demanding that he be admitted. The crowd taunts him and mocks him, and he defies all those who revile him. A man who identifies himself as Miles Hendon, and whose clothes have seen better days, takes up the prince's cause. And it is well that he does, for had he not done so, the crowd would have beaten the poor prince. Hendon's sword gives the two breathing room for awhile, but matters continue to look grim until a king's messenger and his troops scatter the mob. Hendon then grabs the prince and takes him away from the danger.

In the Guildhall, a messenger proclaims that the king is dead; this news shocks the crowd into momentary silence. In the next moment, however, they stretch their arms toward Tom and shout, "Long live the king!" Tom is confused, but he suddenly realizes something momentous; turning to the Lord Hertford, he asks if his word is now law—if it is true that whatever he commands must be carried out. Assured that this is so, Tom proclaims, "Then shall the king's law be a law of mercy, from this day, and never more be a law of blood! . . . To the Tower and say the king decrees the Duke of Norfolk shall not die!"

Commentary

In contrast to the pauper, who was described at length as he tried to adjust to the role of being a prince, attention is now shifted to the trials and tribulations which the Prince of Wales encounters as a common citizen. Interestingly, in a later chapter we will hear the prince express the concept that all kings should be forced to live the life of a common citizen in order to understand the problems that the common man faces. For the present, however, the first thing that the young prince learns, as a commoner, concerns the absolute brutality of life itself. Having shifted from living a life of luxury, with over three hundred servants to wait on him, the prince now finds that the life of a pauper offers a fearsome contrast. Furthermore, Twain underscores the contrast in life-styles by elaborately detailing the royal pageantry described in Chapter 9, with all of its sumptuous luxury, and then starkly focusing on John Canty, dragging the prince through Offal Court.

The existence of the prince is compared to that of an animal, and whereas Tom Canty himself is considered mad, the real prince is likewise considered to be mad. Tom's mother, for example, thinks that her son has read so much that this "foolish reading hath . . . taken [his] wit away." The father, John Canty, also considers his son to be too much involved in "fine mummeries" and "foolery." Here, Twain is emphasizing the central contrast between the prince and the pauper: Tom Canty is believed to be the mad Prince of Wales; yet, because he is believed to be mad, he is coddled and protected and given every possible consideration. On the other hand, the Prince of Wales, believed to be a pauper, is treated brutally by his "father" and "grandmother" and receives no sympathy whatsoever.

In terms of Twain's plotting, we learn in Chapter 10 that Tom's mother devises a test whereby she thinks that she can discern whether or not this young lad is truly her son or not. The test involves an automatic reflex that Tom Canty always does when he encounters something unexpected. Yet after three trials by Mrs. Canty, the woman is not convinced of anything certain, and she still questions whether or not the boy is really her son. In Chapter 31, when Tom Canty is on his way to be crowned king and the procession passes Offal Court, he sees his mother unexpectedly in the crowd and "up flew his hand, palm outward, before his eyes—that old involuntary gesture, born of a forgotten episode, and perpetrated by habit."

The test that Tom's mother performs should be contrasted with the suspicion that both the Lord St. John and the Lord Hertford have concerning the true identity of the Prince of Wales. Twain's point is clear: despite even a slight difference in the character and personality of a person, his clothes ultimately determine his status as an individual; unfortunately, a pauper is a pauper because he wears a pauper's *clothes*, and a prince is a prince merely because he wears a prince's *clothes.*

Likewise, in terms of Twain's plot devices, it should be noted that John Canty accidentally strikes a stranger in the mob; the stranger turns out to be old Father Andrew, now dying. The death of Father Andrew makes it imperative for the Cantys to flee and makes it impossible, therefore, for the real Tom Canty to know where his family is. In particular, the ease with which the Cantys are able to leave Offal Court is contrasted with the pomp and circumstance of the royal court and the virtual "imprisonment" that Tom Canty finds himself in as Prince of Wales.

Another major plot element involves the prince's escape from John Canty. The loving cup, the one offered to John Canty, has to be held with both hands, or else the tradition is not considered to be an honorable one. Thus, when John Canty takes the loving cup in both hands, it allows the prince to escape. The prince's intentions are, of course, to return to court and make himself known. He is furious and vows to use his royal prerogative to see to it that Tom Canty is "hanged, drawn, and quartered." However, after the Prince of Wales has lived as a commoner for a time and is finally restored to his rightful kingship, his many and varied experiences as a pauper will have taught him great compassion and tolerance.

In Chapter 11, note the magnificence of the royal barge procession, the rich clothing, and the luxurious pillows on which Tom and his companions recline while they view the pageantry; all of this provides an effective contrast with the conditions that the real prince experienced in Chapter 10. The pageantry of royalty is a constant preoccupation of Twain's; he glories in describing its magnificence, but, at the same time, he mocks this great show of ceremony in several ways later in the novel.

The motif of the loving cup also appears in Chapter 11, when Tom and Elizabeth drink from one at the royal feast. This time, however, both of them are willing to drink (unlike Canty and the insistent waterman), and the mood here is celebratory. Indeed, this ceremony is followed by still further pageantry and by festive dancing by the court nobles.

It is somewhat ironic that in the midst of this celebration, feting the health and well-being of the Prince of Wales, the *real* Prince of

Wales is outside the gates demanding entrance and, as a result, is very nearly beaten for his seeming foolishness and arrogance. It is also ironic that the news of the king's death is announced in the midst of all this festive celebration, for note that as soon as Tom Canty learns that the king is dead, he wonders whether it is true that if *he* gives a command, it will be obeyed. Assured that his word is indeed law, his first decree is that "the Duke of Norfolk shall not die." Thus the pauper, acting as the new King of England, performs the first in a series of humanitarian acts and establishes a reign of decency and mercy and justice, qualities that should, of course, be found in any king. A great cheer greets the end of the reign of blood (during which Henry VIII killed approximately 60,000 people and imprisoned 70,000 more—for religious reasons).

Chapter 11 also introduces Miles Hendon, a good example of the best of English common sense and common "nobility," even though his *clothing* has seen better days and belies his true nature. Hendon is immediately attracted to the Prince of Wales—not because he is a prince but because Hendon is able to see that despite the outward facade of pauper's clothes, the young boy has true nobility of character. Throughout the rest of the novel, Miles Hendon never really believes that the lad is the true prince, but nonetheless he seeks ways to help the lad recover from his "delusions," and he remains a loyal friend to him.

Chapters 12 and 13

Summary

As Miles Hendon takes Edward away from the Guildhall and toward London Bridge, they move quickly through the streets, the prince feeling the loss of his father keenly. Tears come to his eyes, especially when the crowd yells, "Long live King Edward the Sixth." Despite his sorrow, however, Edward is thrilled that—despite everything—he is now King of England.

London Bridge is a village unto itself, packed with shops and family dwellings above them; in short, it is a place where people live their entire lives, and Hendon's lodgings are in a small inn on this bridge. Before they reach these lodgings, however, Hendon and Edward are stopped by John Canty, who reaches out for the prince and threatens to beat him for escaping. Hendon again intercedes, threatening Canty with his sword, and Canty slinks away, "muttering threats and curses."

In Hendon's apartment, the prince falls asleep on the bed immediately, leaving orders to be awakened when food arrives. Hendon is amused by the boy's actions—which are, however, truly in character with his claim to be Prince of Wales. Already, Hendon has become fond of the boy, and he resolves to humor him and care for him, even if it means acting as the boy's "retainer."

The prince is awakened by the noise of someone departing after food has been brought in, and he expects to be waited on—with water, so that he can wash himself and with a towel so that he can dry himself. In addition, the prince reprimands Hendon for sitting, while in the prince's presence. Hendon humors the boy without a word, although he is silently amused.

Refreshed by the food and drink, Edward asks Hendon for his story. Hendon tells the prince that he is the middle son of a baronet in Kent. His older brother is gentle and generous, but his younger brother is a mean and vicious rascal. Although his older brother, Arthur, has been betrothed to the Lady Edith since childhood, he loves another. Miles Hendon himself is in love with Edith, and she with him, and Arthur has assured them that things will work out satisfactorily. However, the younger brother, Hugh, wants to marry Edith for her fortune. To get his way, Hugh conspired against Miles and managed to have him banished. While fighting in a war on the Continent, Miles was captured and lay in a dungeon for seven years. He escaped only a short time before and is now on his way home to Kent.

The prince proclaims that he will set matters right. Then he tells Hendon about his own adventures. Although the prince has clearly accepted Hendon's story as truth, Hendon cannot do the same for the prince's story, yet he renews his resolve to protect the boy and, hopefully, help him regain his sanity.

The prince then says that Hendon deserves some reward for the service he has rendered. Even though he is startled by such news, and even though he does not believe that the prince is really the Prince of Wales, Hendon thinks carefully about the matter. Finally, he requests that he and his heirs have the right to sit in the presence of the king. Edward grants this request, naming Hendon as henceforth "Sir Miles Hendon, Knight." Hendon cannot believe what he hears; he tells himself that he is, alas, a "knight of the Kingdom of Dreams and Shadows." Nonetheless, he is content.

The prince suddenly feels extremely sleepy, and he orders Hendon, as though Hendon were his valet, to remove the rags he is wearing. Hendon strips the boy; then the prince notices Hendon's obvious perplexity about where he is to sleep. Edward tells his "knight" that he can sleep "athwart the door." Hendon does so, without complaint, and falls asleep near dawn.

Waking up near noon, Hendon measures the still-sleeping prince and sets out to buy better clothing for the boy. Gone less than an hour, Hendon returns and begins to mend the secondhand clothes he has bought. As he works, he sings and muses upon all that has happened. All this time, he has taken care not to awaken the prince.

When he finally does go to rouse the prince, he discovers to his amazement that the boy is gone. He accosts a servant, who tells him that another boy came for the prince and took him toward the Southwark area of the bridge. They were joined by a man who looked like a ruffian, and the three of them continued on toward Southwark. Hendon realizes that the man is no doubt the very one who stopped them the night before—John Canty—and he plunges out of the inn, resolved to scour the countryside until he finds the boy once again.

Commentary

In Chapter 12, when the Prince of Wales hears the cry, "Long live Edward the Sixth," he is immediately filled with immense grief for the death of his father and, at the same time, he is thrilled with immense pride at now being King of England, even though he is treated as a mere pauper. Edward's view of his father as a kind and loving person contrasts, of course, with the views of others in the story; Henry VIII had, for example, inspired great fear in the Lord Chancellor in Chapter 8, and he has been responsible for the deaths and imprisonments of tens of thousands of English citizens.

In this section of the novel, Twain interrupts the narrative flow of the novel in order to give a historical description of the famous London Bridge, largely so that he can create a sense of historical accuracy for his novel. Then he resumes his story, and we learn that while on the bridge, Hendon and Edward encounter John Canty, a pattern which occurs often throughout the novel: Hendon will lose the prince to Canty and then regain him. Miles Hendon's admiration for the boy increases as a result of the plucky courage which Edward exhibits when he confronts the threats and curses which John Canty hurls at him.

In this particular scene and throughout the novel, Miles Hendon's response to the prince is more like the royal court's response to Tom than like the rabble's response to the prince. Hendon seems genuinely concerned for the boy's well-being, and he is determined to protect him and do everything necessary to help the boy be cured of his madness. Thus, Hendon again and again demonstrates for us his true nobility of spirit.

But in spite of his admiration for the young boy's spirit and his recognition of the prince's essential "nobility," Miles Hendon is unable to accept in any way the prince's tale of his past adventures. This, of course, contrasts with the prince's ready and swift acceptance of Hendon's adventures and family difficulties. The prince's response to Hendon's story also demonstrates his quickness in promising to right all wrongs and his willingness to reward Hendon's service and loyalty. These characteristics which are displayed by the prince are clearly parallel to similar circumstances and characteristics shown by Tom Canty when he pardons the Duke of Norfolk.

Miles Hendon's request to Edward, when he is given the opportunity, is a very practical one. Foreseeing that he will be required to—literally—stand a great deal if he continues his association with this boy, Hendon simply asks for permission to "sit" in the presence of the "king." Once this favor is granted, Hendon is allowed far more rest than he would have otherwise have had; also of note, here, it is important that in the novel's last chapter, as a test to determine whether or not the person on the throne of England is indeed the little waif whom Hendon rescued so often, Hendon makes reference to this permission to "sit" in the king's presence.

Chapter 13 is primarily devoted to reestablishing the next steps of Twain's plot—that is, it establishes that the prince is gone, recaptured by John Canty apparently, and it also establishes Hendon's firm decision to follow the boy and recapture him. One other important feature of this chapter is the irony of Hendon's statement that he makes about the Prince of Wales. Hendon says, "Dear heart, he should have been born a king!" Little does he know that the boy asleep on the bed is indeed the true King of England. It is no wonder, therefore, to us, that Edward "playeth the part to a marvel."

Chapters 14-16

Summary

Near dawn, on the same morning as the prince's disappearance, Tom Canty awakens in his royal bed. After a few moments of confusion, he calls for his sisters to come to him so that he can tell them about his strange dream. The person who comes to Tom, however, is a stranger and asks what Tom's "commands" are, reminding him that he is Edward, King of England. This greatly upsets Tom, but he manages to go back to sleep and to dream a pleasant dream about a dwarf who shows him where to dig for twelve pennies every week, enough to satisfy his father and still have some left over to give to the priest and to his mother.

In the midst of Tom's dream, he is awakened and must submit to the process of being dressed, with each item of clothing passed from one person to the next in a long line of serving men. Once dressed, he is then officially washed and dried and given over to the Hairdresser-royal. He is allowed to eat, and he is then taken into the throne room, with much ceremony and with many officers and other functionaries attending him. There, he must hear and approve many tedious reports, assisted by his "uncle," the Lord Hertford. When he learns that the king is to be buried later in the coming month, he is surprised and wonders if the body will "keep." When he learns of the expenses of the royal household for the past six months and of the fact that most of it has not been paid, he bursts out, "We be going to the dogs, 'tis plain." He then begins to outline means of economizing (taking a smaller house, releasing servants, and so forth), but he is brought up short by pressure on his arm from the Lord Hertford. The assembled company seems to notice nothing, and as business continues, Tom learns that the king made a provision in his will to raise the Lord Hertford to the ducal degree and to raise Sir Thomas Seymour, his brother, to the peerage, and that both grants were accompanied by grants of money. He is about to blurt out something about the propriety of paying the late king's debts, but a touch from his advisor saves him from such indiscretions. Finally, all of this business of state so wearies Tom that he falls asleep, letting the business of the kingdom come to a standstill for the moment.

Later that morning, Tom spends an enjoyable hour with the Lady Elizabeth and the Lady Jane Grey, and he also has a brief and unpleasant interview with his older "sister," later known as "Bloody Mary."

After these young women have left, a boy of about twelve is shown in. This boy is Humphrey Marlow, the royal "whipping-boy." It takes Tom some time to figure out that Humphrey is actually paid money to take the punishment that would be meted out to the prince. In his talk with Humphrey, Tom shows signs of realizing what is expected of him, as he leads Humphrey to believe that he is helping the prince regain his memory.

Humphrey has two requests. The first is that Tom will intercede so that the punishment that is to be meted out to him on this day be annulled; Tom grants this request quickly. Humphrey's second request is that he not be turned away, now that the prince is King of England and will no longer need a whipping-boy. Being a whipping-boy is Humphrey's only means of support for himself and his sisters, he explains, so Tom makes him and his heirs "Hereditary Grand Whipping-Boy to the royal house of England!"

Once these requests are granted, Tom keeps Humphrey with him, encouraging him to talk with him. As he does so, Humphrey notices that Tom's memory has "improved" markedly after he has had several incidents "recalled" for him. Tom, in turn, resolves to visit with Humphrey as frequently as possible.

After Humphrey leaves, the Lord Hertford enters to tell Tom that the Council has decided that Tom should eat in public so as to dispel all rumors of his madness, and in the course of "reminding" Tom of what is expected of him, Hertford discovers that Tom's memory has "much improved." The Lord Hertford is encouraged, therefore, and he tries other areas; here, too, Tom's earlier conversation with Humphrey stands him in good stead. When Hertford asks about the Great Seal, however, Tom asks what it looks like. Hertford takes this as a sign that the prince's wits "are flown again" and, rather than answering the question, he begins speaking of other matters, diverting Tom's attention from the Great Seal.

On the following day, the foreign ambassadors come to pay their respects to the new king. The scene is splendid and Tom enjoys the ceremony, but eventually it becomes tedious and wearies him. As far as he is concerned, the day has been wasted—except for the hour he spent with his whipping-boy; during that hour, he gained enjoyment and information, and he was not constrained by ceremonial rituals.

Tom's third day at court is very much like the second, except that he is becoming more accustomed to all the pageantry and ceremony. Even though he often wishes to be back on the streets in familiar surroundings, there are times when he forgets these things and enjoys his present circumstances. Tom's fourth day would perhaps have seen further adjustment to his station, but the matter of the approaching dinner and the fact that he must eat in public is distressing. Tom's apprehension leaves him "low-spirited and absent-minded," and his "sense of captivity" weighs heavily upon him.

While in this mood, Tom wanders to a window to look out and get some sense of the freedom of those who are not confined within the palace walls. He becomes interested in a "hooting and shouting mob" approaching. He gives orders for someone to find out what this is all about, and word is brought back that the mob is following a man, a woman, and a girl who are about to be executed for their crimes.

Filled with pity for these poor people and never thinking about the laws they might have broken, Tom orders them to be brought before him so that he might find out more about them and their crimes. When he does, he sees that his commands are instantly carried out. He marvels at the absolute power he has.

The three doomed people are brought before him, and Tom recognizes the man, after a moment's thought, as the man who saved one of Tom's comrades on New Year's Day. Tom's first question is whether or not the crime the man is accused of has been "proven upon him." When assured that it has, Tom sighs and is about to send the man to his doom when the man unexpectedly asks a boon—that he be hanged for his crime. When Tom asks why he wishes this as his boon, the man tells him that "it is ordered that I be *boiled alive*!" Tom is horrified by this order, and when he is told that such is indeed the law of the land, he demands that the law be changed immediately.

After learning of the punishment that was to be inflicted upon the man, Tom inquires more closely into the crime that the fellow allegedly committed. Tom is told that the man entered the house of a sick man in Islington; within an hour after the man left, the man who was ill died in a manner that the doctors believe could only have been caused by poison. Furthermore, Tom is told that the entire crime had been foretold. At this point, the prisoner claims that at the time he was supposed to be killing the man, he was actually saving a life. Hearing this, Tom asks when the so-called crime took place. Learning that it supposedly took place on New Year's Day, the very time when the man was saving Tom's comrade's life, Tom declares that the man should be freed, and he says, "It enrageth me that a man be hanged upon such idle, hare-brained evidence!"

His questioning of the man, of the sheriff, and his decisive action in the case, bring forth admiration from all those in the audience. Indeed, there are those who feel that if Tom is "mad," it is certainly an improvement on the normal state of affairs.

Next, the woman and the young girl (her daughter) are brought before Tom; they are accused of having sold their souls to the devil and of bringing down a storm that laid waste to the entire region around them. This "crime" has been proven, it is charged, by people who saw them going into a ruined church and by others who experienced the storm. Tom's first question is whether or not the woman also suffered from the storm; when told that her home was swept away, Tom comments that this suggests that perhaps she is mad and did not know what she was doing; therefore, she could not be guilty.

When Tom asks how the woman is supposed to conjure up such storms, he is told that she does so by "taking off her stockings." He then tells her that he would like to "see a storm." He says that if she conjures up a storm for him, he will let her and her daughter go free. The woman pleads with him, telling him that she would raise the storm to save her daughter, but she cannot. Tom accepts her story and he gives them both a full pardon.

The experiences of the morning boost Tom's self-confidence so thoroughly that he finds that he no longer dreads the state dinner which he must attend. He is beginning to adjust to his new role, and he is doing so very admirably.

The royal dinner, like all things involving the king, is splendid and picturesque. Twain describes the costumes as all being magnificent, and the movements of all—servants and nobility alike—are all carefully orchestrated. Tom, for his part, "bore himself right gracefully, and all the more so because he was not thinking of how he was doing it, his mind being charmed and occupied with the blithe sights and sounds about him."

He eats with not the least embarrassment during the dinner, even though he is conscious that all eyes are upon him. He makes sure that he does nothing for himself; he lets the servants all wait on him, and he is particularly careful to take his time doing everything expected of him. As a result, he feels triumphant. He could, he thinks, endure this several times a day if he could avoid certain other requirements of his office.

Commentary

Chapter 14 again focuses on Tom Canty, the pauper who has been suddenly thrust into the role of a prince. As Edward Tudor did, while he was awakening in the hovel occupied by the Canty family, Tom awakens and calls for familiar people, especially his sisters. This scene reflects the difference between dreams and reality, a motif that frequently appears in the novel. In all cases, the dreams are wonderful, and the experiences on awakening to reality are depressing and frightening. Once, Tom Canty dreamed of being a prince; now, after he has seen what it is like to actually *be* a prince, he dreams of being back with his own family, even though he would have to endure the dismal conditions under which they live.

When Tom is finally awakened to begin the day, the process of dressing takes up a good deal of time. Undoubtedly, this process was lengthy enough in real life, but Twain has added as many retainers as he could and has lengthened the process even more to satirize all the pomp and circumstance involved. Unlike the pageantry of the river trip into the city, which allowed the citizens a chance to see their prince and to find some reason to celebrate, the "pageantry" of dressing is useless and unproductive, in Twain's eyes.

Once again, the difference between the way the prince is treated as a commoner and the way the pauper is treated as a prince is contrasted. Both are believed to be mad, but whereas the prince is laughed at, scorned, and beaten for the "errors" he makes in his "madness," Tom is given every consideration; everyone at court is willing to overlook all his mistakes and to help him regain his sanity. As noted before, Tom learns quickly, and it does not take him long to learn to use his madness as a tool so that he can find out the things that he needs to know. For example, in his conversation with his whipping-boy, Tom decides to use his "loss of memory" as an aid in gaining information; he says, " 'Tis strange how my memory doth wanton with me these days. . . . But mind it not—I mend apace—a little clew doth often serve to bring me back again the things and names which had escaped me." The thought of helping his king regain his memory thrills Humphrey and gives him an added incentive to continue talking with Tom.

The institution of the whipping-boy interests us almost immediately. The doctrine, of course, is that the prince, a son of the king, is sacred; death is the reward for anyone who so much as touches this sacred person. Thus, any punishment due the prince is meted out to his stand-in—the whipping-boy. Note throughout the novel that the prince threatens many people with death simply for laying a hand on him. Humphrey accepts the beatings that he takes in the prince's stead with some pride. Although the beatings undoubtedly are painful, he is useful to his prince; more important, these beatings are the means by which he supports himself and his two sisters. Considering the beatings that Tom received in Offal Court, Humphrey's life cannot be worse than that; indeed, it is better in many ways than the life Tom is used to. Nevertheless, Tom is horrified by the thought of someone *voluntarily* taking a beating. Like the prince, Tom is willing to prevent cruelty and to reward service and need; as the prince made Hendon a knight, so Tom makes Humphrey Marlow "Hereditary Grand Whipping-Boy to the royal house of England."

The theme of Tom's fascination with pageantry, mingled with the tedium of the ritual performance of duty, appears again in Chapter 14: "The splendors of the scene delighted his [Tom's] eye and fired his imagination, at first, but the audience was long and dreary, and so were most of the addresses; wherefore, what began as a pleasure, grew into weariness and homesickness by and by." Nevertheless, as Tom learns more and more of what he is expected to do and say, he becomes more comfortable in this new role. Indeed, one of the contrasts in this novel is the way that Tom moves easily into his new role of being a prince, while the true prince resists any suggestion that he adapt to the life that he finds himself in. Of course, Tom's new life is far more pleasant—even with the tedium of all of the royal ritual—than the prince's new life is. Tom, therefore, has far more incentive to adapt, while the prince has far more incentive to try and fight his way back to his rightful position.

Tom's quick wit and native intelligence, as well as his humanity and decency, are clearly in evidence in this chapter—especially when his curiosity and desire for a diversion lead him to inquire about the nature of the mob and to have the prisoners brought before him. Tom, like Huck Finn in one of Twain's later novels, responds to the innate goodness of the prisoners and is offended by the harsh injustice of the country's laws. Consequently, Tom is creating a superb reputation for himself as the King of England. The people who have heard rumors that the king is mad begin to wonder: if this be madness, what indeed is sanity?

In Chapter 16, because of Tom's success in dispensing law and dealing with prisoners and diplomats, he gains enough confidence in his own judgments that he feels that he can now go to the state dinner with much more assurance and ease. The chapter also provides another "history lesson" in its description of the pageantry of the state dinner. Twain was obviously well-read in the history of this period and his knowledge is quite apparent in the abundant descriptions of historical details.

Chapters 17-22

Summary

Miles Hendon follows the tracks of the persons he is seeking part of the way through Southwark, but there all traces end. He returns to his lodgings, therefore, to rest so that he can scour the town thoroughly the next day. As he lies in bed, he decides that the prince is likely to have headed toward Hendon Hall, and he resolves to go that way, looking carefully along the way.

In the meantime, the boy who came to fetch the prince leads him through Southwark and onto the road beyond; the ruffian, the fellow who had seemed ready to join them, follows at a distance. When the prince balks at going any farther, he is told that a friend of his lies wounded in a wood ahead, news which speeds him on. He is brought to a decaying barn and the ruffian, who is actually John Canty in disguise, takes charge, making it clear that the prince is once again his prisoner.

While Canty and Hugo, the youth who brought the prince to the barn, confer, the prince withdraws to a pile of hay at the far end of the barn and falls asleep after crying over the death of his father, whom the prince loved very much. As he sleeps, the rest of the vagabonds—a grim and motley group of society's outcasts—come into the barn. Eventually their rowdiness awakens the prince, and he realizes that they have feasted and drunk a good deal. He listens as "John Hobbs," the name John Canty is now using, is brought up to date about the lives of the comrades he once had in this group before he went to live in London. Although he remains quiet, the prince is attentive and serious as he listens to the tales and hears of the ways that the laws of the land affect these people. For example, he hears about a farmer who was turned from his place, reduced to beggary, lashed through three towns, had his wife and children killed, had his ears chopped off, was whipped, and was finally sold as a slave. By this time, the prince is horrified and can keep silent no longer, and he proclaims an end to the law that allows such things to happen. When asked who he is, he answers, "with princely dignity, 'I am Edward, King of England.' "

This, of course, sets the crowd to laughing uproariously. Furthermore, everything the prince does amuses them, until a tinker in the group proclaims Edward to be "Foo-Foo the First, King of the Mooncalves!" The group crowns him with a tin basin, robes him in a tattered blanket, enthrones him upon a barrel, and gives him a soldering-iron as a scepter. They then fling themselves upon the floor before him and mock him:

"Be gracious to us, O sweet king!"

"Trample not upon thy beseeching worms, O noble majesty."

"Pity thy slaves, and comfort them with a royal kick!"

This mockery continues for some time, and the prince's eyes are filled with "tears of shame and indignation." He feels that they could not be any more cruel to him if they tried; he offered to do a kindness for them and was repaid with unjust ridicule.

Early the next morning, the troop of vagabonds sets out; it is a grey and chilly day, and the entire troop is sullen and thirsty. As the day warms, however, they become more cheerful and begin to insult those they meet along the highway. They snatch things from the hedges, but the size of the troop protects them from any reprisal. They eat a farmer's larder bare, insult his wife and daughters, bedevil the farmer and his sons, and threaten to burn the house with the family in it if any word of their passing comes to the ears of the authorities.

Late in the morning, the vagabonds reach the outskirts of a large village. The prince is sent with Hugo to steal something, but since they find no opportunity to do this, Hugo decides that they will beg instead. The prince, however, stoutly asserts that he will do no such thing, and a spirited argument follows. Before Hugo falls upon the prince to beat him, a gentleman suddenly appears. Hugo quickly instructs the prince as to how he should act and then starts moaning and reeling about; when the gentleman comes closer, Hugo sprawls on the ground. The man is very much concerned, and he is very nearly taken in by Hugo's act until the prince tells him that Hugo is a beggar and a thief. When he hears the prince confess the truth, Hugo leaps to his feet and runs away, with the gentleman following and raising a great hue and cry.

Left by himself, the prince quickly flees in the opposite direction, moving as far and as fast as he can. Several times, he stops at farm houses for food, but he is driven away before he can even make a request. He keeps moving until well after dark, when he sees a lantern by the open door of a barn. He steals into the barn, quickly hiding himself when he hears voices. While the laborers do their chores, he looks about the barn, noting the position of a stall, as well as a pile of horse blankets.

After the men leave, he creeps to the stall and arranges the blankets so that he can sleep between them. Just as he is about to doze off, however, he feels something touch him. He is frightened, but he lies there, waiting to see if anything stirs. When it does not, he begins to drop off to sleep once more—and again something touches him. This time, he slowly and cautiously reaches out. After several moments of absolute dread, the prince discovers that a calf is sharing the stall with him. His first feeling is shame for having been so frightened, but then he grows delighted at the company. As he strokes the calf's back, it occurs to him that the calf can provide warmth and comfort. Thus he snuggles up to the calf, falls asleep, and he is not disturbed, despite the moaning and whistling of the wind and the creaking and groaning of the barn.

In the morning, the prince awakens to find a rat sleeping on his chest. He takes this as a good omen; his fortunes, he reasons, can go no lower than this, so things must be about to turn for the better. A short time later, two little girls come into the barn. When they see him, they stop and look at him for a time; then they begin to discuss him. Finally, they ask who he is. He tells then that he is the king and, after a brief discussion of whether this can possibly be true, they calmly accept his word. They then bring him to their mother, who does not believe him, of course; she assumes, naturally, that he is a demented boy who has wandered away from his keepers. She tries to find out where he came from, but to no avail. The prince clearly has no idea of where the places are which she mentions. She continues trying to speak to him, describing various activities, trying to see if he has been apprenticed. But she remains disappointed, since Edward knows nothing of the things she talks about.

Finally, the good aroma in the kitchen and the prince's hunger inspire him to discourse upon a variety of fine dishes; the woman leaps to the conclusion that perhaps he has helped in a kitchen some time or other. To test her theory, she leaves him to watch the food that is cooking, suggesting that he might create a few other dishes. Recalling that King Alfred once performed a similar task, the prince agrees, and he tries his best, but the woman's experiment is a disaster.

Finally, the prince, the woman, and the two girls sit down and eat together, and Edward does not insist that they stand and serve him, since he feels that he must somehow atone for having failed the woman. For her part, she does not put him in a corner, as she would do to any other common tramp. She feels a bit guilty herself that she scolded him so harshly for his failure with the food. Neither one, however, realizes that the other has made an exception to his or her usual practice.

After the meal is finished, the woman sets the prince to washing dishes. Once again, the example of King Alfred leads him to do the job, which he finds much more difficult than he had thought that it would be. When he completes this task, he is set to paring apples, which he does so badly that he is given a knife to sharpen. Next, she gives him wool to card, and he begins to think that King Alfred's example has been followed long enough.

After the noon meal, the prince is given a basket of kittens to drown. He is about to refuse to do this task, when he sees John Canty and Hugo approaching the front gate. He takes the kittens out the back way, and leaving them in an outhouse, he hurries down a narrow lane, away from the house.

As soon as the high hedge hides him from the house, the prince runs as quickly as he can toward a woods. When he is just about to hide within its shelter, he looks back and sees two figures in the distance. He turns and races even faster into the woods and only when he is far within it does he feel that he can safely stop and rest.

Although he had planned to stay where he was the rest of the day, the chill in the air forces him to move on to keep warm. As he travels, the woods become denser, and night begins to fall. Fearing that he will be left in the open after it becomes too dark to travel, he is gladdened when he sees a light ahead. He finds a hut and looks in. It is a simple place inhabited by a hermit, a situation which the prince considers most fortunate. He knocks on the door and is invited in. When he is asked who he is, he answers simply that he is the king. The hermit welcomes him, seats him by the fire, and, pacing the floor, talks about his life as a hermit. He lapses into muttering for some moments, and then he comes over to the prince and whispers, "I am an archangel!"

Becoming more energetic, he tells the prince how he was made an archangel. Then he angrily asserts that he should have been pope, instead of a mere archangel; had it not been for the king, who cast him from his religious home, he would have become pope. He continues ranting and raving about this injustice for an hour, and the prince can only sit there, listening to the hermit's ravings. Then, as suddenly as it appeared, the hermit's frenzy leaves him, and he gently tends the prince's wounds and feeds him. After the meal, the hermit puts the prince into bed and then sits by the fire, musing. When the prince is almost asleep, the hermit starts up and asks the boy if he is truly a king. When he hears that his guest is not only a king, but the King of England, and that Henry VIII is dead, a frown crosses the hermit's face, and "he clenched his bony hands with a vindictive energy."

He softly asks the boy if he knows that it was Henry who turned him and his brethren out of the monasteries. When he discovers that the prince has not heard him, that the boy has fallen asleep, the hermit smiles, listens carefully for a time, and begins searching for something. When he finds an old, rusty knife and a whetstone, he sits by the fire and begins sharpening the knife. As he sharpens it, he mutters to himself, occasionally revealing that he plans to do to the boy what he would have liked to have done to Henry VIII.

When the prince stirs, the hermit leaps to the bedside, knife upraised; then, when the boy once again resumes his deep sleep, the hermit leaves his side. Noting the time, however, he decides that it would be best if his victim did not make any noise to attract a chance passerby. Therefore, the hermit stealthily binds up his captive as he sleeps. When he is finished, the hermit again sits by the fire and softly begins to whet the knife again, mumbling and gloating to himself.

When he discovers that his victim is awake and staring at him wide-eyed, the hermit asks the prince if he has prayed. The boy struggles to get loose of his bonds, and the hermit tells him to pray his last prayer. As the day begins to dawn, the hermit kneels by the boy, knife in hand. Just as he is about to plunge the knife into Edward's body, voices are heard outside the hut, followed by a thunderous knocking on the door. A voice calls for the door to be opened, and the prince feels that there is hope once again, for the voice is that of Miles Hendon.

The hermit talks with Hendon, telling him that the boy has been sent on an errand and will return shortly. The prince tries to make some kind of noise that will attract Hendon's attention, but the hermit attributes it to a noise in a nearby grove. Finally, Hendon grows impatient and says that he would like to follow the prince and find him. The hermit decides to lead Hendon away. As soon as Hendon and the hermit leave, the door opens. In walk John Canty and Hugo, and the prince is even glad to see them. They soon free him and, each taking an arm, hurry him through the forest.

Hugo takes some joy in finding small, unobtrusive, and "accidental" ways of making the prince uncomfortable. For example, Hugo "accidentally" steps on the prince's toes three times. The first two times, the prince ignores it; the third time, however, he seizes a cudgel and proceeds to beat Hugo with it, using his skills in weaponry which he learned from his masters at court. This brings him high esteem from the rest of the vagabond troop. Yet they are confused by the boy's actions: he refuses to steal, he refuses to beg, and he refuses to do any work of any kind. In addition, he takes every possible opportunity to try and escape.

As a result of his trouncing, Hugo plans to get even with the prince. His first attempt is to put a "clime"—a poultice that painfully induces a rather ugly sore—on the prince's leg. Although he and a tinker, whom the prince had once held at bay with a soldering iron, manage to put the "clime" on the prince's leg, it is removed by another of the troop before it can take effect. Hugo's next plan is to pin a crime on the prince, making sure that he is captured.

In a neighboring village, Hugo looks for a good opportunity to deliver his charge over to the law, while the prince looks for a good opportunity to escape again from Hugo and the vagabond troop. Hugo's opportunity arrives first. Hugo sneaks up behind a lady, grabs a large package out of the basket she is carrying, and races back past the prince, thrusting the package into the prince's arms. The prince throws the bundle to the ground and stands there—but not for long; the woman grabs him with one hand and retrieves her package with the other. A crowd gathers and threatens the boy, calling him foul names; one of the crowd, a blacksmith, would have trounced the prince if Miles Hendon had not suddenly arrived at that very moment, taken charge of matters, and used his sword to enforce his will.

Commentary

This large middle portion of the novel largely focuses on Twain's social criticism of monarchy and any other form of government in which the common man is at the mercy of dictatorial authority. In these chapters, the prince experiences the life of the lowest stratum of English society as he tries to free himself from John Canty. He must fend for himself and make his way through the English countryside, which is filled with people who are hostile to anyone whom they do not know. While he is a part of the troop of vagabonds and while he is alone, trying to fend for himself, the prince hears many tales of the cruelty of English laws and of many types of injustices throughout the land. These injustices he hears about, and witnesses, continue and will culminate and receive their greatest impact when Edward finds himself and Miles Hendon in prison in Chapter 27.

Throughout this section, there is also an emphasis by Twain on disguises. In a sense, this theme was introduced near the beginning of the novel, when the prince and the pauper exchanged clothes. Now, however, Twain focuses on the vagabonds, who use disguises in order to dupe people who have more money than they have and then, after robbing them, successfully escape from the clutches of the law. For example, John Canty is shown in this section in his disguise as a lame ruffian-beggar. Later in the chapter, a blind man casts off the patches from his "excellent eyes" and, in addition, a man with a peg leg unstraps his real leg and is revealed to be as fit as the rest of the troop. Finally, the prince is mockingly dressed—in disguise—as "Foo-Foo the First, King of the Mooncalves"; the prince, who was in disguise as a pauper, is now metamorphosed into a make-believe king.

Returning to Twain's main emphasis in this section, note particularly that when the prince is introduced to the dregs of his country's society for the first time, he sees the savage effects that his father's laws have had on ordinary citizens. Many in the vagabond band tell tales of harassment by law enforcement officers, and these tales climax with Mr. Yokel's story: once he was a prosperous farmer, but suddenly—because he was hungry and tried to feed himself and his family—he was hunted down by the law, his wife and children are now dead, his ears are chopped off, and he was sold as a slave— all because "it [is a] crime to be hungry in England."

The prince is shocked by this recital and bursts out with the proclamation that "this day the end of that law is come!" While the proclamation shows the prince's indignation and determination to ease the suffering of his people and abolish English injustice, his attempts earn him only mockery. His anger and his disappointment at being mocked, however, suggest that he has not yet fully learned the effect of English law on the people in this stratum of society.

In Chapter 18, Twain contrasts the treatment of vagabonds as a troop and as individuals. When they are gathered together as a band, no one is willing to cross them; insults, theft, and physical discomfort to their victims are suffered without comment. However, when one of them is perceived to be a lone vagabond, the very least he can expect, as the prince finds out, to his dismay, is to be threatened with a severe beating. After he has escaped from Hugo, for instance, the prince tries to find food and shelter but because people think that he is merely another vagabond, he is chased away again and again; in fact, Edward is quite fortunate that he is *only* chased away and does not have to endure physical punishment.

In this same chapter, Twain also illustrates the prince's continual refusal to make no concessions to his condition or to the people who hold him captive. Not only will he *not* steal or beg, he will not cooperate in any way with Hugo when Hugo tries to make him steal. As an example, when Hugo effectively gulls a passerby out of some money, the prince proclaims loudly that Hugo is a vagabond and a thief. As a result, Hugo is pursued and the prince is able to escape a second time from John Canty.

Slowly, the prince begins to learn to be extremely cautious and to control his fears. When he spies a light in a barn, he approaches slowly and makes sure that he is hidden when he hears voices. Later, when he feels something suddenly touch him in the dark, he is terrified, but he controls his fears and forces himself to find out what it is that touched him. His discovery that it is only a calf is a relief, and the animal provides him with warmth for the night. Only with difficulty, though, is Edward learning to mature in the ways of the "real world." For a good number of years, he has been taught to think that he has royal rights and privileges.

One of Twain's favorite themes in his novels is the innate goodness of children, as contrasted with the fear and suspicion of adults. Here, in Chapter 19, Twain dwells on that theme. The two girls who find Edward quite readily accept his story about his past, and they believe his assertion that he is a king. Indeed, Edward finds it a great relief to pour out his tale to someone who finally accepts everything he says as true. The girls' mother, however, thinks that the boy is either mad or a liar, and she tries every possible means to discover where he is from or who he is running away from. And here one should note that the prince, for all his sterling ideals about fighting to right the wrongs of his country, is reluctant to do "common tasks." He has never had to; yet he does *try* to do kitchen work for the woman by rationalizing that King Alfred himself did kitchen work at one time. In this way, Edward has yet other experiences of the common life of his country—far more than he would ever have had otherwise, and thus he learns that it is much more difficult to do such a simple task as wash dishes than he would have believed; he always took such work for granted. But his willingness to perform these tasks and his failure to insist on his "royal" prerogative as king earn him better treatment than he has received since he impulsively left the palace gates. Throughout the novel, whenever Edward asserts his "prerogatives" as king, he is treated harshly; when he does not, he is treated more kindly.

In Chapter 20, Twain focuses on the prince—alone and cold, but Twain's message here is that the prince is learning to be wary of all situations; the safety of the royal apartments, where he spent his early life cannot be compared with the dangers of the countryside, especially at night. Edward is learning to fend for himself and he is earning for himself esteem and courage. And Edward needs all of his new-found courage, especially when he meets a hermit who readily accepts Edward's assertion that he is king; unfortunately, of course, the hermit is mad, and he considers himself to be an archangel—and an archangel is superior to a king; therefore, the young king is at the mercy of this mad hermit. This time, Twain's theme, or motif, of madness becomes a very real danger to young Edward.

When the prince becomes astute enough to realize that the hermit blames Edward's father, Henry VIII, for the hermit's not being pope, we are inclined to chuckle, but we, like Edward, suddenly realize that this man is dangerously mad. Yet here also, the prince is still learning about the effects of royal edicts on ordinary people of the kingdom. Historically, one should note that Edward's father, Henry VIII, did indeed proclaim a royal edict establishing the Church of England as separate from Rome and that he closed many monasteries.

When this mad monk kneels beside the prince with an upraised knife, it is only his desire to gloat an extra moment that saves the prince—because Miles Hendon, John Canty, and Hugo raise such a row that the hermit hesitates a moment too long. Yet even in his madness, the hermit is sly and he manages to lure Miles Hendon away from the hut, thus allowing John Canty and Hugo to take the prince as a prisoner once again. So, once again, the prince is at the mercy of old John Canty and the evil Hugo. This time, however, the prince's "pluck and spirit" win him the admiration of the troop of vagabonds—except for John Canty and Hugo. But the prince is finally able to retaliate against the petty harassments of Hugo, and the troop allows the prince and Hugo to fight a duel to settle their argument. Unlike Twain's other situations in which the prince is at odds with a commoner, his royal training in this instance stands him in good stead, for he has been taught to handle weapons with ease, including the single stick and quarter staff. As a result, he soundly trounces Hugo.

Despite his learning experiences, which are many and varied, the weariness, sordidness, meanness, and the vulgarity of this common life often depresses the young prince. He dreams of being back on "this throne and master again." (Likewise, in the royal apartment, Tom Canty has moments when he wishes for the freedom that he had when he was a mere pauper.) Indeed, Edward's life as a commoner depresses him so much that he thinks it might have been better to have suffered death at the hands of the mad hermit. However, he never dwells long on this self-pity, nor does he ever forget his experiences when he is finally returned to the throne.

The difficulty that the prince causes Hugo makes the villain look for ways to revenge himself on the prince. And certainly he does try, but his attempt to put a "clime" on the prince's leg is thwarted by another of the troop who admires the prince's spunk. But Hugo does try again—and the prince finds himself at the mercy of a mob—alone—and once again he realizes the actualities of law are quite different from law as theory. For example, because the prince is alone and has the appearance of guilt, these facts are sufficient for the mob to take the law into its own hands. And in this, one might want to note that the mob here is like the prince himself who, as regent, can always take the law into *his* own hands. Note, too, that when Hendon interposes himself between the prince and the mob, the prince begs Hendon to "carve me this rabble to rags!" Twain takes great pains not to idealize or sentimentalize the young prince.

Chapters 23 and 24

Summary

After being called "Sir" Miles, Hendon has to force back a smile because he still is amused at what he considers to be his young friend's gentle madness in pretending to be Prince of Wales. But as far as a title is concerned, Hendon thinks: "An empty and foolish title is mine, and yet it is something to have deserved it, for I think it is more honor to be held worthy to be a spectre-knight in his Kingdom of Dreams and Shadows, than to be held base enough to be an earl in some of the *real* kingdoms of this world."

As a constable comes to take them away, and as the prince is about to resist, Hendon, playing along with the prince's "madness," reminds the prince that the laws are, after all, *his* laws: "your laws are the wholesome breath of your own royalty; shall their source resist them, yet require the branches to respect them? Apparently, one of these laws has been broken; when the king is on his throne again, can it ever grieve him to remember that when he was seemingly a private person he loyally sunk the king in the citizen and submitted to its authority?" The prince agrees with Hendon that even the king himself should obey the king's laws. This is great wisdom for a young boy to consider and agree to.

When the woman is called to testify to the worth of the pig (the contents of the stolen bundle), she tells the judge that it is worth three shillings and eightpence. At this announcement, the judge has the court cleared. Then the judge asks if the woman is aware that if the pig is indeed worth that much, the young lad must hang for his crime, for it is the law of the land that if someone steals property worth more than "thirteen pence ha'penny," one must hang. Immediately, the woman is horrified at the idea of so young a person being hanged, and she announces that the pig is worth only eight pence, in reality. As she is leaving, the constable offers to buy the pig for the eight pence. When she refuses, he blackmails her by threatening her with perjury—punishable by death. She then lets the corrupt constable have the pig for eight pence. In the meantime, Hendon has been concealed, listening to the entire transaction. The judge then gives the prince a short lecture and sentences him to a minor jail sentence, to be followed by a public flogging. As the prince is about to resist, Hendon steps forward and stays his young friend's objections. As the constable is leading the prince off to jail, Hendon asks for a word with the official; Hendon asks the constable to allow the boy to escape. The constable balks indignantly, of course, until Hendon tells him that he witnessed the constable's blackmailing the woman and getting her pig for only eight pence.

The constable maintains that he was only "jesting" with the woman, but Hendon threatens to consult the judge about the penalty for such "jesting." The constable despairs; he is well aware that the judge does not allow such abuses of the law. Hendon explains, furthermore, that such a crime is called "*Non compos mentis lex talionis sic transit gloria Mundi*"—legalistic Latin claptrap, of course, a favorite comic device of Twain. Furthermore, says Hendon, the punishment for such "jesting" is death—"death by the halter, without ransom, commutation, or benefit of clergy."

The constable is horrified and promises to "turn [his] back" while the young boy escapes. In fact, he will even spend the night battering down a door to make it seem as if the lad escaped; that way, the judge won't mind because "the judge hath a loving charity for this poor lad."

Commentary

Edward Tudor continues to be exposed to various types of injustices that are rampant through his kingdom. That there should exist a law that demands that a person be put to death if he, or she, steals anything worth thirteen pence ha'penny is unjust, for the sum is a pittance. Yet since Edward cannot prove his claim to royalty, he is almost put to death—and would have been were it not for the leniency of the judge and the humanitarian feelings of the old woman who cannot conceive of so young a boy being put to death for so trivial a crime. Yet it is because of her humanitarianism and "humanitarian" blackmail that *she* is cheated out of the pig—when the constable threatens to have *her* put to death if she does not sell the pig to him, and *he* is threatened if he does not release Edward.

Twain's point throughout these chapters is that all kings and rulers (and presidents, we can presume) would do well to travel throughout the country disguised as an ordinary citizen. In this way, they could realize the effect of the laws of the land in all their forms—both just and unjust. However, note here that if Hendon had not overheard the constable blackmailing the old woman, *he* would not have been able to threaten the constable and thus attain the prince's freedom.

In addition to the bad laws and the unjust application of some of the laws, the prince does occasionally, it should be pointed out, meet upright Englishmen of fine mettle. The judge in this town is one of these men, and when the king regains his rightful throne, he will see to it that this particular judge, and others like him, are fully rewarded for their attention to, and execution of, justice in its highest sense. But, plotwise, once again were it not for a series of lucky coincidences and circumstances—a generous old woman, a lenient and just judge, the corruptness of the constable, and the shrewdness of Miles Hendon—the prince would have found himself in jail, an indignity that Twain saves for a later, more climactic chapter.

Chapters 25 and 26

Summary

Hendon tells the young king to wait outside of town while he settles his accounts at one of the inns, and Edward is content to do so, for now he is warm and comfortable in the new clothes which Hendon brought him. Hendon is greatly concerned that harsh treatment is bad for the boy's "crazed mind, whilst rest, regularity, and moderate exercise would be pretty sure to hasten its cure, [and] he longed to see the stricken intellect made well again and its diseased visions driven out of the tormented little head."

On the road, they travel slowly for several days; at nights, Hendon allows the boy to sleep in the bed, and he sleeps on the floor. Finally, on the last day of their trip, Hendon becomes ecstatic as they approach Hendon Hall. He points out all the old familiar sights and then finally welcomes his friend to Hendon Hall itself, assuring the "king" that he will receive a warm welcome from all. Hendon then rushes to embrace his brother Hugh, telling him to "call our father, for home is not home till I shall touch his hand, and see his face, and hear his voice once more."

Hugh Hendon is horrified and comments, "Thy wits seem touched, poor stranger." He wonders who Miles Hendon conceives himself to be, for a letter arrived some six or seven years ago, telling of the death of Miles Hendon, and upon close scrutiny, Hugh Hendon can see no relationship between this demented stranger and his brother Miles. Hendon calls for his father and for his brother Arthur, but learns that both are long since dead. The Lady Edith is alive, but only five of the old servants are alive, and they are all scoundrels. Hendon is saddened and incensed, but the young prince reminds him, "There be others in the world whose identity is denied, and whose claims are derided. Thou hast company." Hendon begs the prince not to doubt him, and the prince responds, "I do not doubt thee." Then he asks Hendon, "Dost thou doubt *me*?" Fortunately, Hendon does not have to answer the question because the Lady Edith suddenly arrives, looks at Hendon, and announces, "I know him not!" The servants arrive and, in unison, all deny that they know Hendon. The greatest shock of all, however, is when Miles learns that the Lady Edith is now Hugh's wife. Sir Hugh orders the servants to apprehend Miles, and when they hold back, he departs to fetch the authorities to arrest this "imposter."

Edward comments that things are most strange, and as Hendon is about to agree, Edward says that he is referring to the fact that the royal couriers of the land are not out looking for him and that proclamations have not been sent out concerning his royal person. It is a "matter for commotion and distress that the head of state is gone." He then offers a plan: he will write to his Uncle Hertford in Latin, Greek, and English; Hendon will take it to London and deliver it to the Lord Hertford in person and then all will be well. Hendon watches the boy begin to write, and he feels that "there's no denying it, when the humor's upon him he doth thunder and lighten like your true king. . . ." After Edward finishes the letter, he gives it to Hendon, whose thoughts are, at the moment, wholly on the Lady Edith. He cannot understand her actions. He is convinced that she is incapable of lying. At this moment, she enters and urges Miles to flee as quickly as possible. She tells him that even if he *is* Miles, it would still be best to flee. Sir Hugh, she says, is a "tyrant who knows no pity." She herself is "his fettered slave." She offers Miles all of the money she has if he will leave immediately. Miles asks one favor; he asks her to rest her eyes on him and tell him that he is indeed Miles Hendon. She refuses to acknowledge him and impores him to leave: "Why will you waste the precious time? Fly and save yourself." It is too late; at that moment, officers of the law burst into the room, arrest Miles, and Edward is likewise bound and taken to prison.

Commentary

These two chapters present a reversal of the young king's situation. He is aware by now that not even Miles fully believes that he is the true king; now he witnesses a situation in which no one believes that Miles is who he says that he is. Miles has told Edward fantastic stories about Hendon Hall; he fully expects to be welcomed at his home with open arms and he will then be able to take care of his sick young friend. All during their journey to Hendon Hall, Miles told Edward about his family; yet in his excitement, he temporarily forgot that earlier he let Edward (and the reader) know that his youngest brother Hugh was a horribly mean person. Consequently, the reader is somewhat prepared for Hugh's rough and brusque treatment of Miles.

The first words which are addressed to Miles are ironic: "Thy wits seem touched, poor stranger." Although there is no reason for Edward to assume that Miles has been telling the truth, the young king has believed his friend completely; certainly this has not been the case with Edward, however. No one, not even Miles, truly believes that young Edward is King of England.

The most puzzling aspect of the chapter concerning Miles's homecoming centers around the Lady Edith's denial of Miles. This mystery is not cleared up until a later chapter, when old Blake Andrews reveals that the Lady Edith lied *not* to save herself, but to save Miles; she was threatened that if she did not deny knowing Miles, Hugh would torture Miles. Thus, out of great concern for Miles, the Lady Edith was forced to lie.

The concern on young Edward's part that royal couriers are not searching for him carries forward the plot line of the novel. Edward writes a letter in Latin, Greek, and English, and he asks Miles to deliver it to the Lord Hertford, but because Miles is so distracted with the disturbing events of Hendon Hall, he shoves the letter into one of his pockets, and it is not discovered again until Miles is arrested later in the novel. It is, therefore, through the discovery of the letter that Miles and the king are reunited, for then Miles will test the king—who looks like Edward—by sitting in his presence, a foolish little bit of ceremonial business that Miles agreed to long ago so that he would be able to get some rest, if he were to spend considerable time in the king's company.

Chapter 27

Summary

Edward is bitter about being placed in prison; the cells are overcrowded and filthy, the food is inedible, and there is continuous fighting among the prisoners. A week passes, during which time, people are sent in to confirm that Miles Hendon is indeed an imposter. Then one day an old man arrives whom Hendon recognizes as a "good old honest soul"—Blake Andrews. He is confident that this man will identify him. However, even old Andrew denies him, but stays behind when the jailer leaves; he wants to give the imposter "a piece of [his] mind."

As soon as they are alone, the old man drops to his knees and praises God that Sir Miles is still alive. If Sir Miles so desires, Andrews will go forth immediately and "proclaim the truth" throughout the land, even though he knows that he will be strangled for doing so. Hendon will not let the old man sacrifice himself, but the old servant does make himself useful because he is able to smuggle in some good food for the young king and bring Hendon an accurate account of the things that have happened during Miles's absence. First, Miles's brother Arthur died; Miles's father weakened and insisted that Hugh marry the Lady Edith. She protested as long as possible but finally the marriage took place at the old man's death bed.

Old Andrews also brings more news: it seems as though there is a "rumor that the king is mad." But he says that it means "death to speak of it." Upon hearing this, young Edward Tudor rouses up and announces that "the king is *not* mad." Andrews then reports that Henry VIII will soon be buried and that the new king will soon be crowned. Sir Hugh will attend the coronation. Edward then learns that "the new king" has won the hearts of the people by saving the Duke of Norfolk from death and that now he is "bent on destroying the cruelest of the laws that harry and oppress the people." Hearing this, Edward's captivity becomes almost unbearable to him. Nothing Miles can do comforts the young boy, however.

One day, two women are brought in chains and thrown in prison; they take pity on little Edward, and he discovers that they were arrested simply because they are Baptists. One day, they are gone, and he hopes they have been freed. He could not be more wrong, for he finds them chained to posts, fagots piled about them, and in an instant they are burned alive, while their daughters plead for mercy. The world is "drowned under a volley of heart-piercing shrieks of mortal agony." The young king says: "That one little moment will never go out from my memory, but will abide there, and I shall see it all the days, and dream of it all the nights, till I die. Would God I had been blind!"

Miles feels somehow pleased that the king is growing gentler and that his "disorder" is mending; once, he would have rushed forth and demanded that the women be released. That same day Edward witnesses more acts of injustice, including meeting an old lawyer who was thrown in prison because he wrote about the injustice of English laws. "The world is made wrong," Edward realizes. "Kings should go to school to their own laws, at times, and so learn mercy."

Commentary

From the social point of view, a large part of the novel has been leading up to this central, climactic chapter. The real king of England is now in one of his own prisons and is treated like a common prisoner. Prior to this scene, Miles Hendon said many times that a king should always be subjected to his own laws. Hendon, speaking for Twain, said that if the laws are too severe for a king to be subjected to them, they are too severe for the king's subjects. If the laws are good laws, then no person, however high in power, should be exempt from good and just laws. Laws that are made *only* for common people should be disobeyed, for they are barbaric and should be done away with.

Young Edward is now at his lowest ebb, yet these experiences will cause him to vow to change all of the cruel, unjust laws of his land. Ironically, the surrogate king, Tom Canty, is now in the royal mansion, and he himself is already changing many of the laws that are unjust. Yet even he is unaware that the true king is suffering unjustly.

It is clear that Twain's chief concern, here, is on the gross injustices which the king, like his subjects, must suffer. For example, even though Edward learns that the "new king" has already instituted a system of reforms designed to rid the nation of injustices, still two women are brought in and jailed, merely because they are Baptists. Edward cannot believe that his kingdom can jail someone for his or her religious views. Yet such is the case, as he sees. Twain, of course, was damning any government that would restrict a man's freedom to worship, according to his conscience. These two women are compassionate, good women; they are especially kind to young Edward, and he is shocked beyond belief when he suddenly must witness their burning at the stake. Tom Canty may be on the throne of England, humanely trying to save lives, but the *real* king is in prison and witnessing the unjust execution of two good women—for their religious views.

Among the other injustices which the young king finds it difficult to fathom is the treatment meted out to an old lawyer whose crime was that he wrote a "pamphlet against the Lord Chancellor, accusing him of injustice." As a result, the old lawyer became the victim of just such injustice as he decried. As soon as the young king is rightfully restored to the throne, he vows to correct such an injustice, and others like it, suggesting that there will be much more freedom of dissent and freedom of speech. Twain's major point here is that all rulers and kings should always know how their subjects live and how the laws of the land are administered.

Chapters 28 and 29

Summary

Miles is growing impatient with his confinement as the day of his sentencing finally arrives. He has to sit two hours in the pillory, while the king is almost condemned to the stocks for keeping such bad company. Edward is dismissed with only a lecture, however; but when he sees Hendon in such a humiliating position, he begins once again to assert his royal indignation. Hendon tells the guard to "mind him not . . . he is mad." Sir Hugh then suggests that the little rascal be given half a dozen lashes for being so impertinent. Edward is seized and suddenly decides to take a beating rather than beg for mercy; it would be unseemly for nobility to beg. Hendon, however, asks that he might be allowed to take the lashes and, consequently, he is removed from the pillory and is given twelve lashes.

Edward responds deeply to this sacrifice in his behalf—not only because Hendon saves him from pain, but also because Hendon saves "the royal person" from *shame*. After the beating, the young king comes to Hendon and dubs him an earl. Hendon is touched but muses that if "this goes on, I shall presently be hung like a very maypole with fantastic gauds and make-believe honors. But I shall value them, all valueless as they are, for the love that doth bestow them."

After Miles's punishment, he is ordered to leave the land, and he wonders how he can ever gain redress for all the injustices perpetrated against him. It is then that he remembers that old Andrews gave him reports concerning "the young king's goodness and his generous championship of the wronged and unfortunate." The question, however, is: how can a *pauper* gain an interview with a *prince* or a *monarch*? Hendon also remembers that his father's old friend, Sir Humphrey Marlow, might be able to help. But the most important matter concerns poor young Edward. Miles fears that life in London might cause his madness to increase. Yet when Hendon inquires of Edward where they should go, the king answers, "To London!" and off they go, making the entire journey without incident. They arrive on the eve of Coronation Day and find a great deal of celebrating going on. Unfortunately, during the celebrating Hendon and Edward become hopelessly separated from one another.

Commentary

In Chapter 28, when Sir Hugh orders that the young king be given some lashes and the boy is seized, note that the boy decides that it is more befitting his royal status to accept the beating than to beg for mercy; no English king has ever begged for anything. Through his study of history, Edward should have known that Henry II requested and accepted a lashing on the steps of Canterbury for a rash remark he had made, which in turn cost the life of another man (Thomas à Becket). But Twain's point is clear: the young king possesses those qualities that will make him a good monarch, despite his faulty knowledge of English history.

Furthermore, when Hendon volunteers to take the lashes (which are doubled) upon his own back, we should remember that Hendon still considers the young king to be a mad young lad who might not be able to withstand the severity of the lashing. After all, earlier, while they were in prison, Hendon made sure that the young king got the choice morsels of the food they were given to eat. Many people might volunteer to be beaten so as to impress a king, but Miles Hendon does it not for the king, but for the sake of a young lad whom he cares deeply for. As a result, the young king understands that Miles Hendon saves him not merely from physical pain, but also from shame and, as a result, he raises Miles to the rank of an earl.

In Chapter 30, Miles Hendon, who is certainly a victim of injustice and who has heard that the new king is correcting all sorts of injustices, decides that he will try to arrange an audience with the king. The main problem, however, is: how can a pauper gain admission to see a king? Twain is drawing his plot to an end by bringing all of the principals to the coronation in England. Edward, of course, is anxious to go, but there is a bit more of Twain's plot to develop before the final unraveling: young Edward and Miles Hendon are separated in the crowd as it gathers for the coronation, and in the midst of all this confusion, it seems doubtful if they will ever see one another again.

Chapters 30-32

Summary

While Edward, the true king, is wandering about London on Coronation Day being mistreated, Tom Canty is just beginning to enjoy and deal effectively in his new position as king. With the help of his so-called whipping-boy, he has lost most of his early fears: "his misgivings faded out and died; his embarrassments departed, and gave place to an easy and confident bearing." In fact, Tom has learned to actually enjoy the splendid clothes, the grandeur, the attention, and the other royal privileges attendant upon his being considered royalty. For example, once when the Lady Mary argued with him over the wisdom of pardoning so many people who would otherwise be hanged, he "was filled with generous indignation, and commanded her to go to her closet, and beseech God to take away the stone that was in her breast, and give her a human heart."

This was not always so, obviously. At the beginning of the novel, Tom Canty had many painful thoughts about Edward, the real prince, but these thoughts eventually faded; likewise, at first, he sorely missed his poor mother and sisters, but later the very thought of their appearing in rags before him made him shudder.

At midnight, on the eve of his coronation, Tom Canty goes to sleep in his splendid bed, watched over by "loyal vassals." At the same time, the true king—"hungry and thirsty, soiled and draggled, worn with travel, and clothed in rags and shreds . . . [is] wedged in among a crowd of people who [are] watching with deep interest" the final preparations for the coronation of the young boy king.

On the morning of the coronation, Tom Canty finds himself once more the center of what he thinks must be the most marvelous pageant in the entire world. Nothing has been spared to make this occasion the richest and most splendid of all coronations. As the procession winds its way through the city, he suddenly realizes that he is once again in the neighborhood of Offal Court, and he catches sight of some of his old comrades, some who played the game of "royalty" with him only a short time ago. Twain reveals Tom's inner thoughts: "Oh, if they could only recognize him now!" As the ride through the crowd continues, Tom hears people shouting for "a largess! A largess!" and Tom scatters handfuls of coins among them.

At one point during the procession, he is suddenly struck dumb as he recognizes his mother! Up flies his hand, palm outward before his eyes—that old, involuntary gesture, "born of a forgotten episode and perpetrated by habit." Almost immediately, his mother, recognizing the gesture, breaks through the crowd and embraces one of the lad's legs; she lifts up to him a face transfigured with love and joy. Tom looks at her and says, "I do not know you, woman!" His mother is snatched away, and a great shame instantly falls upon Tom's heart; all of the grandeur now seems as worthless as the rotten rags he once wore; royalty has lost its "grace and sweetness"; its pomp has become a reproach, and remorse is eating his heart out. He cries out for God to free him from his "captivity!"

As the procession continues, Tom Canty becomes so dejected that he slouches foward as though his soul had been struck with a funeral bell. His attendants try to encourage him to lift up his head, to shed the clouds from his face and to smile upon the people, but

Tom can only respond that "she was my mother!" The duke attending Tom is horrified, and he assumes that the king "is gone mad again!"

Meanwhile on this Coronation Day, we learn that many people in the town have been awake and busy since early in the wee hours of the morning. And besides all the poor folks who anticipate the pomp and ceremony, there are just as many nobles and their ladies who also look forward to the coronation. Indeed, the vast sea of diamonds and other jewels glitter so brilliantly that one can hardly see. Finally, in all of this grand ceremony, the Archbishop of Canterbury finally lifts the crown above the head of the "trembling mock-king" and, at that moment, from a hiding place, a boy appears; he is "bareheaded, ill-shod, and clothed in coarse garments." He delivers this note of warning: "I forbid you to set the crown of England upon that forfeited head. *I* am the king!" The young fellow is instantly apprehended, but Tom Canty orders that Edward be turned loose, proclaiming loudly that Edward is indeed the king. There is sudden panic everywhere. Then the Lord Protector recovers his self-control and instructs the assembly to "mind not his majesty, his malady is upon him again—seize the vagabond." Tom Canty then countermands the order, and there is even more confusion. Tom Canty then approaches Edward and swears fealty to him. It is then that the Lord Protector and others notice the amazing similarity between the two boys. The Lord Protector then has an idea: he asks Edward—if he be king—the whereabouts of the Great Seal of England which has never been found, for, he says, ". . . *only* he that was the Prince of Wales *can* so answer!" This is a simple question; the young king explains that there is a secret compartment where the Seal is kept—known only to him and his carpenter, and he instructs them where to find it. After awhile, however, the Lord St. John returns with horrifying news: "Sire the Seal is not there!" Edward, the real king, is about to be taken away when Tom suddenly realizes what the object is that they are looking for. He asks Edward to recall the first day that they met and to remember *all* the details about that day. The king can remember almost everything, but he has to be prompted on a few details. For example, Tom reminds him how they exchanged clothes and, afterward, when the king noticed Tom's injured hand, he rushed forth from the royal palace. But before he did so, he looked for a place to put the Great Seal. It is then that the young king remembers where he put the Seal! He instructs the Lord St. John to go to the Milanese armor and look in the arm piece; there, he will find the Great Seal.

The Lord St. John leaves, returns with the Seal, and everyone acknowledges Edward as the "true king." When Tom Canty begins to shed his royal garments, the Lord Protector orders that "the small varlet be stripped and flung into the Tower." But the new and true king will not have such. He reminds his uncle, the Lord Protector, that his conduct is not becoming to him because it was through Tom Canty that he became a duke and, tomorrow, he must "sue to me, *through him*, for its confirmation, else no duke, but a simple earl, shalt thou remain."

Edward then turns to Tom and asks him how he knew where the Great Seal was; Tom blushes and explains that without realizing its true function, he had been using it all this time as a nutcracker!

Commentary

These chapters shift attention away from the young king and, instead, focus on Tom Canty the pauper. Twain points out how magnificantly the young pauper has adapted to the regality of his new life; again, he suggests that there is very little difference between a prince and a pauper—except for the clothes they wear and the company they keep.

Chapter 31, in particular, emphasizes the basic, good qualities of Tom Canty; in spite of his having enjoyed the great wealth which has surrounded him, the sight of his mother and his horribly cruel rejection of her cause Tom to long to be a pauper again; he truly wishes that it were possible for him to put aside all of his new splendor and riches and rejoin his family, becoming simple Tom Canty once again. His royal role is empty, compared to the love he found with his mother and sisters.

In Chapter 32, perhaps the true climax of the novel occurs. Recall that the prince and the pauper exchanged clothes early in the novel as a joke; now the rightful ruler must be restored to the kingship, and Tom must be allowed to return to being a simple citizen once again. During the course of the novel, the many and varied experiences of the boys will have their effect on them forever. For example, Tom learned much about royalty, but—more important—

young King Edward learned even more about his subjects, about justice and injustice, and, in general, he learned how he should properly rule a kingdom.

The seeming possibility of a prince being able to swap places with a pauper occurred, and it caused such consternation that even the royal and supposedly learned authorities could not tell the difference. They simply are inclined to believe that one—or both—of the boys is mad: no king would willingly give up his throne to become a pauper! Yet, that is exactly what Tom Canty proposes. The irony here is that he—as *king*—must be obeyed. And the lords don't know which boy is the real king. If they obey the person who looks like the king, they could lose their heads. If they obey the person who looks like a pauper, they will seem ridiculous. Consequently, the plot device introduced at the beginning of the novel has now become the means whereby the identity of the true prince is discovered. Dramatically, the whereabouts of the Great Seal of England is known only to the Prince of Wales, but when it is sent for, it is ironically not there; only upon clever prompting from Tom is the true king able to remember where the Great Seal was placed.

Early in the novel, one should recall, the true king threatened several times to punish the vagabond usurper, but when Tom Canty is now ordered to be arrested, the new king forbids it. His many and varied experiences among the people of his realm have taught him valuable lessons in gratitude and justice.

Chapter 33 and Conclusion

Summary

Miles Hendon, looking "picturesque enough," according to Twain, moves through the riot on London Bridge and by the time he emerges, what little money he had on his person has been filched by pickpockets. Nevertheless, he continues his search for his young friend, deciding that perhaps he can find him in the poorer sections of town. After awhile, he realizes that he has walked many miles without success. Noon finds him still looking; however, this time, he is among the rabble that follows the royal procession. He continues on, following the pageant out of town, until at last he lies down and falls asleep under a hedge.

When he awakens the next morning, he moves on toward Westminster, thinking that he can perhaps borrow a few coins from old Sir Humphrey Marlow. As he approaches the palace, the whipping-boy notices him and notes to himself that this man fits the description of the man whom his majesty has been concerned about. When Miles approaches him and asks about Sir Humphrey Marlow, the boy agrees to carry a message, and he asks Miles to wait in a recess sunk in one of the palace walls.

As he sits down, however, a group of halberdiers arrest him as a suspicious-looking character; they search him and find the letter which the king wrote earlier. They hold him while an officer hurries into the palace, and when he returns, he is much more courteous, conducting Miles into the grand entrance of the palace. From there, another official enters and treats him with great respect, leading him through a great hall into a vast room filled with many of the nobility of England. Then he is left in the middle of the room.

While the king talks with someone at his side, Hendon looks about him, and when he sees the king clearly, he is amazed; indeed, he cannot be sure whether he is sleeping or if his eyes have deceived him. To test whether or not this is his old companion, he reaches for a chair and sits in it in the middle of the floor. Keenly, he watches the young king. The ensuing commotion over such unseemly behavior catches the attention of all the nobles, but before anyone can do anything about this "disrespect," the king affirms that Miles Hendon does indeed have the right to sit in the king's presence. In addition, the king affirms Miles's knighthood, his earldom, and sufficient money and lands befitting that station. Miles falls to his knees, swears allegiance to young Edward, and pays proper homage to him.

The king then suddenly sees Hugh Hendon among the many people in the room; he orders him arrested immediately and stripped "of his false show and stolen estates." Next, Tom Canty enters; he is richly dressed and marches down to the king and kneels. Edward tells Tom that he is pleased with the way that Tom governed in his stead. He announces that Tom's mother and sisters will henceforth be cared for throughout their lives at Christ's Hospital, as will Tom himself. In addition, the king gives Tom the "honorable title of the King's Ward" and grants him distinctive dress for affairs of state.

In the concluding chapter, Twain confirms that the Lady Edith repudiated Miles because of a command of his brother Hugh, who threatened both her life and Miles's life if she did not obey him. Neither she nor Miles will testify against Hugh, and so he is not prosecuted for his threats or for usurping his brother's estate and title, but Hugh abandons his wife and goes to Europe where he dies a short time later. And not long after, Miles marries the widow.

Nothing more is heard of John Canty, but Twain tells us that young Edward seeks out many of the people whom he encountered on his travels—the farmer who was branded and sold as a slave, the old lawyer from the prison, the daughters of the Baptist women who were burned, the boy who found the stray falcon, the woman who stole a remnant of cloth, the judge who was kind when the prince was believed to have stolen a pig, and the official who whipped Miles undeservedly. To those who did him a service, he gives aid and comfort. To the officials who misused their power, he orders immediate punishment.

Miles Hendon and Tom Canty remain favorites of the king. But as Earl of Kent, Miles does not abuse his privilege of sitting in the king's presence, and this right is exercised only a few times in the following years. Tom Canty lives to be an old and distinguished looking man, honored throughout his days.

The reign of Edward is short, but he is a worthy ruler—lenient with his people and always doing his best to mend harsh and repressive laws. His is a merciful reign, especially during the difficult times that confronted England.

Commentary

Continuing the contrast between the pauper and prince, Twain focuses on Miles Hendon as yet another pauper; Miles wants to use his friendship with Sir Humphrey Marlow in order to gain access to the new king, who is reported to be very concerned over the many injustices in the land. Miles Hendon, of course, has just suffered a terrible injustice at the hands of his young brother Hugh, but—dressed as he is—his chances of gaining access to a royal audience are very slim indeed. However, in terms of Twain's plot, young King Edward has described in great detail the man known as Miles Hendon, and when a man fitting Edward's description is discovered in the neighborhood of Westminster, it becomes part of the plot that the king's whipping-boy be the one who discovers Miles. Remember that, coincidentally, one of Miles's last acts was to be whipped *himself* rather than have young Edward be whipped. Thus, this royal whipping-boy reports the presence of Hendon, but before he can gain admission to the court, he is arrested again. Luckily, the letter that young Edward wrote—in Latin, Greek, and English—is found on Miles's body and saves him in the nick of time. Even when Miles is finally brought before the king, however, he can still not believe that his "mad young friend" is really King of England—as he insisted all along that he was. For that reason, Miles tries the ruse of sitting in the king's presence; that will be a fail-proof test of the king's identity.

The last chapter of almost all nineteenth-century novels concerns itself with tidying up all the details that were left hanging after the climactic incident of the plot. Twain's novel is no exception. His readers felt almost certain that young Edward would eventually be restored to his rightful place on the throne of England, but no doubt they all wondered if he became a good king. Twain tells us that Edward long remembered all of his experiences when he lived as a pauper among his subjects. He rewarded those who showed honor and mercy and justice, and he punished those who were wicked and cheap and evil. We have witnessed the education of a king—a young boy who passed from innocence as he grew up in the royal apartment and gained further maturity as he was exposed to the very worse extremities of life, living as a pauper, despised and hated by most people. All these experiences made him become a wise and tolerant king, one whose rule, although brief, was always just.

TWAIN'S METHOD OF CHARACTERIZATION

Story, character, setting, and plot are the main elements that combine to form a short story or a novel. These elements, with the language used in presenting them, also combine to create the theme of a work of fiction. Story, character, setting, and plot are always present in any work of fiction, but the emphasis on them varies from work to work. Thus, one work may emphasize the exploration of character, and the other elements will be secondary to that focus. Another work may emphasize the events of the story, while a third may emphasize the setting in which the action takes place.

Of course, theme is important in every fictional work; theme is the basic reason for the existence of a literary work, masterpiece or or otherwise. Still, some works give greater direct emphasis to theme than other works do; when this happens, all other elements in the work are subordinate.

The Prince and the Pauper is one of Twain's most tightly plotted novels. In addition, this novel is strongly thematic. Thematically, Twain is particularly interested in contrasting the lives of the rich with the lives of the poor, the lives of the nobility with the lives of the lower classes. At the same time, however, Twain is also interested in showing that a person of noble birth is not essentially different from a person of common birth, even though their lives may seem to be very different. In other words, he wishes to show that a prince dressed in a pauper's clothing will be treated as a prince; in addition, the pauper can do the prince's job very nearly as well as the prince could, if the pauper is given the chance.

This thematic emphasis requires characters of certain kinds, which means that the themes of the novel establish a set of characteristics that the characters must have. Adding to the limitations of characterization established by the themes of the novel, other limitations are added by the requirements of the plot. That is, the characters in this novel must have certain characteristics that will allow them to participate in the action as it develops.

The two main characters in *The Prince and the Pauper* are, of course, Tom Canty and Edward Tudor. Because these two boys are the main characters, they also carry the main burden of advancing both the theme and the plot. The theme and the plot require that the lives of these boys be contrasting, that the life of one be very different from the life of the other. This requirement is met by having one of the boys a prince, a person whose life has been extremely guarded and luxurious, and having the other boy a pauper, a person from the lowest ranks of society whose life has been very hard. In order to contrast the lives of these two boys most clearly and effectively, then, the natural choice is one boy from each of society's extremes.

In this novel, Edward Tudor has been raised in luxury. He is used to fine foods and magnificent clothing. He is used to being waited on by hundreds of servants. He is used to being protected and to giving commands that others obey quickly. He is used to sleeping in soft, comfortable beds. He is used to these things simply because they are part of the life of a prince. On the other hand, Tom Canty has been raised in extreme poverty. He is used to little food and to saving extra bits of food whenever he finds them. He has one set of rags that he wears until they fall apart. He expects to take care of himself and to do things for himself. He also expects to be beaten if he does not do certain things. He sleeps quite comfortably on straw, tossed in a pile on the floor. He is used to these things—indeed, he does not see any particular problem about living this way; enduring these discomforts is the only way he has lived, and his way of life is exactly like that of everyone around him.

The theme of the novel requires that, although these two characters must be accustomed to different ways of life, they must also be similar in nearly all other respects. Thus, they must look alike, so much alike that people can easily mistake one for the other. Thus, Tom Canty and Edward Tudor have the same coloring, the same height and weight, the same facial features, and so on. If they were identifiably different in their appearances, the events of the novel could not have taken place, and the thematic points could not have been made. If Tom Canty had been dark-haired and dark-complexioned, while the prince was light-haired and had a light complexion, the prince wearing the pauper's clothing might have been put out the gate, but Tom would never have been taken for the prince, even in the prince's clothing. If Tom is not mistaken for the prince, of course, he would have been punished, probably harshly, and a search for the real prince would have been started immediately. A very different novel would have resulted.

In order to stress the idea that rank is not based on essential differences between people, these two boys must also share other characteristics. One of these characteristics is youth. If they had been older, and if they had become more solidified in a particular way of life, they could not have changed positions so easily. If Edward, for example, had been king for, say, a year or two, the difference between his actions and Tom's actions on the throne would have been more pronounced and more likely to cause suspicion. As it is, neither of them has any particular experience, and thus one can slip into the other's role without much difficulty; although Edward had a better background and more training for becoming king, he would have had to grow into the job in the same way that Tom grows into it.

In addition to their youth, this aspect of the theme of the novel requires that they share other characteristics as well. Thus, both Edward and Tom are intelligent and kind-hearted, ready to recognize injustice and cruelty, willing to reward service and alleviate need, and able to learn from their experiences. The theme does not require this particular set of characteristics; it only requires that, whatever the characteristics are, Tom and Edward share them. In other words, if Edward were stupid, Tom would also have to be stupid, and so on. These particular characteristics are, instead, the result of the requirements of the plot. One of the functions of plot is to align the reader's sympathies with one set of characters and against another set of characters. Twain obviously wants the readers of *The Prince and the Pauper* to like these two boys and to identify with them; in order to achieve this effect, positive and favorable characteristics are needed. In addition, the plot requires that certain things happen: if Tom were stupid, for example, he could not have learned what is expected of him as king, and the novel could not have been developed as it was.

In short, each of the characteristics shown by Edward and by Tom is a characteristic required by either a theme or the plot—or by both the themes and the plot.

Miles Hendon is another character whose characteristics meet requirements set by the plot and by the themes of the novel. The plot requires that the prince have a protector to keep an eye on him as he travels through his realm. Miles Hendon is the person who serves this function. In order to protect the prince, this person must have some skill with a weapon or with his fists, as well as a reason, or excuse, for wearing a weapon; Miles Hendon, of course, has been a soldier, which gives him a reason for wearing a sword and a background that would enable him to use it effectively. This protector must also have some kind of motivation for trying to keep the prince—whom he doesn't know is the prince—with him or for trying to find him once they are separated. Hendon, of course, admires the boy's spirit and pluck, and he sympathizes with what he imagines to be the boy's delusion; in short, Hendon is warmhearted, sympathetic, kind, and loyal. These characteristics are among those that would be necessary in a person in order for that person to qualify as a protector for the prince.

It is helpful that Hendon is of a noble background, for this allows him to understand what the prince expects. In addition, this background makes it more likely that Hendon can treat the prince's expectations without resentment. Finally, this background allows

Hendon to be wronged by his brother, thus allowing the prince to show his sense of injustice and his willingness to reward others for service and kindness.

Hendon does not believe that the boy whom he is trying to protect is the King of England; indeed, no adult in the novel believes Edward's claim. Children can readily believe his claim because they can do nothing about it. It is essential to the plot of the novel, however, that those who could help Edward establish his true identity do not believe him, since their belief could change the whole direction and thrust of the novel. It is particularly important that the prince's protector be skeptical of his claims, since he is also the person who could do the most to help him regain his rightful position before the prince has completed the education that he must have before he regains the throne.

The needs of the plot and the needs of the various thematic elements in *The Prince and the Pauper* thus determine the characteristics displayed by Tom Canty, Edward Tudor, and Miles Hendon. Tom Canty is intelligent, perceptive, quick to learn and to adapt, kind-hearted, decisive, young, and low-born. He has these characteristics because they are required by the plot and by the themes; he has no characteristics that are not related either to the requirements of the plot or to the requirements of the themes. Similarly, Edward Tudor is intelligent, perceptive, strong-willed, kind-hearted, decisive, young, nobly-born, and impervious; he has these characteristics because they are required by his role in the plot and in the theme, and he has no characteristics that are not required. Likewise, Miles Hendon has only those characteristics that are required by the plot and by the themes of the novel: he is kind, loyal, considerate, well-born, persistent, and skilled with a sword because these are the qualities necessary for him.

E. M. Forster divided the characters in fiction into two groups, rounded characters and flat characters. Rounded characters are those that have a variety of characteristics, some of which are required by the plot, others of which are required by thematic considerations, but still others of which are simply present to give a character individuality and life-likeness. Flat characters, on the other hand, have only those characteristics required by plot and theme. Rounded characters are found most frequently in novels that focus on the exploration of character, but in any novel, even in those most concerned with this exploration, only a very few characters become fully rounded. Usually only one or two characters are truly rounded in a novel. Most characters in fiction are flat, yet to say this is not to condemn any novel or any novelist's ability to portray character; it is simply to acknowledge the fact that some novels are more concerned with other aspects of fiction than they are with character development; this usually means that the characters must serve the needs of those other aspects, leaving little room, or need, for more rounded characters.

The characters in *The Prince and the Pauper* are flat characters. They were created to advance the plot of the novel and to develop the thematic points that Twain wanted to suggest to his audience. Nevertheless, although they are not rounded individuals, people remember Tom Canty and Edward Tudor because of the characteristics they do have and because of the roles they play in the action of this novel.

QUESTIONS FOR REVIEW

1. Compare and contrast the characters of Tom Canty and Edward Tudor.

2. In what ways do the episodes of traveling with the vagabonds, helping the peasant woman with housework, being held captive by the mad hermit, and sitting in jail with Miles Hendon contribute to the education of Edward Tudor?

3. Why does Twain incorporate passages that are quoted from historical texts into the various chapters of *The Prince and the Pauper*?

4. What means does Tom Canty use to learn how he must act in his role as king?

5. Why does Tom Canty adapt to his role as king more quickly than Edward Tudor adapts to his role as pauper?

6. What does Edward Tudor learn from his travels among his subjects?

7. What practical results does this education produce in the laws of the country and in his treatment of his subjects?

8. Discuss whether or not Tom Canty would have made a good king for England if Edward had not returned.

9. Discuss the advantages that Tom Canty and Edward Tudor see in the life of the other boy before they trade places. Also discuss the differences between their initial ideas and the realities they encounter after exchanging roles.

10. Why is Tom Canty so willing to help Edward regain his throne?

11. What role does Miles Hendon play in this novel?

12. What are the differences between the way in which the common people view Henry VIII and the way in which Edward views him?

13. What details of the novel contribute toward the effort to make the exchange of roles between the prince and the pauper plausible?

14. Discuss the theme of clothes determining the way a person is treated.

15. Discuss the ways in which ceremonial rituals are satirized by Twain, as well as the ways in which they have a positive function.

SELECTED BIBLIOGRAPHY

PRINCIPAL WORKS

The Celebrated Jumping Frog of Calaveras County, and Other Sketches, 1867.

Innocents Abroad, 1869.

Roughing It, 1872.

The Adventures of Tom Sawyer, 1876.

A Tramp Abroad, 1880.

The Prince and the Pauper, 1882.

Life on the Mississippi, 1883.

Adventures of Huckleberry Finn, 1885.

A Connecticut Yankee in King Arthur's Court, 1889.

The Tragedy of Pudd'nhead Wilson and the Comedy of Those Extraordinary Twins, 1894.

The Man That Corrupted Hadleyburg and Other Stories and Essays, 1900.

The Mysterious Stranger, 1916.

BIOGRAPHICAL MATERIAL

BROOKS, VAN WYCK. *The Ordeal of Mark Twain.* New York: E. P. Dutton, 1920. Rev. ed., 1933. An influential study suggesting that the moralistic pressure of family, friends, and American culture affected Mark Twain's genius.

DE VOTO, BERNARD. *Mark Twain's America.* Boston: Little, Brown, 1932. This book gained notoriety for its heavy attack on Van Wyck Brooks's book listed above.

FERGUSON, DELANCEY. *Mark Twain: Man and Legend.* Indianapolis: Bobbs-Merrill, 1943. An excellent biography.

HOWELLS, WILLIAM DEAN. *My Mark Twain: Reminiscences and Criticisms.* Edited by Marilyn A. Baldwin. Baton Rouge: Louisiana State University Press, 1967. An affectionate memorial by an old, loyal friend.

WAGENKNECHT, EDWARD. *Mark Twain: The Man and His Work.* 3rd ed. Norman: University of Oklahoma Press, 1967. Originally published in 1935, this study is still one of the best.

CRITICAL WRITINGS

BELLAMY, GLADYS CARMEN. *Mark Twain as a Literary Artist.* Norman: University of Oklahoma Press, 1950. An early full-length study of Mark Twain.

BLAIR, WALTER. *Mark Twain and Huck Finn.* Berkeley: University of California Press, 1960.

BRANCH, EDGAR MARQUESS. *The Literary Apprenticeship of Mark Twain: With Selections from his Apprentice Writing.* Urbana: University of Illinois Press, 1950. An account of Twain's early career.

CARDWELL, GUY A., ed. *Discussions of Mark Twain.* Boston: D. C. Heath, 1963. A collection of critical material.

COX, JAMES M. *Mark Twain: The Fate of Humor.* Princeton, N. J.: Princeton University Press, 1966. The author's thesis is that Twain's work was successful in his comic writings and unsuccessful in his serious writings.

DE VOTO, BERNARD. *Mark Twain at Work.* Cambridge, Mass.: Harvard University Press, 1942. The volume contains three long essays about Twain.

FERGUSON, DELANCEY. *Mark Twain: Man and Legend.* Indianapolis: Bobbs-Merrill, 1943.

LEARY, LEWIS. *Mark Twain.* Minneapolis: University of Minnesota Press, 1960. No. 5 in the "Pamphlets on American Writers" series.

LONG, E. HUDSON. *Mark Twain Handbook.* New York: Hendricks Houser, 1957. A summary of Twain's life, background, ideas, and reputation.

MARX, LEO. "Mr. Eliot, Mr. Trilling, and Huckleberry Finn," *American Scholar,* XXII (Autumn, 1953), 423-40.

ROURKE, CONSTANCE. *American Humor: A Study of the National Character.* New York: Harcourt, Brace & Company, Inc., 1931, pp. 209-20.

SALOMON, ROGER B. *Twain and the Image of History.* New Haven, Conn.: Yale University Press, 1961. The book covers Twain's historical ideas and writings.

SCOTT, ARTHUR L., ed. *Mark Twain: Selected Criticism.* Dallas: Southern Methodist University Press, 1955.

SMITH, HENRY NASH, ed. *Mark Twain.* Englewood Cliffs, N. J.: Prentice-Hall, 1963. A collection of critical essays.

STONE, ALBERT E., JR. *The Innocent Eye: Childhood in Mark Twain's Imagination.* New Haven: Yale University Press, 1961.

NOTES

NOTES

NOTES

THE RED BADGE OF COURAGE

NOTES

including

- *Chapter Summaries and Critical Commentaries*
- *Biography of Stephen Crane*
- *Critical Analysis of the Novel*
- *Character Analyses*
- *Crane's Style and Technique*
- *Questions for Review*

by
J. M. Lybyer
Washington University

INCORPORATED

LINCOLN, NEBRASKA 68501

Editor

Gary Carey, M.A.
University of Colorado

Consulting Editor

James L. Roberts, Ph.D.
Department of English
University of Nebraska

ISBN 0-8220-1120-4
© Copyright 1964
by
C. K. Hillegass
All Rights Reserved
Printed in U.S.A.

1990 Printing

The Cliffs Notes logo, the names "Cliffs" and "Cliffs Notes," and the black and yellow diagonal-stripe cover design are all registered trademarks belonging to Cliffs Notes, Inc., and may not be used in whole or in part without written permission.

Cliffs Notes, Inc. Lincoln, Nebraska

CONTENTS

THE RED BADGE OF COURAGE

INTRODUCTION

Stephen Crane was only twenty-two and had never witnessed any war when he wrote *The Red Badge of Courage*. On the surface this is a simple story of a young soldier in the Union Army in the Civil War who becomes frightened as he faces battle for the first time but who recovers from this fright as the book progresses. However, what makes this book unique is not the simple outward story. Crane has imagined what is going on in the mind of the youth and chronicles this in great detail. Thus through the eyes of the hero, Henry Fleming, the reader can experience not only the actions of an ordinary soldier but also his thoughts and feelings.

Crane's story is cosmic in scope in spite of its limited viewpoint and concise style because it deals with some of the major agonies facing man. These agonies, which Henry experiences in the book, are extreme isolation from other human beings, the confrontation of death, the lack of self-identity, failure, and guilt. During the course of the book Henry also experiences the opposites of these. He recognizes the brotherhood of man, in this case born of the fact that all face death together in battle. He faces death and finds "that, after all, it is but the great death." His search for self-identity is successful. He discovers that courage is sublime unselfishness. Finally he is able to see all his actions, good and bad, in perspective so that he feels less proud about his good deeds and less guilty about his bad actions.

Crane enriches his story by writing in an impressionistic and symbolic manner using color in a compelling way and creating images which are striking and original. For instance he compares guns to Indian chiefs:

> The guns squatted in a row like savage chiefs. They argued with abrupt violence. It was a grim pow-wow. Their busy servants ran hither and thither.

Underlying the story is Crane's belief in the naturalistic concept of man as insignificant and helpless, driven to action by his instincts and the conditions of his environment. Crane points up the insignificance of Henry by emphasizing the machine-like quality of the army of which Henry is just a small cog and the indifference of nature to his plight.

The story is basically realistic. Crane undercuts the glory of war by writing of the boredom, hardships, and actual dangers of fighting. He emphasizes the simple, awkward actions and talk of his characters even during extremely tense moments. In writing of officers Crane says:

> The officers, at their intervals, rearward, neglected to stand in picturesque attitudes. They were bobbing to and fro roaring directions and encouragements. The dimensions of their howls were extraordinary. They expended their lungs with prodigal wills. And often they nearly stood upon their heads in their anxiety to observe the enemy on the other side of the tumbling smoke.

CHAPTER SUMMARIES AND COMMENTARIES

CHAPTER I

Summary

The chapter opens with a description of an army resting on some hills with the enemy campfires visible in the distance. A tall soldier goes to the brook to wash his shirt. He comes back with a rumor he has heard that the company will move the next day. The other soldiers listen carefully and discuss the possibility of the rumor being true. A loud soldier calls this information "a thundering lie" as he does not think the army will ever move. The tall soldier defends the rumor.

One youthful private listens intently to the discussions and then goes to his shabby little hut to think of the implications of actually being in battle for the first time. He recalls his early dreams of great and bloody battles of far-off times and places. He remembers how he insisted on enlisting despite his mother's wishes because he had read of "marches, sieges, conflicts, and he had longed to see it all," even though he suspected that present-day war would not be the grand struggle it was in other ages.

The youth remembers his mother's farewell talk to him in which she admonishes him to take good care of himself, stay away from bad companions, and not to shirk his duty on her account. He recalls that although the sight of his mother peeling potatoes as she gave him advice irritated him, his last sight of his weeping mother makes him momentarily ashamed of his desire to seek adventure and glory.

He recalls that he has spent several months in camp doing very little but trying to keep himself comfortable and being "drilled and reviewed" over and over again and he has come to the conclusion that he is an insignificant part of a large machine and that war as a glorious heroic endeavor is a thing of the past.

The youth ponders the nature of the enemy for a time but then comes to the conclusion that it does not matter what the enemy is like as long as it fights. The real problem is how he himself will react to a real battle. He becomes fearful as he realizes that he may prove not to be heroic after all. He is afraid that his dreams of glory are just dreams.

After awhile the tall soldier and the loud soldier come to the hut still arguing about the truth of the rumor. The youth asks the tall soldier, Jim, whether he thinks any of the soldiers will run from the battle. Jim replies that probably some will run but most will stay and fight after they once start shooting. Jim says that he will probably do what the majority of men do. If most of the company runs he will run too but if most stay and fight he will stay and fight too. Jim points out that all the new recruits are untried in battle. Jim's words reassure the youth somewhat.

Commentary

The author introduces most of the main elements in the book in the first chapter. He reveals the atmosphere of the book, which is serious and somber, in his opening sentence: "The cold passed reluctantly from the earth, and the retiring fogs revealed an army stretched out on the hills, resting."

The author's technique is impressionistic; that is, he describes scenes, characters, and moods as they appear to him at a particular moment rather than how they are in actuality. For instance in describing the landscape in the early morning as it is getting light he tells how "the landscape changed from brown to green...." Actually the change of light gives this effect at this time. Later the landscape might look blue or some other color.

The chapter reveals that the book has two settings, one physical and one emotional. The physical setting is an army camp on some wooded hills with a brook and river nearby. The arguing, rumbling soldiers seem to be part of the setting. On another level the setting is the mind of the youthful soldier. The boy reacts to a series of impressions gained from his environment, his senses, and his own thinking. For instance his early impression of war as a great and glorious conflict is gained from his early reading, gossip, newspaper accounts, and his own imaginings.

The main character in the book is introduced although we do not learn his full name until later. The author speaks of him as "a youthful private" or "the youth." We learn that Henry Fleming is a farm boy, who, before his enlistment and during the first few days of his service, has created in his mind an illusion about himself and about the nature of war. His illusions reigned over the reality until after he has experienced the monotony and anonymity of being "part of a vast blue demonstration." He has temporarily lost his sense of identity until the rumor of impending battle jolts him back to a consciousness of himself as an individual. Then he turns his attention to the central problem of the book, his behavior in a real battle. Will he fight bravely and honorably or will he cowardly run away?

The other characters in this chapter tend to point up Henry's character and his illusions. It is emphasized that Henry's whole regiment is untried and thus all the men face what he faces. The veterans call them "fresh fish." The tall soldier enjoys being the center of attention when he spreads the rumor. The loud soldier is swaggering and seemingly unthinking. Both are more concerned about the externals of going into battle than their behavior during the fighting. Thus Henry feels alone with his problem.

Crane's realism is apparent in this chapter. The soldiers talk in a dialect which was common in rural areas during the Civil War period. Henry's mother, during the very emotional moments when Henry tells her he is going to enlist and when he says his farewells to her, milks the cows, and peels the potatoes. The tall soldier hears the rumor when he is washing his shirt in the brook. Henry first meets the enemy when he and a rebel soldier are both standing guard duty on opposite sides of a river. They chat amiably and like each other.

The chapter moves ahead through a series of pictures or images. First there is the picture of the arguing soldiers excited by a rumor. Then there is a picture of Henry in his shabby, crowded hut thinking of his past life and what may occur in the future. The two merge in the last picture as the tall and loud soldiers enter the hut still arguing and disturb the youth's reverie. By means of Henry's reverie Crane reveals the background of the youthful hero.

CHAPTER II

Summary

The chapter opens with Henry Fleming learning that the tall soldier's rumor is false, that the company will not move after all. However, the youth is still troubled by the question of whether he will be brave in battle. He thinks about the question constantly and finally comes to the conclusion that he will not know the answer until he actually gets into battle. He becomes eager to fight so that he can prove his courage. He seeks comfort from the other soldiers. The tall soldier, whom he has known since childhood, gives him the most consolation because he feels that he can do what the tall soldier can do. Even so, a battle may bring out hidden qualities in the other man. Henry alternates between thinking his companions are the bravest of men and as frightened and wondering as he, himself, is. He cannot find anyone to confide his fears in as he is afraid of being ridiculed.

One morning the order is given to move. There is much speculation among the men as to where they are going. Henry, however, is lost in his own thoughts. He is depressed while his companions sing and make jokes. A fat soldier battling with a country lass about a horse makes the soldiers forget their big war for the moment.

When the soldiers camp for the night Henry withdraws from his comrades to think his gloomy thoughts. He becomes homesick as he thinks of the farm and the peaceful animals on it. He thinks that perhaps he is not cut out to be a soldier after all.

The loud soldier, Wilson, interrupts his reverie and asks Henry what the trouble is but the youth cannot tell him. Wilson talks happily of the battle and how they will defeat the enemy easily. He swaggers as he talks of the fight ahead, obviously confident that he will fight hard and well. Henry asks him how he knows that he won't run from the battle. Wilson laughs at the thought and refuses to admit that there is even the possibility of such a thing. He becomes angry with Henry for bringing up the question and leaves him again.

Henry feels more alone than ever when Wilson leaves. He goes to bed in his tent but has a hard time going to sleep because of his great fear that he will prove to be a coward. In the background he hears the snoring of the tall soldier and of other soldiers playing cards. He is alone with his mental anguish.

Commentary

On a physical level the chapter finally sees the regiment starting toward a battle. Rumors and speculations are rampant. The soldiers are happy and confident as they look forward to their first battle. The tall soldier seems very matter-of-fact about the engagement. The loud soldier is swaggering and confident.

Henry's battle in his mind continues. He cannot again become part of the anonymity of the "blue demonstration." He no longer just wonders if he will be courageous in battle but now fears that he won't be. He tries to "measure himself by his comrades" but he is not able to sense any insecurity in them. He is homesick, lonely, and unhappy.

One of the most striking images in this chapter is the picture of the marching army as "moving monsters." Crane describes the soldiers as "huge crawling reptiles," "long serpents," and the like. This has the effect of depersonalizing the army and the men in it. The men seem to be part of one moving insect. This is in keeping with the impressionistic method which presents a scene in terms of colorful images.

Crane uses color more like a painter than a writer. He is interested in the effect of light on color as is shown by his pointing out that the soldiers' uniforms before daybreak "glowed a deep purple hue." He speaks of the enemy campfires as "red eyes."

Crane again shows how he can fuse the real with the imaginative and achieve a single effect. While Henry is suffering mental agony in his bunk Crane introduces a background of relaxed soldiers playing cards. Both of these are in contrast to the poetic image of the "red, shivering reflection of a fire on the white wall" of Henry's tent. The three elements point up Henry's suffering and insecurity.

CHAPTER III

Summary

The chapter opens with the troops crossing the river and then camping for the night. The next morning they start their march again. The regiment begins to lose some "of the marks of a new command," although they still do not look like veterans. They begin to get rid of the non-essential items in their knapsacks.

The regiment rests briefly again. One morning early Henry is awakened by the tall soldier and he finds himself running along a path in the woods. Presently his regiment is joined by other regiments and Henry realizes that the time has finally come, that he is about to be tested. He thinks of running away but realizes that he can't as he is surrounded on all sides by the regiment. He feels as if he is "in a moving box." He forgets momentarily that he voluntarily enlisted and blames a cruel government for what he considers to be a death march.

As he marches toward the front line the youth is, at first, curious and tries to see all he can. He is fascinated by the skirmishers in front of him who shoot into bushes and trees in the distance. He encounters his first corpse and stares at it curiously. However, his curiosity soon is satisfied and he feels more alone than ever. He becomes obsessed with the thought that the troops are marching into a trap and that none of the leaders know it. He wants to warn his companions but doesn't for fear of ridicule. The regiment halts in a forest and the men busily dig trenches but are soon moved to another position and then another. The youth feels the strain of the waiting; he is eager to fight to prove to himself that his doubts about his courage are false—"The youth had been taught that a man became another thing in battle."

The tall soldier accepts the situation calmly, in an uncomplaining manner, and eating whenever he can. As the afternoon wears on, Henry feels "stupid and incompetent" again but this time does not try to fight his fears. He decides that perhaps death is the best solution to his problem but the sight of fighting ahead drives the thought out of his mind.

The loud soldier, at the sight of the fighting, becomes depressed and feels certain that he will be killed. He gives Henry a yellow envelope to deliver to his family after his death.

Commentary

This chapter is concerned with the march toward the front where the fighting is taking place. There is a feeling of movement throughout the chapter. The infantry gets rid of excess baggage so it can move more efficiently. The chapter ends when the regiment finally reaches the front.

In Henry's mind there is also a feeling of movement as he goes forward to meet his challenge. His thoughts are always concerned with his problem but he reacts to it in different ways as he moves along. At one moment he feels trapped by the regiment unable to escape if he wants to. Even the landscape seems hostile to him. Sometimes he forgets his fears in the face of his curiosity about war. At other times he looks forward to death as a possible solution. For the most part he is eager for the battle so that he can prove to himself that he is courageous.

There are many contrasts between illusion and reality. For instance, a "house standing placidly in distant fields" looks "ominous" to Henry. He has the illusion that he was forced to join the Army and to fight although actually it was entirely his own doing.

Crane's realism is shown often in the chapter. One example is the description of the dead soldier. He is presented very realistically pointing out the horror of war.

It is significant to note that the tall soldier and the loud soldier are changing their attitudes. The tall soldier seems less concerned with rumors and tactics. He still argues with the loud soldier but defends his leaders. New soldiers cannot see the whole picture of the war and thus cannot see the reasons for the many moves and delays. He is calm and does not object to the hardships of marching.

The loud soldier is still complaining and swaggering until the regiment gets to the front and he sees the fighting. Then he loses his cocky pose and becomes frightened, upset, and unsure.

CHAPTER IV

Summary

The brigade is hiding near the edge of a grove of trees with their guns pointing toward the open fields. They look out through the haze of gunsmoke and see running men and also hear them gossiping about the battle. Although they are not yet fighting, bullets whiz over their heads causing twigs and needles to come down on their heads. The lieutenant gets shot in the hand and the captain binds it up with his handkerchief. They watch a regiment retreat amidst catcalls from the veteran regiments on either side of it. The retreating men frighten Henry's regiment and make them want to run too. However, they all stay where they are. Henry realizes that he has not seen the enemy yet. He thinks that once he has seen the enemy, he, also, will be very ready to run away.

Commentary

The regiment is waiting in a grove of trees to be called to join the fighting. This is a time of quiet after the continuous move in the last chapter. The retreat of another regiment shows the recruits the reality of war. Their side cannot always win and not all men can fight off an attack. Henry and his comrades are almost at the point of being in battle themselves.

CHAPTER V

Summary

The chapter opens with the regiment still waiting to be called into battle. Someone calls out, "Here they come!" and the soldiers prepare themselves for the fight. The general appears on his horse and tells the colonel that the line has to hold the enemy back. All the officers look agitated.

Henry takes his rifle and starts shooting at the enemy. He forgets himself for awhile, forgets that he is an individual and feels that he is a part of the common personality of his regiment. He is always conscious "of his comrades about him." He feels "the subtle battle brotherhood more potent even than the cause for which he was fighting." After a time he feels the physical effects of fighting, burning sensations in his eyes and roaring in his ears. He then develops a "red rage" and feels frustrated because he does not have the power to make a grand gesture and subdue the enemy all at once. He feels almost suffocated from the smoke of the gunfire.

There are no "heroic poses" or "picturesque attitudes" on the part of the soldiers and officers. They are fighting intently in every conceivable posture. The officers are running "to and fro roaring directions and encouragements." Several men are killed; others are wounded.

At last the fighting stops. The youth realizes that he and his comrades have repulsed the attack. He, at last, takes a drink of water and surveys the scene around him. He sees the motionless forms of the dead and the slow procession of the wounded as they move away from the battlefield. He hears the sounds of fighting coming from all directions and for the first time realizes that the fighting is going on in other places and not just where he is.

Commentary

This is the first picture of an actual battle in the book. War is presented with moving realism. The soldiers are intent on what they are doing. They suffer from heat, smoke, noise, and exhaustion.

The Army is again presented as a single entity, but this time as a person rather than an insect. Henry forgets that he is an individual and is "welded into a common personality...dominated by a single desire." When the wounded men start to leave, Crane speaks of their procession as "a flow of blood from the torn body of the brigade."

The grim picture of warfare is contrasted with a serene, unblemished nature. The youth is amazed to look up and see a "blue, pure sky and the sun gleaming on the trees and fields."

One good example of impressionism in this chapter is the comparison of guns to Indians as follows:

> The guns squatted in a row like savage chiefs. They argued with abrupt violence. It was a grim pow-wow.

The youth does not consider his state of mind in this chapter. Crane suggests that Henry is in "his battle sleep" and is not fully aware of all that he is doing.

CHAPTER VI

Summary

The youth wakes up from his "battle sleep" and considers himself and his reaction to the battle. He is delighted with himself and feels that he has fought well and heroically. He feels that he has passed the test. He displays a new interest and good will toward his companions and chats sociably with them.

But suddenly to the regiment's amazement the enemy reappears. The men are tired and cannot stand the thought of more fighting. The youth feels that it must be a mistake. He is on the verge of total exhaustion. He exaggerates in his mind "the endurance, the skill, and the valor of those who are coming." The man next to him suddenly stops shooting and runs away howling. The youth sees other men fleeing. He feels that perhaps he is being left behind by his regiment to fight the enemy alone.

Suddenly the youth becomes panic-stricken and runs away from his post. He is so frightened that he loses all sense of direction. He becomes more fearful as he runs and imagines that he is being chased by the enemy. He narrowly misses being hit by a stray shell in a little meadow. He comes across a battery of six gunners and feels sorry that they soon will be killed by the enemy who is chasing him. He sees a fresh brigade marching toward the fighting.

As he moves away from the noise of the fighting he slows down his pace. Presently he comes upon a general seated upon a horse conferring with his staff who are also on horseback. The youth hangs around to see if he can learn anything. He discovers that his comrades have held the line, that there was no general retreat after all.

Commentary

The first five chapters have led up to the moment in this chapter when the youth's worst fears are realized and he runs away from his battle post. While he can see his comrades at his side fighting steadily he, too, is molded into the common person of the regiment and can fight. However, when he is cut off briefly from the other men he feels alone and he panics. Physical fatigue also plays a part in his inability to fight in the second round of fighting.

The differences between illusion and reality are again brought out. For instance, he feels that he is better able to understand what is going on in the battle than the general and his staff of officers who are experienced and who have access to information concerning the battle in all its parts. The youth is not aware how inexperienced he is and how limited is his viewpoint.

CHAPTER VII

Summary

The youth is smitten with shame when he hears that his comrades have held the line. At first he is amazed that they have been able to do what he felt was impossible. Then his surprise turns to anger against "his fellows, war in the abstract, and fate...." He tells himself that he has acted with wisdom and from good motives in running away while his fellows have been foolish to stay and fight. He begins to pity himself because of the injustice of his position. He dreads their scornful remarks when they next see him.

He leaves the fields and the sounds of the guns and fighting and goes into the deep woods where he can be by himself. At first the peaceful landscape reassures him. He throws a pine cone at a squirrel which runs away chattering with fear. Henry feels that this is a sign showing that all living things try to preserve themselves from harm by running away from danger.

The youth moves ever deeper into the woods. He comes upon a lovely spot where the boughs of the trees form a chapel-like area with brown pine needles for the carpet. To his horror he finds inside a ghastly corpse with small ants crawling on the face. He screams when he sees it and gazes at it for some moments before he gathers the strength to run away. He flees afraid that the dead man is pursuing him in some manner. Finally he stops and listens to see if the corpse is calling "horrible menaces" after him.

Commentary

There is a great feeling of loneliness in this chapter. Henry is alone with the problem of his cowardice. He tries to find solace in two different ways neither of which are satisfactory. First, he tries to justify his actions intellectually by trying to convince himself that he has acted with great wisdom in running away and in accord with the basic natural law of self-preservation as was exemplified by the squirrel who ran away from danger. However, he still feels ashamed and cannot bear to face his comrades because of their probable derision. Second, he seeks refuge from the war and from his own thoughts by going deep into the woods. For a short time he is soothed by the peaceful landscape and the feeling that the war is far off. However, he comes upon a ghastly ant-eaten corpse which frightens him terribly and causes him to blindly flee again. He feels that the corpse is deriding him for his cowardice. He finds that he is unable to run away from his problem.

The naturalistic belief in the indifference of nature is clearly emphasized in this chapter. Henry does not find solace in nature.

CHAPTER VIII

Summary

Henry finds himself near the fighting again after his flight from the corpse. The "crimson roar" of the musketry and artillery lead him to believe that a battle of cosmic proportions is in progress. He begins to run toward the noise as he does not want to miss witnessing such a great conflict.

He begins to think that perhaps the battle in which he took part was an insignificant prelude to the real fighting. He can see the humor in his and his comrade's former attitude that the fighting in which they were engaged would decide the outcome of the war.

As he moves toward the edge of the forest he imagines that nature is hostile to him, that the trees are spreading out their branches to keep him from passing. He wanders around near the rear of the fighting fascinated by the sights and sounds.

He joins a group of wounded soldiers who are marching away from the battle. The soldiers react in various ways to their wounds. One laughs hysterically; one blames the commanding general for his wound; one has the "gray seal of death already upon his face"; some are angry and sullen.

A tattered soldier, wounded in the arm and head, trudges along beside Henry. At first we see him agog at the lurid exaggerated tales of fighting told by a bearded sergeant. After a time he tries to make friends with Henry even though the latter obviously gives him no encouragement. He remarks how none of the boys on their side ran away and what great fighters they were. Then in a loving and brotherly fashion the ragged soldier turns to Henry and asks him, "Where yeh hit, ol' boy?" Henry panics at this question, turns away from his inquisitor, and disappears into the crowd.

Commentary

Crane again points up the difference between the reality of the war and the illusions in Henry's mind. Although before he had witnessed the corpse in the deep forest he had imagined that nature was soothing and comforting toward him, now nature seems hostile. Actually nature is not a person with attitudes and feelings. Also, he imagines that the battle has assumed heroic proportions because of the extremely loud noise it is making.

It is significant that Henry teams up with the wounded men. He is no longer alone.

For a short period the author shifts the focus from Henry to the tattered soldier who seems to be an embodiment of Henry's early idea of himself as a great and glorious war hero. In response to the sergeant's lurid tales.

> he was like a listener in a country store to wondrous tales told among the sugar barrels. He eyed the story-teller with unspeakable wonder. His mouth was agape in yokel fashion.

This sounds very much like Henry before he entered the Army. However, the tattered soldier, unlike Henry, has been wounded in two places, the head and arm. Thus he is a reproach to Henry even before he begins to question him. The inevitable question as to his own wound again causes Henry to panic. He cannot of course bring himself to answer that he has no physical wound but has a deeper, shameful wound in his mind.

CHAPTER IX

Summary

The youth falls back in the line until he can no longer see the tattered soldier and walks along with the other soldiers. However, he is surrounded by soldiers with wounds and he feels that his own shame and guilt are visible to them. He envies them their wounds and wishes that "he, too, had a wound, a red badge of courage."

Henry finds himself walking by the "tall soldier," Jim Conklin, who, though obviously mortally wounded and in great pain, marches steadily onward brushing aside the offers of help from his fellow soldiers. Henry is very much shaken by his friend's plight and walks along with him offering to take care of him. Suddenly Jim turns to Henry and confesses his one great fear, that he will fall down in the road and that the artillery wagons will run over his body. Henry promises to drag his body off the road if this should happen. Then Jim seems to forget about his fears and marches stonily onward.

Presently the youth hears a voice telling him softly that he had better lead his friend out of the road and into the fields as Jim will be dead within five minutes and an artillery battery is coming. Henry turns and sees that it is the tattered soldier talking.

Henry, with the tattered soldier following, leads Jim into the fields. Then Jim starts running toward some bushes. Henry tries to stop him but he shows a purpose in his face and body to get to the bushes before he dies and refuses to listen to his friend. "There was something ritelike in these movements of the doomed soldier." Finally he gets to the clump of bushes and stands quietly waiting for his death spasm which shortly comes. He dies horribly but with dignity in spite of his terrible contortions.

Henry watches with great interest as well as agony the death ceremony at the "place of meeting." When it is over he gazes at his friend and then turns and shakes his fist at the battlefield.

Commentary

This chapter is mostly concerned with the death of Henry's friend, Jim Conklin, and its effect on Henry. Jim, although certainly not a great deal older than Henry, has been a childhood friend. Henry, earlier in the book, looks up to him and seeks reassurance from him. He seems to represent the comfort and authority of those persons whom he has known and loved in his childhood. Thus his death leaves Henry even more alone with his problem. One more source of comfort is gone. In the past two chapters Henry has tried to find comfort and justification for his action in the realization that "self-preservation is a basic natural law," by turning away from the battlefield and his companions and seeking solace from nature, by marching along with wounded soldiers who seem to represent his early thoughts of battle, and finally by his meeting with Jim. All have failed him.

Crane's realism is at its best in this chapter. Henry is obviously very much moved by his meeting with the doomed Jim. However, he does not express his emotion in a sentimental way. He awkwardly screams, "Gawd! Jim Conklin!" Jim gives him "a little commonplace smile" and says, "Hello, Henry." Jim Conklin, though wounded so badly that his side looked "like it had been chewed by wolves," only says, "An', b'jiminey, I got shot—I got shot. Yes, b'jiminey, I got shot."

On another level this chapter is concerned with wounds as symbols of courage. Before Henry meets Jim he envies the wounded men around him and imagines that all it takes to be happy is a "torn body." He conceives of a wound as "a red badge of courage." Then he watches Jim suffer and finally die from his wounds. Jim seems to embody courage at its finest. Crane ends the chapter with a single powerful image, "The red sun was pasted in the sky like a wafer." Thus the sun seems to be a symbol of Jim's wound and of courage.

It is significant that the tattered soldier who seems to represent Henry's idealized self returns in time to tell him to lead Jim into the fields to die. Although the youth is awkward about it he does stay with Jim until his death and at least tries to help him.

There are religious overtones in the death-scene. Jim, when he sees a clump of bushes in the distance, feels that this is the place that he is destined to meet with death. He shows his sense of purpose by running to the place in spite of Henry's efforts to stop him. Crane points out that his movements are "ritelike" and that he shows "a resemblance...to a devotee of a mad religion, blood-sucking, muscle-wrenching, bone-crushing." When he reaches the spot his face becomes peaceful as he waits for his "rendezvous with death." Henry tries to discover what Jim has in his mind but is unsuccessful. However, there seems to be a link in Crane's mind between death and religion; in Chapter VIII he has Henry discover a ghastly corpse in a natural chapel deep in the forest.

CHAPTER X

Summary

Henry is dumb with grief at the death of his friend. The tattered soldier suggests to Henry that they move on, that he is beginning to feel worse. Henry looks up and notices that the tattered soldier is beginning to weaken from his own wounds and is turning blue. He tells Henry that he can't die yet as he has children at home who need him. He begins to talk incoherently and confuses Henry in his thoughts with another of his friends.

After a time the tattered soldier again starts questioning Henry about his wounds. The soldier's curiosity stirs up Henry's shame and dread of being discovered. He becomes furious with the soldier and gives him looks "of hatred and contempt." Finally in spite of the fact that the tattered soldier is obviously dying he leaves him alone in the field, wandering aimlessly about muttering to himself.

Henry now wishes that he were dead and envies those soldiers who have died. He is very upset by the questions of the tattered man. It seems to him now that all of society is determined to know his shameful secret. He feels that he is unable to keep his secret to himself any longer.

Commentary

In the last chapter Jim Conklin who represented Henry's childhood died. In this chapter the tattered soldier representing Henry's idealized self is dying. But before he can die Henry deserts him. Thus symbolically he is deserting the image of himself that he had before he joined the Army. On a physical level he is deserting a wounded comrade and this adds a new offense for him to bear along with his cowardice in battle.

The tattered soldier's off-hand questions about his wound have upset Henry so much that he wishes he were dead. Crane is careful to make his tattered soldier more than just the embodiment of an idea. This is in keeping with his emphasis on realism. The tattered soldier talks of his children and of his desire for "some pea soup an' a good bed."

CHAPTER XI

Summary

Without being aware of it the youth comes nearer to the battlefield. As he comes around a hill he notices that the road is now full of "wagons, teams, and men" retreating from the battlefield. He feels comforted by this sight. He has not been alone in his retreat.

Soon he sees a "forward-going column of infantry" moving steadily toward the battle and he feels depressed again. He feels that he is looking at "a procession of chosen beings." He wishes he could be like them but feels that he never can be. He begins to imagine himself returning to battle and fighting gloriously. He carries on a debate within himself as to whether he should try to find his regiment and fight again. However, he is afraid that his comrades will ask him questions and that he will be ridiculed. Also he is physically in poor shape. He is hungry, tired, and aches all over especially in his feet. He gives up the idea of going into battle and hates himself for this decision. He feels that he is a "craven loon."

He stays "in the vicinity of the battle" as he has a great desire to know who is winning. He wishes for a time that the Army would lose the battle and thus share in his shame. He would then perhaps be looked up to as having great perception in being one of the first to run away just as a prophet foretelling a great flood might be the first to climb a tree. He feels that if the Army does win the battle that he is "a condemned wretch" for life. He feels that he will have to isolate himself from other men.

Before long he turns away from the idea that his salvation lies in the defeat of the Army. He does not really think that the Army can be defeated. He has been too well trained in the idea that the Army is certain to be successful. Again he momentarily wishes he were dead.

He tries to make up an excuse for his disappearance to take back with him to his regiment. However, he cannot think of anything which sounds plausible. He suffers agonies as he imagines the whole regiment discussing his cowardice and making fun of him.

Commentary

This chapter takes place almost entirely in the mind of the youth who is struggling with many conflicting emotions. At first he wishes that the Army would be defeated so that he would not stand alone in his shame. Then he gives up this idea and wishes that the Army would win but that he would die. Finally he speculates on returning to his regiment but is overcome by his fantasy of the whole regiment making fun of him.

Henry's feelings seem stronger and there is a sense of approaching crisis in this chapter. Obviously Henry cannot go on the way he is much longer. Something is going to happen.

CHAPTER XII

Summary

Suddenly a group of frightened retreating soldiers come sweeping down into the field where Henry is. Henry is "horror-stricken" as he feels that the war has been lost. He tries to question the men but they pay no attention to him. Finally he grabs the arm of one of the men to try to get him to answer his questions. The frightened soldier swings his rifle and smashes it down on Henry's head. Then the soldier runs on.

Henry falls to the ground in agony. As soon as he can he gets up and walks along "tall soldier fashion." After a time his wound pains him less. He wanders along aimlessly and thinks of home, his mother, and her cooking. He remembers how he and his school companions would swim in a shaded pool after school.

He becomes very weary and has an argument with himself as to whether he should lie down and sleep or keep going until he reaches an unknown haven. Presently he hears a cheery voice near his shoulder. The owner of the voice takes his arm and walks with him toward his regiment threading "the mazes of the tangled forest with a strange fortune." He manages to avoid guards and patrols and at the same time carries on a monologue which is almost incoherent. At last he and Henry reach the campfire where his regiment is resting for the night and the owner of the cheery voice bids farewell to Henry and disappears into the night without Henry's having seen his face.

Commentary

The climax of the book occurs in this chapter when Henry finally gets a wound, "a red badge of courage," ironically not from the enemy but from one of his own comrades who is fleeing in panic just as Henry did in Chapter VI. The frightened soldier seems symbolic of Henry himself. Henry is now face to face with his own image. He is seeing the reality of his cowardly act without explanations or justifications. Crane says that he "threw aside his mental pamphlets on the philosophy of the retreated and rules for the guidance of the damned." The result of this wound is a change in the direction of the story. Henry now starts his journey back to his regiment.

It is important that the strong trooper who takes Henry back to the regiment is nameless and faceless. He appears from nowhere to lead Henry back to camp and disappears as suddenly. His incoherent monologue on the way points up the aimlessness and meaninglessness of war:

> There was shootin' here an' shootin' there, an' hollerin' there, in th' damn darkness, until I couldn't tell t' save m' soul which side I was on.

Thus on one level Henry's journey back to camp is a journey of self-discovery. He does not have a saviour to whom he can give thanks. He is himself responsible for his cowardice, for his wound, and for his decision to return to his regiment. There is no one he can lean on except himself.

CHAPTER XIII

Summary

The youth goes slowly toward the fire as he is exhausted and needs food and rest. He is still afraid of being ridiculed but has no strength to go further or to invent a plausible lie. However, he soon finds that he does not have to say much. His friend, Wilson, the former loud soldier, is on guard duty. He is delighted to see Henry whom he has believed to be dead. He assumes that he got cut off from his regiment in the confusion of the fighting and easily accepts Henry's explanation that his head wound has been caused by a bullet. He and the corporal nurse Henry's wound, give him hot coffee, and put him to bed in Wilson's blankets.

Commentary

Henry is no longer alone. He is now back in camp with those who care about him and his comfort. He is obviously happy to be back. When Wilson tells him to lie down and go to sleep he "stretched out with a murmur of relief and comfort. The ground felt like the softest couch."

The change in Wilson is very noticeable. He is no longer loud and swaggering. He is very thoughtful and loving in his care of Henry even to giving him his own bed to sleep in though this means he will have to sleep on the ground himself.

CHAPTER XIV

Summary

The chapter opens with the youth awakening after a good night's rest. At first he has a fantasy that the sleeping men surrounding him are corpses but then he comes back to reality as he hears the crackling of the campfire and sees a few figures bustling about. The drums and bugles wake up the rest of the men.

Wilson comes over to him, examines his wound, and then encourages him to come to the fire for some breakfast. Henry is very much struck by the change in Wilson. He has become quiet, considerate, and reliable. Henry talks to him about it and Wilson admits that he was "a pretty big fool in those days."

The two friends discuss the battle and their chances of defeating the enemy. Henry tells Wilson that Jim Conklin is dead. Wilson is visibly moved. Shortly Wilson acts as peacemaker and keeps three soldiers from fighting over a trivial matter. Henry points out that a couple of days before, Wilson, too, loved to fight over trivial matters.

Wilson tells Henry that over half of the men in the regiment had been lost the day before. Many had returned during the night just as Henry had done.

Commentary

This is a time of recuperation for Henry. His sleep has been deep and restful. He enjoys his breakfast and companionable conversation with Wilson. He does not think of his former shame.

The most important element in this chapter is the picture of the new Wilson. In the last chapter we saw the change in him as he took care of Henry when he returned to camp wounded. In this chapter he is one of the first to get up and help others with their breakfasts. His role of peacemaker is new as is his modesty in his conversation with Henry. We see this as a possible foreshadowing of Henry's change from immaturity to maturity.

CHAPTER XV

Summary

The chapter opens with the regiment in formation waiting for orders to march to battle. Henry remembers the yellow packet which the loud soldier gave him before battle on the previous day to give to his family if he should die in battle. He calls to Wilson intending to give it back to him with a sarcastic remark. However, Wilson looks so meek that Henry does not wish "to deal the little blow" and so does not say anything.

Henry has been afraid of his friend because he feels that he may ask him for details of his adventures of the day before. However, he feels that with the packet in his possession he can deride Wilson at the first signs of any questioning.

Henry's self-pride is restored now that he realizes that nobody knows of his disgraceful behavior of the day before. "He had performed his mistakes in the dark, so he was still a man." He feels superior to his friend and speaks to him in a condescending though pleasant manner. He does not think about the battles which lie ahead of him. He has painfully learned that he doesn't have to plan his attitudes toward them. He feels that chance enters into the matter a great deal. Also he is beginning to feel more self-confident. He imagines now that he is "chosen of gods and doomed to greatness." He feels scornful of the men who had run from the battle the day before. He imagines that he has fled "with discretion and dignity."

Finally Wilson interrupts Henry's daydreaming by nervously asking for the packet which he had entrusted to his care. Henry returns it without making any comment and feels that he is a very generous fellow. Wilson's obvious shame at his behavior of the day before makes Henry feel stronger.

He starts daydreaming about how he will return home and tell his family and friends wonderful stories of the war. "He saw his gaping audience picturing him as the central figure in blazing scenes." He is now beginning to think like a veteran.

Commentary

Henry, now that he realizes that his cowardice is not going to be discovered, realizes that he has learned a truth about life. Neither bravery nor cowardice matters if neither is noticed by others. There is little purpose in trying to look into the future. What happens to a man is largely governed by chance. If things go well for him he can be glad of it. If things do not go well for him he has to do the best he can under the circumstances.

> In the present, he declared to himself that it was only the doomed and the damned who roared with sincerity at circumstance. Few but they ever did it. A man with a full stomach and the respect of his fellows had no business to scold about anything that he might think to be wrong in the ways of the universe, or even with the ways of society. Let the unfortunates rail; the others may play marbles.

The above reflects Crane's naturalistic concept of man's actions being largely governed by the circumstances of his environment and by his instincts responding to these circumstances.

Henry also realizes that real war is not the same as he had imagined it. "He had been out among the dragons...they were not so hideous as he had imagined them." This gives him self-confidence.

However, he still shows his immaturity by again building a false hero-image of himself in his mind. He imagines that he is favored by Fate and has acted wisely the day before.

CHAPTER XVI

Summary

The chapter opens with the youth's regiment marching to relieve a command which has been fighting in some damp trenches. The sound of the gunfire is everywhere so that conversation is impossible. At last the guns do stop momentarily and the men start spreading rumors, most of them being "stories of disaster." As the regiment is moving to another spot Henry forgets his behavior of the day before and lengthily condemns the commanding officers of the forces. Wilson gloomily defends the officers.

Henry gets carried away and continues his harangue even though he is "secretly dumbfounded" at his own words: "Well, don't we fight like the devil? Don't we do all that men can?" Finally a sarcastic soldier deflates Henry's ego with the remark, "Mebbe yeh think yeh fit th' hull battle yestirday, Fleming." The youth feels threatened by "the man's words" and after this he is silent. "He became suddenly a modest person."

The troops continue marching and talking until they finally reach a clear space in the woods where they stop and wait for further orders. There is much grumbling. Henry seems to sum up the frustration of all when he says:

> Good Gawd...we're always being chased around like rats! It makes me sick. Nobody seems to know where we go or why we go. We just get fired around from pillar to post and get licked here and get licked there, and nobody knows what it's done for. It makes a man feel like a damn' kitten in a bag.

The lieutenant, inwardly dissatisfied himself, silences the men.

Finally there is a lull before the battle. The men are tense, worn, and exhausted from the trials of the day before and stand "as men tied to stakes" waiting. Suddenly the shooting begins.

Commentary

There is a feeling of movement again in this chapter. The men are being marched to take part in another battle. The naturalistic doctrine is emphasized in this chapter. The men sense their helplessness. They have no choice but to obey orders even though they can see no sense in them. The individual person is frustrated in asserting his will against the collective person which is the regiment. Henry in the passage quoted above in the summary very aptly sets forth his personal frustration at being treated like a helpless animal, a "kitten in a bag," who is imprisoned and unable to act on his own. The lieutenant expresses the naturalistic doctrine in his answer:

> You boys shut right up! There no need' a your wastin' your breath in longwinded arguments about this an' that an' th' other ...All you got to do is to fight....

His answer means that all the grumbling and arguing does no good. In the end the men have to bend their own wills to that of the composite body of the regiment and so fighting it does no good.

Henry learns modesty in this chapter. He starts out being loud and brash, passing on rumors which he has heard from others without thinking about their meanings. This is in contrast to his behavior earlier in the book when he would hear a rumor and then ponder its significance silently in his own mind without saying anything. Although he is secretly appalled at what he is saying he is very much like the loud soldier at the beginning of the book. However, a sarcastic soldier's caustic remark brings him to his senses. The loud soldier has changed so much that he is actually defending those in authority in this chapter.

CHAPTER XVII

Summary

Before the battle begins Henry feels great rage and exasperation toward the enemy. He feels the need of rest and the enemy is making him fight. The day before he hated the universe but now he hates the "army of the foe." He crouches behind a tree "with his eyes burning hatefully and his teeth set in a curlike snarl." He daydreams that his foes are "flies sucking insolently at his blood." He feels the desire to revenge himself on them.

When the fighting begins, Henry loses sight of everything but his great feeling of hate. He fights as hard as he can, unaware of discomfort from the hot smoke and the heat of the rifle barrel. He and his companions cause the enemy to retreat but Henry continues to fire until a companion points out that he is shooting at nothing.

Much to Henry's surprise the men now regard him as "a war devil." The lieutenant is delighted with him and remarks, "By heavens, if I had ten thousand wild cats like you I could tear th' stomach outa this war in less'n a week!" Henry realizes that he is now a hero "and that he had not been aware of the process. He had slept and, awakening, found himself a knight."

Commentary

In this chapter Crane shows us what he conceives courage to be. It is simply doing what has to be done. Henry can now fight because he is reconciled to his own character and doesn't have to think about it. Therefore all his anger and imagination is focused on the enemy. Without realizing what he is doing he fights heroically. Crane suggests that Henry is half-asleep during the fighting. By this he means that Henry is simply not aware of himself.

CHAPTER XVIII

Summary

This chapter covers a few minutes respite in the fighting. One of the men, Jimmy Rogers, who has been shot, writhes in the grass. Henry and Wilson secure permission to get water for him. They think there is a stream nearby but are unable to find it. However, they are able to see more of the battlefield and thus gain a slightly wider view of the struggle in which they are engaged.

While they are retracing their steps back to their regiment they come upon the general, who is the commander of their division, and his staff. They linger nearby to overhear the conversation in the hopes that "some great inner historical things would be said." Much to their amazement they hear their regiment referred to as "a lot 'a mule drivers." They learn that they are going to take the offensive and charge themselves against the enemy and that not many of them can expect to survive the attack.

The youths hurry back to their regiment and tell the others the news they have heard about the charge. Most of the men believe them and start discussing and thinking about it. The officers bustle about getting the men set for the charge ahead.

Just before the fighting starts, Henry and Wilson look at each other remembering the remarks about the "mule drivers" and that not many of them would get back. They had not shared this information with the rest ot the men. However, neither hesitates. Meekly and without argument they accept the dangers of the battle ahead.

Commentary

This chapter illustrates further the naturalistic belief in the unimportance of individuals in the large scheme of things. Henry's regiment has just fought well and repulsed an attack. Yet the general who only knows the regiment by a number refers to it as a bunch of "mule drivers." It is unimportant that most of the men will be killed. A job needs to be done.

Henry's change of attitude is shown in this chapter. He accepts what the officers say about his regiment and their plans for it without comment or rebellion. He agrees with the meek soldier who says, "We'll git swallowed," but he doesn't try to fight it. He does not agonize in his own mind as to how he will react to the danger. He simply is ready to do what must be done.

CHAPTER XIX

Summary

The charge begins. Henry at first doesn't understand that the line is moving ahead as there is so much pushing and jostling. However, he soon lunges ahead and runs toward a distant clump of trees as fast as he can. He believes that the thing to do is to try to get over "an unpleasant matter as quickly as possible." The enemy shoots at the regiment from the woods. Henry, though not realizing it, is in the lead. His senses are unusually acute; he is aware of each blade of green grass and of the rough texture of the bark on the trees. "His mind took a mechanical but firm impression, so that afterward everything was pictured and explained to him, save why he himself was there."

There is a quality of frenzy to this rush. The men cheer insanely as they move forward, arousing each other to great excitement. For a brief moment they forget they are men and they believe no enemy can stop them no matter what the odds are against them. However, after a time they begin to tire and "become men again." Their pace slows down and they begin to be cautious again. Henry feels that he must have run miles and thinks that he is in "new and unknown land." The men gaze around at the wounded and dying men underfoot and appear "dazed and stupid."

Soon the lieutenant urges the men to come forward again. He shouts and swears at them. Finally Wilson is aroused and fires a shot at the woods. This spurs the other men to action. They begin to shoot and move forward again but more slowly this time. Finally they come to a spot where there is a large open space between them and the enemy line. The lieutenant swears at them trying to get them to cross the open space. Once he grabs Henry by an arm and tries to drag him forward. Henry is furious and shakes him off. However, the two men with Wilson close behind run in front of the regiment leading the way across the open space. They yell, "Come on, come on" in front of the colors. The man with the flag starts toward them and the rest of the regiment follows. The youth runs as fast as he can so that he can reach a tree before he can be hit by a bullet.

While he runs he suddenly feels a great love for the flag which is near to him. To him it symbolizes "beauty and invulnerability." When the sergeant holding the flag is hit by a bullet, Henry grabs the pole to keep the flag from falling to the ground. At the same time Wilson grabs it from the other side. The dead man who has held the flag does not let go and the men have to wrench it from him.

Commentary

Crane continues to emphasize the naturalistic concept of the insignificance of the individual when he shows us that Henry is aware of everything that is going on except the reason for his being where he is. He is being driven by the circumstances of his environment.

Crane defines courage in a passage that explains why Henry was leading the attack. It is "a delirium that encounters despair and death, and is heedless and blind to the odds. It is a temporary but sublime absence of selfishness."

Crane shows Henry thinking of the flag symbolically in terms of "beauty and invulnerability." Ironically, the sergeant holding the flag dies from a bullet just at the time that Henry is feeling that the flag does have the power to keep the men from harm.

CHAPTER XX

Summary

The two youths have a small argument over who should keep the flag. Each really doesn't mind the other having it but each wants to prove his courage by being willing to carry it. Henry finally keeps it.

The regiment retreats back to the trees and pulls itself together for another attack. Most of the men are tired, stunned, and discouraged. However, the officers keep urging them on.

Now Henry feels a great hatred toward the officer, "who, not knowing him, had called him a mule driver." He had felt that he and his companions would show this man what great fighters they really were. However, now he feels ashamed at the small retreat they have made and wonders if they can really win this skirmish after all.

Finally Henry's pride gets the best of his other emotions and, holding the flag high, he harangues and appeals to his comrades to start fighting again. He feels a subtle brotherhood with the lieutenant and supports him in his pleas. "But the regiment was a machine run down." The soldiers who did have the courage to proceed were continually aware that many of their fellow soldiers were silently slipping away to the back lines. "It was difficult to think of reputation when others were thinking of skins."

Suddenly Henry realizes that the enemy has gathered its forces together and is about to attack his regiment. The men become panic-stricken. They wonder if one of their own regiments could possibly have gotten lost and be coming in the wrong direction. There is so much smoke that it is impossible to see anything very clearly. Men run around trying to find a way of escape. "With serene regularity, as if controlled by a schedule, bullets buffed into men."

Henry calmly walks into the middle of the mob and stands quietly holding the flag high. Finally the officers get the men in shape to fend off the attack. The enemy is almost upon them before the serious shooting begins. They exchange rapid gunfire at very close range. The regiment holds the line and repulses the enemy.

When it is apparent that the enemy has retreated the men in Henry's regiment stand up and dance for joy. Although they have burning eyes and dry throats they feel enthusiastic and proud again. They feel a new trust in themselves and their weapons.

Commentary

This chapter is mainly important as it shows the continuing change in Henry. He is calm and brave in the face of great danger.

Crane emphasizes again the image of the armies as machines. When the men are tired he talks of a "machine run down." Bullets from the enemy buff into the men "with serene regularity, as if controlled by a schedule."

CHAPTER XXI

Summary

The fighting has stopped for the time being. The men who are left gather together for the final march. Some are fearful who have not been so before. Veterans from another company who are resting taunt the battered regiment. These taunts hurt the war-weary men. Henry is amazed when he sees what a short distance has been covered by the recent charge and realizes that the elapsed time has been short also. He begins to think that perhaps the veterans are right.

Henry, for the first time since the charge, has time to review his own actions in his mind. He is pleased with his recollections.

The officer who had called the men "mule drivers" comes along and reproaches the officers of the regiment for not having gone far enough. He had expected them to go one hundred yards farther. The men, at first, cannot believe that "their efforts have been called light," but when they do finally believe it they "were like cuffed and cursed animals, but withal rebellious."

Henry and Wilson discuss the matter. Henry develops "a tranquil philosophy" and decides that the officer hasn't seen the fighting himself and just concludes that the men have not fought well. Wilson comments that "there's no fun in fightin' for people when everything yeh do—no matter what—ain't done right." Henry soothes his friend by reminding him how well the two of them have fought.

Several men come hurrying up to the two youths and tell them that the colonel and young lieutenant have been discussing the bravery and good fighting of Fleming and Wilson. They tell them that the colonel has said that they deserve to be "major generals." The boys, though embarrassed, are delighted and exchange happy looks. They quickly forget their disappointment in the veterans and the general and think with great affection of the colonel and lieutenant.

Commentary

This is a time of rest for the men between rounds of fighting. There is a contrast between what the men think of themselves and what the veterans and senior officers think of them. The men judge themselves by how hard they have fought. The officers judge them by how much territory they have gained.

Although the focus is still on Henry we are now aware of Wilson and the rest of the fighting men too. Henry is definitely a part of his regiment and is proving to be a leader in it also.

CHAPTER XXII

Summary

The chapter opens with the enemy again coming out of the woods. Henry is standing where he can see some of the fighting of the other regiments and he watches with interest the two lines of men weaving "perpetually backward and forward in riotous surges."

Henry's regiment is again undaunted in its fighting. The lieutenant calls forth "from a hidden receptacle of his mind new and portentous oaths" with which to urge his men on. Henry, still holding the flag, is an interested spectator. A group of enemy soldiers now come into range and the fighting begins in earnest.

Remembering that the general had called them "mud diggers" the soldiers now fight with a new savageness and swiftness apparent both in their movements and in the expressions on their faces. Henry is determined not to move backward from the place where he is standing. He feels now that his best revenge on the general is simply to die here on the field. He thinks that his corpse will be a reproach to the general for his unkind and unjust words.

The men continue fighting but the casualties are heavy and they begin to weaken. "The robust voice, that had come strangely from the thin ranks, was growing rapidly weak."

Commentary

The battle continues. Henry gets a wider view of the fighting. His horizons are expanding.

There is some humor in connection with the lieutenant's swearing. Apparently when he is most excited and most anxious to inspire his men to move forward he swears. "Strings of expletives he swung lashlike over the backs of his men, and it was evident that his previous efforts had in nowise impaired his resources." Also this passage shows Crane's realism. In the traditional literature of warfare an officer would inspire his men by saying noble and uplifting words. In actuality an officer gets his men to move by swearing at them.

Obviously the regiment cannot stand much more fighting. The men are brave and undaunted but the casualties are heavy and the men who are left are weakening from their tremendous efforts.

CHAPTER XXIII

Summary

The chapter opens with the colonel and other officers running along near the back of the line telling the men to take the offensive and charge the enemy. Henry considers the order and agrees that it is the only thing to do as they will all be killed if they stay where they are or retreat. They must move forward and push the enemy away from the fence.

Henry expects that his companions will have to be driven to do this. To his surprise he notices that they are agreeing to the charge. When the command is given the soldiers run forward with eager cries.

> It was a blind and despairing rush by the collection of men and dusty and tattered blue, over a green sward and under a sapphire sky, toward a fence, dimly outlined in smoke, from behind which sputtered the fierce rifles of enemies.

Henry keeps the flag with its bright colors near to the front and shrieks and urges the other men on. However, he does not need to do this for the men are again united in an unselfish, enthusiastic, unthinking mob which fights recklessly against the enemy. Henry feels "the daring spirit of a savage religion-mad." He feels that he is capable of sacrificing himself for the glory of the endeavor.

Henry strains himself to the utmost. He begins to imagine what it will be like when the "two bodies of troops crash together." However, he finds that the gray line gives away in most points so that the two lines do not meet in a terrible clash.

In one spot though several of the enemy refuse to run. They keep shooting and yelling at the regiment. Their flag flutters over them. Henry looks with longing at the other flag, which to him expresses "bloody minglings, near blows." He starts toward the group with the idea of capturing the other flag. He sees now that the man carrying the enemy flag has been hit by the last volley of gunfire. He watches his struggle to stay alive and take the flag to a safe place. However, he is too badly hurt to do what he wants. Wilson leaps over the fence and grabs the flag from his dying hands.

The men go wild with joy at having routed the enemy from their line at the fence. Four men are taken prisoner. They soon are surrounded by "blue men" who are curious and want to question them. The prisoners react to their predicament in different ways.

One shows his resentment by looking at his captors and swearing at them. Another talks of "battles and conditions" in a calm and pleasant manner. Another is depressed and the last is deeply embarrassed at having been caught.

After the men have celebrated their victory they sit down in the grass to rest. Henry and Wilson sit together and congratulate each other.

Commentary

Crane again defines courage for us as he shows the men united in an unselfish, unthinking, and enthusiastic brotherhood.

The enemy comes into sharper focus in this chapter. Now Henry and his comrades can see the enemy at the fence and watch their actions. They find that the enemy is not endowed with supernatural powers as the veterans have suggested but that the Confederate soldiers are very much like themselves, men with a job to do.

CHAPTER XXIV

Summary

The chapter opens with the noise of gunfire slowly dying out until finally all is quiet. Henry and Wilson look up and notice that there is some movement going on among the troops. Shortly they receive the order to go back across the river to where they had started out the morning before. The soldiers grumble over this just as they would have grumbled over an order to attack again.

The regiment joins other groups of soldiers and all retrace their steps toward the river.

Henry feels "a subtle change" going on in his mind. He is casting off his battle mind and trying to resume his normal way of thinking. Finally he realizes that he is leaving the battlefield with its upheavals, strange passions, and fighting and he is leaving it alive. He feels very happy about this.

Later he reviews "his deeds, his failures, and his achievements" with some degree of accuracy. He is "gleeful and unregretting" about his public deeds which his companions had seen. They were truly joyful to think about. He had been brave and his companions were aware of this and had spoken to him about it. However, he still feels ashamed about his flight from his first encounter in battle. Also, the memory of the tattered soldier and his treatment of him comes to mind to irritate and agonize him. He remembers that he deserted this dying comrade who had been solicitous of his supposed wounds, leaving him to die alone in the field. This remembrance "darkened his view of these deeds in purple and gold."

After a time he manages to put this sin into some perspective and also his pride in his great deeds. His eyes "seemed to open to some new ways. He found that he could look back upon the brass and bombast of his earlier gospels and see them truly." He now feels that he is a man. He feels sturdy and strong but not assertive and loud. "He had been to touch the great death, and found that, after all, it was but the great death."

The chapter and book ends with the youth moving along in the procession of mumbling weary soldiers away from the heat and violence of battle. Henry smiles to himself "for he saw that the world was a world for him." His mind now turns to images of peace such as "tranquil skies, fresh meadows, cool brooks...."

Commentary

The battle is over. Ironically the men are ordered back to the spot they started from two days before. All the fighting and bloodshed has had little purpose behind it.

However, Henry has changed and he knows it. He can look at his sins and his heroic deeds now in perspective and not feel too proud about one nor too guilty about the other. He is glad to be alive and feels that the world is a good place for him to be. "He was a man."

Crane emphasizes the change from war to peace by means of

images, taken from nature, "tranquil skies, fresh meadows, cool brooks...." Henry's mind, the soldiers in general, and the environment are all at peace at last.

BIOGRAPHY OF STEPHEN CRANE (1871-1900)

Stephen Crane was born at Newark, New Jersey, November 1, 1871, the fourteenth child of a Methodist minister. He suffered from poor health in his youth but always had high spirits. He attended several schools including the Pennington Seminary and the Hudson River Institute at Claverack, New York. Although extremely brilliant he was not studious and was mainly interested in unusual words and baseball. In 1890 he went to Lafayette College for two terms and then attended Syracuse University for one year. Here he preferred to read books which were not related to his courses and to engage in athletics. After he left college he went to New York and worked for a short time in a business office but soon left this to devote his full time to writing. He was a reporter for two New York newspapers and also wrote free lance articles. During this time he suffered severe privations due to his extreme poverty.

His first significant piece of writing was *Maggie: A Girl of the Streets* which so shocked the publishers because of its naturalism that Crane had to have it printed himself. It deals with a girl who was overcome by her environment and committed suicide. The environment is the Bowery of New York City in Crane's time.

In March, 1893, Crane wrote the first draft of his novel, *The Red Badge of Courage*. It first appeared in a Philadelphia newspaper as a serial and was published in book form in the fall of 1895. It is said that he wrote the original draft in only ten days. The book was an immediate success and established Crane's literary reputation.

Crane continued to write prolifically. He published four volumes of short stories and two volumes of poetry. Probably his best short story is "The Open Boat" which is based on an experience he had when a boat he was on was shipwrecked enroute to Cuba. He was one of only three survivors. His poetry is free in form and contains unusual images. In 1925-1926 his *Collected Works* were published in twelve volumes.

Besides working on the writing mentioned above, Crane also traveled to Greece to write of the war with Turkey for periodicals in England and America. Later he went to Cuba to report on the Spanish-American war for several New York newspapers.

While he was in Greece he married Cora Taylor, whom he had known in Florida. He and his wife rented a large Elizabethan mansion, Brede Place, in England where he lived for two years except for trips to Cuba. He was overly generous and hospitable and attracted all sorts of people, some of whom took advantage of his generosity.

Crane had never enjoyed robust health and his adventures and hard work weakened him so that he contracted tuberculosis. He and Cora left England for Germany where he hoped to regain his health in the dry climate of the mountains of the Black Forest. However, he did not recover and died June 5, 1900, at the age of twenty-eight. He was buried in his family plot in New Jersey.

During his lifetime, Crane attracted the attention of many of the leading authors of his day. William Dean Howells was one of the first to discover him; Hamlin Garland was an early admirer. In England Crane was a close friend of Joseph Conrad and his family, and of Robert Barr, and Harold Frederic, to name but a few.

CRITICAL ANALYSIS

STRUCTURE

General Remarks

The Red Badge of Courage is, in many ways, more like a short story than a novel. It is compressed and unified so that nothing extraneous is included.

The book is organized around the life of an ordinary soldier, Henry Fleming, just before and during a Civil War battle. Henry is introduced on the second page of the book and is constantly "on stage" throughout the book. The other characters – Henry's mother, the tall soldier, the loud soldier, the tattered soldier, the officers – are important partly because they reflect or point up certain attitudes and emotions in Henry. The tall soldier and the loud soldier face the same problem Henry faces and gain maturity as the book progresses just as Henry does. All the characters in the book, with the exception of the mother who gives the reader valuable insight into Henry's childhood and upbringing, are considered in terms of their behavior just before, during, and after fighting in battle. This gives the characters a direct relationship to Henry and gives the book a tight unity.

The book also has unity of setting. The setting, on one level, is a battlefield of the Civil War. The book opens with the troops resting on a hill near a river. The book ends with the troops marching back to the same spot they started from. In the meantime they move into fields, through forests, up hills, and down again. During most of the book this landscape is torn by the strife of battle. On another level the setting is the mind of the untried and youthful private with all his emotions, impressions, attitudes, and thoughts.

The book also has unity of time. The first three chapters cover the time just before Henry is to take part in his first battle with a flashback telling of the circumstances of his enlistment and early days in the service. The remaining twenty-one chapters deal in detail with the two days of the fighting.

Themes

Several themes run through the book and add greatly to its unity.

COURAGE

The most important underlying theme is the nature and meaning of courage. Crane poses the question early in the book by having Henry think that he must discover whether he is brave or not. Henry learns that courage is "a temporary but sublime absence of selfishness" in which men for a short time become united in a comradeship which leads them to heroic actions. While they are being courageous they do not think of themselves as individuals.

WAR

Crane is disillusioned as to the purpose of war. There is no feeling of a great or noble cause which might make it worthwhile for men to give up their lives. No great leaders are shown inspiring their men to great valor. The leaders treat their men almost like animals. After brave and successful fighting a general calls the men in Henry's regiment "Mule Drivers."

Crane is disillusioned as to the consequences of war. After a bloody two day battle the men march back to their starting place. There is no feeling of having gained anything in the two days of hard fighting. War seems purposeless and meaningless.

However in spite of the above points, Crane thinks of war as a great adventure for an individual man, a test of his courage and stamina. Crane values the little man who faces almost unbearable danger in battle.

The theme of war is, of course, closely tied to the theme of courage. War provides the setting for an individual to prove that he is courageous.

FEAR

Crane also considers the effect of fear. Henry's two great fears in the book are death and ridicule. He runs from battle because he is afraid of being killed. Later in the book he wishes he were dead because he fears that his comrades will discover his cowardice and ridicule him.

Story

Crane has avoided using a tightly knit plot in this book. The story is in essence a psychological study of the mind of a youth, Henry Fleming, who faces death for the first time. He becomes frightened in battle and runs away. Later he overcomes his fright and fights bravely and well. In the process, he matures and becomes aware of himselt as an individual. The book is chiefly concerned with chronicling the tensions, anxieties, moods, thoughts, and impressions of Henry as he progresses through the series of episodes which make up the book. Thus Crane simultaneously tells two stories, one, of the outer action of Henry before and during the battle, and the other, the effect of this action on his mind and emotions. Crane is successful in fusing the two planes of the story into one unified impression.

The action of the book can be divided into five parts.

1. Henry before the battle: Chapters I-IV

2. Henry during the first fighting: Chapters V-VI

3. Henry's flight: Chapters VI-XI

4. Henry's wound and his return to his regiment: Chapters XII-XIV

5. Henry in battle again: Chapters XV-XXIV

1. *Henry before the battle:* Chapters I-IV

   These chapters serve as an introduction to the rest of the book. On a physical level the reader is introduced to the main character, Henry Fleming, who is an inexperienced young farm boy who joins the Union Army. As his regiment is about to move into action, he is fearful that he will prove to be cowardly in battle. He tries to find other soldiers who are as frightened as he is but he cannot break through the reserve which each soldier has built up around himself. He becomes increasingly disturbed as his regiment gets nearer to the fighting.

   On an emotional level the reader becomes acquainted with the mind of Henry Fleming. The story moves ahead in terms of the images in Henry's mind. First there is the image he had of himself before he joined the Army and in his early days after enlistment. He thought of himself as a hero who would do "breathless deeds." After a time he loses his hero image and becomes an anonymous member of the Army. However, when his regiment is about to get into actual battle he again thinks of himself as an individual and wonders whether he is cowardly or heroic. He tries to answer this question by comparing himself to other soldiers but finally comes to the conclusion that he won't know until he actually starts to fight.

2. *Henry during the first fighting:* Chapters V-VI

On a physical level Henry and his comrades repulse the first attack of the enemy. However, when the enemy attacks again Henry becomes panic-stricken and runs away. On an emotional level Henry is successful in fighting at first because in his mind he has again become an anonymous member of the "blue demonstration." In the second round of fighting he has an acute awareness of his individuality and has a vision of himself being deserted by his comrades and having to face the enemy alone. This is too much for him and he runs away.

3. *Henry's flight:* Chapters VI-XI

Henry runs aimlessly for awhile. Then he unsuccessfully seeks comfort in the dark forest. Finally he joins a group of wounded soldiers who are marching away from the front lines. He meets a tattered soldier, badly wounded, who causes him great anguish by asking casually where he has been wounded. He finds his old childhood friend, Jim Conklin, who after suffering terribly from his wounds, dies in front of Henry. Henry next deserts the tattered soldier who is about to die and wanders off by himself.

On an emotional level Henry tries to find consolation in nature. The scene in the forest when Henry unexpectedly comes across a ghastly corpse in a natural chapel is a grim reminder that nature is not a person with feelings and thoughts. Next Henry tries to take refuge in the idea of himself which he had before entering the Army, personified by the tattered soldier. But he is tormented by the questioning as to his own wounds. He deserts this idealized self as he is about to die in the fields. He meets Jim Conklin who seems to represent Henry's childhood, and who consoled him earlier in the book. Henry watches him die an agonizing death. Henry's emotions get more and more unsettled. Once he wishes that the Army would be defeated so that others would share his feeling of guilt. But he gives up this idea because he cannot really believe that the Army can be defeated. Several times he wishes he were dead as he cannot bear to face the ridicule of his company when they find out how cowardly he has been.

4. *Henry's wound and his return to his regiment:*
Chapters XII-XIV

Henry runs into another group of soldiers who are fleeing from the front in panic. When he tries to stop one of them to find out what is happening at the front, the man, overcome with terror, hits Henry on the head with the butt of his rifle. He stumbles around, not seriously hurt but in pain, until a cheerful soldier comes upon him and leads him back to his own regiment. There to his relief, his comrades assume that he got separated from them during the fighting and that his wound was caused by an enemy bullet.

On an emotional level Henry at last faces the reality of his act of cowardice. The fleeing soldier is just what he was himself when he fled from his first fighting. Thus in a sense as the refugee is symbolic of himself, he wounds himself. This is the turning point in the book. Now that he starts his journey back to his regiment. At first he wanders around aimlessly thinking of home. Then he meets a cheerful soldier who leads him back to his regiment which now represents not only a return to duty but also a return to companionship. Henry has experienced agonizing loneliness which is now over. The soldier who leads him back to camp is without a name or face. Thus in a sense Henry's journey is one of self-discovery. Crane points this up by not revealing Henry's full name until he returns to his regiment.

Henry returns to his campfire fearful of the ridicule of his comrades. When they assume that he has been wounded by an enemy bullet and lavish attention on him, he discovers that cowardice, if it is not discovered, does not matter. "He had performed his mistakes in the dark, so he was still a man." He now realizes that he does not have to worry about how he will act in future battles. He can face losing his individuality temporarily in battle because he has come to grips with his own character.

5. *Henry in battle again:* Chapters XV-XXIV

The next day there is more fighting. This time Henry fights recklessly and well. He keeps the flag from falling into enemy hands and later leads a charge in such a rash manner that the regimental commander comments on his daring and bravery. At the end of a day of hard and often confused fighting the regiment is ordered back from its new position for no reason apparent to the soldiers.

This part of the book shows the change in Henry as he is not only personally courageous but also urges others to heroism. Crane points out that Henry is not aware of what he is doing in battle. He "had proceeded sheeplike." When the battle is over Henry is happy with his public behavior in battle. Crane shows us the new mature Henry in a passage during the march of troops away from the battlefield.

> And at last his eyes seemed to open to some new ways. He found that he could look back upon the brass and bombast of his earlier gospels and see them truly. He was gleeful when he discovered that he now despised them.
>
> With the conviction came a store of assurance. He felt a quiet manhood, non-assertive but of sturdy and strong blood. He knew that he would no more quail before his guides wherever they would point....

SETTING

The Civil War had long interested Stephen Crane when he wrote *The Red Badge of Courage,* thirty years after the end of the war. He had heard veterans expound on their experiences, and had read some of the memoirs of former soldiers which were printed in Century Magazine's series, "Battles and Leaders of the Civil War." However, it is significant that Crane not only had not fought in the Civil War but at the time he wrote the book had never fought in nor witnessed any war at all. By means of his imagination he used the information he had gained from his reading and listening to create one of the most realistic accounts of warfare that has ever been written.

Specifically he was writing about the Battle of Chancellorsville, one of the bloodiest conflicts in the Civil War. However he does not name the battle in the book. The crash of artillery and other noises of battle are part of the background throughout most of the episodes.

The time was 1861. This was before the Industrial Revolution when the nation was largely agricultural. The rural people worked hard on their farms. Their lives were simple and sometimes dull. Although they were poorly educated for the most part, they held strong and simple beliefs. The hero, Henry Fleming, came from this kind of background.

The Confederate and Union armies are part of the setting. The strong social order in the book is the Army. Crane depicts the Army as an insect, machine, or a person. The individual soldiers are part of the corporate body of the Army. They fight best when they accept their place in the scheme of things. However, the daily life of the soldiers is also part of the setting. Crane shows the soldiers huddled around their campfires eating, talking, and sleeping. He shows them marching, fighting, getting wounded, and dying.

The countryside where the battle takes place is also part of the setting. Crane describes wooded hills, streams, valleys, fields, and a river. This peaceful countryside points up the bloody battle taking place on it. The reader sees the dead and wounded in the fields, the bullet marks in the trees, and the marching of soldiers and artillery on the narrow dirt roads. These seem like a temporary intrusion on the naturally peaceful land.

On another level the setting is the mind of the young soldier, Henry Fleming. Every impression, thought, and emotion reveal this imaginative world of fear, violence, and isolation.

On a universal level the setting is any conflict or battle. Men in any battle or conflict seek danger, try to avoid it, or accept what comes along stoically.

THE CHARACTERS

Henry Fleming

Henry is the most important character in the book and the most completely presented. The book is basically the story of his successful search for self-identity and maturity during the period just before and during the Battle of Chancellorsville in the Civil War.

Crane does not mention Henry's exact age but he emphasizes his youth and inexperience in several ways. In a flashback in the first chapter Crane makes the reader aware of Henry's immaturity before he joined the Union Army. He spent a good deal of time dreaming of battles and imagining his heroic actions in them. He thrilled over the accounts of battle experiences which he read and had an insatiable appetite for hearing of the "breathless deeds" of war. He wanted to join the Army so that he could, firsthand, experience the magnificent struggles he envisioned. He enlisted in spite of his mother's practical common sense arguments that he was needed more on the farm than in the Army. He was thus showing a youthful rebellion against authority. When he first got his uniform just before he left for his training period, he spent an afternoon saying goodbye to school friends and showing off in his newly gained regalia. There is no mention of any great cause or ideal that he wants to fight for. He simply wants to find in real life the adventures he has dreamed about having.

Henry is a typical youth of his time and place. He has grown up on a small inland farm helping with the chores and also attending school in a nearby town. Apparently his father is dead and Henry has been raised by his mother who is devoted to him. She has strong simple beliefs about life which she has tried to impart to Henry. When he is about to leave her for the first time she seems mainly concerned about his not drinking or swearing, but she also mentions that he must always do his duty.

Henry does not seem to be deeply religious. He does not try to seek comfort in religion when he is faced with the problem of his cowardly behavior in battle. However, he does show his moral upbringing by feeling guilty when he deserts his post in battle and when he deserts a wounded comrade in the field.

Henry, in spite of his illusions about war and about himself is basically an honest person. Even in his early days when he is dreaming of the glories of war he, in his more rational moments, knows that such wars do not exist any more. "From his home his youthful eyes had looked upon the war in his own country with distrust. It must be some sort of play affair." Even though he hangs on the words of the veterans as they tell him of the terrible enemy he feels that "he could not put a whole faith in veterans' tales, for recruits were their prey."

Henry is basically an introspective person. He feels that he must find out all that he can about himself. Thus all through the book after he has been through an experience, he stops and analyzes his thoughts, emotions, and actions. Even at the end of the book after he has fought bravely and well he stops "...to study his deeds, his failures, and achievements."

The book is more concerned with Henry's reactions to what happens to him than the actions themselves. For instance in the first few months of Army life Henry looks out for his own comfort and endures the constant drilling and reviewing. The result of this is that he loses his sense of identity and grows "to regard himself as a part of a vast blue demonstration." However, when he hears that his regiment is about to go into battle for the first time he regains his feeling of individuality and begins to ponder on how he will react to the challenge. He unsuccessfully tries to measure himself against the veterans who make him feel inferior and against his fellow recruits who are also untried in battle.

Henry's character goes through various phases as the book progresses. When the book opens Henry is a young untried soldier about to face death for the first time in battle. At first he is just unsure of himself. Then he has agonies of doubt about himself. He has to obey commands that he cannot understand. He has to behave in ways that he hates. He has no built-in reactions to the situations he faces. At first he forgets about himself and fights well but in the second attack by the enemy he becomes panic-stricken and flees, thus proving to himself that he is a coward.

For quite some time he flees from facing the truth about himself. This is a spiritual as well as a physical flight. He shows that he is not only frightened but also pretentious. He wavers between pretending to himself that he has acted in accordance to nature's law of self preservation and wishing he were dead because of his cowardly behavior. He pretends he has a physical wound when he joins the line of the wounded soldiers leaving the front. Actually his wound is in his soul. However, eventually Henry faces his cowardly act openly and returns to his duty. When he meets the enemy again the next day he proves to be extremely heroic. His character has changed from the insecure, frightened, cowardly boy of the day before to an active, unafraid, secure man. He is tinged with sin but has established a pattern for his maturity. His new code of behavior is based on what he learned the day before in his disgrace. He realizes now that the kind of war he imagined does not exist. He does not have to fight the enemy alone. All he has to do is to accept each situation as it occurs calmly and to do the best he can in it. He still has to obey orders he cannot understand. He still has to fight until he is physically exhausted. He still remembers his cowardly action of the day before both in battle and when he deserted the badly wounded soldier in the field. However, now he can look at all of this objectively. "He has been to touch the great death, and found that, after all, it was but the great death. He was a man."

Mother of Henry Fleming

Henry's mother appears only briefly in the book in Chapter I when Henry recalls the circumstances of his enlistment in the Union Army. However, the farewell scene between Henry and his mother is one of the most moving in the book.

Henry's mother is a hard-working, uneducated farm woman. She is deeply religious as is shown by her response, "The Lord's will be done, Henry," when he tells her that he has enlisted against her wishes.

She is simple, kind, and obviously loves her son dearly. When he is going off to war she knits him eight pair of socks and puts blackberry jam in his knapsack because he is fond of it.

Although she is probably not highly educated she has a great deal of common sense. She understands that Henry wants to enlist because of his unrealistic dreams of the glories of war. She tells him what he finally learns the hard way on his own:

> Don't go a-think' you can lick the hull rebel army at the start, because yeh can't. Yer jest one little feller amongst a hull lot of others, and yeh've got to keep quiet an' do what they tell yeh.

She aids the realistic tone of the book. In contrast to Henry's romantic imaginings she is very down to earth. When he returns from enlisting she is milking the cows. In her farewell talk with him she peels potatoes.

She also represents universal motherhood. Mothers parting from their sons for the first time in every age are concerned with the same things about which she is concerned. She cautions Henry to take care of himself physically and to stay away from bad companions who might lead him astray. She tells him to "do no shirking" on her account, but if he is killed "the Lord'll take keer of us all."

The conflict between Henry and his mother also suggests a universal conflict between two generations. The older generation is more conservative and can see life more realistically. The younger generation is full of dreams and eager for adventure.

The Tall Soldier–Jim Conklin

The tall soldier is the first character in the book to whom we are introduced. He comes "flying back from a brook" where he has been washing his shirt with the rumor that the regiment is going to move the next day into battle. This causes much speculation among his comrades and he is forced to defend the rumor particularly from the loud soldier who seems to doubt everything he says. He shows that he is youthful by his complete acceptance of the rumor and his joy in elaborating on it and causing a commotion among his comrades. This incident is important to the book because this rumor starts Henry thinking about the problem of courage which is the central theme of the book.

That night Henry asks the tall soldier if he thinks he might run away in battle. Jim answers honestly that it is a possibility but he believes basically in himself and the other men to stay and fight. His answer reassures Henry somewhat as Jim did not quote the "correct confidence" which Henry expected to hear.

During the first part of the book Jim imagines that he can understand the strategy of the war with his limited viewpoint as a private. As he gets nearer to the fighting he becomes philosophical about all the moves he and the soldiers are required to make without any understanding at all. He defends the leaders and calmly does what he is told.

Henry meets Jim again in Chapter IX among the procession of wounded soldiers who are leaving the battle area. Jim is obviously mortally wounded but shows great courage as he marches forward looking for the place where he feels he is to make his "rendezvous with death." He is glad to see Henry and for a time clings to him. Finally Henry at the suggestion of the tattered soldier leads Jim into the fields and there Jim breaks away and runs to some nearby bushes and dies alone in a "solemn ceremony" of "ritelike movements." He exhibits courage at its finest.

Jim is important to the book for several reasons. His growth from immaturity to maturity precedes a similar change in Henry. At the beginning of the book he is young, inexperienced, and gets his pleasure from spreading rumors. However, when there is a job to do he does it without complaining. Although somewhat bewildered, he accepts his agonizing wounds and death calmly and bravely.

In a way he symbolizes Henry's youthful background. Henry and Jim have been childhood friends and Henry looks to Jim for comfort when he first begins to ponder the problem of courage. Thus in Chapter IX when Henry meets Jim when the former is fleeing from his battle post one might expect Henry to seek comfort from him. Jim's death cuts off one possible refuge for Henry and forces him to resolve his own problem.

Jim points up Henry's character by the contrast of his own reactions. First, when Henry is worrying about how he will behave in battle, Jim is quite unconcerned about the problem. He feels that he will probably do all right and does not worry about his actions ahead of time. During the long and tedious march to the front Henry rebels in his mind against following orders he cannot understand. Jim calmly follows orders and stands up for those in authority. The most striking contrast is in Chapter IX when Jim and Henry are in the procession of wounded soldiers. Henry has no physical wound while Jim has been wounded so severely that his "side looked as if it had been chewed by wolves." Thus he is a silent reproach to Henry.

Jim also greatly aids the realism of the book. Crane is trying to dispel the romantic illusions about war. Jim personifies great courage yet he speaks and acts in a commonplace manner. When he is marching along in great agony from his wounds he simply comments, "An', Lord, what a circus! An', b'jiminey, I got shot—I got shot. Yes, b'jiminey, I got shot."

The Loud Soldier—Wilson

The loud soldier is actually only loud during the first part of the book. In Chapter I he refuses to believe the tall soldier's rumor and scoffs at everything he says. In Chapter II he repeats the soldier's traditional illusions about battle, "We've got 'em now. At last, by the eternal thunders, we'll lick 'em good!" Henry asks him if he thinks he might run away in battle. Wilson answers, "Run?—of course not!" Thus his view is in contrast to Henry's worries about courage and the tall soldier's acceptance of what may happen.

During the march to the front Wilson complains about those in authority. He shows his youth and inexperience by looking at the war from a very limited viewpoint. Later in the book Henry has this attitude also.

Just before the first part of the battle begins Wilson panics and is certain that he will be killed. He gives a packet to Henry to deliver to his folks after he is dead. Despite his earlier brave talk now he says, "It's my first and last battle, old boy." This panic precedes Henry's panic in Chapter VI.

Wilson next appears in Chapter XIII when Henry returns to his regiment after his wanderings behind the line. Wilson shows a great change in his character. He is loving and kind to Henry, letting him sleep in his blankets even though this means that he will have to sleep on the cold ground.

Chapter XIV is almost completely concerned with showing the reader the new mature Wilson.

> He seemed no more to be continually regarding the proportions of his personal prowess. He was not furious at small words that pricked his conceits. He was no more a loud young soldier. There was about him a fine reliance. He showed a quiet belief in his purposes and his abilities.

Henry notices the change and sees "that ever after it would be easier to live in his friend's neighborhood."

In Chapter XV Wilson asks Henry to return the packet which he gave him to give to his folks before the initial battle. He is very ashamed of his panic of the day before and acts in an embarrassed manner. This is in contrast to Henry's assured manner and shows great irony. Wilson and Henry both were frightened of the battle. However, Wilson's fear was mild compared to Henry's which caused the latter to flee his post. However, Henry knows about Wilson's weakness and so feels superior to him while Wilson does not know about Henry's mistakes and so feels inferior to him.

When the fighting begins again Wilson and Henry team up and together fight equally bravely and well. Both receive the commendation of commanding officers for their daring. At last their attitudes and performances are almost the same.

Throughout the book Wilson reflects briefly many of the attitudes of Henry, which indicates that the attitudes are not unique to Henry and also in one way makes Wilson almost seem like an extension of Henry.

The Tattered Soldier

The tattered soldier appears only briefly in Chapters VIII, IX, and X, and yet he is important to the book. He is described as "a tattered man, fouled with dust, blood and powder stain from hair to shoes, who trudged quietly at the youth's side." He listens with great eagerness to a sergeant's lurid tales of battle, "his mouth agape in yokel fashion." He thus reflects Henry's early attitude toward war. Henry, too, listened "yokel fashion" to the glorious descriptions of battle in the country store before he joined the Army. The tattered soldier is badly wounded in two places, the head and the arm, and seems to be the embodiment of Henry's ideal of a wounded veteran. At the time Henry is very much wishing that he were wounded as a wound is to him a symbol of courage.

The tattered soldier is also a reproach to Henry who is not wounded. His casual but searching questions about Henry's wounds cause Henry to desert this idealized self twice, once in the procession of wounded soldiers and again in the field when he is about to die.

The tattered soldier appears when Henry and Jim Conklin are walking together and suggests that Henry take Jim into the fields so that Jim can die in peace away from the other soldiers. He stays with Henry until after Jim's death when Henry leaves him to die in the fields alone.

Although the tattered soldier appears only briefly and seems to be mostly symbolic in character, Crane has portrayed him as a real person also. He speaks of his children whom he loves and of his wish for a clean bed and some pea soup for supper. He shows a loving concern for his comrades particularly for Henry and Jim Conklin.

The Soldiers as a group

Veterans: Crane has characterized the veterans as an experienced group of soldiers who are tattered and torn in appearance, and who love to spin tall tales about their battle experiences particularly for the benefit of the recruits whom they call, "Fresh Fish." They provide a contrast to the inexperienced, unsure recruits and also provide them with an example which they try to emulate.

Recruits: As a group the recruits spend most of their time moving from one place to another and grumbling and mumbling about every move and every order they receive. They do not understand what they are doing most of the time. They see the war from a very limited viewpoint. In battle they do what they must and fight even though they suffer from fatigue and wounds and do not understand why they are fighting. Only the dead, the severely wounded, and the panic-stricken soldiers stop fighting. By the end of the book the recruits, as a result of their battle experiences, are veterans also.

Officers: The officers are not much different from the ordinary soldiers in their language and attitudes. They are not noble and do not provide inspired leadership. They get their men to fight by swearing at them. When one lieutenant gets the order to charge he says, "Charge? Well, b'Gawd!" He does not understand the reason for the order but he carries it out anyway. The senior officers are concerned with the job to be done and do not consider the men as individuals. Shortly after Henry's regiment has successfully repulsed an enemy attack a general calls the regiment a bunch of "mule drivers."

STYLE AND TECHNIQUE

Crane wrote in a style that was a departure from the usual good writing of his day and which, even today, sounds modern to the reader. He influenced many writers who came after him.

Crane's vocabulary is simple but he uses it with great control and skill for the effect he has in mind. Actually there are two styles in the book, one used for the dialect of the characters and the other for the narrative and the descriptions.

The dialogue of the characters is written in a simple and accurate dialect which was the prevalent way of talking in the small Eastern American towns of the Civil War period. Crane reproduced accurately the language heard at that time. For instance Henry's mother in her farewell address to him says:

> You watch out, Henry, an' take good care of yerself in this here fighting business—you watch out, an' take good care of yerself. Don't go a-thinkin' you can lick the hull rebel army at the start, because yeh can't. Yer jest one little feller amongst a hull lot of others, and yeh've got to keep quiet an' do what they tell yeh. I know how you are, Henry.

In the above passage the final "d's" and "g's" are omitted in many of the words. Crane used such words as "yerself" and "hull." This accuracy of detail in the dialect of the time is in the "local color" tradition of Mark Twain and other writers.

Crane's dialogue is often irrelevant. As the men are marching along toward the front Henry hears his comrades whisper the following sentences:

> Say—What's all this—about?...What th' thunder—we skedaddlin' this way fer?...Billie—keep off m' feet...Yeh run—like a cow.

The above sentences are simply part of the background of the army. They are not important in themselves. There is a good deal of seemingly irrelevant conversation in the book.

Most of the humor in the book comes from the language of the soldiers. This is the humor of exaggeration, of great impatience, and of a kind of leanness in the use of words. For instance in Chapter VIII when the tattered soldier is listening to a sergeant paint a vivid, terrible picture of war with his mouth "agape," the sergeant makes a comment, "Be keerful, honey, you'll be a-ketchin' flies."

Crane's style for the narrative and the descriptions is marked by original and unusual figures of speech. For instance in writing of the army marching along he says:

> It was now like one of those moving monsters wending with many feet. The air was heavy, and cold with dew. A mass of wet grass, marched upon, rustled like silk.

Crane uses simple declarative sentences which do not seem formal. However, the abrupt almost nervous style conveys a sense of deliberateness and conscious effort. The sentence, with its unusual images, rather than the paragraph dominates his work.

> At nightfall the column broke into regimental pieces, and the fragments went into the fields to camp. Tents sprang up like strange plants. Camp fires, like red, peculiar blossoms, dotted the night.

Crane sometimes uses adjectives in an unconventional way. In the following sentence he uses the word, "bubble," as an adjective rather than as a noun. "The mournful current moved slowly on, and from the water, shaded black, some white *bubble* eyes looked at the men."

Crane, in his descriptions, often uses an impressionistic technique, that is, he writes his impression of a scene as he imagines it at a given moment rather than as it actually is. For instance in telling of the army's march he says:

> But the long serpents crawled slowly from hill to hill without bluster of smoke. A dun-colored cloud of dust floated away to the right. The sky overhead was of a fairy blue.

Thus Crane rather than writing a literal description gives the reader an impression of a moving army. A more complete discussion of impressionism can be found in the separate section entitled "Impressionism."

Crane uses color in a compelling manner. In the first paragraph of the book the rising sun changes the landscape "from brown to green," the river waters are "amber-tinted," and the enemy camp fires have a "red, eyelike gleam." He speaks of the Federal troops as the "blue demonstration." He also writes of the blue sky, blue smoke of battle, and the blue steel. Green foliage sometimes appears blue in the distance. Red is the most important color in the book. It is related to battle as it symbolizes the blood lost, the rage which a soldier feels, and the color of the flag. It also seems to be related to any strong emotion such as hate.

There is a strong sense of rhythm in the book. Part of this is due to the frequent repetition of thoughts and ideas. For instance in Chapter I Henry tells of his early feeling that war was glorious in olden days and in other countries. He does not think such a struggle can exist now in this country.

> He had long despaired of witnessing a Greeklike struggle. Such would be no more, he had said. Men were better, or more timid. Secular and religious education had effaced the throatgrappling instinct, or else firm finance held in check the passions.

After he had been in the Army several months he had the following thought:

> He was brought then gradually back to his old ideas. Greeklike struggles would be no more. Men were better, or more timid. Secular and religious education had effaced the throatgrappling instinct, or else firm finance held in check the passions.

In between he had the illusion that war could be glorious and grand in our country and so had enlisted in the Army. He was gradually disillusioned and came back to his old ideas.

Part of the rhythm comes from the movement of the troops which is almost constant throughout the book. Much of the time the men are moving aimlessly but they are moving either toward the battlefield, away from the battlefield, or on it.

NATURALISM

Naturalism is a theory of fiction which approaches life with a detached, objective, almost scientific outlook. Man is portrayed as an insignificant and helpless creature who acts according to his instincts in response to the conditions of his environment. He does not exercise his individual intelligence and free will to any great extent. He is like a puppet at the mercy of the physical conditions which surround him.

Nature is conceived of as being serene and indifferent to the troubles of mankind. Nature is not a person with attitudes, feelings, and intelligence. It is simply the natural environment and the physical forces which surround man.

Crane reflects these naturalistic concepts in *The Red Badge of Courage*. To Crane war is part of nature, a condition that is part of the physical environment. Crane many times repeats the idea that the individual loses his identity in the collective regimental personality. He writes of the military units as insects or machines. In the early march to the front Henry wants to run away but cannot do so.

> He saw instantly that it would be impossible for him to escape from the regiment. It enclosed him and there were iron laws of tradition and law on four sides. He was in a moving box.

Henry discovers, in his flight from the battlefield, that he cannot find refuge and consolation in nature. He goes into the dark forest seeking comfort. Instead he comes upon a ghastly corpse hidden in a "natural chapel" made of the boughs of trees. As he runs away from the scene panic-stricken, the bushes and trees seem to him to be impeding his progress. Here is a picture of a youth who is helpless against his environment which is indifferent to his problems.

Crane points out the serenity of nature in contrast to the fighting that is taking place.

> As he gazed around him the youth felt a flash of astonishment at the blue, pure sky and the sun gleaming on the trees and fields. It was surprising that Nature had gone tranquilly on with her golden process in the midst of so much devilment.

Crane has attempted to portray a "natural" man in the person of Henry Fleming, and "natural" actions. Henry follows his instincts when he runs from the battlefield. He later discovers that no harm was done by this action as no one knows about it and he comes to the following conclusion:

> In the present, he declared to himself that it was only the doomed and the damned who roared with sincerity at circumstance. Few but they ever did it. A man with a full stomach and the respect of his fellows had no business to scold about anything that he might think to be wrong in the ways of the universe, or even with the way of society. Let the unfortunates rail; the others may play marbles.

Later when Henry acts with great bravery he discovers that the heroic actions, too, are natural. In looking back at his actions he reflects the naturalistic concept.

> He had fought like a pagan who defends his religion. Regarding it, he saw that it was fine, wild, and, in some ways, easy. He had been a tremendous figure, no doubt. By this struggle he had overcome obstacles which he had admitted to be mountains. They had fallen like paper peaks, and he was now what he called a hero. And he had not been aware of the process. He had slept and, awakening, found himself a knight.

REALISM

Realism is a type of literary composition in which the author attempts to present life as it actually exists rather than tinged with idealism or romanticism. Crane, in his writing, attempted to portray people in real situations. He was not interested in social questions as such.

In this book Crane handles one of the most universal of all subjects, war, realistically. He writes of war as an ordinary private experiences it and tells in detail what he thinks and feels as well as what he does during the course of one two-day battle.

Before the fighting begins Henry finds that life in the Army consists mostly of being drilled and reviewed endlessly. His main concerns are to keep warm and to get enough to eat. In battle the soldiers experience fatigue and fear as they face death for the first time. They act in a casual, natural way during the fighting. They sweat from their exertions, their throats are dry, their eyes burn, their ears roar from the incessant noise, they swear when they are shot, and the most heroic deeds are accomplished with great awkwardness. He did not flinch from showing death in its ghastly reality. His description of the corpse in the forest chapel is one of the most moving in the book:

> He was being looked at by a dead man who was seated with his back against a columnlike tree. The corpse was dressed in a uniform that once had been blue but was now faded to a melancholy shade of green. The eyes, staring at the youth, had changed to the dull hue to be seen on the side of a dead fish. The mouth was open. Its red had changed to an appalling yellow. Over the gray skin of the face ran little ants. One was trundling some sort of a bundle along the upper lip.

The realism of the book is aided by Crane's ability to visualize his background—the peaceful wooded hills, small streams, and a river disrupted for a time by the noises of battle, gunsmoke, and the wounded and dying men. The reader can smell, hear, and see the sounds and sights of the battlefield as it existed in the Civil War.

The men and officers talk in a simple and unaffected manner such as was used in the rural areas of that time. This is more fully discussed under the section entitled "Style."

Crane emphasizes the commonplace and unglamorous actions. For instance the tall soldier hears the rumor that the regiment will soon move into battle while he is unheroically washing his shirt.

Henry's mother delivers her farewell address to him while she is peeling the potatoes for supper. Just as the Confederates are about to attack, a soldier ties a red kerchief around his throat. These trivial actions help keep the book on a realistic level. They keep the war from assuming a "larger than life" aspect.

The book is not basically humorous. Yet there is a kind of commonplace, rowdy, natural humor in the soldiers' actions and talk. The soldiers forget their war for a time as they delightedly watch a soldier battle lightly with a country girl over her horse. Henry, like Tom Sawyer, sometimes relishes the overwhelming tragedy of his own death. Other times he looks forward to returning home and expounding his adventures with great exaggeration like the veterans to whom he used to listen.

IMPRESSIONISM

Impressionism is a method of writing in which the author presents characters, scenes, and moods as he visualizes them at a particular moment rather than as they are in reality. The term comes from the French impressionist painters who painted an object in a few strokes thus suggesting the form rather than delineating it realistically. They were chiefly concerned with the effect of various kinds of light on an object or scene.

Crane was one of the chief impressionists of his day. Like the painters he had little sense of line. He characterized his people by giving an impression of a loud soldier, a tall soldier, a tattered soldier, or a cheerful soldier. Although the reader knows a great deal about Henry Fleming he does not know what he looks like physically.

Crane had the same concern as the painters for the effect of light on color. In the book the landscape and objects change their colors as the light changes. A river is "amber-tinted" in the early morning. Green trees and bushes appear blue in the distance. Crane describes troops on the battlefield as follows:

> These battalions with their commotions were woven red and startling into the gentle fabric of softened greens and browns.

Crane has used impressionism as a painter but he also has carried this art beyond the physical level by creating images which are impressions of the mind rather than just impressions of line and color. Many of the seemingly disconnected images in the book are relevant to the emotional experiences of Henry. For instance in Chapter II Crane repeatedly creates the image of the regiment as an insect.

> It was now like one of those moving monsters wending with many feet.

> There was an occasional flash and glimmer of steel from the backs of all these huge crawling reptiles.

> They were like two serpents crawling from the cavern of the night.

> But the long serpents crawled slowly from hill to hill without bluster of smoke.

Henry, as part of the "moving monster," feels very much alone with his thoughts and problems. The army is like a monster to him which forces him to be part of it against his will and which makes him obey orders he cannot understand.

SYMBOLISM

In its broadest sense a symbol is anything which stands for an object, an idea, or an emotion, other than itself. Thus language is symbolic of the objects or ideas which it expresses. However, the term in connection with literature generally means the use of imagery and imagination. An author may endow an object with qualities not inherent in it so that it represents an abstraction such as a philosophical idea. Also he may give universal meaning to an experience or an emotion.

Crane uses symbols in many different ways and on many different levels. On almost every page of the book Crane has created unusual and compelling images each of which is symbolic in some way. The following passage is just one instance of this:

> From across the river the red eyes were still peering. In the eastern sky there was a yellow patch like a rug laid for the feet of the coming sun; and against it, black and pattern-like, loomed the gigantic figure of the colonel on a gigantic horse.

The above is a descriptive passage which occurs in the book just before Henry's regiment receives its orders to march into battle. It suggests the imminent battle. The "red eyes" are the enemy campfires which are symbolic of the hostility of the opposing side. The exaggerated figure of the colonel on his horse seen as a pattern against the rising sun is symbolic of the aggression which is soon to occur. Several times in the book the horse is used as a symbol of aggression.

Crane uses colors symbolically. For instance, red suggests the emotions connected with battle as well as the wounds suffered there. The title of the book, "The Red Badge of Courage," refers to the bloody wounds received in battle. These wounds are symbolic of courage. In Chapter IX after Jim Conklin has just died in a courageous manner from his wounds, Crane writes, "The red sun was pasted in the sky like a wafer." Thus the sun is symbolic of Jim's death and of his wound.

Often Crane symbolizes the state of mind of Henry Fleming by means of the landscape. For instance near the end of the book after the battle in which Henry has acted so heroically, the author points out that Henry's mind is muddled from the battle. "Gradually his brain emerged from the clogged clouds...." He then is able to see the events of the past two days in perspective. "His eyes seemed to open to some new ways." The landscape reflects this awakening in the last sentence of the book, "Over the river a golden ray of sun came through the hosts of leaden rain clouds."

Crane also uses symbolism in connection with his characters. On one level all his characters are symbolic of various aspects of Henry Fleming. This is discussed in the section entitled, "The Characters." Crane calls many of his characters by a particular aspect of their personalities which he is emphasizing. For instance Wilson, the loud soldier, symbolizes the person who protects himself from having to face his self-identity by acting in a swaggering, unthinking, and boastful manner. Henry acted in this manner several times in the book and more specifically the loud soldier symbolizes this aspect of Henry.

Perhaps the most unique symbolism lies in having the outer action of the book symbolic of the inner conflict in Henry's mind. This is discussed in detail in the section entitled "Structure, The Story."

QUESTIONS

Note: The section or sections indicated in parentheses below each question contain information which will help answer the question.

1. Discuss the themes which appear throughout the book thus helping to unify it.
   (Critical Analysis: Structure, Themes)

2. Discuss the ways the characters, setting, and duration of time in the book contribute to the book's unity.
   (Critical Analysis: Structure, General Remarks)

3. What are the two stories within the book and how are they related to each other to form one unified impression?
   (Critical Analysis: Structure, Story)

4. Discuss the setting of the book on the realistic and emotional levels. How are they related to each other?
   (Critical Analysis: Setting)

5. Discuss the character of Henry Fleming paying particular attention to how his character changes during the course of the book.
   (Critical Analysis: Structure, Story and Critical Analysis: The Characters, Henry Fleming)

6. How does the portrayal of Henry's mother aid the realism in the book?

(Critical Analysis: The Characters, Mother of Henry Fleming and Chapter I, Commentary)

7. What is the importance of the tall soldier, Jim Conklin, to the book?
(Critical Analysis: The Characters, The Tall Soldier)

8. Compare the character of the loud soldier, Wilson, with the character of Henry Fleming paying particular attention to the similarities.
(Critical Analysis: The Characters, The Loud Soldier – Wilson and Chapters XIII-XIV, Commentaries)

9. Discuss the function of the tattered soldier in the book.
(Critical Analysis: The Characters, The Tattered Soldier and Chapters VIII, IX, and X, Commentaries)

10. Discuss the characterization of the soldiers as a group. How do they contribute to the realism of the book?
(Critical Analysis: The Characters, The Soldiers as a group)

11. What are the main elements in Crane's style of writing? Quote examples to prove your points.
(Critical Analysis: Style and Technique)

12. Is there any humor in the book? If there is, in what does it consist?
(Critical Analysis: Style and Technique and Critical Analysis: Realism)

13. Crane has been called a prose painter. How does his use of color justify his having this title?
(Critical Analysis: Style and Technique and Critical Analysis: Impressionism)

14. What is the theory of Naturalism and how does Crane express it in this book?
(Critical Analysis: Naturalism and Chapter XV, Commentary)

15. Define Realism and show how Crane writes in this manner

by finding examples of it in the book.
(Critical Analysis: Realism)

16. Discuss Crane as an impressionist.
(Critical Analysis: Impressionism)

17. Discuss the meaning of the title of the book, "The Red Badge of Courage."
(Critical Analysis: Symbolism and Chapter IX, Commentary)

18. How does the landscape sometimes symbolize the state of Henry Fleming's mind?
(Critical Analysis: Symbolism)

19. What are some of the major agonies which confront the characters in the book?
(Introduction)

NOTES

THE ADVENTURES OF TOM SAWYER

NOTES

including

- *Introduction*
- *Brief Summary*
- *List of Characters*
- *Chapter Summaries and Commentaries*
- *Character Analysis*
- *Critical Analysis*
- *Review Questions*

by
Marion P. Thayer

REVISED EDITION

INCORPORATED
LINCOLN, NEBRASKA 68501

Editor

Gary Carey, M.A.
University of Colorado

Consulting Editor

James L. Roberts, Ph.D.
Department of English
University of Nebraska

ISBN 0-8220-1301-0
© Copyright 1964,1967
by
C. K. Hillegass
All Rights Reserved
Printed in U.S.A.

1990 Printing

The Cliffs Notes logo, the names "Cliffs" and "Cliffs Notes," and the black and yellow diagonal-stripe cover design are all registered trademarks belonging to Cliffs Notes, Inc., and may not be used in whole or in part without written permission.

Cliffs Notes, Inc. Lincoln, Nebraska

CONTENTS

The Adventures of Tom Sawyer

INTRODUCTION

Samuel Langhorne Clemens, who wrote under the pen name Mark Twain, was born in the little town of Florida, Missouri, on November 30, 1835, shortly after his family had moved there from Tennessee. When he was about four, the family moved again, this time to Hannibal, Missouri, a small town (about five hundred persons) on the Mississippi River some eighty miles from St. Louis. Hannibal was dusty and quiet, with forests nearby. The steamboats which passed daily were its main contact with the outside world. Samuel Clemens spent his boyhood in Hannibal and immortalized this sleepy little village as St. Petersburg in *The Adventures of Tom Sawyer.*

Clemens' father was from Virginia originally. He was a lawyer by profession but was unsuccessful at this and also at land speculation, by which he hoped to become wealthy. He was highly intelligent, but stern, and had little rapport with his son Sam. Clemens' mother, a Southern belle in her youth, had a natural sense of humor, was emotional, and was particularly fond of animals and unfortunate human beings. Although the family was very poor, Sam had a generally happy childhood.

The characters in *The Adventures of Tom Sawyer* are drawn from Clemens' boyhood world. Judge Thatcher is based on his father, Aunt Polly on his mother. Mary and Sidney are patterned after a sister and a brother, Pamela and Henry. Huck Finn is drawn from Tom Blankenship, the son of the village drunk. Injun Joe was a local person of disrepute. Becky Thatcher is modeled on an early sweetheart, Laura Hawkins. Tom Sawyer is drawn from Sam himself and two of his friends.

Thus Twain has written an autobiographical novel, using a setting he knew intimately, characters drawn from his family and friends that he grew up with, and incidents that really happened. However, the book is much more than just a record of a boy growing up in a small river town of the 1840s. Twain took ingredients from his youth and constructed one of the most entertaining and delightful volumes ever written. It transcends time and place and becomes universal in its revelation of human nature and its creation of a boy world, with fears, fantasies, and limited viewpoint. Twain tells excellent stories, accurately describes nature, and warmly satirizes accepted institutions in a style that is noteworthy for its clearness and readability.

It is hoped that the commentaries to each chapter and the critical analysis at the end will point up some of the elements in the book worth noting and thus make the experience of reading it richer and more satisfying.

BRIEF SUMMARY

About two decades before the Civil War, Tom Sawyer is living in St. Petersburg, a small Missouri village on the Mississippi River. Tom's mother is dead and he lives with his Aunt Polly, whose anxious efforts to rear the youngster firmly are hampered by her tender-hearted affection for the boy. Other members of the household are Tom's gentle cousin Mary and his deceitful half-brother, Sidney.

Tom is a keen-minded boy of normal impulses. He groans under the restrictions of school, from which he often flees with an easy conscience to glory in the freedom of the woods and the river. He feuds constantly with his half-brother and has a distaste for boys who are representative of big-city ways or standards of model deportment. In his frequent encounters with the adult world, Tom commonly outwits his adversaries.

For choosing to go swimming when he was supposed to be in school, Tom is sentenced by Aunt Polly to spend Saturday whitewashing a long, high board fence. By means of some shrewd applied psychology, Tom induces various other boys to do the work—and to pay for the privilege.

After a game of war with his friend Joe Harper, Tom passes the Thatcher residence and, at first sight, falls in love with the pretty Becky. When he lingers about her house later in the day, his ardor is dampened by a sudden deluge of water.

In Sunday school the next day, Tom receives a Bible upon presenting the tickets that would be awarded for memorizing 2,000 verses. Only Tom has acquired the tickets by bartering, and his ignorance of scripture is mercilessly exposed. In church, the proceedings are enlivened when Tom's pinch bug gets away from him and stirs up a wandering dog.

On Monday, Tom's faked illness fails to save him from school. On the way to that place of torture, Tom tarries with Huckleberry Finn, and they make plans to take a dead cat to the cemetery at midnight as a wart-cure. Because he is late Tom is ordered to sit in the girls' section, where the only vacant seat is alongside Becky Thatcher. But the courtship gets off to a bad start, and Tom and Joe Harper take another holiday from education.

In the cemetery that night, Tom and Huck come upon Dr. Robinson, Injun Joe, and Muff Potter digging up a recently buried corpse. There is a quarrel and Injun Joe stabs the doctor to death after Potter has been knocked unconscious. Afterward the horrified boys take an oath never to reveal what they have seen.

The town is in an uproar the next day after the murder is discovered and Injun Joe names Muff Potter as the killer. Tom is almost sick with apprehension for fear that Injun Joe will learn of the witnesses to his crime.

Tom, Huck, and Joe Harper decide to become pirates and they establish themselves on Jackson's Island in the Mississippi, where they enjoy a carefree outing. It was believed that cannon fire over water would bring up bodies, so when a ferryboat steams past shooting, the boys realize that they are presumed to be drowned. Tom sneaks home at night to leave Aunt Polly a note explaining that they are safe. But he changes his mind when he overhears that church services for the boys will be held Sunday if they are not found by then. The scheduled funeral is disrupted when the three "deceased" calmly stroll down the aisle.

Back in school, the romance between Tom and Becky has its stormy moments. Then Tom finally wins her heart completely by heroically suffering punishment for her misdeed. The exercises of the last day of school provide the boys with an opportunity to take revenge on their tormentor, the schoolmaster, by exposing his gilded bald head to public view.

It has generally been accepted that Muff Potter killed Dr. Robinson. However, Tom is produced at the trial as a surprise witness and relates what actually happened. Injun Joe makes his escape through a window.

While Tom and Huck are on a treasure hunt, they explore an abandoned house. They are trapped upstairs by the arrival of two men. One of them has appeared in town as a deaf and dumb Spaniard, but when he speaks the boys recognize Injun Joe in disguise. The two accomplices take a box of silver coins from concealment and then, by chance, dig up a horde of gold that evidently had been buried by some other outlaws. It is decided to take the treasure to Injun Joe's "Number Two" hangout. The terrified boys narrowly escape detection and the men leave, after Injun Joe has spoken ominously of remaining in the vicinity until he has accomplished vengeance.

Tom and Huck figure out that Number Two is a room in the "Temperance Tavern." Their reasoning proves to be correct, and they find that Injun Joe is hiding out there with an abundant supply of whiskey.

On a picnic excursion Tom and Becky become lost in McDougal's cave. That night Huck follows two men toward Cardiff Hill. He hears that Injun Joe intends to inflict injury on the Widow Douglas because her husband had once had the half-breed publicly horsewhipped. Huck hastens to inform Mr. Jones of the plot, and the Welshman and his sons drive off the vicious pair. Huck becomes ill and the Widow Douglas comes to the Welshman's house to care for the homeless boy.

When it is discovered that Tom and Becky had not spent the night with friends, a thorough search of the cave is carried out, but the children cannot be found. At one point during their ordeal, Tom catches sight of Injun Joe in a passage. After they have been underground for three days, Tom finds an opening miles from the main entrance of the cave, and he and Becky make their way back to town.

Two weeks later Tom is appalled to hear that Judge Thatcher has had the mouth of McDougal's cave sealed. Only then does Tom disclose that Injun Joe is in the cave. The half-breed's body is just inside the door of the cave; his partner had already been found dead in the river.

Tom and Huck later go back to the cave and recover $12,000 worth of treasure, and it is invested for them. Huck is taken into the home of the Widow Douglas, who intends to educate him and train him in the habits of normal living. Huck finds this almost unbearable but agrees to endure it in return for being admitted to the robber gang that Tom is organizing.

LIST OF CHARACTERS

Tom Sawyer

The hero of Twain's story is a typical boy of his time and place. He is mischievous, imaginative, and active.

Aunt Polly

The sister of Tom's mother loves her nephew tenderly and feels keenly the responsibility for his upbringing.

Sidney

Tom's half-brother plays the part of an obedient good boy to cover up his tricky disposition.

Mary

Tom's cousin is a kind, gentle girl who patiently attempts to guide him.

Huckleberry Finn

The abandoned son of a drunkard, Huck leads a seemingly carefree life that makes him the envy of other boys.

Joe Harper

Tom's friend shares many of his activities but is less daring than Tom.

Willie Mufferson

The "Model Boy" is the joy of all mothers and the despair of all other boys.

Alfred Temple

The new boy from St. Louis is an outsider regarded with suspicion by the local boys.

Amy Lawrence

Tom's first love ceases to interest him after his first glimpse of Becky Thatcher.

Becky Thatcher

The heroine is a lovely blue-eyed blond who is somewhat temperamental but resolute in a crisis.

Judge and Mrs. Thatcher

Becky's parents are highly esteemed residents of the county.

Lawyer Thatcher

A St. Petersburg attorney who is Jeff's father and the brother of Judge Thatcher.

Mr. Walters

The Sunday school superintendent performs his job earnestly.

The Reverend Mr. Sprague

The pastor of the village church excels at lengthy prayers and tedious sermons.

Mr. Dobbins

The village schoolmaster, who had hoped to become a doctor, makes life miserable for his pupils.

Dr. Robinson

The young doctor is murdered while conducting a grave-robbing expedition.

Injun Joe

A sinister half-breed who is unscrupulous and dangerous.

Muff Potter

A weak man fond of drink who is easily taken in.

Judge Frazer

The judge organizes the Cadets of Temperance to save boys from the evils of liquor, tobacco, and profanity.

Widow Douglas

An attractive, amiable woman who is popular in the town.

Mr. Jones

The kindly Welshman lives on Cardiff Hill near the Widow Douglas.

Major and Mrs. Ward

St. Petersburg residents.

Lawyer Riverson

A St. Petersburg attorney.

Ben Rogers ***Billy Fisher*** ***Johnny Miller*** ***Jeff Thatcher*** ***Johnny Baker*** ***Jim Hollis*** ***Bob Tanner***	St. Petersburg boys
Gracie Miller ***Susy Harper*** ***Sally Rogers***	St. Petersburg girls

CHAPTER SUMMARIES AND COMMENTARIES

PREFACE

In his short preface the author informs the reader that he has used his own adventures and the experience of his boyhood friends as the basis of his story. Thus he is representing a distinct time and place, as well as people he has known intimately. Twain also says the superstitions in the book were commonly believed by children and slaves in the West between 1835 and 1845. That he particularly calls this to the reader's attention illustrates his attempt to provide a historically authentic background for the story and reveals Twain's keen general interest in folklore, particularly superstitions. Finally, he tells the reader that the purposes of his book are to entertain children and to remind adults of their own childhood.

CHAPTER 1

Summary

The chapter opens with Aunt Polly searching for Tom. She discovers that he has been eating jam on the sly. By using his wits, he manages to avoid punishment. The old lady criticizes herself for not being harder on Tom. He avoids doing his household chores by telling the young Negro boy, Jim, of his adventures while Jim does the work. Tom plays hooky from school to go swimming and manages to keep this from Aunt Polly until betrayed by his half-brother, Sid. He then escapes and beats up a nicely dressed boy who is new to the town. In the end, though, Aunt Polly catches Tom. She decides that his punishment shall be to work at home during his Saturday holiday from school.

Commentary

This chapter sets the tone of the book, that of boyhood with its pranks and adventures. Tom, the hero, and his immediate family are introduced. Tom is lazy when there is work to do, full of fun, carefree, quick witted, disobedient, quarrelsome, and self-willed. In his background are a secure home and a loving aunt.

Aunt Polly is described as an old lady, but she has a strong voice and is still able to move quickly. She is a very kind, simple, loving person who tries her best to bring up the elusive and mischievous Tom correctly. She is constantly having to assume a role that is not natural to her, that of a disciplinarian.

The feud between Tom and his half-brother, Sidney, is brought into play. Tom is the typical bad boy of the Sunday school literature who doesn't mind his elders. Sid is the typical good boy who does his chores, goes to school regularly, and minds his elders. The author identifies with Tom, who is presented quite sympathetically. Sid is a prig and a tattler.

Tom is also contrasted to the new boy, who is well dressed. Tom fights, but is fair. When Tom turns his back, the new boy throws a stone and hits him.

CHAPTER 2

Summary

Chapter 2 opens with a description of an idyllic Saturday morning, bright, fresh, and happy. Tom is dejected as he begins his punishment, the whitewashing of a ninety-foot board fence nine feet high. He tries to get Jim to replace him at the fence, but Aunt Polly intervenes and Tom is left with the job.

After Tom has counted his worldly possessions to see whether he has enough wealth to bribe his friends to help, he gets a great idea. Thus when his first critic, Ben Rogers, arrives, he is painting the fence happily and industriously. When Rogers asks if he can have a turn, Tom brings up a great many arguments against it. Finally, Rogers pays him an apple for the privilege of working.

Tom idly eats his apple and plans how he will entice the other boys to help with the whitewashing. The boys arrive to jeer but soon pay a precious belonging to be allowed to whitewash. By the middle of the afternoon, the fence has three coats of whitewash, Tom is wealthy, he has been idle all day, and he has had lots of company.

The author points out that "Work consists of whatever a body is obliged to do and that Play consists of whatever a body is not obliged to do."

Tom meditates a bit on his newly gained wealth and then goes off to report to Aunt Polly.

Commentary

This is one of the most charming episodes in the book and is well remembered by most readers. The author has shown his knowledge of human nature by revealing a basic human weakness: man desires most what it is hard for him to attain.

Tom's character is more fully developed. In the first chapter we saw Tom principally with his family. Here he is seen with his friends in their boy world. That he is emotional is shown by the contrast between his gloom when he starts his work and his joy after he has thought of a way to avoid doing the job. Tom is a fine actor and cleverly uses this ability in handling his friends. And he shows that he is not above bribing others to attain his own ends.

Small details add to the impression that this is a boys' world. Jim is interested in Tom's sore toe. Ben impersonates a steamboat instead of merely walking along. The other boys' wealth includes a piece of chalk, orange peels, a knife handle, a doorknob, and the like.

Twain often makes a point more vivid by means of contrast. In this chapter, the bright, fresh morning described in the opening paragraph is in direct contrast to Tom's gloom as he begins his punishment.

Chapter 2 is also a good example of Twain's literary style at its best. He presents the essential heart of experience without submerging it in nonessentials. He has painted a picture which is authentic in all details and which the reader can clearly understand.

CHAPTER 3

Summary

The chapter opens with Tom reporting to Aunt Polly on the completion of his work. She is amazed to see that he has stuck with the job and has done it magnificently. She rewards him with an apple and tells him he can go play. Before leaving, he takes revenge on Sid for getting him into trouble the night before, throwing several dirt clods at him. Then he joins his friends for a game of soldiers, in which he is one of the generals who conduct the battle.

On his way home, Tom sees a pretty new girl and immediately forgets his former love, Amy Lawrence. He tries to gain the girl's admiration by various "showing off" antics, and the girl shows her approval by throwing a pansy to him before going into the house. He is overcome with joy and stays near the fence until nightfall.

During supper, Tom is at first in high spirits because of his success with the girl, but his joy turns to a deep melancholy when Aunt Polly punishes him unjustly for an accident which Sid has with the sugar bowl. Aunt Polly does not tell Tom that she is sorry for her mistake. He goes off alone and wishes he would die.

Tom finally wanders to the new girl's house and lies on the ground beneath a lighted second-floor window thinking morbid thoughts. An unexpected deluge of water recalls him from his melancholy reverie and he dashes home to bed. Sid notices but does not mention Tom's wet state.

Commentary

In this chapter, the characters of Aunt Polly, Sid, and Tom are further developed. We see that Sid, although outwardly good, is sly, no above letting his brother take his punishment for him, and furtive in observing Tom.

There is a mental struggle between Aunt Polly and Tom. When Aunt Polly has wrongly punished Tom, she feels remorse but does not want to say so because she thinks that to admit an error would weaken her role as disciplinarian. Tom knows his aunt is sorry, but he refuses to see the signs that she wants to make up with him. He enjoys playing the martyr. Thus Tom can knowingly make his aunt suffer because she is so fond of him.

We also see that Tom's world of boyhood is not all joy and pranks. Being punished unjustly and being drenched with water are a part of this boy world, too.

Although the reader may not be aware of it at this point, Becky Thatcher, the heroine of the book, is introduced to us. All we learn of her is that she is pretty, dainty, and not averse to Tom. However, her impact on him is so strong that we can predict she will figure again in the story.

CHAPTER 4

Summary

Chapter 4 begins with a description of the prayers and sermons delivered by Aunt Polly on a peaceful Sunday morning. Mary bribes Tom to learn his Bible verses for the day—after he has been unable to learn them without this incentive—and forces him to wash properly and put on his hated Sunday clothes. Then the children go off to Sunday school.

At Sunday school, Tom starts collecting red, blue, and yellow tickets by trading for them the wealth he has accumulated the day before. The tickets are earned by the children for reciting Bible verses, and the prize for ten yellow tickets, which represent memorizing two thousand verses, is a Bible. Few students can accomplish this.

The Sunday school scene is described in some detail, with emphasis on the typical restless, noisy, quarrelsome little boys and the oversentimental and boring superintendent. The arrival of the Thatcher family, which includes an out-of-town judge, throws everyone into an unnatural state, and all show off for one anothers' benefit. Tom claims the prize of the Bible, much to everyone's amazement, especially the superintendent's. Tom basks in his glory until his cheating is exposed when he cannot answer the simplest question about the Bible.

Commentary

The chapter is primarily a description of Sunday in the life of Tom, his family, and his friends, with particular attention to Tom's efforts to liven up the day with his pranks. Early family worship, learning Bible verses, getting dressed up, and going to Sunday school and church are apparently part of regular Sunday routine in families of this small town.

The author begins with an episode in Tom's family and then moves to a wider facet of Tom's world, the Sunday school. Twain is at his best in his description of the Sunday school, with its undisciplined, troublesome little boys; its stiff, correct, and mawkishly sentimental superintendent; and its teachers, who are self-conscious in their behavior when an important guest is present. Twain understates the climax when Tom's cheating is discovered. Having thoroughly filled in the background, he lets the reader's imagination do the rest.

The character of Mary, Tom's cousin, is introduced. Like Sid, she is outwardly good, but, unlike him, she is also loving and good at heart. She is more like Aunt Polly, but doesn't have Aunt Polly's sharp tongue. She tries to get Tom to behave through gentleness, love, and bribery, although she can be firm, as is shown when she washes him thoroughly before Sunday school.

The heroine, Becky Thatcher, is reintroduced briefly in this chapter. We learn her name, that her father is an important judge, and that her uncle is a local attorney. Thus we know she is from one of the more prominent families in the county. We again see her effect on Tom, who shows off as soon as he sees her.

Tom continues in his role as a mischievous boy. His trading for yellow tickets the wealth he acquired on Saturday from his friends for the privilege of whitewashing his fence ties this chapter to Chapter 2. We do see, however, that Tom feels embarrassed, ashamed, and ridiculous when his cheating is exposed. This is in line with the author's attempt to present a complete boy who is both good and bad.

CHAPTER 5

Summary

The chapter begins with the congregation gathering for the Sunday morning church service and sermon. Twain describes the various members of the congregation as they arrive at church. These include the postmaster, the mayor, the justice of the peace, a lawyer, the best hostess in town, the belle of the village and other pretty young girls, all the young clerks in town, and the model boy, who always brings his mother to church and carries a white handkerchief.

The minister reads the hymn in a manner thrilling to all the ladies. Then come the notices of meetings, followed by a very long prayer. Tom catches a fly, but is forced by Aunt Polly to release it.

The minister begins his sermon, which is of the "fire and brimstone" type. Tom involuntarily flips his pinch bug (a beetle) into the aisle when it pinches his finger. A poodle idles along and goes through all sorts of antics with it—to the delight of most of the bored congregation. Finally the dog unwittingly sits down on the beetle, is pinched by it, yelps, and is thrown out the window by its master, with the beetle still attached. By this time the whole congregation is full of suppressed laughter, and all attempts to listen to the sermon have been given up. Tom goes home concluding that church is not so bad after all. He does wish, though, that the dog had not disappeared with his pinch bug.

Commentary

The author does two things in this chapter. First, he describes accurately and with humor the congregation and minister. There are in the congregation many types of persons who can be found in any church or town. Second, Twain entertains the reader with a very funny incident involving the poodle and the pinch bug. Tom, although he is the instigator of the incident, does not figure largely in this chapter. Here again, Twain's writing is brief and to the point but very rich in essential detail.

CHAPTER 6

Summary

Chapter 6 opens with Tom's attempt to discover an illness that will keep him from school. Tom's groans fool Sid, but not Aunt Polly. Tom does discover a loose tooth, which Aunt Polly extracts. On the way to school, Tom is the envy of his friends, for the loss of the tooth enables him to spit in a different and admirable way.

Tom meets Huckleberry Finn, son of the town drunkard, on the way to school. Huck is a homeless boy who sleeps in hogsheads or on doorsteps. Huck's clothes, which are discarded men's clothes, do not fit him and are in rags. He does not wash, does not go to school or church. He can go swimming or fishing whenever he wishes. The mothers of the town's boys hate and fear Huck because they feel he is idle and bad. All the boys envy Huck. Although Tom has been forbidden to play with Huck, he joins Huck at every opportunity.

Tom and Huck discuss various cures for warts. These include using a dead cat, spunk water, or a bean. They also discuss the power of witches and devils. They agree to visit the cemetery that night to try out a cure for warts, using Huck's dead cat. They promise to meet at the signal of a cat's "miaow." Tom notices that Huck has a tick and talks him into trading it for the newly extracted tooth. Tom puts the tick in his percussion-cap box and goes on to school.

The schoolmaster asks Tom to explain his tardiness. Tom notices that the only vacant seat on the girls' side of the room is next to the new girl, Becky Thatcher. He tells the truth: he has been talking with Huck. The schoolmaster whips him soundly and makes him sit next to Becky. Tom attracts Becky's attention by giving her a peach and drawing a picture for her on his slate. They exchange names and agree to meet at noon so that Tom can give Becky a drawing lesson. He writes "I love you" on his slate and shows it to her. By this time, the schoolmaster has noticed Tom's behavior, and he rudely returns Tom to his proper seat again.

Tom is exultant over his success with Becky. He tries to study now but he is too upset emotionally to keep his mind on his work and fails miserably in all his subjects.

Commentary

An important character, Huckleberry Finn, is introduced in thi chapter. There are basic differences between Tom and Huck, but thei friendship and influence on each other are important to the story. Tor has a secure, love-filled home with a family who care for his physica intellectual, emotional, and spiritual needs, perhaps not wisely, bu conscientiously. Huck has no home, no family to care for him. His father is the town drunkard. His life is free and uncomplicated. He has no ambition to better himself. He does not wish to be respectable and lead the kind of life the other boys in town lead. He is satisfied with his lot.

Tom envies Huck greatly. As we have seen, Tom hates to wash, go to school, attend Sunday school and church, do chores, and obey grown-ups. Huck's free and easy life seems idyllic to him.

In his preface, Twain mentions that he has introduced superstitions that were actually believed by children and slaves during the period covered by the story. In this chapter, the boys discuss many of them. In addition to various cures for warts, we learn that devils go to the graveyard to get a dead person who has been wicked. One can't see devils, but one can hear them rustle like the wind. When a witch is "witching you," she stares at you and mumbles the Lord's Prayer backward.

These superstitions are interesting historically. Tom's and Huck's belief in ghosts, witches, devils, and other spirits indicates the primitive state of their boy minds. They differ somewhat in their beliefs. Huck, with no formal education, knows a great deal more about the world of spirits than does Tom. Also, he is less critical and tends to believe in a superstition if he hears of it. Tom, on the other hand, asks questions to see whether a certain belief is really true. He is more educated and thus somewhat more critical.

The superstitions are also important to the plot because Tom and Huck plan to visit the graveyard at midnight, believing they can get rid of warts by taking a dead cat to the cemetery and waiting near a fresh grave. When a devil comes to take the corpse away, the cat will follow the devil, and the wart will follow the cat. The boys' trip to the graveyard sets off an episode which is one of the key adventures in the book.

The story of Tom and Becky continues in this chapter. Although they have noticed each other on two previous occasions, the two have not spoken to each other as yet or become acquainted. In this chapter they exchange names and arrange for a future meeting, and Tom declares his love to Becky. The author does not want us to forget that they are children. Having them meet in school and communicate by means of writing on a slate and whispering seems appropriate to their ages and situation. Becky's responses to Tom, which alternate between being shy and being eager, seem typical of a young schoolgirl.

CHAPTER 7

Summary

This is a continuation of the preceding chapter. Tom finds it impossible to keep his mind on his books. The day is sleepy and Tom is bored. As he tries to think of a way to liven things up, he remembers the tick in his pocket. He releases the tick onto his desk, and Tom and his best friend, Joe Harper, who is sitting next to him, devise a game with the tick. Before long, they are quarreling over it. This attracts the attention of the schoolmaster, who punishes the boys.

Tom and Becky slip back to the empty school at noon. Tom shows Becky how to draw a house, and then they discuss rats, chewing gum, and circuses. Tom tells Becky that he wants to be a clown when he grows up. At last he tells her of his love for her and proposes to her. She is shy, but confesses that she loves him, too, and they become "engaged." They kiss and agree to walk together to and from school "when there ain't anybody looking." All is going well until Tom inadvertently mentions his former love, Amy Lawrence. Becky becomes hurt and angry and weeps. She repulses Tom's efforts to make up. Tom gives her his best possession, a brass knob, but she throws it to the floor. Tom leaves her then, not to return to school that day.

After Tom has gone, Becky recovers from her grief and calls Tom to make up. But he has gone, and she must spend the rest of the afternoon hiding her grief from her classmates. She feels very lonely and sad.

Commentary

In this chapter, we are introduced to Tom's best friend, Joe Harper and we are amused by another of Tom's mischievous experiences. Th character of the schoolmaster becomes clearer also. In Chapter 6 w suspected that he was a man who punished severely and often. Now thi is borne out: Tom has been punished three times in one morning. Th teacher is shown to be somewhat brutal, and there is no sign that he i an intelligent and interesting person who might inspire his pupils t intellectual endeavor.

The stormy course of Tom and Becky's love is important to the plc When Tom is spurned by Becky, he runs away. Tom's relationship t Becky shows another side of his character. He has, of course, been u true to Amy, and he has been rather ungainly in his wooing of Beck

However, in the space of three days since he first saw her, he has wooed and won her, and much of this has taken place in front of a roomful of students. This shows he has handled the matter with finesse—until the blunder of mentioning Amy's name.

The reader learns more about Becky in this chapter. She is a sweet, somewhat shy girl who has not had a serious boy friend before Tom. She is jealous, quick to anger, and slow to forgive a supposed wrong. It is to be assumed that her pride and Tom's pride will cause more complications in the course of their romance.

CHAPTER 8

Summary

Tom's mood is one of blackest melancholy, and the weather, hot and oppressive, seems to match it. He has run away from school and Becky to the woods. At first he contemplates dying, but decides that his Sunday school record is not good enough to risk it. Then he thinks of running away to be a clown, soldier, or Indian chief, but finally decides that a pirate would lead the most thrilling life.

Tom decides that he will leave home the next morning to be a pirate. Meanwhile, he will gather his belongings together to take with him. Tom uncovers a marble under a rotten log and throws it away in disgust. One of his superstitons has failed him: he expected to see all the marbles he ever lost sitting with the one marble he buried. He makes a test with a doodlebug and concludes that a witch has been responsible for the failure.

A blast on a toy trumpet by Joe Harper calls Tom to play Robin Hood. He forgets his melancholy and his desire to be a pirate in the thrill of playing Robin Hood. Tom has a tin trumpet, bow and arrows, and sword, all hidden behind the rotten log. He answers Joe's blast, gives orders to his imaginary men, and arranges his clothes to look like Robin Hood. Tom and Joe impersonate the characters in the story of Robin Hood, which they know by heart. At the end of the afternoon, the boys hide their weapons, get dressed, and go home, mourning the fact that there are no real outlaws any more.

Commentary

Tom's melancholy at the beginning of this chapter is very much like his mood in Chapter 3 when he has been punished unjustly by

Aunt Polly. Here he feels that Becky has treated him harshly. It is interesting that Tom is most affected emotionally by the women he loves, Aunt Polly and Becky. The displeasure and even cruelty of the schoolmaster do not seem to bother him.

The romantic side of Tom's nature is shown clearly when he is considering the various occupations which he might follow. He does not consider any solid profession, such as doctor or lawyer, but thinks only of the illustrious careers which might bring him glory, such as clown, soldier, Indian chief, or pirate. He wants to have adventure and at the same time to impress others with his glory.

In the scene with the marble, we again see the superstitious world which is part of Tom's boyhood. There seems to be a connection between the forest and superstitious beliefs. Huck and Tom plan to test the dead-cat cure for warts in the graveyard, away from town, just as Tom has tested the marble theory in the forest, away from home, school, and town.

That Tom is an avid reader is shown by his intimate knowledge of the story of Robin Hood, including the exact language used. The play with Joe shows the friendly relationship between the two boys and their agreement that Robin Hood is one of the most glorious of heroes.

CHAPTER 9

Summary

The chapter opens with Tom listening to the sounds of the night while he waits for Huck Finn's call. Finally, in spite of his struggle to stay awake, he dozes, but awakes at Huck's signal, and the two boys go to the graveyard, which is a mile and a half from the village. It is unkempt, with grass and weeds everywhere. The graves are sunk in the ground and there are no tombstones. The boys hide themselves behind three elm trees near the grave of Hoss Williams, who has recently died. They hold a conversation about dead people.

Three men approach the grave. At first the boys think they are devils, but then recognize them as Muff Potter, who is drunk, Dr. Robinson, and Injun Joe. Dr. Robinson watches as Potter and Injun Joe dig up the corpse. Potter asks the doctor for more money to haul it away. Injun Joe, because of an old grudge, threatens the doctor. The doctor knocks Injun Joe to the ground. Potter starts to fight the doctor now, and the doctor knocks Potter unconscious. Injun Joe takes Potter's knife and murders the doctor. At this point, the two frightened boys run away.

Injun Joe robs the body and puts the knife in Potter's hand. When Potter wakes up, Injun Joe tells him that he has murdered the doctor. Potter is confused about his guilt. He doesn't remember killing the doctor, but he has been drinking, so he believes Injun Joe's false story. Injun Joe promises not to tell anyone of Potter's guilt. Potter runs away, leaving his knife. Injun Joe leaves two or three minutes later.

Commentary

Chapter 9 marks a new beginning in the book. Up to this point, Tom has been a mischievous boy playing pranks and dreaming of glory and great adventures. The reader has met his family, schoolmates, and girl friend. Tom has been seen at home, at school, at Sunday school, and at play in the forest. However, he is now experiencing a real adventure, one that is frightening and full of violence. Many of the chapters of this book will be concerned with the story of what happened as a result of this night's experience.

The two characters of Injun Joe and Muff Potter are introduced. Injun Joe is not just dishonest; he is truly wicked. Not only does he rob a grave, but he also kills a man for a trivial reason and then puts the blame on an innocent man.

Muff Potter, a weak man hired to rob Hoss Williams' grave, ends up believing he has killed Dr. Robinson. That Muff is not very bright is shown by Injun Joe's success in making him pick a quarrel with the doctor and later making him believe that he has killed the doctor.

Superstitions concerning dead people are discussed by Huck and Tom. We learn that devils, like cats, can see in the dark. And the spirits of the dead can hear the boys talking.

CHAPTER 10

Summary

Huck and Tom flee to the tannery in a state of panic and horror at what they have witnessed. They discuss the murder and decide to keep silent because of their fear of Injun Joe. The boys know that Injun Joe would not hesitate to kill them if they tell the townspeople what they have seen. Injun Joe is a formidable character and might escape from jail even if he were apprehended for the crime. The boys take a secret oath on a pine shingle, sign it in blood, then bury the shingle.

Unnoticed by the boys, a figure creeps into the other end of the building. The boys are fearful because of the howling nearby of a stray dog. They feel better when they see that the dog has his back to them.

The boys hear someone snoring, and upon investigating, they discover Muff Potter sleeping in the tannery. They realize now that the stray dog is facing Potter as he howls. They discuss the possibility that howling dogs do not always foretell death.

The boys return to their homes. Tom feels confident that his escapade is not known, but actually Sid is awake and has noticed Tom's absence and return. Sid apparently tells Aunt Polly because the next morning, Tom is treated in a solemn and silent manner by his family. Aunt Polly weeps over his wickedness. Tom is affected by her tears as he is not affected by a flogging. At school he and Joe Harper are whipped for playing hooky the afternoon before. As a final blow, Becky returns his brass knob. Tom is miserable, gloomy, and suffers keenly.

Commentary

In this chapter, the reader sees the reaction of Tom and Huck to the dreadful crime they have witnessed. It is boyish, for they are mainly concerned with their own horror and fear. When they decide not to tell what they have seen for fear of revenge on themselves by Injun Joe, they devise an elaborate way of taking an oath of silence, one which will involve both writing and blood to suit the solemnity of the occasion. This also injects humor into the situation: there is comic illogic in the boys' behavior.

The author has contributed to the boys' feeling that they are in a dark, lonely world full of horror by providing an appropriate setting. The tannery is lonely, dark, and secret. The sounds of the howling dog and Muff Potter's snoring add to the eeriness.

Huck and Tom again show they are superstitious by their faith in a blood vow and by their fear that a howling dog foretells coming death. Taking the blood vow is also important to the plot because Tom is later very hesitant to break his vow and testify against Injun Joe.

We have noticed in earlier chapters how easily Tom's melancholy moods change to those of happiness. However, in this instance, Tom is not revived by his family, school, or girl friend. Instead of meting out her usual robust and good-natured punishment, Aunt Polly weeps over him, which is much more upsetting to him. He is flogged in school, but he barely notices it, for his mind is on more serious matters. Becky's return of the brass knob is the last straw. Tom's happy world has collapsed for the time being.

CHAPTER 11

Summary

The townspeople learn of the murder and are very much excited and interested. The schoolmaster dismisses school for the afternoon. Muff Potter is immediately suspected, since his bloody knife is found near the slain doctor. Potter has also been observed washing himself in the early morning hours, a highly suspicious act, for he is not in the habit of washing. A search for Potter is launched, and the people drift toward the graveyard.

Tom and Huck meet at the cemetery and hear the accusation against Potter. The sheriff brings Potter to the scene. Muff protests his innocence at first, but then tells Injun Joe to tell all. Injun Joe, in front of Tom and Huck, tells his story, placing the guilt on Potter. The boys decide that Injun Joe has sold his soul to the Devil, and they resolve to watch him nights in order to catch a glimpse of his master, about whom they are curious.

Tom's conscience disturbs him the following week. Sid becomes suspicious when Tom mutters in his sleep about blood. Aunt Polly saves Tom from Sid's questions by admitting that she dreams about the murder, too, every night. For a time Tom is tormented by his friends' interest in inquests on dead cats. Sid notices that Tom avoids these play inquests, but says nothing.

Tom eases his conscience by taking small treats to Muff Potter in jail. Injun Joe, in his statement, has been careful to begin with the fight with the doctor and has not confessed the grave robbery which preceded it. The villagers realize that Injun Joe had been involved with the grave robbing before the fight, but, because of their fear of Injun Joe, do not press the case against him. It is decided not to try the case in court until later.

Commentary

The great excitement of a murder in the lives of persons dwelling in a sleepy, humdrum village is described by the author. In Chapter 5, we saw the villagers in church and shared their delight and amusement in the incident between the poodle and the pinch bug. A murder, of course, is much more entertaining and interesting to them, as is shown by the fact that school is dismissed and the people all drift toward the scene of the crime.

The characters of Muff Potter and Injun Joe are developed further in this chapter. Potter is pictured as fearful, hopeless, unnerved, haggard, and shaking. He is weak, and the villagers are quick to take advantage of his weakness and condemn him on the basis of rumors before a formal accusation is made against him. Injun Joe, on the other hand, is ruthless, fearless, wicked, and full of confidence. The villagers are quick to believe his story and do not wish to condemn him of the relatively minor crime of grave robbery for fear of retaliation on his part.

Tom is obviously uncomfortable over his decision to remain silent about the murder. That his conscience is bothering him is shown by his talking in his sleep, his taking small comforts to Potter in jail, and his avoidance of games which involve the murder. Thus we see that Twain is portraying a real boy, one who is both good and bad. He is also setting the stage for Tom's later reconsideration of his decision to keep quiet.

Sid continues to be a sneaky, prying individual who knows that Tom has a secret and tries to discover what it is. When Tom ties his jaws at night so that he won't talk in his sleep and thereby reveal the secret, Sid removes the bandage and listens for a while in the hope of learning something concrete.

CHAPTER 12

Summary

As the chapter opens, Tom is distracted from his secret about the murder by Becky Thatcher's illness. He hangs about her house, tries to get news of her, and loses interest in all his favorite pursuits. He becomes pale, dejected, and melancholy. Aunt Polly is convinced that Tom is ill and tries all sorts of quack medical treatments on him. Finally she discovers a new medicine, called "Painkiller," which is "simply fire in a liquid form." Tom pretends to like it, but really pours his doses down a crack in the floor. One day he feeds his aunt's cat, Peter, a dose. Peter goes into a frenzy and races around the house causing much damage in the process. Aunt Polly discovers the reason for the cat's wild behavior. Tom defends his act by comparing his aunt's concern for his well-being with his concern for the cat's well-being. Aunt Polly sees that what is cruel behavior toward a cat may also be cruel behavior toward a boy. She regrets that she has given Tom such harsh medical treatments and stops them.

Tom continues in low spirits as he goes to school early to watch for Becky. She finally appears and Tom's behavior becomes uncontrolled because he is so happy. He desperately tries to gain her attention and approval with his antics. Becky, however, reamins indifferent to him until he falls down right under her nose. Then she criticizes him for being such a show-off. Tom's spirits are crushed by her attitude.

Commentary

This is a transitional chapter. The author is going to drop the Muff Potter story for a while and he must provide the motivation for doing so. Thus he briefly resumes the story of Tom and Becky. Tom shows how much he still cares about Becky by his deep melancholy when she is ill and his joyful, ungainly antics when she recovers. Her rejection of him leads to the Jackson's Island adventure, which begins in Chapter 13.

The humorous incident concerning the effects of the painkiller on the cat chiefly entertains the reader, but it also points out the conflict between Tom and his aunt over the various medical treatments which she insists on trying out on him. With his clever replies to Aunt Polly's questions, he makes her feel guilty enough to cause her to stop the treatments.

Aunt Polly's character is further revealed to us as we see her foolishness over quack health remedies and patent medicines. The author satirizes both her gullibility in believing the conflicting advice in her health journals and the journals and treatments themselves.

Becky is shown to be unforgiving and unyielding as she refuses to make up with Tom.

CHAPTER 13

Summary

As the chapter opens, Tom justifies his decision to run away by reminding himself that he is forsaken, friendless, and unloved. His mood is gloomy and desperate. He blames others, not himself, for the necessity of his leading a life of crime.

He meets Joe Harper, who has just been punished unjustly, and they decide to run away together and become pirates. They select Jackson's Island as their hiding place because it is uninhabited and not too far away. They invite Huck Finn to go with them. The three boys agree to meet at midnight at a lonely spot on the riverbank.

The boys arrive at the appointed place about midnight with their provisions: a side of bacon, ham, a skillet, some half-cured leaf tobacco, and other supplies. They "capture" a small log raft and drive it downstream, grounding it on the bar close to the island. After unloading their provisions, they build a fire and prepare a meal of bacon and corn pone, which they devour speedily. They discuss hermits and pirates before becoming drowsy. Huck has no trouble falling asleep, but both Tom and Joe are kept awake for a time by conscience. They feel uneasy about having run away from home, and are particularly concerned over "hooking" the bacon and ham. They ease their minds by resolving not to steal again, and soon fall asleep.

Commentary

The story moves out of the little town of St. Petersburg to nearby Jackson's Island—long, narrow, wooded, uninhabited, with a shallow bar at its head. It is an ideal setting for the boys' pirate play.

Tom's dreams of glamorous adventure come alive for him in this chapter. Although he runs away because of Becky's rejection and Aunt Polly's overcautious care, he decides to become a pirate strictly because it is the most glorious occupation he can think of. He wants to be a hero among his contemporaries. He pictures himself performing brave and daring deeds as a pirate, which, of course, will make him the envy of all his friends. In Chapter 8 he threatened to run away and become a pirate, but he got sidetracked and played Robin Hood instead.

Tom has stylized ideas of what pirates are like from the books he has read, so each of the trio has a pirate name. Tom is the "Black Avenger of the Spanish Main," Huck the "Red-Handed," and Joe the "Terror of the Seas." They give the countersign, "Blood," when they meet at the riverbank. They take the arduous way down the cliff to the river because pirates value difficulty and danger. Even though the boys simply row the raft across the river, they use nautical terms, such as "luff," "aye-aye, sir," "steady it is," "tops'ls," and "flying jib," for their "style." Tom tells Huck and Joe how pirates capture ships and burn them, take treasure from the ships and bury it, kill all the men, and carry any women aboard to their island. He points out that pirates wear gaudy clothing and gold, silver, and precious jewels.

The contrast between Joe and Tom, with their standards of respectability, and Huck, who has not been brought up with such standards, is well defined here. Tom and Joe are basically alike because they have had the same kind of upbringing. They have guilty consciences over stealing food for the outing, and they say their bedtime prayers to themselves before going to sleep. This is in direct contrast to their boastful talk of capturing ships and killing men.

Huck, on the other hand, doesn't have pangs of conscience. He doesn't feel that he must live by society's standards or by the book. He is happy on Jackson's Island because he is getting more to eat than he usually gets and because there is no one to pick on him. He does look up to Tom, however, because of Tom's literary knowledge, and asks him questions about what pirates do and how they dress. Tom and Joe admire Huck because he smokes. Thus the boys respect one another partially because of their differences.

It is interesting to note that Huck and Tom seem to have forgotten the grim aspects of the grave robbery and murder. They do not mention this incident or their oath, and there is no feeling of terror and little talk of superstitions on Jackson's Island.

CHAPTER 14

Summary

The chapter opens with a description of the early morning hours and the activities of birds and insects. The boys have an idyllic morning – swimming, fishing, eating the fish, exploring the island, and taking delight in the beauties of nature.

In the middle of the afternoon, the boys hear the booming cannon of the ferryboat and realize that the townspeople think they have drowned and are searching for their bodies. The boys are overjoyed at the thought of causing talk and envy in the town. Joe suggests that perhaps they should go home, for he realizes how much grief his disappearance is causing his family. However, Tom and Huck talk him out of it.

After Huck and Joe are asleep, Tom gets up and writes two notes on the bark of a sycamore tree. He puts his boyish treasures—chalk, ball, fishhooks, and a marble—in Joe's hat with one of the notes. Then, with the other note in his jacket pocket, he departs toward the sandbar.

Commentary

There is a feeling of intimacy with nature here. When Tom awakens before Huck and Joe, he gets a thrill from watching the antics of the small insects and birds. The boys enjoy their swimming and exploring. An atmosphere of calm, quiet joy is apparent, whether the boys are chasing each other around in the water or cooking freshly caught fish or exploring the island.

The sounds of the ferryboat searching for the boys' bodies provides a change in mood. Society is not as far away as the boys have been pretending. They have already been missed, and family and friends are grieving for them. The boys' reaction is one of joy, since they feel they are truly heroes. They like the idea of being cried over and of causing suffering to those who have been mean to them. However, it is not long before Joe and Tom suffer a little themselves, for they know how grieved their families are.

Tom talks Joe out of going home, but steals away himself. We do not know yet why he has left his friends, and the chapter ends with an element of mystery.

CHAPTER 15

Summary

Tom wakes and swims to the Illinois shore, hides on a ferryboat to recross the river, and finally arrives home. He sneaks into the sitting room, where Aunt Polly, Sid, Mary, and Mrs. Harper are talking, and hides under the bed. Aunt Polly and Mrs. Harper show their grief as they tell each other how goodhearted and unselfish their boys really were. Sometimes the boys were mischievous and unthinking, but never bad. Tom learns that the villagers think the boys drowned and that their funerals will be preached the following Sunday morning. Finally, Aunt Polly and Joe's mother have a good, consoling cry, after which Mrs. Harper goes home and Sid and Mary go to bed. Tom sheds tears as he hears Aunt Polly pray for him. After Aunt Polly has gone to sleep, Tom starts to leave the bark note by her bed, but changes his mind and puts it back into his pocket. He leans over the bed and kisses his aunt before going back to the island.

Tom announces his return to Huck and Joe at a dramatic moment in their conversation: they are telling each other that they can keep his belongings if he is not back before breakfast. Tom gives an exaggerated account of his adventure during the meal, then sleeps while the other boys fish.

Commentary

Tom is shown to be very plucky. Alone, he makes a somewhat arduous trip to town and back, all in one night. This means that he has had to go without sleep after having been active all day.

Although the scene with Aunt Polly and Mrs. Harper is humorous because we know Tom and Joe are still alive, there is an underlying pathos which is stronger than the humor. The grief is real, as is shown by Tom's being so moved by it that he weeps. Aunt Polly reveals her love for Tom by her remarks about his fine qualities and by her prayers for him, as well as by her manifestations of grief. Tom shows his love for Aunt Polly by making the trip to give her the note telling her he is safe, by weeping at her grief, and by kissing her before he returns to the island.

The author does not explain why Tom did not leave the note. However, we learn later that Tom had an idea which kept him from doing so. It provides one of the funniest episodes in the book.

CHAPTER 16

Summary

The boys amuse themselves Thursday night and Friday morning by hunting turtle eggs on the bar and feasting on them. They also swim, play circus, and shoot marbles. After a while, the boys begin to get homesick. Tom tries to hide his feelings, but Joe admits that he longs to see his mother again. Finally, Joe and Huck start home, but Tom stops them by telling his secret. The prospects excite Joe and Huck, and they are happy once more.

After dinner, Tom and Joe decide to try smoking. They smoke for a while, then hurry off to conceal their sickness from Huck. They later refuse another smoke.

An approaching storm awakens Joe about midnight, and he gets the other boys up. They take refuge under their tent until it blows away, then huddle under an oak tree. Finally, the fierce storm abates and the drenched boys return to camp to find that the sycamore under which they had been sleeping has been demolished by lightning. They are thankful they were not under it when this occurred.

The boys coax back their fire, which has almost been put out by the storm, and dry off a bit. Later they sleep and get thoroughly dry in the sun on the sandbar. Tom can feel more homesickness coming on, and so suggests that they play Indians instead of pirates. Huck and Joe are delighted with the idea, and the three have a gory and very satisfactory imaginary Indian battle.

The boy savages return to camp about dinner time and, despite some reservations by Joe and Tom, smoke the peace pipe. To their amazement and great delight, they can now smoke without feeling sick. The author remarks that he is leaving the boys to smoke and chatter for the present.

Commentary

The author does three things in this chapter. First he presents an idyllic picture of the boy world of Tom and his friends. The descriptions of the boys playing circus with all of them being clowns, of their playing Indians with all of them being chiefs, of their rough play in the water, and of Tom's and Joe's first smoking experience remind adults of their own childhoods. This is a world of carefree, imaginative play.

Second, we see that the boys do get homesick away from their families. Joe remarks that it is more fun to go swimming if there is someone to tell him he cannot go. Tom writes Becky's name in the sand. Only Tom's secret, which we do not know as yet, keeps the boys from returning home.

Third, the author gives us a most beautiful description of a fierce storm. The calm before the storm, the building up of the storm to its height, the gradual diminishing of it, and the results to the camp and to the boys are told in exquisite prose. Also, there is a great contrast here between the wild storm and the peaceful, sunny days which preceded and followed it. The author shows that even an idyllic spot can be dangerous and thus makes the adventure seem more realistic.

The differences between Joe and Tom are revealed in this chapter. Joe is somewhat more dependent upon his family and home than Tom. Joe gets much more homesick, perhaps because he is the only one of the three boys who has a mother. Tom is again shown to be a leader as he bucks up his companions when they are lonely and keeps suggesting new games and occupations to keep them happy and interested in staying on the island.

CHAPTER 17

Summary

Back in town, on Saturday, preparations are being made for the boys' funerals. Becky mopes about the empty schoolhouse and yard, reliving her experiences with Tom and regretting her behavior. The persons who last saw the boys alive are envied and made to feel important.

On Sunday, after Sunday school, the funeral services begin with the tolling of the church bell. The boys are eulogized by the minister, who extols their great virtues. Finally, the minister and most of the congregation are weeping. In the middle of this, the door opens and the three boys march up the aisle. The congregation rises and stares at the supposedly dead boys. The boys' families give the boys loving attention, and Aunt Polly even smothers Huck with affection. The minister leads the congregation in the hymn "Praise God from Whom All Blessings Flow." The congregation, although knowing that it has been made to look absurd, is glad the boys are safe and is moved by the resounding singing of the last hymn. For the rest of the day, Tom receives "cuffs and kisses," alternately, from Aunt Polly.

Commentary

This is one of the most humorous episodes in the book. Again Twain underplays the scene and lets the reader's imagination have free rein after he has set the scene.

Twain sets the scene for the funerals by relating the regrets of various persons. Becky is sorry that she did not keep Tom's brass knob, for she now has nothing to remember him by. The people in the congregation regret that they have not been able to see the boys' true values and virtues while they were alive, but have only seen faults and rascally behavior. Tom is mourned, not only by Aunt Polly and Becky, but also by his playmates and the villagers as a whole.

To have the boys listen to their own funeral sermon in the gallery and then walk up the aisle is a dramatic and theatrical gesture on the boys' part. The humor lies in the surprise and suddenness of their appearance. It is a grand joke and a fitting climax to the generally idyllic Jackson's Island adventure. The affectionate welcome the boys receive shows that the boys' families and the townspeople truly do care for them.

CHAPTER 18

Summary

The author backtracks a little and explains that Tom's secret, which kept the boys from leaving the island sooner, was his plan for them to return unnoticed and attend their own funerals. The boys crossed the river on a log on Saturday night, slept in the woods until almost morning, and then crept to the church, where they hid in the gallery.

At breakfast on Monday morning, Aunt Polly and Tom discuss whether his treatment of her has been kind. She is delighted to have him back, but feels that he should have let her know that he was just playing and not dead so that she wouldn't worry about him. Tom insists that he loves his aunt. To prove this, he tells her of a "dream" he has had. He tells her all the details of his secret visit, pretending that he has dreamed it. Aunt Polly is amazed and delighted with the dream, embraces Tom, and forgives him. She rebukes Sid for making a doubting remark. Sid still doubts the dream because all the facts are accurate, but he says nothing and the children go off to school. Aunt Polly goes to visit Joe's mother to tell her of Tom's dream.

Tom is the hero, which he longed to be, to his friends at school. Smaller children follow him and Joe, and their contemporaries try not to show their great envy and admiration. Tom and Joe become conceited and swaggering. Tom decides that he will live only for "glory" and will ignore Becky. Thus when she arrives, he pays no attention to her, and, in fact, gives special attention to her rival, Amy Lawrence. Becky tries to get Tom's attention by showing off, by looking at him and sighing, and then by inviting the other children to her picnic. Tom continues to ignore Becky and she goes off by herself and weeps. After a while, she stops feeling injured and decides to seek revenge on Tom.

At recess time, Tom is still giving Amy special attention, but Becky is flirting with Alfred Temple, the well-dressed boy from St. Louis. Now it is Tom's turn to suffer. He finds Amy's company, with her incessant chattering, intolerable. He engages in an imaginary battle with Alfred and, of course, utterly defeats him.

Tom goes home at noon because he can bear no more of Amy's happy company, nor can he bear to see Becky and Alfred together. Becky begins to regret her behavior and dismisses Alfred. Alfred realizes now that Becky has only flirted with him to spite Tom, and he feels angry and humiliated. In revenge, he pours ink on the page in Tom's spelling book, which contains the day's lesson. Becky observes this through the window, but decides to say nothing and let Tom be punished.

Commentary

There is another conflict between Tom and Aunt Polly in this chapter. As we have noticed earlier, Tom usually comes out ahead in these struggles because he has a quicker mind than his aunt and because she is so fond of him that she wants to believe the best of him. Here she is not certain that Tom is as fond of her as she would like. She feels that if he truly loved her, he would have given her some sign that he was still alive. Tom does not want to tell her of his secret trip, but does want to reassure her of his love for her. So he tells her of his trip but pretends he has dreamed it. She is gullible enough to believe this, even though Sid raises some doubts about it.

The story of Becky and Tom continues. At first, Becky is eager to make up, but Tom spurns her advances. He acts this way because the glory he is feeling at being a hero has gone to his head, and he feels that he can get along without Becky. Later, when he sees Becky with Alfred Temple, he regrets his earlier behavior.

The character of Becky is developed a little more fully in this chapter. First, she acts like a little girl with her awkward bids for attention. Then she cries because she feels sorry for herself. Finally, she resolves to have revenge on Tom because of his treatment of her. Her flirtation with Alfred, her resolve to let Tom take the blame for the ink in the spelling book, and her decision to hate him forever show her revengeful feelings toward Tom.

CHAPTER 19

Summary

Tom is in a melancholy mood as he goes home for lunch. Aunt Polly confronts him with the news that she has learned the truth about the dream from Mrs. Harper. Tom explains that he did not make the trip in order to laugh at the family's sorrow, but to reassure her that he was all right. He tells his aunt that he did not leave the note on the bark because he got the idea of the boys' appearing at their funerals and did not want to spoil the fun. Tom tells her that he wishes now that she had awakened when he kissed her so that she would have been spared so much grief. Aunt Polly cannot quite believe Tom, but sends him back to school with a kiss.

After Tom has left, Aunt Polly goes to the closet and takes out his jacket. She decides not to look in the pocket, for she cannot bear to be disillusioned about Tom again. She puts the jacket away, but reaches for it again twice before finally putting her hand in the pocket and finding the bark. The note on it completely restores Aunt Polly's confidence in Tom.

Commentary

This is a rather touching scene between Tom and his aunt. There is pathos in evidence. Aunt Polly can stand any number of Tom's pranks and sins if only she can truly believe that he loves her. Tom sees how his smartness and ingenuity, if carried too far, can be mean and degrading. Being able to understand another person's feelings is a step toward maturity. The test of Tom's love which Aunt Polly makes, and her emotions while making the test, again show the reader her basic honesty and goodness. She wants to know the truth, even if it is painful.

CHAPTER 20

Summary

Aunt Polly's kiss sweeps away Tom's melancholy mood, and when he sees Becky on the way to school, he apologizes for his earlier conceited behavior. Becky scorns him, however, and the two exchange several angry retorts. They are furious with each other, and Becky can hardly wait for Tom to be beaten for the ruined spelling lesson.

The author comments that Becky will soon be in trouble herself. The schoolmaster, because of a secret ambition to be a doctor, keeps a textbook on anatomy locked in his desk, studying it in his spare time. Becky finds the drawer unlocked, opens it, examines the book, and accidently tears one of the pages. Tom sees her tear it. Becky puts the book back and rebukes Tom for watching her. She fears that he will tell on her and that she will be whipped. She goes outside, crying. Tom considers Becky's predicament and decides that, although he will not tell on her, he will let her solve the problem of escaping punishment by herself.

When school starts again, Tom finds that he cannot keep his mind on his studies because of Becky's troubled face. Soon the ink spots in the spelling book are discovered, and Tom is accused and whipped, even though he denies having done it. Becky is not as happy about this as she thought she would be, and has the impulse to reveal that Alfred is guilty.

Later, the schoolmaster gets out his anatomy book and discovers the torn page. Tom realizes that something must be done, but cannot think fast enough to accomplish anything. The schoolmaster questions each student, finally coming to Becky, whose guilty face is about to give her away. To keep Becky from being punished, Tom quickly volunteers that he has torn the page. The schoolmaster whips Tom severely and makes him stay two hours after school. Becky waits for Tom, and they become reconciled. Tom plans revenge on Alfred after Becky tells him the whole story, not sparing her part in the incident. Tom goes to sleep that night with Becky's words of admiration, "Tom, how could you be so noble!" lingering in his ears.

Commentary

This chapter is important because in it, Becky and Tom are reconciled. Although Becky has earlier spurned Tom's efforts to make up, when he takes her punishment for her, she is ashamed of her earlier behavior. When the chapter ends, all is well in Tom's world. Aunt Polly and Becky have forgiven him, and both love him.

There is a parallel between the two incidents of the spelling book and the anatomy book. Tom is falsely accused of spilling ink on his spelling book. Becky, knowing that Alfred is guilty, could easily tell the truth and save Tom from punishment, but she remains quiet. Tom could have let Becky take her deserved punishment, but he cannot bear to have her distressed and humiliated and so, nobly, takes her punishment for her. Becky thus seems less kind and more spiteful than Tom.

CHAPTER 21

Summary

As summer vacation approaches, the schoolmaster becomes more exacting and severe, for he wants his students to make a good showing at the public "Examination Day." He administers severe whippings to most of the younger students vigorously and frequently. The smaller boys rack their brains to think of a suitable revenge and finally conceive a plan. They enlist the help of the sign painter's son, since the schoolmaster boards with the boy's family.

The night of the exercises arrives, and the hall is lavishly decorated with flowers and greenery. Students, parents of students, and the town dignitaries, all dressed in their Sunday clothes, are present. The author describes various poorly executed declamations, reading exercises, and a spelling bee. The highlight of the evening is the reading of original compositions by the older girls. These all have melancholy themes, have no new ideas in them, use over-refined and gushy language, are sentimental, and end with a moral. The effect is insincere, and the author is very critical of them. A particularly melancholy composition entitled "A Vision" wins the grand prize for excellence.

The schoolmaster, now feeling quite happy, turns his back on the audience and starts to draw a map of America on the blackboard. He has fortified himself with some drink, so his hand is not quite steady. Some of his students titter as he tries to draw the map. He corrects his mistakes, but the tittering continues. Unbeknown to the schoolmaster, a cat is being suspended through a trapdoor in the ceiling just above his head. Finally, the cat snatches the schoolmaster's wig and is then quickly jerked up to the attic again. The teacher's head shines like a star: "the sign painter's boy had *gilded* it" while the schoolmaster was asleep. The boys are happy and satisfied with their revenge.

Commentary

Chapter 21 does not contribute to the structure of the book, nor are any of the main characters involved in the episode. Tom appears briefly to give a declamation as part of the program, but he does not distinguish himself.

The author does three things in this chapter. First, he paints a realistic picture of Tom's world, an important part of which is the school. The exercises mark the end of the school year, and the description of them adds to the realism of the book.

Second, Twain entertains us with the amusing and satisfying incident of the cat, the wig, and the gilded bald head of the schoolmaster. It is an imaginative and inspiring revenge of the younger and weaker boys against their tyrannical schoolmaster.

Third, the author uses the exercises as a vehicle for his satire. He is particularly critical of the melancholy, sentimental schoolgirl themes and poems which always end with a sermon. He notes that he has taken the various pieces from a book, *Prose and Poetry, by a Western Lady,* and says they are more illustrative of schoolgirl writing than any imitations he could devise.

CHAPTER 22

Summary

The chapter opens with Tom joining the Cadets of Temperance because he likes the gaudy uniforms. He promises not to smoke, drink, or swear while he is a member. Tom discovers a basic human truth: "that to promise not to do a thing is the surest way in the world to make a body want to go and do that very thing." Tom suddenly has overwhelming desires to drink and swear. Judge Frazer is gravely ill, and Tom knows that the Cadets will parade at his funeral. Thus he stays in the Cadets until the judge is pronounced out of danger. Disappointed, Tom resigns, but that night, the judge gets worse and dies. Tom is envious of the Cadets' showing at the funeral, but is glad to be free again. He discovers that he no longer wants to drink or swear.

Tom is disappointed in his summer activities. Becky Thatcher is away on vacation. The secret of the murder preys on his mind. A Negro minstrel show, a circus, a phrenologist, and a mesmerizer provide entertainment for a few days. It rains on the Fourth of July, and the United States senator who comes to speak is not as grand as the boys have imagined.

Finally, Tom gets a bad case of the measles and is very sick for two weeks. While he is ill, a religious revival takes place in the town. When he recovers, he finds that all his former friends, even Huck, have become depressingly religious. He feels completely alone and forsaken.

Tom thinks that he alone in the town is doomed, and that night, when there is a fierce thunderstorm, he hides his head and waits for death. He is certain that his wickedness is the cause of the thunderstorm. When the storm dies down, Tom considers reforming and repenting, but decides to wait and see if there are more storms before taking such a drastic step. He has a relapse and is sick another three weeks. When he recovers, he finds that his friends have got over their religious fervor and have returned to their normal pursuits.

Commentary

This chapter covers several weeks in Tom's life during the summer. It is important to the realism of the book that Tom have some ordinary experiences. He cannot have exciting adventures all the time, nor can he constantly think up mischievous pranks to play on others. Because he is being treated like a real boy, there must be periods of boredom and illness. Chapter 22 treats of such a period.

The mention of Becky's being away on vacation is significant because it helps the reader to remember that she still is important to the story. At this point, she and Tom remain on good terms.

The revelation that Tom is still very much concerned about Muff Potter and the murder is important because this story will be continued in the next chapter.

The author satirizes the Cadets of Temperance. He shows that boys like Tom join the Cadets only because of the showy aspects of the group's uniforms and parading, not because of a belief in temperance. Also, Tom's wanting Judge Frazer to die so that he can parade at the funeral shows a childlike and limited viewpoint. The episode is very funny. The author points out the human truth, as he did in the whitewashing episode, that people always want to do what they are forbidden to do.

Twain also pokes fun at the religious life of Tom and his friends. We see how the religious revival has a great effect on the boys for a week or two, just as the circus or traveling minstrel show has an effect for a few days. However, natural boy instincts are much more genuine, and they take over after a short time. Tom's fear of the thunderstorm shows that he has a conscience that begs for attention from time to time. However, his fear lasts just about as long as the storm.

CHAPTER 23

Summary

The murder trial is about to begin, and Tom becomes increasingly uneasy about his secret. He talks with Huck, who assures him of continued silence, and the boys swear another oath not to tell the truth because of their fear of Injun Joe. They discuss all the talk they have heard in the village about Muff Potter. They are sorry that he is being abused, and they remember all the kind things he has done for them. Then they hang around the jail for a while, hoping that some miracle will save Potter, but nothing happens. The boys give Potter some tobacco, as they have done before, and the prisoner's gratitude makes the boys feel miserable and guilty.

During the first two days of the trial, the boys hang around the courtroom but don't go in it. They avoid each other. However, they keep their ears open and follow the case closely. Potter seems doomed. There is no evidence to cast a doubt on Injun Joe's story.

On the night of the second day of the trial, Tom is out late and comes home through the window. He is so excited that he gets very little sleep.

The next morning, the court assembles. Besides the spectators, there are present the jury; lawyers; the judge; the sheriff; Potter, looking haggard and hopeless; and Injun Joe, impassive as usual. Witnesses are called by the prosecution to testify against Potter, and the defense attorney refuses to question them. The villagers, although convinced that Potter is guilty, are dissatisfied that his counsel is making no attempt to save him. The prosecuting attorney makes his final accusation of Potter, and Potter groans. Many of the spectators feel compassion and weep.

The counsel for the defense now arises and changes his tactics: he calls Tom to the stand. Tom, haltingly at first, tells the story of what happened the night he was at the graveyard, not mentioning Huck's name. Injun Joe listens until he hears Tom say that the half-breed murdered the doctor; then Injun Joe jumps through a window and escapes.

Commentary

This is the climax in the story of Tom and Muff Potter. Muff, who is innocent, is accused of murdering the doctor and he himself thinks he may be guilty. All the evidence seems to prove his guilt. Tom and Huck, the only persons who know the truth, have decided to remain silent out of fear of Injun Joe. Near the end of the trial, Tom identifies Injun Joe as the murderer and saves Potter. Tom's evidence is presented in a very dramatic way. Injun Joe escapes, just as Tom feared he might. Thus we have a very dramatic and suspenseful episode.

This incident is important to the development of Tom's character. He originally went to the graveyard with Huck and a dead cat because of a childish superstition. Until the last day of the trial, Tom's chief concern was for his own safety. However, in this chapter, we see Tom's increasing concern for Potter. First, he talks with Huck to make sure that Huck isn't weakening in his decision not to talk, for Tom knows that he himself is weakening. He even takes another oath to bolster his courage in this decision. He takes gifts to Potter. At night he has nightmares. During the first days of the trial, he hangs around the courtroom. Finally, he can stand it no longer and he tells the truth on the witness stand in spite of his great and reasonable fear of what Injun Joe will do to him. This is a mature and courageous action.

It is interesting to note that the author does not describe the entire trial in detail. He is letting us see the trial through Tom's eyes. Thus he presents a great deal of information about Tom's feelings and actions during the trial so that Tom's appearance in court will seem well motivated.

However, Twain does give an accurate picture of a small-town trial. The courtroom, jury, witnesses, prisoner, counsel, and spectators are aptly described, and one feels the atmosphere of the trial and what it means to the town.

Potter and Injun Joe are again contrasted. Potter is pictured as pale, weak, haggard, and hopeless. Huck and Tom consider helping him escape, but give up the idea because they know he would be caught again almost immediately. Injun Joe, on the other hand, is a confident man of action. When he realizes he has been identified as the murderer, he wastes no time looking mournful or being scared. He simply escapes as rapidly as possible. We suspect that he will not be easy to capture.

CHAPTER 24

Summary

Tom is again the hero of the village, "the pet of the old, the envy of the young." His name appears in the village paper, and some people think he may be President some day. The villagers treat Potter with great kindness and lavish attention on him.

Tom is still terrified of Injun Joe and has nightmares about him almost every night. He refuses to leave home after dark. Huck, too, is afraid, even though Tom did not mention his name in court. The defense counsel knows the truth, and although he has promised not to tell, Huck has no faith in such a promise after Tom's breaking two solemn oaths of silence. Potter shows Tom his gratitude daily, and this makes Tom glad that he has saved Potter from the gallows. However, at night, when he is awakened by nightmares of Injun Joe, he regrets that he has spoken.

Rewards are offered for the capture of Injun Joe. An out-of-town detective arrives and discovers a "clue," but Injun Joe is not found.

Tom's fears and tenseness gradually lessen as time passes and nothing happens.

Commentary

In this chapter, Tom's insecurity and fear of Injun Joe are revealed by his nightmares and his refusal to leave the house after dark. He becomes more fearful when rewards and a professional detective's efforts do not reveal Injun Joe's whereabouts. However, as time passes, Tom relaxes somewhat. It is apparently impossible for a young boy to remain highly anxious for too long a time.

The fickleness of the townspeople is shown. Ordinarily, Tom is considered a young scamp, but now he is so well thought of that he is mentioned as a possibility for President someday. Before Tom's testimony, the villagers spoke against Potter and spread all sorts of ugly rumors about him. Now that they know Potter is innocent, they reverse their opinion of him and have nothing but good things to say of him.

Huck becomes a little wiser in this chapter. Until Tom broke his two solemn oaths and testified in court, Huck had implicit faith in the efficacy of oaths. Now, however, he is completely disillusioned, and his faith in oaths—in fact, in human beings in general—is gone. Now he doesn't trust anyone. He has become less gullible and more mature.

CHAPTER 25

Summary

As the chapter opens, Tom is hunting for a companion to dig for buried treasure. He bumps into Huck, who agrees to go with him. The boys talk about buried treasure and then walk three miles to a special spot to begin their digging. First they discuss how they will spend the money if they find it. Huck will have pie and soda pop every day and will go to the circus frequently. Tom will buy a drum, a sword, a red necktie, a bull pup, and use the rest to get married. Huck is appalled at Tom's wish to get married someday. The boys dig for an hour with no results, then try another spot. Finally, they decide to dig under the tree behind the Widow Douglas' house, but to wait until midnight to do so. They hide their tools in the bushes.

The boys meet that night about midnight at the appointed spot, which is lonely and eerie. They wait until they think it is exactly midnight and then dig where the shadow of the tree limb falls. Tom finally decides that they are digging in the wrong spot again. Huck is nervous digging at midnight with witches and ghosts possibly being around. The boys discuss dead people, treasures, and a haunted house. They decide to try digging in a haunted house next, but to wait and try it in the daytime. They pass the haunted house on their way home. It is almost in ruins, the fences are down, and the whole yard is overrun with weeds.

Commentary

In this chapter, Tom and Huck begin a boyish search for buried treasure. Although the reader does not know it yet, this is the start of a new and exciting adventure which will involve them and Injun Joe again.

Tom and Huck are contrasted in the discussion of how they will spend their money if they find treasure. Huck will spend it all as fast as possible to have a good time. He sees no point in saving money for the future, since his father might return to town and take the money from him. Tom, although wanting to spend some money on boyish desires, such as a drum and a puppy, wishes to save the bulk of his money for his marriage. Tom, then, is thinking and planning for a future with Becky, which shows a sense of security and a more mature outlook on life.

Again the author is interested in the hour of midnight. Tom and Huck went to the graveyard where the murder occurred at night. The three boys met to go to Jackson's Island at the same hour. Now Tom and Huck meet to dig buried treasure, believing that midnight is the most auspicious time. This is a time of fear of robbers, a haunted house, a skull, witches, dead people, blue lights, and ghosts. This fearful, midnight, superstitious time is a part of the boy world of Tom and Huck.

CHAPTER 26

Summary

The boys meet at noon the next day to get their tools so they can go to the haunted house and dig for buried treasure. They decide not to go to the haunted house after all because it is Friday and Huck has had a dream about rats, which portends danger. The boys play Robin Hood the rest of the day, although they do give some attention to the haunted house as they play.

The next day, Saturday, the boys again meet at the dead tree and dig a little more just to be certain there is no treasure. Then they go to the haunted house, which seems so eerie and lonely that they hesitate to go in. They creep to the door and look in. They see "a weed-grown, floorless room, unplastered, an ancient fireplace, vacant windows, a ruinous staircase." The boys finally enter and examine the house. While they are upstairs, two men arrive. The boys throw themselves on the floor and watch the men through knotholes.

One of the pair is an old deaf and dumb Spaniard they have seen in town once or twice. He has long white hair, a bushy white beard, wears a serape and green glasses. When he begins to talk, the boys recognize him as Injun Joe in disguise. The other man is ragged and unpleasant looking, but the boys have not seen him before. The men discuss plans for another robbery and "revenge" job, then have supper and a nap. The boys are afraid to leave their hiding place.

While hiding a small bag of coins, Injun Joe discovers a box filled with gold coins. He opens it with the boys' pick, which he discovers in a corner. Joe is concerned because the pick has fresh earth on it. He decides not to rebury the money at the haunted house, but to take it to his den "Number Two." He decides to search for the owner of the pick before leaving. He starts up the stairs, but his weight is too much for the rotten wood, the stairs collapse, and he falls to the ground. He and his friend decide not to search further, and they leave with the treasure, heading for the river.

Tom and Huck, much relieved, leave the house and go home, regretting their bad luck in leaving the pick where Injun Joe could see it and thus deprive them of the opportunity to get the treasure. They decide to keep a lookout for the Spaniard when he comes to town to do his "revenge" job and perhaps follow him to his Number Two. The boys are fearful that perhaps the revenge that Injun Joe plans is on themselves, or at least on Tom.

Commentary

This is a continuation of the adventure begun in Chapter 25. The boys learn that the Spaniard whom they have seen in town a few times is really Injun Joe. Thus the mystery of what has happened to him is cleared up. Much to everyone's amazement, Injun Joe discovers treasure. Another of Tom's fantasies is coming alive. What started out as a game no more serious than playing pirates or Robin Hood is now a serious thing. The boys know that a murderer, who has reason to hate them, is free. They narrowly escape death only because a rotten staircase gives way. They see treasure richer than what they dreamed of in their play. They have a chance to steal this treasure if they can discover where Injun Joe hides it.

The author's descriptions of the haunted house, with its unkempt, ruinous, spooky looks, and of the boys' feelings and actions on entering the house are excellent.

Two superstitions, the belief that Friday is an unlucky day and Huck's dream about rats, are important here because they keep the boys from going into the haunted house on Friday and thus meeting Injun Joe there.

Injun Joe's character is more fully revealed in this chapter. Up to now, we have seen him in connection with the doctor and Muff Potter. Now we see that he is plotting another crime, which involves both robbery and revenge. He continues to be clever. He notices that the boys' pick has fresh earth on it and deduces that someone may be upstairs spying on him. When he is prevented from inspecting the second floor, he takes no chances and carries the treasure to another hideout.

CHAPTER 27

Summary

Tom dreams about the treasure Injun Joe found. Tom has had no experience with money, and even though he has talked in terms of hundreds and thousands of dollars, he has actually been thinking of treasure in terms of "a handful of real dimes and a bushel of vague, splendid, ungraspable dollars." Tom hunts up Huck to reassure himself that the experience with the robbers has been real. The boys discuss their adventure in the haunted house and decide to try to find a way to Injun Joe's Number Two. Tom decides that Two refers to a room in one of the two taverns in town, since none of the houses are numbered. Tom visits the taverns and learns from the young son of its owner that Room No. 2 in the poorer of the taverns is kept locked at all times. No one comes out of it or goes into it except at night. There was a light there the night before. Tom devises a plan whereby they will take all the door keys they can find and, on the first dark night, try them on the door of Room No. 2. Also, if either boy sees Injun Joe, he will follow him to see where he goes.

Commentary

This is a continuation of Chapter 26. The important thing here is that Tom figures out where Injun Joe's Number Two may be and devises a plan to find out whether he is correct in his deductions and also to get the treasure if possible. Tom's desire for the treasure is stronger than his fear of Injun Joe, as is shown by his plans to follow Injun Joe if he sees him.

Tom and Huck are again contrasted. Tom has dreamed about the treasure, but he so often dreams of fanciful things that he cannot be certain that he did not dream the whole adventure. Huck, on the other hand, dreams not of treasure but of being killed by Injun Joe. He has no doubt that the adventure really happened.

CHAPTER 28

Summary

The boys keep watch near the tavern for three nights, and, although they do not see anything, the nights are too bright to try the keys. On Thursday night, the boys decide to try the keys, for it is very dark and they have not seen anyone entering or leaving the alley where the door to Room No. 2 is. Huck stands guard while Tom, carrying a lantern wrapped in a towel, creeps to the door to try the keys. Huck is anxious for Tom's safety. After a while, Tom runs by Huck as fast as he can, telling Huck to run with him.

They enter a deserted slaughterhouse just as a thunderstorm breaks. Tom tells Huck that he took hold of the door knob because the keys he was trying were making so much noise and that the door opened because it wasn't locked after all. He went in, took the towel off the lantern, and almost stepped on Injun Joe's hand. Injun Joe was lying on the floor asleep, probably drunk, since there was an empty liquor bottle near him and the room was full of liquor. Tom grabbed the towel and ran away as fast as he could.

The boys decide not to try to get the box until Injun Joe leaves the room. Huck will watch the room every night and call Tom if he sees anything. Huck mentions that he can sleep in Ben Rogers' hayloft during the day because he has been befriended by Uncle Jake, the Negro servant of Ben's father. Tom promises not to disturb Huck in the daytime unless he has to.

Commentary

Tom is again shown as a very plucky youth. He knows he will be killed if Injun Joe finds him out alone at night, yet he goes to what is probably Joe's hideout to try to find the treasure. He is, of course, terrified when he sees Injun Joe lying asleep on the floor, and runs away. However, he is not so scared that he gives up his plan to search for the treasure, although he will wait until Injun Joe leaves the room.

The author has again used a thunderstorm to point up the boys' fears. After running from Room No. 2, they hide in an abandoned slaughterhouse to talk over what Tom has seen. During the time they are in the slaughterhouse, there is a heavy storm, which subsides as they finish talking. Twain has also used thunderstorms in the Jackson's Island episode and after Tom's measles to point up the anxieties of Tom and his friends.

The author satirizes "Temperance Taverns" by having Tom discover that liquor is kept in a locked room of a supposedly "dry" tavern.

Huck's human nature is shown in this chapter. He almost faints from fear for Tom while Tom is trying keys at Room No. 2. Furthermore, in an era when Negroes and whites did not form friendships, he becomes friendly with Uncle Jake, a Negro servant.

CHAPTER 29

Summary

The chapter opens with Becky and her family returning from their summer vacation. Tom is overjoyed, and for the moment, Injun Joe and the treasure do not seem as important as being with Becky again. Becky's picnic is planned for the next day. The picnickers gather the next morning about eleven at the Thatchers' house. The children are under the care of several young adults rather than their parents. An old steam ferryboat has been chartered to take the guests to the picnic spot. Because Becky will be getting home late, her mother tells her to stay all night with Susy Harper, who lives near the ferry landing. Tom persuades Becky to go to the Widow Douglas' home for ice cream after the picnic instead of directly to the Harpers'.

The children arrive at the picnic spot and have a grand time playing until lunch time. After lunch, they go to McDougal's Cave with candles to explore it. The mouth of the cave, which is up a hill, is shaped like the letter A. Its large wooden door is not barred. Inside is a small, cold, gloomy, limestone room very romantic to look at. Leading off this room are many small crooked passageways, some of which do not lead anywhere. Only a small part of the cave is "known," and the children are careful to explore only the parts of the cave with which they are familiar. Finally, the group leaves the cave and returns to the ferryboat for the trip home.

In the meantime, Huck, who knows nothing of the picnic, is watching the alley. Shortly after eleven that night, the door of Room No. 2 closes softly and two men carrying something brush past Huck. Huck realizes that he has no time to call Tom, since the men will have disappeared by the time he can get him. So Huck follows the men cautiously and quietly. They go up the river street three blocks, up a cross street, to the path that leads up Cardiff Hill, then up the hill past the Welshman's house and the quarry to the summit. They stop on a path between the tall sumac bushes. Huck is terrified, but stands still and listens. He overhears Injun Joe planning to take revenge on the Widow Douglas because her husband, who before his death was justice of the peace, had once had Injun Joe horsewhipped in front of the jail. He plans to "slit her nostrils" and "notch her ears like a sow." The two men see a light in the widow's window and think that she has company. They decide to wait until the light goes out to attack the widow.

Huck cautiously creeps away from the two men and runs to the Welshman's house, which is not too far away. He tells the Welshman and his sons what he has heard, but makes them promise not to tell who told them. They rush to the sumac bushes. Huck follows them part of the way, then hides behind a rock and listens. He hears shots. Huck waits no longer, but runs away as fast as he can.

Commentary

There are two parts to this chapter. In the first, the story of Tom and Becky is continued. Becky's return makes Tom less interested in Injun Joe and the treasure. He is happy to play childish games with her and to enjoy the special picnic with her. Although the reader is not yet aware of it, the setting for Tom's most perilous adventure, and the only one involving Becky, is being laid. The description of the cave, with its many passageways and unknown areas, is important for this reason.

The author's description of the picnic itself is in keeping with his attempt to show Tom's various activities. We have seen Tom's school, his Sunday school, his church services, his games with friends, and now we see a grand boy-girl picnic party, with its old ferry steamboat, its games, its delicious food.

It is important that Becky's mother should think Becky has spent the night at the Harpers', because the next day Becky and Tom are not missed until church time. Tom's suggestion that they visit the Widow Douglas after the picnic for ice cream adds mystery; the reader may think they are the visitors at the house when Injun Joe and his companion appear to take revenge on the widow.

In the second part of the chapter, the story of Huck and Injun Joe is continued. Tom is out of this story for the time being. When Tom is around, he is the leader of the two and makes the plans. Huck is very amenable to Tom's suggestions and does what Tom wants him to do. However, now that Huck is on his own, we see that he is both brave and resourceful. Although it is dangerous and he is frightened, he follows the men and overhears their plans to harm the Widow Douglas. Even though he is not welcome at the townspeople's houses, he goes to the Welshman's house to tell him what he has heard. Thus we see Huck doing the "right" thing in a tight situation because he is fond of the widow and does not wish to see her hurt.

The extreme wickedness of Injun Joe is stressed again. His robber companion does not want to injure the widow, but Joe threatens to kill him if he does not go along. The widow is not responsible for her husband's actions against Injun Joe, yet Joe feels a need to harm an innocent woman to get his revenge.

It is interesting to note how often the plot is dependent upon what the boys overhear or what they see on the sly. Huck and Tom witness the murder at the graveyard. Tom overhears Aunt Polly telling of the plans for the funerals. In the haunted house, Tom and Huck see Injun Joe find the treasure and overhear his plans for robbery and revenge. In this chapter, Huck again hears Injun Joe making plans. The device is an important one.

CHAPTER 30

Summary

The chapter opens with Huck returning to the Welshman's home to discover what happened the night before. The Welshman tells him that he and his sons crept to the spot in the sumac bushes where the robbers were. Unfortunately, the Welshman sneezed at the wrong time and the robbers ran away. The Welshman and his sons fired at the spot where they heard the rustlings and chased the men but did not catch them. Then they notified the sheriff, who organized a posse to hunt for the robbers.

Huck describes the men to the Welshman and explains that he saw them in town and followed them because they were carrying something he thought they had stolen. Huck tries to keep from telling that the Spaniard is Injun Joe, but finally discloses this without wanting to. The Welshman promises not to tell who told him.

Huck has breakfast with the Welshman, and they continue their conversation. Huck shows a great interest in the bundle which the Welshman found the night before where the robbers were. The Welshman tells him that it contained burglar's tools. He wonders why Huck is so concerned about the bundle, but concludes that he is not well after the excitement of the night before and needs rest.

After breakfast, the Widow Douglas and a group of citizens arrive to hear the story of what has happened the night before. The widow is full of gratitude for not having been harmed. She says she fell asleep while reading. The Welshman tells her that someone other than himself deserves most of the credit for saving her but refuses to disclose the person's name.

Becky's and Tom's families finally miss them after church and deduce that they are still in the cave. Two hundred men immediately go to the cave to start the search. The Welshman, one of the searchers, comes home toward Monday morning exhausted and finds that Huck is still at his house, delirious with fever. The Widow Douglas comes to care for Huck. The search for Becky and Tom continues, with no success. Becky's mother is beside herself with grief. Huck, although very ill, asks the widow whether anything has been found at the Temperance Tavern, and she tells him that liquor has been found. He asks if Tom Sawyer found it, and can't understand why she cries at this. He is too sick to be told that Tom is missing. Three days pass without a trace of Becky and Tom. The Widow Douglas despairs that the search cannot go on much longer, for men do not have the hope or the energy to keep on looking.

Commentary

Chapter 30 continues the two stories which filled Chapter 29. Tom and Becky are missed, and an intensive three-day search in the cave fails. The townspeople are important here. It is impressive that two hundred men, probably most of the able-bodied men in the village, drop everything to search for the children. We see, as we did at Tom's funeral and again when he testified at Potter's trial, that the citizens care deeply for Tom and the town's other children.

Huck's character is revealed more fully. We see how he responds to kindness and attention. The Welshman greets him eagerly and gives him a hot breakfast. When the old man says "welcome" to him, Huck "could not recollect that the...word had ever been applied in his case before."

When Huck becomes ill and the doctors are busy at the cave, the Widow Douglas comes to care for Huck because "whether he was good, bad, or indifferent, he was the Lord's." At this point, she does not know that Huck saved her from Injun Joe. Thus she is revealed as a good-hearted and kind woman who is not afraid to befriend Huck even though he is homeless and lacking in ambition.

Huck, well or ill, cannot get the treasure out of his mind. He almost gives the secret away when he avidly questions the keen Welshman about the robbers' bundle. Even when he is very ill, he questions the widow about what has been found at the Temperance Tavern.

CHAPTER 31

Summary

The author takes us back to Becky and Tom, who are in the cave, at the time of the picnic. They wander along with the other children, staying in the known portion of the cave. Tom, however, when he sees a "natural stairway" behind a waterfall, cannot resist playing explorer and seeing where it leads. Becky willingly accompanies him. They see beautiful things, such as stalactites and natural springs, as they wander more deeply into the cave. Some bats chase the children, and in fleeing from the bats, they stop making marks to guide them back, thus getting completely lost. They try to find their way out, cheerfully at first. Finally, they admit that they are lost, and Becky sinks to the ground and cries uncontrollably. Tom tries to comfort her, blaming himself for their predicament. She stops crying and insists that it is just as much her fault as his.

The children again move aimlessly through the cave, trying to find a familiar landmark. Tom blows Becky's candle out to conserve their slim resources. Finally, Becky can go no further, and the children sit down. Becky falls asleep, and Tom sits and gazes at her. He finds solace in her peaceful face.

The children get up again and wander. Finally, they search for and find a spring of water, and Tom explains that they must stay near the spring because their last candle is almost gone. Tom shares a piece of cake from the picnic with Becky. The children discuss the possibility of being found by searchers soon, but Becky becomes frightened when she realizes that they won't be missed until late Sunday morning, for she was to have spent the night at the Harpers'.

The children sleep again and awake to their miseries. They share the last bit of cake. They hear voices and start toward the sound, but a deep chasm keeps them from going farther, so they return to the spring and rest again.

Tom decides to explore some of the passages nearby, using his kite line as a guide. At the end of one corridor, he sees a human hand holding a candle. He yells as loud as he can, but then sees that the hand belongs to Injun Joe. The shout frightens Injun Joe, and he runs away. Tom does not tell Becky about Injun Joe, but decides to stay near the spring in order not to risk seeing Injun Joe again.

After another long wait at the spring, Tom is so hungry that he decides to explore another passage in the hope of finding an exit, in spite of his fear of Injun Joe. Becky is now too weak to go with him, and stays by the spring. She feels that she will die soon and makes Tom promise that he will return to her and hold her hand when the dreadful moment arrives. Tom kisses her and tries to act brave as he leaves her to try, once more, to find a way out of the cave.

Commentary

This is a rather detailed description of the cave and Becky's and Tom's experiences in it. They face several dangers. The overwhelming one is the threat of starving to death. They have only a small piece of cake between them, and no way of getting more food. Fortunately, there are natural springs to satisfy their thirst. There is also danger in bats, from which they escape. Still another threat is Injun Joe, who, by coincidence, is hiding in the cave and narrowly misses recognizing Tom when they meet in a passageway.

Tom shows maturity after he realizes that he and Becky are lost. He takes full blame for their predicament and tries to bolster Becky's spirits. He conserves their candles for as long a time as possible. Then he insists that they camp by a spring so they will have a supply of water. He explores from the spring by using his kite string as a guide. In spite of weakness and, later, a fear of Injun Joe, he does not give up. He proves again that he is plucky and resourceful.

Becky shows that she, too, is a good sport. Although she weeps and despairs at times, she does not blame Tom for their situation. She feels that she is just as much to blame. She does what Tom tells her to do. At the end of the chapter, she faces death calmly.

The brief introduction of Injun Joe into the adventure of Tom and Becky is important because it ties the two stories of Tom and Injun Joe and Tom and Becky together. This adds unity to the book. Moreover, the appearance of Injun Joe adds suspense to the children's predicament. Will he find them and recognize Tom? In a future chapter, the author will show the effect of Tom and Becky's adventure on Injun Joe.

CHAPTER 32

Summary

It is Tuesday, and the villagers are suffering over the loss of Becky and Tom. Mrs. Thatcher is ill, and Aunt Polly's hair has turned white. In the middle of the night, Tom and Becky return to the village, and the rest of the night is spent in joyous celebration. A messenger goes to the cave to tell Becky's father the news. He and a handful of men are still searching, but can be found by "twine clues." Tom tells how he finally found an opening in the cave, went back for Becky, and how they had come out five miles below the mouth of the cave. Two men passing by in a boat saw them and took them to a house for food and rest before returning them to their homes. Becky and Tom are ill after their experience, but Tom is well by the following Saturday. It takes Becky a long time to recover.

Tom learns that Huck is ill and goes to see him, but the Widow Douglas won't let Tom tell him of his adventure in the cave until Huck is better. Tom hears of the Cardiff Hill episode and learns that the "ragged man" had drowned in the river, probably while trying to escape.

About two weeks after the cave adventure, Tom drops by the Thatchers' to see Becky. The judge mentions that he has had the cave locked and is keeping the keys so that children will not be able to get into the cave again and possibly get lost. Tom turns pale and announces that Injun Joe is in the cave.

Commentary

The author underplays the children's escape from the cave. He spent a long chapter describing their struggles to survive and find a way out. He also described in some detail the townspeople's attempts to find Tom and Becky and their horror and grief when they are unsuccessful. However, in one paragraph, Tom tells of their escape and rescue. Because the scene has been so thoroughly set, the reader can imagine the details of their escape and homecoming.

It is interesting to compare Tom's supposed death after the Jackson's Island episode with his possible death after being lost in the cave. In both instances, there is pathos. However, in the first instance there is an underlying humor because the reader knows that Tom is alive. In this episode the reader knows that Tom is in serious danger and may not live. Thus the mood and attitude are different.

Becky's character is developed a little more in this chapter. When Tom goes back to her after discovering a way out, she at first refuses to go with him. She has resigned herself to death and does not have the strength or desire to leave. Tom convinces her to leave, and later she is extremely happy to be out. It takes her a long time, though, to get over her harrowing experiences.

Tom is brought up to date on what happened at Cardiff Hill while he was in the cave. This prepared him to continue the treasure hunt in the next chapter.

Chapter 32 ends on a note of horror when Tom tells the judge that Injun Joe is still in the cave, which has been sealed for a fortnight. Tom, although fearing Injun Joe, turns pale when he realizes that Injun Joe has suffered the fate which he so narrowly escaped.

CHAPTER 33

Summary

The chapter opens with a rescue party, including Tom, going to McDougal's Cave to search for Injun Joe. They find his body at the entrance when they open the door. He had tried to cut through the door with his bowie knife, but to no avail, and had starved to death. Tom feels sorry for the man, for he knows from experience how much Joe has suffered. However, he also feels a great sense of relief and freedom from fear for the first time since he testified against Joe in court.

People from several small towns nearby come to Injun Joe's funeral, he is buried near the cave opening. His death puts an end to a petition, drawn up for the governor, asking for Joe's pardon in spite of his having killed five persons. The author satirizes the petition.

The next morning, Tom and Huck have a private talk. Huck asks Tom if he was the person who told of the liquor in the locked room at the tavern, and Tom says no. Huck tells Tom of his part in the Cardiff Hill episode but that he does not wish it known for fear of reprisal by Injun Joe's friends. Huck feels that he and Tom will not now be able to find the treasure. Tom tells Huck that he is certain that Injun Joe left the treasure in the cave, and the boys decide to try to find it.

The boys gather the supplies they need, "borrow" a skiff, and go to the spot where Tom and Becky escaped from the cave. They discuss the possibility of later becoming robbers and using the cave as a hideout. The boys enter the cave, and Tom leads Huck to the spot where the cross is. Huck is afraid to dig because of Injun Joe's ghost, but Tom reassures him by telling him that a ghost wouldn't get near a cross. After much searching and digging, Tom finds the treasure box. The boys put the money into two bags, put the bags into the skiff, and go back to their starting point, arriving just after dark. Tom finds a small wagon. The boys load their treasure in it and pull it as far as the Welshman's house. There they meet the Welshman, who offers to help the boys pull the cart. They tell him that it is full of old metal. He leads the boys to the Widow Douglas' house. Huck is apprehensive about going there, but the Welshman calms his fears.

The Welshman pushes the boys into the Widow Douglas' drawing room. Most of the people of note in the village are there. These include the Thatchers, the Harpers, the Rogers family, Aunt Polly, Sid, Mary, the minister, and the newspaper editor. The widow takes the boys to a bedroom and gives them new clothing, which she tells them to put on after washing.

Commentary

There are two main parts to this chapter. In the first, Injun Joe is found dead in the cave and is buried. Tom has mixed feelings: he is happy to be rid of his fear of Injun Joe, but he also feels compassion for Joe's ordeal, which he can well understand. The author points out the fickleness of some people. Injun Joe is a hardened criminal who has murdered at least five persons and is hard to keep under lock and key, yet many persons sign a petition asking the governor to pardon him.

In the second part of the chapter, Tom and Huck continue their search for the treasure. Tom's boy world is emphasized again. In his behavior in the cave with Becky, Tom has acted maturely, but here Tom and Huck happily talk of playing robbers, following the rules of the books and collecting ransoms. Huck's childish belief in ghosts almost keeps them from digging for the treasure after they get to the cave.

Chapter 33 is important to the plot. Injun Joe has played an important part in two of the boys' adventures, first the story of the murder, culminating in the trial of Potter, and second the story of the buried treasure, which included a plot against the widow and which is almost finished in this chapter. Injun Joe is dead and cannot now take revenge on the boys, nor can he involve them in furthur adventures. Both boys have matured as a result of these two adventures. Tom managed to overcome his fear of Injun Joe enough to testify against him in the murder trail. Huck has become more a part of the town as a result of his having followed Injun Joe to Cardiff Hill. He now has a staunch friend, the Welshman, and is becoming more attached to the widow.

The chapter ends on a note of suspense, for the author does not explain why the important townspeople are gathered at the widow's house nor why they have been looking for Tom and Huck.

CHAPTER 34

Summary

The chapter opens with the boys getting dressed in the bedroom. Huck's first impulse is to climb out the window and flee, but Tom reassures him about meeting the crowd downstairs. Sid appears and tells them that the gathering is a party which the Widow Douglas is giving for the Welshman and his sons for saving her from Injun Joe and his companion. Sid predicts that the party will be a failure because the Welshman, Mr. Jones, plans to surprise the people by telling them of Huck's part in the rescue. Sid claims that all the people, including the widow, already know of it. Tom accuses Sid of telling the secret and boxes his ears, kicks him several times, and dares him to tell Aunt Polly.

In due time, the Welshman gives his little speech, springing his surprise about Huck's efforts in the widow's behalf. The widow pretends to be surprised and thanks Huck effusively. She tells Huck that she plans to have him live with her permanently, attend school, and eventually go into a modest business for himself. Tom interrupts her by telling all present that Huck is wealthy in his own right. Since no one believes him, he goes and gets the treasure and pours it out on a table. He tells the gathering that half is his and half is Huck's. Tom tells how he and Huck discovered the treasure. Mr. Jones comments that the little surprise he planned is small compared to the surprise the boys produced. The money is counted and is found to be about twelve thousand dollars, more than anyone present has ever before seen at one time.

Commentary

Huck continues to become more a part of respectable society. The widow offers to give him a home with her permanently, educate him, and set him up in business. He is publicly honored as being brave and honest.

Tom and Huck are again contrasted. Tom does not mind facing the large crowd of people, while Huck is miserable at the thought. Tom enjoys any attention and admiration given to him, but Huck is uncomfortable when the Welshman tells of his bravery in tracking Injun Joe and even more so when the widow thanks him.

CHAPTER 35

Summary

The author opens the chapter with a description of the villagers' reaction to the boys' treasure. The villagers admire, stare at, and talk about Tom and Huck and get so excited over the treasure that many of them, grown men as well as boys, begin hunting for treasure seriously and methodically.

The Widow Douglas and Judge Thatcher invest the boys' money for them, and Tom and Huck receive a substantial weekly income from it. Judge Thatcher's already good opinion of Tom for getting Becky safely out of the cave grows when Becky secretly tells him of Tom's taking her punishment for her at school. He hopes that Tom will be a great soldier or lawyer someday and plans his education accordingly.

Huck enters upon a new life. He lives with the widow and unhappily settles down to a sterile, civilized existence for about three weeks. Then he disappears. Tom discovers Huck in his old haunt, an empty hogshead, behind the deserted slaughterhouse. Huck tells Tom that he cannot stand the regularity of life with the widow. He hates washing, wearing tight-fitting clothes, sleeping in a bed, going to church, praying, and wearing shoes on Sunday. Also, school is about to open, and Huck does not want to go to school. Tom tries to persuade Huck to return to the widow by telling him that he is having to do only what the other boys have always had to do. He does not convince Huck, however, until he makes respectability a requirement for membership in his gang. Huck wants to be a member of Tom's gang, so he agrees to return to the widow for a month's trial. Tom promises to ask the widow to ease up a little bit on Huck. The chapter ends with Huck feeling thrilled over Tom's exciting plans for his robber gang.

Commentary

Again the author gives the reader a picture of the villagers, this time describing their excitement over the boys and the treasure.

Judge Thatcher enters the story more positively as he takes a real interest in Tom as an individual. At Aunt Polly's request, he invests Tom's money for him. He also makes tentative plans for Tom's future. Thus Aunt Polly will have help in influencing and guiding Tom in the future.

The author satirizes the accepted civilized ways of the townspeople by looking at respectable behavior through Huck's eyes. Huck says: "Looky-here, Tom, being rich ain't what it's cracked up to be. It's just worry and worry, and sweat and sweat, and a-wishing you was dead all the time."

Huck feels a conflict between the freedom of the river and woods, which he can enjoy to the fullest if he lives outside society, and his desire for the companionship of Tom and other boys in their imaginative play. In the end, he agrees to give up his freedom in order to be accepted by society, but the reader wonders whether he can live up to his decision.

That Tom asks Huck to become respectable shows that Tom is turning his back on the freedom he has been seeking. Tom has always professed to hate all the things which Huck hates, but it is his way of life and he basically does not wish to get away from it.

The book closes with a return to the boy world of Tom and Huck and their make-believe play. They are making plans to form a gang of robbers, who will be initiated at midnight.

CONCLUSION

The author points out that he has ended the book because it is the story of a boy and if he continues much longer, the boy will be a man. He says that he may write about the same characters again someday.

CHARACTER ANALYSIS

Twain is a master at creating character, either in an individual or a whole town. For the most part, his characters are presented realistically and convincingly. His people are kind and loving, but also cruel, stupid, and hypocritical at times. The only completely evil character in the book is Injun Joe.

TOM SAWYER

Tom is the most important character and the most completely presented. The book is basically the story of his growth and development during one spring and summer in the dusty little village of St. Petersburg.

Twain does not tell us Tom's age, but in his conclusion he says that he must stop the book or the boy will become a man. This would indicate that Tom is in his early adolescence. Twain is writing of events that happened over a ten-year period in his youth. Thus some of Tom's behavior, such as swiping jam, seems quite youthful, while other acts, such as camping out for several days on Jackson's Island, seem quite mature.

Tom is a typical boy of his time and place. He has a loving, happy home, with a devoted aunt to care for him. He is restricted by the home routine of prayers, meals, chores, bedtime, and the like, but the beauties of the nearby river and woods are always there, and if civilized life seems unbearable, Tom can and does escape to nature. His daily life includes regular attendance at school, Sunday school, and church. These are dull, but Tom manages to liven them up with his pranks.

Religion is an important part of Tom's life. Even though he rebels against memorizing Bible verses and attending Sunday school and church, he does have a conscience and believes what he has been taught about God and the Devil—sometimes. He feels guilty about his decision not to tell the truth about Injun Joe after Dr. Robinson's murder. He feels guilty about having stolen meat to take to Jackson's Island. He says his prayers on Jackson's Island, even though there is no one there to force him. When he has the measles, he thinks that the thunderstorm is heralding his own death, since he has been so wicked. Twain does not moralize about sin, but he does show us Tom meeting moral problems on his own level.

Twain summarizes Tom as follows: "He was not the Model Boy of the village. He knew the model boy very well though—and loathed him." Tom plays boyish pranks on Aunt Polly, Sid, his friends, the schoolmaster, the Sunday school superintendent, and the village as a whole. He steals, lies, plays hooky, fights, swipes doughnuts, and goes swimming on the sly. But Twain admires him and presents him sympathetically. Mischievous pranks are one way of developing the individual. He is what a normal boy should be. Most of the pranks occur in the first third of the book.

Although Tom hates school and plays hooky frequently, he is an avid reader and acts out the romantic adventures he has read about. He knows the story of Robin Hood by heart, including the exact language used, as he shows in his play with Joe Harper. He also knows exactly what robbers and pirates do, although he may not know their reasons for doing it. Throughout the story, he shows his knowledge of famous literature.

Tom's great love of adventure leads to many of the incidents in the book. His desire to be a pirate leads to the Jackson's Island incident. Tom's wish to be an explorer is responsible for his getting lost in the cave with Becky. His desire to find buried treasure is the cause of his and Huck's adventure with Injun Joe.

Tom is a clever, imaginative boy who has a good knowledge of human nature and uses it. He outwits Aunt Polly much of the time. He persuades other boys to do his work for him (in the whitewashing scene) without their being aware of it. On Jackson's Island, he devises entertainment for Joe and Huck to keep them happy.

Tom's greatest wish is to be a celebrity and attract attention and be talked about. He joins the Temperance Cadets so he can parade at funerals in a flashy costume. After the Jackson's Island episode, he enjoys being the center of attention.

Tom is unusually plucky. Even though he has excellent reason to fear Injun Joe, he goes to the Temperance Tavern, where Injun Joe may be hiding, to try to find the treasure. In the cave with Becky after he has seen Injun Joe, he risks meeting him again in order to find a way out of the cave.

Tom has fears, too. He is afraid, at various places in the book, of being harmed by Injun Joe, of starving to death with Becky in the cave, of witchcraft, and of death during the thunderstorm when he is ill with measles. Some of his fears are based on real danger, and some are just in his mind. Partially by luck and partially by using his mind and courage, Tom triumphs over these fears.

Tom, although usually of a sunny nature, periodically goes off by himself to think melancholy thoughts and to wish he were dead. Usually, these dark moods last for only a very short time. For instance, after being spurned by Becky, Tom goes off into the woods to make plans to run away. However, a call by Joe Harper to play Robin Hood makes him forget his melancholy.

Although Tom likes to rebel against society and its restrictions, he is basically respectable. He is the nephew of a woman who is the soul of propriety and who has instilled in him her own values. Tom calculates his pranks and adventures in terms of society's reactions. Wanting to be a hero in Sunday school leads him to cheat about the number of Bible verses he has learned. At the end of the story, he persuades Huck to become respectable by telling him that he won't let him join his robber gang "if you ain't respectable." Thus he shows that he is a part of the society in which he lives.

Tom's character grows in the book. In the four main stories, Tom starts out acting childish and irresponsible and ends up acting more mature and responsible. The story of Muff Potter begins with Tom and Huck going to the graveyard because of a superstitious belief. It ends with Tom defying superstition and fear of bodily harm by testifying against Injun Joe in court, thus freeing Muff Potter.

The first part of the story of Tom and Becky begins with Tom's desertion of his sweetheart, Amy Lawrence, when he sees the pretty Becky in the Thatcher yard. Tom and Becky's feud is petty and childish. In the end, however, Tom keeps Becky from harm by taking her whipping for her in school. Tom and Becky get lost because of Tom's childish wish to be an explorer, but he later shows maturity and courage in taking care of Becky in the cave and then finding a way to get her out.

The Jackson's Island story begins with Tom running away from Aunt Polly and Becky to play pirate. However, he and his friends manage to camp out for several days, feeding themselves, amusing themselves, and in one instance avoiding being hurt in a terrible storm. Tom shows his concern for Aunt Polly's feelings by sneaking off the island one night to let her know that he is safe. Because he cannot bear to spoil the fun of appearing at his funeral, she does not learn of his concern until later, but he at least does have the thought.

The story of Injun Joe begins with Tom and Huck digging for buried treasure. The development of the story concerns Huck more than Tom, but when Tom and the rescue party find Injun Joe dead in the cave, "Tom was touched, for he knew by his own experience how this wretch had suffered." Thus he shows the ability to consider the feelings of even an evil person like Injun Joe.

Although Tom is portrayed as a real boy living in a real time and place, he is also a symbol of eternal boyhood. Tom's dreams are the dreams of all boys: to find buried treasure, to save his beloved from death, to triumph over his enemy, and thus to be a hero in the eyes of the world. Tom's dreams come true in the book, and he enjoys the admiration of the people in his world.

AUNT POLLY

Aunt Polly is shown to be an old lady, but one who is still full of vigor and has a sharp tongue. She is simple, kind, and adores her mischievous nephew, but has a difficult time bringing him up properly because of his elusive and quick-witted ways. She tries her best to be a good disciplinarian, but Tom gets the better of her most of the time.

Tom's aunt is deeply religious. She has family prayers on Sunday morning for the entire household and requires the children to learn Bible verses, pray every night, and attend Sunday school and church.

Almost fanatic about health remedies, Aunt Polly subscribes to fraudulent "health" magazines and tries all the suggested treatments on her family and friends. She also buys all the new patent medicines she hears about. In Chapter 12 she lovingly persecutes Tom with all sorts of treatments and finally ends up dosing him with "Painkiller," which "was simply fire in a liquid form."

Tom has a closer, more loving relationship with Aunt Polly than anyone else in the book. He becomes melancholy when she scolds him unjustly or when she weeps at his wickedness. Aunt Polly can stand any amount of mischief as long as she can be certain that Tom loves her. After the Jackson's Island adventure, she feels fully confident of Tom's love for her when she discovers the bark, with its note reassuring her, in Tom's jacket pocket.

SIDNEY

Sidney is Tom's half-brother. Sid is outwardly an unbelievably good boy who loves going to school and church, does his chores without being reminded, and obeys his elders. However, we soon discover that Sid is really a prig, a tattler, and an eavesdropper. He tells Aunt Polly of Tom's mischief at every opportunity. He lets Tom take his punishment for breaking the sugar bowl, saying nothing. When Tom is suffering pangs of conscience over Muff Potter, Sid listens at night to his mutterings in the hope of learning something. He also tells the Widow Douglas of Huck's part in her rescue from Injun Joe, thus spoiling the Welshman's surprise party for Huck.

Tom and Sid carry on a feud in this book. They share a bedroom, so Sid manages to keep fairly good track of Tom's nocturnal goings and comings via the window. However, Tom manages to get the best of

Sid at the end of the story when he cuffs him and kicks him for telling the Welshman's secret.

MARY

Mary, Tom's cousin, is outwardly good like Sid, but unlike him, she is kind and loving at heart. Mary is a very minor character in the book. Although she does not appear often, she is part of Tom's family and thus part of his world. The longest scene in which she appears is the one in which she gets Tom ready for Sunday school and helps him learn his Bible verses. She treats him with gentleness and love.

HUCKLEBERRY FINN

After Tom, Huck is the most carefully drawn character in the book. He is introduced in Chapter 6 and plays an important role in three of the main stories: the Muff Potter story, the Jackson's Island adventure, and the story of Injun Joe and the treasure. He is not involved in Tom and Becky's story, nor with most of Tom's pranks.

Huck is a homeless boy who sleeps in hogsheads or on doorsteps. He fears his father, the town drunkard, who is absent during the period of this story. He remembers little about his mother except her fights with his father. Huck wears the discarded clothing of grown men; it does not fit him. He lives without washing, wearing clean clothes, sleeping in a bed, or eating regularly. He does not attend school or church, nor does he have chores to do. He swims and fishes when he wishes and smokes regularly.

Huck is a threat to the mothers of the town, for their sons envy him and would like to live as he does. The mothers feel that Huck is idle and bad, so they forbid their sons to have anything to do with him. However, the boys—and Tom in particular—play with him at every opportunity.

Huck is generally satisfied with his lot. He leads a free and uncomplicated life and has no wish to better himself and become respectable. He does not feel that he must live by society's standards or by the book.

Since Huck has had no formal education, he looks up to Tom because of Tom's knowledge of books. However, Huck knows the world of superstition well, and Tom relies on him for knowledge of the supernatural. Huck knows various signs and omens and understands the power of witches and devils.

Throughout the book, Huck appears more realistic than Tom except for his superstitious beliefs. He enjoys himself on Jackson's Island because he has more to eat than usual and there is no one to pick on him. After the boys have watched Injun Joe find the treasure, Tom wonders whether he dreamed the whole thing. Huck, on the other hand, knows that the adventure was real and dreams of being killed by Injun Joe.

Huck, however, like Tom, grows during the narrative. In the Muff Potter story, Huck begins by believing implicitly in the blood vow that he and Tom take to keep silent about what they have seen at the graveyard. When Tom breaks the vow and testifies in court, Huck is disillusioned about the power of a vow and thus becomes a little wiser.

In the Jackson's Island episode, he finds that he is a little more dependent on the society of the town than he has realized. He gets lonesome on the island for his familiar hogsheads and doorsteps.

Huck has a chance to prove his pluck and resourcefulness without Tom when Tom is in the cave with Becky. Although Huck is frightened because of the very real danger of being discovered, he follows Injun Joe and his companion when they leave the Temperance Tavern and overhears their plans to harm the Widow Douglas. It is significant that he does not merely run away and keep this information to himself, as he did after witnessing the murder of Dr. Robinson. He immediately runs to the Welshman's house to tell him of Injun's Joe's revenge plans. Thus he shows more maturity and social responsibility than he did at the beginning of the book.

Huck becomes more a part of society as the story progresses, although he is uncomfortable about it. He makes friends with the Welshman as a result of his adventure with Injun Joe. The Widow Douglas takes care of him when he is ill, although she does not know of the part he played in her rescue, and becomes fond of him. After he and Tom find the treasure, Huck goes to live with the widow.

There is a conflict within Huck between his desire for the freedom of action, which he can enjoy if he lives outside society, and his desire for acceptance by Tom and his friends in their imaginative games. In the last chapter of the book, Huck runs away from the Widow Douglas. He cannot stand being respectable and rich. He hates the regularity and lack of freedom in his life with the widow. Tom persuades him to return for another month's trial, for Tom doesn't want Huck in his robber gang unless Huck is respectable. Huck agrees to try again to live with the widow, and the book ends with Huck getting excited over Tom's plans for the robber gang. However, this decision seems to go against his nature, and the reader expects that he will run away again.

JOE HARPER

Joe is Tom's best friend among the respectable boys in town. Joe is not an original character like Huck. He has a background similar to Tom's, and he reflects the same attitudes and desires. Like Tom, he is mischievous, plays in school, and plays hooky if he feels like it. He and Tom play with a tick in school one morning and later play hooky from school and play Robin Hood in the woods.

Joe is one of Tom's companions on Jackson's Island. He gets more homesick than either Tom or Huck, but stays on the island in order to surprise the townspeople at the funeral. He enjoys all the games which Tom devises, but is not original himself in thinking up things to do.

He is important to the book because his similarity to Tom shows that Tom is a typical boy in his behavior, interests, and wishes. However, by contrast to Joe, Tom definitely shows more intelligence, pluck, resourcefulness, and qualities of leadership.

BECKY THATCHER

Becky is the heroine of the book. In Chapter 3, Twain describes Tom's first sight of her as follows:

> ...he saw a new girl in the garden—a lovely little blue-eyed creature with yellow hair plaited into two long tails, white summer frock, and embroidered pantalettes. The fresh-crowned hero fell without firing a shot.

Although Becky is involved in at least part of eleven chapters, her character is not fully developed. Twain shows her effect on Tom, and we just catch glimpses of her in the book. However, Tom's love for her is one of the elements that unify the book. The stormy course of Tom and Becky's romance runs through the story until Chapter 20, when they are finally reconciled after Tom saves Becky from a whipping in school. However, nearly all we learn about her up to this point is that she is from one of the important families in the county, she is very pretty, she is attracted to Tom, and she is proud and jealous.

Becky becomes a different kind of person in her adventure with Tom in the cave. There she is gentle, sweet, submissive, fearful of their predicament, but trusting in Tom; she does not blame him for their situation. She shows more stamina than one would expect under the circumstances. She faces death calmly and bravely.

INJUN JOE

Injun Joe is the villain. His character is well drawn, and he is involved in two of the main stories in the book.

Joe is clever, dishonest, wicked, brave, ruthless, resourceful, and formidable. He kills Dr. Robinson, puts the blame on Muff Potter, and makes Potter believe that he may be guilty. He convinces the villagers that his story is true. His formidable character is shown by the townspeople's fear of apprehending him for the crime of grave robbery for fear of retaliation on his part. When Tom tells the truth about him in court, he shows his strength by escaping from the courtroom.

He next shows up, disguised as a deaf and dumb Spaniard, in the haunted house, where, with a companion, he plans robbery and revenge. He cleverly notices that there is fresh dirt on the pick he finds, and so realizes that other persons may be in the house. He is wise enough to remove the treasure from the haunted house to a safer hiding place. He displays his extreme cruelty again when he tells his companion that he plans to harm the Widow Douglas by slitting her nostrils and notching her ears and that he will kill his partner if the latter refuses to help him.

In the end, Injun Joe has the reader's sympathy, for he slowly starves to death in the cave. Even here he shows his ingenuity and energy: he catches bats to eat and tries to cut through the door of the cave with his knife in order to save himself.

Injun Joe's chief importance in the book is his effect on Tom and Huck. He is partly responsible for the steps they take toward maturity as the book progresses. He also provides horror and suspense in a book which is otherwise quite idyllic. Horror, fear, suspense, and violence are part of Tom's world because they are part of life, and they are embodied in the character of Injun Joe.

MUFF POTTER

Muff Potter is a weak man who is hired to rob a grave and ends up believing he has killed a man. He is not very bright, as is shown by

Injun Joe's ability to convince him that he has killed Dr. Robinson. Potter is pictured as being fearful, hopeless, nerveless, haggard, and shaking. The villagers take advantage of his inherent weakness by condemning him on the basis of rumors before he has been formally accused. He is too weak to consider escaping from jail.

Potter's importance in the book is twofold. His weakness brings out strength in Tom, so that Tom is able to overcome his fear of Injun Joe and testify against him in court. Also, his weakness contrasts with and points up the strength of Injun Joe.

THE VILLAGERS

Twain gives character to the townspeople by describing their actions on several different occasions. He shows them at church, first being moved by the minister's thrilling way of reading, then laughing at the incident of the poodle and the pinch bug. Next, they get so excited by the murder of Dr. Robinson that they stop their usual activities, go to the scene of the crime, and spread all sorts of rumors. They appear again at the funeral of Tom, Huck, and Joe and almost convince themselves that the boys were noble rather than mischievous. They come to the school's Examination Day and are taken in by silly, sentimental writing. At Potter's trial, they spread ugly rumors until he is proved innocent, whereupon they reverse themselves and have nothing but praise for him. When Becky and Tom are lost in the cave, the men of the village drop everything and spend several days and nights looking for them. After Huck and Tom find the treasure, many of the villagers attempt to find treasure themselves and go so far as to tear up abandoned houses.

As portrayed by Twain, the villagers are important for two reasons. First, they give substance to Tom's world. Tom is a member of a particular social group which reacts in predictable ways because of similar backgrounds and mores. He grows up within a group framework. Second, the villagers reveal human qualities and action which are common to people wherever or whenever they may live. Thus they add realism to the book.

Mr. Dobbins, the Schoolmaster

Mr. Dobbins rules St. Petersburg's one-room school, which Tom and his friends reluctantly attend. He is pictured as a harsh man who punishes his pupils at any excuse. Although the schoolmaster is a minor character, he is important for two reasons. First, the reader can see what a typical teacher and school were like in a small river town of that period and can understand why boys like Tom hated school and played hooky often. Moreover, the schoolmaster's frustrated wish to be a doctor is indirectly the cause of Tom and Becky's final reconciliation. Tom wins Becky's love and gratitude by taking her punishment for her after she has accidentally torn the teacher's anatomy book. He also is the excuse for a very funny prank in Chapter 21 involving a cat, his wig, and his bald head.

Widow Douglas

The Widow Douglas is a generous, attractive, and wealthy woman who lives in a mansion on Cardiff Hill and loves to entertain her friends. She is kind and goodhearted. She is important to the narrative for two reasons. She enters into the Injun Joe story because she is Injun Joe's intended victim, but she is saved by Huck and the Welshman. Thus she is a plot character. Also, she befriends Huck when he is ill and later takes him to live with her. Although she is kind and loving, she leads a regulated existence, with meals, prayers, and sleep scheduled at certain set times. To Huck, she is the embodiment of the restraint of respectability.

Mr. Jones, the Welshman

Mr. Jones is a neighbor to Widow Douglas. It is he whom Huck calls upon for help when he discovers Injun Joe's evil plan for the widow. He chases the robbers away, then befriends Huck, who is not used to being welcomed in the homes of the villagers. He lets Huck stay at his home while Huck is ill and later plans a surprise party to honor him publicly for his bravery in tracking Injun Joe to the widow's house. The Welshman is warm, kind, and brave.

Judge Thatcher

Judge Thatcher is Becky's father. He is a minor figure, but he is characterized rather well. He is an important man in the county, well educated and knowledgeable. He is a very loving father, as is shown by his refusing to give up the search in the cave until the children are found, even though most other persons have long ago given up hope. After Tom finds the treasure, the judge takes a personal interest in him and makes tentative plans for Tom's education and future. At Aunt

Polly's request, he invests Tom's money for him. Thus as the book ends, the reader has the impression that Aunt Polly will no longer have the burden of raising Tom completely on her own shoulders, but will have substantial help from the judge.

CRITICAL ANALYSIS

STRUCTURE

Although Mark Twain has been criticized for the loose structure of his novels—and there is certainly no attempt to conform to a tightly knit plot in *The Adventures of Tom Sawyer*—there is a good deal of structure apparent in this work. Generally, it has unity of time, place, and character. The book is organized around the life of Tom Sawyer in the town of St. Petersburg over a period of several months during one spring and summer. Most of the story is told in chronological order, although occasionally the author will backtrack; for instance, he backtracks when he has the boys turn up unexpectedly at their funerals after the Jackson's Island sojourn and then in the next chapter tells how they got off the island and to the church. In the first eleven chapters of the book, Twain tells in some detail of six days in Tom's life. Then moves time ahead more quickly until the Jackson's Island adventure, when he again presents several consecutive days. Throughout the book, he tells of a particular adventure or prank in great detail, then summarizes a longer time rather briefly, as he does in Chapter 22 when he tells of Tom's summer activities before Muff Potter's trial begins.

There are four main stories within the book. The first is the story of Tom and Becky, which is really two stories: their courtship and their adventure in the cave. Of the thirty-five chapters in the book, their story occupies at least a part of twelve. Their courtship also contributes motivation to other major episodes. The story starts in Chapter 3 with Tom falling in love with Becky the first time he sees her. He performs awkward antics in Chapters 3, 4, and 6 to gain her attention, and finally wins her in Chapter 7. However, Tom almost immediately mentions his former sweetheart, Amy Lawrence, and the course of Tom and Becky's love becomes stormy until they finally reconcile in Chapter 20 when Tom nobly takes her punishment for her in school. In between, Becky's rejection twice motivates him to run away and become a pirate. The first time, he does not get very far because he forgets his melancholy in the thrill of playing Robin Hood with his friend Joe

Harper. The second time, however, he does run away and, with Huck and Joe, spends several days on Jackson's Island.

After Chapter 20, Tom and Becky's love remains constant, and their story concerns their adventures in the cave when they become separated from the rest of their friends and are hopelessly lost for several days. Tom takes good care of Becky in the cave and finally gets her out.

The second major story in the book is the Jackson's Island adventure, which occupies six chapters. Tom, unhappy over Becky's rejection of him and Aunt Polly's treatment of him, runs away with Huck and Joe Harper to Jackson's Island to play pirate. The boys' appearance at their own funeral is a humorous climax to the story. A terrible thunderstorm and a secret trip by Tom to alleviate his aunt's worry about him contrast with the rest of the carefree, idyllic existence on Jackson's Island.

The third major story concerns Tom, Huck, and Muff Potter and is told in six chapters. Tom and Huck go to the graveyard because of a superstition involving warts and a dead cat. They witness a murder committed by Injun Joe but blamed on the weak drunk, Muff Potter. Tom and Huck decide not to tell what they have seen because they fear Injun Joe. However, Tom's conscience gets the best of his fear, and he finally testifies in court against Injun Joe, who escapes from the courtroom.

The fourth story in the book is the story of the buried treasure and Injun Joe. It occupies parts of ten chapters. Huck and Tom go off to search for buried treasure. While they are exploring a haunted house before beginning to dig there, Injun Joe and a companion appear and, with the boys as eyewitnesses (unknown to the two men), discover treasure. The boys narrowly escape, and Injun Joe takes the treasure away to a new hideout. During part of this story, Tom is lost in the cave with Becky, and Huck carries on alone. Huck follows Injun Joe to Cardiff Hill and saves the Widow Douglas from Injun Joe's revenge. Later, Tom sees Injun Joe in the cave. After Injun Joe is found dead in the cave, Huck and Tom go there alone and find the treasure.

In addition to the four stories mentioned above, Tom's pranks form a fifth part of the book. They occupy most of the first eight chapters. Tom plays hooky from school and goes swimming, steals jam, tricks his friends into whitewashing the fence for him, tricks the Sunday school superintendent into giving him a Bible, causes a funny incident in church with his pinch bug, plays with a tick in school, and plays Robin

Hood when he should be in school. In Chapter 12 he feeds "Painkiller" to Aunt Polly's cat.

Some of these episodes touch on the main stories. For instance, in Chapter 12, Tom is depressed because Becky is ill. Aunt Polly thinks Tom is ill and feeds him Painkiller. He gives a dose to the cat, and this causes a great commotion in the house. However, the prank would not have occurred if Tom had not made himself ill over Becky's condition.

Many of the incidents are not important in themselves and could have been left out and others substituted. In particular, the episodes of the Sunday school prize, the battle between the poodle and the pinch bug, Examination Day at school, and the temperance pledge are unrelated to the main stories. However, they add realism to the book and give Twain good material for satire.

In addition to the unity he gains by having one setting (the land in and near St. Petersburg), a short time span (a few months), and one major character (Tom, who is involved in most of the action of the book), Twain introduces several recurring themes which help tie the book together. Midnight seems to be a favorite hour with Twain. The following all occur at midnight: Tom and Huck meet to go to the graveyard; Huck, Tom, and Joe meet to go to Jackson's Island; an approaching storm awakens Joe on Jackson's Island; Huck and Tom meet to dig for buried treasure; Huck and Tom plan to have the initiation into Tom's robber gang at midnight.

Twain uses thunderstorms several times in the story. A terrible one on Jackson's Island nearly harms the boys. A bad one coincides with Tom's relapse after he has had the measles. A brief storm lasts as long as Tom and Huck's conversation after they have found Injun Joe at the Temperance Tavern.

Twain repeats the device of spying or overhearing conversations throughout the narrative. Tom and Huck witness the murder of Dr. Robinson while hiding in the graveyard. Tom spies on Aunt Polly and Mrs. Harper from under the bed and overhears plans for his funeral when he is presumed dead during the Jackson's Island adventure. Tom and Huck overhear Injun Joe's plan for robbery and revenge and see him discover treasure while they are hiding upstairs in the haunted house. Huck overhears Injun Joe's plan to harm Widow Douglas on Cardiff Hill. Sidney overhears the Welshman tell Aunt Polly of Huck's part in the widow's rescue from Injun Joe.

Related dreams and superstitions also appear throughout the book. Tom and Huck go to the graveyard because of a superstition concerning a dead cat. Tom tries a superstition to recover all the marbles he has ever lost. The boys fear that a howling dog foretells death for Muff Potter. Tom and Huck do not enter the haunted house on Friday because the day is unlucky and because Huck has dreamed of a rat. The boys almost fail to dig for the treasure in the cave because they fear Injun Joe's ghost. However, they finally decide that a ghost would not be found near a cross. Besides affecting their actions, superstitions are often in the boys' thoughts. They discuss ghosts, witches, devils, and other spirits and their supposed habits.

SETTING

Mark Twain spent his boyhood in the little town of Hannibal, Missouri, on the Mississippi River about eighty miles from St. Louis. At that time, it had a population of fewer than five hundred people and was principally a farmers' village. It was near beautiful forests, where a boy could play Robin Hood or go off by himself and dream of great adventures. The river kept Hannibal from being isolated from the rest of the world, for steamboats bearing travelers and goods daily passed the town's wharf. The boys used the river for swimming, fishing, boating, and would sometimes visit small islands situated in it. The children loved to explore a cave on the riverbank a few miles from the town.

The time was the 1840s. This was before the Civil War and before the industrial revolution had reached the Missouri. A sleepy Southern atmosphere prevailed most of the time, but the violence and roughness so characteristic of the frontier would sometimes come to the foreground, showing that the town had not been civilized long. Slaves were part of the social structure, but primarily as household servants rather than laborers in the fields.

Life was uncomplicated, relaxed, and sometimes a little dull. The children lived close to nature and were relatively free. They were required to go to church, school, and Sunday school, and to do chores, but they enlivened these obligations with their pranks. The children possessed few clothes and toys, but they had loving homes and plenty to eat.

Twain described this place and time in three of his books, *The Adventures of Tom Sawyer, The Adventures of Huckleberry Finn,* and

Life on the Mississippi. He has written of the era with both realism and nostalgia, so that the reader becomes intimately acquainted with it and eventually enamored of it.

St. Petersburg

Hannibal becomes St. Petersburg in *The Adventures of Tom Sawyer.* This shabby little village where Tom Sawyer, his family, and friends live is the principal setting in the book.

The town and its institutions are important because Tom grows up within the framework of his home, the village school, Sunday school, church, jail, courthouse, Temperance Tavern, and the homes of the Widow Douglas, the Welshman, and the Thatchers. Of the thirty-five chapters in the book, the scenes of twenty-one are set in the town, and Tom is at home in at least part of eleven chapters.

The hauntingly beautiful forests nearby are the setting for much of Tom's imaginative play. There he plays Robin Hood and digs for buried treasure. The river, with its boats and rafts, is referred to often and is used by Tom in connection with his Jackson's Island episode and also for one of his treasure-hunting expeditions. Twain uses the eerie, rundown graveyard, the abandoned tannery, and the ramshackle haunted house as settings for four of his chapters. These point up the mystery, melancholy, and sometimes violence which is also a part of this world.

Cardiff Hill, on the outskirts of town, plays a part in the story. The Welshman and the Widow Douglas live there. A quarry is located on the hill, and the area is thick with sumac bushes. There Huck overhears Injun Joe's plan to harm the widow.

Jackson's Island

Jackson's is an uninhabited island near St. Petersburg where Tom, Huck, and Joe Harper stay for several days playing pirate. It is long, narrow, and wooded, with a shallow bar at its head. It seems isolated to the boys, and they have a grand time fishing, swimming, exploring, playing games, and generally living close to nature. It is the most idyllic setting in the book.

McDougal's Cave

McDougal's Cave is located on the river bank a few miles from St. Petersburg. The mouth of the cave, which is on a hillside, is shaped like the letter A. Its large wooden door is not barred. Inside is a small, cold, gloomy, limestone room that is very romantic to look at. Leading off this room are many small crooked passageways, some of which do not lead anywhere. There are many stalactites and natural springs. Tom and Becky are lost in the cave for several days, and later Tom and Huck find Injun Joe's treasure there. And Injun Joe meets his death there. Thus the cave is another important setting in the book.

World of Boyhood

On another level, the setting of the book is the world of boyhood. Twain has portrayed it just as realistically as he has described historical and geographical setting. It is universal and transcends time and space. Twain creates this world by showing what it is like to be a boy, how a boy acts, what he dreams of doing, and what his fears are.

Mischief is part of the boyhood world. Twain shows boys outwitting their elders in original and humorous ways. For instance, the schoolboys pay the schoolmaster back for his cruel ways by having a cat snatch his wig at the Examination Day exercises, revealing a gilded bald head.

Small actions of the boys reveal this world. Tom, for example, is excited over the loss of a tooth because he can now spit in a new and admirable way. Ben Rogers does not merely walk down the street; he pretends he is a steamboat and makes appropriate gestures and noises. One of Tom's most prized possessions is a brass knob.

A boy's fantasies are part of the boyhood world. Dreams of glorious adventure, of saving a loved one from death, of finding buried treasure, and of overcoming a wicked and dangerous villain are universal. Twain has emphasized these childhood fantasies by making them come alive. Tom actually lives his dreams.

Superstition plays a part in this world, too. A boy fills in the gaps of his knowledge with beliefs in ghosts, witches, devils, and the importance of certain omens and signs. Tom always wears a good-luck charm when he swims.

STYLE

Bernard DeVoto says that "Mark Twain wrote one of the great styles of American literature, he helped develop the modern American style, he was the first writer who ever used the American vernacular at the level of art."[1] Twain is writing realistically, from personal experience, of a boy growing up in a small Mississippi River town before the Civil War. He uses simple, clear English, which reflects the simple, common river folk about whom he is writing. He uses the idioms and vocabulary of their time, place, and condition in life. For instance, when Tom, Joe, and Huck are playing pirate on Jackson's Island, the boys talk among themselves as follows:

> "*Ain't* it gay?" said Joe.
> "*It's Nuts!*" said Tom. "What would the boys say if they could see us?"
> "Say? Well, they'd just die to be here—hey, Hucky!"
> "I reckon so," said Huckleberry; "anyways, *I'm* suited. I don't want nothing better'n this. I don't ever get enough to eat, gen'ally—and here they can't come and pick at a feller and bullyrag him so."

Twain narrates his story in the third person, and there is an oral character about his prose. His sentences and diction are simple, but he has a feeling for the beauty of language and uses it rhythmically and sensitively. Twain's description of the boys swimming off the bar at Jackson's Island shows these qualities:

> And now and then they stooped in a group and splashed water in each other's faces with their palms, gradually approaching each other, with averted faces to avoid the strangling sprays, and finally gripping and struggling till the best man ducked his neighbor, and then they all went under in a tangle of white legs and arms, and came up blowing, sputtering, laughing, and gasping for breath at one and the same time.

Twain's manner is informal. He writes in a neighborly, friendly tone, even when discussing serious matters. His purpose is to please and entertain the reader, and thus his manner is light, informal, and lively. An example of this is the description of Tom's and Huck's reactions to Injun Joe's accusation of Muff Potter at the graveyard the morning after the murder:

> Then Huckleberry and Tom stood dumb and staring, and heard the stonyhearted liar reel off his serene statement, they expecting

[1]*Introduction to The Portable Mark Twain,* edited by Bernard DeVoto (New York: The Viking Press, 1946), p. 26.

> every moment that the clear sky would deliver God's lightnings upon his head and wondering to see how long the stroke was delayed....

Twain generally does not intrude himself directly into his narrative. In a few places, however, he plays the kindly philosopher and makes a few comments, such as after the whitewashing episode, when he says:

> If he [Tom] had been a great and wise philosopher, like the writer of this book, he would now have comprehended that Work consists of whatever a body is obliged to do and that Play consists of whatever a body is not obliged to do.

Twain is usually realistic in his description of nature. He is accurate and precise in his choice of details. Obviously, he has the gift of keen observation. His description of some ants on Jackson's Island shows these qualities:

> Now a procession of ants appeared from nowhere in particular, and went about their labors; one struggled manfully by with a dead spider five times as big as itself in its arms, and lugged it straight up a tree trunk....

Occasionally, Twain introduces a personification of nature, which seems out of keeping with his usual writing and is in the romantic tradition. An example of this is the opening sentence in Chapter 4: "The sun rose upon a tranquil world, and beamed down upon the peaceful village like a benediction."

Twain is a master of dialect. Throughout the narrative, he uses a dialect that is common to the area and the time. However, he also makes a distinction between class and racial dialects. The only Negro appearing directly in the book is Aunt Polly's Jim, who appears briefly in the whitewashing episode. His dialect is distinct, as is shown in his reply to Tom's request for help with the whitewashing:

> "Can't, Marse Tom. Ole missis, she tole me I got to go an' git dis water an' not stop foolin' roun' wid anybody...."

Tom and Huck have different dialects, since Tom is more educated then Huck and is also an avid reader, which has affected his manner of speaking to some extent. Witness this example of their speech habits as they discuss whether they should follow Injun Joe when he leaves the Temperance Tavern (Huck speaks first):

"Lordy, I don't want to foller him by myself!"

"Why, it'll be night, sure. He mightn't ever see you—and if he did, maybe he'd never think anything."

"Well, if it's pretty dark I reckon I'll track him. I dono—I dono. I'll try."

"You bet *I'll* follow him, if it's dark, Huck. Why, he might 'a' found out he couldn't get his revenge, and be going right after that money."

"It's so, Tom, it's so. I'll foller him; I will, by jingoes!"

In the passages above, Tom says "follow" and Huck says "foller." In another scene, Tom and Huck are about to dig for buried treasure and Tom asks Huck whether he is going to save some of the money if they find the treasure. Huck answers as follows:

"Oh, that ain't any use. Pap would come back to thish yer town someday and get his claws on it if I didn't hurry up, and I tell you he'd clean it out pretty quick. What you going to do with yourn, Tom?"

"I'm going to buy a new drum, and a sure-'nough sword, and a red necktie and a bull pup, and get married."

Judge Thatcher, probably the most educated person in the town, talks very much like Twain. He tells Tom that he won't be able to go to the cave again in the following words:

"Well, there are others just like you, Tom. I've not the least doubt. But we have taken care of that. Nobody will get lost in that cave any more."

Aunt Polly reveals her character and a colorful dialect when she says, in a monologue:

"I ain't doing my duty by that boy, and that's the Lord's truth, goodness knows. Spare the rod and spile the child, as the Good Book says. I'm a-laying up sin and suffering for us both, *I* know. He's full of the Old Scratch, but laws-a-me! he's my own dead sister's boy, poor thing, and I ain't got the heart to lash him, somehow...."

Twain has the ability to present the essential heart of an experience without introducing extraneous material. His technique is to describe the background of a scene thoroughly and then tell his story quickly. For instance, when the boys appear at their funeral after the Jackson's Island episode, the scene has been so well set with descriptions of the villagers' changed feelings about the boys, and of the service itself, that the reader's imagination can finish the incident. Twain presents enough detail to make his point, but does not labor it.

Twain's style is basically humorous as well as realistic. He uses humor as a device for presenting his story and for commenting on persons, manners, and institutions. His humor is in keeping with the informal, regional style he has chosen. For instance, Twain tells of Tom's disappointment in a visiting United States senator because "he was not twenty-five feet high, nor even anywhere in the neighborhood of it."

Twain is witty in his choice of words. For instance, when Tom joins the Cadets of Temperance because of the flashy uniforms, Twain speaks of his finery as "shackles." This refers, not to the uniform, but to the freedom to swear and smoke which Tom has given up in order to be a member. And when Tom recovers from the measles, he discovers that all his friends have become religious because of a revival meeting held while he was ill: "Tom went about, hoping against hope for the sight of one blessed sinful face...." There is a play of words here on *blessed.* Usually, *blessed* refers to holy persons, but here it is used ironically to mean the opposite and also to imply that Tom would feel blessed if he could find another sinner.

In conclusion, Twain's style is basically realistic, informal, and humorous. He wrote in simple, clear, beautiful English and introduced dialects suitable to the characters using them. He was able to get to the heart of experience without using extraneous words to present his narrative. His style has influenced many later writers, including Ernest Hemingway.

HUMOR AND SATIRE

Twain is writing about personal experience in *The Adventures of Tom Sawyer*, and his method of handling his material is humorous. An example of this is the description of Tom's efforts to learn his Bible verses.

> Then Tom girded up his loins, so to speak, and went to work to "get his verses." Sid had learned his lessons days before. Tom bent all his energies to the memorizing of five verses, and he chose part of the Sermon on the Mount, because he could find no verses that were shorter. At the end of half an hour Tom had a vague general

> idea of his lesson, but no more, for his mind was traversing the whole field of human thought and his hands were busy with distracting recreations.

The passage above also illustrates how humor expresses the individuality of Twain himself and his unique comic outlook on the world. He looks at a small boy trying to memorize something which has no meaning in his boy world. Twain sees the humor in this situation and manages to convey it to the reader.

By means of humor, Twain distinguishes between the superficial aspects of life and the heart of existence. He recognizes human values, understands human nature, and exposes the incongruities in both. For the most part, he does this charitably and in good humor.

Human qualities are the basis of a good deal of Twain's humor. For instance, Aunt Polly is basically concerned over the health of her family, a normal "worry" for most women. Her preoccupation with quack health remedies, as suggested in her health magazines, is foolish and an exaggeration of the universal concern about hea th. Twain points out that "she never observed that her health journals of the current month customarily upset everything they had recommended the month before."

Twain uses many humorous devices in the book. Exaggeration is one of his favorites. For instance, Tom joins the Cadets of Temperance because of their flashy uniforms and their parading. Twain exaggerates this desire on Tom's part to "show off" by having Tom follow the day-to-day progress of the illness of Judge Frazer, whom he hopes will die so that he can parade at the judge's funeral. Twain also uses a type of humor which depends on sudden revelation for its impact. An example of this is the boys' sudden and unexpected appearance at their own funeral when they have been presumed dead. Some of Twain's humor is almost slapstick, such as the antics of the poodle and the pinch bug and the cat's behavior after receiving the Painkiller.

Satire uses humor and wit to criticize human institutions, manners, and persons. Twain is usually good-natured about this criticism, and does not seem to dislike actively what he is satirizing. For instance, he describes the choir in the church as follows:

> ...then a solemn hush fell upon the church which was only broken by the tittering and whispering of the choir in the gallery. The choir

> always tittered and whispered all through service. There was once a church choir that was not ill bred, but I have forgotten where it was, now. It was a great many years ago and I can scarcely remember anything about it, but I think it was in some foreign country.

Twain's lengthiest satire in the book is directed against the schoolgirl compositions read on Examination Day. These were melancholy, flowery, insincere, and "marked and marred" by the "inveterate and intolerable sermon that wagged its crippled tail at the end of each and every one of them."

In the last chapter, Twain satirizes the social values of respectable society when Huck finds his wealth and new place in society oppressive and wishes to give up the new life and return to his former free, impoverished, familiar, and comfortable state.

REVIEW QUESTIONS

1. Discuss ways in which Twain brings unity to the loose structure of the book.

2. What are the four main stories within the book and how are they related to each other?

3. What is Twain's purpose in introducing incidents which do not contribute to one of the four main stories?

4. Discuss Twain's use of superstition, including his reasons for using it, how it affected the action, and what it revealed about Huck and Tom.

5. Discuss the importance of Twain's early life to the setting, characters, and action of the book.

6. Describe St. Petersburg and the surrounding area, including Jackson's Island and McDougal's Cave.

7. What is meant by the "world of boyhood" and how has Twain conveyed this world to the reader?

8. Discuss Tom's character in terms of his typical, universal, and unique qualities.

9. Compare Tom and Huck in terms of their homes, families, education, place in society, habits, speech, etc.

10. Discuss the ways in which Tom's character develops during the course of each of the four main stories.

11. Describe Sidney, Tom's half-brother, and his feud with Tom.

12. What human qualities does Aunt Polly exhibit in her behavior toward Tom?

13. Discuss Huck in terms of his freedom from the restraints of society.

14. Discuss Becky's influence on Tom's feelings and actions.

15. Compare the characters of Injun Joe and Muff Potter.

16. Discuss Injun Joe as the embodiment of evil in the book.

17. In what way is Twain's portrayal of the villagers important to the book?

18. Why is each of the following minor characters important to the book? (1) Mr. Dobbins, the schoolmaster; (2) the Widow Douglas; (3) Mr. Jones, the Welshman; (4) Judge Thatcher.

19. Discuss Twain's literary style, including his realism, his informal manner, and his use of dialect and humor.

20. Discuss ways in which Twain uses his understanding of human qualities and values as the basis of much of his humor.

21. Discuss Twain's use of satire in the book, including his attitude toward it.

22. What is the effect of Tom's reading on his actions and speech?

23. What is Twain's attitude toward nature?

NOTES

NOTES

NOTES

NOTES

NOTES

UNCLE TOM'S CABIN

NOTES

including

- *Life of the Author*
- *List of Characters*
- *Brief Plot Synopsis*
- *Summaries and Commentaries*
- Uncle Tom's Cabin *as Melodrama*
- *Outline of the Melodrama*
- *Essay Topics*
- *Select Bibliography*

by
Gary Carey, M.A.
University of Colorado

INCORPORATED
LINCOLN, NEBRASKA 68501

Editor

Gary Carey, M.A.
University of Colorado

Consulting Editor

James L. Roberts, Ph.D.
Department of English
University of Nebraska

ISBN 0-8220-1313-4
© Copyright 1984
by
C. K. Hillegass
All Rights Reserved
Printed in U.S.A.

1990 Printing

The Cliffs Notes logo, the names "Cliffs" and "Cliffs Notes," and the black and yellow diagonal-stripe cover design are all registered trademarks belonging to Cliffs Notes, Inc., and may not be used in whole or in part without written permission.

Cliffs Notes, Inc. Lincoln, Nebraska

CONTENTS

UNCLE TOM'S CABIN
Notes

LIFE OF THE AUTHOR

Because *Uncle Tom's Cabin* is written so emotionally, most readers assume that Stowe is an evangelical Southerner. They are surprised to discover that Stowe's roots are deep in Yankee soil. She was born in 1811 in Litchfield, Connecticut, into a minister's family, and when she was four, her mother died, and she was reared by an elder sister, Catharine. Catharine founded a school in Hartford, and Stowe received her education there; afterward, she became a teacher at the school.

When Stowe was twenty-one, her father became president of a theological seminary in Cincinnati, Ohio, and she and Catharine moved to Ohio with him. Catharine set up one of the first colleges for women, Western Female Institute, and Stowe began teaching once more.

Her interests broadened as she talked to the people of Ohio. Cincinnati is just across the river from Kentucky, then a slave state, and there, Stowe heard many tales of slavery and runaway slaves. There also, she met and married Calvin Stowe, a minister and one of the professors at the seminary. After the marriage, Calvin encouraged his new bride to continue writing; she had begun winning prizes two years earlier and was grateful for her husband's attitude, which wasn't wholly unselfish. The newlyweds were very poor and, in this way, Stowe could supplement the family income.

Stowe lived eighteen years in Ohio, unconsciously collecting data and impressions about slavery. Then in 1850, Calvin accepted a professorship in Maine and so Stowe moved her family there. The following year, she began writing about a vision she had had of a ragged old slave being beaten. She submitted a selection of her writing to the *National Era*, and they agreed to publish it as a serial. It was an immediate success, and in 1852, it was issued in book form as *Uncle Tom's Cabin.* Ironically, the firebrand abolitionists did not think that the novel sufficiently exposed the evils of slavery as thoroughly as it could have. Nonetheless, Stowe mailed her novel abroad and, in a short time, *forty* different publishers in England had issued it, and it had been translated into twenty languages. Stowe found herself world famous. Accordingly, she traveled to England and was courted by politicians, intellectuals, and royalty. Not long afterward, literary gossip has it that on meeting Lincoln, the president remarked, "So this is the little lady who started this big war!"

The novel was dramatized, and the play was a huge success. Traveling companies across the nation produced it, and "Tom shows," in fact, owe their genesis to this novel.

Stowe continued writing for the rest of her life, but nothing else she produced approached the drama of *Uncle Tom's Cabin*–nothing, that is, unless one considers *Lady Byron Vindicated*, a didactic book that almost buried Stowe in bad reviews. Written with the best of motivation–a belief that she could gain sympathy and understanding for her old friend, the poet's widow–Stowe revealed that Lady Byron had told her in confidence that she had broken with the poet because of his incest with his sister, Augusta. Critics charged her with publishing cheap rubbish and exploiting a revered name. Seemingly, these charges were false, but certainly Stowe's literary reputation suffered as a result of this book.

Nonetheless, Stowe was undaunted. She continued writing for over twenty years more, publishing *Poganuc People* in 1878, a remembrance widely hailed as accurately and honestly capturing a portrait of a Yankee community–in this case, a thinly disguised rendering of the people who once lived in Stowe's hometown of Litchfield, Connecticut.

After Calvin died in 1886, Stowe moved to Hartford and lived there in seclusion until she died in July, 1896. Modern literary critics have downplayed *Uncle Tom's* literary merit, which may not be wholly inaccurate, but if *Uncle Tom* is not a great novel, certainly it is, without question, one of the major documents of American history.

LIST OF CHARACTERS

Uncle Tom

Unfortunately, the term "Uncle Tom" has taken on negative connotations in today's society; to be called an "Uncle Tom" is to be labeled a lackey, a doormat. Therefore, when we read Stowe's novel, we feel a sense of joy when we discover what the original Uncle Tom was like. Superficially, one might say that, at times, Uncle Tom seems to be too passive. Similarly, one could say the same thing about Jesus. Stowe's Uncle Tom is clearly a Christ-figure, just as her novel is a book that was clearly written to be a didactic document that would show her readers that Christianity and slavery were antithetical.

Above all, Stowe's portrait of Uncle Tom stresses his boundless goodness, his love for *all* people, and his determination to better himself, within the bounds imposed by Southern society. When we first meet Tom, he is laboriously practicing his penmanship, just as he will later read and re-read, with difficulty, his Bible, for Tom wants to become not only a better man, but a better *Christian* man. Ironically, his vision of Christianity is that of Christ's, while his white masters' vision of Christianity is satanic because of their belief in the concept of slavery as being right and natural.

Among the other slaves on the Shelby plantation, Tom serves as a kind of spiritual father. They gather to his cabin for prayer. According to Stowe, "nothing could exceed the touching simplicity, the child-like earnestness" of his prayers. It is this child-like earnestness that causes Tom to be uncompromisingly loyal to whomever his "Mas'r" might be. Tom recognizes the terrible injustices that are inflicted on him and his fellow blacks, but his firm belief in the Bible will not allow him to rebel. His role models are the saints and Christ, who also suffered and died for their beliefs.

Tom is flogged to death, but before he dies, he tells young George Shelby that he is "going into glory," and that despite everything, he "loves 'em all!" Stowe meant for her readers to identify Tom with Christ, and because of her dramatically effective depiction of Tom's unjust murder and his unyielding goodness, her novel became a sort of Bible for the Abolitionists. Uncle Tom's death served as the graphic epitomy of her indictment against slavery. She believed that it was impossible to be a true Christian and also a slave owner. Tom was a victim of the evil Simon Legree, but, by extension, all slaves were victims of a "Christian" social system that allowed a master/slave relationship. To Stowe, slavery was a poison in the body of America, and her country could only be purged of this inhuman cancerous evil by a re-examination of Christianity and a renewed dedication to Christ's principles.

Arthur Shelby

He functions as Stowe's concept of the "good" Southern gentleman-type of plantation owner. One of the reasons why Stowe wrote this novel was to point out that although men of this type are basically "good," they do not recognize the fact that blacks are as "human" as whites are. These men are kind and generous to their black slaves as long as the economy and their own personal finances are solvent, but if they are faced with a financial crisis, as Arthur Shelby is when the novel opens, they will sell even their most beloved and trusted black slaves, if their debts can be paid off. They have been so thoroughly "brainwashed" by the Southern code of master/slave that although they consider themselves to be Christians, they feel that, basically, the blacks belong to a separate and inferior race, that blacks are not truly members of the human race.

Mrs. Shelby (Emily)

Arthur Shelby's wife. Like her husband, she is fond of Uncle Tom and Eliza and little Harry. She cannot imagine her husband's selling them, and she is disturbed that he is even talking to the "ungentlemanly" slave trader, Mr. Haley. She is horrified when she discovers that her husband has sold Uncle Tom and Harry; she feels like a guilty hypocrite. She has considered herself to be a Christian woman, and all these years, she has rationalized that as long as she was good and kind to their slaves, God would not censure her. Now because of what her husband has done, all of her "Christian goodness" has been undone. She realizes that slavery is unfair and unjust and, most of all, that it is unchristian. She finally cries out, "God's curse on slavery!" She says that slavery is "a curse to the master and a curse to the slave. . . . I never thought that slavery was right – never felt willing to own slaves." This insight and loud denunciation is unique among the white characters in the novel. Only Stowe herself is more stern and emotional in condemning slavery.

Eliza

A beautiful young quadroon woman who works for the Shelbys. When she overhears Mr. Shelby tell his wife that he has sold Eliza's little five-year-old son, Harry, to a slave trader, she escapes with Harry in the night, hoping to reach Canada. Her husband, George Harris, has already escaped from his plantation master, and he is also heading toward Canada. Eliza barely manages to elude Mr. Haley, for when she reaches the Ohio River, it is turbulent and filled with large cakes of floating ice. In desperation, Eliza leaps from one ice floe to another, cutting her feet, and almost falling into the icy river.

She is helped ashore by a kindly man who takes her and Harry to a Quaker settlement; by coincidence, Eliza's husband has also taken refuge in the community. One night, the family tries to slip out, aided by the Quakers, but they are ambushed by two slave hunters, who have been hired by Haley. When they are safe at last, they are put on board a ship sailing for Canada. There, Eliza is reunited with her mother, and George is reunited with his sister. A few weeks later, they all settle in Liberia.

The two traits which best characterize Eliza are her courage and her fierce love for her family.

Eva St. Clare ("Little Eva")

The young daughter of the wealthy and kindly plantation owner, Mr. St. Clare. Eva takes an immediate liking to Uncle Tom when they meet on a steamboat bound for New Orleans, and before they reach their destination, Uncle Tom has saved Little Eva from drowning, and Mr. St. Clare has bought Tom from the evil Mr. Haley. Eva is described as looking like an angel, with golden hair, a beautiful face, and violet, spiritual eyes. She lives in a happy dream of bountiful goodness; love seems to radiate from her.

Her early death scene is well-known in literature. Eva has boundless affection for her father's slaves, and she has them gather at her deathbed. There, she gives each of them a lock of her golden hair and prays for them. She tells them that she is going to heaven and that they must become Christians so that they can all see one another again. After they all leave, Uncle Tom stays with Little Eva until she dies, soothing the deep sorrow of Eva's distraught father. Little Eva's last words are: "O! love,–joy,–peace."

Topsy

Mr. St. Clare buys Topsy for his sister, Miss Ophelia, after he brings Ophelia down from Vermont to help manage the plantation.

Miss Ophelia finds so much fault with the "Southern" ways of doing things that Mr. St. Clare thinks that if Ophelia has someone whom it is her specific responsibility to educate and train, then perhaps there will be more peace in the house.

At first, Miss Ophelia is horrified by little Topsy: "so heathenish" is all she can utter. Topsy could care less. She has a gaiety that cannot be suppressed. She's been treated like a dog, but it has not extinguished her spirit. She sings, she dances, and she doesn't care if white folks like her or not. Love from other people is alien to her. She doesn't know when she was born, and she doesn't care. She learns how to do chores, but does them only when she's in the mood. And she is usually in the mood to play. She's like a cute, but ornery kitten—hence, a delight to those who have patience and a good sense of humor, two qualities which Miss Ophelia lacks during most of the novel.

Topsy's "soul" is finally touched by Eva's continual declarations of love for her. It is as though Topsy at last truly realizes what love is and that it exists for her. When Eva's love is released within Topsy, the little black girl kneels, puts her head between her knees, and sobs, as Eva bends over her "like a bright angel stooping to reclaim a sinner." Obviously, Stowe inserted Topsy into the novel as a counterpart to the "perfect" Little Eva and to show us Eva's unique power to convert others, even mischievous sprites, to Christianity.

Simon Legree

To most Americans, Simon Legree and the word "villain" are synonymous, yet curiously, Legree does not make his appearance in this novel until it is almost three-fourths finished.

Legree, a Yankee living in the South, buys Tom from the widow of Augustine St. Clare. St. Clare has been a kind slave owner to Tom, and both St. Clare and his daughter, Little Eva, have been particularly fond of Tom. Mrs. St. Clare, however, is an imaginary invalid, and after her husband's death, she decides to sell a number of the plantation's slaves, including Tom.

In the slave auction scene, Stowe describes Legree as being a "short, broad, muscular man," dressed in clothes "much the worse for dirt and wear." Legree appears to possess "gigantic strength," and Stowe is careful to emphasize his "bullet head" and his "large, coarse mouth," distended with chewing tobacco. He is brutal with Tom from the first moment he sees him, inspecting his mouth and examining his muscles.

Legree's plantation is as squalid as he is. Dirty clothes, spoiled food, and piles of stray hounds clutter his house, and it is clear that Legree does little else but beat his slaves, force them to work long hours, and drink himself into one stupor after another. Legree is an alcoholic, and his villainy is therefore worse. He is often so drunk and senseless that he doesn't realize how brutal he really is. He has a particularly pathological dislike for Uncle Tom because Tom submits to Legree's floggings and beatings without seeming to hate or resent Legree. Legree *needs* to see his Negroes grovel so that he can feel that he is the Master. And if they lash back at him, he has an excuse for being even more brutal and bestial.

Legree can be manipulated by only one person, a slave named Cassy, who tries as best she can, to take care of Uncle Tom. Cassy makes Legree believe that she has supernatural powers. But even Cassy cannot finally save Uncle Tom from Legree's beatings. Uncle Tom offers absolutely no resistance to anyone, and thus one day, Legree flogs Tom until the old black man lies dying.

Harry ("Jim Crow")

A beautiful and talented little black child; he sings, dances, and mimes excellently. His parents are George and Eliza Harris. He is sold to Mr. Haley, but Eliza manages to escape with him and flee to safety in Canada.

Mr. Haley

A cruel Southern slave trader; ironically, he considers himself a "humanitarian" slave trader. Most people who are only vaguely familiar with this novel believe that it is Simon Legree who chases Eliza across the ice floes on the Ohio River; it is not; the hunter is Mr. Haley.

Aunt Chloe

The plump, cheerful wife of Uncle Tom; she is an excellent cook and housekeeper.

George Shelby

Mr. and Mrs. Shelby's young son; when he is thirteen years old, he patiently teaches Uncle Tom how to read and write. At the end of the novel, he locates Uncle Tom and manages to talk with him a few moments before Tom dies. Afterward, George buries Tom in a shady knoll.

Mose and Pete

"A couple of wooly-headed boys with glistening black eyes and fat, shining cheeks"; sons of Uncle Tom and Aunt Chloe.

Polly

A toddler; the daughter of Uncle Tom and Aunt Chloe.

George Harris

Eliza's husband; he escapes from a neighboring plantation and, disguised as a Spaniard, he reaches Ohio; after he and his family are reunited, they find safety in Canada.

Sam and Andy

Two blacks on the Shelby plantation who are ordered to help Haley track down Eliza and Harry. They scheme, instead, how to *appear* to do so and, at the same time, they cleverly manage to avoid doing so.

Mr. Symmes

A man who knows the Shelbys and who helps Eliza escape onto the bank of the Ohio River.

Tom Loker

A massive and burly slave hunter hired by Shelby to track down Eliza and Harry.

Marks

Tom's sidekick; a weasel-like, unscrupulous slave hunter.

Senator John Bird

Basically, the senator is a good man, but he votes for an Ohio law that prevents residents of Ohio from aiding runaway slaves. He did it, he says, "to quiet the excitement" stirred up by the "reckless Abolitionists."

Mrs. Mary Bird

She is small in stature and is best characterized by her gentle and sympathetic nature. When Eliza and her son appear at the Birds' door and Eliza faints, both Senator Bird and his wife take pity on them and give them comfortable beds and food.

Old Cudjoe

A Negro jack-of-all-trades who works for the Birds. He takes personal charge of little Harry while Eliza and her young son stay with the Birds.

Old Aunt Dinah

A black servant of the Birds.

Van Trompe

An old client of Senator Bird; originally from Kentucky, he set all his slaves free. Senator Bird takes Eliza and Harry to Van Trompe's house for safety.

Mr. Wilson

Former employer of George Harris in a factory. He says that George was the best worker he ever had and tells a group of bigoted slave owners about George's ingenious invention.

Rachel and Simeon Halliday

An elderly Quaker couple who give room and board and genuine compassion to Eliza and Harry; they urge them to stay in the Quaker settlement instead of trying to escape to Canada.

Mr. St. Clare

A young New Orleans gentleman of great fortune and family who is a passenger on the same boat with Haley and Uncle Tom. He purchases Uncle Tom after Tom saves St. Clare's daughter, Eva, from drowning, and Eva begs him to do so. He becomes very fond of Uncle Tom, and when the boat docks at New Orleans, he makes Tom his head coachman. He promises Tom his freedom, but unfortunately, St. Clare is fatally wounded trying to settle a drunken brawl, and Tom is sold to Simon Legree by St. Clare's widow.

Lucy

A slave whom Haley buys on his way to New Orleans. He plans to have her cook for him. When Haley sells Lucy's little son, she drowns herself in the Mississippi River.

Ruth Stedman

A Quaker friend of the Hallidays.

Mrs. St. Clare (Marie)

A Southern belle who was once beautiful and popular. After her marriage to St. Clare, however, she became bored, and so she began to invent various illnesses in order to get attention. She cares for no one but herself and her creature comforts.

Miss Ophelia St. Clare (Miss Feely)

St. Clare's sister; he brings her from Vermont to New Orleans to help him manage his large estate. Ophelia, however, never adjusts to the slow pace of the South. Her constant complaining finally drives St. Clare to buy a little black girl for Ophelia to have sole charge of. His plan works. At first, Ophelia is repulsed by Topsy, but gradually Topsy wins her over and returns with Ophelia to Vermont at the end of the novel.

Adolph

An old distinguished black doorman for the St. Clare mansion.

Mammy

An old black retainer who looks after Marie St. Clare's continuous wants and ailments.

Phineas Fletcher

A Quaker friend of the Hallidays; he offers to help George, Eliza, and Harry escape and vows to protect them until they are safe on a road leading to Canada.

Jim Selden

A black man who accompanies Fletcher during Fletcher's attempt to help George, Eliza, and Harry escape. He too hopes to escape, along with his very old and feeble mother.

Michael, Stephen and Amariah

Quakers to whom Fletcher entrusts George, Eliza, and Harry.

Grandmam Stephens (Dorcas)

She nurses Loker (the slave hunter) because of her basic Christian goodness.

Old Dinah

Head cook for the St. Clares.

Prue

Black neighbor of the St. Clares who sells hot rolls and rusks.

Jane and Rosa

Two of Marie St. Clare's chambermaids.

Alfred St. Clare

Augustine's twin brother, a diametrically opposite type of plantation owner. In St. Clare's words, Alfred is "as determined a despot as ever walked."

Henrique

Alfred's son; a princely boy, possessed with vivacity, spirit, and a fiery, mean temperament. He is fascinated "by the spiritual graces of his cousin Evangeline."

Scipio

A "regular African lion" of a slave whom Alfred brings to St. Clare "to tame." St. Clare dresses Scipio's wounds and gives him his freedom papers. In town, Scipio tears the papers in two and becomes "trusty and true as steel."

Dodo

A mulatto slave boy of thirteen; Dodo is cruelly beaten by Henrique when he lies about brushing down Henrique's imported Arabian horse.

Mr. Skeggs

The keeper of a depot who oversees the first lot of the St. Clare slaves until they can be sold at auction.

Susan and Emmeline

Susan is a mulatto slave between forty and fifty; Emmeline is Susan's daughter, a quadroon. Both mother and daughter are beautiful women and are waiting to be sold in the same lot as Uncle Tom and the other St. Clare slaves.

Sambo and Quimbo

Legree's two lackeys; they obey his every word. In return, Legree allows them to get drunk with him. They are loathed by the other plantation slaves, and they "cordially" hate each other.

Lucy

An ill slave whom Tom tries to help pick cotton. He is severely punished for doing so.

Cassy

A tall, slender, formidable slave woman who belongs to Legree; her eyes flash with pride and defiance. She helps Tom pick cotton, and after Tom is beaten for helping Lucy, Cassy comes to bind up Tom's wounds. Long ago, both of Cassy's children were taken from her and sold. It turns out that Cassy is Eliza's mother, and she is finally reunited with her daughter in Canada.

Emmeline

Another of Legree's slaves; she escapes with Cassy.

Madame de Thoux (Emily)

By coincidence, she is on the same ship that Cassy, Emmeline, and George Shelby board to escape from Legree. Talking with Madame de Thoux, they discover that she is George Harris' sister.

BRIEF PLOT SYNOPSIS

The novel opens on the Arthur Shelby plantation in Kentucky, a few years before the Civil War. Seemingly, Shelby's plantation is an efficient, pleasant, and humane plantation, for Mr. Shelby is not a cruel slave owner. However, Mr. Shelby has incurred serious debts, and now he must sell some of his slaves in order to pay his bills. Discussing the matter with Mr. Haley, a villainous Southern slave trader, Haley chooses, first, Uncle Tom, Shelby's favorite and most loyal slave, and then Haley chooses little Harry, a beautiful and talented child about five years old. Shelby is deeply reluctant to sell Uncle Tom, and he dislikes separating Harry from his mother, but because of his enormous debts, he has no other choice.

Eliza, Harry's mother, overhears Mr. Shelby and his wife arguing over the "rightness" of what Shelby must do, and so Eliza decides to do what *she* must do: she gathers little Harry up, slips out into the night, and stops at Uncle Tom's cabin and tries to convince Uncle Tom that he must come with her. Together, she says, they can try and escape to Canada via the "underground railroad," a secret network of good people who help runaway slaves find safety in the North; already, Eliza's husband, George, has fled to Canada. But Eliza fails to convince Tom to come with her and Harry. Tom feels that, above all, he must be loyal to his "Mas'r." Sadly, Eliza leaves, heading toward the Ohio River.

Haley tries to follow Eliza and Harry, but Eliza reaches the river before he can catch her. When she arrives, however, she finds that the river is filled with large, flat ice floes; it looks impossible to cross, but Eliza has no choice except to leap onto one of the slab-like ice floes. She almost topples off, but regains her balance and then, leaping from one ice slab to another, slipping and cutting her feet, she at last reaches the other side and is assisted ashore by a man who has seen her peril.

It seems like an act of God that Eliza is saved, because this particular man, Mr. Symmes, loathes slave traders. Thus, he takes Eliza to the home of Senator Bird and his wife. There, Eliza and Harry are given a good bed and some food, and the senator, even though he has just voted for a bill that forbids whites from aiding fugitive slaves, is so touched by Eliza's plight that he takes her and her son to a Quaker settlement. There, Eliza finds kindness and hope while she stays with a Quaker family, the Hallidays. She also discovers that her husband, George, has also come to this kindly Quaker community for safety, and so the family is reunited.

But Haley is still determined to have little Harry; therefore, he enlists the help of two vicious slave hunters, Loker and Marks, and they almost succeed in capturing Eliza and her family, but again, Eliza is helped by the Quakers, and soon the little family is aboard a ship bound for Canada.

At this point, Haley has no alternative but to return to the Shelby plantation and take Uncle Tom to New Orleans. Tom's departure is felt deeply by the other slaves, but Tom is stoic throughout: he has his Bible, and on the steamboat he takes it out and reads it as well as he can, for he has spent many hours with Mr. Shelby's son, George, trying to learn to read.

During the steamboat trip, Tom is discovered by a little girl about five years old. She has golden hair and is dressed all in white; she looks and acts like an angel. Her name is Eva St. Clare, and she and Tom immediately become fast friends. He carves her little trinkets, she slips food to him and talks with him, and before they reach New Orleans, Uncle Tom has saved Little Eva from drowning, and she has convinced her father that he must buy Uncle Tom for their plantation.

At the St. Clare plantation, life is extremely pleasant. Tom is head coachman for the St. Clares, but he finds that he spends most of his time with Little Eva. He almost worships this child, for all she speaks of is love and goodness. She is like a ray of heavenly light on the St. Clare plantation, and she manages to infuse her love and warmth into everyone; she even touches the heart of a very mischievous and clever little black girl, Topsy. Topsy is about Eva's age, but, unlike Eva, she has no morals, no training, and can't believe that people could possibly love her; she is an imp and a scamp. Yet, Eva's patience and her declarations of love for Topsy finally convince Topsy that she is a person worthy of being loved. This is Eva's special quality; she can make people see their inner worth and the worth of others and convince them to share their goodness with one another. Eva even manages to charm the stern Miss Ophelia, St. Clare's sister, whom he brought from Vermont to manage his mansion, since his wife is continuously ill with one imaginary ailment or another.

Days pass, and Eva grows paler and paler; she senses that she is dying, and so she asks for the slaves to be brought to her bedside. She gives each of them one of her golden curls and prays for them. She even makes her father promise to set Tom free after she has gone to heaven.

After Eva's death, however, St. Clare is desolate; he fully plans to free Tom, but he never does it, legally, and one day while he is in a cafe, he tries to settle a brawl between two drunken men and is fatally wounded.

St. Clare's wife recovers from her hypochondria sufficiently to settle her husband's debts by selling most of the slaves. Tom is put up for auction, and he is purchased by the most infamous villain in American literature: Simon Legree.

Legree lives on a large, squalid plantation; he drinks to excess, and he beats his slaves until they drop. One of his slaves, however, defies him and taunts him that she has otherworldly powers. Legree is terrified of her and drinks even more when she threatens to work her voodoo on him. This slave, Cassy, takes pity on Uncle Tom, and she does her best to help him, but Tom is a fierce pacifist. He will not use force against anyone, and so he suffers terribly from Legree's bestial beatings and brutality. Finally, Cassy can take no more, and she convinces another slave, Emmeline, to hide with her in Legree's attic, and together they "haunt" the drunken Legree.

One day while Legree is drunk, George Shelby arrives; he has traced Uncle Tom to Legree's plantation, and he offers to buy Uncle Tom. Legree laughs wickedly. Tom, he says, is probably dead, and if he isn't dead, then he's probably dying. And, indeed, Tom is very near death when George finds him.

After Tom dies, George sees that he is buried in a peaceful, shady spot, and then he boards a steamboat, bound for Kentucky. On board the ship, he meets Cassy and Emmeline, who have fled Legree's plantation. They, in turn, meet a Madame de Thoux, and they all discover that Madame de Thoux is George Harris' sister, and that Cassy is the mother of Eliza, who was snatched away from Cassy and sold years ago.

Shelby leaves the steamboat in Kentucky and returns to his plantation and frees his slaves. The rest onboard ship travel on to Canada where they are all joyfully reunited. George Harris and his family eventually travel to Liberia, along with Cassy; Topsy returns to Vermont with Miss Ophelia, and Stowe ends the novel with a long chapter about the cruel and unchristian institution of slavery.

SUMMARIES AND COMMENTARIES

PREFACE

There are two key points in Stowe's Preface: first, she makes it very clear that her purpose for writing this novel is to enlighten the public about the true worth of "a race hitherto ignored by the associations of polite and refined society." Stowe is referring, of course, to the black race, which in her day was believed to be inferior to the so-called "polite and refined" white society. Stowe intends to write an exposé of how the blacks have been unjustly and unfairly treated by the whites.

Second, she states that this novel is *not* a novel. Stowe calls the volume a collection of "sketches." That is, her book is not meant to be read for light entertainment, as were many novels of that day. Her sketches were meant to be read for *enlightenment,* hoping to correct a social injustice that had existed for much too long.

For the purposes of these Notes, however, we shall refer to *Uncle Tom's Cabin* as a novel because it is commonly referred to as a novel, and second, because it would be awkward to continually refer to it as a "collection of sketches"; such a lengthy phrase would disconcert the reader from Stowe's message – for that is what the book contains foremost: a message, a message of mistreatment.

Stowe believes that her novel is being written at exactly the right time in history, when poetry and art and "every influence of literature" are beginning to recognize and hear "the great master chord of Christianity" – that is, in her own words, "good will to man." And by *man*, Stowe means *all* people – white *and* black. She is writing this book, hoping that it will contain and spread "the great principle of Christian brotherhood." This point is particularly important to remember because many people today have the notion that Stowe wrote this book as somewhat of a potboiler, with a highly emotional theme, and that it was so accidentally explosive – indeed so much more so than she ever expected – that it caused the Civil War. Nothing could be further from the truth. Stowe's motivation was based on Christian indignation; she hoped to correct a terrible wrong and to alert and enlighten the reading public as to the tragic distresses of the "lowly, the oppressed, and the forgotten" black people.

Stowe is a didactic deliverer of a "message," but she is also a romantic; one should not forget this latter fact while reading the novel. She will try and squeeze every bit of melodramatic sympathy and pathos that she can from the reader. For example, note the highly charged language as she describes the black man "bound and bleeding at the foot of civilized and Christianized humanity, imploring compassion in vain." Stowe was sincere, however, even in her melodrama; of this, there can be no doubt – but her prose is more than a little purple, and her melodramatic tone will continue throughout the book. She felt deeply about her topic and her continual "over-writing" is evidence of it.

Stowe is an honest woman. She knows that it is not just the cardboard, plantation-type villains who are to blame for the conditions of slavery. According to Stowe, even the "noblest of Southern minds" have been, in today's jargon, "brainwashed" by tradition, and so she addresses her novel to those minds, as well as to the less educated minds, and also to the readers in the North, who, she realizes, may at first think that she has created caricatures. She insists that what she reveals in her novel is absolutely true; she – and any Southerner with a conscience – has been a witness to the fidelity of her sketches.

This novel is her own meager attempt to right wrongs and expose those wrongs; more important, however, is *God's* role in this condition of oppression. According to Stowe, God is the only one who can truly right the wrongs "in the cause of human liberty." And before she ends her Preface, Stowe quotes a six-line poem dealing with God's delivering the needy and the poor. Then she ends her Preface by evoking the blood that blacks have shed because of their oppressive white masters, blood that is precious "in His sight."

CHAPTER 1

Summary

The novel opens on a chilly February day in Kentucky. Over drinks, two men attempt to strike a bargain concerning the sale of a slave, or slaves, to cancel a debt of Mr. Shelby's, a kindly Southern plantation owner. In order to cancel his debt, Mr. Shelby has decided to sell his most trusted slave, Uncle Tom, and he describes Tom's many good qualities in great detail to Mr. Haley, especially Tom's honesty. But Haley, a slave trader, is not fully satisfied, for he suddenly sees a beautiful little black boy, "Jim Crow," and he immediately wants him; then he sees Jim's beautiful black mother, Eliza, and he wants her too – in addition to Uncle Tom, Shelby's favorite slave.

For the moment, Shelby refuses; he says that after he talks the matter over with his wife, he will give Haley a final decision, between six and seven o'clock that evening. Alone, Mr. Shelby despairs about his vast debts and about the fact that he must part with three of his favorite slaves. He becomes almost furious when he recalls Haley's arrogance.

Upstairs, Eliza (the mother of "Jim Crow," whose real name is Harry) is in a state of despair, for she listened at the door long enough to realize that Mr. Shelby was discussing the sale of her son. Finally, however, Mrs. Shelby is able to calm the young mother. She feels sure that Mr. Shelby would *never* deal with a "Southern" slave trader, much less sell Eliza's son.

Commentary

Here, Stowe focuses on the so-called Southern gentleman, and she makes it very clear that Haley, the slave trader, is *no* gentleman. His inner evil is reflected in his gaudy clothes and his multitude of rings. In contrast is Mr. Shelby, seemingly a gentleman – but one of those Southern men with the "noblest of minds and hearts" (of whom Stowe spoke of in the Preface), but nonetheless a man who owns slaves simply because that is the way plantations are run. Shelby knows no other way of managing a plantation, even in this state of Kentucky, which has, Stowe says, "perhaps the mildest form of the system of slavery." But although Mr. Shelby has a good heart and is generous to his slaves, he feels nevertheless superior to them. For instance, he calls Eliza's son, Harry, by the demeaning nickname of "Jim Crow," and he has him perform a mime and dance for Haley in much the same way that he might bring out a performing monkey. We also know that despite the fact that Shelby does not want to deal with such an unscrupulous "Southern" slave trader as Haley that Shelby *does* buy and sell slaves himself; in short, he does *not* consider black people truly human. Nor does his wife. Mrs. Shelby loves Eliza and Harry very much – but only to a point. These two blacks are pleasant and good people, but their value lies in their usefulness.

On the other hand, we have Haley, a true villain, and Stowe uses all of her satiric tools to fashion this man into the epitome of a villain. First of all, we learn that Haley considers himself a "humanitarian" slave trader. If a family is to be sold in separate units, he makes sure that the wife is *not* present, and he suggests to the seller that the slave woman should receive "some earrings, or a new gown, or some such truck" so that she will not grieve for her husband and children or become insanely angry.

Unashamedly, Haley tells Shelby that Shelby "spiles" his slaves: "These critters ain't like white folks." Haley has sold slaves for a long time and considers himself an expert in doing "the humane thing" when he has to do "onpleasant parts like selling young'uns." He does his best to convince Shelby to sell Jim Crow, emphasizing again, " 'Tan't, you know, as if it was white folks, that's brought up in the way of 'spectin' to keep their children and wives."

This is strong racial prejudice, and Stowe leaves off her narrative here in order to point out that even in Kentucky, where one might witness "the good-humored indulgence of some masters and mistresses," one should not be deceived. A law, she says, exists that declares that blacks are "*things* belonging to a master," and, furthermore, despite the "oft-fabled poetic legend of a patriarchal institution," it is "impossible to make anything beautiful or desirable in the best-regulated administration of slavery." Her didacticism is sharp and to the point. No slave trader nor slave owner, not even the kindly Mr. Shelby and his gentle wife, escapes Stowe's wrath. Both Shelby and Haley consider themselves to be, in different degrees, men of compassion. To Stowe, however, nothing could be further from the truth.

CHAPTERS 2 & 3

Summary

Eliza, Mrs. Shelby's maid, is an unusually beautiful and gracious quadroon (one-fourth black – that is, she had a black mulatto mother and a white father) who is married to George Harris, a handsome and clever mulatto (one-half black; black mother, white father) who works on a neighboring plantation. George is so clever, in fact, that he has invented a machine for cleaning hemp. His master, however, was so outraged when he discovered this fact – "let a nigger alone . . . and they'll invent labor-saving machines" – that he put George to doing "the meanest drudgery of the farm."

We learn that it was while George was working in the factory that he fell in love with Eliza. The couple were married in the Shelbys' parlor, and Mrs. Shelby herself arranged orange blossoms in Eliza's hair. Tragedy soon followed, though, for Eliza and George lost two infant children, and Eliza was so distraught that it was not until Harry was born that she regained her tranquility and poise. George's fate was not so lucky. He continued to live "under the iron sway of his legal owner," who absolutely refused to let George return to the factory.

One afternoon, George walks over to tell Eliza that he has decided to try and escape to Canada. His master has worked him too hard for too long, has drowned his dog, and has now ordered George to marry Mina, a black slave on the master's plantation. George can take no more. He refuses to recognize his master any longer as a superior: "I'm a man as much as he is. . . . I know more about business than he does; I'm a better manager than he is; I can read better than he can . . . and what right has he to make a dray-horse of me?"

Before he leaves, George tells Eliza that she is lucky; she has been "indulged." But he warns her that because young Harry is male, his fate will not be happy. Someday, fate will strike Harry and when that happens, the consequences will pierce through Eliza's soul. With terrible foreboding, Eliza remembers the sinister slave trader in Mr. Shelby's dining-parlor.

Commentary

In these two chapters, Stowe is concerned that we recognize the rightness of George's anger, although it is dangerously intense anger. George is being punished for two reasons only – because he is black and because he is smarter than his master, and both men know it. Additionally ,George dares to ask *the* taboo question: "Who made him my master?" That is, he questions the entire concept of slavery, and for a black man to do that was both revolutionary and, to most whites, blasphemy. Using George as her mouthpiece, then, Stowe is able to shock her readers early in the novel to the terrible and unjust conditions of master-and-slave relationships, a relationship that allowed the slave absolutely no individual, human rights.

In contrast to George's fierce anger is Eliza's attempted calm and her very real fears. She has been brought up a Christian, and she has been taught that she "must obey [her] master and mistress, or [she won't] be a Christian." This dimension of Christianity is one that Stowe also wants her readers to question, for Stowe cannot reconcile the tenets of Christianity and the institution of slavery. To Stowe, one cannot be a true Christian and also be a slave owner. In addition, she wants to show us how Eliza has been "brainwashed" by Christians into accepting – without question – her status as a non-person on the Shelby estate.

Before George leaves Eliza, their parting words concern God – whose prayers God hears and whose prayers He doesn't hear. Then there are "sobs and bitter weeping," two things that Haley has said were *impossible* for black people because the "critters ain't like white folks."

When *Uncle Tom's Cabin* was first published, in 1851, Stowe's portrait of Haley was not inaccurate at all; most Southerners believed as Haley does – and also many Northerners. But this novel revealed to Americans that blacks *were* capable of human emotions and had human worth, and its "sketches" were extremely bold and graphic. In fact, in ten years, a war would be fought that would split Americans into two camps – those who believed in maintaining slavery and those who favored abolishing it forever.

CHAPTERS 4-6

Summary

Uncle Tom's cabin is a small log building not far from the Big House. Tom keeps a neat garden; he is a good gardener and is a great lover of flowers. His small cabin is almost covered with climbing roses and masses of tall, blossoming flowers of all varieties. Inside the cabin, Tom's wife, Chloe, is preparing supper. She wears a starched, checked turban and is busy cooking; she has a reputation for being the best cook in the neighborhood. In one corner of the cabin, Tom and Chloe's two young children are teaching the new baby to walk.

At the dining room table, young thirteen-year-old George Shelby, the master's son, is teaching Uncle Tom how to write. The lessons are interrupted, however, when Chloe announces that she has tall piles of hot cakes for them. Afterward, Uncle Tom capers and dances with Polly, the new baby, and then the merriment is ended because the cabin must be tidied up for a religious meeting.

George Shelby is cajoled into staying and reading from the Bible, and before long the cabin is filled with Tom and Chloe's friends. Before the service, there is much gossiping concerning the white master's doings, and then the service begins. It is a highly emotional religious service; there is a lot of handclapping and crying and laughing, and it is in this scene that we most clearly see Uncle Tom's patriarchal role among the slaves on Shelby's plantation. Tom's prayer hypnotizes them, as it were; his voice is sonorous, earnest, and touching in its simplicity.

Meanwhile, back in the Big House, Mr. Shelby is closing a business deal with Mr. Haley, the slave trader. Money and bills are exchanged, and Mr. Haley becomes the new owner of Uncle Tom and little Harry ("Jim Crow"). Before Haley leaves, however, Mr. Shelby makes him promise not to sell Uncle Tom without knowing for a certainty that Tom will have a gentle and understanding new master. Haley promises, but Shelby is not fully reassured, and, afterward, he retires in solitude with a cigar.

Later, when Mr. Shelby is preparing for bed, his wife asks him what dealings he has just completed with Haley – "that negro-trader," she calls him. Shelby is forced to confess that because of huge debts, he has had to sell Tom and little Harry. Mrs. Shelby is furious with her husband; again and again, he has promised Tom his freedom, she says. Shelby weakly replies that at least he didn't sell Eliza – and he *could have*; he was offered a good sum for her. Mrs. Shelby is totally distraught. Seemingly, there is nothing to be done; Haley has a mortgage to the Shelby plantation, and the sale of Tom and Harry will clear the balance. Shelby pleads with his wife to "see the necessity of the thing"; they have narrowly escaped losing their plantation. Haley will take possession of the slaves in the morning. Shelby advises his wife to take Eliza for a drive so that she won't see Harry carried away.

However, unknown to the quarreling Shelbys, Eliza has been listening in a large closet in an outer passage. Instinctively, she knows what she must do. Hurriedly, she writes a note to Mrs. Shelby saying that she must try and save Harry, then she dresses the little boy and glides out into the night. She stops momentarily at Uncle Tom's cabin and reveals what has happened: Harry and Uncle Tom have *both* been sold to Haley. Aunt Chloe pleads with Tom to go with Eliza, but Tom refuses; he resigns himself to fate. He can't "break trust" with "the master." He feels that somehow "Mas'r ain't to blame." Then he breaks into heavy, hoarse sobs.

Next morning, Mrs. Shelby learns of Eliza's escape. "The Lord be thanked," she sighs. Shelby is angry, and Haley is even angrier. He insults both Shelby and his wife and demands to have some horses to chase the escaping mother and son. But the blacks on Shelby's plantation have a "curiously difficult" time catching the horses: ". . . the horses won't be cotched all in a minit." Mrs. Shelby understands the blacks' strategy and says all that she dares to: "Be careful of the horses; *don't* ride them too fast," she says, hoping to give Eliza as much time as possible to escape. Sam understands her and cleverly causes Haley's horse to bolt and throw him. Several hours later, the horse is caught after it has bounded down a lane, and Sam is able to convince Haley that the horse now needs "rubben down." Haley has no choice but to agree to wait. The blacks are jubilant; they have outwitted the wicked slave trader.

Commentary

This section begins with Stowe's focus on the hero of her novel, Uncle Tom; she also focuses on Uncle Tom's wife, Aunt Chloe. Unintentionally, in her portrait of these two black characters, Stowe created stereotypes that remain largely unchanged today; thus, it is wise to remind oneself that Stowe's primary purpose in writing this novel was "to awaken sympathy and feeling for the African race," and in order to do this, she had to use *all the sentimentality* that was at her disposal. As a result, she oftentimes "humanized" the Negro to excess. She took enormous care to create fictional blacks who were graphically and over emotionally flesh-and-blood, in contrast to the off-handed way that Mr. Haley described them – as being little more than animals.

In order to awaken her readers' Christian conscience, Stowe shows us, first of all, Uncle Tom's log cabin; the logs, however, can scarcely be seen beneath its picturesque blanket of blossoming summer roses and begonias. Happiness itself seems to exude from Uncle Tom's cabin, and, within, Uncle Tom's wife, Aunt Chloe, is beaming with "satisfaction and contentment."

Incidentally, this was new fictional territory for Stowe's readers. Her readers were actually *inside* a slave cabin. And yet there seems to be no cultural shock; Stowe eases us into the cabin. Aunt Chloe's kitchen is a bustle of happiness. It is a slave cabin, but it is homey. It is *not* a squalid hovel. Stowe uses melodramatics, it is true, but her plan is to achieve the utmost sympathy for these human beings. She is not about to show us a heartrending, tragic picture of "poor slaves" immediately. That will come later, and it will be in fierce contrast to the boundless family happiness which we see here. For the present, Stowe wants to show us an abundance of family love and joy so that we can use it to measure the grief and loss that we feel after Uncle Tom is sold to the evil Simon Legree.

In Uncle Tom's cabin, we survey today's stereotypes, stereotypes that have persisted in white minds (and, frequently, in black imaginations) ever since this novel was first published. Aunt Chloe is an Aunt Jemima-type of woman: she wears a starched, checked turban, and she is the best cook in the neighborhood. This is a positive touch. Chloe takes pride in her cooking, yet she is humble enough to cook with "grave consideration," and she refers to her food as being "only something good." Thus, Stowe laces her portrait with humor, commenting that because of Aunt Chloe's culinary expertise, every "chicken and turkey and duck became faint at heart at Aunt Chloe's approach." This overwriting seems excessive today, but when Stowe wrote this novel, she wanted to portray Chloe as humanly as possible. Accordingly, we enjoy meeting Aunt Chloe; she is a good, *human woman*–jolly, immaculate, somewhat overweight, shuffling around, a bit of a fussbudget, and feeling more than a little superior to Uncle Tom, her husband, whom she lovingly refers to as her "ole man."

In contrast, Uncle Tom does not possess the teasing mirth of his busy, bustling wife. He is a large man with a broad chest, and he has "truly African features." His expression is grave and full of good sense, tempered with kindliness and benevolence. Clearly, this is *not* the physical stereotype that blacks and whites have today when they label someone, derogatorily, as an "Uncle Tom." Stowe's Uncle Tom is not the grinning, hat-in-hand, head-bobbing, "Yes, Mas'r"-type of caricature who comes to mind when we hear the term today. Stowe's Uncle Tom is more like "Uncle Ben," kindly and solid as a rock; he is determinedly trying to learn to write, while Aunt Chloe is enjoying entertaining the master's son, young George Shelby, about the "fierce argument" that she and George's mother almost had over whose pie recipe was going to be used for the pie that would be served to General Knox. With mock sassiness, Aunt Chloe says, "I can't do nothin' with 'ladies' in the kitchen." She then recalls, with genuine pride, that because she demanded that *her* recipe be used for the general, he "passed his plate three times for more pie."

Stowe means for us to laugh with Chloe; Chloe isn't an educated woman, but she has a rich, spirited sense of humor, and she also has a pride in herself that is justified. So far, she shows far more integrity than any of Stowe's *white* characters.

Surprisingly, Uncle Tom's role here is relatively minor. He plays with his and Chloe's children before the gospel meeting, and Stowe tells us that he is "a sort of patriarch in religious matters"; we see evidence of this later. It is particularly in his prayers that Tom excels: "nothing could exceed the touching simplicity, the child-like earnestness, of his prayers."

During the gospel meeting in Uncle Tom's cabin, the quality of the blacks' Christianity which Stowe emphasizes most is their passion. The prayer meeting is one of great energy and impromptu singing and jubilation. Two of the key words that are repeated over and over in the hymns are "die" and "glory." The meaning is clear. This life of slavery is one of woe, often ending in early and painful death, but beyond the grave, there is *glory.* Heaven is a reward, and it is a literal heaven that the meeting evokes in order to sustain the slaves during their long days of hard labor. Heaven is a reward; "*glory* is a mighty thing."

The close brotherhood of this emotional gospel scene is in stark contrast to the cold slave-selling scene which Stowe juxtaposes to it: Shelby's selling Tom and Harry to Haley is conducted swiftly. At its core is Haley's vile, ironic statement: "If there's anything that I thank the Lord for, it is that I'm never noways cruel." We are absolutely convinced that nothing could be further from the truth, and Haley's use of the word "Lord" underscores his depraved hypocrisy.

The scene in which Mr. Shelby confesses to his wife that he has sold Tom and Harry is awkward for Shelby. He knows that what he did compromised his promises to Tom, but, within his code as a Southern gentleman (with debts), he *had* to sell the two blacks. To Mr. Shelby, Tom was "property"–loved and valued property, it is true, but ultimately property–and Mr. Shelby had to sell Tom and little Harry in order to save his plantation. He thinks that his hysterical wife is over-reacting when she collapses into sobbing and indignation; he feels that he is *not* "a monster." Trying to defend what he has done, he says, "Everyone sells slaves."

Stowe's portrait of Mrs. Shelby is ambivalent. She is truly grieved about Tom and Harry's fate, but she sees her husband's act as undercutting her own lifetime of good "Christian" deeds. She has "mothered" these "poor, simple creatures," and her husband has now sold them off with as little concern as he would have if he were selling a couple of highly prized farm animals. Mrs. Shelby has genuine, sympathetic feelings for the slaves, but her feelings also contain concern for herself. She has tried to teach these slaves to be Christians and to have a "sense of family," like "white folks" have. But now that Tom and Harry have been sold, she's afraid that the slaves will look on her as a fraud (". . . how can I ever hold up my head again among them?"). It is to her credit, however, that she does finally lash out against the entire concept of slavery: "God's curse on slavery! . . . a curse to the master and a curse to the slave." Here, we hear Stowe's voice–loud and clear: "It is a sin to hold a slave."

Then Mrs. Shelby reveals a naked truth about herself: in her heart, she has *always* known that slavery was wrong, but she thought that she could "gild it over . . . by kindness and care." This is a painful revelation. Ideally, we would like to think that Mrs. Shelby is a "heroine," and she is – of a sort. That is, her ideals are very anti-slavery, but she has hoped that by doing "Christian good deeds and Christian half-measures" in order to "help" the blacks, she could live with her conscience. So far, she has been able to do so – but not now. Clearly, Stowe is using Mrs. Shelby as an example of flawed, Christian "do-good" morality: it isn't enough, Stowe is saying, to be "kind and caring" to one's slaves. Ultimately, she is saying, the entire system of slavery must be done away with.

Privately, Mrs. Shelby would agree, but she is still the wife of a Southern plantation owner, and she has always had to compromise her deep feelings about the abominations inherent in the system of slavery; thus, she has helped perpetuate slavery. She realizes this, and thus we applaud her when she becomes so angry that she finally screams at her husband: "I never thought slavery was right – *never* felt willing to own slaves." Here is one of the many tragedies resulting from slavery: if a white man had a plantation in the South, he was *expected* to own black slaves to farm the plantation; if a woman were married to a plantation owner, she was expected to be silent about how the plantation was managed (regardless of how she personally felt about slavery). Stowe sees this dimension of slavery's tragedy affecting the white population, and she firmly states that no amount of white, "Christian" good deeds can erase or ease the deep pain that black people suffer day after day.

Mr. Shelby is able, to a point, to understand his wife's compassion for their slaves, but he is ultimately blind to the basic inhumanity of slavery itself. He feels that his wife should understand, finally, the "*necessity* of the thing" – meaning, slavery.

Eliza's night flight is reckless, but there is no time for rational weighing of matters. Her beloved Harry's fate is at stake, and here Stowe lingers purposely over the sleeping young boy – the victim of this slave sale. She tugs at our emotions, hoping that we will erupt with fierce indignation that this system of slavery can so cavalierly buy and sell such an innocent "slumbering boy" from his mother. Stowe notes Harry's "long curls falling . . . around his face, his rosy mouth half-open . . . a smile spread like a sunbeam over his whole face." This severing of a child from his mother is one of the worst evils of slavery; a family is being wrenched apart with no more forethought on behalf of the "master" than he would give to selling one of the dray animals. Stowe is outraged, and she wants us to be likewise. Eliza's tears are not really tears, she says; they are "blood." Eliza is "bleeding away in silence." Stowe's prose is soaked in emotion, but she wants to shock us – and she does. She wants to show us, as graphically and as metaphorically as possible, that this is a perversion of the human condition, and she does so by focusing on a mother's love for her child – a love for which a mother will risk everything. This is non-fail dramatic technique; it has affected readers since the very beginnings of literature.

Eliza's single pause before she begins her flight into the frosty, starlit night is to warn Uncle Tom that he too has been sold. Aunt Chloe's common sense echoes Eliza's: Tom ought to try and escape. Tom, however, cannot. His code of honor will not allow him to do so. Thus, we measure his code of right and wrong against that of Mr. Shelby's. Tom's code is idealistic, whereas Mr. Shelby's is realistic. Tom fully realizes the fierce cruelty that awaits him, for he breaks into heavy sobs, but he simply *cannot* run. He is a man, a man with pride, and he is an honorable man; therefore, unlike Mr. Shelby, he cannot break his oath of loyalty.

Eliza leaves, having no real hope that she will find freedom in Canada. She will try, but the "kingdom of heaven" seems more realistic as her final haven of safety than does far-off Canada.

The short chapter that focuses on the Shelbys' discovering that Eliza and Harry have fled is largely comic. Mrs. Shelby is joyous (although she is careful to conceal her feelings), and Haley is furious because throughout the chapter, the blacks manage to foil his every attempt to saddle up and go after Eliza. They frustrate Haley by self-caricaturing themselves as the slow-moving, slow-witted black half-humans that Haley believes them to be. Like a frustrated villain in a "mellerdrammer," Haley stamps and curses and swears. He doesn't know what has happened, but *we* do: the blacks have bested him.

CHAPTERS 7-9

Summary

After leaving Uncle Tom's cabin, Eliza lovingly clutches the still-sleeping Harry to her breast and runs, aimlessly, simply running away, heading North, and praying all the while. Seemingly supernatural strength pours into her, making her "flesh and nerves impregnable." When daylight dawns, she is many miles from the Shelby plantation. By coincidence, she and Mrs. Shelby have been in this area before, and she realizes that if she wants to escape farther North, she will have to cross the Ohio River. Trying to avoid the suspicion that she is a runaway slave, she slows her pace, reluctantly, and puts Harry down and urges him to walk beside her. Harry tries to convince his mother to eat, but she cannot. Fear rises and fills her throat despite the fact that, in theory, both she and Harry are "white enough" not to be identified immediately as "fugitives."

An hour before sunset, she reaches the Ohio River. To her, it seems like the living embodiment of the River Jordan, and the other side, "the Canaan of liberty." The river is swollen with spring turbulence, and "great cakes of floating ice [are] swinging heavily to and fro in the turbid waters."

Discovering that there is no ferry or boat to carry her across, Eliza realizes that she has no alternative: she must cross the ice, but first, she lets Harry rest in the bedroom of a kindly housewife, and it is at this point in the story – when Eliza is lost in confusion and agony – that Stowe leaves her, in a cliffhanger situation, and returns the narrative to Eliza's pursuer, Mr. Haley.

Back at the Shelbys,' Mrs. Shelby and Aunt Chloe are preparing dinner for Haley with an "unusually leisurely and circumstantial manner." The house-help seem to know that on this particular occasion the mistress will welcome "any number of constant accidents which will retard the course of things." And, of course, the slaves are happy to take out their resentment on Mr. Haley. They also deeply resent what Haley has done; one of them remarks, "*His* master'll be sending for him," meaning, of course, God. And whatever punishment is meted out in heaven, Mr. Shelby "will deserve it," adds the usually good-natured Aunt Chloe. Overhearing this bitterness, Uncle Tom pleads with the Negroes to do "as the good book says" – that is, pray for the white folks, for their souls are in "an awful state." What worries Tom most is what will happen to the plantation when he is gone; Tom has been "a-keeping up all the ends," and Shelby doesn't know how, nor do any of the other slaves. Sincerely concerned, Tom is worried that "things will be kinder going to rack." This sentiment is almost saint-like, but Stowe intends it to be.

Haley threatens Tom with what will happen if he should try and escape, and Tom reminds Shelby that Tom held his master in his arms when Shelby was less than a year old: ". . . have I ever broke word with you?" he asks him. Shelby, tears in his eyes, is overcome. With all the "female artifice," she can contrive, Mrs. Shelby tries to detain Haley, as does the Negro Sam, explaining that "der's two roads" to "the underground" (the escape route for the blacks). There are, of course, no two roads, but Haley doesn't know this. Sam also suggests that women are unpredictable: "No telling which road Lizy took."

Finally, Haley plunges his horse forward, down a little-used road, followed by Andy and Sam, until they reach a dead end. Muttering under his breath, Haley backtracks. They arrive finally at a tavern, and Haley spies Eliza trying to flee down the bank of the Ohio River. He follows her as fast as he can, but with "one wild cry and flying leap," Eliza vaults onto an ice raft, far beyond her pursuer. This is an act of despair. Haley, Sam, and Andy all realize it. The ice floe pitches, and Eliza, with wild cries, leaps from one cake of floating ice to another–stumbling, leaping, slipping, clutching Harry to her breast, her feet bloodied, until at last she reaches the Ohio side, and as if Providence placed him there, a stranger reaches out his hand to save Eliza. It is an old friend of the Shelbys, a Mr. Symmes, a man who admires grit. To him, Eliza has "arnt" (earned) her liberty, and so he tells her where to go for safety and shelter.

The baying of the dogs especially angers Symmes: "I don't see no kind of 'casion for me to be hunter and catcher of other folks." Stowe emphasizes that these words are not spoken by a well-bred, schooled "Christian"; Symmes is a "poor and heathenish" man to whom goodness comes naturally.

On the far bank, Haley is thunderstruck by Eliza's good luck: "The gal's got seven devils in her." Sam and Andy can't restrain their happiness. They laugh till tears roll down their cheeks. In frustration, Haley lashes out at them with his riding whip, but they are too quick for him, and "with much gravity," they apologize, then say that they should be leaving so that "the Missis won't be anxious."

Eliza, for the moment, is safe, for Stowe tells us that the "swollen current of the river and the floundering masses of ice present a hopeless barrier between Eliza and her pursuer.

Back at the tavern, though, Haley convinces two slave catchers, Loker and his sidekick, Marks, to track down Eliza and Harry with their fierce dogs, sell Eliza, and return Harry to Haley. To Sam and Andy, who return to the Shelbys, Providence has saved Eliza, and thus they and the other slaves celebrate her escape.

Now, we enter the home of a Senator Bird from Ohio. His wife is fussing over his late arrival home, and she asks what the Senate has been doing. She is aghast to learn that a law has been passed forbidding people to help runaway slaves from Kentucky. She can't believe the severity of so unchristian a law. She vows to break the law, even though her husband says that he voted for its passage. She refers to the Bible, which orders Christians to "feed the hungry, clothe the naked, and comfort the desolate." Her loyalty is to the Bible. Her husband says that his loyalty is to the State.

At that moment, Eliza and Harry appear in the doorway, and Eliza faints. The Birds' black servants immediately surround them and give Eliza and Harry what comfort they can. Within moments, both Eliza and Harry are tucked away, sleeping heavily by the fire, Eliza's arms encircling Harry "with an unrelaxing clasp." When she awakens, Eliza tells the stunned Birds about her escape across the ice floes from Kentucky in order to save Harry.

Finally, Senator Bird softens and agrees to hide Eliza and Harry at an old client's house, a Mr. Van Trompe; in addition, they will provide Harry with clothes that belonged to one of their little boys who died, and they will give some dresses to Eliza. Van Trompe agrees to hide Eliza and Harry, and the senator gives Van Trompe ten dollars to give to Eliza. Van Trompe says that he'll be ready for any slave pursuers and will meet them with his seven six-foot sons.

Commentary

A mother's fierce love for her child is Stowe's initial focus in these chapters; because of her protective love for little Harry, Eliza will dash out into the Unknown, ready to face whomever and whatever – just as long as she can. We admire not only this kind of deep love, but also the courage of this woman. Mrs. Shelby, in contrast to Eliza, never has had the courage to denounce slavery – until now. She has tried to hide behind "Christian" good deeds. She has even convinced Eliza that to be a good Christian, she must be a "good" slave. But Eliza can no longer be a good "Christian" doormat for the Shelbys. She must save her son. The Shelbys have been good friends to Eliza, Stowe tells us, but stronger than friendship is her maternal love for Harry. And so she must leave her "friends," and run, trembling, out into the dark, cold night. And now Stowe emphasizes that Eliza's *only* friend at this point is God: ". . . from her pale lips burst forth, in frequent ejaculations, the prayer to a Friend above–'Lord, help! Lord, save me!'"

In fact, Stowe wants so fervently to arouse our sympathy for Eliza's plight, that she speaks outright to her readers, asking them how fast they would run if *their* child were going to be "torn" from them, especially if the child's head were on their shoulder, "the small, soft arms trustingly holding on to your neck." As we noted, this is melodramatic and didactic, but it is certainly effective in making us cheer Eliza on and in arousing our hatred for Haley and for the concept of slavery.

Then, just before Eliza will make her dramatic crossing of the ice floe-filled Ohio River, Stowe has Eliza pause, making us wait in suspense, while she returns us to the Shelbys. We are not ready to hear more about the Shelbys. They have betrayed Eliza. And yet Stowe makes us rejoice in what we discover when we return to the plantation. Mrs. Shelby and Aunt Chloe have joined forces to thwart Mr. Haley. She even characterizes Mrs. Shelby as a kind of "trader" herself in order to embroider the scene with comedy. She tells us that Mrs. Shelby promised Haley to have dinner put hurriedly on the table, and although she could have done so, "it required more than one to make a bargain." Thus, dinner was prepared "in an unusually leisurely and circumstantial manner"–all in an attempt to keep Haley from taking his "purchases." Once again, Stowe shows that the blacks justify, rightly, what they are doing: Aunt Chloe says that Revelations speaks of souls "a-calling on the Lord for vengeance."

Tom, however, also quotes from the Bible: "Pray for them that spitefully use you," he says. Clearly, Stowe is again emphasizing his goodness and his belief in the tenets of Jesus; that is, Tom is forgiving and compassionate, whatever the circumstances. He is a Christian. To him, "the Lord's grace is stronger" than vengeance. Haley, he says, will have to answer to God for his wickedness. Tom says that he would rather be sold "ten thousand times over" than "have all that ar poor crittur's got to answer for." He understands that "Mas'r couldn't help hisself." This is Christian intuition and exceptional understanding on the part of a man who has just been "sold"–for money–to another man, a stranger, who will, in turn, sell Tom to whomever he wishes.

Then Stowe returns to her mood of comedy as Sam and Andy frustrate Haley in a prelude to the well-known scene of Eliza crossing the ice-packed Ohio River. Surprisingly, the scene is very short. Stowe does not dwell on it until it is lifeless. She narrates it as swiftly as Eliza herself swiftly leaps from one ice floe to another. She emphasizes that Eliza is successful because she is "nerved with strength such as God gives only to the desperate." Haley cannot believe what he sees; he says that Eliza has seven devils in her. We smile at the irony. Stowe has just told us that Eliza was aided by God.

In order to sustain her suspense, Stowe tells us that Eliza is not safe. Haley hires two professional slave hunters. Eliza will still need God's help in order to escape from the evil slave hunters. And God does assist Eliza, for she is taken to the home of the loudly Christian Mrs. Bird; she will *not* abide by the new law which her husband has just voted for, one that forbids Ohioans from aiding runaway slaves from Kentucky. According to her, the Bible commands her to aid these very people. Her husband disagrees–in theory. And then he sees Eliza and her baby on their doorstep and Eliza faints, and his heart goes out to this graphic picture of despair. A mother's anguish touches him, just as Stowe has touched *our* sympathy for Eliza. In fact, it is *Senator* Bird who suggests that some of his wife's dresses might be let down and given to Eliza; and he even suggests that his wife give Eliza an "old bombazine cloak." And it is the senator who suggests that to guarantee Eliza and Harry's safety that he take them to an old client's house, a Mr. Van Trompe, who lived in Kentucky, but who set all his slaves free and moved to Ohio. And it is the senator who asks his wife if they can't give away some clothes that once belonged to their little boy Henry, who died. The senator, says Stowe, is a "political sinner," but that he "was in a fair way to expiate it by his night's penance." What the senator has done has been Christian. For the first time, he has seen the "real presence of distress," and his heart has been filled with true Christian goodness.

CHAPTERS 10-16

Summary

Uncle Tom is not as lucky as Eliza. Haley arrives for him, and

Haley is in a fierce and terrible mood. The blacks all gather round, grieving, as Haley fastens a heavy pair of shackles around Uncle Tom's ankles. "Give my love to Mas'r George," Uncle Tom says, as Haley whips the horses and whirls away.

While Haley makes a quick stop to have some handcuffs adjusted for Tom, the blacksmith laments about Tom's fate on the sugar plantation down South: "They dies thar tol'able fast." Haley's reply is: "They dies so as to keep market up pretty brisk," and off they go after a short, sobbing scene with young George Shelby who, by accident, happens to meet them on the road. As they part, George vows to try and get Tom back.

Meanwhile, George Harris, Eliza's husband, is making his own escape. He is in disguise, in the tavern-inn where he has stopped, and with his regal air and dark Spanish complexion, he fools even Mr. Wilson, his former boss at the factory, where he invented the hemp machine. Later, when George reveals his true identity, Mr. Wilson is very nervous and quotes from the Bible, trying to urge George to return "home." The risk which George is taking is too great, he says. George knows this to be true, but he has two pistols and a bowie knife. He says that he will "fight for [his] liberty with [his] last breath."

On the way to New Orleans, Haley stops and purchases three more slaves, fastening each with a handcuff to a long chain, and a few days later, they all board a boat, bound for Louisiana. A stop is made, and Haley buys two more slaves, Lucy and her child. A stranger, however, finally strikes a bargain and buys the little ten-month-old boy from Haley. Tom watches this "unutterably horrible and cruel" transaction. Stowe says, "His very soul bled." Later, waiting until night, Lucy, the young mother, jumps into the river.

Stowe changes her focus now to Eliza, who is living at the rustic but comfortable Quaker home of an old, white, loving couple, Rachel and Simeon Halliday. As Eliza watches Harry play, we can see that she has changed. Her young heart has grown old and firm. There is a sense of steady resolve that was never there before. By accident, when some of the Hallidays' friends are making small talk, it is revealed that it is possible that George Harris, Eliza's husband, has arrived at this same Quaker settlement. Thus, the family is reunited, and their new white friends genuinely rejoice for them. Stowe says that, for the first time, George felt what the word "home" meant. That night, since the pursuers are still after them, Eliza and George and little Harry set out, fleeing, they hope, toward Canada.

Meanwhile, back on board the ship bound for New Orleans, we discover that the innate goodness of Uncle Tom has even won over the evil that infests Haley, for Haley has now let Tom sleep at night unfettered; furthermore, Tom has won the good will of all on board the ship. We are not truly surprised that when Stowe returns our focus to Tom, we find him in a nook among some cotton bales, studying the Bible, slowly and laboriously re-reading his favorite, marked passages.

Also on board ship is a rich New Orleans gentleman and his daughter, "Eva," short for Evangeline, a child who is the essence of sparkling childhood beauty. Always dressed in white, she seems like an angel of goodness. Even to Tom, she seems almost divine, and she secretly slips Tom and the other slaves candy, nuts, and oranges. In return, Tom gives her little trinkets which he has carved.

One day, when the boat stops at a small landing, Eva slips overboard into the river, and Tom dives in and saves her life. In gratitude, Eva's father, Augustine St. Clare, a kindly, dreamy man, buys Uncle Tom. Then Stowe gives us some background on the St. Clares.

Years ago, St. Clare married one of the most sought-after of all the Southern belles, and he won her, but before long, she became bored and sickly, and she also became afflicted by a variety of "fanciful diseases." She is tended to by Little Eva and by St. Clare's cousin, a Miss Ophelia St. Clare.

St. Clare and Eva arrive at the St. Clare plantation, and Tom is immediately made "head coachman." From the very beginning, Tom and Little Eva are great friends. She decorates him with wreaths of roses around his neck—which makes her mother suddenly fall into another ill spell—the "spectacle" of *her* daughter being so familiar and blithe with a slave! In fact, however, Eva seems not to notice her mother's melodramatic carryings-on. She asks her father to allow Tom to be her special servant, and St. Clare agrees to the suggestion: Tom has orders to let everything else go and attend "Miss Eva" whenever she wants him.

Speaking of slavery one night, Mrs. St. Clare objects to Eva's treating Tom so generously. Slavery, she says, is proscribed by the Bible; her husband disagrees. If cotton prices fell, there would be an entirely *new* interpretation of the Bible, he says. This shocks his wife. Eva states that *she* likes slavery: ". . . it makes so many more round you to love." St. Clare, at this point, praises Tom's prayers, and his wife despairs of her family's sanity.

Commentary

The primary focus in this section is on the first of Uncle Tom's many trials of unjust brutality and Tom's never-ending, forgiving Christian understanding. When Haley comes to take Tom away, Tom is reading the Bible. "I'm in the Lord's hands," he tells Aunt Chloe; he says that he is grateful that it is he who must go with Haley, and not Chloe and the children. And Stowe interrupts her narrative here to explain, as it were, "the nature of the Negro"; for example, she tells her readers that "the instinctive affections of that race are peculiarly strong," and she goes on to add that they are not daring and enterprising, but home-loving and affectionate, and she elaborates on how they fear being sold into slavery from childhood. As pointed out earlier, she felt it to be her mission to give not only a portrait of slavery, but to write, at the same time, a treatise on that subject and on Christianity. She then shows us Tom, being shackled before Haley leaves, and she tells us that "a smothered groan of indignation" arose from the circle of blacks which had gathered. In contrast to them, Tom is silently stoic.

Haley stops at a blacksmith's for handcuffs, and Stowe has the blacksmith comment that on the plantations farther south, "a Kentuck nigger . . . dies tol'able fast." She is guiding our sympathy for Tom, as well as revealing the multitude of horrors accompanying slavery. (Later, she will linger over a scene in which Haley takes a ten-month-old child from its mother, and afterward, in utter despair, the mother leaps to her death in the river.)

When young George Shelby appears, Tom's thoughts are not on his dark future, but on George's bright one. Tom asks George to "'Member yer Creator," and, for the first time, we see Stowe's strong characterization of Tom as a Christ-figure, a portrait that Stowe will continually enlarge on and emphasize.

On board ship, Tom reads his Bible, glancing up to see the fields of slaves, their huts, and the stately plantation mansions. Some tears, Stowe tells us, fall on Tom's Bible. Then she traces his laborious reading, syllable by syllable, as he reads a verse asking for a peaceful heart. She tells us of Tom's unique way of marking passages which "gratified his ear." Here is a man alone, except for his God, whose every word promises everlasting peace, asking only that man forgive his enemies and believe in him. And Tom will fervently continue to try and lead the life that is asked for.

The secondary focus here is on the angelic Little Eva. Stowe goes to great lengths to detail Eva's goodness and the natural affection that exists between the middle-aged black man and the tiny white girl. Our feelings for Tom are high when he is bought by the kindly St. Clare. For a moment it seems as though Tom *will* have a bright future with good people; of course, we know that he has yet to encounter Simon Legree, but because of Tom's Christian goodness, we are grateful that for the present he has Little Eva for a companion and the kindness of St. Clare to shelter him.

CHAPTERS 17-19

Summary

During her family's stay at the Hallidays, Eliza convinces George that he should "try to act worthy of a free man" and that he should also try and *feel* like a Christian. He agrees; in Canada, he assures her, everything will be easier. Word has spread, however, that slave hunters are still trying to track down Eliza, George, and little Harry, and so they decide to leave in the night. But they are not quick enough. They are cornered by Tom Loker and Marks, by two constables, and by a rowdy posse. There is a fight, and George wounds Loker, Marks runs away, and the Hallidays, being Quakers, decide to take Loker with them and give him proper nursing in a clean bed.

Meanwhile, back at the St. Clares, the "Mas'r," Tom complains, is good to everybody–too good in fact. But not good enough to St. Clare himself. St. Clare embarrassedly agrees. At the same time, the womenfolks have their troubles also. Miss Ophelia, with her stern New England ways, finds it difficult to adjust to the way that St. Clare's plantation is run. She finds too much disorder and shiftlessness. There seems, for example, to be too much chaos in the kitchen–but no one is bothered by it except Miss Ophelia. Valiantly, she tries to reform every "department" of the St. Clare house into some kind of systematic pattern, but she fails. Her brother, she realizes finally, is simply too indulgent – especially to the growing friendship between Tom and Little Eva. Thus, St. Clare decides to divert Miss Ophelia's zealous, busybody harping, and so he buys her a little Negro girl about eight or nine years of age; the little girl can be a playmate for Eva, and Miss Ophelia can exhibit some of her ever-quoting missionary zeal on a real live Negro that *she* is responsible for.

Commentary

The first part of this section focuses on George, Eliza's husband; he vows to forget his bitterness of the past and try to learn to be "a good man." Obviously, when Chapter 17 begins, Eliza has been talking to him about what constitutes a good Christian because the first words we hear are George's vow to change his attitude toward life. He admits to Eliza how lucky they are – to be together and have their son. He says that he could "scarcely ask God for any more." He may own nothing – materially – yet he feels rich. Here is evidence that George's relationship with God is changing, as well as his relationship with himself. His self-esteem and sense of self-worth are becoming more positive. Now that the family unit has been restored and George has a chance to be protective and nurturing, he can at last afford the objectivity to realize, in his own words, "what a blessing" it is to *feel* free, even if they aren't yet safe in Canada. For the first time in a long time, George is happy.

Likewise, Tom is happy. Although he is not free, he has all of slavery's emotional shackles removed from him. In fact, he feels uneasy at all of his seeming freedom, especially at the vast amount of trust that St. Clare gifts him with. We are told that if Tom were not a Christian, there would be many times when he would be tempted to be dishonest, but never does he succumb. St. Clare is both careless and extravagant with his money and entrusts dollar bills – without looking at them – to Tom so that Tom can do the marketing, but because Tom has the strength of his Christian faith, he never falls to greed.

Because of his genuine fondness for St. Clare, Tom feels that he can say, frankly, that St. Clare is too generous – especially with his own time. The scene was no doubt shocking in its day – a slave telling his master how to spend his time. But Tom's motives are akin to

Eliza's. Earlier, she chided George for wasting his time in bitterness; now Tom is cautioning St. Clare against drinking and going to the theater and the opera. Tom tells St. Clare that eventually it will mean "the loss of all," and he quotes a Bible passage from memory. Such love touches St. Clare, and he, like George, vows to give up all of this "cursed nonsense."

In contrast to the newfound self-worth of George and St. Clare, Stowe juxtaposes the humorous, exaggerated sense of self-worth of Miss Ophelia, St. Clare's sister. Her missionary zeal descends first of all on Dinah's kitchen, and in a few days, "every department of the house" has been reduced to a systematic pattern. She is appalled by the South's "shiftless confusion." Her Yankee no-nonsense approach to matters parallels her faith's outlook on humanity. It is a cold, stern, unemotional, demanding faith that she has, and because it is so unique in the context of the novel, it seems excessive, unnatural, and, finally, ridiculous. For that reason, St. Clare buys Topsy for her, someone so irrational that Ophelia will have no time to bother the household staff with her squeaky-clean Christian righteousness.

CHAPTERS 20-26

Summary

No one could have been more surprised than the strict, New England-bred Miss Ophelia when St. Clare calls her downstairs one day and introduces her to "a purchase for [her] department"—that is, he is putting Miss Ophelia in charge of educating Topsy, a very black little Negro girl, her eyes glittering like glass beads, mouth open, teeth sparkling, and stray little pigtails sticking out in every direction on her head. Miss Ophelia shudders: "so heathenish." St. Clare then asks Topsy to dance, and she does so—"hands and feet spinning around, doing summersets, then suddenly sitting down with a sanctimonious expression." Miss Ophelia is paralyzed with amazement. St. Clare relishes in her astonishment. "Behave yourself," he teases Topsy, and then leaves. Topsy's eyes twinkle.

The other slaves look askance at this newcomer, and so, very early, it is clear that Topsy is indeed Miss Ophelia's "property" and her responsibility. But soon, when Miss Ophelia gives Topsy a bath, her attitudes soften. Never before has she seen such "great welts and calloused spots."

She crops Topsy's hair closely and dresses her in clean clothing until she looks "more Christian-like than she did." But the veneer is thin indeed. The word "God" means nothing to Topsy. In addition, Topsy doesn't know how old she is; she can't even remember having a mother *or* a father, and she is *sure* that she "never was born." She ponders, then says, "Don't think nobody never made me." She can't sew, she says, but she can "fetch water, wash dishes, and wait on folks."

And so Miss Ophelia begins in earnest to try and rear Topsy according to her own New England Christian teachings, which are continually frustrated by her demand that Topsy "confess." Totally confused, Topsy "fesses" to stealing, but the things which she says she has stolen appear within minutes–Eva's coral necklace is around Eva's neck, and Rosa's ear-bobs are on Rosa's ears. "I couldn't think of nothing else to 'fess," says Topsy. Her absolute innocence and her ignorance of all Christian "rules" awe Miss Ophelia.

Then Stowe contrasts Topsy with Little Eva. Eva is fair, high-bred, and has golden curls; Topsy is black, keen, subtle, and cunning. One, Stowe says, is born "of ages of cultivation, command, and education"; the other, "of oppression, submission, toil, and vice."

Nevertheless, despite all, Topsy touches Miss Ophelia's heart, and Miss Ophelia, in turn, touches Topsy's heart; her "words of kindness are the first" that the child has ever heard in her life. But Miss Ophelia is at a loss as to how she should discipline Topsy, for Topsy *is* mischievous. St. Clare says to beat her if Miss Ophelia must. Topsy, he says, is used to being punished "with a poker, knocked down with a shovel," but, he says, if a human being has to be governed with a lash–"*that* fails." He acknowledges that his slaves "act like spoiled children," but that behavior, to him, is better than "for us both to be brutalized together."

Topsy is like a sprite in St. Clare's house. She is seemingly everywhere–having a talent "for every species of drollery, grimace, and mimicry–for dancing, tumbling, climbing, singing, whistling, imitating." She seems inexhaustible. Eva is fascinated by her–*too* fascinated, Miss Ophelia thinks, but St. Clare is sure that Eva cannot be taught mischief, and we are inclined to agree. The two children are diametrical opposites.

Surprisingly, Topsy quickly learns all the chores of the house: "Mortal hands could not lay a spread smoother, adjust pillows more accurately, sweep and dust and arrange more perfectly than Topsy – when she chose – but she didn't very often choose." Topsy is a rebel, but a charming rebel. Thus, Stowe ends her long introduction to Topsy who, she says, "will figure, from time to time, in her turn, with other performers."

Then Stowe returns us to Kentucky, to the Shelbys. Mrs. Shelby is telling her husband that Chloe has had a letter from Uncle Tom, and that he has been bought by a fine family, but he is anxious to return to his "real home." Shelby still complains of his outstanding debts, and so Mrs. Shelby ceases talking, hoping that her promise to reunite Uncle Tom and Aunt Chloe might be possible soon, but knowing that that hope seems unlikely at present.

Just then, Aunt Chloe appears and convinces Mrs. Shelby to let her go work in a confectioner's store in Louisville. Mrs. Shelby is reluctant to see Chloe go, but she understands: working in Louisville will give Aunt Chloe more money and, most important, she will be nearer, geographically, to Tom. After Chloe has worked two years in the store, Stowe tells us, her "skill in the pastry line was gaining wonderful sums of money," all of which was laid up for Tom's "redemption money."

Tom is ecstatic with George's letter that relates this news; he suggests to Eva that perhaps they should "frame the letter." Clearly, the old black man and the little girl are best friends. Tom buys Eva small, special presents, and together they discuss the Bible and, especially, they discuss heaven. Eva confides to Tom that soon she will be in heaven, and she seeks Tom's assurance that it will be as lovely as the Bible says that it is. It is then that Tom realizes with sudden horror that Eva has indeed grown thinner, that her cheeks and hands are often feverish, and that her cough grows worse every day. Eva's father seemingly refuses to recognize these symptoms; however, privately, he is becoming anxious and growing restless. Mrs. St. Clare takes no notice whatsoever of Eva's growing illness. She worries more about Eva's desire to teach the blacks how to read the Bible. Mrs. St. Clare "always had a headache on hand for any conversation that did not exactly suit her," Stowe remarks.

After a brief visit from St. Clare's brother and his son, Eva's health begins to fail rapidly, then for a brief time, she seems to grow a bit stronger. But, she soon begins talking of dying. She tells Tom that, like Jesus, she would gladly die if her "dying would end all this misery," meaning slavery.

Talking seriously to her father, Eva tells him about her dream of *freedom.* She worries what will happen to the slaves if anything were to happen to St. Clare. She has heard terrible stories about slave owners. She reminds her father that he wants her to have a life free of pain; in contrast, the slaves' lives are nothing but "pain and sorrow, all their lives." She pleads with him to promise that if she should die, that he will free all his slaves, especially Tom. "I will do anything you wish," St. Clare tells his daughter. Then Eva closes her eyes, and St. Clare rocks her in his arms "until she was asleep."

Eva rallies briefly and plays with Topsy, trying to convince the little black girl that she truly and deeply loves her. But Topsy can't believe it: "Nobody love niggers," she says defiantly. Eva asks Topsy to be good – for her sake – for Eva is so very ill and, according to Stowe, "a ray of heavenly love" suddenly touches Topsy, and she weeps and sobs.

Before Eva dies, she asks that all the servants be called to her bedside. She speaks to them of heaven, the new home that awaits her, and she also speaks about Jesus to them. She begs the slaves to all become Christians so that she can see them someday in heaven. Tears and sobs fill the room, then the slaves leave, all carrying with them a lock of one of Eva's golden curls.

Suddenly, Topsy appears; she promises Eva that she "*is* tryin' . . . but, Lord, it's so hard to be good!"

During Eva's last days, Uncle Tom carries her into the orchard so that Eva can smell the blossoms; he sings hymns to her, and at night, he sleeps on the veranda, next to her room. And Tom is there when Eva dies, offering his old black hand to St. Clare, as Eva struggles for her last breaths, whispering that, at last, she has seen a land of "love – joy – peace." Then she closes her eyes, eternally.

Commentary

Topsy is a black Peter Pan. One can't imagine her ever growing up. She is quick and she is restless, never still a moment. In contrast to the corkscrew-curled, Shirley Temple-like Little Eva, Topsy is mahogany-colored, and her hair is braided in short tails, sticking out all over her head. And whereas Little Eva exudes syrupy, rational goodness, Topsy sparkles with unexpected and delightful irrationality. "Never was born!" she says, grinning, "I spect I just grow'd."

It is a credit to Stowe's sense of literature that she allowed herself to create, with humor and love, Topsy – and thus relieve the solemn tone of her crusading message of Christianity. The scenes between Topsy and Miss Ophelia are the stuff of modern "sit-com" comedy. Miss Ophelia is aghast at this black sprite who explodes like a firecracker into song-and-dance acrobatics, then stops, frozen in a pose of mock demureness.

"Heathenish," shudders Ophelia, ". . . a little plague." St. Clare chides his sister's holier-than-thou attitudes. He tells her that he's bought Topsy for *her* to educate, and when Ophelia protests, he says, "That's you Christians all over!" And he goes on to indict her hypocrisy in minute detail.

It is a revelation to see Ophelia gradually soften her tones of prudish racial superiority and become genuinely fond of Topsy. Because of Topsy, Ophelia finally becomes a true Christian, one who recognizes the emotional and physical scars that "the system" (slavery) inflicts on an entire race of human beings.

Stowe balances Topsy's refreshing delightfulness with Little Eva's highly emotional, bathetic death scene, one of the most famous death scenes in American literature. It is a death scene that one feels could have been borrowed from the opera stage.

Little Eva lies dying, her family and the servants all around her. "Has there ever been a child like Eva?" Stowe asks, then tells us, "Yes . . . but their names are always on grave-stones. . . . It is as though heaven had an especial band of angels." Eva tries to talk to them all, tries to tell them how much she loves them – black and white alike – but her confession is interrupted by "groans, sobs, and lamentations." She tries to tell them about heaven, where she is going, "where Jesus is," but she is interrupted again, and she has to gently chide them: "If you love me, you must not interrupt me so."

She tells them that "each one of you can become angels," and that Jesus will help them, "even if you can't read." And then she gives each of them one of her bright, golden curls, as they kneel and kiss "the hem of her garment."

After everyone has gone, Little Eva talks to her father about his faith. She herself loves Christ "most of all," even if she hasn't seen him. That is faith – having no proof of Christ's evidence, yet loving him "most of all."

Afterward, Tom carries Little Eva to the veranda. This scene of

Tom with the dying, frail Little Eva in his arms is the epitomy of this highly sentimental scene. Here is a three-dimensional black man whose heart is aching and torn, full of Christian love for the baby Christ-like Little Eva. Goodness cradling goodness. Eva's last words are words of promise, promises that are the keystones of Stowe's Christian faith: "Love, –joy, –peace!"

CHAPTERS 27-34

Summary

After his beloved Little Eva dies, St. Clare does as she asked: he begins to deeply contemplate setting all of his slaves free. Accordingly, he takes up the Bible and begins reading it. First, he gives Topsy to Miss Ophelia to rear. To Tom, he confesses that "the whole world is as empty as an eggshell."

"I know it, Mas'r," says Tom, and Tom counsels St. Clare to think of heaven, Eva's home. St. Clare pleads with Tom to tell him about Christ. Tom does so, and St. Clare realizes that the old black man sincerely loves him. Tom admits that it is true; he does love St. Clare: "I's willin' to lay down my life, this blessed day, to see Mas'r a Christian." Then Tom gives St. Clare the Bible and prays a long, earnest prayer. Immediately, St. Clare feels closer to his little lost Eva.

Weeks pass, and slowly life settles back to its usual flow on St. Clare's plantation – except that St. Clare is seen reading more and more frequently in Eva's Bible. Then one day, St. Clare tells Tom that he plans to free him – "so have your trunk packed and get ready to set out for Kentuck." But Tom refuses to do so. He has a duty yet before he can leave; he wants to convert St. Clare and insure Christian happiness for him.

Afterward, St. Clare talks to Miss Ophelia about freeing the slaves, and he asks her if she believes that the Northerners will educate and care for them. Miss Ophelia is positive that they will: "I know it is so. . . . there are a many good people at the North, who is in this matter and need only to be *taught* what their duty is."

St. Clare feels relieved and decides to go downtown. He enters a cafe and immediately tries to settle a fight between two drunken men. It is a terrible mistake; almost immediately, he is stabbed, fatally, in his side and carried home. He calls for Tom and asks him to pray.

All of the plantation mourns, except St. Clare himself. He feels that he is "coming home, at last." "At last," he says, "at last!" Then he utters the single word "Mother," and dies.

After her husband's death, Marie St. Clare decides that even though St. Clare had wanted to free the slaves, she cannot do so; it would be wrong. Instead, she orders about a dozen slaves to be sold, and Tom is thus taken to the slave market. There is a public auction, and during the auction, Tom is treated brutally; his jaw is jerked open, his teeth are inspected, and his shirt is torn open to reveal Tom's muscular body. Finally, he is bought by a Mr. Legree, a short, bullet-headed man, a Yankee who moved South to make his fortune in slaves and cotton.

On the riverboat bound for home, Simon Legree orders Tom to strip and put on some dilapidated clothes and some coarse shoes. Then he seizes Tom's hymnal, snarling that he'll have no "bawling, praying, singing niggers on [his] place." He shouts that on *his* plantation, "*I'm* your church – you've got to be as *I* say." Tom, however, hides his Bible from Legree and says, "Let Legree have the hymnal; it is best to say nothing to this man." Then silently, Tom says within himself, "*No!*" And he hears Little Eva's voice, "Fear not!" Legree continues shouting: *he* has no overseers. He prides himself on "*knocking down niggers*" with one single blow of his mighty fist. "Ye won't find no soft spot in me, nowhere. So, now, mind yerselves; for I don't show no mercy!"

Tom quickly realizes that Legree, besides being thoroughly evil, is also a drunk – which makes him twice as dangerous. Legree's plantation can hardly be called a plantation. It has fallen into ruins and looks ragged, forlorn, and decayed. Weeds are everywhere, and windows are broken. Two black men seem to be the principal work-hands and, clearly, Legree has trained them by savagery and brutality.

The slave quarters are little more than crude shanties, with no furniture and only a heap of straw on the floor, which is befouled and dirty. Tom feels empty, utterly alone. But it is not long before the field hands return home, having worked all day "under the driving lash." That night, Tom brings out his Bible. The book is a rare sight for the other slaves; they have only heard of the book. Tom reads selections to them from his favorite passages, then prays for them all.

From the first, Tom works efficiently, and Legree takes silent note of Tom's first-class value. "Yet he felt a secret dislike for him." Tom *could* be an overseer "were he tough," but Legree sees a tenderness in Tom that can never be eradicated.

While Tom toils in the cotton fields one day, he sees a woman kicked in the head; he tries to help her by filling her sack with some of his cotton, but out of fear, she protests. Legree hears about the incident, and he orders Tom to flog the woman. Tom says that he cannot – "no way possible." Legree strikes him across the face and says that Tom *will* flog the woman. Tom still refuses, so Legree has Tom flogged until Tom is unconscious.

As Tom lies groaning and bleeding alone, one of the slaves slips in and tends to him. It is Cassy. She tells Tom of the horrors of her life with Legree. Tom calls on the Lord for help, but Cassy quiets him. God can't help them now, she says. She's suffered too much misery to believe that God cares for the black race. Legree's treatment of his slaves is proof to her that "everything is pushing us into hell." There is no law on Legree's plantation, she says; a black man could be burned alive, cut to pieces, torn apart by dogs – or anything. Legree would – and could – do anything to a black man or a black woman whom he disliked.

Uncle Tom refuses to believe her. He has lost everything, but he won't give up his belief in Christ. He asks that Cassy bring him his Bible. Cassy does so and reads to him about Christ's last sufferings. Finishing some of Christ's final words, "Father, forgive them, for they know not what they do," she sobs aloud. Tom begins praying. "The Lord han't forgot us," he says.

Cassy then tells Tom about her early life of luxury and how her master agreed to free her, but he neglected to do so before he died. Then she was bought by the handsomest man she ever saw. They had two beautiful children, Henry and Elise. "O, those were happy days," she says. Then came the day that Cassy's children were sold to erase her master's gambling debts. She went mad, she supposes, and took up with a Mr. Stuart, bore him a child, and after Stuart died, she was bought by Legree. She loathes Legree: "I'll send him where he belongs – a short way, too – one of these nights, if they burn me alive for it!" Then she collapses in sobs. Recovering slowly, she places water within Tom's reach, then leaves the shed.

Commentary

In this section, we encounter two types of villains – Marie St. Clare and Simon Legree. Before St. Clare died, his wife Marie was merely a whining annoyance. After St. Clare's death, though, she emerges as a thoroughly bitter, wicked woman. The servants immediately sense her "unfeeling, tyrannical character." She orders Rosa to the whipping house when she catches the young quadroon trying on some of her lovely clothes, and whipping houses, Stowe tells us, are run by "the lowest of men" who brutally and shamefully expose, then punish young women. When Ophelia chides St. Clare's widow for being cruel, Marie answers callously that "these creatures get used to it; it's the only way they can be kept in order." We are not surprised when she impulsively decides to sell the slaves at auction, disregarding in particular her late husband's promise to give Tom his freedom.

Thus, Tom encounters Simon Legree, one of the most infamous villains in all of Western literature. Usually, Legree is portrayed in the movies by a lean, tall man. Stowe's Legree, however, is short, broad, and muscular–"of gigantic strength"–and "bullet-headed." Stowe points out that the first thing that Legree does is put chains on Tom's wrists and ankles. She says that Tom and other blacks are treated like chairs and tables when they should not be–simply because "a *man* can feel." Obviously, Legree would disagree; he grabs up Tom's hymnal and says that he'll soon have *that* out of Tom: "I'll have none o' yer bawling, praying, singing niggers on my place. . . . *I'm* your church now!" For Stowe, such a statement was utter blasphemy.

Another of Legree's first acts is to smash his "great, heavy fist" on Tom's hands: "I never see the nigger, yet, I couldn't bring down with one crack." Brutality, then, characterizes Legree's maniacal lust for power. He lives in a run-down, squalid plantation, does not have the respect of other white men, and cannot forget the cruel way he treated his late mother; thus he has turned to alcohol and brutality to his slaves in order to try and obtain some final respect. Ironically, the more brutal he is, the less respect *everyone* has for him. Stowe tells us that one slave buyer looks upon Legree's perverted excesses "with the curiosity of a naturalist studying some out-of-the-way specimen." Another slave buyer sums up Legree succinctly when he tells Legree, "practice has made your heart just like it," meaning Legree's hard fist, which he has been bragging about. One buyer comments that Simon Legrees abound in the South because no one forbids their cruelty: they wouldn't exist "if it were not for your sanction and influence." If other plantation owners would speak up and pass laws, then "the whole system could not keep a foothold for an hour . . . there would be no planters like that one . . . the whole thing would go down like a millstone." It is the silence of timid Southern planters, especially their "respectability and humanity which licenses and protects his [Legree's] brutality." Thus, Stowe again indicts the good, but silent "Christian" plantation owners.

CHAPTERS 35-40

Summary

As this flashback chapter opens, we are in Legree's sitting-room. The wallpaper hangs from the walls, mouldering, torn, and discolored. The room seems unwholesome and smells of decay. Saddles, bridles, and harnesses are scattered chaotically all over the floors, and throughout the rooms, dogs lie amidst overcoats and tossed-off clothing. Legree is mixing himself yet another drink from a cracked pitcher of liquor.

Cassy slips in and startles him. "You she-devil," he snarls at her, "you've come back, have you?"

"Yes, I have," Cassy says, "come to have my own way." It is clear that Legree fears this woman, for he is deeply superstitious. He sees Cassy's eyes flash, wildly and insanely. "I've got the devil in me," she taunts him. Legree slurps his liquor, filled with terror, as Cassy eyes him one final time, then slips out and goes to minister to poor, bleeding Tom.

Large drops of sweat cover Legree's forehead, and his heart beats heavy with fear. He calls loudly for Sambo and Quimbo, fills them both with liquor, and before long the house is filled with loud shrieking and whooping as Legree tries to blot out the memories of how foully he treated his mother. Cassy, meantime, has slipped back from Tom's shed, and she peers through one of Legree's windows: "Would it be a sin to rid the world of such a wretch?" she asks herself.

When morning arrives, Legree awakens with a fierce hangover and immediately pours himself a tumbler of brandy. Cassy is there and tells him to leave Tom alone. Legree says if Tom "begs his pardon," Legree will ease up on him. Cassy says that is impossible; Tom will never do so. Then Legree turns on her savagely: "He'll beg like a dog."

Cassy disagrees, but Legree charges out and heads toward Tom's shed. Inside, he taunts the old black man, kicking him, and calling him a beast. Tom says that he knows Legree can do terrible things to him, but he also knows that there is *Eternity* waiting for him. He speaks the word, and it "thrilled the black man's soul." Then Tom faces Legree and says that he's not afraid to die; the Lord Almighty is beside him.

With one blow of his powerful fist, Legree knocks Tom to the ground. Cassy runs to Tom, as Legree whirls and leaves. She tells Tom that Legree's everlasting wrath is on him, and that it will follow Tom "day in, day out," and she says that it will be as though Legree were "hanging like a dog on your throat – sucking your blood, bleeding away your life, drop by drop."

"I know the man," she adds quietly.

At this point, Stowe leaves Tom and Cassy, and she returns to let us know what has happened to George and Eliza and Harry, who were living in a friendly home when we left them. The Quakers are still nursing Loker, the slave hunter, but, at the same time, they are making plans for George and Eliza's escape. When the two blacks are fully disguised, a Mrs. Smyth, a respectable woman from Canada, helps them on board a ship that takes them to the small town of Amherstberg in Canada. The two stand still, then kneel down and lift their voices in hymns to God for their newfound freedom.

And now that we know that George and Eliza are safe, we are returned to the fate of Uncle Tom. Tom is put to work in the fields before his wounds are healed, but he continues to read secretly from his Bible, praying that someday God will give him deliverance. Meanwhile, Legree taunts Tom to join his "church" of liquor and cruelty, like Sambo and Quimbo have done. Tom says, "The Lord may help me, or not help; but I'll hold to Him, and believe Him to the last."

One night, Cassy calls to Tom. She has drugged Legree, and she and Emmeline are going to escape. But Tom says that he cannot go. He feels that he *must* stay with the rest of these "poor souls" and "bear my cross" with them "till the end." He urges Cassy to try and escape, however. "I'll pray with all my might for you." Then Cassy agrees to go. "Amen!" says Tom. "The Lord help ye!"

Cassy has a wild plan that just might work. She figures that Legree will search the swamps, but he will *not* find her and Emmeline, for they will be hidden in Legree's garret. On the way to the garret, Cassy pockets a roll of bills (". . . that will pay our way to the free states.").

From a knothole, they watch Legree and his dogs floundering in the swamp mud. Then, finally, Legree returns home, vowing dire revenge, and falls into bed.

Next morning, Legree suspects that if any of the slaves knows of Cassy's and Emmeline's whereabouts, it will be Tom. Thus, he has Tom brought before him. Tom admits to knowing *something,* but he says that he will die before he'll reveal it. "I'll *conquer ye, or kill ye!*" cries Legree, "I'll count every drop of blood there is in you, one by one."

My troubles will soon be over," Tom answers, "but if ye don't repent, yours won't *never* end." Suddenly, Tom hears heavenly music. There is a moment of silence. Then Legree, foaming with rage, strikes Tom to the ground. Walking away in a wake of anger, Legree is sure that Tom is dead, but Stowe tells us that "Tom was not quite gone." Tom's words have touched the slaves around him, and they wash his wounds and make him a crude bed. Even Quimbo and Sambo are overcome by Tom's Christian courage and beg his forgiveness, asking to be told more about this Jesus who inspired such strength within Tom. At these words, Tom prays again, asking God to take their souls, and Stowe remarks, "That prayer was answered!"

Commentary

This section centers upon Legree's cruelty to Tom, and Tom's strong faith. Despite Legree's vicious beatings, Tom's faith never falters. It does – for a time – succumb to dejection, but it never wholly despairs. Legree kicks Tom and calls him a beast, tells him to get on his knees and beg for pardon, "striking him with his riding whip." He taunts Tom and considers tying him to a tree and building "a slow fire" around him. Tom's response is merely to say that Legree can kill his body, but after that, "there ain't no more ye can do. And O, there's all ETERNITY to come, after that." Tom tells Legree that he can have all of Tom's time and strength, but not his soul – "my soul I won't give up to mortal man." He says that he isn't "afeared to die. I'd a soon die as not. Yet may whip me, starve me, burn me, it'll only send me sooner where I want to go."

Stowe likens Tom to a Christian martyr who daily, slowly bleeds, "drop by drop, hour after hour." Like those martyrs, she says, when Tom is face-to-face with "his persecutor," his "heart swelled bravely in him." With his vision of Jesus and his knowledge that heaven was "but a step beyond," he can face anyone or anything. And yet, even for Tom, there comes a time when even he is confused by God's silence, in the face of so many "souls crushed and ruined . . . and evil triumphant." For weeks and months, Stowe tells us, "Tom wrestled, in his own soul, in darkness and sorrow." Thus, Legree's wickedness is so terrible that it brings Tom almost to the edge of despair. But when Tom can finally find a moment to return to his worn Bible, his strong faith returns, more powerful than ever.

Legree threatens Tom and spits scornfully at him, but Tom stoically says that "the Lord may help me, or not help; but I'll hold to Him, and believe Him to the last." In a vision, he sees Christ, crowned with thorns, "buffeted and bleeding." And although Stowe does not say so, we feel that Tom must be a counterpart of Christ in this scene and that the two of them are victims of gross injustice. A voice speaks to Tom, telling him that heaven awaits and that soon he will sit on God's throne. Tom's soul-crisis has passed and, once more, Tom is filled with joy. He no longer feels "hunger, cold, degradation, disappointment, and wretchedness." Stowe says that "a quietness which no insult or injury could ruffle seemed to possess him."

Thus, Tom's strength is stronger–even when Legree's hatred descends with all its fury onto him. And when Quimbo seizes him, Tom looks toward heaven and, Christ-like, says, "Into thy hands I commend my spirit." When Legree rages at Tom, "Do you know I've made up my mind to KILL you?," Tom does not fear Legree; instead, he senses only that "the hour of release" is at hand.

Stowe does not tell us, in detail, of the degree of Legree's final cruelty to Tom. She says simply that Legree "smote his victim to the ground," and then she comments that "what man has nerve to do, man has not nerve to hear." And it is to her credit that she does not emblazon her picture of Legree's cruelty with blood and gore. Instead, she focuses on Tom's faith, and tells us that, besides Tom, there has already been "One whose suffering changed an instrument of torture, degradation, and shame, into a symbol of glory, honor, and immortal life." Once more, she parallels Christ and Uncle Tom.

CHAPTERS 41-44

Summary

Mrs. Stowe now returns us to the Shelby household. Miss Ophelia's letter about Tom's being sold after St. Clare's death finally reaches Mrs. Shelby. But by now, Mrs. Shelby is near death. Meanwhile, young George Shelby has grown to manhood, and after his father died, we learn, he and his mother began selling property and settling debts. That task completed, George now decides to go to New Orleans and see if he can find out who bought Uncle Tom. By accident, George meets a man who knows about the sale, and so George takes a steamboat to Red River, certain that he can find and re-purchase his old friend.

George enters Legree's house and asks about Tom, hoping to buy him. Legree's brow darkens. Yes, he has Tom – a rebellious and impudent dog – "set up my niggers to run away, got off two gals, worth eight hundred or a thousand apiece." Then he adds that he has flogged Tom, and now "I b'lieve he's trying to die; but I don't know as he'll make it out."

George runs to the shed and finds Tom, who has lain there for two days. He weeps when he sees Tom's wretched condition. And when Tom is roused to consciousness, he too begins weeping. It is too late, however, he says, for Tom feels that he is dying. His breath rises and falls in heavy sighs, and then he sleeps.

George turns and sees Legree standing sullenly behind him. George offers to buy Tom's body, for he feels that Tom is surely dead, but Legree refuses. George ignores him and has Tom's body loaded in the wagon, then he turns to Legree, "I will proclaim this murder. I will go to the very first magistrate and expose you."

"What a fuss, for a dead nigger," snarls Legree sarcastically. And it is then that George realizes the futility of trying to convict Legree. There is not another white person on the place.

Uncle Tom is buried quietly on a dry, sandy knoll, shaded by a few trees. The Negroes who have accompanied George beg him to buy them. George cannot, he realizes, but he vows to do "*what one man can* [do] to drive out this curse of slavery from my land!"

Back at Legree's, legends of ghosts have begun to haunt the place. The "ghosts," of course, are Cassy and Emmeline, still hiding in the attic. George helps them escape – which is not too difficult – since Legree has begun drinking more than ever.

Yet another adventure awaits the women. On a boat headed north, they meet a woman named Madame de Thoux. It seems that she is George Harris' sister, and it is discovered that George's wife,

Eliza, is Cassy's daughter. It takes some time, but finally all of them are reunited, and they all kneel together and pray. Back in Kentucky, George Shelby frees his slaves after a magnificent welcome home dinner, especially prepared by old Aunt Chloe. He frees his slaves, in the name of Uncle Tom, for he vowed on Tom's grave never to own another slave. "Rejoice," he says, "in your freedom and be as honest and as faithful a Christian as Tom was."

Commentary

When at last George finds Uncle Tom, Tom is near death. He is roused almost reluctantly, then he sobs: "Now I shall die content." Clearly, Tom knows that he is dying, and he is prepared for his death. "The Lord's bought me," he says, using what is to him a most natural analogy–that of master and slave–and, he says further, "I long to go. Heaven is better than Kintuck." George calls him "Poor, poor fellow," and Tom chides him for doing so: "Don't call me poor fellow. . . . I *have* been a poor fellow; but that's all past and gone, now. I'm right in the door going to glory! . . . I've got the victory."

Like George, we are awestruck at Tom's newfound "vehemence and power, with which these broken sentences [are] uttered." Tom's thoughts, though, are not wholly on heaven. He asks George not to tell Chloe about his wretched state: "Only tell her ye found me going into glory." He asks George to tell the Shelbys that he loves them: "'Pears like I loves 'em all! I loves every creature, everywhar!–it's nothing *but* love! O Mas'r George! What a thing 'tis to be a Christian!" We are reminded here of the similarity of this scene to the death scene of Little Eva.

This, then, is Stowe's finished portrait of a Christian who has stood trial for his body and soul, and who has survived–long enough to realize that, although near death, he has been triumphant, and his heavenly award awaits him.

After Tom is buried, Stowe speaks outright to us. She says that there is "no monument" marking Tom's grave. "The Lord," she says, "knows where he lies." She asks us not to pity Tom, just as Tom asked George not to pity him, and then she closes the section with a quotation from the Bible: "Blessed are they that mourn, for they shall be comforted."

CHAPTER 45

Summary

In Stowe's concluding remarks, she says that she has given only "a faint shadow, a dim picture, of the anguish and despair that are at this very moment, riving thousands of hearts, shattering thousands of families, and driving a helpless and sensitive race to frenzy and despair." She calls upon all the men and women of America – even those in Massachusetts, New Hampshire, Vermont, and Connecticut – to listen to her. She calls upon the mothers of America, who have sat beside their children's cradles, to heed her story. "Pity," she says, "those mothers that are constantly made childless by the American slave-trade!" She indicts the North because the people of the free states have "defended, encouraged, and participated; and are more guilty for it, before God, than the South, in that they have *not* the apology of education or custom."

To fill Africa with "an ignorant, inexperienced, half-barbarized race, just escaped from the chains of slavery" would solve nothing, she says. "Let the church of the North receive these poor sufferers in the spirit of Christ . . . until they have attained somewhat of a moral and intellectual maturity, and then assist them in their passage to those shores, where they may put in practice the lessons they have learned in America." She calls, first, for education. A day of vengeance is upon America, she believes, and both North and South are "guilty before God." The Christian church, she says, has "a heavy account to answer." If the injustice of slavery continues, she warns, its cruelty will bring down "the wrath of Almighty God!"

Commentary

In her final chapter, Stowe takes on the role of crusader again. What her readers have read, she says is *not* fiction. Either she herself or her personal friends have observed "the separate incidents that compose the narrative." Living witnesses "all over our land," she says, can testify to parallels of other Uncle Toms. Nothing, she stresses, can "protect the slave's life, but the *character* of the master." Brutality and injustice, she emphasizes, are "*inherent* in the slave system – it cannot exist without them."

She asks the men and women of the South to examine their

consciences—"Have you not, in your own secret souls . . . felt that there were woes and evils in this accursed system?" She appeals to a mother's compassion everywhere not to condone, in silence, this cruel buying and selling and breaking-up of families. She states that Christians everywhere owe the African race some reparation for the wrongs committed by America. Liberia, she says, has been provided by God himself as a refuge for the black race, but it would be wrong to fill Liberia with black people until America has taken them into her churches and into her schools. In order to sever the "chains of slavery," it is necessary to ensure that those who settle in Liberia are educated Christians who can put an end to suffering and hopelessness. These people have talents, minds, and souls that need to be encouraged to mature and, thereby, eradicate the curse of slavery.

Stowe herself has known emancipated slaves; their first desire is for education. With opportunity and encouragement, these people can become highly respected men and women. Now, however, they are a persecuted people. Stowe wonders how much has been lost—for the sake of mankind—all because the Christian church hasn't seen that it has an obligation to free, then educate, these people. The Kingdom, she says, is coming. Christians cannot waste time. A day of vengeance is approaching. Only one day of grace remains. Both North and South are guilty of injustice and cruelty to the black man: "The *Christian church* has a heavy account to answer." She pleads for positive, decisive action. She prays for the black man's freedom.

UNCLE TOM'S CABIN AS MELODRAMA

In the nineteenth-century theater, little attention was paid to consistency or unity of plot or characterization. What would play—that is, what appealed to the audience—was more important than any attempt to write good or unified drama. Today, most of nineteenth-century drama is officially called melodrama or, derogatorily, meller-drammer. What the nineteenth-century audience took seriously, often crying real tears, is today laughed at, and in the modern tradition, it is exaggerated so out of proportion that the audience is expected to participate by throwing popcorn at the villain, hissing him, and cheering the hero.

Of all the plays that have come out of the nineteenth century,

Uncle Tom's Cabin was the most popular; there were numerous touring companies and in almost every large city, one could often find a production of it. At one time, in New York City alone, *Uncle Tom's Cabin* was playing eighteen times a week to sold-out houses. Every famous actor and actress eventually opted to play one of the plumb roles – Uncle Tom, Simon Legree, Topsy, Eliza, Gumption Cute (*not* a character in the novel), or "Feely" (Miss Ophelia).

An important fact to be mentioned is that in spite of the extreme popularity of the play – often shortened to be called "A Tom Show" – all types of liberties were taken with the novel, such as adding characters, or omitting large scenes or characters. And Mrs. Stowe never realized a cent of profit from any of the productions. In fact, she was of a religious persuasion that forbade her to even *enter* a theater – much less write for it. Therefore, due to the popularity of the novel, an early version of the play, written by Charles W. Taylor, appeared shortly after the novel's publication. In this version, we have a happy ending, for at the time abolition was not a popular subject for the theater, and, additionally, it would have been shocking for the audience if they were to see Negroes on the stage. It should also be pointed out (or emphasized) that the Negro characters were played by **white** people in black face. At the time, it was unheard of to use a real Negro actor, even if one could be found.

The first version was soon followed by others, but soon an actor named George L. Aiken, thinking that his troupe, especially since it included his own daughter as Little Eva, could make the play a successful one, wrote the play which is outlined here; ever since its publication, it has been the only version of the play ever presented. It has been estimated that this play has had over half a million performances in various parts of the world, and this in spite of the fact that Mrs. Stowe never received a cent of royalty nor did she ever see a performance of the play.

The play is more a series of scenes than a consistent drama with motivation. There is virtually no cause-and-effect relationship between the parts; the play skips haphazardly from Eliza's plight, to Uncle Tom's plight, to Miss Ophelia, and the setting shifts from either Louisiana, or Vermont, or to Simon Legree's plantation.

Like the novel, the play does concern itself – partially – with the plight of the slaves. But whereas Stowe's novel was a plea for the abolition of slavery, the play often stresses other matters, especially religion. Of the two most famous scenes in the play—that is, Eliza crossing the ice with bloodhounds chasing her, and the final scene with Little Eva in heaven, welcoming her father and Uncle Tom—the emphasis is on two main concerns—slavery and religion.

OUTLINE OF THE MELODRAMA

ACT I. Scene 1 *A Plain Chamber:* Eliza and George Harris discuss the difference between George's vicious master and Eliza's seemingly good master, Mr. Shelby. George is determined to escape to Canada.

Scene 2 *A Dining Room:* Mr. Shelby discusses a slave trade with the slave trader Haley. Mr. Shelby must sell his most reliable and respected slave, Uncle Tom, in order to settle debts or else lose the plantation. Haley also wants to buy Eliza and her five-year-old son, Harry.

Scene 3 *A Snowy Landscape in Front of Uncle Tom's Cabin:* Eliza tells Uncle Tom and his wife, Chloe, about the sale. Eliza reveals her plans to run away, but Uncle Tom feels that he must remain behind to be sold so as not to betray the trust his master has in him.

Scene 4 *A Tavern by the River:* Eliza and Harry are befriended by a Quaker named Phineas until the ferry boat arrives. First, Marks and then Loker, two notorious slave tracking bounty hunters come in. Haley soon follows, and Eliza overhears their plans to capture and sell her and her son, Harry. She decides to escape over the ice—better to drown than to be captured.

Scene 5 *Snowy Landscape:* Eliza is seen fleeing, pursued by Haley, Loker, and Marks.

Scene 6 (This scene, printed below in its entirety, requires elaborate and intricate staging. It is by far the most famous scene in all of nineteenth-century

American drama, and all restraints were let loose in staging this scene, which included the entire stage area being flooded with ice, live bloodhounds loosed upon the stage to chase Eliza and Harry, lighting effects, winds, howlings, and all types of mechanics to thrill and excite the audience.)

Scene 6

"The entire depth of the stage, representing the Ohio River, is filled with floating ice.

— — — — — — — — — —

(Eliza appears, with Harry, on a cake of ice, and floats slowly across. Haley, Loker, and Marks on the bank observing. Phineas on the opposite side.)"

ACT II. Scene 1 *A Handsome Parlor:* St. Clare arrives home with his daughter Eva (Evangeline), his cousin Ophelia, and Uncle Tom, whom St. Clare has bought after Uncle Tom saved Eva when she fell overboard. Marie (Mrs. St. Clare) is too busy with her imaginary illnesses to be concerned with their arrival.

Scene 2 *A Garden:* Uncle Tom and Eva are playing, to the delight of St. Clare and to the disgust of Miss Ophelia, who loathes blacks, while being indignant about their being slaves. St. Clare reveals that he has bought Ophelia a slave, Topsy, for her to educate. Upon questioning, Topsy reveals that she has no parents and is a wicked girl.

Scene 3 *A Tavern by the River:* Phineas has been sent to find Eliza's husband, and it happens that George is in this very tavern in disguise. Suddenly, the slave traders appear, and George Harris has to make a hasty retreat, vowing to die before being captured.

Scene 4 *A Plain Chamber:* Topsy is telling Little Eva about some of the wicked things she has recently done. Eva is shocked and tries to convince Topsy that she is loved and that she should *try* to be good.

Scene 5 *A Chamber:* George, Eliza, and Harry have been reunited, but they must move on to Canada because there are so many bounty hunters along the border states. Phineas enters with news that the bounty hunters are close behind. George takes out pistols to defend them, and they leave for safer grounds.

Scene 6 *A Rocky Pass in the Hills:* As the bounty hunters close in, they have to approach single file through the rocks. When Loker charges, he is wounded by George, and the others flee in terror.

ACT III. Scene 1 *A Chamber in St. Clare's House:* Uncle Tom pleads with St. Clare to mend his ways, to quit drinking and be converted to Christianity. Meanwhile, Miss Ophelia despairs of ever teaching Topsy anything. When Topsy leaves, Miss Ophelia admits that all blacks make her feel repugnant, but she will try to emulate Little Eva, who loves everyone – even Topsy.

Scene 2 *Underneath a Tree, beside a Lake:* Eva looks up at the clouds in the sky and tells Uncle Tom that she will soon be going up there. Eva extracts a promise from her father that when she dies, he will set Uncle Tom free.

Scene 3 *A Corridor next to Little Eva's Room:* When questioned by Miss Ophelia, Uncle Tom explains that he is sleeping on the floor to be near the dying Little Eva.

Scene 4 *Eva's Chamber:* Everyone is gathered next to Little Eva's death bed, and when her father asks her what she sees, she responds: "Oh! love! joy! peace!" and then dies.

ACT IV.	Scene 1	*A Street in New Orleans:* Gumption Cute (a character who does not appear in the novel) is looking for Miss Ophelia to claim a dubious kinship and to sponge off of her. He meets Marks, the bounty hunter, who wants Cute to become his new partner in slave hunting, but Cute thinks that it is too dangerous an occupation.
	Scene 2	*A Gothic Chamber:* Uncle Tom is still trying to convert a doubting St. Clare to Christianity. St. Clare tells Tom that he plans to give him his freedom. Tom is ecstatic. Even though he has been treated well by St. Clare, he would rather be poor and free than to belong to someone else. Miss Ophelia drags Topsy in and accuses her of stealing. When confronted, Topsy reveals that she is concealing a lock of hair that Little Eva gave her just before she died.
	Scene 3	*A Front Chamber:* Topsy is confused because she hasn't done anything wicked since Little Eva died. Miss Ophelia, who has now learned to love Topsy, decides to take her back to Vermont. At that moment, Uncle Tom enters with the news that St. Clare has been fatally wounded.
	Scene 4	*St. Clare's Chamber:* St. Clare is dying and is deeply troubled because he never got around to signing Uncle Tom's freedom papers, and before he can call his wife, he dies, calling out Little Eva's name.
ACT V.	Scene 1	*A Slave Auction Mart:* Uncle Tom is now up for sale. He and a fifteen-year-old quadroon, Emmeline, are sold to the evil and vicious Simon Legree.
	Scene 2	*The Garden of Miss Ophelia's House in Vermont:* Miss Ophelia and Deacon Perry discuss the loss of his wife eighteen months ago, and as he is about to propose, Topsy rushes in and is introduced as an adopted daughter. Left alone on stage, Topsy encounters Gumption Cute, who is still looking for Miss Ophelia to sponge off of her.

Scene 3 *A Rude Chamber in Simon Legree's Place:* When the new slave Emmeline is repulsed by the touch of Simon Legree, he orders Uncle Tom to flog her. When Uncle Tom refuses, Simon Legree first strikes him with a whip and then has two other slaves flog Uncle Tom within an inch of his life.

Scene 4 *A Chamber in Miss Ophelia's House:* Topsy reports the arrival of Gumption Cute, who tries to claim kinship with Miss Ophelia. She is not impressed. When she leaves to tend to some household chores, Deacon Perry arrives, and Gumption Cute, fearing a rival, insults the gentleman. When Miss Ophelia returns and hears the insults, she orders Gumption Cute out of the house.

ACT VI. Scene 1 *An Old Roofless Shed:* The slave Cassy brings Uncle Tom some water, and she explains how isolated and miserable they all are, and how they are all constantly mistreated by Simon Legree. When Uncle Tom says that he relies on God for succor, Cassy says that she feels that God has deserted everyone on Legree's place.

Scene 2 *A Street in New Orleans:* Young George Shelby, now grown, has come to New Orleans to repurchase Uncle Tom and reunite him with his wife and family. He meets Marks, the bounty hunter, who for a price will conduct George to Simon Legree's plantation.

Scene 3 *A Rough Chamber at Simon Legree's.* Sambo, one of Simon Legree's slaves, brings in a "magic charm" that he found around Uncle Tom's neck. When Legree unties the bundle, Little Eva's lock of hair seems to burn Simon Legree's hand. He explains that his dying mother had tried to reform him in his youth by sending him a lock of her hair which he burned and, since then, he has dedicated his life to sin and evil.

Scene 4 *A Street in New Orleans:* Gumption Cute meets the bounty hunter, Marks, who tells him that when St. Clare interfered in a fight between Cute and Simon Legree, St. Clare died of a knife wound. Since the two were the only eyewitnesses, they plan to blackmail Legree.

Scene 5 *A Rough Chamber at Simon Legree's:* Simon Legree sends for Cassy and hears that both Cassy and Emmeline have run away. Legree sends for the dogs and blames Uncle Tom for the escape. Uncle Tom is dragged in, but he refuses to say anything, and although Uncle Tom is almost dead, he is violently beaten. George Shelby, Gumption Cute, and Marks arrive, and George immediately tries to comfort Uncle Tom. Meanwhile, when Marks and Gumption Cute try to arrest Simon Legree, he resists and begins to beat them. Marks then kills Simon Legree. George Shelby tries to further comfort Uncle Tom, but it is too late, and Uncle Tom dies in George's arms.

Scene 6 Scene 6 concludes the play and since this scene is so famous for its staging and spectacle and because it so enthralled the audience with its transcendant beauty, the entire scene is reprinted.

"Gorgeous clouds, tinted with sunlight. Eva, robed in white, is discovered on the back of a milk-white dove, with expanded wings, as if just soaring upward. Her hands are extended in benediction over St. Clare and Uncle Tom, who are kneeling and gazing up to her. Impressive music.—Slow Curtain."

ESSAY TOPICS

1. Define the values of the typical Southern, white planter/plantation owner during the era of *Uncle Tom's Cabin*.

2. Critics have said that *Uncle Tom's Cabin* is "the most influential novel ever published in the United States." Account for such a statement.

3. Would Stowe be considered a liberal today? Why or why not, making references to the novel.

4. What was Stowe's attitude toward Liberia?

5. Consider Stowe's message about slavery in terms of one of the principles upon which America was founded – that is, all men are created equal.

6. What new information about slavery and slave owners did Stowe furnish the readers?

7. Define Uncle Tom in terms of his Christianity.

8. How does Stowe present the breakup of a family as being one of the cruelest evils of slavery?

9. Discuss Little Eva's goodness and her naiveté.

10. What role do Christians have in making restitution to the black race?

SELECT BIBLIOGRAPHY

ALLEN, JAMES LANE. "Mrs. Stowe's Uncle Tom at Home in Kentucky," *Century,* October, 1887.

BALDWIN, JAMES. "Everybody's Protest Novel," *Partisan Review,* June, 1949.

BANCROFT, FREDERICK. *Slave-Trading in the Old South.* Baltimore: J. H. Furst Company, 1931.

BIRDOFF, HARRY. *The World's Greatest Hit: Uncle Tom's Cabin.* New York: S. F. Vanni, 1947.

BONTEMPS, ARNA. *Story of the Negro.* New York: Alfred A. Knopf, 1951.

BROWN, HERBERT ROSS. *The Sentimental Novel in America 1789-1860.* Durham: Duke University Press, 1940.

BULLARD, F. LAURISTON. "Uncle Tom on the Stage," *Lincoln Herald,* June, 1946.

CASH, W. J. *The Mind of the South.* Garden City: Doubleday Anchor Books, 1954.

CLARK, THOMAS D. "An Appraisal of Uncle Tom's Cabin," *Lincoln Herald,* June, 1946.

COBBETT, ELIZABETH. "Uncle Tom Is Dead," *Theater Guild Magazine,* June, 1931.

COLEMAN, J. WINSTON, JR. "Mrs. Stowe, Kentucky, and Uncle Tom's Cabin," *Lincoln Herald,* June, 1946.

DAVIS, J. FRANK. "Tom Shows," *Scribner's,* April, 1925.

EASTMAN, MRS. MARY H. *Aunt Phillis's Cabin: or, Southern Life as It Is.* Philadelphia: Lippincott, Grambo & Co., 1852.

FOSTER, CHARLES H. *The Rungless Ladder: Harriet Beecher Stowe and New England Puritanism.* Durham: Duke University Press, 1954.

GILBERTSON, CATHERINE. *Harriet Beecher Stowe.* New York: D. Appleton-Century Company, 1937.

HILL, WALTER B. "Uncle Tom without a Cabin," *Century,* April, 1884.

ISAACS, EDITH J. R. *The Negro in the American Theatre.* New York: Theatre Arts, 1947.

JORGENSON, CHESTER E., ed. *Uncle Tom's Cabin as Book and Legend.* Detroit: The Friends of the Detroit Public Library, 1952.

KAYE, JOSEPH. "Famous First Nights: 'Uncle Tom's Cabin.'" *Theatre Magazine,* August, 1929.

MATTHEWS, ESSIE COLLINS. *Aunt Phebe, Uncle Tom and Others: Character Studies Among the Slaves of the South, Fifty Years After.* Columbus: The Champlin Press, 1905.

MCCRAY, FLORINE THAYER. *The Life-Work of the Author of Uncle Tom's Cabin.* New York: Funk & Wagnalls, 1889.

MOODY, RICHARD. "Uncle Tom, The Theatre, and Mrs. Stowe," *American Heritage,* October, 1955.

NELSON, JOHN HERBERT. *The Negro Character in American Literature.* Lawrence: *Bulletin of the University of Kansas,* XXVII, No. 15, September 1, 1926.

NICHOLSON, KENYON AND JOHN GOLDEN. *Eva the Fifth: The Odyssey of a Tom Show in Three Acts.* New York: Samuel French, 1928.

NYE, RUSSEL B. "Eliza Crossing the Ice – A Reappraisal of Sources," *Historical and Philosophical Society of Ohio,* April, 1950.

POLK, WILLIAM T. *Southern Accent: From Uncle Remus to Oak Ridge.* New York: William Morrow and Company, 1953.

STOUT, WESLEY WINANS. "Little Eva Is Seventy-Five," *Saturday Evening Post,* October 8, 1927.

WARNER, CHARLES DUDLEY. "The Story of Uncle Tom's Cabin," *Atlantic Monthly,* September, 1896

WASHINGTON, BOOKER T. *The Story of the Negro: The Rise of the Race from Slavery.* New York: Doubleday, Page & Company, 1909.

WESLEY, CHARLES H. "The Concept of Negro Inferiority in American Thought," *Journal of Negro History,* October, 1940.

WILSON, EDMUND. "Harriet Beecher Stowe," *New Yorker,* September 10, 1955.

WILSON, FORREST. *Crusader in Crinoline: The Life of Harriet Beecher Stowe.* Philadelphia: J. B. Lippincott Company, 1941.

WOODSON, CARTER G. *The Mind of the Negro as Reflected in Letters Written during the Crisis 1800-1860.* Washington, D.C. : The Association for the Study of Negro Life and History, Inc., 1926.

WOODWARD, C. VANN. *The Strange Career of Jim Crow.* New York: Oxford University Press, 1955.

NOTES

NOTES

TITLE INDEX

This is the TITLE INDEX, indexing the over 200 titles available by Series, by Library and by Volume Number for both the BASIC LIBRARY SERIES and the AUTHORS LIBRARY SERIES.

TITLE INDEX (cont'd)

TITLE INDEX (cont'd)

TITLE INDEX (cont'd)

TITLE	SERIES	LIBRARY	Vol
Lost Horizon	Basic	English Lit	5
"Love Song of J. Alfred Prufrock, The" (in T.S. Eliot's Major Poems and Plays)	Basic	English Lit	6
Love's Labour's Lost (in Comedy of Errors....)	Basic	Shakespeare	1
	Authors	Shakespeare	8
Lysistrata & Other Comedies	Basic	Classics	1
Macbeth	Basic	Shakespeare	2
	Authors	Shakespeare	9
Madame Bovary	Basic	European Lit	1
Main Street	Basic	American Lit	3
	Authors	Lewis	7
Man and Superman (in Shaw's Man and Superman)	Basic	English Lit	6
	Authors	Shaw	11
Manchild in the Promised Land	Basic	American Lit	7
Mayor of Casterbridge, The	Basic	English Lit	3
	Authors	Hardy	4
Measure for Measure	Basic	Shakespeare	1
	Authors	Shakespeare	8
Medea (in Euripides' Electra & Medea)	Basic	Classics	1
Merchant of Venice, The	Basic	Shakespeare	1
	Authors	Shakespeare	8
Merry Wives of Windsor, The (in All's Well....)	Basic	Shakespeare	1
	Authors	Shakespeare	8
"Metamorphosis, The" (in Kafka's Short Stories)	Basic	European Lit	2
Middlemarch	Basic	English Lit	4
Midsummer Night's Dream, A	Basic	Shakespeare	1
	Authors	Shakespeare	8
Mill on the Floss, The	Basic	The English Lit	4
Misanthrope (in Tartuffe....)	Basic	European Lit	1
Miss Lonelyhearts	Basic	American Lit	5
Moby Dick	Basic	American Lit	1
Moll Flanders	Basic	English Lit	1
Mother Night (in Vonnegut's Major Works)	Basic	American Lit	7
Mrs. Dalloway	Basic	English Lit	5
Much Ado About Nothing	Basic	Shakespeare	1
	Authors	Shakespeare	8
"Murder in the Cathedral" (in T.S. Eliot's Major Poems and Plays)	Basic	English Lit	6
My Antonia	Basic	American Lit	3
Mythology	Basic	Classics	1
Native Son	Basic	American Lit	5
New Testament	Basic	Classics	4
Nichomachean Ethics (in Aristotle's Ethics)	Basic	Classics	1
Nineteen Eighty-Four	Basic	English Lit	6
No Exit	Basic	European Lit	1
Notes from the Underground	Basic	European Lit	3
	Authors	Dostoevsky	2
O'Connor's Short Stories	Basic	American Lit	7
Odyssey, The	Basic	Classics	1

TITLE INDEX (cont'd)

TITLE INDEX (cont'd)

AUTHOR INDEX

This is the AUTHOR INDEX, listing the over 200 titles available by author and indexing them by Series, by Library and by Volume Number for both the BASIC LIBRARY SERIES and the AUTHORS LIBRARY SERIES.

AUTHOR	TITLE(S)	SERIES	LIBRARY	Vol
Aeschylus	Agamemnon, The Choephori, & The Eumenides	Basic	Classics	1
Albee, Edward	Who's Afraid of Virginia Woolf?	Basic	American Lit	7
Anderson, Sherwood	Winesburg, Ohio	Basic	American Lit	3
Aristophanes	Lysistrata * The Birds * Clouds * The Frogs	Basic	Classics	1
Aristotle	Aristotle's Ethics	Basic	Classics	1
Austen, Jane	Emma	Basic	English Lit	1
	Pride and Prejudice	Basic	English Lit	2
Beckett, Samuel	Waiting for Godot	Basic	European Lit	1
Beowulf	Beowulf	Basic	Classics	3
Beyle, Henri	see Stendhal			
Bronte, Charlotte	Jane Eyre	Basic	English Lit	3
Bronte, Emily	Wuthering Heights	Basic	English Lit	4
Brown, Claude	Manchild in the Promised Land	Basic	American Lit	7
Buck, Pearl	The Good Earth	Basic	American Lit	4
Bunyan, John	The Pilgrim's Progress	Basic	English Lit	2
Camus, Albert	The Plague * The Stranger	Basic	European Lit	1
Carroll, Lewis	Alice in Wonderland	Basic	English Lit	3
Cather, Willa	My Antonia	Basic	American Lit	3
Cervantes, Miguel de	Don Quixote	Basic	Classics	3
Chaucer, Geoffrey	The Canterbury Tales	Basic	Classics	3
Chopin, Kate	The Awakening	Basic	American Lit	2
Clark, Walter	The Ox-Bow Incident	Basic	American Lit	7
Conrad, Joseph	Heart of Darkness & The Secret Sharer * Lord Jim	Basic	English Lit	5
Cooper, James F.	The Deerslayer * The Last of the Mohicans	Basic	American Lit	1
Crane, Stephen	The Red Badge of Courage	Basic	American Lit	2
Dante	Divine Comedy I: Inferno * Divine Comedy II: Purgatorio * Divine Comedy III: Paradiso	Basic	Classsics	3
Defoe, Daniel	Moll Flanders	Basic	English Lit	1
	Robinson Crusoe	Basic	English Lit	2
Dickens, Charles	Bleak House * David Copperfield * Great Expectations * Hard Times	Basic	English Lit	3
	Oliver Twist * A Tale of Two Cities	Basic	English Lit	4
	Bleak House * David Copperfield * Great Expectations * Hard Times * Oliver Twist * A Tale of Two Cities	Authors	Dickens	1

AUTHOR INDEX (cont'd)

AUTHOR	TITLE(S)	SERIES	LIBRARY	Vol
Dickinson, Emily	Emily Dickinson: Selected Poems	Basic	American Lit	2
Dostoevsky, Feodor	The Brothers Karamazov * Crime and Punishment * Notes from the Underground	Basic	European Lit	3
	The Brothers Karamazov * Crime and Punishment * Notes from the Underground	Authors	Dostoevsky	2
Dreiser, Theodore	An American Tragedy * Sister Carrie	Basic	American Lit	3
Dumas, Alexandre	The Count of Monte Cristo * The Three Musketeers	Basic	European Lit	1
Eliot, George	Middlemarch * The Mill on the Floss * Silas Marner	Basic	English Lit	4
Eliot, T.S.	T.S. Eliot's Major Poets and Plays: "The Wasteland," "The Love Song of J. Alfred Prufrock," & Other Works	Basic	English Lit	6
Ellison, Ralph	The Invisible Man	Basic	American Lit	7
Emerson, Ralph Waldo	Emerson's Essays	Basic	American Lit	1
Euripides	Electra * Medea	Basic	Classics	1
Faulkner, William	Absalom, Absalom! * As I Lay Dying * The Bear * Go Down, Moses * Light in August	Basic	American Lit	4
	The Sound and the Fury * The Unvanquished	Basic	American Lit	5
	Absalom, Absalom! * As I Lay Dying * The Bear * Go Down, Moses * Light in August The Sound and the Fury * The Unvanquished	Authors	Faulkner	3
Fielding, Henry	Joseph Andrews	Basic	English Lit	1
	Tom Jones	Basic	English Lit	2
Fitzgerald, F. Scott	The Great Gatsby	Basic	American Lit	4
	Tender is the Night	Basic	American Lit	5
Flaubert, Gustave	Madame Bovary	Basic	European Lit	1
Forster, E.M.	A Passage to India	Basic	English Lit	6
Fowles, John	The French Lieutenant's Woman	Basic	English Lit	5
Frank, Anne	The Diary of Anne Frank	Basic	European Lit	2
Franklin, Benjamin	The Autobiography of Benjamin Franklin	Basic	American Lit	1
Gawain Poet	Sir Gawain and the Green Night	Basic	Classics	4
Goethe, Johann Wolfgang von	Faust - Parts I & II	Basic	European Lit	2
Golding, William	Lord of the Flies	Basic	English Lit	5
Greene, Graham	The Power and the Glory	Basic	English Lit	6
Griffin, John H.	Black Like Me	Basic	American Lit	6

AUTHOR INDEX (cont'd)

AUTHOR	TITLE(S)	SERIES	LIBRARY	Vol
Haley, Alex see also Little, Malcolm	The Autobiography of Malcolm X	Basic	American Lit	6
Hardy, Thomas	Far from the Madding Crowd * Jude the Obscure * The Mayor of Casterbridge	Basic	English Lit	3
	The Return of the Native * Tess of the D'Urbervilles	Basic	English Lit	4
	Far from the Madding Crowd * Jude the Obscure * The Mayor of Casterbridge The Return of the Native * Tess of the D'Urbervilles	Authors	Hardy	4
Hawthorne, Nathaniel	The House of the Seven Gables* The Scarlet Letter	Basic	American Lit	1
Heller, Joseph	Catch-22	Basic	American Lit	6
Hemingway, Ernest	A Farewell to Arms * For Whom the Bell Tolls	Basic	American Lit	4
	The Old Man and the Sea	Basic	American Lit	7
	The Sun Also Rises	Basic	American Lit	5
	A Farewell to Arms * For Whom the Bell Tolls The Old Man and the Sea The Sun Also Rises	Authors	Hemingway	5
Herbert, Frank	Dune & Other Works	Basic	American Lit	6
Hesse, Herman	Demian * Steppenwolf & Siddhartha	Basic	European Lit	2
Hilton, James	Lost Horizon	Basic	English Lit	5
Homer	The Iliad * The Odyssey	Basic	Classics	1
Hugo, Victor	Les Miserables	Basic	European Lit	1
Huxley, Aldous	Brave New World & Brave New World Revisited	Basic	English Lit	5
Ibsen, Henrik	Ibsen's Plays I: A Doll's House & Hedda Gabler * Ibsen's Plays II: Ghosts, An Enemy of the People, & The Wild Duck	Basic	European Lit	4
James, Henry	The American * Daisy Miller & The Turn of the Screw * The Portrait of a Lady	Basic	American Lit	2
	The American * Daisy Miller & The Turn of the Screw * The Portrait of a Lady	Authors	James	6
Joyce, James	A Portrait of the Artist as a Young Man * Ulysses	Basic	English Lit	6
Kafka, Franz	Kafka's Short Stories * The Trial	Basic	European Lit	2
Keats & Shelley	Keats & Shelley	Basic	English Lit	1
Kesey, Ken	One Flew Over the Cuckoo's Nest	Basic	American Lit	7
Knowles, John	A Separate Peace	Basic	American Lit	7

AUTHOR INDEX (cont'd)

AUTHOR INDEX

AUTHOR	TITLE(S)	SERIES	LIBRARY	Vol
Shakespeare, William	Troilus and Cressida * Twelfth Night * The Winter's Tale	Basic	Shakespeare	1
	All's Well that Ends Well & The Merry Wives of Windsor * As You Like It * The Comedy of Errors, Love's Labour's Lost, & The Two Gentlemen of Verona * Measure for Measure * The Merchant of Venice * Midsummer Night's Dream * Much Ado About Nothing * The Taming of the Shrew * The Tempest * Troilus and Cressida * Twelfth Night * The Winter's Tale	Authors	Shakespeare	8
	Antony and Cleopatra * Hamlet * Julius Caesar * King Lear * Macbeth * Othello * Romeo and Juliet	Basic	Shakeapeare	2
	Antony and Cleopatra * Hamlet * Julius Caesar * King Lear * Macbeth * Othello * Romeo and Juliet	Authors	Shakespeare	9
	Henry IV Part 1 * Henry IV Part 2 * Henry V * Henry VI Parts 1,2,3 * Richard II * Richard III * Shakespeare's Sonnets	Basic	Shakespeare	3
	Henry IV Part 1 * Henry IV Part 2 * Henry V * Henry VI Parts 1,2,3 * Richard II * Richard III * Shakespeare's Sonnets	Authors	Shakespeare	10
Shaw, George Bernard	Man and Superman & Caesar and Cleopatra * Pygmalion & Arms and the Man	Basic	English Lit	6
	Man and Superman & Caesar and Cleopatra * Pygmalion & Arms and the Man	Authors	Shaw	11
Shelley, Mary	Frankenstein	Basic	English Lit	1
Sinclair, Upton	The Jungle	Basic	American Lit	3
Skinner, B.F.	Walden Two	Basic	American Lit	7
Solzhenitsyn, Aleksandr	One Day in the Life of Ivan Denisovich	Basic	European Lit	3
Sophocles	The Oedipus Trilogy	Basic	Classics	1
Spenser, Edmund	The Faerie Queen	Basic	Classics	4
Steinbeck, John	The Grapes of Wrath *	Basic	American Lit	4
	Of Mice and Men * The Pearl * The Red Pony	Basic	American Lit	5

AUTHOR INDEX

AUTHOR	TITLE(S)	SERIES	LIBRARY	Vol
Steinbeck, John	The Grapes of Wrath * Of Mice and Men * The Pearl * The Red Pony	Authors	Steinbeck	12
Stendhal	The Red and the Black	Basic	European Lit	1
Sterne, Lawrence	Tristram Shandy	Basic	English Lit	2
Stevenson, Robert Louis	Dr. Jekyll and Mr. Hyde *	Basic	English Lit	3
	Treasure Island & Kidnapped	Basic	English Lit	4
Stoker, Bram	Dracula	Basic	English Lit	3
Stowe, Harriet Beecher	Uncle Tom's Cabin	Basic	American Lit	2
Swift, Jonathan	Gulliver's Travels	Basic	English Lit	1
Thackeray, William Makepeace	Vanity Fair	Basic	English Lit	4
Thoreau, Henry David	Walden	Basic	American Lit	1
Tolkien, J.R.R.	The Lord of the Rings & The Hobbit	Basic	English Lit	5
Tolstoy, Leo	Anna Karenina * War and Peace	Basic	European Lit	3
Turgenev, Ivan Sergeyevich	Fathers and Sons	Basic	European Lit	3
Twain, Mark	A Connecticut Yankee * Huckleberry Finn * The Prince and the Pauper * Tom Sawyer	Basic	American Lit	2
	A Connecticut Yankee * Huckleberry Finn * The Prince and the Pauper * Tom Sawyer	Authors	Twain	13
Virgil	The Aeneid	Basic	Classics	1
Voltaire, Francois	Candide	Basic	European Lit	2
Vonnegut, Kurt	Vonnegut's Major Works	Basic	American Lit	7
Walker, Alice	The Color Purple	Basic	American Lit	7
Warren, Robert Penn	All the King's Men	Basic	American Lit	6
West, Nathanael	Miss Lonelyhearts & The Day of the Locust	Basic	American Lit	5
Wharton, Edith	Ethan Frome	Basic	American Lit	3
Whitman, Walt	Leaves of Grass	Basic	American Lit	1
Wilder, Thornton	Our Town	Basic	American Lit	5
Williams, Tennessee	The Glass Menagerie & A Streetcar Named Desire	Basic	American Lit	6
Woolf, Virginia	Mrs. Dalloway	Basic	English Lit	5
Wordsworth, William	The Prelude	Basic	English Lit	2
Wright, Richard	Black Boy	Basic	American Lit	4
	Native Son	Basic	American Lit	5

INDEX OF SERIES

BASIC LIBRARY (24-0)

THE SHAKESPEARE LIBRARY: 3 Volumes, 26 Titles (25-9)
- V. 1 - The Comedies 12 titles (00-3)
- V. 2 - The Tragedies, 7 titles (01-1)
- V. 3 - The Histories; The Sonnets, 7 titles (02-X)

THE CLASSICS LIBRARY: 4 Volumes, 27 Titles (26-7)
- V. 1 - Greek & Roman Classics, 11 titles (03-8)
- V. 2 - Greek & Roman Classics, 2 titles (04-6)
- V. 3 - Early Christian/European Classics, 7 titles (05-4)
- V. 4 - Early Christian/European Classics, 7 titles (06-2)

ENGLISH LITERATURE LIBRARY: 6 Volumes, 55 Titles (29-1)
- V. 1 - 17th Century & Romantic Period Classics, 7 titles (07-0)
- V. 2 - 17th Century & Romantic Period Classics, 7 titles (08-9)
- V. 3 - Victorian Age, 11 titles (09-7)
- V. 4 - Victorian Age, 10 titles (10-0)
- V. 5 - 20th Century, 10 titles (11-9)
- V. 6 - 20th Century, 10 titles (12-7)

AMERICAN LITERATURE LIBRARY: 7 Volumes, 77 Titles (33-X)
- V. 1 - Early U.S. & Romantic Period, 11 titles (13-5)
- V. 2 - Civil War to 1900, 11 titles (14-3)
- V. 3 - Early 20th Century, 9 titles (15-1)
- V. 4 - The Jazz Age to W.W.II, 11 titles (16-X)
- V. 5 - The Jazz Age to W.W.II, 10 titles (17-8)
- V. 6 - Post-War American Literature, 13 titles (18-6)
- V. 7 - Post-War American Literature, 12 titles (19-4)

EUROPEAN LITERATURE LIBRARY: 4 Volumes, 29 Titles (36-4)
- V. 1 - French Literature, 12 titles (20-8)
- V. 2 - German Literature, 7 titles (21-6)
- V. 3 - Russian Literature, 7 titles (22-4)
- V. 4 - Scandinavian Literature, 3 titles (23-2)

AUTHORS LIBRARY (65-8)

- V. 1 - **Charles Dickens** Library, 6 titles (66-6)
- V. 2 - **Feodor Dostoevsky** Library, 3 titles (67-4)
- V. 3 - **William Faulkner** Library, 7 titles (68-2)
- V. 4 - **Thomas Hardy** Library, 5 titles (69-0)
- V. 5 - **Ernest Hemingway** Library, 4 titles (70-4)
- V. 6 - **Henry James** Library, 3 titles (71-2)
- V. 7 - **Sinclair Lewis** Library, 2 titles (72-0)
- V. 8 - **Shakespeare** Library, Part 1 - The Comedies, 12 titles (73-9)
- V. 9 - **Shakespeare** Library, Part 2 - The Tragedies, 7 titles (74-7)
- V. 10 - **Shakespeare** Library, Part 3 - The Histories; Sonnets, 7 titles (75-5)
- V. 11 - **George Bernard Shaw** Library, 2 titles (76-3)
- V. 12 - **John Steinbeck** Library, 4 titles (77-1)
- V. 13 - **Mark Twain** Library, 4 titles (78-X)

Moonbeam Publications ISBN Prefix: 0-931013-

CLIFFS NOTES

HARDBOUND LITERARY LIBRARIES

INDEX OF LIBRARIES

This is the INDEX OF LIBRARIES, listing the volumes and the individual titles within the volumes for both the BASIC LIBRARY SERIES (24 Volumes, starting below) and the AUTHORS LIBRARY SERIES (13 Volumes, see Page 6).

BASIC LIBRARY SERIES (24 Volumes)

THE SHAKESPEARE LIBRARY: 3 Volumes, 26 Titles

Vol 1 - The Comedies (12 titles)
*All's Well that Ends Well & The Merry Wives of Windsor * As You Like It * The Comedy of Errors, Love's Labour's Lost, & The Two Gentlemen of Verona * Measure for Measure * The Merchant of Venice * A Midsummer Night's Dream * Much Ado About Nothing * The Taming of the Shrew * The Tempest * Troilus and Cressida * Twelfth Night * The Winter's Tale*

Vol 2 - The Tragedies (7 titles)
*Antony and Cleopatra * Hamlet * Julius Caesar * King Lear * Macbeth * Othello * Romeo and Juliet*

Vol 3 - The Histories; The Sonnets (7 titles)
*Henry IV Part 1 * Henry IV Part 2 * Henry V * Henry VI Parts 1,2,3 * Richard II * Richard III * Shakespeare's Sonnets*

THE CLASSICS LIBRARY: 4 Volumes, 27 Titles

Vol 1 - Greek & Roman Classics Part 1 (11 titles)
*The Aeneid * Agamemnon * Aristotle's Ethics * Euripides' Electra & Medea * The Iliad * Lysistrata & Other Comedies * Mythology * The Odyssey * Oedipus Trilogy * Plato's Euthyphro, Apology, Crito & Phaedo * Plato's The Republic*

INDEX OF LIBRARIES (cont'd)
BASIC LIBRARY SERIES

THE CLASSICS LIBRARY (cont'd)

Vol 2 - Greek & Roman Classics Part 2 (2 titles)
*Greek Classics * Roman Classics*

Vol 3 - Early Christian/European Classics Part 1 (7 titles)
*Beowulf * Canterbury Tales * Divine Comedy - I. Inferno * Divine Comedy - II. Purgatorio * Divine Comedy - III. Paradiso * Doctor Faustus * Don Quixote*

Vol 4 - Early Christian/European Classics Part 2 (7 titles)
*The Faerie Queene * Le Morte D'Arthur * New Testament * Old Testament * The Prince * Sir Gawain and the Green Knight * Utopia*

ENGLISH LITERATURE LIBRARY: 6 Volumes, 55 Titles

Vol 1 - 17th Century & Romantic Period Classics Part 1 (7 titles)
*Emma * Frankenstein * Gulliver's Travels * Ivanhoe * Joseph Andrews * Keats & Shelley * Moll Flanders*

Vol 2 - 17th Century & Romantic Period Classics Part 2 (7 titles)
*Paradise Lost * Pilgrim's Progress * The Prelude * Pride and Prejudice * Robinson Crusoe * Tom Jones * Tristram Shandy*

Vol 3 - Victorian Age Part 1 (11 titles)
*Alice in Wonderland * Bleak House * David Copperfield * Dr. Jekyll and Mr. Hyde * Dracula * Far from the Madding Crowd * Great Expectations * Hard Times * Jane Eyre * Jude the Obscure * The Mayor of Casterbridge*

INDEX OF LIBRARIES (cont'd)
BASIC LIBRARY SERIES

ENGLISH LITERATURE LIBRARY (cont'd)

Vol 4 - Victorian Age Part 2 (10 titles)
*Middlemarch * The Mill on the Floss * Oliver Twist * The Return of the Native * Silas Marner * A Tale of Two Cities * Tess of the D'Urbervilles * Treasure Island & Kidnapped * Vanity Fair * Wuthering Heights*

Vol 5 - 20th Century Part 1 (10 titles)
*Animal Farm * Brave New World * Cry, The Beloved Country * The French Lieutenant's Woman * Heart of Darkness & The Secret Sharer * Lord Jim * Lord of the Flies * The Lord of the Rings * Lost Horizon * Mrs. Dalloway*

Vol 6 - 20th Century Part 2 (10 titles)
*Nineteen Eighty-Four * Of Human Bondage * A Passage to India * A Portrait of the Artist as a Young Man * The Power and the Glory * Shaw's Man and Superman & Caesar and Cleopatra * Shaw's Pygmalion & Arms and the Man * Sons and Lovers * T.S. Eliot's Major Poems and Plays * Ulysses*

AMERICAN LITERATURE LIBRARY: 7 Volumes, 77 Titles

Vol 1 - Early U.S. & Romantic Period (11 titles)
*Autobiography of Ben Franklin * Billy Budd & Typee * The Deerslayer * Emerson's Essays * The House of Seven Gables * The Last of the Mohicans * Leaves of Grass * Moby Dick * Poe's Short Stories * The Scarlet Letter * Walden*

INDEX OF LIBRARIES (cont'd)
BASIC LIBRARY SERIES

AMERICAN LITERATURE LIBRARY (cont'd)

Vol 2 - Civil War to 1900 (11 titles)
*The American * The Awakening * A Connecticut Yankee in King Arthur's Court * Daisy Miller & The Turn of the Screw * Emily Dickinson: Selected Poems * Huckleberry Finn * The Portrait of a Lady * The Prince and the Pauper * Red Badge of Courage * Tom Sawyer * Uncle Tom's Cabin*

Vol 3 - Early 20th Century (9 titles)
*An American Tragedy * Babbitt * Call of the Wild & White Fang * Ethan Frome * The Jungle * Main Street * My Antonia * Sister Carrie * Winesburg, Ohio*

Vol 4 - The Jazz Age to W.W.II Part 1 (11 titles)
*Absalom, Absalom! * As I Lay Dying * The Bear * Black Boy * A Farewell to Arms * For Whom the Bell Tolls * Go Down, Moses * The Good Earth * The Grapes of Wrath * The Great Gatsby * Light in August*

Vol 5 - The Jazz Age to W.W.II Part 2 (10 titles)
*Miss Lonelyhearts & The Day of the Locust * Native Son * Of Mice and Men * Our Town * The Pearl * The Red Pony * The Sound and the Fury * The Sun Also Rises * Tender is the Night * Unvanquished*

Vol 6 - Post-War American Literature Part 1 (13 titles)
*100 Years of Solitude * All the King's Men * The Assistant * The Autobiography of Malcolm X * The Bell Jar * Black Like Me * Catch-22 * The Catcher in the Rye * The Color Purple * The Crucible * Death of a Salesman * Dune and Other Works * The Glass Menagerie & A Streetcar Named Desire*

INDEX OF LIBRARIES (cont'd)
BASIC LIBRARY SERIES

AMERICAN LITERATURE LIBRARY (cont'd)

Vol 7 - Post-War American Literature Part 2 (12 titles)
*The Invisible Man * Manchild in the Promised Land * O'Connor's Short Stories * The Old Man and the Sea * One Flew Over the Cuckoo's Nest * The Ox-Bow Incident * A Separate Peace * Shane * To Kill a Mockingbird * Vonnegut's Major Works * Walden Two * Who's Afraid of Virginia Woolf?*

EUROPEAN LITERATURE LIBRARY: 4 Volumes, 29 Titles

Vol 1 - French Literature (12 titles)
*Candide * The Count of Monte Cristo * Cyrano de Bergerac * Les Miserables * Madame Bovary * No Exit & The Flies * The Plague * The Red and the Black * The Stranger * Tartuffe, Misanthrope & Bourgeois Gentlemen * The Three Musketeers * Waiting for Godot*

Vol 2 - German Literature (7 titles)
*All Quiet on the Western Front * Demian * The Diary of Anne Frank * Faust Pt. I & Pt. II * Kafka's Short Stories * Steppenwolf & Siddhartha * The Trial*

Vol 3 - Russian Literature (7 titles)
*Anna Karenina * The Brothers Karamozov * Crime and Punishment * Fathers and Sons * Notes from the Underground * One Day in the Life of Ivan Denisovich * War and Peace*

Vol 4 - Scandinavian Literature (3 titles)
*Giants in the Earth * Ibsen's Plays I: A Doll's House & Hedda Gabler * Ibsen's Plays II: Ghosts, An Enemy of the People & The Wild Duck*

INDEX OF LIBRARIES (cont'd)
AUTHORS LIBRARY SERIES (13 Volumes)

AUTHORS LIBRARY

Vol 1 -Charles Dickens Library (6 titles)
Bleak House * *David Copperfield* * *Great Expectations* * *Hard Times* * *Oliver Twist* * *A Tale of Two Cities*

Vol 2 - Feodor Dostoevsky Library (3 titles)
The Brothers Karamazov * *Crime and Punishment* * *Notes from the Underground*

Vol 3 - William Faulkner Library (7 titles)
Absalom, Absalom! * *As I Lay Dying* * *The Bear* * *Go Down, Moses* * *Light in August* * *The Sound and the Fury* * *The Unvanquished*

Vol 4 - Thomas Hardy Library (5 titles)
Far from the Madding Crowd * *Jude the Obscure* * *The Major of Casterbridge* * *The Return of the Native* * *Tess of the D'Urbervilles*

Vol 5 - Ernest Hemingway Library (4 titles)
A Farewell to Arms * *For Whom the Bell Tolls* * *The Old Man and the Sea* * *The Sun Also Rises*

Vol 6 - Henry James Library (3 titles)
The American * *Daisy Miller & The Turn of the Screw* * *The Portrait of a Lady*

Vol 7 - Sinclair Lewis Library (2 titles)
Babbitt * *Main Street*

INDEX OF LIBRARIES (cont'd)
AUTHORS LIBRARY SERIES

Vol 8 - Shakespeare Library, Part 1 - The Comedies (12 titles)
*All's Well that Ends Well & The Merry Wives of Windsor * As You Like It * The Comedy of Errors, Love's Labour's Lost & The Two Gentlemen of Verona * Measure for Measure * The Merchant of Venice * A Midsummer Night's Dream * Much Ado About Nothing * The Taming of the Shrew * The Tempest * Troilus and Cressida * Twelfth Night * The Winter's Tale*

Vol 9 - Shakespeare Library, Part 2 - The Tragedies (7 Titles)
*Antony and Cleopatra * Hamlet * Julius Caesar * King Lear * Macbeth * Othello * Romeo and Juliet*

Vol 10 - Shakespeare Library, Part 3 - The Histories; Sonnets 7 titles)
*Henry IV Part 1 * Henry IV Part 2 * Henry V *Henry VI Parts 1,2,3 * Richard II * Richard III * Shakespeare's The Sonnets*

Vol 11 - George Bernard Shaw Library (2 titles)
*Pygmalion & Arms and the Man * Man and Superman & Caesar and Cleopatra*

Vol 12 - John Steinbeck Library (4 titles)
*The Grapes of Wrath * Of Mice and Men * The Pearl * The Red Pony*

Vol 13 - Mark Twain Library (4 titles)
*A Connecticut Yankee in King Arthur's Court * Huckleberry Finn * The Prince and the Pauper * Tom Sawyer*